SCHOOL ADMINISTRATION
AND SUPERVISION

SECOND EDITION

SCHOOL ADMINISTRATION AND SUPERVISION

LEADERSHIP CHALLENGES AND OPPORTUNITIES

RICHARD A. GORTON

UNIVERSITY OF WISCONSIN, MILWAUKEE

ᴜᴄb

WM. C. BROWN COMPANY PUBLISHERS
DUBUQUE, IA

Formerly entitled: *School Administration: Challenge and Opportunity for Leadership*

Copyright © 1976 by Wm. C. Brown Company Publishers

Copyright © 1983 by Wm. C. Brown Company Publishers

Library of Congress Catalog Card Number: 82–71673

ISBN 0–697–06246–5

Printed in the United States of America
10

Contents

Preface

This book continues to be directed to those individuals who are interested in developing a deeper understanding of the challenges and opportunities for leadership in school administration and supervision. The focus of the text is on principles and theories of administering and improving a school; however, many of the chapters are also relevant for other administrative levels. The intended readership includes prospective as well as experienced principals, assistant principals, district administrators, and persons responsible for preparing or working with school administrators.

In the process of revising the book, the literature on educational administration, supervision, and leadership was extensively and thoroughly reviewed. The review included relevant literature identified in *Education Index, Reader's Guide, Dissertation Abstracts, Books in Print,* and in Educational Resource Information Center, or, as it is commonly known, ERIC. (ERIC reports will be identified by an ERIC number; such reports are available in most university libraries and can be ordered directly from ERIC Document Reproduction Service, P. O. Box 190, Arlington, Virginia 22210). Efforts have been made to utilize important ideas from the past (since much that has been recommended, though not yet implemented in many schools, is still sound) as well as more current concepts and data.

As a result of the revision process, obsolete and less functional content has been omitted; several chapters have been reorganized to provide a more logical presentation of ideas; and the suggested review activities at the end of each chapter have been strengthened. Also, in addition to a general updating of trends and programs, a number of new topics and emphases has been added. These include special professional personnel problems, such as staff and administrator stress, administrator evaluation, employee absenteeism and drug abuse, staff reductions, staff dismissal; the principal and the exceptional education program; in-school suspension and guidelines for administering corporal punishment; barriers, prerequisites and approaches to school-community relations and school-news media relations; school closing and budget reductions; and greater emphasis on the role of the administrator as program evaluator and instructional leader.

In order to minimize the problem of sexism in the use of the book, male and female pronouns are used alternately by chapter: the female pronoun is used in all even-numbered chapters, while the male pronoun is used in the odd-numbered chapters. The only exceptions to this practice are in the case of direct quotations, in which the original pronoun (usually male) is used, and in the last two chapters dealing with career opportunities, in which pronouns of both genders are included.

At this point it might be well to emphasize again that this is *not* a book which extols *present* administrative and supervisory practices in the schools, but rather one which offers recommendations and suggestions for *improving* current practices. Realistically speaking, school administration and supervision are neither as bad as some of their critics have claimed nor as good as many of their defenders would have us believe. However, most people would probably agree that there is room for improvement in school administration and supervision, and it is toward meeting that need that this text is addressed.

Finally, it should be mentioned that the major thrust of the book continues to stress leadership responsibilities and opportunities of the school administrator and supervisor. Although, as the text indicates, administration and supervision should be a team effort and there are others associated with the school who make an important contribution, the proposition is advanced that few problems will be resolved or school improvements initiated unless the school administrator and supervisor exercise leadership. Given proper administrative and supervisory leadership, a school can do much to ameliorate its problems and improve educational services; in the absence of appropriate administrative and supervisory leadership, these goals will seldom be achieved.

It is the author's strong conviction that the way to begin improving education is by improving the administrative and supervisory leadership of the school. Hopefully, this book will make a positive contribution to that end.

Richard A. Gorton

Acknowledgments

An author of a book is usually indebted to many people. For me, this includes the individuals who reviewed earlier drafts of proposed chapters and offered helpful suggestions, and the students who pilot-tested much of the material in the text.

Special appreciation is due my wife, Pat. She has provided essential support, encouragement, and most importantly, love; and it is to her that this book is dedicated.

Meet the Author

Richard A. Gorton received his doctorate from Stanford University, majoring in school administration. His master's degree in counseling and guidance, and his bachelor's degree in political science were conferred by the University of Iowa. Doctor Gorton's experience includes six years as chairman of the Department of Administrative Leadership at the University of Wisconsin-Milwaukee, where he is currently professor of Administrative Leadership and Supervision. A leader in state and national administrator organizations, he has collaborated in a national study of "the effective principal." Because of his expertise and practical experience acquired in several administrative positions in the schools, he is frequently called upon as consultant and workshop leader in the areas of teacher and administrator evaluation and in-service education, program evaluation, instructional supervision, student disciplinary problems, school-community relations, problem solving and conflict resolution. Dr. Gorton has published two textbooks, two monographs, and more than fifty articles on a variety of topics related to educational administration and supervision, as well as education in general. His other book, *School Administration and Supervision: Important Issues, Concepts, and Case Studies,* published by Wm. C. Brown Company, is used in numerous university courses devoted to administrator preparation, and by school districts for administrator in-service education.

1

PURPOSE/DIRECTION/ ACCOUNTABILITY

1

Role of the School in a Changing Society

Cheshire Puss . . . would you tell me, please, which way I ought to go from here? That depends a good deal on where you want to get to. . . .

Lewis Carroll
Through the Looking Glass

The school administrator should not look upon administration as an end in itself, but as a means to an end. That end should be represented by the goals and objectives which the school is trying to achieve. Those goals and objectives give direction and purpose to the people who are associated with a school, and help to identify the various tasks and activities which will need to be accomplished if the school is to be successful in achieving its aims.

An administrator of a school or school district without clear goals and objectives is like a captain of a ship without a rudder. The ship may not sink, but the progress it makes towards its destination will be, at best, uncertain. Therefore, it is in the interest of every administrator to become knowledgeable about the various goals and objectives which have been proposed for the school, and to develop some vision and convictions about the direction that education should, in his estimation, take in the future. A logical way to initiate this process is through the study of various goals and objectives which have been proposed for the school. Too often educators have ignored the wisdom of the past and have, as a result, wasted time and energy reinventing the educational wheel. We will therefore begin our study by considering early concepts of the role of the school and its objectives. (For an excellent treatment of the social history of public schooling during this period, see *Schooled to Order* by David Nasaw, Oxford University Press, 1979.)

EARLY CONCEPTS OF THE SCHOOL'S ROLE

INITIAL FOCUS

The American school was conceived as an institution the main purpose of which was to teach students to read, write, and "cipher," often with a view toward attending college in preparation for the ministry or one of the other professions.[1] Since the primary function of many schools at that time was to prepare one for college, the students generally received an education which was predominantly classical in nature, with strong emphasis on Latin. "Dame School" was the name commonly applied to the elementary school of that day, while the secondary school was frequently titled "Latin Grammar School." Although other types of school existed, Dame Schools and Latin Grammar Schools were most prevalent during the period, 1647–1750.[2]

In 1751 a new secondary school with a different purpose and title was introduced. The new secondary school, called the "academy," was first chartered in Philadelphia in 1751 by Benjamin Franklin.[3] Its primary objective, as contrasted with the purpose of the Latin Grammar School, was to provide students with an education that would be *practical* as well as college preparatory. In the words of Franklin, "As to their studies, it would be well if they could be taught *everything* that is useful and *everything* that is ornamental; But Art is long and their Time is short. It is therefore propos'd that they learn those Things that are likely to be most useful and most ornamental."[4]

Subsequently, additional academies sprang up in other states. In general, their goals also stressed the practical outcomes of education. Perhaps best typifying this priority was a statement (1781) by the donors of the Philips Academy in Andover, Massachusetts, which indicated that the school's objective was to "lay the foundations of a public free School or Academy for the purpose of instructing Youth not only in English and Latin Grammar, Writing, Arithmetic and those Sciences wherin they are commonly taught; but more especially to learn them the Great End and Real Business of Living."[5] The concept of the academy, with its emphasis on a more comprehensive and practical education, later formed the basis for the early high schools, the first of which was instituted in Boston in 1821.

As the purpose of education was gradually changing at the secondary school level after 1750, so changes were also occurring at the elementary level. Education was becoming more utilitarian, and less emphasis was being given to religion. Certainly, after 1750 emphasis shifted to reflect a greater concern with the educating of all the children, and with providing a broader curriculum than previously. But it should be noted that the curriculum of many of these elementary schools, frequently referred to as "common schools," was still largely college preparatory in nature.[6]

A BREAK WITH THE PAST

Although the academy, the early high schools, and the common schools represented attempts to broaden the function of education, the goals and purposes of many schools continued, until the early 1900s, to emphasize students' preparation for college.[7] In 1913, however, the National Education Association appointed a Commission on the Re-organization of Secondary Education that ultimately issued a series of reports clearly indicating a break with the past, insofar as the goals of the secondary school were concerned. Their main report, entitled, *Cardinal Principles of Secondary Education,*[8] stressed the importance of preparing a person to function in a democracy, rather than in college, as the central focus for secondary education.*

In deciding which goals were appropriate for secondary education, the Commission analyzed the activities of the individual and found that seven areas were crucial to his existence and should therefore constitute the basic objectives of education, namely, (1) health, (2) command of fundamental processes, (3) worthy home membership, (4) vocation, (5) citizenship, (6) worthy use of leisure, and (7) ethical character.[9]

While most administrators easily recognize a list of *Cardinal Principles of Secondary Education,* many are not familiar with the Commission's discussion and reasoning in support of each objective. For this reason, among others, implementation of the seven principles has not always been as successful or complete as one might have desired. However, since the *Cardinal Principles of Secondary Education* have formed the basis for later attempts to delineate the objectives of American education, and because the principles, for the most part, appear to be as relevant today as at the time of their issuance, a brief summary of their underlying rational is presented in figure 1.1.[10]

Promulgation of the *Cardinal Principles of Secondary Education* was a landmark event in American education. For example, in 1932 a special Committee for Elementary Education, appointed by the New York State Department of Education, adapted the Cardinal Principles for the elementary school. They proposed that the primary function of the elementary school was to help every child to (1) understand and practice desirable social relationships, (2) discover and develop his own desirable individual aptitudes, (3) cultivate the habits of critical thinking, (4) appreciate and desire worthwhile activities, (5) gain command of common integrated knowledge and skills, and (6) develop a sound body and normal mental attitudes.[11]

---

*It should be emphasized at this point that the reports have also greatly affected thinking about the goals of elementary education as well. As Herrick and others have noted, "Although directed towards secondary education, and the 'educated adult,' the *Cardinal Principles of Secondary Education* have affected the elementary school and its practices as much as, if not more than, those of the secondary school." (Virgil E. Herrick et al., *The Elementary School* [Englewood Cliffs, N.J.: Prentice-Hall, 1962], p. 70.)

HEALTH

In the area of health, the Commission felt that if the individual was to carry out his other responsibilities—family, vocation, citizenship—he needed to be healthy. Health education, to the Commission, included inculcating health habits in the students, organizing an effective program of physical activities, and cooperating with the home and the community in safeguarding and promoting health.

WORTHY HOME MEMBERSHIP

In regard to worthy home membership, the Commission felt that the school should be trying to develop those qualities that would make it possible for the individual to contribute to and derive benefit from membership in a family. These qualities included, for girls, interest and ability in the proper management and conduct of a home, and for boys, appreciation and skill in budgeting for and maintaining a home. Developing wholesome attitudes and relationships between boys and girls, and developing proper attitudes on the part of students toward their present home responsibilities were also considered important aspects of the objective of worthy home membership.

VOCATION

In the area of vocational education, the Commission took the position that the school should help the student to secure those understandings, attitudes, and skills which would make it possible for him to secure a livelihood for himself and those dependent upon him, and to serve society. It specifically stated that vocational education should help the student to find in his future vocation his own best development.

CITIZENSHIP

To achieve the citizenship goal, the Commission felt that the school should develop in the individual those qualities which he would need to function properly as a member of a neighborhood, town, city, state, or nation. The particular qualities which the Commission believed were essential were: "A many-sided interest in the welfare of the communities to which one belongs; loyalty to ideals of civic righteousness; practical knowledge of social agencies and institutions; good judgment as to means and methods that will promote one social end without defeating others; and, as putting all of these into effect, habits of cordial cooperation in social undertakings."

(continued)

Figure 1.1. Cardinal Principles of
Secondary Education

WORTHY USE OF LEISURE

In regard to worthy use of leisure, the Commission believed that education should see to it that an adequate recreation program is provided both by the school and by other appropriate agencies in the community so that the individual could recreate his body, mind, and spirit, and enrich and enhance his personality. The Commission also asserted that education should attempt to foster in each individual one or more special avocational interests which could be used during leisure moments.

COMMAND OF FUNDAMENTAL PROCESSES

This principle included the development of adequate skills in reading, writing, arithmetic, and oral and written expression. This Commission did not look upon the development of these skills as an end in itself, but as an indispensable objective if the individual was to function satisfactorily in school and in later life.

ETHICAL CHARACTER

The final objective the Commission recommended was that of building ethical character. The Commission indicated that education for ethical character should include developing on the part of the student a "sense of personal responsibility and initiative and, above all, the spirit of service and the principles of true democracy which should permeate the entire school. . ." The Commission felt that no other objective was as important as the development of ethical character for, in a real sense, achieving all of the other objectives was dependent on the student's possessing ethical character.

Figure 1.1. Continued

While implementation of the Principles in the different classrooms across the country has been and continues to be uneven and less than complete, it is nevertheless clear that the publication established a new direction for American education.

And, although it is true that certain of the Cardinal Principles, such as the definition of "worthy home membership" now need to be updated to take into consideration changing social mores and expectations, the basic concepts continue to be relevant.

LATER EFFORTS TO DEVELOP SCHOOL GOALS

Since the publication of the *Cardinal Principles of Secondary Education,* numerous attempts have been made to define the goals of American education. These efforts indicate the continuing concern of educators and other Americans about the outcomes of education. This concern seems to reflect the periodic need to establish or, perhaps more accurately, to reaffirm the aims of education, and thus to provide direction and focus in times of turmoil or uncertainty in the larger society. Since one of the purposes of this book is to help the administrator to formulate ideas and convictions about objectives which the school should adopt, four important proposals for goals in education will be presented for consideration. Although these proposals are in a sense historical documents, they deserve the thoughtful consideration of any administrator who hopes to benefit from the wisdom of the past in his efforts to develop school objectives.

THE PURPOSES OF EDUCATION
IN AMERICAN DEMOCRACY

The first major proposal for school goals following the issuance of the *Cardinal Principles of Secondary Education* was entitled, *The Purposes of Education in American Democracy*. This proposal, authored by the Educational Policies Commission in 1938, advanced four basic objectives for American education: (1) self-realization, (2) human relationship, (3) economic efficiency, and (4) civic responsibility.[12] Each of these general objectives was divided by the Commission into subobjectives, examples of which are presented in figure 1.2 so that the reader may better understand and evaluate their merits.

   The Purposes of Education in American Democracy builds and elaborates upon the *Cardinal Principles of Secondary Education*. The document's value derives largely from the fact that it specifies in greater detail and depth the seven areas of school objectives which had been initially formulated in the Cardinal Principles. Its major limitation, like that of the Cardinal Principles, is that the terms used in stating the purposes frequently fail to lend themselves to precise interpretation of meaning, or are stated in such a manner as to make evaluation of the achievement of the purposes difficult. Still, the 1938 statement by the Educational Policies Commission deserves the consideration of the administrator even today. Certainly the statement can be used as a basis for the development or revision of a school's educational objectives. However, for such use, efforts should be made to define terms more precisely so that meaning will be clearer and evaluation of achievement more attainable.

THE IMPERATIVE NEEDS OF YOUTH

Probably one of the most influential documents dealing with the goals of secondary education was published in 1944 by the National Association of Secondary School Principals and was entitled, *The Imperative Needs of Youth*

1. **The Objectives of Self-Realization**
   The Inquiring Mind. The educated person has an appetite for learning.
   Reading. The educated person reads the mother tongue efficiently.
   Writing. The educated person writes the mother tongue effectively.
   Esthetic Interests. The educated person appreciates beauty.
   Character. The educated person gives responsible direction to his own life.
2. **The Objectives of Human Relationship**
   Respect for Humanity. The educated person puts human relationships first.
   Friendships. The educated person enjoys a rich, sincere, and varied social life.
   Cooperation. The educated person can work and play with others.
   Courtesy. The educated person observes the amenities of social behavior.
   Appreciation of the Home. The educated person appreciates the family as a social institution.
3. **The Objectives of Economic Efficiency**
   Occupational Information. The educated producer understands the requirements and opportunities for various jobs.
   Occupational Appreciation. The educated producer appreciates the social value of his work.
   Work. The educated producer knows the satisfaction of good workmanship.
   Consumer Judgment. The educated consumer develops standards for guiding his expenditures.
   Consumer Judgment. The educated consumer takes appropriate measures to safeguard his interests.
4. **The Objectives of Civic Responsibility**
   Social Justice. The educated citizen is sensitive to the disparities of human circumstance.
   Social Activity. The educated citizen acts to correct unsatisfactory conditions.
   Tolerance. The educated citizen respects honest differences of opinion.
   Conservation. The educated citizen has a regard for the nation's resources.
   Political Citizenship. The educated citizen accepts his civic duties.

Used with the permission of The National Education Association.

Figure 1.2. The Purposes of Education in American Democracy

of Secondary School Age.[13] The proposed objectives in the document were based on several assumptions:

1. that education should be planned for all youth
2. that education should be free
3. that all youth have certain educational needs in common, and that education should be adapted to personal and social needs
4. that education should be continuous.[14]

Based on these assumptions, the Association set forth ten important needs of youth to which it felt education should address itself. They are as follows:

The Imperative Needs of Youth of
Secondary School Age[15]

1. All youth need to develop saleable skills and those understandings and attitudes that make the worker an intelligent and productive participant in economic life. To this end, most youth need supervised work experience as well as education in the skills and knowledge of their occupations.
2. All youth need to develop and maintain good health and physical fitness and mental health.
3. All youth need to understand the rights and duties of the citizen of a democratic society, and to be diligent and competent in the performance of their obligations as members of the community and citizens of the state nation, and to have an understanding of the nations and peoples of the world.
4. All youth need to understand the significance of the family for the individual and society and the conditions conducive to successful family life.
5. All youth need to know how to purchase and use goods and services intelligently, understanding both the values received by the consumer and the economic consequences of their acts.
6. All youth need to understand the methods of science, the influence of science on human life, and the main scientific facts concerning the nature of the world and of man.
7. All youth need opportunities to develop their capacities to appreciate beauty in literature, art music, and nature.
8. All youth need to be able to use their leisure time well and to budget it wisely, balancing activities that yield satisfactions to the individual with those that are socially useful.
9. All youth need to develop respect for other persons, to grow in their insight into ethical values and principles, to be able to live and work cooperatively with others, and to grow in the moral and spiritual values of life.
10. All youth need to grow in their ability to think rationally, to express their thoughts clearly, and to read and listen with understanding.

A similar document was published for the elementary school: *Education for All American Children,* by the Educational Policies Commission in 1948. The document proposed that elementary schools attempt to develop fully the capabilities of each child by helping the student to acquire a basic health education; a high degree of skill in reading, writing, and arithmetic; habits of good workmanship; skills of critical thinking, constructive discussion, social responsibility; and cooperative skills.

Publication of the document, *The Imperative Needs of Youth of Secondary School Age,* was an important contribution to the sharpening of the focus of secondary school education at the end of World War II, and was undoubtedly useful to many administrators and school groups who were seeking direction at that time. The educational objectives implied in this statement of the needs of youth were comprehensive, covering many facets of student development. The statement also was visionary in its recommendation that education and the educational objectives set forth should be planned for *all* youth.

Unfortunately, like many statements of proposed goals, implementation has been uneven or lacking in important respects. For example, school groups have had considerable trouble determining which ethical values and principles the committee referred to in Imperative Need #9, and agreement on moral and spiritual values has frequently been difficult to achieve. Also, many secondary schools, if not most, have chosen to ignore the premise that *all* youth possess the ten needs identified and have provided only an elective program for certain of the needs, such as #1, #4, #5, and #7. In addition, it seems clear that, inadvertently or by design, most schools have either rejected or ignored the educational objective implied in #8, that all students need to develop understandings, skills, and attitudes in regard to using their leisure time wisely.

Despite the less than complete implementation of *The Imperative Needs of Youth,* the document nevertheless stands as a useful reference for any administrator who wishes to help establish or revise the educational goals of a school. It is true that the statement and many of its terms need further definition and elaboration, and cannot be simply transplanted into a new school situation. However, the basic outline, orientation, and thrust of the document provide guidelines which are as valuable and relevant today as they were in the mid-forties. Those readers interested in more recent attempts (with results generally similar to past efforts) to develop goals for education should see *What Schools Are For* by John I. Goodlad (Bloomington, Ind.: Phi Delta Kappa Foundation, 1980) and *Measuring and Attaining the Goals of Education* (Alexandria, Va.: Association for Supervision and Curricular Development, 1980).

THE QUESTION OF VALUES

In the proposals on educational aims presented to this point, reference has been made to developing ethical or moral values. The *Cardinal Principles of Secondary Education* referred to education for ethical character. *The Purposes of Education in American Democracy* mentioned "character" and "respect for humanity." *The Imperative Needs of Youth* stated that all youth need to develop insight into ethical, moral, and spiritual values. One problem, however, is that proposals on school goals have not been very specific in stating

(Educational Policies Commission)
   The basic moral and spiritual value in American life is the supreme importance of the individual personality.

   1. Each person should feel responsible for the consequences of his own conduct.
   2. Institutional arrangements are the servants of mankind.
   3. Mutual consent is better than violence.
   4. The human mind should be liberated by access to information and opinion.
   5. Excellence in mind, character, and creative ability should be fostered.
   6. All persons should be judged by the same moral standards.
   7. The concept of brotherhood should take precedence over selfish interest.
   8. Each person should have the greatest possible opportunity for the pursuit of happiness, provided only that such activities do not substantially interfere with the similar opportunities of others.
   9. Each person should be offered the emotional and spiritual experiences which transcend the material aspects of life.

Used with permission of The National Education Association.

Figure 1.3. Moral and Spiritual
Values in the Public Schools.[16]

which ethical, moral, or spiritual values the school should attempt to develop in students. To this omission there has been one notable exception.

In 1951, the Educational Policies Commission published an essay entitled, "Moral and Spiritual Values in the Public Schools," which is still probably the best statement available on this very difficult subject. The most important parts of the essay developed by the Educational Policies Commission are presented in figure 1.3.

While it is true that the moral and spiritual values proposed by the Educational Policies Commission are not stated in behavioral or operational terms, they do offer an administrator rough benchmarks on the basis of which further refinements can be achieved. Moreover, in recent years interest in value education has increased, and several worthwhile proposals have been advanced by Butts and by Thomas.[17] The Talawanda School District in Ohio has also adopted a comprehensive list of values to be added to their educational objectives, including such items as "Having the courage to resist group pressures to do things that we would not do as individuals," and "Treating others as we wish to be treated, recognizing that this principle applies to persons of every class, race, nationality and religion."[18]

However, one problem that will confront schools in their attempt to include the development of student values in their aims or objectives is that everyone does not subscribe to the same set of values. Many people continue

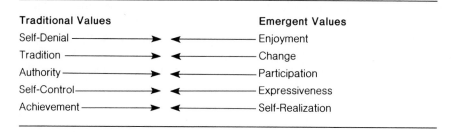

Traditional Values	Emergent Values
Self-Denial ⟶ ⟵	Enjoyment
Tradition ⟶ ⟵	Change
Authority ⟶ ⟵	Participation
Self-Control ⟶ ⟵	Expressiveness
Achievement ⟶ ⟵	Self-Realization

Figure 1.4. Examples of Traditional vs. Emergent Values[19]

to hold what might be referred to as traditional values, while a number of other people espouse what social scientists term "emergent values." The potential conflict between these two sets of values can be seen by examining the examples in figure 1.4.

The problem of conflict between traditional and emergent values cannot be easily avoided by the school. This problem and the questions of how and whether values can and should be fostered will be more fully discussed in chapter 2.

THE CENTRAL PURPOSE OF AMERICAN EDUCATION

In none of the proposals on educational objectives presented thus far has any *priority* of importance been stated or implied. In 1961, the Educational Policies Commission apparently decided that the lack of priority in statements of objectives was a serious omission which needed to be corrected, so the Commission published a document entitled, *The Central Purpose of American Education.* In its statement the Commission took the position that the central purpose of American education ". . . is the development of the ability to think."[20]

It should be noted, as the Commission pointed out, that singling out the development of the student's thinking abilities does not imply that this should be the school's sole objective or that it should be the most important objective in *all* cases. Nevertheless, it is clear from examining the language of the Commission that it considered the achievement of this objective worthy of receiving the highest priority of the school.

The Commission's statement, while accorded general approval by educators, has been attacked in some circles for its failure to address itself to the question of the *purpose* for which the student should use his rational power. Bramheld, for example, criticized the document soon after publication because it did not face squarely the key issue of ". . . whether these powers [thinking abilities] should be used to achieve values and institutions appropriate to an age undergoing, as ours is undergoing, lightning-like change—values and institutions that represent the widest, deepest aspirations of the greatest number of human beings everywhere on earth."[21] While Bramheld's position on the central purpose of education may be that of the minority, the issue has by no means been settled, as the proposed roles for the school, presented in the next section, indicate.

RECENT EMPHASES REGARDING
THE ROLE OF THE SCHOOL

There has seldom been a shortage of proposals from educational leaders, or others outside the field of education, on what the aims of the school should be. Frequently these statements have just reaffirmed positions taken by earlier national groups, but in a number of instances new ground has been broken. Rather than provide an extensive discussion of all of the various recent points of view on school goals, figure 1.5 presents a representative sampling for the reader's consideration and analysis.

Two themes seem to permeate many of the statements presented in figure 1.5: (1) that the school should assign a higher priority to making sure that students develop certain basic skills of learning, and (2) that, important as basic skills development is, the school also needs to provide students with adequate knowledge and understanding for functioning effectively and ethically in a multicultural, ever changing country and interdependent world. Both of these aims, of course, have been proposed for the schools at one time or another in the past, but it would appear that there is currently greater emphasis on these aspects of a student's education than ever before.

Public Expectations

As the school administrator and his staff consider the question of what the role of the school should be, they should also be aware of public expectations. Periodic polls of public attitudes toward education have been helpful in revealing preferences by the public as to the primary goals of education. For example, in a Gallup Poll commissioned by the National Association of Elementary School Principals and the National Association of Secondary School Principals, a representative sample of citizens was asked what they wanted their children to gain from education. The ten most important outcomes, from the perspective of parents, are identified and ranked in figure 1.6.

An examination of figure 1.6 indicates that both public and parochial school parents expect the schools to give a high priority to career education and training, whereas personal development and interpersonal relations seem to receive a much lower priority, particularly from parents of parochial school

1. *Development of Basic Skills*

   A renewed commitment to basic skills proficiency is absolutely necessary. However, to function successfully in society, students must also be taught how to apply these skills to practical tasks and decisions they will face daily.[22]

2. *Humanistic Education*

   Americans have traditionally set loftier goals for education than the acquisition of basic skills alone. . . . As an integral part of their commitment to quality in public and private education, local administrators should maintain in every elementary and secondary school a strong, well-structured curriculum in the humanities and arts.[23]

3. *Intellectual Development*

   Its [the school's] first responsibility is to do those things that are associated in the public mind with the outcomes of schooling, namely, to develop the intellectual prowess of individual children and to help them comprehend their heritage.[24]

4. *Learning How to Learn*

   It is more important for students to learn *how* to learn than to study any specific body of knowledge.[25]

5. *Personality Development*

   The healthy growth of students as persons—with clear understanding of the dynamics of human interaction and in possession of personal skills for living effectively with other people—must find an important place among the primary objectives for today's and tomorrow's schools.[26]

6. *Citizenship Education*

   Education for citizenship is the primary purpose of universal education. . . .[27]

7. *Problem Solving*

   Tomorrow's citizens must be effective problem solvers, persons able to make good choices, to create solutions on the spot.[28]

8. *Global Understanding*

   It is essential that we acquire more knowledge about other peoples and cultures, a greater sensitivity to their attitudes and views, and a clearer understanding of our roles as individuals, as members of various social groups, and as citizens in an interrelated world.[29]

9. *Education for Ethics*

   We need to reemphasize individual ethical conduct as opposed to social ethics which tends to propagate an "ends justify the means" position and a system of "situational ethics" . . .[30]

10. *Multicultural Education*

    . . . School pupils have a moral responsibility to learn, understand, and respect the values inherent in other races and religions and to practice behaviors that will insure human dignity and civil rights to males and females of cultural groups different than their own.[31]

Figure 1.5. A Sampling of Proposed
School Goals

Desired Outcomes of Education	Public School Parents (Rankings)	Parochial School Parents (Rankings)
To get better jobs.	1	1
To be self-supporting.	2	2
Provide a better life.	3	4
Prepare them for the future.	4	3
To get along better with people at all levels of society.	5	8
To stimulate their minds.	6	5
To make more money.	7	8
Become a good citizen.	7	7
Personal growth.	7	6
To attain self-satisfaction.	*	8
To have a better life than parent had.	10	*

*Did not rank in top 10 items.

Figure 1.6. Parent Expectations for School Outcomes for Their Children[32]

students. Somewhat distressing is the rather low priority assigned to intellectual development. However, whether or not educators agree with public expectations, it seems clear that these expectations need to be seriously considered. To paraphrase an important observation made in another context, "The question of what should be the primary function or goals of education is too important to be left solely to educational authorities." The school administrator and associates need to become more aware of the public's point of view, and to utilize data from national polls and local surveys of community attitudes in establishing or revising the goals of education in the school. Since the Gallup Poll is a national survey, school administrators should conduct their own study of their local community if they question the national findings.

EDUCATION AND THE FUTURE

Goal proposals and public expectations are two useful sources of ideas for determining the role of a school. However, the administrator needs to recognize that the students who are now attending school will in all probability be confronted by circumstances and problems when they are adults that will be very different than those faced by adults today. Certainly, if the amount of change which has occurred in the past three decades is any indication, the type of society in which we will be living in the twenty-first century will be much different from that of the twentieth century. Therefore, if one of the functions of the school is to prepare students for the kind of world in which they will be living as adults, then the school administrator needs to become more aware of projections and predictions of what society will be like in the future.

Although there have always been people who have tried to predict the future, it was not until recently that social scientists—particularly those in education—began a systematic effort to project future trends and possibilities and their implications for education. As one might suspect, this has not been an easy task, for as Ziegler has pointed out, ". . . we have no way of validating our predictions until the future becomes present."[33] For this reason and because the field of predicting the future is so new, the predictions advanced by any group or individual are usually very tentative and their implications for education are frequently not specific.* However, based on the author's continuing review of the literature on the subject of the future and its implications for education, it would appear that the school needs to prepare students for a future in which the following abilities will be important:[34]

1. Directing and coping successfully with change in an ever-changing society
2. Conserving the environment and managing resources wisely in a society with increasingly scarce resources and a growing technology capable of destroying larger segments of the environment
3. Pursuing learning continuously in a society in which new knowledge will be coming to the fore constantly and much previously acquired knowledge will become obsolete
4. Developing computer skills for obtaining access to new approaches to learning and sources of print and non-print information
5. Utilizing increased amounts of leisure time wisely
6. Developing and maintaining rewarding human relationships in a society becoming increasingly impersonal
7. Developing and maintaining a set of ethical values and philosophy which will provide an individual with purpose, direction, and a basis for decision making in an increasingly pluralistic and valueless society
8. Perceiving the increasing interdependency of the various parts of the world, and supporting attempts to develop cooperative and peaceful solutions to increasingly difficult world problems

*For a discussion of what appears to be an excellent approach that educators might be able to utilize in gaining insight into what the future may hold, see Christopher Dede and Dwight Allen, "Education in the 21st Century: Scenarios as a Tool for Strategic Planning," *Phi Delta Kappan,* January 1981: 362–66.

It should be noted that many of the abilities which are predicted as necessary in the future, are currently needed and several of them have been recommended for some time. However, if various predictions of the future are correct, then these abilities will be not only desirable but essential for a successful adult life.

Historically, the school has frequently been slow to respond to changes in society and seldom has anticipated change. Generally, the school has tended to *react* to change after it has occurred in the larger society rather than trying to anticipate, plan for, and direct change. As a result, while one could argue that the school has done a good job, its graduates have not been as well prepared as they might have been, had the future and its implications for education been taken into greater consideration.

The school must not only prepare students for current circumstances and challenges but also for their adult life. The school administrator can play a leadership role in achieving that goal by not only considering goal proposals and public expectations for the role of the school, but also predictions, projections, and ideas about the future.*

Review and Learning Activities

1. Why is it in the best interest of an administrator to be concerned about school goals and objectives?
2. In what ways did the purpose and program of the school change between inception and the twentieth century?
3. Discuss the main focus and implications for the school of the following goal proposals:
   a. Cardinal Principles of Secondary Education, or Cardinal Objectives in Elementary Education
   b. The Purposes of Education in American Democracy
   c. The Imperative Needs of Youth of Secondary School Age, or Education for All American Children
   d. Moral and Spiritual Values in the Public Schools
4. Two major themes permeate the goal statements presented in figure 1.5. What are their implications for the school?
5. In deciding the goals and objectives, to what extent should the school consider the expectations of the community?
6. Why is it important for the administrator to become aware of projected future school and societal trends?

*For the administrator who is interested in a magazine which attempts to report predictions about the future, see *The Futurist,* a bimonthly publication of the World Future Society, 4916 St. Elmo Ave., Washington, D.C. 20014.

Notes

1. Ellwood P. Cubberley, *Public Education in the United States* (Boston: Houghton-Mifflin, 1934), pp. 12–25.
2. Ibid., pp. 27–33 for further detail about these schools.
3. H. G. Good, *A History of American Education* (New York: Macmillan, 1956), pp. 72–77.
4. Quoted in Edgar W. Knight and Clifton L. Hall, *Readings in American Educational History* (New York: Appleton-Century-Crofts, 1951), p. 76.
5. Quoted in Elmer E. Brown, *The Making of Our Middle Schools* (New York: Longmans, Green & Co., 1903), p. 195.
6. Cubberley, *Public Education,* p. 330.
7. Ibid., pp. 542–44.
8. *Cardinal Principles of Secondary Education,* Bureau of Education, Bulletin no. 35 (Washington, D.C.: Government Printing Office, 1918).
9. Ibid., pp. 5–10.
10. Ibid.
11. Committee for Elementary Education, *Cardinal Objectives in Elementary Education—A Third Report* (Albany: University of State of New York Press, 1932), pp. 9–16.
12. Educational Policies Commission, *The Purposes of Education in American Democracy* (Washington, D.C.: National Education Association, 1938), pp. 50, 72, 90, 108.
13. National Association of Secondary School Principals, *The Imperative Needs of Youth of Secondary School Age,* Bulletin no. 145 (Washington, D.C.: National Education Association, 1947).
14. Ibid., p. 4.
15. Ibid., p. 43.
16. Educational Policies Commission, *Moral and Spiritual Values in the Public Schools* (Washington, D.C.: National Educational Association, 1951), pp. 18–38.
17. R. Freeman Butts, *The Revival of Civic Learning* (Bloomington, Ind.: Phi Delta Kappa, 1980); M. Donald Thomas, "The Limits of Pluralism," *Phi Delta Kappan* (April 1981): 589–92.
18. "School District Emphasizes Outstanding Social Principles," *NASSP News Leader* (November 1981): 4.
19. Figure 1.4 was developed from an analysis of the ideas expressed in the following sources: Paul Nash, "Student Protest: A Crisis of Values," *Boston University Journal* (Winter 1970): 23–31; Daniel Yankelovich, "New Rules in American Life," *Psychology Today* (April 1981): 35–91. The original source for a discussion of traditional versus emergent values was George Spindler, *Education and Culture* (New York: Holt, Rinehart and Winston, 1967), pp. 132–46.
20. Educational Policies Commission, *The Central Purpose of American Education* (Washington, D.C.: National Education Association, 1961), p. 12.
21. Theodore Branheld, "What is the Central Purpose of American Education?" *The Kappan* (October 1961): 12.
22. Raymond F. Reisler, "An Educational Agenda for the Eighties," *The Kappan* (February 1981): 414.
23. Commission on the Humanities, *Humanities in American Life* (Los Angeles: University of California Press, 1980), pp. 28, 40.
24. Excerpt from an address by Dean J. Myron Atkins, Stanford University, January 9, 1981.
25. Phil Schlemmer, "The Zoo School: Evolution of an Alternative," *The Kappan* (April 1981): 558.
26. Arthur W. Combs, "Humanistic Education: Too Tender for a Tough World?" *The Kappan* (February 1981): 447.

27. R. Freeman Butts, "Curriculum for the Educated Citizen," *Educational Leadership* (October 1980): 6.

28. Arthur W. Combs, "What the Future Demands of Education," *The Kappan* (January 1981): 369.

29. James M. Becker, "Needed: A Global Context for Local Actions," *NASSP Bulletin* (November 1980): 27–28.

30. M. Donald Thomas, "Morals and Ethics: School Responsibility?" *NSBA Newsservice* (August 1979): 2.

31. Gordon Berry, "The Multicultural Principle," *The Kappan* (June 1979): 745.

32. George H. Gallup, *The 13th Annual Gallup Poll of the Public's Attitude toward the Public Schools* (Reston, Va.: National Association of Secondary School Principals, 1981).

33. Warren L. Ziegler, *An Approach to the Future—Perspective in American Education.* (Syracuse, N.Y.: Educational Policy Research Center, Syracuse University Research Corporation, 1970), p. 12.

34. Rather than a list of all the sources consulted by the author, those books and articles which seemed to be most helpful in predicting the future and in provoking consideration about the implications for education are provided below.

Harold Shane, *Education for a New Millenium* (Bloomington, Ind.: Phi Delta Kappa, 1981).

Frank Feather, ed., *Through the 80s: Thinking Globally, Acting Locally* (Bethesda, Md.: World Future Society, 1980).

Thomas E. Jones, *Options for the Future* (New York: Praeger, 1980).

Arthur W. Combs, "What the Future Demands of Education," *Phi Delta Kappan* (January 1981): 369–72.

Alvin Toffler, *The Third Wave* (New York: Bantam Books, 1981).

Walter Marks and Bethene LeMahieu, "The Issue of Theory into Practice is Focused on Anticipating the Future," *Theory into Practice* (Autumn 1981): 213–89.

Gerard K. O'Neill, *2081: A Hopeful View of the Human Future* (New York: Simon and Schuster, 1981).

2

Development of School Objectives

The ideas presented in chapter 1 should be viewed and utilized as conceptual tools for the development of a school's educational objectives. Certainly one of the most significant leadership responsibilities which an administrator and relevant others can perform today is to develop school objectives, including not only the evaluation and revision of current objectives, but also the generation of new objectives. While all of the administrative and leadership activities that will be discussed in this book are important, they will not result in positive contributions to the school if the educational objectives to which they should be related are vague or nonexistent.

In generating school objectives, the administrator and the people with whom she is working will need to understand the context in which, and the process through which school objectives are developed and approved, and they must be prepared to deal with the major issues and problems which can arise during the process. The following sections take up each of these essential aspects.

MAJOR CONSIDERATIONS AND PROCEDURES

ORGANIZATIONAL RELATIONSHIPS AND SOCIAL FACTORS

The development of school objectives does not occur in a vacuum. The school administrator will need to take into consideration certain organizational relationships and social factors as she works with others on this important task.

Organizationally, a school is composed of several subunits and is itself a member of a larger unit, the school district.[1] The relationship between the goals and objectives of these organizational units is depicted in figure 2.1.

The most important organizational fact which an administrator should understand from an examination of figure 2.1 is that a school is not a separate entity but a member of a school district which has a philosophy and set of

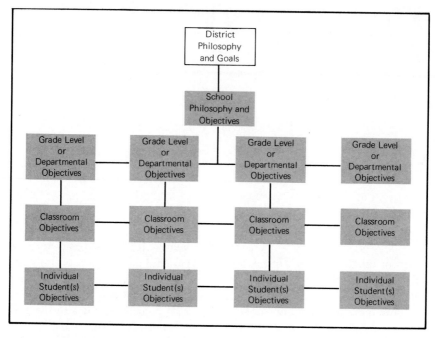

Figure 2.1. Organizational Framework
for School Objectives

goals to which it must adhere. Consequently, the administrator and the professional staff of a school are not free to act unilaterally in developing school objectives, but must work within the philosophical and goal framework set by the school district. Usually the district's philosophy and goals will be stated in general terms—general enough to allow the individual school considerable latitude in developing its own objectives. But regardless of the degree of flexibility in a district's framework, the objectives of an individual school must be compatible with the district's goals.

Secondly, in the development of school objectives the administrator and staff need to be aware of the organizational units within the school and their interrelationships. Most schools are organized according to grade level and, in the secondary school, by department also. Within these organizational units there are individual classrooms. While the emphasis in this chapter and the previous one is on the development of *school-wide* objectives, there should also be objectives for each grade level, department, classroom, and student which are related to the overall school objectives. Therefore, when the school administrator and staff are working on the development of school-wide objectives, they need to consider how these might be implemented at the grade, department, classroom, and student levels. It makes little sense to develop what may appear to be desirable school-wide objectives if, for some reason, they cannot be implemented at more specific levels within a school.

In addition to organizational relationships, the administrator and the staff will need to consider certain major social factors in developing school objectives. These factors are identified in figure 2.2.

As figure 2.2 shows, many social factors can affect the development of school objectives and need to be taken into consideration by the school administrator and staff. While all of the factors identified are important, five of them merit further discussion.

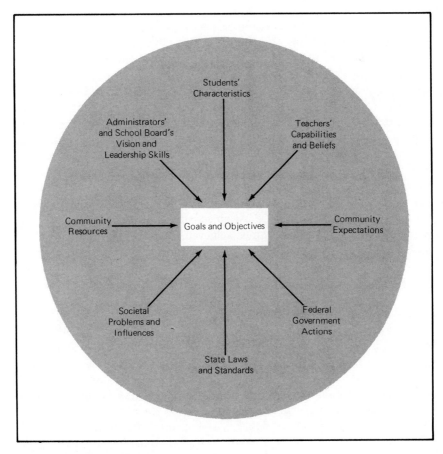

Figure 2.2. Major Social Factors Affecting the Development of Goals and Objectives

The characteristics of students enrolled in a school should be an important source of input to the development of the objectives—perhaps the *most* important source. Objectives which do not take into account the backgrounds, capabilities, and aspirations of students in a school will tend to be unrealistic, and the objectives may not be achieved. Consequently, in developing a school's objectives, the characteristics of students in the school should be identified and defined, and that information should be made available to all appropriate parties.

Community expectations and resources are two important factors which can affect the development of school objectives. For example, a community which believes the school should not become involved in certain innovative aspects of education probably will not support educational objectives which go beyond traditional student learnings. On the other hand, a community that may believe strongly in an enlarged role for the school may lack the financial or human resources to support its commitment. Of course, community resources and expectations can often be changed. State or federal aid may supplement the resources of a local community, and administrative and faculty leadership (or the lack of it) can affect the expectations of a community. However, it seems clear that, in the development of school objectives the administrator and staff will need to consider community expectations and resources.

Two additional factors which are especially significant in establishing objectives for a school are the capabilities and beliefs of the faculty, and the vision and leadership skills of the administration and school board. If the faculty lacks the skills for the achievement of particular school objectives, or doesn't value the importance of those objectives, this situation will need to be rectified before the objectives can be achieved. Certainly, unless the teachers possess both the skills for and commitment to achieving whatever objectives are established in a school, their achievement is unlikely. The objectives may look good on paper, but they are not apt to be reached at the level intended.

It should be emphasized, however, that the capabilities and beliefs of the faculty can be influenced by the educational vision and leadership skills of the administration and the school board. The vision and leadership skills of the latter two groups may help the faculty to acquire increased skill and higher aspirations; conversely, the absence of vision and leadership may result in a stagnant situation. In the case of both the faculty and the community, the educational vision and leadership skills of the administration and the school board are extremely important factors in the development of school objectives.

The remaining factors in figure 2.2—societal problems and influences, federal government actions, and state laws and standards—are also significant, and will be discussed in chapter 4.

WHO SHOULD BE INVOLVED IN DEVELOPING EDUCATIONAL OBJECTIVES?

In the elementary and secondary system of education in the United States, the school board or board of directors makes the overall educational policy in a district; and the aims and objectives of a school constitute policy decisions within the province of a school board.[2] But the board's role is generally one of giving final approval to—or disapproval of—proposed educational objectives for a school. The board does not typically take an active role in initiating or proposing new educational objectives for a school, although there are exceptions. Normally, the school board assumes that the professionals in the school system, particularly the school administrators, will assume the leadership in proposing educational objectives, and the board's role will be that of evaluating such proposals and making final decisions. The main point that the school administrator must remember is that she is not free to implement new educational objectives without securing the final approval of the board of education. It would also be in her best interest to keep the board involved in efforts to develop school objectives.

In the process of developing objectives for a school, the administrator should also consider involving several other groups, which include: (1) the central office staff, (2) the faculty, (3) the parents, (4) the community, and (5) the students. Each of these groups can contribute valuable input to the development of educational objectives, and their support and commitment will be required in most cases if the objectives are to be implemented successfully.

Specifically, the central office staff can be helpful in providing time, materials, budgeting, and consultant assistance; and their understanding and support of the educational objectives ultimately proposed to the school board will be essential. The faculty represent the main vehicle for implementing the educational objectives, and without their understanding and commitment, implementation will undoubtedly be hampered, if not resisted. In addition, the educational backgrounds of faculty members, and their daily contacts with the student body, increase the potential value of their contribution to the development of educational objectives.

While some administrators may question whether parents, the community and students should be involved in the development of school objectives, it would seem that each of these groups can offer unique and frequently useful input.* All three sources represent the layman's point of view, and that kind of a contribution is probably healthy in any discussion of educational objectives. If a school is to implement successfully its educational objectives, it will

---

*For an example of how one school district involved its community in the development of educational objectives, see Robert Lucco and Philip Meekins, *Community Involvement in Instructional Programming: Fact or Fiction?* (Eric Report, Ed–136–388).

definitely need the understanding of parents and students, and such an understanding may be best achieved through their involvement in the process of developing educational objectives. In the case of the community, there are undoubtedly specialized resources such as businessmen, and professional and labor leaders, who could offer valuable insights and whose expertise should be utilized in the development of objectives for a school.

APPROACHES TO THE DEVELOPMENT OF SCHOOL OBJECTIVES

The traditional approach to the development of school objectives is the establishment of a committee which examines various materials and, after considerable discussion and usually some compromise, arrives at a statement of proposed objectives. The main limitations of this approach are that committee discussions frequently generate more heat than light, and the more influential members of the group tend to dominate the discussion and the decision making.

A proposed alternative or adjunct to the traditional approach to the development of school objectives is the Delphi Method. The Delphi Method, which grew out of the work of Olaf Helmer and Norman Dalkey, was originally intended as a tool for the scientific and technological forecasting of the future.[3] It has, however, been adapted for use in generating objectives and in establishing priorities among those objectives.[4] The major steps involved in the method are the following:

1. Identifying those individuals and/or groups whose opinions, judgments, or expert knowledge it would be valuable to obtain in the development of school objectives.
2. Soliciting anonymous recommendations for proposed objectives from those individuals and groups.
3. Compiling a list of the proposed objectives recommended by individuals and groups, and distributing this list to those who participated in step 2.
4. Requesting participants to indicate the importance or priority of each proposed objective on the list, e.g., very important, important, somewhat important, unimportant, no opinion.
5. Summarizing the results of step 4 and distributing data to participants; requesting participants to review the results and indicate any change in their assessment of the importance of certain objectives. The activities of this step are repeated until there is a reasonable consensus on the objectives which a school or school district should try to achieve.

It should be noted that information regarding proposed school objectives and their importance can be gathered and communicated by mailing questionnaires and reports of the data obtained, or the information may be collected and disseminated at a meeting, although the former procedure is more typically used. An important prerequisite or aspect of the Delphi Method, however, is that in the initial stages particularly, the anonymity of any individual or group proposing a school objective or indicating its priority should be maintained. The basic assumption is that an individual or group whose identity is not made known to the other participants is likely to be more candid in proposing school objectives and more flexible in considering and reconsidering their importance. Of course, in later stages of the process, it may be necessary for participants to discuss their differences openly, in order to compromise or arrive at a consensus.

The Delphi Method is an excellent approach for involving a large number of people in the development of school objectives and for minimizing the importance of status factors in deciding which objectives are most important. However, there are potential weaknesses and questions associated with this approach which the administrator and staff may need to resolve.[5] One potential limitation is the time element: if mailed questionnaires are used, difficulty may be encountered in securing an adequate number of responses without too much delay. Also, there is the question of whether the responses to the questionnaires should be the sole basis for determining school objectives or whether they should constitute only one of several bases for making decisions about school goals. And finally, there is the question of who should organize the process of generating objectives and attend to its implementation.

To resolve these problems and questions the administrator and staff may need to establish a committee on school objectives that would plan and implement the foregoing process and which would prepare a report to the school board about the proposed objectives which the school would like to adopt. The committee, which might be composed of representatives from the groups mentioned in the previous section, could also be helpful in generating support for the Delphi Method by providing materials and data for the consideration of participants, and in helping them to resolve problems. In working with the committee, as well as with the other participants, the administrator should utilize her leadership skills to make the entire process more productive.

Of course, there are other approaches to the development of school objectives which deserve the administrator's consideration and merit further investigation. For examle, Phi Delta Kappa's Commission on Educational Planning distributes a manual and materials for developing and stating priorities among school goals and objectives which deserve further consideration by the administrator. The manual and materials can be ordered from Phi Delta Kappan, P. O. Box 789, Bloomington, Ind. 47401. However, regardless of the

method that the administrator ultimately employs, she and all other participants should try to adhere to the following principles proposed by the Joint
Committee on Educational Goals and Evaluation.[6]

1. The goal setting process should be kept open to all points of view
   without domination or intimidation by any special interest group.
2. The purpose of bringing people together is not to dwell on past
   deficiencies or lay blame, but to evolve a philosophy, identify needs,
   determine goals, goal indicators, or sub-goals and program
   objectives, and to establish priorities.
3. Participants should not expect to have everything their way; they
   should come seeking a better understanding of the community, its
   people, and problems.
4. A spirit of cooperation and trust should be established among
   individuals and groups involved in the process.
5. Roles of leadership in school-community planning should be earned
   rather than based on authority.
6. Individuals and groups who are instrumental to the goal setting
   process should provide for the open flow of information.
7. The individual school should be the base of operation for bringing
   people together.
8. In the process of determining philosophy, goals and objectives,
   opinion must be balanced with fact.
9. The interaction process must begin with the concerns which have
   high priority for the people involved.
10. The governing board should commit the resources necessary to see
    the goal setting process through to a satisfactory conclusion; board
    members should be encouraged to participate in the interaction
    process, not as board members, but as private citizens.
11. Teachers, administrators, and classified employees should honor
    their responsibility to the community by taking an active part in
    the goal setting process.
12. A variety of meetings should be held as a part of the goal setting
    process; mixed groups assist consensus building.
13. Inasmuch as the learning process is recognized as being dynamic
    and individualistic, any objectives of education that are established
    should not be so specific or restrictive as to pre-program the
    learning process for any student.
14. To ensure that the philosophy, goals and objectives of public
    education continue to be relevant, a recycling process should be
    designed.
15. The goal setting and planning process should result in observable
    action.

MAJOR ISSUES AND PROBLEMS

ARE SCHOOL GOALS AND OBJECTIVES REALLY FUNCTIONAL?

It would seem that there is no lack of ideas or methods for developing or revising school goals and objectives. In addition, there is a strong professional norm which encourages, if not pressures, people into goal development. As Larson notes, "Goal setting is a time honored organizational activity. . . . Rarely does one encounter an organization that doesn't have a list of goals."[7]

A major problem, however, is that most schools' educational goals or objectives don't seem to provide much direction and a basis for decision-making by those who are associated with the school.[8] It is almost as though goals or objectives are an entity in themselves, existing outside of the reality of what really occurs in a school. Their place seems to be in a handbook or curriculum guide, and their main value seems to be as a showpiece during an accreditation evaluation or to a group of visitors. Unfortunately, school goals and objectives also don't appear to be used very often as a basis for resource allocation or for evaluating school programs.[9] Whether or not their lack of value is an inherent characteristic is debatable, but there seems to be little doubt that, for the most part, they fail to exert a major impact on what goes on in a school.[10]

One important study which shed some light on the question of why more useful educational objectives and goals are not developed was conducted by Larson. He found that there were essentially four reasons why efforts to set functional school goals and objectives have frequently failed:[11]

1. Goal setting was seen by most teachers as an isolated effort, just another one-shot activity on the long list of educational "fads." The predominant attitude [by teachers] was that goal setting was just another fruitless experience.
2. When professional staff did discuss goals seriously, it was with decidedly "here and now" rather than with a future-oriented attitude. Purposes of education were rarely grappled with, an observation substantiated by the fact that in no school were any additions made to the original list of educational goals.
3. Educational personnel were reluctant to rank goals, despite pressures upon schools to sort out priorities. Educators felt strongly that all eighteen goals were important if schools were to fulfill their societal mission.
4. Rating the performance of current programs relative to goals was avoided.

The typical end result of this kind of goal setting is the development of educational goals or objectives that are ambiguous in nature, thereby providing little direction to and generating little commitment by the people who work in the school organization. While it might seem that the remedy to this situation might be greater concentration on making the goals and objectives more definitive (and this aspect will be addressed later), it has been pointed out by March and his colleagues that goal ambiguity may be an *intentional* condition which is sought, or at least permitted, in order to provide greater freedom of choice to those people who work in the organization and to make evaluation of the achievement of educational goals and objectives more difficult.[12] If this is true, then such goals become dysfunctional in terms of the original organizational purpose in generating them, but they may become very functional in meeting the needs of certain people in the organization. In this kind of a situation, goal substitution and goal displacement generally occur.[13]

If school goals or objectives are to become more functional in improving the educational program, it seems clear that the school administrator will need to devote greater efforts to involving the professional staff and relevant others in meaningful decision-making about school goals, and providing better in-service education to help the staff acquire the necessary skills for implementing the goals. (For additional guidelines on how to accomplish this, see Gorton.[14]) The primary purpose of this effort is to develop staff commitment to the goals or objectives. Without commitment, the staff is likely to be satisfied with or even desire goal ambiguity and is unlikely to try to utilize the goals or objectives in planning and evaluating school programs.

WHICH OBJECTIVES SHOULD BE INCLUDED?

Herbert Spencer alluded to the question of which educational objectives should be included in the school's program when he asked in 1880, "What knowledge is of the most worth?"[15] Since that time, and undoubtedly even before then, educators and others have debated the question. Over the years, there has developed rather general agreement that the schools should teach the basic skills of reading, writing, and arithmetic, and the ideas contained in certain subject matter disciplines, such as history and science; but there appears to be little consensus on what else is "basic," and how much emphasis and time should be given to the achievement of various objectives.[16] Therefore the debate continues, ebbing and flowing with the latest social pressures and needs.

A major issue which the administrator will probably face in responding to the question of, "What knowledge is of the most worth?" is whether a school's objectives should be limited to developing students' skills and knowledge, or whether the school should try to enlarge its mission to include the teaching of attitudes and values. As the administrator reviews the various proposed goals and roles of the school presented in the previous chapter, she will note that in most instances a broad and comprehensive role and set of objectives are recommended for the school. And yet, the administrator will probably meet resistance and opposition from particular individuals and groups if she attempts to move the school in the direction of teaching attitudes and values, particularly in a period of concern about student achievement.

For example, some people may question whether the school *should* teach values and attitudes to students. Frequently, this inquiry will be raised in the context of doubt as to whether there is a consensus on the values and attitudes which should be taught, but concern may also be expressed about whether the school knows *how* to teach attitudes and values, such as compassion or integrity.[17] This is a particularly relevant concern, since there is evidence to suggest that many teachers themselves have difficulty in thinking and reasoning about values and morals.[18] These questions raise legitimate issues which require discussion and analysis. However, what needs to be recognized is that the school already teaches values and attitudes, whether or not it intentionally sets out to do so. As Charles Silberman notes:

> And children are taught a lot of lessons about values, ethics, morality, character, and conduct every day of the week, less by the content of the curriculum than by the way schools are organized, the way teachers and parents behave, the way they talk to children and to each other, the kinds of behavior they approve or reward, and the kinds they disapprove or punish. These lessons are far more powerful than the verbalizations that accompany them and that they frequently controvert.[19]

Silberman's observations suggest that the school *does* teach attitudes and values to students, regardless of whether or not explicit objectives and an organized program exist. While there may remain legitimate concerns on the part of educators about how one can teach attitudes and values, there is really no lack of materials and approaches for developing these student characteristics.*

A more serious objection to the school's teaching of attitudes and values is the disagreement over which attitudes and values the school should emphasize. For instance, anthropologist George Spindler has found in his studies of the American culture that a new set of values has surfaced. He calls these "emergent values," and sees a possible conflict between them and the more traditional values that have been espoused in our country.[20] (See the list of traditional and emergent values presented in chapter 1). Spindler has discovered that many communities comprise a mixture of people holding traditional and emergent values, and that such conditions are responsible for many of the conflicts between the school and the community.

---

*For example, see Vincent Presno and Carol Presno, *The Value Realms: Activities for Helping Children Develop Values* (New York City: Teachers College Press, 1980). Also see John Church, *Values Programs;* 440 Bret Harte Road, Sacramento, Calif.

Complicating the problem of achieving agreement on specific attitudes and values that the school should teach is the diversity of cultures and life-styles that can be found in any particular community. Differences in ethnic and racial background, social class, and other personal and social factors all compound the school administrator's difficulty in trying to secure consensus on the attitudes and values that the school should teach to students.[21] (Nevertheless, despite these obstacles the administrator should recognize that there is a considerable consensus that parents do want some type of education for their children in this area, as evidenced by the fact that in a Gallup Poll, 79 percent of the parents surveyed were in favor of instruction in the schools on morals and moral behavior.[22])

In attempting to resolve these problems the administrator and staff would appear to have available at least four main alternatives.[23] (1) They may choose to resolve the problems and issues by focusing on those values which represent dominant values in the local community, (an approach for accomplishing this is described by Thomas and Melvin[24]), ignoring the possibility that a number of students may not stay in the local community; (2) the choice may be made to focus on more generalized values which transcend the local community; (3) they may choose to involve students in an analysis of a variety of values for the purpose of helping students to select those values which are best for them, or (4) the administrator and staff may choose to do nothing. Clearly, staff and community involvement and in-service will be essential if the first three alternatives are to succeed.

While each of these alternatives needs to be examined carefully for its consequences and implications, the administrator cannot avoid a decision in this matter. Even deciding to choose alternative four is a decision to maintain the status quo. This probably means that, although the school will not focus in any explicit way on attitudinal or value objectives, it will continue to "teach" attitudes and values in the ways Silberman noted. Whichever decision is made, it would seem that the question of whether or not a school should concern itself with values and attitudes cannot easily be avoided.

HOW SHOULD SCHOOL OBJECTIVES BE STATED?

In recent years, the question of how school objectives should be stated has become an issue in American education. Ideally, they should be stated clearly so that they communicate and in terms which facilitate the evaluation of progress or achievement. This suggests that school objectives should be operationalized and defined in behavioral terms as recommended by Mager.[25] And yet, the administrator needs to be aware that there continues to be debate on the part of some people about the issue of behaviorally-stated objectives.[26]

Those opposed to behaviorally-stated objectives usually put forth the following arguments:

1. Some objectives are impossible to state in behavioral terms. (The examples used are typically in the affective learning domain.)
2. There are certain objectives that, even if they could be stated in behavioral terms, could not be measured because there are no evaluation techniques available. (Again, the examples used are typically from the affective learning domain.)
3. By emphasizing behaviorally-stated objectives, which are usually developed prior to interaction with the learner, the educator fails to utilize the interests and insights of the learner in developing the objectives, and may easily overlook or ignore objectives which arise spontaneously out of a learning situation for which there was no previously stated goal.
4. The process of operationalizing an objective, i.e., stating it in behavioral terms, is a sterile, mechanistic approach which tends to focus one's efforts on measurable aspects of learning at the cost of ignoring humanistic elements of education.

While it is conceded that these are important concerns, further analysis indicates flaws in the arguments used by those opposed to behaviorally stated objectives.[27] For example, a careful examination of the first two objections to behaviorally-stated objectives would suggest that they are based, for the most part, on inadequate skill or knowledge. While there may be exceptions, the vast majority of objectives in education can be stated behaviorally, and progress or accomplishment can be measured in some reasonable manner.* Therefore, the first two arguments against behavioral objectives should not be posed by an administrator as insurmountable obstacles to defining school objectives in behavioral terms.

Possibly the strongest argument against the use of behavioral objectives is the potential problem resulting from lack of student involvement. Although there is no reason why behavioral objectives could not be developed with the involvement of the learner, this has generally not been the case. Most behaviorally-stated objectives are developed by educators with little or no involvement of the learners who will be expected to achieve the objectives. It should be noted, however, that this characteristic is not unique to behaviorally-stated objectives; it is true of most school goals and objectives, whether or not they are stated in behavioral terms. Whether students *should* be involved in the

---

*For help in this area see Lorin W. Anderson, *Assessing Affective Characteristics in the Schools* (Rockleigh, N.J.: Allyn and Bacon, 1981). Also see Oscar K. Buros, ed., *The Eighth Mental Measurement Yearbook* (Lincoln, Nebr.: University of Nebraska Press, 1978). Also see *Measuring and Attaining the Goals of Education* (Alexandria, Va.: Association for Supervision and Curriculum Development, 1980).

development of school goals and objectives is a separate issue. However, there is nothing inherent in the behavioral objectives approach which precludes student input in their development.

Finally, it may be true that, by developing a behaviorally-stated objective, the achievement of which can be measured, there may be a tendency to overlook or ignore important outcomes which might arise spontaneously from a learning situation for which there were no previously stated goals. It is also possible that the operationalizing of objectives may tend to focus one's efforts on the more measurable aspects of learning to the neglect of education's more humanistic elements. These are not inevitable or predictable consequences of behaviorally-stated objectives, but they are potentialities which the administrator and staff must consider. The resolution of these problems, however, does not lie in the rejection of behaviorally-stated objectives, and reliance on objectives which *cannot* be measured or that arise spontaneously out of a classroom situation (since they may not arise spontaneously). Instead, there should be an awareness by the administrator and staff of potential limitations in the use of behavioral objectives, and a flexibility that will permit the adjustment of objectives when problems occur.

The basic case for behaviorally-stated objectives is that, in contrast to non-behaviorally-stated objectives, the accomplishment of the former can be more easily evaluated while the latter frequently cannot be evaluated at all, or only with great difficulty. Therefore, rather than engaging in nonproductive arguments about whether objectives should or can be stated in behavioral terms, it would appear that the essential task for administrators and others is to address themselves to the process of trying to operationalize school objectives. In pursuing this essential task the administrator should work closely with the professional staff, who (it should be noted) may be ambivalent about the need to develop behaviorally-stated objectives. Still, there are effective ways of working with the staff on this matter, and the school administrator should utilize whatever resources are available.[28] (For an excellent review of research on the effectiveness of behavioral objectives, see the March, 1981, issue of *Educational Technology*.)

WHO SHOULD BE HELD ACCOUNTABLE
FOR ACHIEVING EDUCATIONAL OBJECTIVES?

Accountability has been and continues to be the most controversial and potentially explosive issue concerning school objectives. Simply defined in the context of school objectives, accountability means that *somebody* accepts the responsibility for not only developing and trying to achieve certain educational objectives, but also the negative or positive consequences of failing or succeeding in the achievement of those objectives.[29] For example, under the concept of accountability, it would not be sufficient for a school administrator and staff to *develop* school objectives; both would also be responsible in large part for achieving them and incurring the consequences of the extent of their attainment. An earlier but still relevant illustration of the concept of accountability is presented in figure 2.3.

RECALLED FOR REVISION

By William C. Miller

Many of us who own recent model automobiles have received a communication from the factory, asking us to return the vehicle to the dealer so that defects can be corrected. Although I have gotten used to call-backs initiated by car manufacturers, I must admit I was startled to receive the following letter from my son's high school:

EDSEL MEMORIAL HIGH SCHOOL

. . . . .Anywhere, U.S.A.

August 1, 19

Dear Parents of our Graduates:

As you are aware, one of your offspring was graduated from our high school this June. Since that time it has been brought to our attention that certain insufficiencies are present in our graduates, so we are recalling all students for further education.

We have learned that in the process of the instruction we provided we forgot to install one or more of the following:

. . . at least one salable skill;
. . . a comprehensive and utilitarian set of values;
. . . a readiness for and understanding of the responsibilities of citizenship.

A recent consumer study consisting of follow-up of our graduates has revealed that many of them have been released with defective parts. Racism and materialism are serious flaws and we have discovered they are a part of the makeup of almost all our products. These defects have been determined to be of such magnitude that the model produced in June is considered highly dangerous and should be removed from circulation as a hazard to the nation.

Some of the equipment which was in the past classified as optional has been reclassified as standard and should be a part of every product of our school.

(continued)

Figure 2.3.

Therefore, we plan to equip each graduate with:

. . . a desire to continue to learn;

. . . a dedication to solving problems of local, national, and international concern;

. . . several productive ways to use leisure time;

. . . a commitment to the democratic way of life;

. . . extensive contact with the world outside the school;

. . . experience in making decisions.

In addition, we found we had inadvertently removed from your child his interest, enthusiasm, motivation, trust, and joy. We are sorry to report that these items have been mislaid and have not been turned in at the school Lost and Found Department. If you will inform us as to the value you place on these qualities, we will reimburse you promptly by check or cash.

As you can see, it is to your interest, and vitally necessary for your safety and the welfare of all, that graduates be returned so that these errors and over-sights can be corrected. We admit that it would have been more effective and less costly in time and money to have produced the product correctly in the first place, but we hope you will forgive our error and continue to respect and support your public schools.

Sincerely,

P. Dantic, Principal

Reprinted by permission of Phi Delta Kappa Inc., December 1971.

Figure 2.3. Continued

The movement for school accountability developed in the late 1960s from dissatisfaction on the part of increasing numbers of people in regard to the kind of product (i.e., the student) emerging from the school.[30] Until the latter 70s the primary thrust in the accountability movement was directed at getting school educators—teachers and administrators—to accept greater responsibility for improving the education of students. Educators responded to pressures for greater accountability in a variety of ways, ranging from rejection of the notion that the schools are responsible for any more than providing an *opportunity* for students to learn, to specification of their responsibilities for the achievement of school objectives.[31]

Recently the emphasis in the accountability issue has broadened to include a greater stress on student and parent accountability for the achievement of educational objectives.[32] In the case of parents, this has taken the form of greater efforts by the school to have parents accept more responsibility for monitoring their child's learning and providing better study conditions in the home.* To promote greater accountability by students, a large number of schools and states have developed competency-based educational programs and minimum competency testing programs which students must pass or be retained in the same grade.[33] These programs have been attacked on several fronts.[34] The competency-based educational programs which tend to emphasize, although are not limited to the development of basic skills have been criticized because they ". . . seem destined to divert a significant amount of energy and intelligence away from other more important educational concerns—such as how to make the schools more responsive to the needs of children as children, not children as adults."[35] Minimum competency testing has also come under attack, and there have been charges that the tests are biased, that the school's educational program is not preparing students adequately in order to pass the tests,[36] and perhaps of greatest importance, that minimum competency testing tends to shift the responsibility and accountability for student failure from the school to the student.[37] However, it is worth noting that both opponents and proponents of minimum competency testing agree on several basic points:[38] (1) the practice of social promotion of students is not desirable, (2) testing of students could be useful, (3) a test should not be the only criterion for awarding or denying a high school diploma, (4) the use of competency testing should be phased in over several years, and (5) students who fail the test should be given remedial help and should be provided with several opportunities to pass the test. (A description of various remedial programs is presented in *Education and Urban Society,* November, 1979.)

As the accountability movement has taken different turns and directions, the *basic* issue remains the same and can be stated in three brief questions: Who is accountable? For what? And to whom? While several answers might be given to the first question, the author's position is that accountability for the achievement of educational objectives is—or *should* be—a *shared* responsibility among educators, students, parents, governmental agencies, and the general public. A problem we have experienced in education, however, is that most individuals and groups stress the accountability of the *other* parties while underplaying their own accountability. It would seem that if the concept of accountability is ever going to result in major *positive* changes in education, each group will need to put forth greater efforts to understand and accept its own accountability for the achievement of school objectives, while placing less emphasis on trying to make other groups more accountable.

At this point the reader may be asking, "But what is the basis of the school administrator's accountability?" In the American system of education the local

---

*A good example is a "contract" plan developed in Oakland, California, which involves the parents, school officials, and the student, who agree to perform certain responsibilities in regard to the achievement of educational objectives.

school is a creation of the state, which has delegated certain broad responsibilities and authority to the local school board, elected by the community. In order to accomplish the objectives of the school district, the school board delegates certain responsibilities to the administrators of the district. Therefore, in a real sense, a school administrator can and should be held accountable to the members of the school board, who in turn can and should be held accountable to their constituents, and to the state that gave them a charter and form of organization.

The question of *what* the school (or more specifically, the administrator and the staff) is accountable for is less easily answered. It could be asserted that the staff and the administrator should be held accountable for achieving the educational objectives which the school has set forth. However, this position has been challenged on two grounds: (1) that there are many variables over which the staff and the administrator have little or no control, e.g., home environment of the student, which may affect the achievement of the school's educational goals, and (2) that the accomplishment of many of the school's objectives is a shared responsibility with other agencies or institutions in society, such as the family, and that the staff and administrator should not be held totally accountable for the achievement of school goals.[39]

Although both of these arguments are valid to a point, they leave unresolved the basic issue of the *degree to which* the administrator and staff should be held accountable. If, in fact, the achievement of school objectives depends on many variables over which the administrator and staff have little or no control, does this mean that neither should be held accountable at *all* for the achievement of school objectives? Obviously not, but researchers, educational theorists, and other educators have not been very helpful in identifying *the extent* to which the administrator and staff should be held accountable.*

And if the achievement of many educational objectives is a shared responsibility, what *specifically* is the staff's and school administrator's share, as compared to that of other agencies of society? All too frequently when the argument of shared responsibility is advanced, the end result is that *no one* takes responsibility or accepts accountability for achieving a particular objective. The concept of shared responsibility has merit if it leads to efforts to coordinate resources and activities. But too often, when proposed, it fails to affix a specific degree of accountability to the parties who are responsible for achieving the objective.

Although a definitive answer has not been developed by the education profession (to say nothing of society) to the question of *what* the school should

---

*It should be noted that recent evidence has been developed which seems to suggest that the school may have more significant impact on student learning than was asserted several years ago. For a review of some of this evidence, see Harold Hodgekinson, "What's Right With Education," *The Kappan* (November, 1979), 159–62. Also see pp. 179–83 in the same issue.

be held accountable for, recent research on school effectiveness has identified a number of factors associated with pupil achievement, which merit consideration.[40] These factors are:

- Strong administrative and instructional leadership
- A climate in which administrators and teachers set high standards for students and for themselves.
- An orderly but unoppressive atmosphere
- A high priority given to pupil achievement over other activities
- Redirection of school resources to basic instruction and curriculum
- Frequent monitoring and reinforcing of pupil progress.

Each of these school effectiveness factors is largely under the control of the school, and it seems reasonable to hold a school accountable for its presence. Therefore, each of the effectiveness factors will be discussed in considerable detail in later chapters, e.g., Chapter 11, Instructional Leadership.

It is important that the educators in a school think through their own position on the issue of accountability. In general, it would appear that if the administrator and staff are going to establish certain educational objectives, they should be held accountable for their achievement. If particular conditions will affect the degree to which those objectives can be achieved, then the staff and the administrator have the responsibility of taking this into consideration in stating the objectives.

In regard to the school administrator's own accountability, it would seem that, in addition to being responsible for carrying out the typical duties assigned, she should also be held accountable for:

1. Identifying and clearly defining, with the help of others, the educational objectives of the school.
2. Specifying which teaching, supervisory, or administrative procedures and resources are needed in order to achieve those objectives.
3. Developing and implementing a plan for evaluating the extent of progress or achievement of the school's objectives.
4. Informing the school board and the community periodically about the degree to which objectives have been achieved, and the reasons for problems, if they occur.

The entire issue of accountability is an emotionally charged one. Undoubtedly, several significant factors should be considered in limiting the degree of the staff's and the school administrator's accountability. However, these factors should not be weighed so heavily that they become an argument for avoiding accountability completely or for avoiding the responsibility of making explicit the *extent* to which the staff or the school administrator should be accountable. In a true sense, the extent to which one is willing to be held accountable for achieving an objective is a valid indicator of the degree to which she has a real commitment to achieving that objective, as opposed to merely giving lip service to its importance.

EVALUATING EFFORTS TO ESTABLISH AND IMPLEMENT SCHOOL OBJECTIVES

The end product which should result from consideration and resolution of the various issues and problems discussed in this chapter is the establishment of a set of educational objectives or aims to which the school is committed and which it is prepared to implement. To aid the administrator in evaluating the strengths and weaknesses of the school's educational objectives and plan for implementation, specific criteria stated in question form are presented as follows:

Criteria Questions for Assessing the School's Efforts in Establishing, Implementing, and Evaluating School Objectives

1. Do the school's objectives reflect and maintain an appropriate balance between the needs of the individual and those of society?
2. Are the school's objectives comprehensive, rather than restricted to knowledge and skill outcomes? Is the development of student interests, attitudes, and values also included in the objectives of the school?
3. Does the school make clear which objectives are its sole or primary responsibility and which objectives it shares with other institutions? If the school shares a responsibility with other institutions, does it make explicit the *extent* to which *it* is responsible?
4. Do the school's objectives focus on *student outcomes* rather than school functions, activities, or processes?
5. Are the school's objectives stated clearly and in terms which facilitate the evaluation of progress or achievement?
6. Does the statement of each school objective indicate
   a. the proposed *level* of performance?
   b. *when* the objective will be achieved?
7. Do the school objectives take into consideration individual differences among students as to backgrounds, abilities, interests, and aspirations?
8. Is there a school plan for the continuous development of understanding of and commitment to the objectives on the part of students, teachers, parents, and important others?
9. Is there a formal plan for periodic and systematic evaluation of progress toward or achievement of the school's objectives?

10. Are the objectives re-examined periodically (every two or three years would be desirable) to see whether modification, elimination, or the addition of new objectives is needed?

In too many schools, objectives are developed, published in the school district's or teacher's handbook and remain there year after year, without critical examination as to their relevancy or accomplishment. Utilization of criteria presented in the statement above should help the school administrator maintain a set of relevant and appropriate objectives whose achievement is evaluated.

However in carrying out an examination of a school's efforts in establishing, implementing, and evaluating its objectives, it would be well for the administrator to be aware of certain potentially negative consequences suggested by Larson:[41]

1. Assessing effectiveness and efficiency on the basis of goal attainment may be misleading because multiple goals may be in conflict and hence, inhibit single goal realization.
2. Frequent measurement of goal attainment may lead to an emphasis on more quantitative as opposed to important but more difficult to measure qualitative type goals.
3. Unanticipated demands on an organization may require energy and resources to be expended on problem solving which, although necessary for survival, may not be directly related to any goal.
4. Unless goals are occasionally updated, public or official goals may, over time, be succeeded by new goals which, although important, may not be stated and thus may escape assessment. In such a situation it may seem that the organization is not performing effectively.
5. A commitment on official goals that is too narrowly focused may inhibit the organization from adopting new goals which may be more appropriate for its mission.
6. Overemphasis on attainment of certain goals may divert resources from other vital organizational functions which may not be as clearly linked with the stated goals (e.g., in-service education for staff may be neglected in favor of the official goal of instructional improvement). Also, official goals can divert management's attention from the more immediate personal needs of employees. Personnel relationships are seldom a publicly stated goal, yet failure to attend to them can lead to serious internal motivation and morale problems.

7. Certain goals, although societally sanctioned, may, if publicly pronounced, be unpalatable to segments of the clientele served (e.g., the socialization function of education versus the 3 R's). An unproductive conflict may result which will inhibit the attainment of related goals.

A FINAL COMMENT

It should be emphasized that the administrator must take the initiative to utilize the ideas presented in this chapter (in cooperation with others associated with the school, e.g., teachers, parents) if the formulation and evaluation of achievement of school objectives are to be improved. It will be easy for an administrator to feel that she is too busy to engage in such efforts and that there are other priorities which demand attention. Certainly, the school administrator's job is a demanding one, and there are many problems and issues that compete for her time. However, the development and evaluation of school objectives may very well be the most important task which the administrator can perform, since the objectives chart the direction that education should take in a school.

Review and Learning Activities

1. What are the main organizational and social factors an administrator needs to take into consideration in the development of school objectives?
2. Identify the groups an administrator should involve in the development of school objectives. What contribution can each group be expected to make?
3. What are the major problems and obstacles to developing functional school goals and objectives? What are the implications for the administrator of these possible problems and obstacles?
4. What are the major factors that an administrator needs to consider in resolving the issue of whether or not the school should include in its objectives the teaching of values and attitudes? Now, choose a position and defend it.
5. State the arguments for and against behaviorally defined school objectives.
6. To what extent should the school and the school administrator be held accountable? What are the implications of your position on this matter?

Notes

1. Thomas J. Sergiovanni, et al., *Educational Governance and Administration* (Englewood Cliffs, N.J.: Prentice Hall, 1980), p. 129.

2. Ibid., pp. 130–44.

3. Olaf Helmer and Norman Dalkey, "An Experimental Application of the Delphi Method in the Use of Experts," *Management Science* (April 1963): 458–67.

4. Arlene Hartman, "Reaching Consensus Using the Delphi Technique," *Educational Leadership* (March 1981): 495–97.

5. Norman Hale, "Problem-Solving Techniques for Administrators." An ERIC Report: Ed–151–894. Also see Beverly Carver, "NGT Modified Delphi Technique: Convergence Patterns in Educational Goal Development" (Ph.D. diss., Arizona State University, 1980).

6. Joint Committee on Educational Goals and Evaluation, *Education for the People I,* Guidelines for Total Community Participation in Forming and Strengthening the Future of Public Elementary and Secondary Education in California" (Sacramento: California Legislature, 1972): 21–26.

7. Robert Larson, *Goal Setting in Planning: Myths and Realities* (Burlington, Vt.: Center for Research, University of Vermont, 1980), pp. 1–2.

8. National Institute of Education, *Decision-Making in Educational Organizations.* An ERIC Report: Ed–131–551.

9. Leroy V. Sloan, "Operative vs. Official Goals in Assessing the Effectiveness of Educational Systems." Paper presented at the American Educational Research Association, annual meeting, Los Angeles, 1981.

10. Larson, *Goal Setting in Planning.*

11. Ibid., 18–20.

12. For further discussion of this problem in organizations, see James G. Marsh and Johan P. Olson, *Ambiguity and Choice in Organizations* (Norway: Harold Lyche, 1976).

13. For this problem and others related to goal setting, see Sloan, "Operative vs. Official Goals."

14. Richard A. Gorton, *School Administration and Supervision: Important Issues, Concepts and Case Studies* (Dubuque, Iowa: Wm. C. Brown Company Publishers, 1980), pp. 240–48.

15. Herbert Spencer, *Education* (New York City: D. Appleton and Co., 1880), p. 32.

16. *Critical Issues in Educational Policy Making,* ed. Louis Rubin (Boston: Allyn & Bacon, 1980), p. 408.

17. For a review of these views and the literature on teaching values, see Jack R. Fraenkel, "Goals for Teaching Values and Value Analysis," *Journal of Research and Development in Education* (1980): 93–102.

18. Robert A. Wilkins, "If the Moral Reasoning of Teachers Is Deficient, What Hope for Pupils?" *The Kappan* (April 1980): 548–49.

19. Charles Silberman, *Crisis in the Classroom* (New York: Random House, 1970), p. 9.

20. George D. Spindler, "Education in a Transforming American Culture," *Harvard Educational Review* (Summer 1955): 145–56.

21. R. Pratte, "Cultural Pluralism: Can It Work?" *Theory into Practice* (Winter 1981): 1–72.

22. George H. Gallup, "Gallup Poll of the Public's Attitudes toward the Public Schools," *The Kappan* (September 1980): 39.

23. For an excellent and still relevant discussion of the problem and these four alternatives, see George E. Artelle, "How Do We Know What Values Are Best?" *Progressive Education* (April 1950): 191–95.

24. M. Donald Thomas and Arthur Melvin, "Community Consensus Is Available on a Moral Valuing Standard," *The Kappan* (March 1981): 479–83. Also see Suzanne Burkholder, et. al., "Values, the Key to a Community," *The Kappan* (March 1981): 483–85.

25. Robert Mager, *Preparing Instructional Objectives,* 2nd ed. (Belmont, Calif.: Pitman Learning, 1975).

26. For a good review of this ongoing debate, see Henry A. Giroux, "Overcoming Behavioral and Humanistic Objectives," *The Education Forum* (May 1979): 409–19.

27. J. R. Calder, "In Defense of the Systematic Approach to Instruction and Behavioral Objectives," *Educational Technology* (May 1980): 21–25.

28. For example, see *Educational Goals and Objectives: A Model Program for Community and Professional Involvement* (Bloomington, Ind.: Phi Delta Kappa, Commission on Educational Planning).

29. S. Allen, "Accountability Revisited," *Education Canada* (Winter 1980): 30–34.

30. Leon M. Lessinger, "Accountability for Results: A Basic Challenge for American Schools," *American Education* (June/July 1969).

31. A. Silberman, "Accountability: A Horror Story," *Instructor* (November 1977): 28.

32. See Richard M. Jaeger and Carol Kehr Title, *Minimum Competency Achievement Testing* (Berkeley, Calif.: McCutchan, 1979), Part I.

33. For a description of several of these, see Jaeger and Title, ibid., Part IV.

34. "Competency Evaluations Don't Pass the Test," *Education U.S.A.* (June 1979): 323, 328. Also see William Habermehl, "Competency-Based Education—Will It Rob Peter to Pay Paul?" *NASSP Bulletin* (November 1980): 54–57.

35. John H. Sandberg, "K-12 Competency-Based Education Comes to Pennsylvania," *The Kappan* (October 1979): 119–20.

36. "Debra P.: The End of Competency Testing." *Education U.S.A.* (May 25, 1981): 309.

37. M. S. McClung, "Are Competency Testing Programs Fair? Legal?" *The Kappan* (February 1978): 397–400.

38. "Testing Trial Gives Competencies Passing Score," *Education USA* (July 20, 1981): 357, 362.

39. J. F. Newport, "Who's Kidding Whom? The Feasibility of Accountability Programs," *School and Community* (October 1977): 10.

40. Michael Cohen, "Effective Schools: Accumulating Research Findings," *American Education* (Jan./Feb. 1982): 13–16. Also see *Why Do Some Urban Schools Succeed?* (Bloomington, Ind.: Phi Delta Kappa, 1980) and Cindy Tursman, *Good Schools: What Makes Them Work?* (Arlington, Va.: National School Public Relations Association, 1980).

41. Larson, *Goal Setting in Planning*, 3–4.

PART

2

DIMENSIONS OF ADMINISTRATION

3

THE SCHOOL ADMINISTRATOR
Tasks and Administrative Process

The goals and objectives discussed in chapters 1 and 2 represent the desired outcomes of education in a school. However, these outcomes are not likely to materialize without the organization and administration of human and physical resources. The essential job of the administrator is to organize and administer these resources efficiently and effectively so that the school objectives can be successfully achieved. This will involve an administrator in the performance of many administrative tasks and in the utilization of an administrative process. The following sections will present an introduction to the tasks and process.

ADMINISTRATIVE TASK AREAS

Figure 3.1 presents an overview of administrative task areas and examples of their component activities, based on a synthesis of several studies concerned with identifying the major activities of the school administrator.[1]

I. Staff Personnel

A. Help formulate staff personnel policies.
B. Recruit staff personnel; attract able people to the school staff.
C. Select and assign staff personnel.
D. Schedule teachers' assignments.

E. Communicate the objectives of the school program to the faculty.
F. Observe teachers in their classrooms.
G. Diagnose the strengths and weaknesses of teachers.

(continued)

Figure 3.1. Major Task Areas in School Administration

H. Help resolve the classroom problems of teachers.
I. Evaluate the performance of teachers.
J. Improve the performance of teachers.
K. Coordinate the work of teachers.
L. Stimulate and provide opportunities for professional growth of staff personnel.
M. Maximize the different skills found in a faculty.
N. Develop *esprit de corps* among teachers.

II. Pupil Personnel

A. Provide guidance services.
B. Institute procedures for the orientation of pupils.
C. Establish school attendance policy and procedures.
D. Establish policy and procedures for dealing with pupil conduct problems.
E. Establish policy and procedures in regard to pupil safety in the building and on the school grounds.
F. Develop and coordinate the extracurricular program.
G. Handle disciplinary cases.
H. Arrange systematic procedures for the continual assessment and reporting of pupil performance.
I. Confer with juvenile court, police agencies, etc.

III. Community-School Leadership

A. Develop and administer policies and procedures for parent and community participation in the schools.
B. Confer with parents.
C. Handle parental complaints.
D. Assist PTA and other parent groups.
E. Represent the school in participation in community organizations.
F. Cooperate with other community agencies.

G. Make possible the continual reexamination of acceptable plans and policies for community improvement with particular reference to the services which the schools are rendering.

IV. Instruction and Curriculum Development

A. Help formulate curriculum objectives.
B. Help determine curriculum content and organization.
C. Relate the desired curriculum to available time, physical facilities and personnel.
D. Provide materials, resources, and equipment for the instructional program.
E. Provide for the supervision of instruction.
F. Provide for in-service education of instructional personnel.

V. School Finance and Business Management

A. Prepare school budget at local school level.
B. Provide for a system of internal accounting.
C. Administer school purchasing.
D. Account for school monies.
E. Account for school property.
F. Keep the school office running smoothly.

VI. School Plant

A. Determine the physical plant needs of the community and the resources which can be marshalled to meet those needs.
B. Develop a comprehensive plan for the orderly growth and improvement of school plant facilities.
C. Implement plans for the orderly growth and improvement of school plant facilities.

(continued)

Figure 3.1. Continued

D. Develop an efficient program of operation and maintenance of the physical plant.

E. Supervise the custodial staff.

VII. **General Tasks**

A. Organize and conduct meetings or conferences.

B. Handle delicate interpersonal situations.

C. Direct the work of administrative assistants.

D. Publicize the work of the school.

E. Diagnose the strengths and weaknesses of the school program.

F. Attend school functions, such as assemblies, plays, athletic contests.

G. Respond to correspondence.

H. Prepare reports for the district administration.

I. Attend principals' meetings.

J. Keep school records.

K. Schedule school programs.

Figure 3.1. Continued

It should be pointed out that in most situations one administrator is not solely responsible for carrying out all of the activities listed in figure 3.1. Many of these responsibilities are shared between two or more administrators at the building level, or with other administrative or supervisory personnel at the district office. However, the school administrator is either actually involved in carrying out most of the activities in figure 3.1, or is responsible for making sure the tasks are implemented if the activities have been delegated to someone else. Because the task areas of school administration are so important, an in-depth examination of each of them will be taken up in later chapters.

ADMINISTRATIVE PROCESS: BASIC ELEMENTS

Henri Fayol is generally regarded as the father of the administrative process. In his book, *General and Industrial Management,* he identified and defined the basic elements which he believed made up the process.[2] Later, Gulick and Urwick adapted Fayol's conceptualization to the job of the chief executive,[3] and other writers on administration have attempted to refine or further elaborate the process.[4]

The administrative process consists of the methods which an administrator utilizes to achieve specific tasks and objectives. Writers vary as to the basic elements or methods which they include in the process, but the author of this text believes, based on an examination of the literature, that the thirteen elements identified in figure 3.2 make up the administrative process.

With a thorough understanding of all the elements in figure 3.2 and with appropriate application of those elements, an administrator should be able to accomplish administrative tasks more effectively and should experience greater

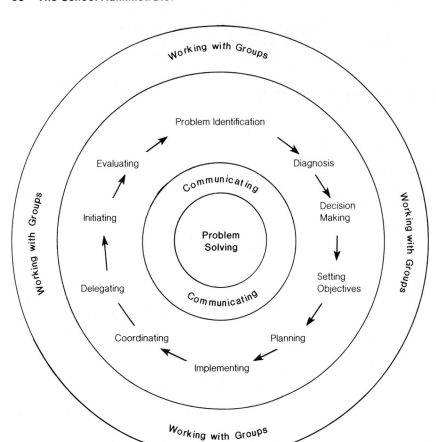

Figure 3.2. Administrative Process

success in achieving objectives. It should be emphasized that the effectiveness with which an administrator utilizes each element is greatly enhanced through the meaningful involvement of significant others, such as teachers.

Rather than trying to discuss all thirteen administrative processes in detail, since entire books have been devoted to most of them, a brief discussion of each will be presented for the purpose of establishing its functions and use. These processes will also be discussed further as they apply to the task areas examined in later chapters. In addition, most of these processes are discussed by the author in considerable depth in another text, *School Administration and Supervision: Important Concepts, Issues, and Case Studies.*[5]

PROBLEM IDENTIFICATION

There is no shortage of problems for which an administrator will be expected to provide solutions. In fact, some administrators—those on the "firing line" particularly—may feel that they need not concern themselves with identifying problems; other people, such as students, teachers, and parents will identify or present them with more problems than they may care to think about. These administrators' motto is, in essence, "Why seek trouble where none exists?" or, "Let sleeping dogs lie!"

Nevertheless, if an administrator wants to avoid going from crisis to crisis, he must begin to identify those underlying problems which will eventually manifest themselves in troublesome behavior, and he must begin to identify potential problem areas which, if not corrected, could ultimately lead to serious consequences for the school. Of course, no one is recommending that an administrator attempt to find or create problems where none exist. But neither can an administrator sit back and wait for a problem to land on his desk, since at that point the problem may have ripened into a crisis and be much more difficult to resolve. Instead, the administrator should engage in the type of behavior observed by Blumberg and Greenfield in their study of effective principals: "She doesn't wait for problems to come to her. Instead, she seeks them out."[6] The administrator who fails to engage in this kind of problem identification will probably continue to be besieged with crises which seem to come upon him suddenly and from which there appears to be no respite.

Although much has been written about the process of problem solving, comparatively little attention has been given to the process of problem identification.[7] Generally, theorists and writers have assumed that a problem already exists, and the main question is how to define and solve it. However, the author's position is that the school administrator should actually spend some of his time trying to *identify* problems of the nature described above that already exist, since without efforts by the administrator to address them, they could eventually evolve into full-blown crises.

To identify problems, the administrator needs to ask questions. Asking the right questions is the key to uncovering potential problems which, if left uncorrected, could lead to serious consequences. It should be pointed out, however, that whether the "right" questions are raised depends, at least in part, upon one's criteria for satisfaction or success, and on whether an assessment is made of performance in a specific area.

For example, if only 35 percent of the parents show up for parent-teacher conferences, the level of attendance may not be perceived as a problem by anyone unless one of the criteria for judging the success of parent-teacher conferences is attendance greater than 35 percent. In addition, if no attempt is made (by the administrator or someone else) to ascertain the percentage of parents who participate in parent-teacher conferences, people will have no basis for determining whether a problem exists. Therefore, before a problem can be identified, criteria must be established for determining whether objectives have been attained, and information must be collected to establish the degree to which the criteria were met. This will involve the administrator in asking value and evaluative questions in order to identify problems. (Mosrie describes the implementation of this process in two schools.[8])

Sample questions which illustrate the kinds of inquiries that an administrator, in cooperation with teachers, students, and parents, might pursue in attempting to identify problems are presented in figure 3.3.

To identify potential problems, then, an administrator should ask two kinds of questions: (1) How well *should* we be doing? and (2) how well *are* we doing?

Criteria Questions	Assessment Questions
A. Students	
1. What *should* be the attitude of students toward the value and usefulness of their school program?	1. What *is* the attitude of students toward the value and usefulness of their school program?
2. What *should* be the level of performance achieved by the students in the school?	2. What *is* the level of performance achieved by students in my school?
3. To what extent *should* students be developing a positive self-concept, self-initiative, and problem-solving skills?	3. To what extent *are* students developing a positive self-concept, self-initiative and problem-solving skills?
B. Teachers	
1. To what extent *should* teachers know and understand the home background and learning strengths and disabilities of their students?	1. To what extent *do* teachers know and understand the home background and learning strengths and disabilities of their students?
2. To what degree *should* teachers individualize instruction and adapt the curriculum to meet the individual needs of students?	2. To what extent *do* teachers individualize instruction and adapt the curriculum to meet the individual needs of students?
3. To what extent *should* teachers go beyond teaching skills and subject matter to developing student attitudes and values?	3. To what extent *do* teachers go beyond teaching skills and subject matter content to developing student attitudes and values?
	(continued)

Figure 3.3. Sample Problem—Identification Questions

C. Parents

1. To what degree *should* the parents understand clearly and accurately the objectives of the school and the programs and activities offered in order to reach those objectives?
2. What *should* be the extent and nature of parent participation and involvement in the school?
3. What *should* be the attitude of parents toward the school program and the professional staff?

1. To what degree *do* parents understand the objectives of the school and the programs and activities offered to reach those objectives?
2. What *is* the extent and nature of parent participation and involvement in the school?
3. What *is* the attitude of parents toward the school program and professional staff?

Figure 3.3. Continued

Of course, these questions frequently are not easy to answer, nor are the answers always pleasing to the administrator. The easiest thing for an administrator to do—at least temporarily—is to *refrain* from asking basic questions or seeking their answers, and instead proceed through the school year, hoping that nothing serious erupts, and delaying any response to a situation until trouble actually develops. Unfortunately, the consequences of this type of behavior is that the administrator seldom deals with problems until they manifest themselves in ways which are frequently difficult to resolve and, as a result, the school fails to function as well as it might. One book that should be of assistance to the school administrator who would like to improve the school's problem-solving capacity has been written by Runkel and his colleagues.[9]

DIAGNOSIS

Why are some students underachieving? Why don't more parents participate in school affairs? Why don't some teachers seem to carry out their responsibilities fully? To answer any of these questions adequately, the administrator must engage in the process of diagnosis—investigating the basic causes of a problem.[10] Diagnosis is concerned with ascertaining the underlying roots of a problem and distinguishing these from its mere symptoms or manifestations. It includes careful, thorough, and objective investigation into the conditions which have led to or created the problem. The process of diagnosis, like that of problem identification, begins with the formulation of questions.

For example, an administrator who is confronted by a growing student attendance problem, might begin his investigation by asking, "Why are so many students truant?" One immediate response to that question could be that "these students are lazy, or they don't have good habits of attendance."

Some administrators would stop at this point, satisfied that they have answered the question, and begin to try to change the students. Other administrators would continue to ask questions, seeking more fundamental causes of the students' misbehavior: "*Why* are the students lazy? *Why* don't they have good habits of punctuality? What is the home situation of these students? Is it possible that the attendance behavior of some or many of these students is affected by learning disabilities, e.g., reading problems, and would the school's cumulative records or diagnostic testing be helpful in checking out this possibility? Is the educational program that the school offers perceived by these students as relevant? Is there anyone in the school with whom these students relate well?"

These are all examples of diagnostic questions seeking the basic causes for the students' misbehavior. Whether these specific questions will uncover the root causes of the problem or whether, perhaps, other questions will need to be raised is not at the issue. The main point is that, if the school administrator is to avoid dealing with only the symptoms of problems, then he must raise questions which attempt to identify the underlying and basic causes of a situation.

The school administrator should engage in the process of diagnosis before he attempts to solve any problem or implement any task. In a sense, the administrator is asking a fundamental question: "What is *really* involved here?" Unless an administrator employs appropriate diagnosis in solving the problems of a school and carrying out his administrative tasks, he is not likely to be successful.

SETTING OBJECTIVES

Administrators who wish to be reasonably effective must set objectives, which represent the outcomes that they want to achieve, and the targets at which they are aiming.[11] The function of objectives is to give an individual or group a direction, purpose, and reason for action.

Objectives may be categorized as individual, group, or program. If, for an example, an administrator is to be productive, he must set *individual* objectives for himself. If the faculty or PTA are to capitalize on their potentialities, then the administrator should work with them in establishing *group objectives*. If the various programs or services which the school offers are to meet the needs of those who they are designed to serve, the administrator should work with the personnel who are involved in the program, helping them to define *program objectives*. Each individual, group, and program in the school should have well-defined objectives of a short and long-range nature.

The administrator needs to ask two basic questions in establishing objectives: "What should we be trying to accomplish?" and, "Have we clearly defined what we want to accomplish?" The first question is designed to stimulate thinking about what the objectives of an individual, group or program should be. The second question is intended to focus efforts on the precise specification of objectives for an individual, group, or program. In essence, the administrator, with the assistance of appropriate others associated with the school, should be trying to arrive at more appropriate and more sharply defined objectives, which can be clearly communicated and can subsequently serve as standards against which progress or achievement will be measured. (Goal setting is also discussed in chapters 2, and 20.)

DECISION MAKING

The administrator engages in decision making perhaps more often than in any other process.

Decision making is basically the process of choosing among alternatives. In most situations there exist two or more alternative courses of action, and an administrator must decide which alternative to pursue. Before making a decision, however, the administrator should engage in diagnosis in order to better understand the nature of the situation calling for a decision, and the alternatives available to him as well. Then he should assess the advantages and disadvantages of each alternative and the probabilities of success in each case. During the process of reaching a decision, an administrator should involve teachers, parents, students, central office supervisors, or others as appropriate, in order to capitalize on any special insights and expertise which they may be able to contribute.

Once a decision has been made, the administrator will need to concentrate on such other administrative processes as planning, implementing, and coordinating the decision. For an extended discussion of decision making, see *School Administration: Important Concepts, Issues and Case Studies;* the reader will also be provided with many opportunities in the remaining chapters of this text to examine and apply the process of decision making.[12]

PLANNING

Like decision making, planning partially overlaps into several other administrative processes. However, much of the planning process occurs *after* goals have been established and decisions made.

Planning is concerned primarily with the question of *how* a goal is to be achieved or a decision implemented.[13] Consideration of the following questions is involved:

1. What needs to be done?   →   *Task definition.*
2. What resources are needed   →   *Definition of resource needs* to do the job, and within   *and time parameters.* what period of time?

3. Who is competent, interested, and available to do the job?	→ *Selection of personnel.*
4. What responsibilities need to be assigned to whom?	→ *Definition and assignment of responsibility.*
5. Which tasks and people need to be related to each other in some manner?	→ *Identification of coordination needs.*
6. Who should be in authority over whom?	→ *Specification of authority relationships.*
7. Who should supervise whom and in which areas?	→ *Specification of supervisory relationships.*
8. Who should communicate with whom and about what?	→ *Specification of communication relationships.*
9. What standards will determine effectiveness?	→ *Establishment of evaluation criteria.*

The process of planning should begin with a definition of the tasks or activities needed to achieve previously approved goals and decisions, and should conclude with the determination of criteria which will be used to evaluate the extent to which the goals are achieved, or the decisions successfully implemented. Intermediate steps include specifying authority, supervisory, and communication relationships between people, and defining the resources which will be required to carry out specific tasks within a certain period of time.

IMPLEMENTING

Once a plan or program has been designed, it must be implemented. Essentially, implementing involves the administrator in the process of making sure that the plan is carried out as intended. This includes providing resources, assistance, and monitoring progress.

While many administrators may believe that once a program is planned, it will be easily implemented, there is now considerable research indicating that program implementation is frequently less than ideal.[14] Generally this is a result of failure to consider adequately one or more of the questions raised in the discussion on planning. For example, Kritek found that efforts to implement innovations typically failed because of goals that were too vague and ambitious, minimal planning to operationalize the innovation and to integrate it into the school, resources that were too limited, and failure to anticipate adequately and deal constructively with the developments that occurred after the innovation was introduced.[15]

Difficulties in implementation can also result from inadequate monitoring of progress and problems after the program has been introduced, incorrect diagnosis of problems, and inadequate efforts to resolve problems.[16] Fortunately, most of these difficulties can be avoided or reduced if the administrator anticipates them and takes corrective action before the problems become major. In anticipating the kinds of problems that could occur during implementation, the administrator would do well to remember two of Murphy's famous laws: "Most things are more complicated than they initially appear to be," and "Most things take longer than originally anticipated."

COÖRDINATING

The school administrator engages in the process of coördinating when he attempts to relate people, tasks, resources, and/or time schedules in such a way that they are mutually supplementary and complementary.[17] A potential need for coördination exists whenever two or more people, activities, resources, and/ or time schedules either operate in conjunction with each other or *should* operate in conjunction with one another. The need for coördination is particularly evident when personnel with different specializations work toward the same or similar objectives. For example, when guidance counselors, nurses, social workers, psychologists, and other pupil personnel specialists are working in the school there is usually a need for coördination. All of these individuals, along with the teachers, are trying to help the student; for total effectiveness, their efforts should be coördinated.

The process of coördinating should occur not only during the planning process, but may also be needed as a plan or decision is being implemented. It is at the latter stage that the blueprint for action starts to take form. People begin to perform tasks, use resources, and interact with each other, based on some kind of a time schedule. While in many situations prior planning for a task or program may obviate the necessity for further coördination, in other instances the administrator may need to become actively involved in the process of coördinating after a program has been introduced.

For example, the administrator may have to redefine roles so that they complement each other better. He may need to restructure tasks so that they do not conflict with or overlap each other; new lines of communication may need to be designated so that there is better coördination of activity or use of resources, and time schedules may need to be rearranged so individuals or groups can work together more easily. In all of these activities the administrator is engaged in the process of coördinating. He is reorganizing people, tasks, resources, and time so that functions proceed more smoothly. As a result the administrator can increase the extent to which an activity or program will be carried out efficiently and effectively.

DELEGATING

No administrator can effectively perform *all* of the various administrative functions and tasks within a school. Therefore, some duties must (or at least, should) be delegated to other people. In certain cases, the administrator may be faced with the problem that, because of financial constraints in hiring assistants or additional staff, there is no one to whom responsibilities can be delegated. However, in many situations, an administrator doesn't delegate responsibilities to an assistant or another person on the staff simply because he either doesn't know how to delegate or has reservations about relinquishing some of the duties.

According to Heyel, who has studied the latter problem, an administrator may be reluctant to delegate responsibility to others when he should, for one or more of the reasons identified below.[18]

1. He has a strong need to be involved in every aspect of administration, and cannot bear to delegate any of his responsibilities to others.
2. He is concerned that others may begin to wonder if he is really capable of handling the job if he attempts to delegate some of the responsibilities to other people.
3. He is not confident that others will do a good job if he delegates certain responsibilities, or at least doubts whether they could do as good a job as he would in carrying out a task.
4. He has a strong need to be recognized as *the* leader in the organization, and is concerned with the possibility that delegation of some of the responsibilities will necessitate the sharing of leadership recognition.
5. He is concerned that by delegating responsibility to someone else, he may be facilitating the advancement of that individual to the point at which the situation could become competitive.

The extent to which an administrator may be influenced by one or more of the considerations suggested by Heyel can be determined only by objective self-analysis. Certainly many, if not most of these factors would affect an individual in a subconscious way that might be difficult to ascertain. At any rate, it seems reasonable to assume that in many instances the lack of additional staff due to financial constraints is not the only factor which would account for the administrator's failure to delegate responsibility.

For some administrators, uncertainty about when or under what circumstances to delegate responsibility may also be a problem. Figure 3.4 presents four general guidelines which should be of assistance to an administrator.

In delegating a task or responsibility the administrator should ask himself, "What would I want to know if my superior were delegating the same

1. When someone else can do the task as well as or better than you can.

2. When you don't have the time to do the job or you have other important priorities.

3. When someone else could do the job adequately, if not as well, but at less expense.

4. When you are attempting to provide orientation and training to someone else who is preparing for a similar position.

Figure 3.4. When to Delegate
Responsibility

kind of responsibility to me?" To answer this question adequately, the administrator should define in considerable detail the nature and scope of the responsibility being assigned, the degree of authority that the individual should be given over others, the extent to which there are supervisory responsibilities associated with the assignment, and the people with whom the individual should communicate in carrying out his new assignment. As a result of carefully defining these factors, an administrator can avoid, or at least minimize uncertainty and unsatisfactory performance on the part of the person to whom an assignment has been delegated.

INITIATING

Administrators engage in the process of *initiating* when they reach the point at which they are ready to take some kind of action individually or with a group.

The school administrator attempts to initiate action on the part of other people in a variety of ways. He requests, instructs, directs, commands, motivates, or tries to persuade others to initiate desired action or activity.[19] In selecting the manner in which he attempts to initiate action, the administrator needs to examine the assumptions he may be making about his authority and power, other people's perception and acceptance of that authority and power, and the kind of an initiating approach that is most likely to be successful in bringing about the desired results.[20] For example, is the administrator merely *assuming* that he has the authority or power to direct, command, or instruct people to do what he wants done in particular circumstances? Or has the authority or power upon which he is basing his attempts to initiate action been explicit delegated to him through school board action or a directive from his superior?

In addition to examining his own assumptions about whether he has actually been delegated the authority to initiate action on the part of other people, the administrator should also attempt to ascertain the extent to which other people perceive and accept the fact that he does indeed possess such authority and power. Even though he may, in fact, validly derive his authority and power from the organization in which he serves, the administrator will undoubtedly experience difficulty in initiating action if the people from whom he is attempting to elicit action don't accept this fact.

And finally, the administrator needs to consider all feasible alternative methods for initiating action. Although he may feel that it is easier simply to issue directives, give commands, and instruct others what to do, there may be additional approaches to initiating action which will be ultimately more successful, particularly in specific situations with certain types of people. For example, requesting or asking others to do something is frequently a productive approach to initiating action. Also, trying to persuade people of the value of taking a particular action is often desirable and may be essential.

Although some administrators may recoil at the notion of trying to *persuade* someone to take action rather than directing him to do it, circumstances can arise in which the former approach is the only viable one, particularly if the administrator's authority or power is lacking or rejected. In addition, if people are persuaded of the merits of taking certain actions, they may be more likely to perform these actions with greater commitment than if they are merely responding to the administrator's authority or power. In any case, the administrator will want to give serious consideration to the advantages and disadvantages of the various approaches he might use in attempting to initiate action on the part of others.

COMMUNICATING

The school administrator is probably engaged in the process of communicating more often than in any other process, with the possible exception of decision making. In order to persuade, instruct, direct, request, present, stimulate, or develop understanding, the administrator must communicate. In order to communicate, he must deliver a *message* via a *medium* which reaches a *receiver* (another person or group) and registers a desired response, e.g., action, understanding.[21]

For example, an administrator may wish to bring to the faculty's attention that there has been too much noise in the hallways during the week, and that the professional staff should increase their efforts to keep noise to a minimum. This, then, is the *message* the administrator wants to deliver to the staff. In delivering the message, he has a choice of several different *media* for communication. He could write a memo, present the message over the public address system, announce it at a faculty meeting, or have an administrative assistant "pass the word" to teachers. Each of these communication media may possess advantages for delivering this particular message, depending on the administrator's skill in communicating, the type of group to whom the message is delivered, and the nature of the circumstances surrounding the message.

But actual transmission of the message by some means, is not the end of the communication process. The message also *must register* with the receiver(s), in this instance the faculty, before the communication can be judged to be effective. They must, first, become more aware of the noise problem in the hallway, and second, that the administrator wants them to take action to reduce the noise level. If, after the message is delivered, the faculty isn't any more aware of the noise problem and the administrator's expectation that they take action to reduce the level of noise in the hallways then the administrator hasn't communicated effectively. He may have *attempted* to communicate, but unless the message has registered, communication hasn't really taken place.

Whether the faculty *will* take action to reduce noise in the hallway, depends, of course, on factors beyond that of whether the administrator has communicated effectively with them. The faculty may clearly understand what the administrator wants and yet not accept it. On the other hand, if the purpose of the administrator's communication was to *initiate* action on the part of the faculty, then he hasn't "successfully communicated" with them unless they take such action.

Communicating is one of the most important administrative processes. By the very nature of his job the administrator communicates with a variety of people, including students, teachers, parents, and central office personnel, about a wide range of items during the course of a school year. The administrator's success in working with these people and in productively carrying out his other responsibilities will be greatly influenced by the extent to which he is an effective communicator.[22] Examples of the use of communication concepts and examples will be provided in later chapters.

WORKING WITH GROUPS

Most school administrators spend a considerable amount of their time working with various groups in different types of group settings. Administrators interact with the faculty, the parent organization, and the student body, as well as with other kinds of smaller groups, ranging from student clubs and organizations to the individual departments or grade units within a school. These groups differ in many important respects, particularly in size and degree of organizational structure and purpose, but they all possess certain basic characteristics in common which the administrator needs to recognize. These characteristics are presented in figure 3.5.

Formal Characteristics	Informal Characteristics
1. A group is originally organized to accomplish a particular objective(s).	1. The objective(s) which the members of the group presently feel to be important may not be the same as the one(s) for which they were originally organized.
3. A group has an appointed or elected leader.	2. There is usually one or more individuals in a group to whom the members of the group look for informal leadership.
3. A group has formally defined roles and tasks.	3. A group generally develops norms and expectations for what constitutes appropriate behavior for its members and others who interact with the group.
4. A group has a prescribed and defined system of communication among its members and its leader.	4. An informal system of communication usually develops within a group which may not be readily apparent to those who are not accepted members of the group.

Figure 3.5. Common Characteristics of Most Groups[23]

Since most school administrators are aware of the formal characteristics of the groups with whom they have contact, the informal characteristics are the ones to which administrators need to become more sensitive. If an administrator, in working with a group, proceeds only on his knowledge of its formal characteristics, real problems could result.

For example, he may assume that a group has a certain organizational objective, the original one for which it was organized, when in reality the group may have developed a different kind of objective. Or the administrator may assume that the appointed leader of a group, such as a department head, is the actual leader of the department, when in reality there is another individual in the department to whom the members actually look for leadership. In another situation, an administrator may determine the tasks for a group to perform, but if he fails to understand group norms and expectations toward the accomplishment of these tasks, they may not be performed well or may not get done at all. Knowledge of the informal characteristics of a group can facilitate the administrator's efforts with that group; lack of such knowledge can constitute a major handicap for him.[24]

In addition to being knowledgeable about the informal characteristics of a group, the school administrator will need to be competent in functioning as a group leader and in helping a group to work together effectively, since he will be the appointed leader in many situations. How the administrator performs as a group leader will be influenced in large part by his own conception of how a leader should behave, and his perceptions of the needs of a group. If the administrator sees his leadership role in working with the members of a group as that of instructing, directing, or ordering them, he will probably tend to play a very dominant, perhaps authoritarian, leadership role. In response to this type of leadership, the behavior of the group may tend to be either passive, restive, or perhaps hostile to his efforts to lead.[25]

If, on the other hand, the administrator sees his leadership role as being a consultant, resource person, or facilitator of group discussion and decision making, he is more likely to work with the group as one of its members than as the individual in charge. Under this kind of leadership there is apt to be greater participation on the part of the members and more group cohesion and *esprit de corps.*

In working with a group the school administrator needs to be aware of the fact that most groups when first formed go through certain stages in their development and enact particular behavior at their meetings, characteristic of their stage. These various stages are described in figure 3.6.

During the first two stages the members of a group do not really function very well together, and the cause can be detected from the nature of the comments which are made. In the last two stages group members begin to perform better as they develop greater purpose and focus, become better acquainted with each other, resolve major differences, and define more functional relationships.

1. *The "Groping" Stage.* It is characterized by comments such as "What are we supposed to be accomplishing?" "Who is supposed to do what? "Who is really in charge here?"
2. *The Griping Stage.* This is a period during which the members of a group find it difficult to adjust to the task of the group or the role which has been assigned to them.
3. *The Consolidation Stage.* This is the stage during which efforts are made to develop group harmony and avoid conflict. Members of the group begin to be more comfortable with each other and their roles in the group.
4. *The Solidifying Stage.* The group is now functioning well, and all members are performing their roles and cooperating easily with each other.

Figure 3.6. Stages in Group Development[26]

As an administrator interacts with a group, he should attempt to behave in ways which will tend to help the group to work cooperatively together and to accomplish their objectives. These behaviors, revealed in a study of group leadership, are enumerated and identified as follows.[27]

Group Leadership Behavior

1. Help members of the group to define their goals and delineate their problems.
2. Establish a cooperative, permissive atmosphere which puts the participants at ease so that they contribute their best thinking to the solution of the group's problems.
3. Utilize the various talents and knowledge of the members of the group in arriving at decisions.
4. Show a genuine regard and appreciation for the worth of each individual and a willingness to understand and accept each one at his own level of growth.
5. Enlist the help of outside resources. Don't always give answers but help to provide experiences through which teachers and lay groups can find their own answers.
6. Plan the procedures, the timing, and the situation so that the group members will be comfortable, have sufficient time, and have opportunity to participate.
7. Allow sufficient time for group thinking so that the participants do not have too many hurdles to surmount at one time.
8. Practice the technique of acceptable group procedures by becoming a listener, teller, questioner, and silent partner as your leadership and expertness merge with the best interests of the group.
9. Instill in others the desire to belong, to participate, and to take responsibility for and pride in the work of the group.
10. Discover skills, competencies, interests, and abilities so that each individual, while taking part in group processes, gains the maximum security which results from having a part to play and a contribution to make.
11. Relinquish leadership to other members of the group when appropriate, but continue to serve as consultant and adviser, to clear obstacles, and revive flagging enthusiasm.
12. Provide materials and resources and make available research studies and data to aid the group in their work.
13. Evaluate yourself continually to see that your purposes are valid, that human relationships are observed, that the steps in group processes are followed, that you are not moving too fast for the group, and that the work of the group is in keeping with the overall program of the school.

14. Be sensitive to group techniques and to human relationships between teachers and administrators, among teachers, administrators, and supervisors.

The behaviors of an effective group leader which are identified in the preceding enumeration need not be restricted to the school administrator. These are behaviors which can be initiated by any member of a group and should be so encouraged by the administrator. The important factor is not *who* enacts the behavior but that it is initiated by someone in the group and at the appropriate moment. Stimulating other people in the group to engage in leadership-type behavior may be the most important group process skill which an administrator can exercise.

EVALUATING

Evaluating represents one of the most important processes that a school administrator can employ, but one which, unfortunately, seems to be among the least frequently utilized. Evaluation can be defined as the process of examining as carefully, thoroughly, and objectively as possible an individual, group, product, or program in order to ascertain strengths and weaknesses.[28] The school administrator should engage in the evaluative process in relation to the following three areas: (1) evaluation of others, e.g., teacher evaluation, (2) evaluation of a school product, process, or program, and (3) evaluation of self.

Observation would suggest that school administrators spend the greatest proportion of their evaluation time focusing on assessment of staff, and the least amount of time on self-evaluation. While it appears that in response to pressures for greater school and administrator accountability the administrator is spending more of his time on product, process, and program evaluation, most of these efforts could be characterized as unplanned, superficial, and sporadic. (It is true that there are notable exceptions to this criticism.) In most schools there is virtually no carefully planned, in-depth attempt to evaluate the various programmatic aspects of the school on a regular basis. And the same criticism could be made about administrators' attempts to engage in self-evaluation.

Although a lack of evaluation skills may act as a deterrent, perhaps the main barrier to more extensive evaluating is that it is potentially threatening to the administrator. Despite this obstacle, the administrator needs to recognize that in the absence of a carefully planned, in-depth evaluation in the three areas previously identified, little significant improvement is possible. For this reason then, the need for evaluation and specific ideas for engaging in evaluation will be stressed throughout the book.

PROBLEM SOLVING

Problem solving can be thought of as a separate process or, perhaps more appropriately, as the effective utilization of most if not all of the administrative elements previously described. Whether or not an administrator employs all of these administrative elements will depend in most circumstances on the nature of the problem. But certainly it is likely that before most problems can be solved, the administrator will need to take the steps of identifying and diagnosing the problem, setting goals and making decisions; and he will also need to plan, implement, initiate, communicate, and coordinate the action. Additionally, in many situations the administrator will need to delegate responsibilities before a problem can be resolved, and frequently his problem solving will involve him with groups. Finally, before he can know whether the problem has been successfully resolved, he will have to evaluate.

So in a real sense, problem solving is not a separate or unique process but a synthesis of many different but related steps or subprocesses. When problems are not solved, the difficulty can frequently be traced back to a failure to engage in or enact effectively one or more of the subprocesses.

It should be noted that administrators differ in their approaches to problem solving.[29] Some administrators respond to a problem by immediately "jumping at a solution," while others take considerable time to seek information which will enable them to define more adequately the nature of the problem as a basis for deciding on possible alternative solutions. Administrative styles in problem solving also differ and can range from authoritarian to democratic to laissez-faire.[30]

While there may be no one "best" approach to problem solving which would cover every problem, circumstance, and individual, the effective problem solver bases his actions on the following principles, extracted from a review of the educational and social science literature:

1. Doesn't wait for problems to manifest themselves. Tries to *anticipate* problems or identify potential problem areas which, if not given attention, may result in significant trouble.
2. When faced with a problem, seeks more information about its causes, nature, and severity. Avoids leaping to quick or easy solutions.
3. Searches for more than one or two alternative solutions to a problem. Avoids settling on the first possible solution that is apparent, or viewing any proposed solution as the only one possible.
4. Evaluates carefully the consequences—both positive and negative—of each of the alternative solutions under consideration.

5. Utilizes the insights, perceptions, and assistance of relevant others throughout the problem-solving process. Avoids the assumption that the administrator possesses all the wisdom and/or expertise for solving a problem successfully.
6. Recognizes that adopted solutions to a problem must be thoughtfully implemented and eventually evaluated. Evaluation is particularly important if future mistakes are to be avoided and effective problem-solving approaches utilized.

Successful problem solving is rarely easy. It usually requires perceptive anticipation, careful analysis, thorough planning, and the involvement of people who can offer useful information, ideas, and constructive assistance. There is no shortcut or easy way to successful problem solving.

A FINAL NOTE

By now it should be clear to the reader that the job of the school administrator is a multifaceted one composed of many tasks and different elements. While some tasks or elements may be more important than others, depending on the nature of a situation, an administrator should attempt to master all of them so that when the need arises, he can respond competently. If an administrator can effectively perform the tasks and elements identified in this chapter, he should be in a good position to meet the problems and challenges which may confront a school.

Review and Learning Activities

1. Compare the job description for the principal in your district with the task areas identified in figure 3.1. To what extent are certain task areas not reflected in the job description? Why not?
2. Read the case study presented below. Then assume that you are the principal and indicate how you would use *each* of the basic elements of the administrative process described in the text, e.g., problem identification to help avoid or resolve the problems explicitly *and* implicitly presented in the case study. If you feel that a basic element of the administrative process could *not* be used, explain why.

FACULTY MEETING AGENDA

It was 15 minutes before the faculty meeting was scheduled to begin, and the principal quickly reviewed his agenda for the meeting.

Faculty Meeting Agenda
November 5

I. Announcements
   A. The deadline for 9-week grades (Principal)
   B. United Fund Drive (Principal)
   C. Request from P.T.A. concerning the need for greater teacher involvement (Principal)
   D. Reemphasis of the Superintendent's Bulletin concerning physical examinations for teachers (Principal)
   E. Deadline for teachers' dues (Chairman of the Faculty Social Committee)
II. Topics for Discussion
   A. Is there too much noise in the corridors?
   B. Are we assinging too much homework?

The principal thought to himself that it looked like a rather lengthy agenda, but perhaps the announcements wouldn't take too much time. He hoped that he and the faculty could soon get down to the real problems which seemed to be affecting the operation of the school. Anyway, there didn't seem to be any good way to limit the number of announcements, and they all seemed quite important. He had considered putting the information in a written bulletin to the teachers, but when he had tried this procedure in the past, many of the teachers had apparently failed to read the bulletins carefully, if at all.

The principal glanced over the agenda a final time. He had spent at least an hour in the early part of the afternoon making up the agenda, and he didn't think that he had missed anything. The agenda appeared to be ready to distribute to the teachers at the beginning of the meeting.

As he walked toward the room where the faculty meeting was to be held, he hoped that he could develop more faculty interest and participation than in the past. For some reason, the teachers always seemed to be rather apathetic. In fact, he could count on the fingers of one hand those teachers who ever took the initiative to contribute anything to the discussions in the faculty meetings. He realized that teachers were often tired at the end of the day, but there should be some way to get them more involved. He felt that the topics to be covered during this afternoon's meeting were very important, as the hallways had been particularly noisy this week, and he had received several complaints from parents about the amount of homework being assigned. These were problems that affected every teacher in the school, and he certainly hoped that the faculty would respond with concern and involvement.

[For additional case studies that can be related to other concepts presented in the text, see *School Administration and Supervision: Important Issues, Concepts and Case Studies* (Dubuque, Iowa: Wm. C. Brown Company Publishers, 1980.]

Notes

1. The following major sources of ideas were used in the development of figure 3.1: Robert S. Fisk, "The Task of Educational Administration" in *Administrative Behavior in Education,* ed. by Roald F. Campbell and Russell T. Gregg (New York: Harper and Row, 1957), chapter 8; *Performance Objectives for School Principals,* ed. Jack A. Culbertson, Curtis Henson, and Ruel Morrison (Berkeley: McCutchan Publishing, 1974); Richard A. Gorton and Kenneth McIntyre, *The Effective Principal* (Reston, Va.: National Association of Secondary School Principals, 1978); Donald Walters, *Perceptions of Administrative Competencies.* An ERIC Report: Ed–172–361.

2. Henry Fayol, *General and Industrial Management,* trans. Constance Storrs (London: Pitman, 1949).

3. Luther Gulick and L. Urwick, eds., *Papers on the Science of Administration* (New York: Institute of Public Administration, Columbia University, 1937), p. 13.

4. Robert Owens, *Organizational Behavior in Education* (Englewood Cliffs, N.J.: Prentice Hall, 1981). Also see Alan C. Filley, et al., *Managerial Process and Organizational Behavior* (Glenview, Ill.: Scott, Foresman, 1976).

5. Richard A. Gorton, *School Administration and Supervision: Important Issues, Concepts and Case Studies* (Dubuque, Iowa: Wm. C. Brown Company Publishers, 1980).

6. Arthur Blumberg and William Greenfield, *The Effective Principal* (Boston, Mass.: Allyn and Bacon, 1980), p. 49.

7. John K. Hemphill, "Administration as Problem Solving," in *Administration as Decision-Making,* ed. A. W. Halpin (Chicago: Midwest Administration Center, 1957), p. 96.

8. David Mosrie, "Assessing School Needs: A Practical Approach," *NASSP Bulletin* (November 1980): 64–66.

9. Philip J. Runkel, Richard A. Schmuck, Jane H. Arends and Richard P. Francisco, *Transforming the School's Capacity for Problem Solving* (Eugene, Oreg.: Center for Educational Policy and Management, 1979).

10. See chapter 13 in this text for a further description of the process. Also see Alvan Elbing, *Behavior Decisions in Organizations* (Glenview, Ill.: Scott, Foresman, 1978), chapter 4; and Raymond L. Calabrese, "The Problem Identification and Classification Process," *NASSP Bulletin* (February 1982): 10–15.

11. Culbertson et al., *Performance Objectives for School Principals,* chapter 1.

12. Gorton, *School Administration and Supervision,* chapter 7.

13. William Cunningham, *Systematic Planning for Educational Change* (Palo Alto, Calif.: Mayfield Publishing, 1982).

14. William J. Kritek, "Lessons from the Literature on Implementation," *Educational Administration Quarterly* (Fall 1976): 86–102.

15. Ibid.

16. Gorton, *School Administration and Supervision,* pp. 306–7.

17. Ernest Dale, Management: *Theory and Practice* (New York: McGraw-Hill Book Company, 1978), pp. 161–71.

18. Carl Heyel, *Organizing Your Job in Management* (New York: American Management Association, 1960), pp. 126–35. For further guidelines in delegating, see Walter St. John, "Effective Planning, Delegating, and Priority Setting," *NASSP Bulletin* (February 1982): 16–23.

19. Gorton, *School Administration and Supervision,* chapter 10.

20. For an excellent description of a principal engaging in the process of initiating, see William W. Wayson, "A New Kind of Principal," *National Elementary Principal* (February 1971): 9–19.

21. Gorton, *School Administration and Supervision,* chapter 8.

22. Ibid.

23. On formal characteristics, see W. W. Charters, Jr., "An Approach to the Formal Organization of the School," in *Behavioral Science and Educational Administration,* ed. Daniel F. Griffiths (Chicago: University of Chicago Press, 1964), pp. 243–44. For informal characteristics, see Lawrence Iannaconne in the same source, pp. 233–42.

24. For additional discussion of the informal characteristics of a group and the effects of these characteristics upon the operation of the school, see Gorton, *School Administration and Supervision,* chapter 13.

25. Kurt Lewin et al., "Patterns of Aggressive Behavior in Experimentally Created Social Climates," *Journal of Social Psychology* 10 (1939): 271–99.

26. Adapted from material developed by Russell D. Robinson, Professor of Educational Leadership, University of Wisconsin-Milwaukee.

27. Adapted from a list of leadership behavior performed by supervisors in a group setting. *See Group Processes in Supervision* (Washington, D.C.: Association for Supervision and Curriculum Development, 1958), p. 128.

28. Evaluation will be emphasized throughout the book. However, the following references may provide supplementary sources of ideas: *Using Evaluation: Does Evaluation Make a Difference?* (Los Angeles: The Center for the Study of Evaluation, 1979); *Standards for Evaluation of Educational Programs* (New York: McGraw-Hill Company, 1980); *Handbook of Teacher Evaluation* (Beverly Hills: Sage Publications, 1981).

29. Ray Cross, "A Description of Decision-Making Patterns of School Principals" (Paper presented at A.E.R.A. Annual Meeting, New York, February 1971). Also see Ray Cross, "A Description of Decision-Making Patterns of School Principals," *Journal of Educational Research* (January/February, 1980): 154–59.

30. Gorton, *School Administration and Supervision,* chapter 9. Also see Jacob W. Getzels, et al., *Educational Administration as a Social Process* (New York: Harper & Row, 1968).

4

THE SCHOOL ADMINISTRATOR
Roles, Expectations, and Social Factors

During a school year an administrator performs a number of different roles.[1] At one point she may act as instructional leader, at another point as conflict mediator, and at a later date may need to perform a different role. In each situation the decision to adopt a particular role will be greatly influenced by the following aspects: (1) the administrator's own needs and attitudes, (2) the expectations of important others, and (3) various social factors.[2] In this chapter the major roles which might be performed by a school administrator will be presented first, followed by a discussion of the various expectations and social factors that may influence an administrator's role behavior.

MAJOR ROLES OF THE SCHOOL ADMINISTRATOR*

There is no shortage of opinions, proposals, or conceptualizations regarding the role of the school administrator.[3] A review of the literature on the subject reveals that, at one time or another, six major roles have been proposed: (1) manager, (2) instructional leader, (3) disciplinarian, (4) human relations facilitator, (5) evaluator, and (6) conflict mediator. While it is unlikely that an administrator will be required to enact all six of these roles simultaneously, she should attempt to become competent in each role so that she can perform it effectively when and if the situation requires.

The following summary descriptions are intended to provide the administrator with a brief introduction to each of the six roles; other chapters of the book will present related discussions of these roles, and references are listed at the end of this chapter for further study.

*Most of the discussion in this chapter relates more to the principalship than to other positions at the middle management level. The other positions will be discussed in the next chapter.

MANAGER

In the eyes of many people, the school administrator is first and foremost a manager. It was based on this general concept that the position originated in the 1800s,[4] and though other roles have since been proposed, the concept of the administrator as manager has persisted.

As manager, the school administrator is expected to procure, organize, and coordinate both physical and human resources so that the goals of the organization can be attained effectively. Her main role is to develop or implement policies and procedures which will result in the efficient operation of the school. In fact, the popularized notion of a manager is, "one who keeps things running smoothly."

It should be noted that the term "manager" conveys a negative connotation for certain individuals.[5] Many administrators, in particular, don't like to think of themselves as managers; the term "leader," which will be discussed later, is perceived by them as a more attractive appellation. However, a school administrator should recognize that when different people and resources are brought together in one location (in this case, a school building or district), there is a need for someone to organize, schedule, and coordinate the entire operation. That "someone" at the building level has typically been the school administrator.

Consequently, rather than resisting the role of manager, the school administrator should accept and implement the role in such a way that the school is efficiently managed, yet she is in a position to be available for other role options. By successfully performing the role of manager, an administrator can help others to accomplish tasks and goals, and in the process can generate a more positive attitude toward her contribution to the school. The school administrator's role as manager is further discussed in other chapters, particularly the chapter on budget and plant management.

INSTRUCTIONAL LEADER

The role of the school administrator as an instructional leader has had a long history.[6] Although the school administrator was at first more a manager than a leader, it wasn't long before the instructional leadership dimensions of the position began to be emphasized in the educational literature and at various professional meetings which administrators attended.[7] It is probably safe to say that leadership, often referred to as "educational leadership," or "instructional leadership," has been widely accepted by administrators as the raison d'être for the continued existence of their position at the building level.

But one of the problems in connection with the proposed role of the school administrator as instructional leader is that people define the role in different ways and with varying degrees of precision, thereby creating confusion for the administrator who is expected to carry out the role.[8] For example, to some, the principalship is a leadership position, and *any* activities in which the principal engages in order to improve instruction are leadership activities. To others, there are *certain* types of activities or actions, such as classroom observation, in which the principal is expected to participate if she is to function as an instructional leader. Compounding the problem is the fact that the principal is frequently encouraged to be an instructional leader and yet may not be perceived by teachers as possessing the subject matter expertise necessary for helping them to improve.[9] This problem and other aspects of the role of the administrator as an instructional leader will be explored in chapter 11.

DISCIPLINARIAN

The importance of the disciplinary role of the school administrator has been revealed by several studies. For example, when teachers and parents are asked to comment on the role which they expect the school administrator to play in the school, disciplinarian is usually cited as a major—perhaps even the *most* important role.[10] Students also tend to see the school administrator as a disciplinarian (although there is some doubt as to whether they approve of this role.)[11]

On the other hand, principals tend to reject the idea that being a disciplinarian is their major role, and frequently assign this responsibility to the assistant principal, if available. However, research has shown that an increasing number of assistant and vice-principals also seem reluctant to accept the disciplining of students as the primary responsibility of their position.[12]

Generally, school administrators resist or reject the role of disciplinarian because of the negative connotation of the term and because the duties associated with the role are frequently frustrating, irritating, and unpleasant to perform. The term, "disciplinarian," traditionally has implied one who *punishes* someone else: in this case, usually a student.

Punishing students can be a very vexing and frustrating job, as anyone knows who has had to assume this responsibility. Although modern concepts of discipline emphasize more positive approaches to improving student conduct, the fact remains that working with student misbehavior problems represents a difficult assignment with few rewards, which may explain administrators' negative reactions to the role. Nevertheless, it should be pointed out that student conduct still constitutes a major problem in many schools, and important reference groups who are associated with the school will probably continue to expect the principal and/or an assistant to play the role of disciplinarian. This role is discussed in considerable depth in chapters 13 and 14.

FACILITATOR OF HUMAN RELATIONS

The human relations role of the school administrator originated in the early 1920s and was given initial impetus by the publication of a book by Mary Parker Follett[13] entitled *Creative Experience.* In this book and in her other writings, Follett emphasized the importance of an administrator's concentrating as much on meeting the personal needs of employees and developing cooperative and harmonious relationships among them, as on achieving the productivity goals of the organization. Later studies by Elton Mayo provided empirical support for Follett's approach,[14] and books by Griffiths and others attempted to incorporate concepts of human relations into the theory of school administration.[15]

The school administrator should, of course, practice good human relations in all aspects of her job, and in relationships with people generally. However, the two areas in which this becomes particularly important are in the developing of high staff morale, and a humanistic school environment. The specific human relations skills involved in achieving these two goals will be identified in the chapter on staff relations.

EVALUATOR

Increased emphasis on school accountability has placed added importance on the role of the school administrator as evaluator. A large number of parents and other members of the public are apparently no longer satisfied with the *opinion* of the administrator that everything is satisfactory with the schools; the public wants to see evidence of effectiveness or attempts to improve a situation.[16]

In order to provide evidence of effectiveness or improvement, the school administrator will need to perform the role of evaluator. This role in most cases tends to center on the evaluation of staff and on program evaluation. In addition, it may involve the administrator in the evaluation of student performance, as well. It is likely in many of these situations that the administrator will need to utilize the expertise of others to help with the evaluation process.

Essentially the role of evaluator involves the following aspects:

- Determining who should be involved in the evaluation.
- Establishing evaluation criteria.
- Selecting methods of evaluation.
- Collecting data.
- Analyzing data.
- Drawing conclusions and developing recommendations.
- Reporting findings.
- Implementing recommendations.

The importance of evaluation and specific evaluation approaches are discussed throughout the text. In addition, the reader is directed to an excellent text on evaluation by Edward F. DeRoche. See *An Administrator's Guide for Evaluating Programs and Personnel* (Boston: Allyn and Bacon, 1981).

CONFLICT MEDIATOR

The role of the school administrator as conflict mediator is of recent origin. Although administrators have always been faced with the need to adjust differences, it wasn't until the mid-sixties that the need to mediate conflict became a major aspect of the school administrator's role. Since that time she has been confronted with, among others, conflicts associated with student disruption, teacher militancy, and parental and community demands for greater involvement in school decision making.

At the present time, conflict resolution comprises a major part of the administrator's job. In the role of conflict resolver, the school administrator acts basically as a mediator.[17] She attempts to secure all of the facts in a situation, as well as the perceptions each party to the dispute has of one another and of the issues in conflict. Generally, the administrator's major goal is for each side to recognize some validity in the other party's position, so that compromise can take place and the conflict can be resolved. As the administrator works with all parties to a dispute, whether they be students, teachers, parents, or others, she needs to develop an understanding on their part that neither side is totally right, and that some "give and take" will be necessary before the conflict can be resolved.

When one views the turmoil surrounding education today, it is clear that the role of conflict mediator is an essential one for the school administrator. For an extended discussion of conflict and the role of the school administrator as a conflict mediator, see Gorton.[18]

ROLE VARIABLES INFLUENCING AN ADMINISTRATOR'S BEHAVIOR

For every administrative position in an effectively managed organization, there are written job descriptions or policy statements, emanating from a governing board, which embody the formal expectations of the organization. In addition, in every organization there are usually implicit, frequently unexpressed expectations for an administrator's behavior, which originate with the various individuals or groups with whom she comes into contact. Together, both sets of expectations comprise a behavioral definition of the role which different individuals or groups—both formal and informal—believe the administrator *should* perform in a particular situation. As Getzels has observed, "The expectations define for the actor [administrator], whoever he may be, what he should or should not do as long as he is the incumbent of the particular role."[19] The expectations also serve as "evaluative standards applied to an incumbent in a position,"[20] and therefore can represent a powerful source of potential influence on any administrator's behavior.

However, the Getzels model[21] hypothesizes that the behavior of an administrator is also affected by her own attitudes toward the role she should play. These attitudes constitute the administrator's self-expectations and may be more important than the expectations of others in determining the role she will take in a given set of circumstances. For example, if an administrator feels that she should play the role of manager, she may become involved in activities designed to bring about a more efficiently operated school, despite the fact that contrary expectations for her role are held by other individuals or groups.

Figure 4.1, which is based on the Getzels model, illustrates the major role variables that can impact on an administrator.

In the following sections the potential effect of a school administrator's personal disposition on her role, the expectations of important reference groups, and the impact of certain social forces will be discussed.

PERSONAL VARIABLES[22]

Every administrator possesses certain needs, values, and attitudes which potentially can influence her role behavior. These can perhaps be best illustrated by the thoughts expressed by several administrators, along with the attitude or value orientation each represents:

Personal Thoughts	**Type of Attitude or Value**
1. "I wonder about the risks involved in pursuing this particular role."	Risk orientation
2. "If Hank recommends it, I am sure that it is a role that needs to be performed."	Attitude toward people
3. "I question whether adopting a 'far out' innovation like the open classroom is good education."	Educational philosophy
4. "This is the type of role that an educational leader would adopt."	Concern about status
5. "It seems to me that if I adopt this role, I can no longer 'call the shots' in that area."	Concern about authority and control

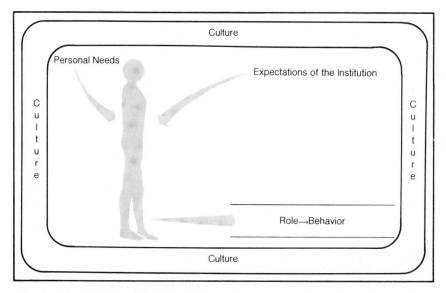

Culture

Personal Needs

Expectations of the Institution

C
u
l
t
u
r
e

C
u
l
t
u
r
e

Role→Behavior

Culture

Figure 4.1. Major Factors Which
Influence an Individual's Behavior

These five examples, of course, are merely illustrative of a wide range of possible values and attitudes which any administrator might possess and which could have a major influence on the type of role she adopts.

As Lipham and Hoeh have perceptively observed,

> . . . Values serve as a perceptual screen for the decision maker, affecting both his awareness of the problematic state of a system and his screening of information relative to the problem. Second, values condition the screening of possible alternatives. . . . Finally, values serve as the criteria against which higher-order goals are assessed and projected. . . .[23]

While an administrator probably cannot avoid the influence of values and attitudes in making decisions about roles, she should attempt to become more aware of the ethical nature of those values. In a study of chief school administrators, Dexheimer discovered that they were more inclined to engage in nonethical forms of accommodations in critical decision-making activities than ethical forms.[24] Although it appears that the study has not been replicated with similar or other administrative positions, it points up the need for every administrator to consider carefully whether the attitudes and values that are influencing her on a particular decision about the role she should play are morally and ethically defensible. This will not be an easy task for the decision maker since most individuals are not very conscious of their values and attitudes or how they are affected by them, and lack criteria and standards for evaluating them. However, the reader is referred to an excellent review on this subject by Ostrander and Dethey[25] and to the statement of *Ethics for School Administrators* developed by several national administrator associations.[26]

A related problem in regard to the influence of attitudes and values in decision-making about roles is the extent to which they can play a dominant role in compromising the objectivity of the decision maker and thereby short-circuiting the decision-making process. For example the administrator who has the attitude that, "If Hank recommends it, I am sure that it is a role which needs to be performed," is revealing a strong, positive attitude or bias toward the person, Hank. Because of the administrator's attitude in this situation, she will probably find it difficult to be objective about evaluating Hank's recommendation or any competing alternative. As a result, the administrator may not engage thoroughly in the various steps of the decision-making process, which should include identifying and evaluating objectively all possible alternatives.

Although the administrator's attitude in the above example is a positive one—at least toward Hank, in another situation involving someone else it may be negative, with the same potential results of compromised objectivity and a superficial decision-making process. Of course, it is not axiomatic that such a decision about roles will be a poor one, and it is recognized that the press of time on an administrator may require a "short-cut" through the decision-making process. However, it is because of the bias of the decision maker and such "short-cuts" that poor decision making frequently results. Therefore, an administrator should make every effort to become more aware of her attitudes and values, and their influence on the type of decision she makes about the roles she should perform, attempting to reduce that influence when it could compromise her objectivity or result in a less thorough and thoughtful decision-making process.

REFERENCE GROUPS' EXPECTATIONS FOR THE SCHOOL ADMINISTRATOR'S ROLE

If a school administrator is to make a wise decision about the role she should adopt in a particular situation, she will need to be knowledgeable about the expectations held by various reference groups. These groups include students, teachers, parents, and others who may be associated with the school. Figure 4.2 identifies a number of groups who hold expectations for the role of the school administrator.

While it may be impossible for a school administrator to become knowledgeable about the expectations for her role held by *all* the different groups who are associated with the school, it would appear essential that she become so in the case of four of the groups with whom she has direct contact: students,

At the Building Level	At the District Level
1. Teachers and other members of the faculty	1. The superintendent
2. Other administrative personnel in the school	2. Central office administrative/supervisory staff
3. Students	3. The school board
4. Clerical and maintenance staff	4. Administrators in other schools

Local and State Groups

1. Parents	4. State department of public instruction
2. Parents' organizations	5. Professional organizations
3. Social, labor, and business organizations	6. Accreditation agencies

Figure 4.2. Reference Groups Who Hold Expectations for the Role of the School Administrator

teachers, parents, and the school administrator's superiors. Although the specific expectations of any of these groups may vary according to the nature of the group, and the local situation, research studies have provided information which should be useful in helping the administrator to develop an understanding of the general orientation of these groups. (The following sections are presented so that an administrator may better *understand* the expectations of certain reference groups; no inference should be drawn that an administrator must conform to those expectations or that all the people in a specific reference group will hold identical expectations.)

Students' Expectations for the School Administrator's Role

Many students have probably never even thought about the role of the school administrator, while others may possess well-conceived ideas about what she should be doing in the school.

A review of the research on students' expectations for the role of the school administrator shows that this area of inquiry has not attracted much interest from researchers. However, some indication of students' expectations can be gleaned from a study by Taylor.[27] This researcher asked students what kinds of changes they would make in the school if they were the "Boss." Elementary students who participated in the study showed most concern about such changes as employing nicer people in the cafeteria and keeping buses cleaner; junior high students had little to say about facilities but they wanted to change human relations by allowing students more influence in administering the school and by establishing fewer and more reasonable rules; and senior high students wanted improvements in such areas as textbook review, scheduling, and teacher evaluation. Taylor's study suggests that as students grow older, they become more and more interested in how a school is administered.

In a study by Pederson an attempt was made to identify the specific kinds of behavior on the part of a school principal that students feel are effective, and those behaviors perceived as ineffective.[28] Pederson's study of a random sample of students was conducted in twenty-five schools. In essence, he asked 1,645 students to describe behavior or actions of their principal which were (1) effective or worthy of praise, and (2) ineffective or deserving of criticism.

The behavior or actions of the principal which students mentioned most frequently as effective were concerned with the principal's *personal* relationships with them. These actions took place in situations in which the principal expressed friendship, courtesy, sincerity, consideration, praise, encouragement, interest toward students, and support of pupils, faculty, and all phases of the school program. Such personal relationship behavior was mentioned by students four times as frequently as any other behavior (of those perceived by the students as effective) on the part of the principal, and therefore strongly indicates the main nature of their expectations for the role of the principal.

Reinforcing the importance of personal relationships between the principal and students were the data on students' perceptions of *ineffective* behavior by the principal. The behavior mentioned most frequently by students as ineffective was also concerned with the principal's personal relationship with students. It involved situations in which the principal had acted in an unfriendly, humorless, discourteous, affected, phony, insincere, inconsiderate, critical, disinterested, or opposed manner towards pupils, faculty, and all phases of the school program.

The importance of the administrator's personal relationship with students was also verified by the National Study of School Evaluation, in which it was found that the most prevalent concern of students regarding administrators was an uncertainty that administrators were interested in them as individuals.[29]

Although there is little doubt that the principal's personal relationship with students is the most important aspect of students' expectations for his role, Pederson's study produced additional findings which suggest that students also expect the principal to[30]

1. Organize advisory groups which represent the viewpoints of all persons interested in the school. Actions by the principal which treat groups partially would be perceived as ineffective by students.

2. Seek and utilize the recommendations of individuals and all advisory groups in the study and solution of school problems. Failure by the principal to seek or utilize the recommendations of individuals and all types of advisory groups in the study and solution of school problems would be perceived by students as ineffective. Also perceived as ineffective would be neglect by the principal in taking action or following up on proposals or recommendations of official groups or committees.

3. Act immediately to stop the misbehavior of individuals or groups. Excessive delay and inappropriate attempts to correct misbehavior of pupils would be perceived as ineffective action by the principal.

4. Reprimand individuals or groups in a calm, mature, and friendly fashion without harshness or threats. Reprimanding individuals or groups in an unfriendly fashion with harshness or threats, or exercising judgment without all of the facts and without listening to the other side of the story would be perceived by students as ineffective behavior.

5. Explain school policies, practices, procedures, regulations, and facts regarding rumors for the entire student body. Failure by the principal to adequately explain and consistently apply school policies, practices, procedures, and regulations would be perceived by students as ineffective behavior.

6. Refrain from censoring student publications, assemblies, discussions, books, and films.

7. Assist pupils directly with individual and group learning projects.

8. Intercede with higher authority on behalf of pupils.

9. Write or speak to the entire student body, stimulating their best efforts.

10. Provide time, equipment, and facilities for the educational program.

11. Safeguard the health and welfare of pupils and school personnel.

Perhaps the most startling finding of Pederson's study was that approximately half of the students rarely observed the principal working on the job. And in a related study by McAulay, over 60 percent of the students could identify no clear function for the elementary principal.[31] These findings may be interpreted in various ways, but one point is certain: the school administrator needs to become more visible to students if she is to be perceived by them as performing an important role in the school.

Teachers' Expectations for the
School Administrator's Role

Perhaps more than any other reference group, teachers have the opportunity for interaction with the school administrator and are therefore in a better position to develop expectations for her role. As a consequence, research studies on teachers' expectations for the role of the school administrator have been numerous. These studies in general indicate three major expectations which an administrator may anticipate that teachers will hold for her role:

(1) **The school administrator should support her teachers on issues and problems of student discipline.**

Several studies have documented this particular expectation of teachers. Becker, for example, found that teachers wanted the school administrator to support them in discipline cases *no matter who was at fault.*[32] In a similar vein, Willower discovered that the strongest teacher expectation was to the effect that the school administrator always back them in matters involving discipline;[33] and Bridges reported that the administrator's support of teachers in regard to their problems with pupils was valued by teachers more than anything else she could do.[34] Further, a study by Brumbaugh and Skinkus,[35] as well as periodic surveys of teachers,[36] provides additional evidence of the importance to teachers of their principal's support in situations involving student discipline.

It would appear from studies on teachers' expectations that teachers believe it is less crucial that the school administrator be a strong disciplinarian (although this may be important) than that she back or support the teachers regardless of the nature of their approach to discipline. However, it needs to be emphasized that meeting this latter expectation will not always be possible or even desirable in certain situations, as further discussed in the chapter on student misbehavior.

(2) **The school administrator should treat teachers as professional colleagues with different but equal roles, rather than as subordinates in a bureaucratic relationship.**

Teachers have improved their educational and professional status in recent years, and research studies have long pointed to the fact that many of them don't recognize the traditional superior-subordinate relationship between the administrator and teachers that existed in the past.

Scully, for example, found that teachers wanted the school administrator to cooperate with them and to regard them as fellow workers, rather than as subordinates.[37] Bidwell's study discovered that teachers expected the school administrator to set clear and fair standards for teachers' behavior.[38] Chase's research revealed that teachers expected the school administrator to show understanding and respect for their competency and work,[39] and Sharpe noted that teachers expected the school administrator to communicate with them frequently and to refrain from curtailing their individual initiative or freedom.[40] These researchers' findings continue to be confirmed by opinion polls and articles in teacher association journals.[41]

In summary, the main implication of these studies is that teachers expect to be recognized as professionals and to be treated accordingly.

(3) **The school administrator should provide a meaningful opportunity for teachers to participate in school decision making and should include a significant role for teachers in the making of final decisions about those activities directly affecting them.**

All of the studies on teacher expectations that were reviewed point to the desire of teachers for a significant role in school decision making. Chase, for instance, found that teachers expected the school administrator to provide opportunities for their active participation in curriculum development, determination of grouping and promotion, and control of pupils.[42] In addition, teachers emphasized that if they were to serve on a committee, the committee must have the power to make decisions rather than mere recommendations on questions already decided by the principal. Sharma discovered in his study that teachers wanted shared responsibility in all areas of the school program except instructional activities, wherein they wanted total responsibility.[43] The literature continues to show a strong expectation by teachers that the school administrator take an active role in involving them in those decisions which affect the teacher in some professional way.[44]

Whether or not the school administrator should meet all or any of the three main expectations by teachers for her role depends, of course, on many factors. Obviously, it will not always be possible and may not even be desirable for the administrator to meet all of the teachers' expectations. However, she needs to be aware that important consequences are associated with the extent to which she meets teachers' expectations.

Horalick, for example, found that in regard to teachers' evaluation of the principal as a leader, it was more important to adhere to certain faculty norms and role expectations than to follow a particular leadership style in interacting with the faculty.[45] Expectations which the faculty held for the principal included the following:

1. She should "back up" teachers in front of parents, even when she considers the teachers to be wrong. If the principal criticizes a teacher, it should be done privately.
2. She should "back up" teachers in front of pupils. If the principal believes that a student is right, the teacher should be told so privately and should never be criticized in the presence of a pupil.
3. The principal should be a good disciplinarian.
4. She should exhibit democratic behavior.

Adherence by the principal to these expectations was associated with high faculty evaluation of the principal as a leader; a lack of adherence was associated with low faculty evaluation of the principal as a leader.

A major implication of Horalick's research is that the school administrator may not be able to gain acceptance or exert effective leadership with teachers until she meets *or* changes their expectations in regard to her role in the school.

Parental Expectations for the
School Administrator's Role

Parents constitute an important third group that holds expectations for the role of the school administrator. Perhaps more than any of the other groups discussed thus far, parents are heterogeneous in their expectations. Therefore, it is more difficult to generalize about the expectations of any single parents' group, to say nothing to parents' groups in different communities. In addition, there has been surprisingly little research on the expectations of parents for the role of the school administrator. Still, some useful findings can be gleaned from the few studies that have focused on parents' expectations for the school administrator's role.

Drake, for example, found in a study of PTA officers that they identified the following five expectations for the principal as carrying a high priority:[46]

- Initiating improvements in teaching techniques and methods
- Making certain that curricula fit the needs of students
- Directing teachers to motivate students to learn at their optimal levels
- Affording teachers the opportunity to individualize programs
- Directing teachers to coordinate and articulate the subject matter taught on each grade level.

The low-priority expectations which PTA officers held for the principal included:

- Becoming involved in community affairs
- Keeping a school maintenance schedule
- Scheduling the activities of the school
- Maintaining school records
- Performing other administrative duties assigned by the superintendent.

It seems clear from examining these two sets of expectations that the PTA officers surveyed are more concerned with the role of the principal as instructional leader than that of school manager.

Another study which focused more on parents' expectations for the principal in regard to working with parents and students was conducted by Buffington.[47] This researcher found in his study of parental expectations for the role of the principal that parents expected the principal to engage in the following kinds of behavior.

Parents' Expectations for the Role of the Principal

  I. Develop relationships with parents' groups and the community
     A. Organize parents' groups
     B. Work with parents' groups
     C. Interpret the school to the community
 II. Know and help individual parents
     A. Meet parents' complaints
     B. Establish friendly relations with parents
     C. Report to parents on progress of children
III. Work with and care for children
     A. Maintain discipline
     B. Show personal interest in children
     C. Protect health and safety of children
     D. Work with atypical children

As one can see from an examination of the expectations revealed by Buffington's study, they fall into three categories: (1) working with parents' groups, (2) interacting with parents on an individual basis, and (3) working with and showing concern for children. While most administrators would probably feel that the kinds of behavior listed under each of these categories are desirable, there are indications that many parents are not satisfied with the extent to which their expectations have been met by administrators. Although this problem is discussed more fully in the chapters on school-community relations, it seems that administrators—with few exceptions—need to become more aware of the expectations by parents for the role of the administrator, as well as more knowledgeable about the extent to which parents feel that administrators are not meeting their expectations. (For further evidence and discussion of the expectations of parents, the reader should consult the chapters on school-community relations.)

Superiors' Expectations for the School Administrator's Role

Probably many school administrators consider the most important expectations for their behavior to be those held by their superiors.[48] They are the individuals who had an important role in hiring the school administrator, and they will play a major role in determining her salary, retention, and status in the district, as well as other matters. For these reasons alone, the school administrator will have a tendency to weigh heavily the expectations of her superiors.

In addition, in a bureaucratic organization such as the school, which is operated according to principles of line and staff, the administrator is responsible to and accountable to her superiors. Therefore, it is only natural to give a higher priority to the expectations of superiors than to the expectations of other reference groups. (But a problem for the school administrator arises when her expectations conflict with those of his superiors. The nature of these conflicts and possible resolutions are discussed elsewhere, and the reader is encouraged to pursue these readings.[49])

Perhaps the best study of superiors' expectations for the role of the school administrator was conducted by Moser.[50] His research showed that superintendents expected their principals to engage in the following kinds of behavior: (1) lead forcefully, (2) initiate action, (3) accomplish organizational goals, and (4) emulate the nomothetic behavior of their superiors.

Nomothetic behavior can be defined as actions which seek to meet the expectations of the institution in which an individual works.[51] As applied to the school administrator-superior relationship, nomothetic expectations mean that the administrator's superiors expect her to pay greater attention to the expectations of the organization for which she works than to her own personal needs or the personal needs of others with whom she may be associated at the building level.

Whether a school administrator will always be able to meet the expectations of her superiors will depend on many factors, including the extent to which the expectations are realistic. Certainly she should attempt to change the expectations of her superiors if she feels that they are not in her best interest or in the best interest of the school. Her success in this endeavor will depend as much on her own skill and perseverance as on the receptivity of her superiors for change. In any event, it would be to the advantage of the school administrator to make sure that she accurately understands the expectations of her superiors and considers carefully the consequences of not meeting those expectations.

Agreement among Reference Groups

Although there is considerable evidence that the expectations of others for the role of the school administrator frequently conflict with each other, a study by Clifford Campbell suggests some common ground.[52] In Campbell's investigation of the expectations of teachers, parents, PTA presidents, nurses, custodians, and secretaries for the role of the school administrator, all of these groups agreed that the following behavioral characteristics were important for the administrator: (1) show interest in work, offer assistance; (2) praise personnel; (3) back up personnel; (4) assume authority, stand by convictions; (5) allow self-direction in work; (6) make clear her feelings; (7) allow participation in decisions; (8) be a good disciplinarian; be considerate of work load; (9) possess good personal characteristics, and (10) be well organized.

While some of the above-mentioned expectations seem contradictory, and the school administrator cannot realistically expect that reference groups' expectations will always be in agreement, Campbell's research suggests that compatability may be achievable to a large extent. The most important step the administrator can take to reach this goal is to make sure that she understands accurately the expectations of reference groups. For, as Roald Campbell has perceptively pointed out,

> An understanding of these expectations, often conflicting in nature, may appear most frustrating. Only by such understanding, however, can the administrator anticipate the reception of specified behavior on his part. Such anticipation seems necessary if the area of acceptance is to be extended and the area of disagreement minimized. Moreover, such understandings are necessary if a program of modifying expectations is to be started.[53]

SOCIAL FACTORS AFFECTING THE SCHOOL ADMINISTRATOR'S ROLE

The job of the school administrator, has, of course, seldom been without problems. But in the last two decades several social factors have emerged which have made the job one of the most challenging in education today. While observers may differ on the nature of the impact, there appears to be fairly general agreement that five factors in particular have affected the role of the school administrator: (1) demographic changes, (2) the state of the economy, (3) collective bargaining, (4) the influence of federal and state government, and (5) the influence of news media and educationally adapted technology.

DEMOGRAPHIC CHANGES

The role of the school administrator has frequently been influenced by demographic changes of one kind or another. For example, the rising birth rates after World War II resulted in the need for school administrators to place increased emphasis, for a considerable period of time, on hiring additional teachers and on planning for the construction of new school buildings.

However, it would appear that in the last two decades tremendous demographic changes have occurred which have impacted on the role of the school administrator, and it is likely that most if not all of these demographic trends will continue for some time.

A major demographic change has been the significant decline, during the past two decades, in the birth rate, which has led to declining student enrollments in many school districts.[54] As a result, administrators have been forced to reduce staff, close some school buildings, and deal with the problems of lower staff morale, an older staff, excess building space, and community opposition to the closing of schools.[55] Declining enrollments have also, according to a study by the Association for Supervision and Curriculum Development, resulted in administrator layoffs, reassignment of administrators to other schools, assignment of more than one school to an elementary school principal, cutback of in-service education, decreased use of student teachers, fewer courses in the curriculum, and excess buildings, or building space being sold or leased.[56]

The characteristics of the family have also undergone major changes in the last decade. The divorce rate more than doubled between 1970 and 1980;[57] the percentage of children born out of wedlock increased 50 percent;[58] and the proportion of single-parent households increased nearly 80 percent during the 1970s.[59] In addition, the proportion of married women who work outside the home for wages increased about 10 percent during the 1970s, and currently more than half of all married women hold paying jobs outside the home.[60]

These changes in family characteristics have impacted on schools and their administrators. For example, a study which was jointly sponsored by the National Association of Elementary School Principals and the Institute for the Development of Educational Activities found that, as a group, children in one-parent families presented more discipline problems, were more frequently tardy and absent, and achieved less in school than did their classmates.[61] In addition, the high rate of divorce in families, the increased number of children born out of wedlock, and the trend toward both parents (or, in the case of one-parent familes, the family head) working outside the home have placed greater pressures on the students coming from these situations and have made it difficult in many circumstances for the school administrator to communicate with and gain support from the home.[62] These difficulties were exemplified, from the single parent's perspective, in a study by the National Committee for Citizens in Education, which discovered that single parents were generally dissatisfied with the way schools treated them, particularly regarding the times that parent conferences were scheduled, the lack of childcare at school during the conferences, the lack of information sent or made available to the noncustodial parent, and the negative attitude of school personnel toward single-parent situations.[63]

Other demographic changes have also impacted on the schools. For example, migration from the large cities to the suburbs, to rural areas, and from the East and Midwest to the Southwest and the West continues to increase, causing the paradox of increased enrollment in some school districts amidst an overall national decline in student enrollment.[64] Immigration, both legal and illegal, has increased greatly during the last decade, bringing with it children with problems of cultural assimilation and special educational needs.[65] The proportion of the population aged 65 and older has increased and is likely to grow substantially in the future, constituting a sizeable percentage of the adult population in many communities, thereby compounding possible problems of financial support for the schools.[66] The increasing number of older people in a community whose children are no longer in school has placed and will continue to place a higher priority for school administrators to communicate with this group of older citizens in order to gain their understanding and support of the goals of the school and the importance of education. The increased role of the school in adult education for senior citizens is another possible implication. (Chapters 6, 8, 17, and 18 present ideas that can be helpful in responding to demographic changes.)

THE STATE OF THE ECONOMY

A second major social force that can affect the role of the school administrator is the state of the economy.[67] A growing, noninflationary economy tends to result in low unemployment, stable prices, high tax revenues, and reduced resistance from tax payers regarding school spending. Unfortunately, the United States has not experienced that kind of economy for the past decade. Instead, our economy has gone through a period of "stagflation," in which growth has been minimal; unemployment, inflation, and taxes have remained high; and tax revenues have been reduced because of increased unemployment.[68] As a result of some of these circumstances, school costs have risen, and taxpayer's resistance to the increased costs of education has risen tremendously.[69]

Resistance by taxpayers to the costs of education (as well as other sources of higher taxes) has taken various forms. In California and Massachusetts, for example, taxpayer pressures have resulted in changes in the way that education is financed, and in the amount of revenue available for education that have caused severe financial problems for many schools.[70] Also, in a number of communities local bond referendums have been rejected by taxpayers, thereby delaying capital improvements; and tax-increase requests for education have been rejected, resulting in some cases in the closing of schools. In Michigan, for example, several school districts have been forced to close school temporarily because of taxpayers' unwillingness to approve increases or even renewals of local property tax levies that provide much of the support for public education.[71] Even in the case of approving the yearly operating budget, many school districts are encountering increased taxpayer scrutiny of individual items in the budget.[72] Energized by high inflation, high unemployment, high taxes, and rising school cost, taxpayer resistance has created a serious dilemma for school boards and administrators who are not opposed to economizing but who are concerned that continued budget reductions will seriously damage the quality of education provided to students.

Although school boards and administrators have attempted to economize in order to reduce increases in the costs of education, they have been confronted with the reality of the spiraling rate of inflation which affects school costs, as well as increased costs due to federal and state mandates for new programs, such as special education, parental resistance to the elimination of reduction of favorite programs, and the fact that most of the school budget is concentrated in the area of personnel salaries and fringe benefits, which are hard to cut because of contractual agreements.[73] In addition, as mentioned earlier, many school boards and administrators believe that they have reached the point at which continued reduction in schools costs would begin to erode severely the quality of education. Unfortunately, no easy answers present themselves for the solution of these problems because most of the economic factors which impact on school administrators, such as inflation and unemployment, are beyond their control, although these factors can be changed by the actions of federal and state officials. What an administrator *can* do, however, is to manage the educational enterprise as efficiently as possible, work to develop a better understanding on the part of the public regarding goals and values of education, and identify clearly the consequences of arbitrary reduction in the financial support of education. These topics are further addressed in chapters 6, 9, and 18 of the text.

COLLECTIVE BARGAINING

There seems to be little doubt that collective bargaining has changed the role of the school administrator, at least in her relationship to teachers. According to the Educational Research Service, "Many observers would agree that collective bargaining has affected the process of decision making and school governance more than any other single development in the mid-twentieth century."[74] Prior to collective bargaining the school administrator's relationship with teachers was frequently a paternalistic one. In most situations she had a choice as to whether or not she should consider teachers' grievances, consult with them about work assignments, or involve them in school decision making, and all too often—at least according to teachers' perceptions—she chose not to do so.

The introduction of collective bargaining, however, has meant that in most situations the administrator must consider teacher grievances and must consult with the teachers in regard to work conditions and other matters affecting their welfare. For example, pertaining to the latter, a Rand Corporation study found that collective bargaining in an increasing number of schools has resulted in contract agreements which limit the principal's decision-making prerogatives in such areas as class size; provisions for determining teacher assignments, transfer and reduction in force; the length of the school day;

teacher evaluation and promotion procedures; and the use of school aides.[75] As a result of this kind of collective bargaining, the principal can no longer act unilaterally in situations in which she previously had primary authority, but now are covered by the master contract; instead, she must administer within the framework of a collective bargaining agreement.

While collective bargaining undoubtedly offers advantages as a technique or process for conflict resolution,[76] one negative consequence has been the limitations it has placed on the initiative and flexibility of school boards and administrators to promulgate those personnel policies which they believe to be in the best interest of the school district and the local community. However, another outcome has been a reduction in arbitrariness and insensitivity by some school districts regarding the needs, problems, and aspirations of teachers. Collective bargining has also tended to involve teachers more as partners in the management of a school district. Whether the latter consequence is desirable or not is yet to be determined, but it seems clear that school governance and the administration of school personnel policies in most school districts will continue to be influenced by collective bargaining.[77] (The topic of collective bargaining and contract administration is further discussed in chapter 9; for an extended treatment of these topics, which is beyond the intended scope of this text, see Anthony M. Cresswell, et. al., *Teachers, Unions and Collective Bargaining in Public Education,* published by McCutchan in 1980.)

INFLUENCE OF THE FEDERAL AND STATE GOVERNMENTS

A fourth major social force which has affected the role of the school administrator has been the intervention by the federal and state governments in educational affairs.* This intervention has taken several forms and has posed new problems for school administrators.

For example, in the past the courts did not often attempt to substitute their judgment for that of school officials in the administration of the schools unless, of course, a serious offense was committed.[78] Recently, however, acting in response to challenges by students, teachers, and parents to school authority and decision-making, the courts have laid down a number of rulings which have altered the role of the administrator. These rulings have covered a broad range of areas, including students' due process rights, racial and sexual discrimination, teacher evaluation, reduction in staff, and competency testing.[79]

These court decisions have had important impact on the role of the school administrator. The administrator's authority has been limited, and she is now required to demonstrate that the school has acted fairly and prudently in its relations with others. Although there appear to be many administrators who

---

*An excellent book on this topic has been written by Arthur E. Wise. See *Legislated Learning* (Berkeley, Calif: University of California Press, 1979).

feel that the courts have "interfered" in school affairs and have made the administrator's job more difficult, the overall result in many situations has been to make the school and the relationships within the school less authoritarian and more humanistic. The extent to which the latter result has been achieved, however, has depended as much on the manner and spirit in which the school administrator has implemented the court decisions as on any other factor.[80]

State and federal legislatures have also passed laws and regulations which have tended to increase the difficulty of the administrator's job and alter her role. These laws and regulations have attempted to address such problems as segregation, the disadvantaged student, the handicapped student, the student speaking English as a second language, and a variety of other perceived needs.[81] These efforts, although perhaps needed and commendable in their original intent, have complicated enormously the role of the school administrator. For example, a Rand Corporation study on the effects of federal education programs on school principals revealed that in general, "Principals are now [1980] more constrained by rules, more subject to public scrutiny, and less in control of their own schedules, than they were five years ago."[82] Another study by Hannan and Freement showed that state and federal funds increased administrative loads far beyond the equivalent funds allocated at the local community level.[83] Perhaps in response to these problems, the executive branch of the federal government has recently attempted to reduce and simplify federal regulations, and both the executive and legislative branches of the federal government have tried to reduce the federal role in education.[84] Although these actions have been welcomed by many administrators, it is likely that most of the problems which had led to an increased federal role in education in recent years will be shifted to the state level, and new problems of state control and unmet school and societal needs will emerge as a result.[85]

Whether state and federal laws and regulations on education constitute "interference" in local school affairs can be debated, but it does seem evident that such laws and regulations have increased the difficulty of the administrator's role. However, what administrators need to recognize is that state and federal governments do not usually pass legislation affecting a local school situation unless there is evidence that local initiative is not being exercised to correct a serious problem. The best alternative for school administrators may be to move more quickly to identify and resolve problems on the local level so that state and federal legislative action will be unnecessary.

INFLUENCE OF THE NEWS MEDIA AND EDUCATIONALLY ADAPTED TECHNOLOGY

The news media and several innovations in educationally adapted technology have affected the role of the school administrator, and the prospects are that they will continue to do so in the future.

The news media consist of newspapers, magazines, and radio and television stations which carry news programs.[86] In recent years the news media have "discovered" education, and seldom does a week pass without some major news story on education. The news story may consist of a TV documentary on "What's Wrong with American Education," a magazine article on "Sex Education in the Schools," a radio talk-show interview of a proponent of "A Need to Return to Basics in Our Schools," or a newspaper article on "Violence in the Schools." Regrettably, the focus of much of the news media's coverage of the schools seems to concentrate on problems of American education, although there are exceptions.[87]

The impact of this increased and largely critical news coverage of the schools has yet to be scientifically determined. However, many administrators appear to feel that the news media's coverage of education impacts negatively on public opinion and places them in a defensive, reactive position.[88] Consequently, they often tend to perceive the news media and reporters in particular as adversaries and are ambivalent in responding to their news inquiries. This type of attitude and behavior by administrators, although understandable, is unfortunate and usually counterproductive. The representatives of the news media have a job to accomplish and, while they frequently may not perform their job to the satisfaction of the administrator, a negative attitude and reaction are only likely to make the situation worse. Instead, most administrators need to take the initiative to develop a better relationship with the news media and to initiate improved ways of communication with the public. Ideas and recommendations for achieving those goals are presented in chapter 18.

While the news media have had, at least in the eyes of many administrators, a negative impact on the role of the school administrator, several innovations in educationally adapted technology have exerted a largely positive influence. These innovations include the use of computers for school data processing and scheduling, hand calculators for mathematics, microprocessors for individualized instruction and learning, and video tape recorders, video discs, and cable television for instructional and self-improvement activities.[89]

Although most of these innovations are too recent to determine their eventual use and value, potentially they could dramatically change administration, teaching, and learning. For example, computer-generated master schedules could remove the need for an administrator to know *how* to schedule a school's instructional program;[90] split screen video recorders offer the possibility for improved staff evaluation and instructional supervision by providing the teacher and the administrator with an expanded visual record of a class session, with the opportunity for replay and analysis.[91] Microprocessor computers offer the possibility of diagnosis, remediation, and individualization in a variety of school subjects including English and social studies.[92] They are also being linked to videodiscs and other data sources in order to provide more individualized and enriched learning experiences for students at school and in the home.[93] And cable television offers schools not only the possibility of enriching their curriculum through various programs but also an opportunity to communicate more directly with their publics and to obtain feedback more systematically.[94]

Whether many of these possibilities and opportunities are actually capitalized on will depend in large part on the school administrator. She will need to develop a deeper understanding of the potential and the use of educationally adapted technology. She will also need to develop skills in evaluating software for the educationally-adapted technology,[95] and she will need to provide in-service education for her faculty to help them develop awareness of and skills for using the technology.[96] While most of these increased understandings and skills can be obtained through reading, coursework and special workshops, very little is likely to occur unless the administrator has the vision and takes initiative in this area. Many schools are already underutilizing traditional audiovisual aids, such as the overhead projector, and unless there is more enlightened leadership and initiative with respect to educationally adapted technology, the schools could wind up with a lot of very expensive, underutilized equipment. (For further discussion on how to introduce program change and to plan in-service education for the staff, see chapters 11 and 12. Also, for additional reading in the area of educationally adapted technology, note the references at the end of this chapter.[97])

CONCLUDING NOTE

It may appear to some readers, after finishing this chapter, that the school administrator has an impossible job. This would represent an understandable but incorrect conclusion. There is little doubt that the job of the school administrator is filled with challenges. However, each of those challenges represents an opportunity to exercise *leadership*. By thoroughly understanding the concepts and ideas presented throughout this text, and thinking about and practicing their application, the reader should be able to respond successfully to the various challenges and, in the process, exercise the kind of leadership needed in education.

Review and Learning Activities

1. Which of the six major roles of the school administrator described in the text are you currently *most* competent to perform? Which of the six are you *least* competent to perform? What is the basis of your self-assessment? What are the implications of those assessments?
2. What implications does Getzel's model hold for your role behavior as an administrator?

3. Based on the discussion in the text on personal variables, to what extent is your own behavior as a teacher or administrator influenced by your attitude and values?
4. Examine the reference group expectations presented in the text. How would you go about ascertaining the expectations of the students, teachers, parents, and superiors associated with your own school?
5. To what extent should an administrator meet the expectations of students, teachers, parents, and superiors for her role? What are the advantages and disadvantages of meeting or not meeting the expectations of these groups?
6. After reading the presentation in the text on social factors, attempt to ascertain the extent to which these social factors are impacting on your own school situation. What are the implications for the role of the school administrator, insofar as these social factors are impacting in your local situation?

Notes

1. Arthur Blumberg and William Greenfield, *The Effective Principal* (Allyn & Bacon. 1980).

2. Richard A. Gorton, *School Administration and Supervision: Important Issues, Concepts and Case Studies* (Dubuque, Iowa: Wm. C. Brown Company Publishers, 1980).

3. For example, see Robert Owens, *Organizational Behavior in Education* (Englewood Cliffs, N.J.: Prentice Hall, 1981).

4. Paul R. Pierce, The Origin and Development of the Public School Principalship (Chicago: University of Chicago Press, 1935), p. 12.

5. M. Claradine Johnson, "The Principal in the 1980s: Instructional Leader, Manager," *NASSP Bulletin* (January 1981): 88–90. For a different point of view, see Cheryl Overy, "A Study of the Managerial Role of the Public School Principal" (Ph.D. diss. University of Nebraska-Lincoln, 1981).

6. See Ellwood P. Cubberley, *The Principal and His School* (Boston: Houghton-Mifflin, 1923).

7. Ibid., p. 43.

8. For an elaboration of different definitions of the role, see JoAnn Mazzarella, *Leadership Effectiveness.* An ERIC Report: Ed–176–362.

9. "The Principal's Role: How Do We Reconcile Expectations with Reality?" *R and D Perspectives* (Winter 1982): 1–8. Also see chapter 11 on Instructional Leadership for additional evidence on this point.

10. Clifford Campbell, "The Elementary Principal as Viewed by His Staff and Parent-Teacher Association Presidents" (Ph.D. diss., University of California, 1964), p. 67.

11. John D. McAulay, "Principal: What Do Your Children Think of You?" *National Elementary Principal* (January 1968): 58–60.

12. David B. Austin and Harry L. Brown, Jr., *Report of the Assistant Principal* (Washington, D.C.: National Association of Secondary School Principals, 1970), p. 68.

13. Mary Parker Follett, *Creative Experience* (New York: Longmans, Green, 1924).

14. Elton Mayo, *The Human Problems of an Industrial Civilization* (Boston: Graduate School of Business Administration, Harvard University, 1946.)

15. Daniel Griffiths, *Human Relations in School Administration* (New York: Appleton-Century-Crofts, 1956).

16. See discussion in chapter 2 for a review of the evidence supporting this point.

17. Edgar A. Kelly, "Principles of Conflict Resolution," *NASSP Bulletin* (April 1979): 11–17.

18. Gorton, *School Administration and Supervision,* chapter 12.

19. Jacob W. Getzels, "Administration as a Social Process," in *Administrative Theory in Education,* ed. Andrew Halpin (Chicago: Midwest Administration Center, University of Chicago, 1958), p. 153.

20. Neal Gross et al., *Explorations in Role Analysis: Studies of the School Superintendency Role* (New York: John Wiley & Sons, 1958), p. 58.

21. Numerous studies have been conducted which support the validity of the Getzels model. They are described in *Educational Administration as a Social Process: Theory, Research, and Process,* eds., Jacob W. Getzels, James M. Lipham, and Roald Campbell (New York: Harper & Row, 1968).

22. This section and the previous one were adapted from material in Gorton, *School Administration and Supervision,* pp. 238–40, 313–14.

23. James M. Lipham and James A. Hoeh, *The Principalship: Foundations and Functions* (New York: Harper & Row, 1974), p. 158.

24. Roy Dexheimer, "The Ethics of Chief School Administrators: A Study in Accommodation" (Paper presented at the 101st meeting of the American Association of School Administrators, Atlantic City, N.J., 1969).

25. Raymond H. Ostrander and Roy C. Dethey, *A Values Approach to Educational Administration* (New York: American Book Company, 1968).

26. A copy of this statement may be obtained by writing any of the national administrators' association, such as the National Association of Elementary School Principals or the National Association of Secondary School Principals.

27. Raymond G. Taylor, "If I Were Boss. . . ." *Education* (Fall 1978): 8–9.

28. Monroe E. Pederson, "Pupil Expectations of the High School Principal" (Ph.D. diss., University of Southern California, 1970).

29. Clinton I. Chase, "Teenagers Are Mostly Positive about High School," *The Kappan* (March 1981): 526.

30. Pederson, "Pupil Expectations." For a related study, see James Mundy, "Effective Ways in Which Secondary School Principals Can Relate to Students" (Ed.D. diss., University of Virginia, 1980).

31. McAulay, "Principal: What Do Your Children Think?", 5.

32. H. S. Becker, "Role and Career Problems of the Chicago Public School Teachers" (Ph.D. diss., University of Chicago, 1951).

33. Donald J. Willower, *The Teacher Subculture.* An ERIC Report: Ed–020–588.

34. Edwin M. Bridges, "Teacher Participation in Decision-Making," *Administrator's Notebook* (May 1964): 1–4.

35. Robert Brumbaugh and John Skinkus, *Organizational Control and the Middle School Principal.* An ERIC Report: Ed–180–053.

36. See, for example, Joseph Sjostrom, "Teachers Want More Backing from Better Bosses," *Chicago Tribune* (May 3, 1981), Section 2, p. 10.

37. E. M. Scully, "Personnel Administration in Public Education: A Study in Human Relationship (Ph.D. diss., University of Wisconsin, 1945).

38. Charles E. Bidwell, "Some Causes of Conflict and Tensions among Teachers," *Administrator's Notebook* (March 1956).

39. Francis L. Chase, "The Teacher and Policy Making," *Administrator's Notebook* (May 1952).

40. Russell T. Sharpe, "Differences between Perceived Administrative Behavior and Role Norms as Factors in Leadership and Group Morale" (Ph.D. diss., Stanford University, 1955), p. 159.

41. For example, see recent issues of *Today's Education.*

42. Chase, "The Teacher and Policy Making."

43. G. L. Sharma, "Who Should Make What Decisions?" *Administrator's Notebook* (April 1955).

44. Daniel Duke, Beverly K. Showers, and M. Imfer, "Teachers and Shared Decision-making," *Educational Administration Quarterly* (Winter 1980): 93–106.

45. J. A. Horalick, "Teacher Acceptance of Administrative Action," *Journal of Experimental Education* (Winter 1968): 39–47.

46. Reported in William H. Roe and Thelbert L. Drake, *The Principalship* (New York: Macmillan Publishing, 1980): pp. 132–33.

47. Reed L. Buffington, "The Job of the Elementary School Principal as Viewed by Parents" (Ed.D. diss., Stanford University, 1954), p. 943.

48. Evidence supporting this point was collected in a study by Gorton. See Richard A. Gorton, "Factors Which Are Associated with the Principal's Behavior in Encouraging Teacher Participation in School Decision-Making." *Journal of Educational Research* (March 1971): 325–27.

49. Gorton, *School Administration and Supervision,* chapter 12.

50. Robert P. Moser, "A Study of the Effects of Superintendent-Principal Interaction and Principal-Teacher Interaction in Selected Middle-sized School Systems" (Ph.D. diss., University of Chicago, 1957).

51. J. W. Getzels, James Lipham, and Roald Campbell, *Educational Administration as a Social Process* (New York: Harper and Row, 1968), pp. 145–49.

52. Campbell, "The Elementary Principal."

53. Roald F. Campbell, "Situational Factors in Educational Administration," in *Administrative Behavior in Education,* ed. Roald F. Campbell and Russell T. Gregg (New York City: Harper & Row, 1957), p. 264.

54. *Statistical Abstract of the United States* (Washington, D.C.: U. S. Government Printing Office, 1981); *The Condition of Education* (Washington, D.C.: National Center for Educational Statistics, 1980).

55. See chapters 6 and 9 for a further discussion of these problems.

56. *The Effects of Declining Enrollments on Instructional Programs and Supervisory Practices in Public Elementary and Secondary Schools* (Alexandria, Va.: Association for Supervision and Curriculum Development, 1980).

57. *Marital Status and Living Arrangements: March 1980* (Washington, D.C.: Census Bureau, 1980).

58. "One of 6 Births in U.S. Out of Wedlock," *AP Services* (October 26, 1981).

59. "One-parent Families and Their Children," *Principal* (September, 1980): 31–39.

60. Linda J. Waite, "U.S. Women at Work," *Population Bulletin* (May 1981): 3–30.

61. "One-parent Families and Their Children."

62. John Ourth, "Children in One-parent Homes: The School Factor," *Principal* (September 1980): 40.

63. *Single Parents: Growing Segment Has Special Needs* (Columbia, Md.: National Committee for Citizens in Education, 1980).

64. *School Finance Reform in the States* (Denver, Co.: Educational Commission of the States, 1980). Also see Jeanne C. Bigger, "The Sunning of America: Migration to the Sunbelt," *Population Bulletin* (March 1979): 1–30.

65. Phoebe P. Hollis, "The Student of the Future." An ERIC Report: Ed–195–507.

66. Michael W. Kirst and Walter I. Garms, *The Demographic, Fiscal and Political Environment of Public School Finance in the 1980s* (Stanford, Calif.: Institute for Research on Educational Finance and Governance, 1980). Also see Beth J. Soldo, "America's Elderly in the 1980s," *Population Bulletin* (November 1980): 1–42.

67. Michael J. Bakalis, "American Education and the Meaning of Scarcity," *Phi Delta Kappan* (September 1981): 7–12.

68. G. Ruben, "Industrial Relations in 1980 Influenced by Inflation and Recession," *Monthly Labor Review* (January 1981): 16–20.

69. "Educators Look at the New School Year," *Education USA* (August 31, 1981): 4.

70. B. Anderson, 'Don't Tell This Little California System That Proposition 13 Hasn't Hurt," *American School Board Journal* (April 1980): 40–42. Also see "Prop 2½ Slashes a Town's Teaching Staff," *NEA Reporter* (November 1981): 7.

71. "Michigan's Woes Fall on Schools," *AP News Services* (October 25, 1981).

72. Bakalis, "American Education."

73. Based on an examination of numerous master contracts.

74. Joan P. Sullivan Kowalski, *Negotiating the Teacher Evaluation Issue* (Arlington, Va.: Educational Research Service, 1979): iii.

75. Loraine McDonnell and Anthony Pascal, *Organized Teachers in American Schools* (Santa Monica, Calif.: Rand Corporation, 1979): pp. 89–91.

76. Claude W. Fawcett, *School Personnel Systems* (Lexington, Mass.: Lexington Books, 1979), p. 128.

77. Richard A. Gorton, "School Personnel Policy" in *Encyclopedia of Educational Research,* ed. Harold E. Mitzel (New York: Macmillan Company, 1982).

78. John C. Hogan, *The Schools, the Courts, and the Public Interest* (Lexington, Mass.: Lexington Books, 1974), chapter 2.

79. *Schools and the Courts* (Eugene, Oreg.: ERIC Clearinghouse on Educational Management, 1980). See also the 1980 and 1981 *Yearbook of School Law* (Topeka, Kans.: National Organization on Legal Problems of Education.)

80. See, for example, "Districts' Compliance with Courts—Low," *Institute for Research on Educational Finance and Government* (Summer 1980): 3.

81. "Fragmented Centralization in American Public Schools," *Institute for Research on Educational Finance and Governance* (Autumn 1980): 1, 7.

82. Paul Hill et al., "The Effects of Federal Education Programs on School Principals." An ERIC Report: Ed–191–178. Also see Jackie Kimbrough and Paul Hill, *The Aggregate Effects of Federal Education Programs* (Santa Monica, Calif.: Rand Corporation, 1981).

83. Reported in the article, "Fragmented Centralization in American Schools," p. 7.

84. David G. Savage, "Washington report," *Phi Delta Kappan* (June 1981): 693; and "Limits Placed on Federal Regulatory Powers, Congress Makes Drastic Cuts in Federal Education Spending," *Center for Law and Education, Inc. Newsnotes* (Summer 1981): 1–7.

85. "State Boards, Federal Officials Toss Around Deregulation Ball," *Education USA* (October 12, 1981): 49, 56.

86. Tom Wicker, *On Press* (New York: Viking Press, 1978).

87. Dolly A. Berthelot, "Content Analysis of Education Coverage in Three Influential U.S. Newsmagazines During a Year of Low Public Support for Education" (Ed.D. diss., University of Tennessee, 1981).

88. Richard A. Gorton, "What Do Principals Think of News Media Coverage?" *NASSP Bulletin* (December, 1979): 116–18.

89. Norman Watts, "A Dozen Uses for the Computer in Education," *Educational Technology* (April 1981): 18–22.

90. See, for example, Richard A. Dempsey and Henry P. Travers, *Scheduling the Secondary School* (Reston, Va.: National Association of Secondary School Principals, 1982).

91. William Moritz and Jo Anne Martin-Reynolds, "The Genie in the Bottle," *Educational Leadership* (February 1980): 396–99. See also, Gerald D. Bailey, "Learning How to Self-critique Using Audiotape and Videotape in Teacher Self Assessment," *Educational Technology* (February 1981): 41–45.

92. Ronald Saltinski, "Microcomputers in Social Studies: An Innovative Technology for Instruction," *Educational Technology* (January 1981): 29–32. Also, Ted S. Hasselbring and Cathy L. Crossland, "Using Microcomputers for Diagnosing Spelling Problems in Learning-Handicapped Children," *Educational Technology* (April 1981): 37–39; and Janis Gershman and Evannah Sakamoto, "Computer-Assisted Remediation and Evaluation: A CAL Project for Ontario Secondary Schools," *Educational Technology* (March 1981): 40–43.

93. Allen D. Glenn and Kent T. Kehrberg, "The Intelligent Videodisc: An Instructional Tool for the Classroom," *Educational Technology* (October 1981): 60–63. Also see "Videodisc Report," *New Technology* (April 1981): 1–4.

94. "The Cables Are Humming in Irvine, California," *New Technology* (January 1981): 5–6.

95. See "Computers: Beware of the Software," *Education USA* (October 12, 1981): 52.

96. Sam Petruso, "A Commitment to Computer Education: Introducing Computers into a District," *T.H.E. Journal* (November 1981): 53, 58. Also see Elizabeth Dershimer, "A Study to Identify the Characteristics of Teachers Willing to Implement Computer-Based Instruction Using Microcomputers in the Classroom" (Ed.D. diss., Memphis State University, 1980).

97. F. J. Frederick, *Guide to Microcomputers* (Washington, D.C.: Association for Educational Communications and Technology, 1980); various issues of the journals *Educational Technology* and *New Technology;* and Adeline Naiman, *Microcomputers in Education: An Introduction* (Cambridge, Mass.: Technical Education Research Center, 1981).

5

The Administrative Team

The concept of "team" suggests a group of people working together cooperatively, rather than unilaterally, to achieve a common goal. The main goals of an administrative team should be to develop school policies and procedures, solve common problems, and, in general, to improve education in the schools by utilizing the collective talents and interests of the individual members of the team.[1] The concept is based on the assumption that administrative decision making schould be a joint effort rather than the sole responsibility or province of one individual, such as the principal or the superintendent.[2]

While it may not be possible to establish an administrative team in every school or school district (and evidence presented later shows that many school districts only pay lip service to the concept), the potential advantages of cooperatively pooling human resources to achieve school and district objectives strongly support the need to organize an administrative team, where feasible. An administrative team is particularly important as a means of facilitating school-based management—a concept which is premised on the assumption that the individual school is a more effective unit for administrative decision making than the district.[3] The following sections will discuss, first at the building level and then at the district level, the various aspects of organizing and operating an administrative team.

THE ADMINISTRATIVE TEAM AT THE BUILDING LEVEL

COMPOSITION OF THE TEAM

With few exceptions, the principal should be the one to make the final decision on the composition of the administrative team at the building level. He is the one who is administratively in charge of the school and should, consequently, determine the membership of the team. In determining the composition of the team he should keep in mind that its basic functions are communication and decision making. It would appear, therefore, that those individuals who are key communicators and who are involved or should be involved in school decision-making should be members of the team. This would include, in most situations, the people occupying the positions identified in figure 5.1.

Figure 5.1 shows the proposed composition of the administrative team and its main characteristics. It indicates that the composition of the administrative team at the building level consists of the principal, the assistant and/ or vice-principal, the department heads or unit leaders, program directors, pupil personnel workers, and a central office representative. The latter might be the individual in charge of secondary or elementary school education in the

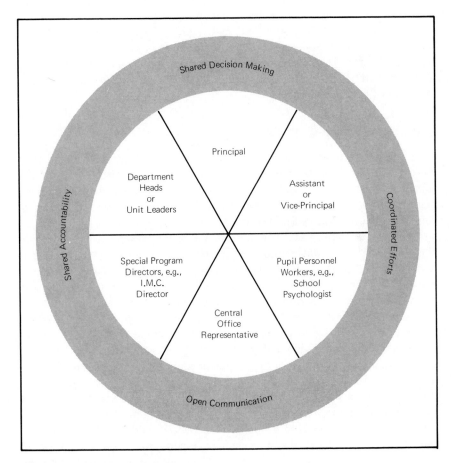

Figure 5.1. Proposed Composition and Characteristics of the Administrative Team at the School Level

district, or someone else who could represent the central administration's point of view, since a number of the topics that the administrative team will discuss are likely to hold implications for the entire district. (Consideration should also be given to adding parent representatives to the team, in order to obtain perceptions, insights and other contributions to effective decision-making and community support that the team might not otherwise receive.)

Note the recommendation that the pupil personnel workers (such as the school psychologist) and the program directors (such as the director of the instructional materials center) should be members of the administrative team. These persons may not be actually administrators or supervisors in the strictest sense of those terms. But at least some of their responsibilities are administrative or supervisory in nature; more importantly, because of their contacts with students, teachers, and parents, they offer a potentially rich source of insights and perceptions that would be useful to the other members of the team. While it may not be possible or even necessary to include these specialists in all of the team meetings, it seems clear that each of them can make a valuable contribution and consequently should be included as members and attend meetings as appropriate.

STRUCTURE OF THE TEAM

Once the composition of an administrative team has been determined, then its structure should be defined, i.e., how each component of the team should function individually and in relationship to the other components. If the principal has not already assigned responsibilities to each member of the term, this should be the team's first priority.[4]

The next objective should be to define the interrelationships which should exist between the various members of the team. If the administrative team is to operate effectively, each member must know about the responsibilities and roles of the other members, and how all team members can help each other and work together cooperatively. In essence, assisting one another and working cooperatively are the keys to a successful team. The type of structure which is initiated must arrive at these outcomes, or the concept of "team" degenerates into a group of individuals merely trying to promote and protect their own selfish interests or those of the people they represent, rather than the common good of the school.

When establishing the structure of an administrative team the issue of the authority relationships within the team should be faced squarely. An initial question which needs to be answered is, who should head the team? Although various arguments could be made in response to this question, it would appear that in most situations the head of the team will be—and should be—

the principal. He is the one who has the overall responsibility for administering the school, and it is he who is held primarily accountable for what goes on in the school.

This does not mean, however, that the principal should play a domineering or controlling role on the administrative team, nor does it mean that he should exercise all of the leadership on the team.[5] On the contrary—the principal's main role should be that of facilitator and resource person for the other team members, as further discussed under "group leadership behavior" in chapter 3. He should try to stimulate their involvement and leadership, and he should attempt to emphasize and encourage cooperation among all members of the team.[6] Although the principal may retain the authority to assign responsibility and then evaluate the performance of the team members, this should be done cooperatively as much as possible.

ADMINISTRATIVE TEAM PROCESSES

An administrative team is functioning successfully if each member is carrying out his responsibilities effectively, and the various members of the team are working cooperatively with each other. Although many of the activities of the team members will take place outside of their formal meetings, it is during the team meetings that most of the important discussions and decisions will take place, and it is during the meetings that members have their greatest opportunity to interact.[7]

Probably the most important step a principal can take to utilize productively the contributions that members offer during a meeting, and to help the group to function as a unit, is to try to maintain an atmosphere conducive to a spirit of cooperation and mutual respect, with an absence of tension or nervousness. In such an atmosphere each member of the team should feel free to contribute ideas and to question other members of the team, including the principal.

The atmosphere at the meetings will depend primarily on what the principal says and does. An organizational structure for the team may have been defined which ostensibly permits a great deal of give and take in discussions. But if the principal dominates and controls discussion during the meetings, it is unlikely that the atmosphere will be conducive to a free exchange of ideas and thoughts by the other members of the team.[8]

The principal will undoubtedly need to exercise authority in certain situations. For example, the other members of the team may wish to make a decision that the principal is not only opposed to but which may even be in an area for which *he* has primary responsible and accountability. The administrator can avoid most of these situations by specifying clearly at the outset the authority of the administrative team and the authority of the principal.

In exercising his authority the principal should also attempt to adhere to the following guidelines developed by Gorton based on an analysis of the social science literature on authority:[9]

1. In deciding on the need for a directive and in its formulation, presentation, and execution, the principal should take into consideration how the order will affect the recipients *personally,* recognizing that people are likely to question or resist directives which they feel are not in their best interest.

2. He should take into consideration the strengths and limitations of those who will be expected to implement a directive. He should avoid issuing orders for which people lack the necessary motivation, skill, or training to carry out.

3. He should explain thoroughly the rationale behind each directive and its relationship to the goals of the organization. He should not assume that people will understand the reasons for an order or that they will necessarily see the logic or value of an order.

4. He should leave room for modifying the original order or its method of implementation. Flexibility and a willingness to compromise when appropriate are key factors in exercising administrative authority successfully.

5. He should issue only those directives which he is relatively sure will either be obeyed or can be enforced if they are resisted. Orders which cannot be enforced in one situation weaken the administrator's authority for successfully issuing orders in other circumstances.

While it may be necessary for the principal to exercise authority upon occasion, his main role should be that of facilitator and resource person.

In order for the administrative team to function effectively, the principal should also establish certain managerial procedures, such as those identified in figure 5.2, which are important to the effective functioning of a group.

The processes recommended in this section are designed to facilitate input from the various members of the team in the development of the agenda, and to provide organization and continuity to the meetings. While one can over-emphasize the need for planning and the follow-through after a meeting, a certain degree of preparation and organization is necessary in order to avoid an aimless discussion and few concrete results. It is primarily the principal's responsibility to make sure that these outcomes do not occur.

A.	B.	C.	D.	E.
Soliciting input from team members for the development of the agenda	Preparing background material on agenda items and disseminating these materials and the agenda several days prior to the meeting	Maintaining a written record of important ideas and decisions made during the meeting	Disseminating written minutes to all appropriate parties after the meeting	Following through on decisions or actions taken during meetings

Figure 5.2. Recommended Processes for Team Meetings

SELECTED MEMBERS OF THE TEAM AT BUILDING LEVEL

For the administrative team to operate successfully, it is essential that the school administrator have a better understanding of the role and problems of each of its members. Since some of these roles will be presented in other chapters, this section will concentrate on the role and problems of the assistant principal, the department chairman, and the unit leader.

THE ASSISTANT PRINCIPAL[10]

For the most part the assistant principalship has not received the attention it deserves in most textbooks on administration and supervision, and in the educational literature. Both national elementary and secondary school administrators' organizations, however, have attempted in recent years to spotlight the role of the assistant principal and several studies have focussed on ascertaining the role and problems of the assistant principal.

For example, one study by Kattman surveyed assistant *elementary* school principals in large city school systems where assistant principals at the elementary level are more likely to be found.[11] An analysis of his data revealed several interesting findings which shed light on the assistant principalship at the elementary level.[12]

One somewhat surprising finding was that a slight majority of the assistant principals were women. Although historical data are not available, it would appear that there has been a substantial increase in the number of women serving in the elementary school assistant principalship. An analysis of mean differences between male and female assistant principals participating in

Kattman's study showed that females were significantly more satisfied in the position than were males, and salary was a less important reason for women to enter administration than for men.

Almost 90 percent of the assistant principals in the study reported that they possessed a Master's degree or higher; approximately 25 percent of the assistant principals had earned an Ed.S. or Ph.D. Most of the assistant principals had been teachers for thirteen or more years, and approximately 60 percent of them were over forty-six years old. The main reason most assistant principals had entered administration was to capitalize on the opportunity to help others, according to the respondents. Most of the assistants were serving in schools with student populations between 600 and 900.

Seventy percent of the assistant principals held full-time administrative positions; 30 percent of the assistants indicated that they also had teaching responsibilities and, of this number, about 19 percent had been given no released time in order to carry out their administrative assignment. The amount of released time from teaching allocated to the assistant principals was significantly related to the extent to which they actually performed a number of important administrative tasks ranging from conducting orientation for new students to evaluating teachers.

Most assistant principals reported that their main responsibilities at the elementary level were (1) administering student discipline, (2) placing substitute teachers, (3) providing instructional materials, and (4) establishing teacher duty rosters. Student discipline appeared to be the dominant responsibility of assistant principals, with three-fourths of the assistants stating that they had been assigned major or total responsibility for discipline. However, in a related analysis, only about one-third of the assistants indicated that they desired to take that much responsibility for student discipline.

What would the assistant principals do if they were not heavily occupied with the responsibility for administering student discipline? Most of them wanted significantly more responsibility than they were currently assigned in the following areas: orientating new teachers, selecting textbooks, administering public relations programs, planning teacher in-service, conducting student orientation, developing the school calendar, administering special education programs, administering guidance programs, developing curriculum, and deciding school policy. The research data do not suggest that most assistant principals want to be totally responsible in each of these areas, but they definitely want more responsibility than the limited amount they are currently assigned.

The elementary school assistant principals who participated in the study were asked to indicate their perception of the severity of certain problems which might be occurring in their situation. Most assistant principals reported that the following possible problems were either *nonexistent* or *very minor:* few opportunities for on-the-job professional growth, no job description, poorly defined responsibilities, little appreciation for contributions, lack of information provided by principal, little or no involvement in decision-making, uncooperative parents, and little or no feedback from superiors on areas in need of improvement. The percentage of assistant principals who felt that these problems were serious or very serious in their situation ranged from 10 to 30 percent. The two problems that were perceived by the assistant principals as *most serious* were (1) insufficient time to do the job, and (2) too many misbehaving students. A majority of the assistant principals viewed these two problems as either moderately or very serious in nature.

All of the problem areas were negatively correlated with job satisfaction. The more serious the assistant principal perceived the problems to be in the school situation, the more likely was the assistant to report a low level of satisfaction with the job. However, it should be noted that most assistant principals indicated considerable satisfaction with their job, although from 28 to 34 percent of them reported a low level of satisfaction with the salary they received, the recognition the job has given them, and the assistance they had received to help improve their effectiveness.

Most assistant principals identified their principal as their main source of help on the job; about 20 percent reported that their principals provided only some or no help. Approximately 60 percent of the assistant principals stated that they received only some or no help from other assistant principals, other principals than their own, or the central office staff. Over three-fourths of the assistant principals indicated that they received no on-the-job help from their university adviser, their state administrators' association or the national administrators' association. The latter results may be related to the finding that most of the assistant principals who participated in the study do not now belong to the state or national elementary administrator organizations, nor do they plan to join these organizations in the future.

What do elementary assistant principals hope to be doing in the future? Almost half of the respondents hoped that in five years they would become a principal; another 29 percent wanted to become central office administrators. Only 25 percent of the assistant principals wanted to continue in the same position either in the same school or a different one.

While the data from Kattman's study of elementary school assistant principals show that most of them are currently satisfied with their job, the majority desire a higher salary, greater recognition, increased responsibility and, eventually, promotion to a higher level administrative position. These latter findings on the desires of assistant principals suggest that if the concept of the assistant principalship as a *career* position is to have any viability, then consideration needs to be given to improving the salary and recognition of the elementary school assistant principals and redesigning the responsibilities of the position.

1. Scheduled detention of a student
2. Discussed with a boy his failure to get a haircut
3. Saw a parent about a car incident involving a student
4. Talked with a boy who had been late for detention
5. Questioned a boy who had no "permission to ride" sticker on his motorbike
6. Inspected the school grounds
7. Supervised the lunchroom
8. Reviewed a recently published student paper
9. Supervised detention hall
10. "Handled" a student fight
11. Distributed memos to some faculty members
12. Checked the rest rooms
13. Checked a locker for stolen materials
14. Supervised students passing in the hall
15. Discussed with the nurse the matter of a boy's broken nose incurred in a fight
16. Notified parents of a student suspension
17. Reviewed the daily bulletin
18. Suspended a boy for taking part in a theft
19. Interviewed a boy who had "sprung" his locker
20. Questioned a girl about tearing pages from a book

From *The Assistant Principalship.* Used with the permission of the National Association of Secondary School Principals.

Figure 5.3. A Day in the Life of an Assistant Principal[13]

At the *secondary* level, several studies have been conducted on the assistant principal. In one study, a diary was kept of the assistant principal's activities during a single day. The activities have been listed in figure 5.3.

An examination of the various activities reported by the assistant principal reveals that student control and discipline are his basic responsibilities.[14] This is not surprising since traditionally, and perhaps typically, the main duties of the assistant principal have been in these areas. In schools having an assistant principal, he is the individual to whom students who are discipline problems are referred. He is also the one who has the responsibility of checking on and working with students who are attendance problems. Although student discipline and attendance duties may be shared with the principal, the assistant principal usually shoulders the major responsibility for these two areas.

It would be misleading, however, to think that supervising student discipline and attendance are the only functions of an assistant principal. While it is true that his duties depend in reality on what the principal assigns to him, most assistant principals are given other kinds of responsibilities in addition to student discipline and attendance.

For example, a study by Stoner and Voorhies[15] found that a majority of assistant principals agreed that the assistant principal(s) in their school perform the following responsibilities, in addition to handling student discipline and attendance:

- Supervise the student activity program
- Supervise teachers through classroom visitations
- Assist in the evaluation of teachers
- Counsel teachers concerning personal or professional troubles
- Prepare daily bulletins or announcements
- Represent the school at community functions.

It should be pointed out, however, that data from other aspects of this research and related studies strongly indicate that handling student discipline and attendance problems continues to be the main responsibility of most assistant principals at the secondary school level.[16]

The responsibilities of working on problems of student discipline and attendance are important ones, and the assistant principal can make a valuable contribution to the school program by carrying out these responsibilities effectively. Nevertheless, it needs to be recognized that frequently these are onerous and frustrating tasks for him, particularly if he is the person primarily responsible. There are many days when an assistant principal may not even be able to leave his office during an entire morning or afternoon because he is seeing students or teachers in regard to student discipline or attendance problems. These typically are not pleasant experiences for an assistant principal, even though he may derive some measure of satisfaction from the feeling that he is trying to help others.

It would seem that the job of the assistant principal at the secondary level would not be a very satisfying position, but research is not conclusive on this point. One study by the National Association of Secondary School Principals found that assistant principals were much less satisfied with their current job than they were when they were teaching.[17] Other studies, however, have concluded that most assistant principals are reasonably well satisfied in their current jobs but, perhaps paradoxically, they don't see the assistant principalship as a lifetime career position.[18] One investigation which attempted to shed some light on sources of dissatisfaction on the part of the assistant principal found that assistant principals were dissatisfied when they were[19]

- Being placed on salary levels similar to those of instructional staff and counselors.
- Completing tasks that require a work day of ten hours or more.
- Functioning in a totally traditional (lacking any particular innovative quality) organizational structure.
- Lacking sufficient secretarial assistance, loyalty, and/or skills.

- Lacking adequate office space, equipment, and privacy.
- Lacking assistance from immediate superiors.
- Being ignored by superiors.
- Having constraints placed upon them by collective bargaining agreements.
- Being perceived negatively by faculty members in reference to the handling of student discipline problems.
- Being perceived by students merely as disciplinarians.
- Experiencing on-going constraints implicit in state and federal policies, in recent student rights and responsibilities documents, and in recent court decisions relative to due process and discipline.
- Having credit for work performed by the assistant principal attributed to superiors.

Assistant principals who are not as satisfied with their current positions as they were when they were teachers are not apt to remain in their present situations if they receive an opportunity to advance. Nor is it likely that these same individuals can operate at their maximum effectiveness in their present job if that job is not giving them the professional and personal satisfaction which they expect and need.

The findings from these studies have raised questions about whether the assistant principalship as it has been set up in many schools is meeting the needs of the individual occupying the position *or* the needs of the school. Consequently, efforts have been made to improve the position, including those by the national elementary and secondary administrators associations who have sponsored a number of conferences for assistant principals. One approach has been to define better the nature of the position. A proposed job description for the assistant principal[20] which was developed after an examination of many job descriptions and which appears quite comprehensive is presented in figure 5.4. (Kreikard and Norton have also developed a competency-based job description for assistant principals, which should be examined.[21])

One approach to making the job of the assistant principal more satisfying and effective has been to divide the responsibilities for student discipline and attendance among two or more assistant or vice-principals, rather than assigning all student discipline and attendance problems to one individual. In this kind of a situation, other tasks such as classroom supervision, curriculum implementation, and administration of student activities are shared by two or more assistant principals, thereby providing each with some variety in his job while utilizing their individual special talents. (Generally this kind of sharing of responsibilities occurs in schools where the administrative team concept is being fully implemented and assistant principals feel that ". . . they are real working partners in the management of the school."[22])

Relationships

The assistant principal is directly responsible to the principal, and is expected to maintain an effective working relationship with other administrators, teachers, maintenance staff, clerical staff, and student personnel.

Duties

Administration

1. Assists in the general administration of the school and serves as the principal when the principal is absent.
2. Operates the school according to the policies established by the principal, superintendent, and the board of education.
3. Participates in the preparation of the annual budget.
4. Assists in preparing district, state, and county reports.
5. Has the responsibility for preparing orientation program for substitute teachers and for assigning them as the situation demands.
6. Prepares the school calendar in cooperation with those responsible for school activity programs.
7. Designs the master schedule for the school.
8. Issues and keeps an inventory of all keys to school property.
9. Supervises the maintenance and cafeteria personnel and originates maintenance requests with the proper authorities.
10. Supervises school security aides.
11. Arranges bus schedules for students.
12. Performs such other duties and assumes such other responsibilities as the principal may assign.

Teaching Personnel

1. Participates in the evaluation of teachers.
2. Assists in the preparation of the teacher handbook.
3. Assists in interviewing and recommending prospective staff members and substitutes.
4. Assists teachers in the improvement of teaching techniques after an assessment of teaching methods.
5. Develops a regular schedule for teacher observation and maintains an accurate record of the observation providing an opportunity for teacher reaction.
6. Serves as liaison, when necessary, between individual teachers and the school principal.
7. Maintains an "open door" policy to all teaching personnel.

Student Personnel

1. Assists those who are responsible for school discipline.
2. Makes disciplinary judgments for students, assigns school detention, or takes other appropriate measures.
3. Establishes a system for keeping detailed records of discipline problems.
4. Assists in the development of the student activities program and is responsible for securing sponsors and supervising the financial aspects of the program.

Figure 5.4. Job Description for the Assistant Principal. *NASSP Bulletin,* May 1980. Used with the permission of the National Association of Secondary School Principals.

5. Supervises guidance functions relating to counseling, testing, college information, etc.
6. Participates in the responsibility for the safety and security of students and all others participating in the educational programs of the school.
7. Schedules time to become known to the students by having visibility in the halls, classrooms, and at school activities.

Curriculum

1. Assists department chairpersons and teachers in curriculum revision and improvement.
2. Attends departmental meetings on a regular basis.
3. Participates in area, district, and other public and professional meetings that concern curriculum improvement.
4. Supervises the mandatory testing programs.
5. Participates in preparation of reports and maintenance of records pertaining to curriculum and instruction.
6. Maintains a constant effort to keep aware of curriculum innovations that surface in areas outside the school's local district.

External Relations

1. Establishes liaison with community agencies (not school financed) that are concerned with the health and welfare of citizens.
2. Attempts to develop good working relationships with the law enforcement and judicial personnel. Works cooperatively with the police and probationary officers.
3. Approves all news releases that deal with the school's operation and establishes a good relationship with the media.
4. Is responsible for developing good articulation programs with feeder schools.
5. Maintains good relationships with service groups that assist handicapped and economically deprived students.

Figure 5.4. Continued

An example of this approach may be found in schools, particularly those with large enrollments, where an assistant principal may be assigned the responsibility for a single grade level, such as tenth grade, or, in the case of the elementary school, three grade levels. Included in this assignment are, typically, the maintenance of student discipline and attendance, and/or classroom supervision, curriculum development and implementation, and administration of student activities. Each assistant principal is responsible for the total program at his grade level(s), and the principal provides the overall coordination and leadership for the school.

Whether it is possible for a school to have an assistant principal for each grade level or set of grade levels depends, of course, on the size of a school and the financial circumstances of the school district. However, it seems apparent that apportioning the responsibilities of student discipline and attendance, as well as some of the other administrative and supervisory tasks, among the administrators of the school is a desirable step toward improving the position of the assistant principal, and is consistent with the team concept described earlier. In defining and allocating the responsibilities of the assistant principal, it would be useful for the principal to keep in mind the following guidelines, developed by the Utah Association of Secondary School Principals, and reported in the *Bulletin of the National Association of Secondary School Principals.*[23]

1. Project a clear picture of what the assistant will be doing and offer some suggestions about how it should be done.
2. Outline carefully how much responsibility and authority will be given, and when responsibility is given, give your assistant equal amounts of authority.
3. Seek the other faculty members' willingness to cooperate with your assistant, and spell out for them the areas of responsibility you have given.
4. Your assistant will do a better job if informed of your plans and problems.
5. Add responsibility gradually. Let your assistant get the feel of the job, then give more responsibility in small doses, to continue to develop capabilities.
6. Hold a loose rein. Constant checking will make your understudy nervous and slow down development. It can also lead to loss of confidence and initiative.
7. If a time limit has been set for the completion of an assignment, expect your assistant to abide by it. Never ignore the failure to complete a task.
8. Praise excellence. When a job is well done or exceeds your expectation, express your compliments. Expressing appreciation motivates one to excel.
9. The accountability for the activities of an assistant cannot be reassigned or relinquished. If an assistant is ineffective, the principal is expected to take remedial action.
10. Periodically review and evaluate your assistant's progress. Be constructive. Your assistant has the right to know of weakness and strength as you see them.

In the final analysis, it is the principal who holds the key to the professional improvement, as well as the morale and satisfaction, of the person who occupies the position of assistant principal.[24] It is generally the principal who delegates to the assistant principal the latter's responsibilities, and it is the principal who provides whatever supervisory help, support, and recognition the assistant principal receives.

While in too many instances the principal still delegates to the assistant principal only those activities and responsibilities that he himself finds less desirable, most principals now seem to recognize that the assistant principalship must become more than just a "dumping ground" for those tasks that the principal doesn't want to handle. If an assistant principal is to become a truly viable member of the administrative team of a school, the principal must provide the kinds of responsibility, support, and recognition which will give the assistant principal an opportunity to make his maximal contribution and meet his professional and personal needs as well.

THE DEPARTMENT CHAIRMAN

A second important member of the administrative team of a school, more typically found at the secondary school level, is the department chairman, often referred to as the department head.

Like the position of assistant principal, the department chairmanship was created in response to increases in the managerial and supervisory functions of the school, but was also a result of the growth of departmentalization in the secondary schools.[25] Once secondary schools became departmentalized, the next logical step was the appointment of an individual to administer the department, and the position of the department chairman came into existence. Although the position is more prevalent in large schools and in departments such as English, social studies, math, and science, there are many schools in which there is a depatment head for every department in the school. Despite periodic predictions of its demise, the position continues to exist in the vast majority of secondary schools in the country.

Similar to the role and responsibilities of the assistant principal, those of the department head are no more or less than the principal defines them to be. Though often proposed by various educational authorities as a position of instructional leadership,[26] the department chairmanship in practice has frequently been grounded in the quicksand of administrative trivia, and handicapped by inadequate released time to carry out instructional improvement activities.

In many schools it is not uncommon for a department head to be provided with only one period of released time, and to be saddled with various kinds of administrative minutiae ranging from inventorying equipment and furniture, to administering a department's supplies and requisition procedures.This is unfortunate since a department chairman potentially can make a major contribution to the improvement of a school's instructional and curricular program because of the subject matter and methodological expertise of the individual occupying that position. However, before that potential can be realized, a school must define the nature of the position and sufficient released time must be provided so that the department head can more reasonably carry out his leadership responsibilities.

Developing a Job Description

The first step toward improving the position of department head in a school is to develop a comprehensive job description.[27] Sample job descriptions for the department chairman which appear to be comprehensive may be found in an excellent book by Sergiovanni, *Handbook for Effective Department Leadership*.[28]

To be functional, a job description should be developed cooperatively by those who will be working in the position and those who will be supervising and evaluating its occupants. In the case of the department chairmanship, this means that the department heads themselves should be directly involved with the principal in any process which leads to the revision of a job description already in use or the introduction of a new one. If the individuals who occupy the position of department chairman are to accept fully their responsibilities, then it is essential to obtain their involvement in defining those responsibilities.

Released Time and In-Service

While a department chairman's job description should meet the criterion of comprehensiveness, it cannot be considered a realistic role description unless he is provided with both sufficient time to carry out his responsibilities and in-service training to help him to acquire the knowledge and skills necessary to function as the educational leader of a department.[29] How much released time* should be provided for the department head is not an easy question to answer, but certainly one period is insufficient (except in very small departments) if the school really expects the chairman to function as the leader of a department.

It would appear that the chairman of a small department should be given at least one period of released time to carry out leadership responsibilities. In departments with more than six to eight teachers, two or three periods of released time should be provided, depending on the relative size of the department.[30] It is recognized that the administration of a school or school district must consider financial factors in deciding about released time. However, unless the department chairman is given adequate time, it is unrealistic to assume or expect that he can truly function as the educational leader of the department.

---

*Released time in this context is time beyond that given to the department chairman for class preparation.

It should also be emphasized that providing sufficient released time will not, of itself, ensure that the chairmen will use the time wisely and productively. Most department heads are good teachers, and some of them are masters of the art. The vast majority of them, however, do not possess the background nor have they received the training necessary to function as educational leaders. They may possess expertise in the methodology and content of their discipline, but they typically lack knowledge and skill in such areas as leadership, classroom supervision, human relations, and curriculum development and implementation.[31]

Before department chairmen will make a maximum contribution to the improvement of the school's educational programs, they will need to be involved in some type of in-service training in the areas just mentioned. Whether this training is conducted by the school district with university assistance or wholly by the school district is not important. What *is* important is that the school or school district provide department heads with *developmental* in-service programs that will help them to acquire the knowledge and skills they need to function as educational leaders.[32] As with released time, the provision of an in-service program has financial implications. But until the department heads are given appropriate training for their responsibilities, they are unlikely to perform them effectively.

Problems

Poorly defined role descriptions, insufficient released time, small salary increment for increased responsibilities, and little or no in-service training for the position represent the major problems that many departments heads experience.[33] However, an additional difficulty that is barely mentioned in the educational literature on department chairman is the problem of role conflict. Role conflict is created when a person has incompatible expectations placed on him by two or more individuals or groups. In the case of the department head, he has expectations placed on him in regard to his behavior by both the principal and the teachers in the department. These expectations may be— and frequently are—incompatible, thereby creating role conflict for the department head.

For example, the teachers in a department typically regard the department chairman as their representative and expect him to be loyal to them and to promote their interests. The principal, on the other hand, is usually the one who has appointed or selected the chairman and consequently generally regards him as the administration's representative to the department, and expects that the chairman will be loyal and promote the administration's interests.

Cognetta found, for example, in his study of department heads, that a stronger relationship existed between the role expectations of the department head toward his responsibilities and his perception of the expectations of his departmental colleagues than between his role orientation and his perception of the expectations of the administration for his role.[34] In essence, this finding means that department heads may be more influenced by their perception of what the teachers expect them to do than by what the administration appears to want.

Although the study did not focus directly on the behavioral outcomes of a conflict in expectations for the department head between the teachers and the principal, the research data suggest that such a conflict would be resolved in favor of the teachers. This is most likely to occur under conditions in which the conflict in expectations is not highly visible to the administration, or the administrator lacks the authority or power to back up his own expectations for the role of the department head. In any event, it would appear that role conflict is a major and perhaps inescapable part of the job of the department chairman, and one about which the administrator needs to be more sensitive.

THE UNIT LEADER

In elementary schools which have been organized along multi-unit lines, the unit leaders in the building should be included on the school's administrative team.[35]

Each unit in a multi-unit elementary school is headed by a unit leader who is also a member of the instructional improvement committee of the school. Although the Wisconsin Research and Development Center, which originated the position, has stated that, ". . . the responsibility of the unit leader is instructional, not administrative or supervisory," they have gone on to say that "He serves as a liaison between the unit staff and the principal and consultants, and he coordinates the efficient utilization of the unit staff members, materials, and resources."[36] Since all of the latter tasks are administrative in nature, it is recommended that the unit leader be included in the administrative team at the elementary level.[37] (For further information on the responsibilities of the unit leader, write the Wisconsin Research and Development Center, Madison, Wis.)

THE ADMINISTRATIVE TEAM AT THE DISTRICT LEVEL

Although our focus thus far has been on the concept of the administrative team at the building level, the idea originated at the district level, primarily in response to problems created by teacher militancy.[38]

Beginning in the late 1960s, administrators began to find themselves being squeezed out of teachers' organizations. At the same time, more and more pressure was being placed on administrators by both school boards and superintendents to decide whether they were management or "something else." This was not an easy decision for many administrators, who were concerned that the lines of difference between management and teachers were being drawn too rigidly. However, for most school administrators there was little choice: the teacher groups appeared to want them only on terms that were perceived as unfavorable by most administrators, and superintendents and school boards moved quickly to introduce the concept of the administrative team, which seemed to offer a logical or useful home base in the district. Since that time the record of the administrative team at the district level has been a mixed one, and problems have surfaced that will be discussed later. However, because few people disagree with the *concept* of a district administrative team, and since the problems can be resolved, given the right kind of commitment and educational vision, we will begin our examination of the district team by first looking at the proposed objectives of the team.

OBJECTIVES OF THE DISTRICT ADMINISTRATIVE TEAM

A review of the literature on the district administrative team suggests that it has two main objectives: (1) to develop and present a unified front in collective bargaining with teachers and in the implementation of the master contract, and (2) to utilize collectively the talents and interests of individual administrators and supervisors to solve problems and improve education within the district. While writings on the concept of the district administrative team no longer emphasize the first objective, there is little doubt that it remains an important goal of most district teams. However, the most important objective of an administrative team should be the second one. The full sense of what the achievement of this goal implies, at least to building administrators, was stated in *Management Crisis: A Solution,* a booklet published by one of the national principals' associations, and the statement continues to represent the most tenable rationale for a district administrative team.[39]

> An administrative team represents a means of establishing smooth lines of organization and communication, common agreements, and definite patterns of mutuality among administrators and the Board of Education as they unite to provide effective educational programs for the community. There are two primary parties involved in the leadership of a school district, namely, the board of education whose responsibility is policy-making, and the administrative team (including all administrators) whose major responsibilities include first advising the board in establishing district policies and then guaranteeing their effective implementation. A close, harmonious working relationship between these two parties is obviously vital to the successful operation of a school district.
>
>   It should also be clear that an effective administrative team has, in addition to its assigned legalistic and primary role of policy implementation, a vital leadership function to perform. Never before has more interest and concern been raised about the need for strong

and united educational leadership. An effective administrative team provides a collective means of strengthening school district leadership, giving individual administrators needed assistance, opportunities, and job satisfaction.

COMPOSITION AND STRUCTURE OF THE DISTRICT ADMINISTRATIVE TEAM

A *district* administrative team should be composed of all of the principals and assistant principals in a district and all of the central office supervisors and administrators.[40] Department heads are not usually included in a district administrative team, nor are other individuals identified in a school's administrative team except as specifically mentioned in this section.

The district team is, of course, headed by the superintendent. Although the responsibilities of a district superintendent would vary somewhat, depending on the size of the district and the expectations of the school board and community, the job description, presented in figure 5.5, is illustrative of the kinds of duties expected of most superintendents.[41] (For additional information on the superintendent's role and relationships, see *Roles and Relationships: School Boards/Superintendents,* published by the American Association of School Administrators in 1981 at Arlington, Va.)

The job of an administrator is seldom a particularly easy one, but various studies have shown that the position of superintendent is especially demanding and frequently of short duration. For example, Dolce sees the superintendency under a great deal of stress because of numerous special interest groups.[42] And a study by Pitner and another by Ogawa found the superintendent frequently

---

Basic Responsibility

The Superintendent is Chief Executive Officer, responsible for overall planning, operation, and performance of the district. He provides staff support and recommendations to the Board with respect to decision-making policies and planning, and is the Board's agent in all relationships with the staff. He selects, organizes, and gives leadership to the management team, oversees planning, staff development, and reward systems throughout the district, and ensures adequate operational and financial control.

Reports to	Board of Education
Supervises	Associate Superintendent(s)
	Director of Planning and Analysis
	Director of Public Relations
	Administrator of Business Services
	Administrator of Educational Services
	Principals

Figure 5.5.

Primary Duties

1. Establish and maintain a constructive relationship with the Board of Education based on appropriate performance and financial information. Guide and aid the Board in its effective operation through competent staff support and through development of his and the Board's skills in working together effectively.
2. Establish programs and practices for the constructive relationship of the district with its community on a school and district level.
3. Direct and coordinate district planning to ensure educational programs and performance in line with community needs and desires. Ensure sound planning of financial, facility, and enrollment requirements for the future. Prepare and recommend an annual budget consistent with long-range plans and appropriate to community financial resources.
4. Recommend district purposes, objectives, policies, and decisions as required, supported appropriately with information, analysis and conclusions presented to the Board and to the public.
5. Organize, staff, and give leadership to the management team as required to meet district objectives. Plan and execute a management development program appropriate to realizing the district's educational objectives.
6. Establish and maintain constructive relationships throughout the district at all levels, including community, parents, students, teachers, staff, and Board.
7. Ensure the development and operation of adequate recruiting, selection, appraisal and compensation systems to meet district objectives.
8. Develop the competence of teachers, staff, and management to the maximum extent possible in the best interests of the individuals involved and to meet district objectives.
9. Establish a performance monitoring system incorporating test data results and consumer judgments to meet the needs for performance information throughout the organization.
10. Establish financial and operating controls adequate to safeguard the district against misuse of funds or unnecessary operations, and to ensure fair value for all expenditures.
11. Provide leadership to the district and community in developing, achieving, and maintaining high educational standards, sound programs, and good performance.
12. Ensure that district operations meet all legal requirements.
13. Oversee staff negotiation and contract administration.

Key Working Relationships

1. Work with the Board of Education to ensure effective Board operations, district policies, objectives, decisions, and performance in line with the public interest.
2. Maintain effective relationships with and among staff at all levels of the organization.
3. Ensure a healthy relationship of the district with its community.
4. Represent the district as required and appropriate in various community, association, and government activities.

Figure 5.5. Continued

bogged down by telephone calls, petty problems and mundane activities.[43] However, due to the size of the sample in these studies, we cannot be sure that the findings are representative of most superintendents. On the other hand, observation would suggest that the job of the superintendent is indeed a challenging one.

While the superintendent is undoubtedly the most important member of the administrative team at the district level, there are other members such as the building principals, assistant superintendents, and program directors, who make up the team.[44] And, although it is difficult to generalize, it seems clear that the other members of the team in many school districts are not of equal status, regardless of what the promotional literature about the team may suggest. Central office administrators, such as assistant superintendents and directors, seem to have greater status on the district administrative team than do principals, and principals seem to be accorded greater status on the team than supervisors. The hierarchical nature of a district administrative team does not mean, however, that the team cannot work together cooperatively and effectively *if* the status differences between the various members of the team do not inhibit or restrict input from the members of the team, and if each person on the team is given a role in which he can make useful contributions and from which he can derive adequate satisfaction.

While there are a number of important principles which should be followed in operating and evaluating a district administrative team, those presented in question form in figure 5.6 are recommended. These same principles

---

1. Are the roles and responsibilities of each member of the team, and of the team as a whole, clearly defined?
2. Does the team provide adequate involvement for all members in the development and evaluation of school and district objectives, policies, and procedures?
3. Does the team work on the problems that individual schools are experiencing, as well as on districtwide problems?
4. Does the team provide assistance and help, when needed, to the various members?
5. Do the team philosophy and objectives permit diversity and individual initiative when, in the eyes of the building administrator, such efforts would improve education in an individual school?
6. Is there periodic evaluation of team effectiveness?
7. Is there truly a spirit of good will and cooperation on the part of the various members of the team?

Figure 5.6. Principles for Operating and Evaluating the District Administrative Team

can be adapted for use in operating and evaluating the administrative team at the building level.

PROBLEMS OF THE DISTRICT ADMINISTRATIVE TEAM

A building administrator has much to gain from and a great deal to contribute to the district administrative team. However, the team concept at the district level is not without its problems, according to the reports of principals.[45] As implemented in some school districts, the administrative team has stifled creativity and initiative at the school building level, and has provided individual school administrators with little or no involvement in developing, as contrasted with implementing, school policies and procedures.

For example, the objective of some district administrative teams seems to be to promote uniformity in school curriculum, teaching, and rules and regulations among all of the schools of the district. Individual differences are frowned upon. School administrators who attempt to develop a different kind of curriculum for their students or who try to operate their schools in a somewhat different way than the other schools in the district are informed that they are not performing as team members should and that individuality is not desirable or possible under the team concept.

Of course, it should be noted that the issue of centralization and uniformity versus individualization and diversity is not a new problem in education. There has always been some tension, and sometimes a great deal, between the central administration and its desire to achieve district objectives with articulation and correlation among various schools, and the individual school administrator who seeks the autonomy to develop the best educational program possible for "his kids," even if that program differs from the educational program in the other schools of the district. However, the team concept, as it has been implemented in some school districts, has tended to accentuate this tension and has caused significant problems for some building administrators.

A different kind of problem, but an equally important one, which has confronted some school administrators who have tried to work cooperatively on the district administrative team, is their limited role. Building administrators may be regarded by other members of the administrative team as only the implementers of school board policies and procedures. Frequently they are not given an adequate opportunity to participate fully in the development of recommended policies and procedures, and often their involvement could be characterized as "too little, too late." As a result, building administrators in a number of states have pressured their state legislature to pass collective bargaining statutes authorizing middle management personnel to organize themselves into collective bargaining units.[46] A corollary development has been the establishment of administrator unions in a number of districts, particularly more populous ones.[47]

ADMINISTRATORS' UNIONS

According to the Educational Research Service, the main causes of middle management unionization are

1. Inadequate communication with the superintendent and the school board
2. Unclear role information
3. Desire for improvements in salaries and fringe benefits
4. Lack of influence in decision making
5. Erosion of authority through teacher negotiations.[48]

With regard to the fifth cause, Sladky found in a study of the role of the principal on the school district management team that principals did *not* perform a significant role in decision making about teacher-board negotiations. In general, principals were limited to being reactors to the impact of contract language on administering the school; they were not involved at all in the decision making process to establish school district priorities for bargaining with teachers.[49]

When middle management personnel have organized themselves into collective bargaining units, they have concentrated in their bargaining on securing protection from the adverse effects of unilateral and bilateral decisions by the school board and superintendent that have tended to erode the authority and professional security base of principals and supervisors.[50] A study by Pisapia and Sells on collective bargaining agreements between administrators and school boards found that these protections fell into three areas.[51]

Administrator Collective Bargaining Protection	*Example*
1. Protection of middle management's traditional right to participate in decision making.	In staffing for a school, the principal has the right to define the position and shall have the primary responsibility for recommending the hiring of all personnel.
2. Protection against arbitrary or capricious actions affecting the job security of middle management personnel.	The school board will refrain from making involuntary transfers, and when transfers are made, will transfer to a position of equal or higher status.
3. Protection against arbitrary or capricious acts against middle management personnel's character, integrity, physical well-being, and personal property.	The principal shall have the availability of grievance procedures and shall be given the opportunity to become knowledgeable about all adverse items placed in his/her personnel file.

As can be seen from an examination of these protections, most if not all of them should not require administrators' collective bargaining but should result from the full implementation of the concept of the administrative team discussed previously in the chapter. The fact that many administrators have felt a need to bargain for these protections suggests that in many school districts the superintendent and the school board are giving only lip service, if even that, to the concept of the administrative team. That this is occurring is suggested by a publication of the American Association of School Administrators, which states:

> The superintendent who tries to go it alone in this increasingly complex world is riding for a fall, and the school board that insists on it is only fooling itself. . . . Meanwhile administrator groups around the country are making noises ominously like those of teacher organizations. . . . They feel that they are "management" in name only. . . . They are turning more to the negotiations arena to resolve their identity crises.[52]

What the future holds for administrator collective bargaining is uncertain. Many people oppose it because of its potential divisiveness. Paul Salmon, executive director of the American Association of School Administrators, expressed this view when he said:

> Collective bargaining, as a process, is adversary in essence. Being a bilateral procedure, it pits party against party. Divergence, proposals, counter proposals, and compromise are its character. In actuality it isolates the superintendent from his team members and requires him (or his designated representative) to function as an adversary at the bargaining table.[53]

While it would appear that national principals' associations would prefer the administrative team rather than collective bargaining as a vehicle for advancing their members' interests and securing their protections, their position is likely to change if the authority of the principal in more and more districts continues to erode, and school boards and superintendents don't use the administrative team to provide principals with necessary protections.[54] Specifically, what do school boards and superintendents need to accomplish? Dillion recommends the following.[55]

1. Extend to your principals and supervisors real and meaningful authority over the selection and direction of personnel for whom they are responsible.
2. Give your building administrators or others with similar responsibility an opportunity to participate in the budgeting/ planning process and to develop priorities for the purchasing of equipment and supplies which they require to carry out the educational program.

3. Before making concessions at the bargaining table, seek the advice and counsel of those who must serve on the front line administering and implementing the terms of the contract.
4. Finally, let the economic benefits which you offer them and the status and support which you give them be such that they will feel no need or reason to bargain collectively.

Although it would seem that the implementation of these recommendations would give real substance to the concept of the district administrative team, the most important ingredient of all is the need for mutual trust and respect among administrators, the superintendent, and the school board. As McNally has perceptively observed, ". . . An administrative team's success depends above all on the existence of an atmosphere of mutual trust, cooperation, and open communication among team members."[56] Unless the superintendent and the school board can create and maintain this type of an atmosphere, it seems likely that building administrators will choose to organize a separate bargaining unit, rather than to become members of a district's administrative team.

A FINAL NOTE

There is little doubt that the administrative team approach is potentially a valuable mechanism for facilitating cooperation among administrators, and for better utilizing their individual interests and talents. Whether that potential is realized or not, however, will depend in large part on the extent to which the concept is fully implemented in practice, and on the degree to which all members of the team strive to work together cooperatively in a spirit of mutual trust and confidence. The alternative, at least at the district level, to an effective administrative team is likely to be pressure for administrators' collective bargaining and the establishment of collective bargaining units.[57]

Review and Learning Activities

1. What are the purposes and advantages of the administrative team?
2. What factors should an administrator consider in defining the composition and structure of the team?
3. How can the administrator increase the effectiveness of team meetings?
4. Discuss the main duties and problems of the assistant principal. How can the problems perhaps be ameliorated?
5. What are the purposes, composition, and problems of the district administrative team? How can the problems be best solved?

6. Why have some administrators chosen collective bargaining rather than the administrative team to protect and promote their interests and concerns? What are the implications of collective bargaining for administrators, in regard to their relationship with the superintendent, the school board, and teachers?

Notes

1. For a review of the origins of team management, see J. S. Swift, "Origins of Team Management," *National Elementary Principal* (February 1971): 26–35.

2. Kenneth A. Erickson and Robert L. Rose, *Management Teams in Educational Administration: Ideal? Practical? or Both?* (Eugene, Oreg., Oregon School Study Council, 1973), p. 1.

3. Ruben L. Ingram, "The Principal: Instructional Leader, Site Manager, Educational Executive," *Thrust for Educational Leadership* (May 1979): 23–25.

4. Thomas Holland, et al., "A Scheme for School-based Change and Decision Making," *NASSP Bulletin* (October 1977): 31–40.

5. For a good description of the reasons for this approach, see Remsis Likert, *The Human Organization* (New York: McGraw-Hill, 1967).

6. For a good approach to achieving these goals, see Joseph A. Young and Jerry Sturm, "A Model for Participatory Decision Making," *NASSP Bulletin* (April 1980): 63–66.

7. For an excellent discussion of the various administrative processes that are involved in operating a team outside of meetings, as well as during meetings, see Richard Wynn, *Theory and Practice of the Administrative Team* (Washington, D.C.: National Association of Elementary School Principals, National Association of School Administrators, and National School Public Relations Association, 1973), pp. 23–35.

8. Although focused on the informal leader, an article by Bradford is well worth reading, as the topic of "hidden agenda" might apply to the principal and team meetings. See Leland P. Bradford, "The Case of Hidden Agenda," *National Elementary School Principal* (October 1957): 23–28.

9. Richard A. Gorton, *School Administration and Supervision: Important Issues, Concepts and Case Studies* (Dubuque, Iowa: Wm. C. Brown Company Publishers, 1980), pp. 280–81. For a fuller discussion of concepts and issues associated with authority, power, and influence, see chapter 10 in that same text.

10. Although some may associate the position of assistant principal primarily with the secondary school, it has long existed at the elementary level as well. For example, see Esther L. Schroeder, "The Status of the Assistant Principal in the Elementary School," in *The Elementary School Principalship: The Instructional and Administrative Aspects,* Fourth Yearbook of the Department of Elementary School Principals, ed. Arthur J. Gist (Washington, D.C.: National Education Association, 1925), pp. 389–400.

11. Robert Kattman, "Characteristics, Role, and Problems of the Elementary School Assistant Principal" (Ph.D. diss., University of Wisconsin-Milwaukee, 1982).

12. Ibid., chapter IV.

13. David Austin, *The Assistant Principalship* (Reston, Va.: NASSP, 1970), p. 5. For a more recent look at the workday, see Penny McDonald, "An Observational Study of the Workday of the Urban High School Assistant Principal" (Ed.D. diss., Portland State Univ., 1981.)

14. More recent reports indicate that the job of the assistant principal at the secondary level has improved some but not significantly. See May 1980 issue of the *NASSP Bulletin.*

15. Lee H. Stoner and William T. Voorhies, "The High School Assistant Principalship in NCA Schools in Indiana," *The North Central Association Quarterly* (Spring 1981): 408–13.

16. Ibid. Also see Alice Black, "Clarifying the Role of the Assistant Principal," *NASSP Bulletin* (May 1980): 33–38; and John C. Croft and John R. Morton, *The Assistant Principal: In Quandary or Comfort?* An ERIC Report: Ed–136–392.

17. Austin, *The Assistant Principalship,* p. 72.

18. For example, see Stoner and Voorhies, "High School Assistant Principalship."

19. Robert Garawski, "The Assistant Principal: His Job Satisfaction and Organizational Potency," *The Clearing House* (September 1978): 9.

20. "Job Description for the Assistant Principal," *NASSP Bulletin* (May 1980): 50, 51–55.

21. John A. Kriekard and M. Scott Norton, "Using the Competency Approach to Define the Assistant Principalship," *NASSP Bulletin* (May 1980: 1–8).

22. Richard A. Gross, et al., "How the Management Team Concept Can Succeed," *NASSP Bulletin* (May 1980): 26.

23. "Taking the Pressure Off," *NASSP Bulletin* (December 1980): 128.

24. Jerry Valentine, "Preparing Your Assistant for the Principalship," *NASSP Bulletin* (May 1980): 40–43.

25. An early report of this process can be found in Preston W. Search, "The Larger High Schools," *School Review* (April 1900): 225–27. For an early study of the position of department chairman, see Harlan C. Koch, "Some Aspects of the Department Headship in Secondary Schools," *School Review* (April 1930): 263–75.

26. Thomas J. Sergiovanni, *Handbook for Effective Department Leadership* (Rockleigh, N.J.: Allyn & Bacon, 1977), chapter 1a.

27. Robert L. Buser and William Humm, "The Department Head Revisited," *Journal of Secondary Education* (October 1970): 281–84.

28. Sergiovanni, *Handbook for Effective Department Leadership,* chapters 1b and 2a.

29. James M. Gallagher, *How to Make Better Use of Department Chairmen.* An ERIC Report: Ed–136–366.

30. For evidence on the importance of adequate released time so that the department chairman can perform effectively as an instructional leader, see James A. Hoeh, "The Effectiveness of Department Chairman in the Improvement of Instruction" (Ph.D. diss., University of Michigan, 1969).

31. Frances Weaver and Jeffrey Gordon, *Leadership Competencies for Department Heads: Needed Areas for Inservice Education.* An ERIC Report: Ed–168–197.

32. For an example of such a program, see Samuel Kostman, "On-the-job Training for Classroom Supervisors," *NASSP Bulletin* (December 1978): 44–50.

33. See Lewis M. Ciminillo, "The Department Heads' Perception of the Functions and Characteristics of Their Position" (Ed.D. diss., Indiana University, 1966).

34. Randall A. Cognetta, "The Relationship of Selected Organizational and Personal Variables to the Behavior of High School Department Heads" (Ed.D. diss., Stanford University, 1967).

35. The Multi-Unit School was pioneered by the Research and Development Center at the University of Wisconsin, and its operation is now rather widespread. For more information about the multi-unit school, see Herbert J. Klausmeier, "The Multi-Unit School and Individually Guided Education," *The Kappan* (November 1971): 181–84.

36. Herbert J. Klausmeier et al., *Individually Guided Education and the Multi-Unit Elementary School* (Madison, Wis.: Wisconsin Research and Development Center, 1971), p. 31.

37. Ibid., pp. 32–34.

38. *The Administrative Team* (Washington, D.C.: American Association of School Administrators, National Association of Elementary School Principals, National Association of Secondary School Principals, and Association of School Business Officials, 1971).

39. *Management Crisis: A Solution* (Washington, D.C.: National Association of Secondary School Principals, 1971), pp. 3–4.

40. For an earlier concept of the administrative team, which excluded building administrators, see *Profiles of the Administrative Team* (Washington, D.C.: American Association of School Administrators, 1971).

41. Fredrick and Allen J. Klingenberg, *Effective Schools through Management* (Springfield, Ill.: Illinois Association of School Boards, 1978), pp. 62–63.

42. Carl Dolce, *Superintendents Under Seige—Get the Leader.* An ERIC Report: Ed–122–362.

43. Nancy J. Pitner and Rodney T. Ogawa, "Organizational Leadership: The Case of the School Superintendent," *Educational Administration Quarterly* (Spring 1981): 45–65.

44. *Selecting the Administrative Team* (Arlington, Va.: American Association of School Administrators, 1981), chapter 5.

45. Norman Hale, *The Management Team* (Eugene, Oreg.: ERIC Clearinghouse on Educational Management, 1978).

46. John Pisapia, "The Legal Basis of Administrator Bargaining," *NOLPE School Law Journal* (1980): #1: 61–84.

47. B. Cooper, "Collective Bargaining for School Administrators Fours Years Later," *Phi Delta Kappan* (October 1979): 130–31.

48. Educational Research Service: *Collective Negotiation Agreements for Administrators: An Analysis of 100 Contracts* (Arlington, Va.: Educational Research Service Inc., 1976).

49. Robert Sladky, "The School Principal and the District Management Team," *Association of Wisconsin School Administrators Bulletin* (May 1980): 22–26.

50. John R. Pisapia and Jack D. Sells, "Administrator Protections in Negotiated Contracts," *NASSP Bulletin* (November 1978): 43–54.

51. Ibid.

52. The American Association of School Administrators, *The Administrative Leadership Team* (Arlington, Va.: AASA, 1979).

53. Paul B. Salmon, "Are the Administrative Team and Collective Bargaining Compatible?" *Compact* (June 1972): 3.

54. "Management Team: An Idea Whose Time Has Passed?" *Education U.S.A.* (February 26, 1979): 200.

55. John Dillon, "Alleviating Administrator Unionism" (Paper presented at the 112th annual meeting of the American Association of School Administrators, Anaheim, California, 1980).

56. Harold J. McNally, "A Matter of Trust," *National Elementary Principal* (November/ December 1973): 23.

57. Milton Bonzell, "A Study and Analysis of Attitudes toward Administrative Bargaining Units Among California Elementary School Principals" (Ed.D. diss., University of San Francisco, 1981).

6

Budget and Plant Management

In recent years budget and plant management have assumed greater importance in education. Although the economic situation and public opinion will influence the priority an administrator will give to these two administrative responsibilities, in a period of inflation and reduced resources the efficient and effective management of the budget and the school plant becomes *essential*. Without efficient and effective budget and plant management, it is likely that a school district will go from one budget crisis to the next, and the physical facilities of the district will not be used economically. Therefore, any administrator who wishes to manage the school's financial and physical resources efficiently and effectively will need to understand major concepts of school budget and plant management.

BUDGET MANAGEMENT

A short but useful definition of the budget is ". . . the blueprint of what the educational program will be and what it will cost."[1] The school administrator's role in relation to the budget consists of three tasks: (1) developing the budget, (2) administering the budget, and (3) evaluating the efficiency and effectiveness of the services and products funded by the budget. A discussion of the concepts, practices, and problems associated with each of these tasks will follow.

DEVELOPING THE BUDGET

The school administrator's role in developing a budget may be a limited or an important one, depending on the degree to which the budget process in a school district is centralized.[2] In a centralized budget process the school administrator's responsibility is typically restricted to reporting to the district office data relative to the number of students and teachers who will be assigned to the school for the following year, and the extent to which capital improvements are needed for the building. The central office of the district then develops the budget for each school based on preëstablished formulae which determine the allocations for the various budget categories.[3] For example, the district budget formula for library books may be $10.00 for each student enrolled in a school. Thereby, a school of 750 students would receive a budget allocation of $7,500 for the purchase of library books, whereas a school of 1,000 would receive $10,000.

Under a centralized budget making process, the role of the school administrator is a very limited one. However, the advantages of this approach are that the allocation criteria are applied objectively and evenly, and the development of the budget proceeds efficiently.

In a *decentralized* budget process the administrator is assigned responsibility for developing the budget for a school, based on the unique characteristics of the students and/or the educational program in the building.[4] This type of budget approach is frequently referred to as "site level budgeting," and it seems to be on the increase in certain parts of the country. It is based on the following principles:[5]

- Funds are allocated to schools on the basis of the needs of the children in the schools.
- The specific educational objectives of a school are set by people associated with the school.
- Decisions about how funds are to be spent for instruction are made at the school level.
- Parents participate in school decision-making.

In this approach, the administrator is encouraged to involve teachers, parents, and even students in developing the budget for the school. Each of these groups may be requested to identify and define their needs relative to the replacement and/or addition of products and services. Throughout the process there is emphasis on involving a wide variety of people and developing a budget which will reflect the unique needs of a particular school.

Although a budget developed under a decentralized process is seldom accepted without some changes by the district administration, proponents of this budgeting process generally feel that it is more likely to reflect the needs of each school than is a centralized approach. It is also argued that the greater involvement of teachers, parents, and students which is encouraged under a decentralized method capitalizes on their insights and helps them to understand the problems and parameters of budget making. And, as Glass observes, "Perhaps one of the most effective ways in which a district can obtain legitimate and direct participation in the school district is by involving them in the district budgeting process, preferably at the local neighborhood school level."[6]

(For assistance in helping parents to understand the budget process, see *The School Budget: It's Your Money and Your Business,* published by The National Committee for Citizens in Education.) The disadvantage of a decentralized budget process, according to Candoli and associates, is that it may result in a situation in which, "Each school becomes a small kingdom within itself and cooperative efforts among and between schools can become difficult."[7]

Of course, the budget-building process in many schools is neither totally decentralized nor centralized, but a combination of the two. For example, one pattern is for the central office to determine the initial budget allocations for each school, based on preëstablished formulae, giving each administrator an opportunity to present a case for *raising* the budget allocation to accommodate any specific category for a school. The salient advantage of this budget system is that it establishes a degree of equity among schools in terms of budget allocations, while providing for additional financial support for any school which can demonstrate that due to certain conditions or circumstances it merits a higher budget allocation than the district standard formula allows. The disadvantages of this method are that (1) the budget is still formulated largely on the basis of the central office's assumptions about the needs of each school rather than on an assessment by the people at the building level, and (2) there is a tendency for building administrators to accept the district office's determination of their budgets, in order to avoid the arguments and "hassles" which may be required to secure a higher budget allocation for their schools.

It should be noted that any budget process will have disadvantages as well as advantages, and the only purpose of this analysis is to explore several alternatives.

PPBS

One systematic approach to budget building about which the school administrator should be knowledgeable is PPBS: Planning, Programming, Budgeting System.[8] Simply defined, PPBS is ". . . a management tool that can be used to plan and arrange a district's activities and resources."[9] While traditional approaches to budgeting also emphasize planning and programming, these budgeting processes are not organized to the same degree around programs and program objectives as are those in PPBS,* nor is evaluation emphasized to the same extent.

*This budget process has been referred to as PPBS. PPBES (Planning, Programming, Budgeting, Evaluating System), and ERMS (Educational Resources Management System). The latter term and concept (ERMS) are used most typically by school business managers. An important book prepared by the research staff of the Association of School Business Officials entitled, *Educational Resources Management System,* is recommended reading for all school administrators. (It is published by the Research Corporation of the Association of School Business Officials, Chicago, IL.)

PPBS	The Traditional Approach
Stages:	Stages:
1. Assess educational needs.	1. Ascertain teacher needs in the areas of supplies, books, etc.
2. Define educational objectives and the criteria and methods to be used in evaluating the objectives.	2. Determine the merits of teachers' budget requests on the basis of perceived need.
3. Determine programs and priorities to achieve objectives.	3. Estimate the cost of teacher requests.
4. Ascertain and cost-estimate the resources needed to carry out programs	4. Organize the budget around categories of needs, e.g., instructional supplies, books, etc.
5. Organize the budget around program areas and objectives.	

Figure 6.1. PPBS vs. the Traditional Approach: The Process [10]

Perhaps the best way for the school administrator to understand PPBS is to compare this budget process with the traditional approach and to see an example of how the budget is organized under each. Figure 6.1 presents an outline of the process of PPBS along with the traditional approach.

As one can see by comparing the two approaches shown in figure 6.1, PPBS places a much greater emphasis on defining and evaluating program objectives and on relating the funds which the school purportedly needs to the achievement of those objectives, rather than to the nature of the items being funded. For an example of how the budget is organized and presented under the two approaches, see figures 6.2 and 6.3.

Although PPBS appears to represent a more logical and effective method of budget building, it has been adopted in only a minority of school districts. Experience has shown that the process can be extremely time-consuming. Also, it places an emphasis on relating budget allocations to definable objectives, and defining certain educational objectives has proved to be a difficult and frustrating task.[11] Still, when one considers both the advantages and disadvantages, it would seem that PPBS offers the school administrator a very good conceptual tool for the budget building process.[12] And it is likely that declining availability of resources and increased pressure for school accountability will force more school districts to adopt some variation of this budget model.

School _____ Date _____

Current Enrollment _____ Anticipated Enrollment _____

Resources Needed

	Account No.	Current Costs	Projected Costs
Personnel Certified	_____	_____	_____
Personnel Noncertified	_____	_____	_____
Instructional Supplies	_____	_____	_____
Noninstructional Supplies	_____	_____	_____
Capital Equipment	_____	_____	_____
Maintenance	_____	_____	_____
Food Services	_____	_____	_____
Transportation	_____	_____	_____

Figure 6.2. Traditional Budget Format: An Example[13]

Program Title _____ Program Level _____ Program No. _____

For period beginning _____ and ending _____

Program objective(s) _____ (The space on this form is less than

_____ would be needed in actual practice) _____

Program Description _____

_____

Program Criteria and Evaluation Methods _____

_____

_____

Anticipated Enrollment _____ Personnel Assigned _____

(continued)

Figure 6.3. Example of a PPBS Format[14]

Resource Requirements	Current Year	Next Year	Following Year	Following Year
Salary and Teacher Fringe Benefits	_____	_____	_____	_____
Supporting Staff	_____	_____	_____	_____
Textbooks	_____	_____	_____	_____
Supplies	_____	_____	_____	_____
A.V.	_____	_____	_____	_____
Maintenance	_____	_____	_____	_____
Capital	_____	_____	_____	_____
Other	_____	_____	_____	_____

Figure 6.3. Continued

PROBLEMS OF BUDGET BUILDING*

Since the school administrator's responsibility in the budget-building process is greater when a decentralized approach is utilized, it would be advisable for her to be aware of problems she might encounter in implementing this method. These problems are not necessarily inherent in the decentralized approach to budget building, nor do they occur in all schools, but they may arise if the administrator fails to take certain safeguards. These problems, and recommended precautionary measures, fall into several areas.

BUDGET REQUESTS BASED ON ACQUISITIVENESS OR LACK OF KNOWLEDGE

The school administrator who involves teachers and others in the budget-building process will sometimes receive budget requests from people who don't actually need what they are requesting or who don't know very much about the item they are requesting or how they are going to use it. For example, the administrator may receive a request from a grade-level chairman who would like an additional typewriter which would be used by six teachers who already have access to another typewriter. Or, the administrator may receive a request

*For some reason, the role of the school administrator and the problems she encounters in developing the budget are given limited attention in the educational literature. Therefore, the ideas presented in this section are based primarily on the experiences of a number of principals who have been interviewed, and a useful study by Brian Caldwell, "Implications of Decentralized School Budgeting." An ERIC Report: Ed–161–148.

from the math teachers to include in the next year's budget a computer terminal which would be installed in one of the mathematics classrooms. In this case the math teachers may be convinced about the educational value of a computer terminal but may lack the knowledge or skills for effectively utilizing the computer terminal in the math program.

One of the best safeguards for preventing problems of acquisitiveness or lack of knowledge from affecting the budget process is to require those individuals who submit budget requests to state in writing the rationale for proposing each item, how it will be used, and the extent to which those who will be using the item possess or will need to acquire additional knowledge and/or skill for effective utilization. The school administrator should also require any person making a budget request to indicate in the rationale whether the proposed item is desirable or essential. A "desirable" item might be defined as one that would improve a situation, but that failure to purchase would not be detrimental to the educational process; an "essential" item could be defined as something that is necessary in order to prevent a deterioration of a situation, or to implement a particular program successfully. A suggested format for securing this kind of informrmation will be included in the discussion of the next problem in budget building.

LACK OF SPECIFICITY ON HOW THE PROPOSED BUDGET ITEM WILL INCREASE STUDENT LEARNING

Budget requests may be for replacement or additional items. Proposed additional items may reflect increased enrollment, or they may represent projected improvements in the program of the school. A problem is created when the school administrator receives budget requests that are unrelated to increased enrollment or do not clearly specify either how the proposed item will improve student learning or how such an improvement in student learning would be assessed. The individuals or groups who propose improvement items which are additions to the budget may believe that the items are necessary for a better school program, but unless that belief can be translated into a statement of how the improvement will come about and how it will be assessed, the administrator will be in a poor position to make a judgment on the validity of such budget requests. Questions for which the adminisrator must obtain answers from the proponents of new budget improvement items are, "How will the new item(s) help the students, and how will we determine whether or not the improvement has been achieved?"

A budget proposal form which the school administrator might consider using to ameliorate the problems discussed in the previous two areas is presented in figure 6.4.

Name _____ Subject _____ Date _____

Budget Classification No. _____ (Check appropriate spaces)

_____ Replacement _____ Desirable

_____ Enrollment _____ Essential
addition

_____ Improvement addition

Description of Item _____

_____

_____ Unit Price: _____

Justification: _____

_____

_____

(Include in your justification the reasons why the item is needed, why it is desirable or essential, how it will improve learning opportunities, and how the improvement can be assessed before the next budget year.)

Figure 6.4. Budget Proposal Form

Although the budget request form recommended in figure 6.4 may seem complicated and imposing, it asks only for the type of information that an administrator needs in order to evaluate a budget request properly. If a person making a budget request has carefully and thoroughly considered all of the various implications of the request, she should have little difficulty in completing the form. The advantage of this kind of a budget proposal form is that it increases the probability that there will be adequate investigation and consideration supporting each budget request.

NEED FOR BUDGET REDUCTION

Legislative mandates, citizen initiatives, the state of the economy, and declining enrollment have, from time to time, created a need for reduction in the overall budget of a school or school district. And for the foreseeable future, educators will probably have to cope with the reality of less available resources and greater pressures for accountability.

Reducing the budget from the level of previous years is seldom an easy task. When programs are modified or eliminated, staff members laid off, and maintenance work and capital improvements delayed, the potential for frustration, disillusionment, and low morale is great. While not all of the debilitating effects of budget reductions can be avoided, their effects can be minimized if the budget approach utilized is rational and fair. One budget approach that seems to meet these criteria and which has proven to be very useful in situations involving the need for budget reduction is what is referred to as Zero-Based Budgeting. (It should be noted that Zero-Based Budgeting is not limited to the need for budget reduction, but its applicability seems most relevant to this kind of situation.)

Zero-Based Budgeting (ZBB) originated in the federal government and has now been introduced in a number of school systems.[15] Its primary purpose, according to Hartley, is " . . . to exert greater control over budgets by requiring justification for *every* proposed expenditure, beginning theoretically from a base of zero."[16] This includes current expenditures, as well as proposed new expenditures. In other words, in Zero-Based Budgeting, each year the school administrator must provide justification for every single item in the proposed budget. This justification must include " . . . a rationale, objectives, evaluation criteria, and needed resources for alternative levels of service for each program."[17] An adaptation of figures 6.3 and 6.4 could be used for this purpose.

While Zero-Based Budgeting may offer an excellent approach for providing needed information so that decision makers can make more rational and fair budget reductions, it should be emphasized that the system does require increased competency on the part of the budget makers, and that a lot of hard work lies ahead for individuals and groups involved in the process.[18] And when certain programs are cut and/or staff reduced, these actions will impact negatively on the people affected. However, despite these possible limitations, ZBB offers a better approach to reducing a budget than across-the-board cuts or other less systematic or more political methods.[19]

LACK OF EXPERTISE IN EVALUATING BUDGET REQUESTS

The typical school administrator is a generalist working with a group of teachers who are subject matter specialists. The administrator may have specialized in some aspect of the school program such as social studies or mathematics as an undergraduate. But it is unlikely that the administrator possesses a very thorough understanding of all of the subject disciplines which comprise the educational program. Consequently, during the budget-building process the administrator will receive requests to include in the proposed budget certain items about which she may know very little.

For example, an administrator may receive from the science teachers a request to order a number of lab kits. The administrator may have taken only one or two college courses in science and may have no idea whether these particular kits are essential or even desirable. She may be able to ask the science teachers a few general questions about the lab kits, but unless the administrator is personally knowledgeable about the subject, she will probably be unable to ask the penetrating, probing questions which need to be raised in evaluating the request.[20]

In this kind of a situation an administrator has three main alternatives. Since the teachers are in a better position to know what they need than she is, she can accept the science teachers' recommendation that they need the lab kits, although this procedure can result in the administrator's becoming a rubber stamp for budget requests rather than an evaluator of them.

Another alternative for the administrator is to try to become more knowledgeable in the area for which the budget request is being made. But while this approach is feasible to a limited extent and should be utilized as much as possible, it is not a complete answer to the problem, in light of all of the other responsibilities that an administrator must perform.

A third alternative for the administrator is to utilize consultant help from a department chairman, a subject-matter supervisor in the district office, or perhaps even someone at the university or state department level to help with evaluating budget requests of a specialized nature. Assuming that such consultant help is available (a condition not always existent), the administrator should be careful in selecting the consultant to make sure that the latter will be objective in making assessments. The contribution of the consultant will be of inverse value if she has a vested interst in "building an empire" in the subject area.

REQUESTS FOR A SPECIFIC BRAND OF AN ITEM VS. CENTRALIZED BIDDING

Many individuals who request a budget item don't want just any make of the item, but desire a particular brand or model. For example, the teacher who feels that a 3-M model of the overhead projector is superior does not want any other brand. Or the orchestra instructor may request a musical instrument manufactured by a certain company. The problem is that the desire to specify a particular brand of an item is antithetical to the purchasing procedures of many school districts which believe in, and may be required to solicit bids on budget items, and then select the company submitting the lowest bids. Therefore, teachers are seldom encouraged to specify the particular make of the item that they request.

School districts are, of course, obligated to obtain the best price possible in purchasing products and services. However, the primary factor determining whether a particular product or service should be purchased should be the extent to which the item will be effectively utilized. Durability and cost are other important factors. Still, it makes little sense for a school district to purchase low-priced items if teachers or students will not utilize them effectively.

Also, as one budget expert observed, "It is a principle of good management, as well as of good human relations, that the people who are to use equipment and facilities be given some voice in suggesting the materials they believe would be most effective to carry out the job."[21]

On the other hand, there is a certain amount of teacher turnover which makes the policy of always budgeting and purchasing the exact brand of an item that a teacher requests a risky one. Perhaps the best resolution of this overall problem is for a school district to involve teachers and students—the users and consumers of the products and services—to a greater extent in establishing the *criteria* for budgeting and purchasing items. This procedure would increase the possibility that factors in addition to cost and durability would be given consideration in the budgeting and purchasing of products and services, and should result in greater utilization of these items.

INADEQUATE CONSULTATION BETWEEN THE DISTRICT OFFICE AND INDIVIDUAL SCHOOLS

Because the budget-building process is a complex operation, it requires a great deal of consultation. Consultation is, of course, important in all aspects of administration, but is of extreme importance in the budget-making process. If the district's central office and the individual schools do not consult sufficiently and coordinate their efforts effectively, the process of developing the budget may become disjointed and frustrating for many of those involved. Unfortunately, in all too many cases the latter consequences are prevalent.

A lack of consultation between a district's central office and the individual schools can occur at two main points during the budget process: (1) at the beginning and (2) after the school budget is delivered to the central administration. At the beginning of the budget process the school administrator needs to know certain basic facts about the budget situation in the district. For example, she needs to know of any financial parameters under which the district and/or school must operate for the coming year. She needs to know the program priorities of the district and the expectations of the district's central office for program development in the school. She needs to know the extent to which she is free to involve teachers, students, and parents in the budgeting process for the school, and whether there are any budget limits under which they must work. The problem is that, in many districts, the school administrator is not consulted at all in regard to this kind of information, or the consultation is such that the information given to her by the district is vague or inaccurate in light of what eventually happens when the proposed budget is sent to the district's central office.

It is after the budget is sent from the individual school to the district office for review and final approval that the second type of inadequate consultation may occur between district administrators and school level administrators. At this point, in too many instances, the proposed school budget is modified and changed by the district administrators without anything more than *pro forma* consultation with the school administrator. Proposed items are cut and substitutions are made, but the school administrator may not discover that these changes have been made until the approved budget is returned later in the year. The inadequate consultation, if acknowledged at all by the district office, is typically justified on the basis of insufficient time and "no other choice."

It would be unfair to indict district administrators totally for the problem of inadequate consultation between them and the school level administrators. The school administrators themselves have not always taken the initiative to consult with the district administration, or taken advantage of the opportunity to consult. For example, it is particularly important for the school administrator to confer with the district business manager during all aspects of the budget process.

Also, in regard to inadequate consultation, it needs to be recognized that district administrators are not free agents in making budget decisions; they are subject to many pressures from the school board and other groups. It is additionally true that consultation with school administrators is difficult to achieve in districts with a large number of schools. However, despite these obstacles, greater effort should be made by all concerned to increase the extent of consultation between the central office and the individual school in all phases of the budget-building process. Through better consultation, the ambiguities and frustrations of the budget-building process could be considerably reduced, thereby contributing to a more constructive and acceptable budget.

ADMINISTERING THE SCHOOL BUDGET

RESPONSIBILITIES AND PROBLEMS

Once the proposed budget is finally approved by the school board, the administrator's main responsibilities relate to purchasing and accounting procedures. Typically, these procedures are predetermined by the district office and implemented by the schools.[22]

The school administrator is usually given the responsibility of making sure that the school operates within its allocated budget and does not overspend in any of the budget categories. To carry out this responsibility effectively, the administrator needs to obtain periodic (at least monthly) budget status reports. These reports should provide information on how much money has been spent up to a certain date, how much money has been encumbered (designated for purchase of products or services but not actually spent), and how much is left in each budget account.

In most medium and large school districts a budget status report is provided periodically to each school administrator. In those districts which don't provide that kind of a service for the administrator, she will need to instruct the school secretary or bookkeeper to prepare budget status reports. Without such reports, the school administrator cannot effectively monitor the spending of funds. It should be noted that even in those districts which provide budget status reports to the school administrators, the reports are usually a month behind the expenditures. This means that it may be necessary, toward the end of the budget year, for the school administrator to keep some type of internal accounting of the money spent, so that the allocated budget will not be exceeded.

As a school administrator manages the budget during the year, she may encounter problems which have occurred in many school districts. First of all, certain people in the school, perhaps even the administrator, may want to purchase an item which has not been included in the budget. Or individuals or departments may want to borrow from one budget account (e.g., capital expenditures) to supplement another budget account (e.g., instructional supplies) which was inadequately budgeted.

Generally, district accounting and purchasing philosophies and procedures tend to discourage, if not actually prohibit, budget transfers from one account to another. The rationale usually given to the school administrator is that she should have budgeted for the item desired, and if permission is given for one school to engage in this practice, other schools may want to do the same thing, and budget planning would become meaningless. There may also be city or state governmental regulations which make budget transfers impermissible.[23]

Despite the need to exercise control over the expenditure of funds previously approved by the school board, it would nevertheless appear that insofar as possible there should be flexibility in the spending of those funds. The school administrator should not be permitted to exceed the total amount budgeted for the school, but she should be allowed some flexibility to adjust the funding in budget categories to meet new situations. The sums of money in the various budget accounts should not be perceived as limits, but as guidelines which can be changed if the situation warrants revision, so long as the administrator does not exceed the total amount in the budget.

This solution would also resolve another problem which has frustrated many school administrators. The difficulty occurs when funds left unspent by a school during one budget year must revert back to the agency that authorized the funds, i.e., the school board or city hall, instead of being credited to the school for the ensuing year. If school administrators were given greater flexibility in adjusting budget accounts, the money which was not used during the year for one budget account could be applied in areas where the need is greater than anticipated, and the unused funds would not be "lost," as far as an individual school is concerned. Of course, such flexibility could be misused, in that administrators might not plan their budgets carefully enough, knowing that they could adjust budget accounts later. However, this is not an inevitable disadvantage and could be avoided with appropriate in-service education and close monitoring. (An article describing how one school district returned to the individual schools' budgets eighty cents for every dollar saved is presented in *The Kappan,* April 1980.)

ADMINISTERING THE STUDENT ACTIVITIES ACCOUNT

The student activities account is one aspect of the budget which deserves special attention, since it is a potential trouble spot. This account usually is not a part of the educational budget previously discussed and is administered primarily at the school level with district supervision. The account involves the funds collected and disbursed for various extracurricular and student activities. Included are monies derived from fees charged for athletic events, plays, concerts, the student newspaper and the annual, extra-class activities, and special fund-raising projects.

The total sum of money in the activities account in any one year can be large, and there have been criticisms of the way the money has at times been spent and the way the account has been administered. While the activities account is usually audited by an independent agency, the principal of a school is relatively free to authorize the expenditure of funds for purposes she thinks important. This practice has led in some instances to the expenditure of money for items which would not have been approved if submitted in the educational budget. In other situations it has resulted in some very large activities funds, the monies of which were put into savings accounts, thereby earning interest. Although seldom has there been anything illegal about the principal's action in relation to the student activities account, administration of the account has frequently been sloppy; therefore better guidelines and supervision would appear to be needed.

First of all, the school administrator needs to recognize that the monies collected and disbursed are *public* funds, and the courts have ruled that "the proceeds of those activities belong to the board of school directors and must be accounted for in the same manner that the other funds of the school district are accounted for."[24] The school board may delegate to the school administrator the responsibilities of collecting and disbursing the funds, and if so, she is accountable for the manner in which she carries out these responsibilities.

Secondly, the school administrator needs to design and implement a responsible system for collecting, disbursing and monitoring the spending of student activities monies. Such a system should include the following characteristics:[25]

1. School board authorization for the collection of student activities fees.
2. The involvement of students and teachers in determining the establishment and size of student activities fees and in decisions about how monies are to be spent.
3. The maintenance of school records of monies collected and disbursed, showing that the procedures enumerated below are being followed:
   a. a receipt is issued to the individual from whom money is received,
   b. a deposit receipt is obtained from the bank, indicating that all monies have been deposited upon being received,
   c. the amount which is deposited is recorded in a student activities account under the appropriate fund,
   d. a requisition form, requiring the signature of the activity sponsor, is used to initiate purchases, with purchases involving large sums of money requiring the approval of the principal additionally,
   e. school checks are used to expend monies and to pay student activities bills,
   f. all expenditures are recorded in the student activities ledger, under the appropriate fund.
4. The provision of a budget-status report for each activity sponsor and for the school administrator, on a monthly basis.
5. A yearly audit and review of the purposes for which student activity monies have been spent, conducted by the district office with the involvement of the school administrator and activities' sponsors.

As one might suspect, administering the student activities account can be very time-consuming, and this responsibility might be delegated to the school's business manager or another member of the staff. However, even if the responsibility is delegated, the final accountability is still that of the school administrator. The administrator is the one who is ultimately responsible, so she must be sufficiently knowledgeable and involved to explain the transactions that occur.

EVALUATING BUDGET UTILIZATION: EFFECTIVENESS, EFFICIENCY

A third function of the school administrator in relation to the budget is to evaluate its effectiveness and efficiency.[26] Budget effectiveness is determined by evaluating the extent to which the funds allocated for each of the programs in the school are achieving their objectives. Budget efficiency is determined by evaluating the extent to which the products and services purchased with budget funds are purchased at the lowest price consistent with the items' usability, durability, and reliability. It also involves the monitoring of products and services utilization. Budget effectiveness and efficiency should both be important concerns of the school administrator, particularly in a time of limited funds.

Until recently it was difficult, if not impossible, to talk meaningfully about evaluating budget effectiveness and efficiency. Budgets were organized according to account categories which, in most cases, bore little if any relationship to school programs or objectives. However, with the advent of PPBS (Planning, Programming, Budgeting System), it is now possible for the administrator to evaluate more accurately the effectiveness and efficiency of the budget. Under PPBS the budget is organized according to educational programs whose objectives have been defined, and for which criteria and methods of evaluation have been identified.

Under this system, if the administrator wants to find out whether or not the funds for a particular program are being utilized effectively, she can evaluate the extent to which the objectives are being achieved, and then make a judgment about whether or not that achievement is sufficient, considering the funds allocated.[27] It should be emphasized that part of the basis for that judgment must relate to whether or not increased funding of the same program or funding of a different program to reach the same objectives would result in *greater* achievement of those objectives. A program should not be judged as effective or ineffective by itself, but only in comparison to what an alternative may cost and achieve.

For an example of how PPBS can be used to evaluate budget and program effectiveness, see figure 6.5.

Once the budget has been approved by the school board, the school administrator's role in evaluating budget efficiency is generally limited to monitoring and preventing wasteful use of funds.[28] Any product or service which is inefficiently utilized, either because of wastefulness or underutilization, merits the administrator's attention. She especially needs to watch for excessive use of supplies, underutilization of equipment, and inefficient use of time and personnel. Evaluating the efficiency of the expenditure of funds is never a popular task. But in situations of limited financial support for education, a school administrator cannot abdicate this important responsibility.

Program Alternatives for Teaching Remedial Reading
to a Class of 9th Grade Students

	Class Size	Personnel	Equipment	Total Estimated Costs	Per Student Cost	Predicted Results
Program Option No. 1	10	1 teacher	None	$20,000	$2,000	Increase one grade level
Program Option No. 2	20	1 teacher	Overhead Projector	$20,500	$1,025	Increase ½ grade level
Program Option No. 3	40	1 teacher, 1 aide	None	$32,000	$800	Increase ¼ grade level

Figure 6.5. Cost Effectiveness Analysis[29]

SCHOOL PLANT MANAGEMENT

Winston Chruchill is said to have observed, "We shape our dwellings and then our dwellings shape us." The physical environment in which we work can and does influence what we do and how we feel. For example, it can affect our flexibility in teaching, our communication patterns, the amount of noise and extent of discipline problems in the school, and many other facets of the total educational enterprise. A well-maintained, bright, sparkling, flexible, physical facility suggests a school that people care about. Such a school does something positive for the spirit of the individuals who occupy the building.

On the other hand, a school which is poorly maintained, institutional-looking and inflexible in its structure tends to dull the spirit of the people who must spend their work days, weeks, and months there. It suggests a school in which people have lost interest and lack pride. Although the importance of the school plant's appearance and flexibility can be overemphasized, there is little doubt that they do affect the feelings and behavior of the people who occupy the building.

In addition, a school building can, over the years, develop a special attraction for and loyalty from the people in the community, particularly parents. This is most evident when a school closing is being considered.

In the following sections four major responsibilities of the school administrator will be discussed: (1) maintenance of the school plant, (2) scheduling facilities, (3) school plant planning, and (4) school closing.

MAINTENANCE OF THE SCHOOL PLANT

The administrator is not, of course, responsible for personally maintaining the school plant. The school district has hired custodians and related workers to perform the actual tasks of keeping the school clean, bright, energy efficient, and in good repair.[30] However, the school administrator cannot assume that these tasks will be carried out effectively without some supervision on her part. The administrator, or someone to whom this responsibility is delegated, will need to supervise the custodians and monitor their work as it relates to energy conservation and the general appearance and condition of the building and grounds. If the school administrator is fortunate enough to have a conscientious head custodian, the supervisory responsibility of the administrator will be greatly reduced. But it should be noted that such custodians are not always available, and in many schools some supervision and monitoring by the school administrator will probably be required.[31]

While the nature and extent of the administrator's responsibilities for supervising the custodians and monitoring the maintenance of the school plant and grounds will vary, depending on local conditions, the following general responsibilities are proposed:

1. *Keep informed about the work schedule and specific responsibilities of each member of the custodial staff.* The school administrator should know the work schedule of each person on the custodial staff and should be knowledgeable about who does what.

2. *Tour the school building and grounds regularly for the purpose of observing the extent to which they are being kept clean, neat, energy efficient and in good repair.* Admittedly, the administrator may have other higher priorities, leaving limited time for this kind of activity. But if she cares enough about the appearance and energy efficiency of the school building and grounds, she will try to schedule such tours every week or two. They can be veritable "eye openers."

3. *Conduct, with the assistance of appropriate help, a comprehensive audit of the energy needs and excesses of the school/district, and design and implement energy conservation practices.* Energy to operate the schools is likely to be in short supply in the foreseeable future, and therefore expensive. The administrator should take steps to improve the energy efficiency of the school. These steps might include (a) carrying out a full energy use audit of all school facilities, (b) establishing appropriate temperature control in all classrooms, (c) conducting regular inspection and maintenance of all heating, cooling, and ventilating systems, (d) reducing all unnecessary lighting, and (e) eliminating all unnecessary use of

water. Of course, these steps are just a beginning, and there are many other actions which need to be considered, as identified in the references listed at the end of this chapter.[32] It should be emphasized that in order for most of these actions to be effective, the understanding and cooperation of teachers and students will be needed, so orientation and in-service meetings should be initiated to achieve these objectives.[33]

4. *Design some method or procedure for students, teachers, or others to bring to the attention of the head custodian and/or the school administrator any problems in plant and grounds maintenance, appearance, or energy loss.* A form could be developed for this purpose, or perhaps the administrator could simply point out to students and teachers the procedure to follow when a problem occurs. (It should be noted that there will be students and teachers who will be reluctant or won't take time to report a problem directly to the custodians.) There may also be value in the practice of the administrator's receiving the reports, or at least a copy of the reports, so that she can become better informed about the maintenance and energy problems in the building.

5. *Develop a good working relationship with all of the custodial staff, particularly the head custodian.* The custodial staff should be treated with the same respect and human relations approach as any other group of employees in the school. They perform an important job and, if dissatisfied, can make things difficult for the school administrator and teachers.

The appearance and energy efficiency of the school plant and grounds should, of course, be the concern of everyone, including students and teachers. However, the administrator must assume the overall responsibility for making sure that the school plant and grounds are kept clean, neat, in good repair, and energy efficient. This responsibility is one which the administrator should not avoid and for which she should rightly be held accountable.

SCHOOL PLANT SCHEDULING

Facilities scheduling is a second major component of plant management. Someone must be responsible for scheduling facilities in a way that will promote appropriate and maximum usage. That person is frequently the school administrator, although the responsibility may be delegated to someone else in certain situations.

School facilities must be scheduled to accommodate (1) the regular educational program of the school, (2) the school's student activities program, and (3) requests of people who would like to use the building at night, on weekends, or during the summer for recreational or adult programs.

There are many different approaches to scheduling the regular educational program of a school, and references are provided for the reader who wishes to explore this subject in depth.[34] However, relatively little attention has been paid in the educational literature to facility scheduling for the extracurricular program or for the recreational and adult programs at night and on weekends.[35] If the administrator finds that there is considerable demand for the use of the school facilities after the end of the school day, she will probably need to assign to a staff member the responsibility for setting up and administering a system for handling requests and scheduling facilities. This system should be coordinated with the custodians' work load and schedule, if problems are to be avoided. In a small school, the individual who has overall responsibility for facilities scheduling may well have to be the principal herself. In a larger school, the principal can delegate this responsibility to an assistant principal, or it may be assigned to the head custodian.

Facility scheduling may not be regarded as a particularly interesting or rewarding aspect of school administration. Nevertheless, it is a task requiring effective performance, though it need not become a time-consuming or frustrating experience if approached in an organized manner.

SCHOOL PLANT PLANNING

The administrator's major responsibilities for school plant planning are two-fold: (1) planning for changes in the existing structure, such as remodeling or additions, and (2) planning for a new facility or the closing of a school.[36]

In a time of educational change, many school plants simply do not provide sufficient flexibility or comprehensiveness to accommodate the various proposals for improving the educational program of the school, and modernization of old buildings is a constant need. Not all communities can afford to build a new school, so an administrator may need to consider ways in which the present facility can be remodeled or expanded.* For example, changes in facilities may be needed in order to accommodate handicapped students.[37] (For answers to questions about how to provide access for handicapped students in the school building, call the National Center for a Barrier Free Environment, 1–800–425–2809.) In addition, modification may be needed to increase the facility's energy efficiency.[38]

Since form should follow function, the administrator should first determine, in cooperation with relevant others, the kind of educational program to be implemented in the school, and then consider needed changes in the physical plant. Having ascertained the type of educational program which the school

---

*For those administrators in a district or school with a declining enrollment, the report *Fewer Pupils/Surplus Space* provides helpful suggestions on how to make good use of surplus space. The report is published by the Educational Facilities Laboratories, 477 Madison Ave., N.Y. 10022.

should implement, the administrator can logically move to the next step—analyzing the physical facilities required by that program and then identifying the need for remodeling or expanding the present school plant. In taking this step the school administrator will want to consult with appropriate facilities specialists in the district office, at the university, and at the state department of public instruction. Assistance in estimating the cost of making changes in the physical plant should also be secured. As a result of conferring with various experts the school administrator should be in a position to submit to the school board for its consideration (1) a document which describes the type of educational program that will be possible with the modification of facilities; (2) preliminary sketches showing the proposed change; and (3) the estimated cost to the district.[39]

School plant planning for remodeling or expanding takes time and preparation. However, there is little doubt that many of our school plants need remodeling or expansion if they are to accommodate needed improvements in the educational program and energy efficiency.[40]

Planning a New Facility

While most school administrators are more likely to participate in planning for facility remodeling or expansion, some administrators will be fortunate enough to become involved in planning for an entirely new school building. This is a task which will challenge the creativity, patience, and endurance of any administrator. At the same time, it can be a very exciting and rewarding activity.

Instead of a discussion of the innumerable details of planning for a new building, some general principles which should be followed are presented below.[41]

1. *Define the educational objectives which are to be achieved in the new school and the programs and activities which will be implemented in order to achieve those objectives.* This effort should result in a document formally referred to as "the educational specifications" of the school.[42] These educational specifications should be as detailed and precise as needed to enable both the administrator and the architect to understand the type of educational program which the new building is to house.

2. *Involve in the planning of the new facility as many of those people who will occupy the new building as possible, e.g., students, teachers.* It may be more convenient and efficient for an administrator to exclude these people, but this will increase the risk that the new facility will not be functional for their needs. The

administrator may choose to establish committees, solicit recommendations from individuals, or attempt some other alternative in securing input.

Regardless of the approach chosen by the administrator, however, a determination should be made in advance that the ideas and recommendations which are generated from the involvement of teachers, students and others will be carefully considered and will not be rejected simply because they might be more expensive than other ideas. Obviously, there are financial parameters within which the school board and the administrator must operate. However, if the participants in the planning process, particularly teachers, gather the impression that cost is going to be the main criterion in assessing the worth of a recommendation, they are unlikely to contribute their time and effort. A school district does not need to involve many people in the planning of a new facility if the basic objective is simply to build the least expensive plant possible.

3. *Study the educational literature on school plant planning.* It makes no sense to "reinvent the wheel," and many mistakes can be avoided by reviewing the recommendations and experiences of others.[43]

4. *Define the nature and scope of the responsibilities of the architect for the project.* In too many situations the architect's responsibilities, particularly as they pertain to making decisions about the educational program to be housed in the school and the type of physical facilities needed, are not clearly delineated. As a result, the architect may end up making decisions about the nature of the new building which are, in reality, educational decisions.

5. *Devise a master plan and time schedule which will program within a specified timetable the planning and implementation activities that need to be accomplished by a certain date.* Unless an overall plan identifies and sequences the various steps to be carried out within a specific time frame, it is unlikely that the new facility will be completed on schedule. An excellent tool which the administrator should utilize in developing and implementing the master plan is PERT-CPM, i.e., Program Evaluation and Review Technique and Critical Path Method.*

6. *Develop criteria and procedures for evaluating the new facility after it is in operation.* Any new structure, regardless of how well conceived and planned, will have defects or deficiencies which may

---

*For a good explantion of Pert-CPM, see *Educational Management Tools for the Practicing School Administrator,* Chapter 2. (Arlington, Va.: American Association of School Administrators, 1979.)

need to be corrected and which should be avoided in the planning of the next facility. In evaluating a new facility, strong consideration should be given to involving the people who are most affected by it: students and teachers.

The administrator who wishes additional information and discussion on the steps involved in planning for the construction of a new facility or building should examine *Schoolhouse Planning,* published by the Association of School Business Officials.

Closing a School

Educators until recently have not had much experience in closing schools. However, because of declining enrollments and growing taxpayers' pressures for greater economies in education, school officials in a number of communities have had to close some of the schools.[44] These conditions are likely to continue into the foreseeable future.

The task of closing a school is seldom an easy one and frequently has been plagued with controversy and resistance on the part of some people in the community. Some of these problems have resulted from poor administrative planning and problem-solving, but others are a consequence of the strong identification with and loyalty to "their school" that many parents and members of the community possess. While sound planning and effective problem-solving won't avoid all of the problems associated with closing a school, the following guidelines should minimize difficulties:[45]

1. Establish, far in advance of any need to close a school, a committee to develop policy and procedures for school closing. The school board, district office, building level administrators, teachers, students, parents, and the larger community should be represented on the committee. Members of the committee should possess the necessary objectivity, energy level, persistence, and expertise for accomplishing what will probably be a complex and arduous task, as well as a potentially emotional issue.[46]
2. Develop criteria for closing a school. The criteria should include student enrollment, population projections, age of the building, energy consumption, maintenance costs, distance from neighboring schools, and zoning trends. It should be recognized that the criteria selected will represent a combination of technical factors and value preferences, but to the greatest extent possible, they should emphasize the former.
3. Develop understanding and support on the part of the community, parents, teachers, students, *and the press* on the idea of the need for school closings. This won't be easily accomplished, but if these groups are involved early in the entire process, and if school

officials are open and candid in meeting the need for information and responding to concerns, many *unnecessary* problems will be avoided.

4. Recognize that closing a school will carry economic, political, and public relations implications, as well as educational consequences.[47] Resistance to the closing of a school may come, for example, from teachers who fear lay-offs, merchants who are concerned about potential business losses, politicians who are being pressured by their constituents, and parents who are worried about transportation and other problems involved in transferring their children to another school. Some of these problems and resistance probably cannot be avoided, but it is important that they be anticipated before they surface so they can be dealt with more effectively.

5. Consider all feasible and reasonable alternatives to closing a school prior to the final decision; make sure the process of considering other alternatives, and the results of the process are clearly communicated to all concerned. These steps will go a long way toward reducing the resistance referred to in guideline 4. If people feel that school officials have fairly examined alternatives other than closing a school, and that the latter is still the best alternative, most individuals and groups will at least resign themselves to a school closing. It is important, of course, that school officials keep an open mind, and that such openness be communicated to the public, before and during the consideration of alternatives to closing a school.

6. Institute follow-up orientation and in-service activities after a decision has been made to close a school. These should include[48] (a) orientation trips for students and parents to visit the new school, where they should be given an opportunity to tour the building, meet teachers and student leaders, and become familiar with the educational program of the school; (b) information distributed about new transportation schedules and routes; (c) continuation of maximum efforts on the part of the principal and staff of the school that is to be closed, to ensure that the best educational program is offered until the school finally closes. This will not be easy, but in fairness to the students and their parents, the effort must be made.

A FINAL NOTE ON BUDGET AND PLANT MANAGEMENT

The school budget and plant represent important vehicles for conserving resources and improving educational opportunities for students. Whether the
full potential of these means is realized will depend in large part on the school
administrator. She will undoubtedly face problems and will need to work within
certain financial and physical constraints. However, in the final analysis, the
administrator's success in providing the best possible budget and physical facilities for the school will depend for the most part on her *knowledge, resourcefulness,* and *persistence.*

Review and Learning Activities

1. What are the steps involved in and the advantages and disadvantages
   of the centralized budget process? The decentralized budget process?
2. Describe the main elements of the Planning, Programming, Budgeting
   System (PPBS). What are its advantages and disadvantages? Compare
   it to Zero-Based Budgeting.
3. Discuss the major problems associated with the process of developing
   the school budget. What are the implications of these problems for the
   school administrator?
4. Identify those factors that characterize the effective administration of
   the budget.
5. Describe the major responsibilities of the administrator in maintaining
   the school plant, scheduling facilities, and school plant planning.
6. Assume that you have been requested to develop a plan for use by a
   school district which wishes to consider the possibility of closing some
   schools. What factors and problems should your plan address?

Notes

1. Leo M. Casey, *School Business Administration* (New York: Center for Applied
Research in Education, 1964), p. 13.
2. Perry E. Burrup, *Financing Education in a Climate of Change* (Boston: Allyn and
Bacon, 1977), p. 294.
3. I. Carl Candoli, et al., *School Business Administration: A Planning Approach* (Boston:
Allyn and Bacon, 1978), p. 147.
4. Ibid., pp. 148–49.
5. Ervin Decker, et al., *Site Management, An Analysis of the Concepts and Fundamental
Operational Components Associated With It* (ERIC Report Ed–150–736:). Also see *Florida
Education Finance Program: State Support for Public Schools, 1976–1977* (Tallahassee:
Florida Department of Education, 1977); Brian J. Caldwell, *Implementation of Decentralized
School Budgeting* (ERIC Report: Ed–161–148).

6. Thomas E. Glass, "Developing the District Budget through Direct Citizen Participation," *School Business Affairs* (February 1979): 12–14.

7. Candoli, et al., *School Business Administration.*

8. Three excellent books for in-depth study of PPBS are S. A. Haggart, et al., *Program Budgeting for School Planning* (Englewood Cliffs, N.J.: Educational Technology Publications, 1971); Robert F. Alioto and J. D. Jungherr, *Operational PPBS for Education* (New York: Harper and Row, 1971); Stephen J. Knezevich, *Program Budgeting* (Berkeley, Calif.: McCutchan, 1973). Also see *A PPM Primer.* An ERIC Report: Ed–169–623.

9. Thomas F. Koerner, *PPBS and the School: New System Promotes Efficiency, Accountability* (Washington, D.C.: National School Public Relations Association, 1972), p. 6.

10. PPBS process adapted from Aliota and Jungherr, *Operational PPBS for Education,* p. 52.

11. For additional information on problems associated with PPBS, see Willian A. Jenkins and Greg O. Lehman, "Nine Pitfalls of PPBS," *School Management* (January 1972): 1–6. Also see Michael W. Kirst, "The Rise and Fall of PPBS in California," *The Kappan* (April 1975): 535–38; Paul Goldman and Sandra Gregory, "Instituting PPBS in Schools," *Urban Education* (April 1979): 76–90.

12. For additional information on PPBS, see I. Carl Candoli et al., *Operational PPBS for Education.*

13. Adapted from several school districts' budget worksheets.

14. Adapted from one school district's budget worksheets.

15. For a discussion of the origins of zero-based budgeting, see Allen Schick, "The Road from ZBB," *Public Administration Review* (March/April 1978): 177–79.

16. Harry J. Hartley, "Zero-Base Budgeting for Secondary Schools," *NASSP Bulletin* (December 1979): 22–23.

17. Ibid., 23.

18. Ross A. Hodel, "Budgeting—A Management Approach for the 80s," *School Business Affairs* (February 1980): 24–25.

19. For additional information on ZBB and related management tools, see *Educational Management Tools for the Practicing School Administrator: A Handbook for School Administrators Who Wish to Plan, Organize, Allocate Resources, and Control Educational Programs* (Arlington, Va.: American Association of School Administrators, 1979).

20. For help in regard to this problem, see R. Louis Bright, *Should Educators Generate Specifications for the Purchase of Equipment?* An ERIC Report: Ed–039–736.

21. New York State University, *School Business Management Handbook: Budget* (Albany: State Education Department, 1956), p. 41.

22. Burrup, *Financing Education,* p. 298.

23. Candoli et al., *School Business Administration,* pp. 185–213.

24. See re German Township School Directors, 465 and C, 562 (1942).

25. For a good study containing a number of excellent recommendations for sound financial business principles in the management of student activities, see Rod Lincoln, "Current Practices in the Administration of Student Activity Finances in Selected Montana Public Secondary Schools" (Ed.D. diss., University of Montana, 1981).

26. For a review of theory and research on this aspect, see David H. Monk, "Toward a Multilevel Perspective on the Allocation of Educational Resources," *Review of Educational Research* (Summer 1981): 215–36.

27. For a good description of one model that appears to be useful in this area, see Jim E. Kim, *A Cost-Effectiveness/Benefits Analysis Model for Improving Educational Program Management.* An ERIC Report: Ed–170–870.

28. Candoli, et al., *School Business Administration,* pp. 252–57.

29. For further elaboration and discussion of the concepts leading up to figure 6.5., see *Educational Resources Management System* (Chicago: Research Corporation of the Association of School Business Officials, 1971), pp. 241–65. Also see I. Carl Candoli, et al., *School Business Administration.*

30. Richard Tonigan, "Do-It-Yourself Ideas for Principals Facing Plant Management Problems," *School Management* (June 1972): 35.

31. For an excellent study of administrative policies and procedures in this area, see Joseph F. Frola, "Administrative Policies and Practices for the Selection, Training and Supervision of School Custodians and Their Relationships to the Quality of Custodial Services in Selected School Districts" (Ph.D. diss., University of Pittsburgh, 1971).

32. See *Field-Proven Programs to Conserve Energy in Schools* (Park Ridge, Ill.: The Association of School Business Officials, 1980); John H. Fredrickson, "Facilities Recycling for Energy Conservation," *National Association of Secondary School Principals Bulletin* (May 1979): 59–65; Ralph J. Askin, et al., *California School Energy Concepts* (Sacramento, Calif.: Bureau of School Planning, California State Department of Education, 1978); Robert M. Jones and John E. Steinbrink, "Developing Energy Conservation Programs," *NASSP Bulletin* (April 1980): 76–82; *Energy Audit Workbook for Schools* (Washington, D.C.: Office of State and Local Programs, Department of Energy, 1978). Also see January and February 1980, issues of *School Business Affairs* for additional ideas.

33. See the chapter on instructional leadership for in-service concepts and alternatives.

34. Richard A. Dempsey and Henry P. Travers, *Scheduling the Secondary School* (Reston, Va.: National Association of Secondary School Principals, 1982).

35. One exception would be John Greenhalgh, *Practitioner's Guide to School Business Management* (Boston, Mass.: Allyn and Bacon, 1978), chapter 17.

36. Basil Castaldi, *Educational Facilities: Planning, Remodeling and Management* (Boston, Mass.: Allyn and Bacon, 1982).

37. For suggestions, see Thomas L. Erekson, "Identifying, Removing Architectural Barriers for the Handicapped," *NASSP Bulletin* (January 1980): 102–8.

38. Thomas Tiedeman, *An Energy Conservation Retrofit Process for Existing Public and Institutional Facilities* (Washington, D.C.: Public Technology, Inc., 1977).

39. For some good ideas in this regard, see McLeod, Ferrara, and Ensign, *School Renewal* (New York: Educational Facilities Laboratories, n.d.) Also see ERIC Report: Ed–143–138.

40. Castaldi, *Educational Facilities,* chapters 15 and 16.

41. Useful literature on new school plant planning includes Candoli, et al., *Educational Facilities,* Part III, and James J. Morisseau, *Design and Planning: The New Schools* (New York: Van Nostrand Reinhold, 1972).

42. For a comprehensive review of the literature on this topic, with sources on ideas for developing educational specifications for the elementary, middle, junior high, and high schools, see Philip K. Piele, *Educational Specifications.* An ERIC Report: Ed–058–620.

43. The ERIC Clearing House on Educational Management at Eugene, Oregon, is a good source for reviewing the literature on school facilities and school plant planning.

44. William Gordon and Larry Hughes, "Consider This Before Closing Schools," *The American School Board Journal* (February 1980): 31–33.

45. The ideas for these guidelines come from an analysis of the articles in *School Closing—the Best of ERIC* (Eugene, Oreg.: Clearinghouse on Educational Management, 1979), and those articles referred to later in the guidelines. For further information on school closings, contact The Center for Community Education Facility Planning, 29 West Woodruff Ave., Columbus, Ohio 43210, and Clearinghouse on Educational Management, Eugene, Oregon 97403. Also see *Declining Enrollment/Closing Schools: Problems and Solutions* (Arlington, Va.: American Assn. of School Administrators, 1980).

46. For further discussion of important prerequisites to involving others, see Richard A. Gorton, *School Administration and Supervision: Important Issues, Concepts and Case Studies* (Dubuque, Iowa: Wm. C. Brown Company Publishers, 1980), pp. 243–46.

47. For an example, see Leonard Bornstein, *Before You Close a School: Economic and Political Factors: Resource Guide—Declining Enrollments.* An ERIC Report: Ed–149–448.

48. M. Donald Thomas, "Administrative Leadership in School Closures," *NASSP Bulletin* (November 1980): 23.

3

STAFF PERSONNEL AND INSTRUCTIONAL/ CURRICULAR LEADERSHIP

7

STAFF RECRUITMENT, SELECTION, AND INDUCTION

Davis and Nickerson have observed that, "The education of children is the central purpose of any school, and the teacher is the most important single resource in producing a quality education."[1] Therefore, every school administrator should be interested in improving the quality of the professional staff. Three important processes by which an administrator can take a major step toward the achievement of this goal are personnel recruitment, selection, and induction. Although the availability and turnover of personnel will tend to influence the priority given to these three processes, they still represent significant means by which an administrator can improve the quality of the staff.

STAFF RECRUITMENT

Staff recruitment may be defined as the active pursuit of potential candidates for the purpose of influencing them to apply for positions in the school district. The goal of a school's or district's staff recruitment program should be to attract applications from the best people available, both beginning and experienced.[2] Although a surplus of candidates for a position may decrease the difficulty of finding a qualified candidate for a vacancy, the administrator should not limit himself to minimal standards of qualification. Instead, the objective of a district's recruiting should be to attract the *most* qualified and outstanding individuals.

Since most staff recruiting programs are centralized at the district level, either in a personnel office or under the jurisdiction of a central office administrator, the focus in this section will be on ways in which a school administrator can most effectively work with the central office in the recruitment of staff.

159

ASSESSING NEEDS

The first important way in which a school administrator can help the district administration in the recruitment of staff is by providing them with data on personnel needs for the school.[3] There are at least three major categories of staff personnel needs for which a school administrator should provide data to the central office:

1. Increased or decreased enrollment which creates a need for more staff or a reduction in staff.
2. Changes in the educational program which necessitate additional or differently trained staff.
3. Staff resignations or transfers which may create a need for new personnel.

For recruitment to be effective, the district office must receive data about all three categories of staff needs, at the earliest possible date during the school year. By studying the enrollment figures for his own school and its feeder schools, and by estimating from census figures and the previous years' student turnover, an administrator should be able to project to the central office by January any staff needs related to potential increases or decreases in the student enrollment in the school for the following year.

Estimating the need for new staff due to changes in the educational program will not be easy. But if the school administrator approaches the change process systematically, target dates can be established which will permit the administrator to indicate to the district office by early spring the existence of vacancies for additional or specially trained staff. Although it may be difficult for the administrator to meet these target dates, it should be recognized that the later personnel needs are reported to the district office for the purpose of recruiting, the harder it will be to find highly qualified staff still available.

The administrator may also encounter considerable difficulty in estimating staff needs which may be created by resignations or transfers. Some districts require that staff transfers from one school to another within the district take place by a certain date, but resignations can and frequently do occur late in the spring, and even into late summer. Some administrators try to survey their staffs in March or April to ascertain who may be leaving but the data obtained are not always valid or reliable. Teachers who will eventually resign may not want the administrator to know that they are even thinking about resigning, until they have actually secured another job. The best the school administrator can do in these circumstances is to "keep his ear to the ground," and report staff needs to the district office as soon as he can.

AVOIDING EMPLOYMENT DISCRIMINATION

In the development of personnel recruitment and selection policies and procedures, it has become increasingly important for school districts to take into
consideration federal laws, regulations, and court cases on discrimination in
employment.[4] A school district should take certain steps to avoid any charges
of job discrimination in the recruitment and selection of applicants. First of
all, a school district should develop a clear policy statement regarding equal
employment opportunities. An example of such a statement is provided by
Harris and his colleagues.[5]

A school district also should develop and implement an affirmative action
employment program. As defined by the federal government, affirmative action refers to ". . . employer initiated development of a set of specific results-
oriented procedures to ensure that job applicants and employees are treated
without regard to race, color, religion, sex or national origin."[6] According to
McCune and Matthews, an affirmative action plan should include a statement
of policy and purpose, a work force utilization analysis, a set of procedures
for identification and modification of present procedures and practices which
have discriminatory impact or which perpetuate past discrimination, and a
statement establishing affirmative action goals and timetables. Guidelines for
developing these elements are provided by McCune and Matthews.[7] The reader
is also referred to *Affirmative Action Guidelines*,[8] in which technical amend-
ments to the procedural regulations may be found.

The main purpose of an affirmative action plan, with regard to personnel
recruitment, should be to ascertain the need to correct past discrimination in
employment and, if discrimination is found to have been present, to take positive corrective steps to aggressively recruit women and minority members for
staff vacancies. While a high priority should be given to developing a policy
on nondiscrimination in employment and an affirmative action plan to carry
out that policy, an equal amount of attention should also be directed toward
monitoring and assessing the degree to which the policy and plan are actually
being implemented. And although governmental laws and regulations addressing this problem may be reduced, no administrator should be comfortable with less than a vigorous program to eliminate employment discrimination.

THE ADMINISTRATOR'S ROLE IN RECRUITING

The actual recruitment of staff, as mentioned earlier, is typically organized
by a personnel office in larger school districts or by a district administrator,
such as the superintendent or an assistant, in smaller school districts. Two
methods are generally used by school districts to recruit personnel: (1) the
dissemination to university, state, and private placement bureaus of brochures
describing the district and its employment opportunities, and (2) visitations

by district recruiting teams to personnel placement offices. The latter approach tends to be used primarily by those districts with increased enrollment and personnel needs.

It would appear that the school administrator could make a useful contribution to both of these recruiting approaches. Certainly the administrator should, at the minimum, be involved in reacting to the strengths and weaknesses of the district's current brochures, or in helping to develop proposed brochures which will be sent to teacher placement bureaus and to candidates who inquire about the district. For most potential candidates, the district's brochures are the first tangible information they receive about a school system, and the likelihood that they might be interested in exploring staffing opportunities at a particular school will be influenced by the quality of the brochures.

The school administrator should also be involved in orienting the district's recruiting team to the school's particular staffing needs. In the past, building administrators were often included on districts' recruiting teams, but currently this practice is less typical. Although the school system's team is recruiting for the entire district (not just for one administrator's school), if the team is to be maximally effective it will need to be aware of and give attention to the specific staffing needs of individual schools. In order to accomplish the latter objective, the recruiting team will need to be oriented by the principal and, to the extent possible, by the faculty, about the school in which the vacancy has occurred. If the district's philosophy or procedures do not provide an opportunity for such orientation, the school administrator should take the initiative to bring about changes in this regard. A perspective must be developed to the effect that the district should be recruiting teachers to meet the needs of *individual* school programs, staffs, and clienteles, rather than just hiring teachers "at large," or as interchangeable components.

Perhaps the best way a building administrator can develop this perspective is to work closely with the district recruiting team in the development of position descriptions pertaining specifically to the vacancies in the school, which can then be disseminated to all interested candidates, and subsequently used in the interviewing process. A position description usually contains the title of the vacant position, its primary function, major responsibilities, qualifications, special assignments, and the organizational relationships of the position.[9] There need not necessarily be a separate position description for each vacancy in an administrator's school. However, to the extent to which a vacant position is unusual, a position description should be developed. A sample position description is shown in figure 7.1. Phelps provides some excellent guidelines for developing job descriptions.[10]

Title: Diagnostic Teacher (Certificated)
Suggested Position Level: Teacher Basis
Days Per Year of Employment: 200 (Full-time)
Reports to: Project Director, Educational Resource Team, and the Principal
Supervises: Project Teacher and Aides (Functionally)
Major Duties and Responsibilities:

1. Diagnoses children referred for learning problems.
2. Assists in diagnosis of children referred for behavior problems.
3. Assesses the needs of children referred for learning problems.
4. Trains project teachers in the use and interpretation of individual standard and nonstandard tests.
5. Trains project teachers and paraprofessionals in individual analysis of student needs.
6. Correlates educational activities of cooperating school teachers with those of project teachers relative to referred children.
7. Works with individual children referred with the intention of confirming diagnoses.
8. Works with the language curriculum specialist in developing recommendations of specific educational programs and techniques.
9. Provides relevant information based on observation and evaluation to the behavioral counselor, to facilitate planning of behavioral approaches.
10. Attends all staffings on referred children both in cooperating school and project setting.
11. Maintains written records on all referred children.
12. Conducts, together with the language/curriculum specialist, in-service sessions.
13. Assists with functional responsibilities in the absence of the project director.
14. Assists in maintaining ongoing internal program continuity and acts as liaison between cooperating school and project director.
15. Assists project director in planning and developing orientation and program structure of proposed implementation of P.E.R.T.

Figure 7.1. A Sample Position Description[11]

THE ADMINISTRATOR'S MAJOR CONTRIBUTION

It should be pointed out that probably the most important contribution which a school administrator can make to the effective recruitment of staff is to help the school develop an excellent educational program and good working conditions. Obviously, potential candidates may also weigh other factors in deciding whether to pursue a staff vacancy, such as the size of the school and community, and cultural opportunities. But a school or district which becomes recognized in the state as a leader in education and a good place to work (or known to be *striving* toward these goals) will thereby do more to improve its success in staff recruiting than perhaps anything else it could do.[12]

On the other hand, a school or district with a fair, poor, or possibly even no image or reputation for being a good place to work and for offering a quality educational program will probably be hampered in its recruiting efforts. Therefore, the most important steps that a school administrator can take in helping the district office to recruit staff, is to concentrate initially and continuously on the improvement of the educational program and working conditions within the school. While to many this may seem obvious, it needs to be emphasized, since regardless of what else a school administrator or school district might do by way of recruitment, there must be a solid basis in working conditions and in educational accomplishments before recruitment of quality candidates will show significant success.

STAFF SELECTION

Although the school administrator is generally involved to only a limited extent in staff recruitment, he should play a major role in staff selection.

However, it should be noted that in some school districts, usually those in large cities, the school administrator's role in staff selection can be described as peripheral. In these situations the personnel department of the district selects new staff for the schools, and the building administrator may not find out who will be joining the staff until just before classes begin. While it is true that in many of these circumstances the school administrator has been given an opportunity to specify to the personnel department the kinds of new staff needed, it is the personnel department rather than the school administrator who ascertains and decides whether or not candidates for a particular vacancy meet the appropriate prerequisites.

In spite of what may seem to be advantages in efficiency when a personnel department (or, for that matter, other central office administrators) selects the staff, it would appear that as long as the building administrator is held accountable for the performance of the staff, he should be directly involved in the staff selection processes. As Corbally and his colleagues have emphasized,

> He [the principal] is in the best position to know his personnel needs, and no one else is better able to provide an analysis of the responsibilities to be taken over by the new person. . . . And because the principal is most directly connected with future orientation and development of the person, by participating in the selection he automatically assumes some of the responsibility for assuring the success of the teacher.[13]

It would seem that there is sound rationale for the proposition that the building administrator should be given an opportunity to interview and recommend candidates for employment and assignment at the school.[14] The administrator should also be able to appeal (to the superintendent) a directive from the district office to assign to the school an individual not wanted on the staff by the administrator. It is recognized that these recommendations define a major role for the school administrator in staff selection and, by implication, a lesser role for the personnel department. However, the contributions of both are important, and the building administrator should attempt to capitalize on the expertise of the personnel department whenever possible.

STAFF SELECTION PROCESS AND TEAM

Staff selection can be conceptualized as a process consisting of a series of sequentially interdependent steps, as depicted in figure 7.2.

The first step in the staff selection process is to define the characteristics of new staff members the school seeks to employ. Ideally, this should have been accomplished at the beginning of the recruitment process, but many schools and districts limit themselves to merely identifying the grade level or subject to which the teacher will be assigned, e.g., third grade, science. They may have other criteria in mind when they identify the vacancy, and they frequently apply additional criteria in making the final selection decision, but initially there appears to be a lack of specificity or comprehensiveness.

A major problem which is associated with the first step in the selection process is the determination of relevant and valid selection criteria. The administrator must ask, "What personal qualities and professional capabilities should candidates possess?" Research suggests that little consensus exists among school districts in regard to this matter. For example, one study identified nineteen items that were perceived as "very important" to "essential,"

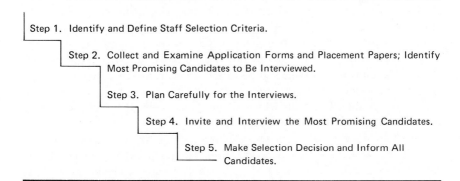

Figure 7.2. The Staff Selection
Process

including health, cooperative attitude, neatness, and dress and grooming. An additional twenty-seven items were ranked as "important" to "very important."[15]

Another study identified appearance and/or size, and sense of humor as attributes that carried greater import than level of education and writing skills.[16] A study of Illinois administrators found that the top four factors considered in selecting teachers were (1) emotional stability and maturity, (2) professional conduct during the job interview, (3) self-expression, and (4) appearance. The quality of a candidate's student teaching was ranked seventh.[17]

In an assessment of the preferences of 140 suburban Chicago superintendents in 1963 and 1973, Endicott noted that personal factors continued to be given greater weight in hiring than was competence.[18] However, in a study of the criteria preferences of administrators, teachers, and parents, Wester concluded that the characteristics given most weight in hiring were reasoning ability, basic speaking and writing skills, emotional stability, common sense, knowledge of subject, and attitude and interest toward students. Those factors considered least important were sex, race, bilingual ability of the candidate, grades, scores on teacher tests, references, and experience.[19] And Grohe found that the three most important and frequently used final screening factors were effective teaching, effective oral communication skills, and likeable personality. High academic competency was reported as one of the least used screening factors.[20]

The tentative conclusion emerging from an examination of studies on personnel selection criteria in education is that a wide range of variables is considered important, with an emphasis on personal factors. For the most part, high academic achievement does not seem to be regarded as an essential selection criterion, although its lack of priority may change in response to growing public concern about teacher competency. Nevertheless, the basic problem with personnel section criteria utilized by school districts is that they seem to be based on subjective impressions rather than on valid research and theory. And, while questions continue to be raised about research on teacher effectiveness,[21] a number of recent studies reviewed in the chapter on staff evaluation have produced findings which should be considered by school districts in the development of personnel selection criteria.

To help identify and define the selection criteria, an administrator should consider establishing a *staff selection team*. The team might include such individuals as a department head or unit leader, a team leader or grade level coordinator, and an assistant principal.[22] Identification of those for whom involvement on the team would be relevant will depend on the nature of the vacancy, but for certain openings, guidance counselors, students, and even parents could make a valuable contribution to defining the selection criteria, interviewing candidates, and even making staff selection recommendations.[23] It should be recognized that the school board has the authority to make final decisions on staff selection, and the building administrator may want to reserve the final determination on who to recommend to the superintendent and, ultimately, the school board. But this should present no real barrier to the nonadministrative members of the staff selection team as long as they understand their role and that of the building administrator.

In defining staff selection criteria, the school administrator and the selection team should give consideration to the following questions:

1. Is it important that the candidate believe in a particular kind of educational philosophy? If so, what are the specifics of that philosophy?
2. What kinds of teaching techniques should the candidate be qualified to use, e.g., inquiry method, discussion leader?
3. What should be the candidate's approach to student discipline and control?
4. How important is it that the candidate be able to work effectively with others, e.g., colleagues, students?
5. What kinds of personal characteristics do we want the candidate to possess, e.g., type of personality, appearance?
6. What kinds of educational background and training do we expect the candidate to possess, e.g., degree, teaching experience?
7. What evidence is available that would provide significant support of the staff selection team's answers to the first six questions?

The final question will undoubtedly be the most difficult and frustrating one for the school administrator and staff selection team to answer, but it is an extremely important question and should be raised at each point at which responses to the other questions are being considered. It seems likely that most schools or districts define their staff selection criteria on the basis of personal preference and experience rather than on a systematic investigation of research on teacher effectiveness. While the former factors are not unimportant, the staff selection criteria should, so far as possible, be based on factors which research has demonstrated to be related to teaching effectiveness. And Grohe's research indicates that all too frequently this is not the case.[24]

ANALYZING PLACEMENT PAPERS

After the selection criteria have been defined, then the staff selection team needs to identify and employ procedures for collecting and examining candidates' data which pertain to the criteria. The two procedures most typically utilized by schools or districts are an examination of applicants' placement papers and a personal interview with candidates. Although these procedures possess certain advantages, each also has certain weaknesses of which the school administrator needs to be more aware.

An examination of placement papers has as its main purpose the screening of applicants so as to determine which ones should be invited for personal interviews. A candidate's placement papers may contain a great deal of useful information, depending on how the forms are designed. But the person or team who examines this information needs to keep in mind that the primary objective of the individual who completes a written application and submits placement papers is to project a favorable image. It is also unlikely that a candidate will knowingly reveal in a statement of philosophy anything which might impair the possibility of securing a job. Certain information requested on an application form is factual, of course, such as the number of years taught, but most of the content of an application form or placement papers is subjective and therefore should not be accepted at face value. Furthermore, school administrators need to exercise care about legal restrictions governing what information can and cannot be elicited on an application form. Data which should not be requested, according to Schustereit, are such items as family status, age, religion, national origin, facts about pregnancy, and nonjob related handicaps.[25]

Transcripts of a candidate's academic work are also generally requested as part of placement papers, and they can offer a potentially useful source of information for screening clearly inferior candidates. However, Harris and his colleagues wonder about the extent to which transcripts are actually utilized,[26] and Lyon questions whether they are really trustworthy indicators of academic performance or predictors of job success because of the problem of grade inflation.[27]

Letters of recommendation are probably perceived with greater confidence in the initial screening process than any other factor,[28] but their utility has also been questioned by Harris and others.[29] Letters of recommendation seldom mention weaknesses or provide a comprehensive analysis of a candidate's strengths. Since the vast majority of letters of recommendation are highly positive, they offer little basis for differentiating among applicants. Moreover, any assessment or description of a candidate's strengths is usually limited by a lack of knowledge of the frame of reference and value system of the individual who has provided the recommendation. Evaluating recommendations has also been potentially limited by the Buckley Amendment, which permits a candidate access to his placement file and to letters of recommendation therein.[30] Individuals who are writing letters of recommendation are aware of which persons have access to their own file, and may therefore temper analyses of those candidates' weaknesses. Many employees seem to be aware of the possible impact of the Buckley Amendment on letters of recommendation, judging from a study by Bryant and others. They noted that over 58 percent of the superintendents participating in the research had indicated a preference for confidential letters of reference in candidates' placement files, i.e., in closed rather than open files.[31]

It is useful to keep in mind while examining recommendations or ratings of candidates that the frame of reference of the person writing the statement or making the recommendation is generally unknown and consequently, one can seldom be absolutely sure what the ratings or recommendations mean. Also, a rater or person writing a letter of recommendation for an employee may not convey his true feelings for fear of losing the employee (or for fear of *not* losing him!) For these reasons, then, the administrator should carefully scrutinize the data contained on application forms and placement papers, and should exhibit considerable caution in drawing firm conclusions about candidates, based only on such data. Perhaps the best use of placement credentials is to develop hypotheses and questions about candidates, which can later be explored during a personal interview. (This recommendation is buttressed by evidence from a study by Arend, who found that, for the most part, candidates' placement papers did not differentiate between effective and ineffective teachers.[32])

Because application forms, transcripts, and letters of recommendation are beset by so many limitations and yet are used so often in the initial screening process, it has been recommended that telephone inquiries be initiated to help clarify and validate the information provided by a candidate or another party.[33] Additionally, a relatively new method for assessing the entry level competencies of beginning teachers, called *Proposition Four,* should be considered.[34] Proposition Four consists of an audiovisual portfolio which includes a student teaching notebook, a slide/narrative program detailing significant experiences of the candidate, audio cassette tapes of lessons taught during student teaching, and a videotape showing the candidate in practice teaching. The portfolio, assembled by the candidate, could be requested by a school district. Administrators interested in this rather promising approach should initiate exploratory discussions with university placement officers.

THE PERSONNEL SELECTION INTERVIEW

The key selection technique in the selection process is the interview.[35] Such important characteristics as personality and attitude are believed by many employers to be best observed and ascertained during a personal interview with the candidate.[36] However, despite its extensive use in personnel selection, the interview has come in for its share of criticism. According to Harris and his colleagues, the personal inerview represents the most used and abused selection technique.[37] The problems apparently stem from inadequate planning, unconscious bias during the interview, and the absence of follow-up after the interview for the purpose of validating the interviewer's procedures and conclusions.[38]

A number of recommendations, based on research and criticism of job selection interview techniques, have been offered for improvement. Greene, for example, has suggested that the variables or characteristics evaluated during an interview exclude those that are difficult to assess reliably and validly in such a process, such as leadership; that the number of variables assessed be few; that more than one person conduct the interview, and that a rating scale or written checklist be used by the interviewers for recording comments and judgments about a candidate.[39] Engel and Friendrichs have identified a number of basic steps that an interviewer should take in *planning* for an interview;[40] Carlson and his colleagues have reviewed research indicating that structured interviews are more effective than unstructured ones;[41] and Hobart has provided guidelines for conducting a structured interview, offering examples of questions that might be used.[42] A type of structured interview referred to as a *Teacher Perceiver* has been used in many school districts, and has been described by Chalker.[43]

In addition, school districts need to consider the federal laws and various court cases which apply to interviews. Schustereit has identified several areas or specific aspects of a candidate's background which, due to federal laws and court cases, no longer are valid areas for inquiry during an interview. These include but are not limited to the candidate's marital and family status, age, religion, national origin, arrests, pregnancy, and nonjob-related handicaps.[44] The latter prohibition is particularly important, inasmuch as Public Law 93–112, Section 504, disallows discrimination in the employment of any handicapped person.[45] In order to reject a handicapped candidate, an employer must demonstrate that the person is not only unqualified but that the reasons why the person is not qualified are unrelated to the handicap of the person, and that those reasons could not be removed by restructuring the job, changing the facilities, purchasing new equipment, or employing an aide. Weisenstein provides a good discussion of traditional barriers and myths that have led to the unemployment and underemployment of the handicapped.[46]

PLANNING AND CONDUCTING THE INTERVIEW

After application forms and placement papers have been examined by the staff selection team, a decision should be made to invite for interviews those individuals who seem to meet the selection criteria to the greatest extent. The team may interview each candidate, the administrator may decide to conduct the interview unilaterally, or another type of interviewing arrangement may be implemented. Regardless of who is conducting the interview, however, careful planning is a key to its success, as pointed out earlier.

The importance of planning for the interview was also underscored in a study by Clower, who found that (1) most interviews were not effective in revealing a candidate's ability to teach, his philosophy of education, or his basic preparation for teaching, and (2) applicants were leaving the interviews with only a hazy idea regarding possible employment.[47] Apparently, more thorough planning for the staff selection interview is needed if it is to accomplish its intended purpose. Planning for a staff selection interview should include consideration of questions identified in figure 7.3.

During the interviews, the staff selection team should attempt to convey an atmosphere of friendliness and warmth, but team members should recognize that their primary objective is to determine candidates' suitability for a particular staff vacancy. This means that the selection team will need to ask penetrating questions of each candidate to reveal individual strengths *and* weaknesses, since many if not most candidates will attempt to project their best image and will seldom volunteer information or be very open about their limitations.

In asking questions the administrator should try to avoid six common errors in interviewing: (1) posing questions that can be answered by "yes," or "no," thereby eliciting little information from the candidate, (2) asking unimaginative questions for which the astute applicant already has prepared answers, (3) asking leading questions which suggest the "correct answers," (4) asking questions which reveal the interviewer's attitude on the questions, (5) asking questions which are unrelated to the task, and (6) asking questions which were already answered on the candidate's application form or resume.[48] Instead, the administrator and the staff selection team should concentrate on asking questions which require candidates to discuss in depth their background, qualifications, and interest in the vacancy.

---

1. What are the objectives of the interview? What do we hope to accomplish?
2. How can we best establish rapport with the candidate at the beginning of the interview, to facilitate communication and candor?
3. What kinds of questions should be asked during the interview to ascertain what we want to know or confirm about the candidate? How should these questions be sequenced?
4. What are likely to be the objectives of the candidate during the interview? What does he/she hope to achieve?
5. What kinds of questions is the candidate likely to ask?
6. What kinds of information or knowledge do we want to be sure that the candidate has been given before leaving the interview?

Figure 7.3. Key Questions in Planning for an Interview

After an interview the members of the staff selection team should discuss their impressions, and then attempt to rate the candidate on the extent to which he met the previously defined selection criteria. Perhaps at this point a decision will be made to hire or reject a particular candidate, although there is value to interviewing all candidates scheduled for conferences before a final decision is made. It is important that the selection team be sure to maintain a *written* record summarizing impressions of the rating given to each candidate. Such a record will be helpful later, when a final decision on hiring must be reached, or in the eventuality that any question may be raised about the selection process.

When all of the candidates scheduled for conferences have been interviewed and evaluated, the selection team should be ready to make a final decision on the individual whom they will recommend for employment. At this stage the administrator and the selection team should be aware of the degree to which their own personal biases may potentially influence their decisions.

For example, a study by Merritt disclosed that principals are more attracted to candidates with attitudes about education that are similar to their own, than to candidates with dissimilar attitudes.[49] This finding would not appear to possess any special significance unless one also knows that the principals in the study preferred candidates with attitudes similar to their own *regardless* of whether the candidates had high or low qualifications. Highly qualified candidates were selected by the principal only when they possessed attitudes about education similar to his own, and candidates with low qualifications were selected over more highly qualified candidates when the former possessed attitudes about education which were similar to those of the principal.

A major implication of Merritt's study is that an interviewer's attitude can exert an important influence on the evaluation of a candidate—an influence which could result in the rejection of a highly qualified individual in favor of one who may be less qualified. Awareness of this possibility by the administrator and the selection team, and a conscious attempt toward greater objectivity should help a great deal to avoid this pitfall. While it is certainly important that there be a reasonable degree of attitude similarity between new staff and the administrator in regard to how they view education, improving educational opportunities for students will hardly be achieved by rejecting highly qualified candidates in favor of those with lower qualifications but with attitudes more similar to those of the administrator. In selecting staff, a certain amount of diversity in thinking is desirable and perhaps should even be deliberately sought by a school administrator.

TEACHER COMPETENCY TESTING

The perceived inadequacy of previously described personnel selection proce-dures has led to the use of competency or performance testing for the selection of teachers.[50] Although the use of competency testing in the selection of school personnel has been limited, its use may spread if public concern continues about the quality of teachers.[51] Teachers' associations seem divided on the issue of using competency tests to select teachers,[52] but school boards appear to favor the procedures.[53] As yet, little research has been conducted on the use of tests in personnel selection in education, but an analysis by Levin showed that the level of a teacher's verbal ability correlated more highly with teaching effectiveness than did any other factor, and that this variable could be validly measured by a test.[54]

Another study, by Andrews and his colleagues, found significant rela-tionships between supervisors' ratings of practice teachers and these prospec-tive teachers' scores on the National Teacher Examination.[55] Research by Piper and O'Sullivan has also tended to support the value of the NTE in the selec-tion of teachers.[56]

While there is not a large body of research available on the effectiveness of using tests in the selection of school personnel, the weight of evidence to date suggests that standardized tests may provide useful information about candidates, particularly when combined with other kinds of selection ap-proaches. However, the available research on this selection method does not justify relying solely on tests in hiring school personnel. Those districts or ed-ucational agencies which are considering using tests in personnel selection need to seek information about the reliability, validity, and potential racial or cul-tural bias of any test, and should make sure that the examination which is utilized for personnel selection is clearly job-related.[57] It has been ruled by several courts that unless a test has been proven to be directly related to im-portant aspects of a job, it should not be used in personnel selection.[58] One testing program that appears to meet these standards has been described by Ellett and his colleagues.[59]

Due to concern about the validity of personnel selection procedures and prior discrimination in personnel selection, the federal government has pub-lished a document entitled, *Uniform Guidelines on Employee Selection.*[60] An addendum to the original publication which includes certain questions raised in regard to the guidelines should also be studied by every school district and educational agency involved in personnel selection.[61] The guidelines apply to all personnel selection procedures, including application forms, tests, inter-views, and evaluation of performance. The guidelines do not require validated selection procedures, but if the procedures are legally challenged as discrim-inatory, the employer must then present validation evidence supporting the selection procedures, as well as proof that they did not discriminate on the basis of race, color, sex, religion, or national origin. In the event of such a legal challenge, employers are required to do more than *assert* the validity of their procedures; they must provide evidence as to that validity. To provide evidence of the validation of personnel selection procedures, employers must demonstrate the job-relatedness of a selection procedure, and the ways of doing so are described in the *Uniform Guidelines.*

Even though the extent to which school districts attempt to validate their personnel selection procedures is uncertain, research suggests that much remains to be done. Grohe found, for example, that most school districts in her study had established no procedures or plan for validating their selection criteria or process.[62] Arend[63] and Merritt,[64] in studies discussed earlier, uncovered findings about school districts' selection procedures which raise serious questions about their reliability and validity. Consequently, from the available research, it must be concluded that most school districts and other educational agencies involved in personnel selection could benefit from a careful study of the appropriate government documents on employee selection procedures and from an assessment of the current selection procedures, developing more valid ones where the need is evident.

STAFF INDUCTION

After the new members of a staff have been hired, the process of induction or orientation should begin immediately. Staff induction is a process by which recently employed individuals are helped to become oriented to a new environment, which includes the community, the school system, the teaching position, and the people with whom they will be working.[65] The importance of the process is underlined by the observations of McCleary and Hencley:

> Orientation requires sensitive planning and careful execution. It is during the orientation period that new staff members gather their first impressions concerning the school's policies, objectives, leadership, and method of operation. Moreover, it is at this time that initial acquaintance is made with colleagues and with the community inhabitants, characteristics, agencies, and services. Since first impressions are often lasting, every effort should be expended during orientation to assure that new staff members gain correct understanding of the many facets of school and community life.[66]

PROBLEMS OF NEW STAFF

To plan an effective orientation program for new staff, the administrator will need to be knowledgeable about the problems they may encounter. An analysis of research on the problems of beginning teachers in adjusting to their new environment suggests that they can experience difficulties in the following major areas during their first year of teaching: (1) knowing what is expected of them, (2) planning and organizing for teaching, (3) motivating and evaluating students, (4) controlling and disciplining students, (5) establishing friendly and cooperative relationships with other members of the school or district, (6) communicating with parents and the community, and (7) achieving personal and professional self-confidence.[67]

Whether the problems experienced by new teachers during their first year result from their own deficiencies or from a poor induction program, or both, is not certain. However, all too frequently, school and district induction programs can be characterized as "too little, too late." Most school districts seem to give considerable emphasis, before school starts, to orienting new staff members to the school district itself; but orientation to the community (particularly the community adjacent to the school), and to teaching in the assigned school, seems lacking. There also appears to be little or no follow-through during the year, once initial orientation activities have been concluded.[68] As a result, many new teachers continue to develop questions and feelings similar to those reported in a survey of beginning teachers after the third week of school, and identified in figure 7.4.[69]

Questions like the ones presented in figure 7.4 support the need for a *continuous* induction program. As the National Education Association has pointed out, "The orientation of teachers is something that cannot be done in a single day or single week or in a matter of weeks."[70]

---

1. "What, exactly, is my total assignment in this school?"
2. "Why don't I have any permanent classroom or office of my own?"
3. "Is everyone as busy during the day and as exhausted at the end of the day as I am?"
4. "What do I do to motivate the kids to learn what I am teaching? And how do I evaluate and grade these kids?"
5. "What do I do about the kids who can't learn? How do I handle the troublemakers in my classes?"
6. "How do I handle this angry parent who keeps calling me to complain about the way I'm treating her child?"
7. "How does one get accepted in this school by the older teachers?"
8. "I am unsure. Do the students and the other teachers really like me, accept me, and think I am a good teacher?"

Figure 7.4. Questions of New
Teachers During the First Semester

A RECOMMENDED INDUCTION PROGRAM

The induction process should actually begin when the new staff member is employed and should continue through the first year until the individual has adjusted successfully to the school environment. The process should include the following steps and provisions:[71]

Phase I. *Before the Beginning of the School Year*
   A. A letter should be sent by the principal to all new staff members, welcoming them to the school and offering to help with any questions or problems they may be facing. The letter should also extend an invitation to come to the school to confer about questions or problems. If possible, the new staff member should be informed in the letter about his specific teaching assignment and schedule, and told how to secure a copy of text material to use in class.
   B. The new staff member should be sent any material which would help orient him to the school or community prior to the preschool workshop, e.g., teacher handbook.
   C. An experienced staff member should be identified and assigned to help the new member of the staff become orientated to the school, and to aid the beginner with any special problems that may arise during the school year, either in or out of the classroom. It should be noted that one study found that beginning teachers would seek assistance from an experienced teacher only if the latter taught the same subject or grade *and* appeared open to friendship.[72] If feasible, the experienced staff member should be given released time to carry out this responsibility of helping a beginning teacher, and new staff should be given a reduced teaching load until they get "their feet on the ground."

Phase II. *Initial School Workshop and New Staff Orientation*
   A. New staff members should be introduced to the entire faculty at the first meeting.
   B. Separate meetings for new staff members during the initial school workshop should be scheduled which focus on the following topics:
      1. nature of the student body and the surrounding community
      2. school philosophy and objectives
      3. overall school operating policies and procedures
      4. the role of supporting personnel in the school or district, e.g., guidance counselor, and appropriate referral procedures
      5. discipline policies and procedures
      6. attendance policies and procedures
      7. requisitioning procedures and the use of supplies

During these separate meetings, new staff members should be
encouraged to ask questions, and time should be provided at later
meetings, if necessary, for questions to be raised which may not
have been answered in exploring the above topics. The goals of the
initial workshop in regard to inducting new staff members should
be to help them begin to function effectively in a new setting and to
become known and accepted by the total school faculty. A
publication developed by NEA, entitled *The Beginning Teacher: A
Practical Guide to Problem Solving,* would appear to be
particularly useful in a workshop setting.[73]

Phase III. *Follow-Up Induction Activities*

As indicated earlier, staff induction should not be a "one-shot affair"
during the initial school workshop, but should be a continuous process
during the entire first year of the new staff member's employment.
Although certain new faculty members may need less orientation and
in-service help than others, the following activities should be beneficial
to most of the new staff during the first year:

A. Monthly "rap sessions" with the principal and other appropriate
   individuals for the purpose of discussing the questions, problems,
   and experiences encountered by new staff members.
B. Individual conferences, as needed, with the principal and the
   assigned "buddy" teacher. The availability of these conferences
   will need to be made explicit and their use periodically encouraged
   before they will be utilized by new staff members to the degree
   desired.
C. Interclass and interschool visitations to observe the demonstration
   of various teaching techniques.
D. Specific supervisory assistance early in the year with attendance,
   discipline, and grading. These three areas seem to give the greatest
   problems to new staff members, and they will appreciate concrete
   suggestions from the administrators of the school.

Phase IV. *Evaluation of the Induction Program*

The induction program is no different than any other program, in that
it must be evaluated if it is to be improved. An important source of
assistance in evaluating a program is its users, which in this case are
the new staff members. Therefore, the school administrator should
attempt during the year (particularly toward the end of the year) to
obtain evaluative feedback from the new members of the staff about
the strengths and weaknesses of various components of the induction
program, with recommendations for improvement. By securing such
feedback, the administrator will not only convey the fact that he cares

about the feelings and perceptions of new staff members, but he will also be in a much better position to improve the school induction program for the following year.

A FINAL NOTE

In many school systems, the building administrator's involvement in staff recruitment, selection, and induction is limited. This is regrettable, since there is a long and continuing tradition of holding the administrator accountable for the performance of the professional staff in the school. It would appear reasonable that if the building administrator is to be held accountable, he should play a significant role in the recruitment, selection, and induction of the professional staff. Certainly no other administrator is in a better position to know the needs of the school. Therefore, an important prerequisite for any effective staff recruitment, selection, and induction program is the major involvement of the building administrator.

Review and Learning Activities

1. What is the main purpose of the district's recruiting program? Describe the ways in which an administrator can make an important contribution to that program.
2. Why is it important for the building administrator to be involved directly in the process of staff selection?
3. Identify the steps involved in the staff selection process. How might the use of a staff selection team help with the process?
4. Describe the factors an administrator should consider in determining staff selection *criteria* and in analyzing placement papers.
5. Discuss the factors an administrator should consider in planning for and conducting the staff selection *interview*.
6. What is the main purpose of a staff induction program? What types of problems do many beginning teachers encounter, and what kinds of steps should a school take to prevent and/or ameliorate these types of problems?
7. Interview the beginning teachers in your school to ascertain the kinds of problems and concerns they have, and the entent to which the program of induction recommended in the text has been implemented.

Notes

1. D. E. Davis and N. C. Nickerson, *Critical Issues in School Personnel Administration* (Chicago: Rand McNally, 1968), p. 17.

2. Ibid., p. 28.

3. Ben M. Harris et al., *Personnel Administration in Education* (Boston: Allyn and Bacon, 1979), pp. 147–49.

4. For a review of these, see Richard A. Gorton, "Personnel Policies," in *The Encyclopedia of Educational Research,* ed. Harold E. Mitzel (New York: Macmillan, 1982). A major part of this chapter has been adapted from this source.

5. Harris et al., *Personnel Administration in Education,* p. 223.

6. S. McCune and M. Matthews, *Programs for Educational Equality: Schools and Affirmative Action* (Washington, D.C.: U. S. Government Printing Office, 1975), p. 1.

7. Ibid.

8. *Affirmative Action Guidelines* (Washington, D.C.: Equal Employment Opportunity Commission, 1979).

9. Harris et al., *Personnel Administration in Education,* pp. 149–50.

10. Vaughn Phelps, *How to Develop Job Descriptions.* An ERIC Report: Ed–154–526.

11. Adapted from a Position Guide of Milwaukee Public Schools, Milwaukee, Wis.

12. Robert J. Babcock, "How to Hook Those First-year Teachers," *School Management* (March 1968): 60–63.

13. J. E. Corbally et al., *Educational Administration: The Secondary School* (Boston: Allyn & Bacon, 1961), pp. 149–50.

14. This principle has long been supported by the American Association of School Administrators, which has stated that, "Since principals have a big stake in the outcome, they should have a voice in the selection of candidates." American Association of School Administrators, *Staff Relations in School Administration* (Washington, D.C. 1955), p. 35.

15. R. E. May and E. G. Doerge, *An Analysis of the Informational Items and Procedures Used in the Selection of Teachers in the Public School Systems of Louisiana.* An ERIC Report: Ed–070–180.

16. Wisconsin Association of School Personnel Administrators, *The Teacher Selection Process in Wisconsin Public Schools* (Madison: Wisconsin Association of School Personnel Administrators, 1979), p. 14.

17. B. Seiferth and T. D. Purcell, *Administrators' Criteria for Hiring Practices.* An ERIC Report: Ed–177–096.

18. F. S. Endicott, "Who Gets a Teaching Position in the Public Schools?" *Association for School, College, and University Staffing* (1979): 15–17.

19. S. J. Wester, "The Perceptions of Selected Personnel Administrators, School Administrators, Parents and Teachers Concerning the Criteria for Selecting Public School Teachers in a Large Metropolitan Area" (Ph.D. diss., East Texas State University, 1979).

20. Barbara Grohe, "School Districts' Teacher Selection Criteria and Process in Wisconsin, and Related Demographic Factors" (Ph.D. diss., University of Wisconsin-Milwaukee, 1981).

21. H. Coker, D. M. Medley, and R. S. Soar, "How Valid Are Expert Opinions about Effective Teaching?" *The Kappan* (October 1980): 131–34, 149.

22. Dale Bolton, *Selection and Evaluation of Teachers* (Berkeley, Calif.: McCutchan Publishing, 1973).

23. See, for example, Nicholas A. Fischer, "Parents: Effective Partners in Faculty Selection, Hiring," *Phi Delta Kappan* (February, 1981): 442.

24. Grohe, "Teacher Selection Criteria and Process."

25. R. C. Schustereit, "Feeling Secure in an Employment Interview," *The Kappan* (February 1980): 403–6.

26. Harris et al., *Personnel Administration in Education,* p. 156.

27. G. Lyon, "Why Teachers Can't Teach," *The Kappan* (October 1980): 108.

180 Staff Recruitment, Selection, and Induction

28. T. G. Baer and L. Brown, "What Does It Take to Get Your Foot in the Door?" *Association for School, College and University Staffing* (1979): 6–7.

29. Harris et al., *Personnel Administration in Education*, p. 154.

30. D. R. Shaffer, P. V. Mays, and K. Etheridge, "Who Shall Be Hired: A Biasing Effect of the Buckley Amendment on Employment Practices?" *Journal of Applied Psychology* (1976): 571–75.

31. B. J. Bryant et al., "Employment Factors Superintendents Use in Hiring Administrators for Their Schools," *Association for School, College and University Staffing* (Fall 1978): 19.

32. Paul Arend, *Teacher Selection: The Relationship between Selected Factors and the Rated Effectiveness of Second Year Teachers.* An ERIC Report: Ed–087–102.

33. C. W. Fawcett, *School Personnel Systems* (Lexington, Mass.: Lexington Books 1979), p. 56.

34. E. Williams, "Proposition Four: Evaluating Entry-Level Competencies of New Teachers," *The Kappan* (October 1979): 129.

35. Richard A. Hobart, "Effective Interviewing Key to Selecting Qualified Staff," *NASSP Bulletin* (December 1979): 29–34. Also see Jim Badertscher, *The Employment Interview: An Essential Evaluation Tool* (Eugene, Oreg.: Oregon State Study Council, 1980).

36. B. Johnson, "What Administrators Look for in Teacher Interviews," *The Kappan* (November 1976): 283–84.

37. Harris et al., *Personnel Administration in Education*, p. 156.

38. R. Dipboye et al., "Equal Employment and the Interview," *Personnel Journal* (1976): 520–22.

39. J. E. Greene, *School Personnel Administration* (Philadelphia: Chilton Book Co., 1971), p. 137.

40. R. A. Engel and D. Friendrichs, "The Emergence Approach: The Interview Can Be a Reliable Process," *NASSP Bulletin* (January 1980): 85–91. See also Dorothy Molyneaux and Vera W. Lane, *Effective Interviewing* (Rockleigh, N.J.: Allyn and Bacon, 1981).

41. R. E. Carlson et al., "Improvements in the Selection Interview," in *Perspectives on Personnel/Human Resource Management* (Homewood, Ill.: Richard D. Irwin, Inc., 1978), p. 143.

42. Hobart, "Effective Interviewing."

43. Donald M. Chalker, "The Teacher Perceiver Interview as an Instrument for Predicting Successful Teaching Behavior" (Ed.D. diss., Wayne State University, 1981).

44. Schustereit, "Feeling Secure in Employment Interview."

45. Public Law 93–112, Section 504 (Washington, D.C.: U.S. Department of Health, Education and Welfare, 1975).

46. G. R. Weisenstein, "Barriers to Employment of the Handicapped: Some Educational Implications," *Journal of Research and Development in Education* (Summer 1979): 57–70. Also see *Educators with Disabilities: A Resource Guide* (Washington, D.C.: U.S. Govt. Printing Office, 1981).

47. Helen L. Clower, "The Use of the Personal Interview in the Selection of Teachers" (Ed.D. diss., University of Southern California, 1963).

48. Richard H. Magee, "The Employment Interview—Techniques of Questioning," *Personnel Journal* (May 1962): 241–45.

49. Daniel L. Merritt, "Attitude Congruency and Selection of Teacher Candidates," *Administrator's Notebook* (February 1971); and a study by Perry suggests this situation persists: Nancy Perry, "New Teachers: Do 'the Best' Get Hired?" *Phi Delta Kappan* (October 1981): 113–14.

50. W. E. Hathaway, "Testing Teachers," *Educational Leadership* (December 1980): 210–15.

51. "Help! Teachers Can't Teach," *Time* (June 16, 1980): 54–63.

52. A. Shanker, "The Nonsense of Attacking Educational Testing," *Educational Times* (October 1980): 2.

53. D. Levin, "You Might Be Able to Test Teacher Applicants, But No Board Has Ever Been Able to Test Working Teachers," *American School Board Journal* (May 1979): 33–37.

54. H. Levin, "A Cost-effective Analysis of Teacher Selection," *Journal of Human Resources* (Winter 1970): 24–33.

55. J. W. Andrews et al., "Preservice Performance and the National Teacher Exams," *The Kappan* (January 1980): 358–59.

56. M. K. Piper and P. S. O'Sullivan, "The National Teacher Examination: Can It Predict Classroom Performance?" *The Kappan* (1981): 401

57. W. B. Castetter, *The Personnel Function in Educational Administration* (New York: Macmillan Co., 1981).

58. Harris et al., *Personnel Administration in Education,* pp. 254–56.

59. C. D. Ellett et al., "Assessing Teacher Performance," *Educational Leadership* (December 1980): 219–20.

60. Equal Employment Opportunity Commission, "Uniform Guidelines on Employee Selection Procedures," *Federal Register* (August 25, 1978): 38290–315.

61. Equal Employment Opportunity Commission, "Adoption of Questions and Answers to Clarify and Provide a Common Interpretation of the Uniform Guidelines on Employee Selection Procedures," *Federal Register* (March 2, 1979): 11996–12009.

62. Grohe, "Teacher Selection Criteria and Process."

63. Arend, *Teacher Selection.*

64. Merritt, "Selection of Teacher Candidates."

65. Harris et al., *Personnel Administration in Education,* pp. 180–81.

66. Lloyd E. McCleary and Stephen P. Hencley, *Secondary School Administration: Theoretical Bases for Professional Practice* (New York: Dodd, Mead and Co., 1965), p. 287.

67. Kevin Ryan et al., *Biting the Apple: Accounts of First Year Teachers* (New York: Longman, 1980).

68. Carl A. Grant et al., "In-service Support for First Year Teachers: The State of the Scene," *Journal of Research and Development in Education* (November 1981): 99–111.

69. Richard A. Gorton, "Questions of New Teachers after the Third Week of School" (unpublished study, revised 1980). Also see Jane H. Applegate et al., "New Teachers Seek Support," *Educational Leadership* (October 1980): 74–76.

70. "Editorial: Welcome to the New Teacher," *National Education Association Journal* (October 1963): 10.

71. Adapted from *Guidelines for Principals: Project on the Induction of Beginning Teachers* (Washington, D.C.: National Association of Secondary School Principals, 1969): and K. Zeichner, "Teacher Induction Programs in the U.S. and Great Britain" (Paper presented at American Educational Research Association meeting, San Francisco, April 1979).

72. Janet McIntosh, "The Beginning Teacher's Search for Assistance from Colleagues," *Canadian Journal of Education* (1979): 17–27.

73. Robert J. Krajewski and R. Baird Shuman, *The Beginning Teacher: A Practical Guide to Problem Solving* (Washington, D.C.: National Education Association, 1979).

8

Special Personnel Problems

Not all members of a school's staff will experience the kinds of problems discussed in this chapter. However, in recent years such problems as teacher absenteeism, drug abuse, and reduction in staff have occurred on an increasing basis. When these problems occur, they not only affect the lives of the individuals involved but they can also impact on the rest of the school. Certainly, they represent major personnel challenges for the school administrator. While there are no easy answers to these problems, an important first step for the administrator is to understand better the nature of each problem. Then she needs to develop a policy and program to deal with the current problems and prevent their future occurrence. The following sections are intended to assist the administrator with those objectives.[1]

EMPLOYEE ABSENTEEISM

Employee absenteeism has only recently surfaced as an issue in education although it has raised concern outside the field of education for many years.[2] Now it would appear from available evidence that employee absenteeism will take its place as one of the major school personnel issues of the '80s.[3]

The primary reason that employee absenteeism has attracted attention is that many people, particularly school administrators and school board members, feel that sick leave provisions are being abused by increasing numbers of employees.[4] The abuse has brought about several negative consequences: greater costs for substitute teachers, a feeling that the quality of education decreases when substitute teachers are utilized more frequently, and a concern about the additional time principals must spend in monitoring teacher absences and arranging for substitute teachers.[5] One state, for example, estimated that $888 million per year was being spent for total professional salaries directly attributable to teacher absences.[6] This amount represented a greater percentage of the total budget than was allocated by that state for school health services, student activities, capital outlay, community services, or food services.

A second reason why employee absenteeism is also likely to develop into a major policy issue is that teachers' associations seem to question whether serious abuses are prevalent in the area of teacher sick leaves. It has been contended that most statistics on teacher absences are misleading since they do not make a distinction between excused absences for such activities as professional meetings, legitimate absences for illness, and unexcused absences.[7]

Unfortunately, it has been difficult to ascertain whether absenteeism by school employees represents a serious problem or not. The records maintained by most school districts are not useful in making such an assessment, and there is consequently a paucity of hard data on the extent and severity of the problem.[8] In addition, studies on employee absenteeism have often encountered difficulty in identifying reliable and valid techniques by which to measure absenteeism.[9] For example, how does a school district assess whether employees are actually sick, rather than taking the day off because they don't feel quite up to teaching? Although certain techniques and forms have been developed to help school districts keep better records of teacher absenteeism, such as the one proposed by Harclerode,[10] the problem of verification remains a touchy one.

Even when reasonably useful and objective data on staff absenteeism have been collected, a decision must still be made regarding the level at which employee absences constitute a serious problem. School districts may vary in that determination, but at least two authorities on the subject suggest that a monthly absentee rate exceeding 5 or 6 percent constitutes a matter of great concern.[11] Regardless, however, of the level of staff absences defined as a problem, it needs to be recognized that a determination will be based on a value judgment as much as on absentee data; consequently, differences of opinion will persist regarding whether or not a serious problem actually exists in a locality.

Acknowledging the difficulties that may be involved in obtaining data regarding the severity of employee absenteeism, the fact remains that many people *perceive* it to be a problem, and that perception has stimulated much discussion and investigation into the *causes* of employee absenteeism. For example, over 400 articles and studies on the topic of employee absenteeism have been identified by Educational Research Service.[12] In a comprehensive review of that literature, ERS concluded that research findings have been inconsistent on the relationship between employee absenteeism and education level, salary level, tenure, satisfaction with pay, satisfaction with promotion, employment status, job autonomy and responsibility, satisfaction with sense of achievement, marital status, or family size. ERS's analysis of the literature further revealed the *absence* of any relationship between absenteeism and satisfaction with organizational policies and practices, employee control and participation, organizational climate, group cohesion/satisfaction with co-workers, or satisfaction with the supervisor and employer. However, ERS did find research showing a *consistent association* betweeen employee absenteeism and increased stress and anxiety, job satisfaction, organization size, lenient personnel policies on absenteeism and leave usage, bargaining and union activity, and dissatisfaction with the work itself. In regard to the relationship between absenteeism and job satisfaction, Bridges concluded that such a relationship was more likely under conditions of high work interdependence than under moderate or low interdependence.[13]

Specific studies on teacher absenteeism provide additional insights into possible causes. For example, a relationship between the number of teachers using their sick leave and the nature of teacher personnel policies on teacher absenteeism was documented by at least two studies. Researchers investigating 56 Pennsylvania school systems discovered a positive relationship between liberal personnel policies on sick leave and employee absenteeism.[14] Those school districts that granted sick leave in addition to that required by the state were plagued by higher employee absentee rates than the school districts which provided no additional sick leave days. A related study showed that the type of monitoring and reporting techniques used on teacher absences make a difference.[15] When teachers were required to phone in their sick leave request to their principals, they were much less likely to make the request than when they could simply call an answering service or another supervisor. The *type* of sick leave policy established by a school district has also been found to be related to the level of absenteeism in that district.[16]

Research has also uncovered a relationship between the introduction of collective bargaining and a rise in teacher absenteeism. A study by Bundren discovered that the absentee rate of teachers in one county increased significantly after the enactment of collective bargaining.[17] A significant positive relationship between the introduction of collective negotiations and days absent for illness was also noted in a related study.[18] And a state-wide inquiry in Illinois revealed that teachers in school systems without negotiated master contracts had a lower rate of absenteeism than teachers in school systems with such contracts.[19]

Although studies on teacher absenteeism can be helpful, the reader is cautioned that usually the research on causes of employee absenteeism has consisted of correlational studies that imply but do not demonstrate causality. The samples employed by researchers have also tended to be small and limited, which make generalization difficult; and frequently controls for other relevant variables have not been used. However, it should be emphasized that the research findings presented above are probably at least as reliable and valid as the personal opinion and subjective experiences which seem to form the basis for most personnel policies on this topic. Administrators who question the validity of research findings in regard to their particular school setting should conduct their own study rather than simply dismissing the findings of others and falling back on personal inclinations.

One model which could be helpful to the administrator in understanding the causes of employee absenteeism was developed by Steers and Rhodes, and has been adapted by the author in figure 8.1.[20]

Figure 8.1 suggests that essentially four major sources of factors could influence an employee's attendance: (1) personal characteristics of the employee, such as work ethics, (2) the particular aspects of the job situation itself, such as the amount of stress experienced by the employee, (3) organizational factors, such as the type of personnel policies governing employee absenteeism, and (4) outside personal factors, such as illness or accidents.[21] It should be noted that the factors identified in each part of the figure exemplify the nature of the category and are not intended to depict its full scope.

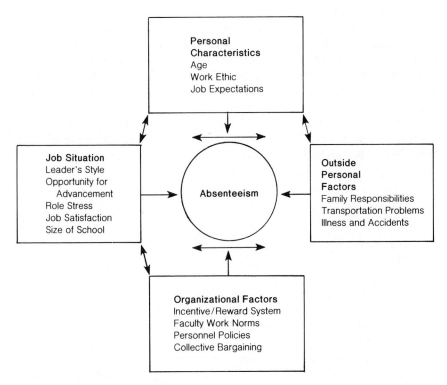

Figure 8.1. Major Factors Influencing
Employee Attendance

While the causes of employee absenteeism are complex and not well understood, there has been no shortage of proposals to control or reduce the problem. These proposals have ranged from a "Let's-get-tough" program to humanistic approaches to teacher absenteeism. One proposed approach, developed by the American Association of School Personnel Administrators, seems especially worthy of consideration. It recommends that a school district[22]

1. Establish an employee monitoring system to ascertain whether the district is experiencing an absentee problem.
2. Develop a policy that sets standards and procedures for governing all aspects of employee absenteeism.
3. Design a program to provide assistance and counseling for those employees whose absenteeism may indicate a particularly serious problem.
4. Offer an incentive program to motivate employees to reduce their absenteeism.

Other proposals emphasize defining the role of the building principal in controlling and reducing teacher absenteeism,[23] and providing training for supervisory personnel that will help them reduce absenteeism.[24] A school program described by Olfson stresses principal awareness and role in reducing employee absenteeism, apparently with considerable success.[25] Other proposals underscore the importance of communicating to all employees the high priority which a district is attaching to the reduction of employee absenteeism.[26]

Generally, experts agree that the starting point in any attempt to improve employee absenteeism is the development of a school board policy on employee attendance. An example of such a policy is presented below.

The board recognizes that good attendance is necessary and expected in order to maintain an efficient school system. Therefore, the board encourages its employees to develop satisfactory attendance performance in pursuance of that goal.[27]

Once a general school board policy has been developed, the next step is to promulgate specific administrative regulations that set forth management's expectations of employee attendance, indicators of unacceptable absenteeism, and procedures for handling employee absenteeism.

Crucial to the success of any school board policy and/or administrative regulations on employee absenteeism is the building principal. Unless the principal is committed to the school board's policy and the administrative regulations, the possibility of their success is uncertain at best. To develop this commitment, school districts need to involve their principals in the development of policy and regulations on employee attendance, and principals need to be provided with in-service education to help them carry out the policy and regulations. As an example, one school district developed the following guidelines for their principals to use in improving employee attendance:[28]

- Gain current knowledge of the problem.
- Recognize excessive and chronic patterns of absence.
- Establish school objectives regarding staff absence.
- Concentrate efforts on employees with excessive absence.
- Review cases requiring special attention with supervisors.
- Make absence records part of the personnel records system.
- Stress the importance of attendance in the pre-employment stages.
- Consider using incentives to encourage good attendance.
- Conduct research dealing with employee working conditions, attitude, and other factors which relate to good attendance.
- Check the school calendar to avoid fracturing the school schedule.

Although principals may need to initiate disciplinary procedures with certain employees who have absentee problems, the recommended approach is to try to provide assistance and counseling for those whose absenteeism may indicate a particularly serious problem. The first step in this approach should be to try to better understand the nature of the problem, and to achieve that objective the administrator should schedule a personal conference with the employee who has an apparent absentee problem, and to seek answers to the following questions:

Is there anything about your assignment that is making the work less enjoyable these days?

Are there any health or personal problems that are affecting your attendance at school?

Are you satisfied with your relationships with students and your colleagues?

Is there anything else in your work environment that is affecting your attendance at school?

Is there anything that I can do to help the situation?

The purpose of such questions would be to gather information which could shed light on the causes of the absences and to show the concern of the administrator about the problem, as well as a willingness to be a source of assistance. Of course, if the administrator's help is rejected and/or the situation doesn't improve, then it may be necessary to take more direct measures to deal with the problem, including disciplinary measures. With regard to the latter, the administrator should check the master contract and board policies before taking action, to make sure of the extent of administrative authority.

Employee absenteeism can be a serious problem, and in some cases it will not be easily resolved. However, the extent and severity of the problem can be reduced as a result of an accurate understanding of the causes of employee absenteeism, a clear school board policy on attendance and absenteeism, specific and reasonable regulations on the implementation of the policy, in-service training for building principals, and a persistent and positive effort by the principal to improve employee attendance. Further proposals and ideas for controlling and/or reducing employee absenteeism are presented in an Educational Research Service publication on the topic.[29]

EMPLOYEE DRUG ABUSE

Chemical dependency, particularly alcoholism, is believed to be a serious employee personnel problem in private industry. During an approximately twenty-five-year period the number of occupational alcoholism programs increased from fifty to an estimated 500, and the number of organizations with some type of program increased to almost 2,400.[30] Unfortunately, few of these programs are in the public sector, and there is little indication that most school districts perceive chemical abuse as a serious employee problem.[31] Cramer, however, asserts that on any given day, in any school system, about 8 percent of the employees will be working while under the influence of alcohol.[32] He feels that the problem of chemical abuse among employees tends to go unrecognized by school districts, since only a few schools have implemented programs that attempt to identify alcohol or other drug problems and to provide treatment. Part of the problem, according to Saltman, is that most employees who work under the influence of alcohol or other dependency-causing drugs try to keep their chemical abuse a secret.[33] In addition, Brooks points out that all too often supervisors ignore or tend to underestimate the extent of employees' drug abuse problems in the hope that such problems will eventually resolve themselves.[34] Despite these obstacles, it seems apparent that sooner or later school districts will recognize the need to pay greater attention to the problem of drug abuse among employees, just as school districts have had to recognize and deal with the problem of drug abuse among students.

While evaluation and research on drug abuse prevention and treatment programs are limited, the National Institute on Alcohol Abuse and Alcoholism states that an effective program should include the following components:[35] (1) a written policy and plan, (2) explicit labor-management involvement and cooperation in program development and operation, (3) description of key organizational personnel to identify and refer employees for appropriate diagnosis, (4) orientation and in-service training for all supervisors and teacher representatives, (5) dissemination of information about the program to all employees, (6) the provision of health insurance coverage for the treatment of alcoholism and related drug abuse, and (7) the assurance of total confidentiality for those identified and referred through the program.

As with employee absenteeism, the initial starting point in drug abuse prevention and treatment is the development of a *formal, written,* school board policy on the matter. While some school districts appear to have an *informal* policy on employee drug abuse, only a formal, written policy is likely to express clearly the school district's attitude and expectations about this problem. Excerpts from several examples of policy statements are provided below.[36]

> We believe that alcoholism or problem drinking is an illness and should be treated as such.
>
> For the purposes of this policy, alcoholism exists when an employee's consumption of any alcoholic beverage repeatedly interferes with job performance.
>
> We believe that the majority of employees who develop alcoholism can be helped to recover, and the organization should offer appropriate assistance.

Although these seem to be clear statements of policy, it is recommended that all policy statements focus on the more general problem of chemical dependency, which includes alcoholism rather than limiting concern to only the latter.

Once a school district has developed a policy on employee drug abuse (and it is recommended that the policy be jointly developed by management and employees), the role of the building administrators in implementing the policy should be specified. Unless the role of the building administrator in preventing drug abuse is made clear and given a high priority, the policy holds little likelihood of being successful. Unfortunately, there is a scarcity of information on this role in an educational setting. However, a proposed role for use by a supervisor in a noneducational setting that appears to be applicable to a school district has been adapted by the author for the latter purpose.[37]

1. Because the chemically dependent employee interprets administrative acceptance of her work record as evidence that her drug abuse is not recognized or is still within acceptable limits, it is extremely important that as soon as substandard or deteriorating job performance is indicated (but well before the situation has worsened to the point that probation, suspension, or termination is needed) the administrator should discuss the problem with the employee in a private conference.
2. At the end of the conference the administrator should inform the employee that, if the decline in performance is caused by a personal problem, the employee may wish to seek counseling and diagnostic services offered by the school district or its health agent.
3. If, after a reasonable time, the employee refuses the school district's help (or declines to seek another source of help with the

problem), and if job performance continues to be unsatisfactory, the administrator should provide a choice of either accepting the service available or accepting the consequences of a negative evaluation of her job performance. If the employee continues to refuse help and her job performance continues to be unsatisfactory, then dismissal procedures should be initiated.

4. If the employee is willing to accept the school district's help, she should be referred by the administrator to a medical agency for diagnosis.
5. If the diagnosis does not indicate drug abuse, but the poor performance seems to result from other personal problems, the administrator should offer counseling assistance or referral.
6. If the diagnosis does indicate a chemical dependency problem, e.g., alcoholism, the administrator should provide information about the school district's plan for rehabilitation or, if the district has no plan, about an outside agency's plan. The school administrator should strongly encourage the employee to seek rehabilitation.
7. During rehabilitation the administrator should attempt to provide continuous encouragement and support, and should try to help the employee in any way that seems reasonable and feasible.
8. If, for some reason, the employee does not seek rehabilitation, drops out of the rehabilitation program, or is not successfully rehabilitated and the employee's job performance continues to be unsatisfactory because of chemical dependency, the school administrator should initiate dismissal procedures.

This approach appears to provide a necessary balance between counseling the employee with a possible drug abuse problem which is impairing her job performance, and taking punitive steps if the offered assistance is declined or rehabilitation is unsuccessful. It should be noted that the policy examples and proposed role appear to make the assumption that the school district does not need to become concerned about the employee's drug abuse problem until that problem begins to impair job performance. The author recommends, however, that school districts adopt a more humanistic policy and role which would involve the district in offering, at the minimum, counseling assistance to any employee who is experiencing a drug abuse problem (whether or not that problem has yet impaired the employee's job performance) and in-service education to all employees regarding the dangers of drug abuse. It is recognized that this recommendation carries financial implications, but it would seem that in the long run, the suggested activities would be a good investment in human resources. (For further discussion of employee assistance program, the reader is referred to the book by Shain and Groeneveld.[38])

MERIT PAY AND FRINGE BENEFITS PROBLEMS

Two other special personnel problem which either have or will be confronting many school administrators are public pressure for some type of merit pay for teachers and growing concern about the increasing cost of employee benefits. An initial factor which administrators in most states will need to take into consideration in attempting to resolve these two problems is the reality of collective bargaining. In states which permit collective bargaining, salary and fringe benefits are usually perceived as part of the working conditions, subject to negotiation between employees and the governing board of a school district. Even in states without collective bargaining legislation there is frequently some type of informal negotiations that influence decisions about personnel salary and fringe benefits.

Whether collective bargaining has resulted in a significant increase in salary and fringe benefits beyond what could have been achieved by employees without collective bargaining is in dispute. At least one study by the Public Service Research Council found that over a six-year period teachers' salaries increased slightly less in states with mandatory collective bargaining laws than in states without them.[39] However, a reading of the publications of the National Education Association and the American Federation of Teachers leaves little doubt that most teachers believe collective bargaining to be essential for obtaining needed salary and fringe benefit increases.

One major policy issue that has surfaced periodically over the years in regard to employee salaries is whether or not employee salary standardization is desirable. Generally, employee salaries and benefits are standardized within a school district.[40] For example, each teacher receives the same fringe benefits provided by the school district, and teachers with identical levels of education and length of teaching experience receive the same salary, regardless of any differences in teaching effectiveness. The absence of any attempt to take into consideration distinctions in job performance when deciding on individual salary levels has troubled a number of people over the years. Consequently, from time to time, merit pay proposals for teachers have been advocated and, in a few districts, implemented.

Simply defined, *merit pay* means determining teachers' salaries according to the effectiveness of their performance.[41] The basic assumption underlying merit pay is that more effective teachers are more valuable to the school and to students than less effective teachers, and the former deserve to be compensated more for their services.[42] While this may seem to be a reasonable assumption, merit pay plans in education have tended to arouse controversy. Major reasons given by teachers opposing merit pay include the belief that the criteria for determining merit were not valid; the evaluators were not competent; the comparisons between teachers were invidious, resulting in lower morale; and salary should be negotiated rather than determined by an evaluator.[43] Merit pay for teachers has, on the other hand, been endorsed by a number of school boards, administrators, and managerial groups, although it appears to be more prevalent as a means for determining administrators' salaries.[44] Advocates of merit pay for teachers believe that employees should be paid according to their effectiveness, that valid criteria of effectiveness can be developed, that competent evaluators can be trained and that invidious comparisons and low morale are not inevitable consequences of merit pay.[45]

As a result of the controversy over merit pay, most school systems have not adopted merit pay plans.[46] Nevertheless, pressures from the public for school accountability, improved teacher competency, and overall cost-effectiveness could change this situation. One basic issue which would need to be resolved before merit pay for teachers could be successfully introduced into a large number of school districts is whether or not the general salary for all teachers in a school district is commensurate with their responsibilities and the cost of living. Recent studies show that the beginning salaries of teachers were lower than that for other college graduates except social workers, and that because of inflation, teachers' salaries overall have increased very little in constant dollar terms during the past decade.[47] As long as these conditions exist, merit pay proposals are unlikely to receive serious consideration by most teachers.

Another difficulty which precludes more favorable consideration of merit pay is the perceived lack of valid and acceptable criteria and procedures for evaluating the merits of teachers. (However, criteria and procedures are presented in the chapter on staff evaluation which appear worthy of consideration.) Teachers would also need to become persuaded of the validity of the premise that more effective teachers *should* be paid higher salaries than their less effective colleagues. In addition, in those states which require collective bargaining, teacher associations are likely to want something in return for their approval of merit pay, and the outcome could be a more costly endeavor than many communities will approve. However, pressures for teacher and school accountability are likely to continue to raise the question of why teachers can't be paid according to their merit.

A related area which is just beginning to surface as a major problem in school administration is the cost of fringe benefits. In recent years the number and cost of fringe benefits in education have increased greatly.[48] In many school districts teachers' associations have concentrated as much on adding to or improving fringe benefits for members as on increased salaries. Fringe benefits now include pension plans, annuity plans, disability insurance, sick leave, personal day(s), life insurance, legal assistance, and health care consisting of medical, dental, and vision insurance.[49] An examination of a number of fringe benefit plans revealed that they also can include tuition reimbursement, longevity payments, severance payments, sabbatical leave, and maternity leave.

As the number of employee fringe benefits has increased, concern has mounted about the cost of these benefits and whether there should be a limit to employee benefits. At least one school district has attempted to control the cost of medical insurance by providing a $500 annual cash incentive for its employees to stay healthy and, at the same time reducing health insurance costs;[50] and a number of other districts are providing their own employee insurance and trying harder to monitor health insurance claims.[51] Because of the continuing increase in the number and cost of fringe benefits, it seems likely that more school districts will need to explore additional ways of monitoring costs and benefits. One school board has concluded after studying the matter that, if current trends continue, expenditures for fringe benefits for school employees will exceed costs for salaries within five years.[52] (For further guidance on this topic, see Ronald R. Booth et al., *Teacher Benefits: How to Compute Costs, Compare, and Evaluate* (Springfield, Ill.: Illinois Assn. of School Boards).

REDUCTION IN STAFF

Throughout the 1960s most school districts experienced increases in student enrollment, program expansion, and a relatively high level of public confidence and financial support. Moving into the 1970s, however, those conditions changed. Many if not most school districts have encountered declining enrollments during the past decade, taxpayers' revolts as exemplified by California's Proposition 13 and numerous defeated bond referendums, along with a loss of public confidence. Whether these trends will continue through the 1980s is still uncertain. But enrollment projections continue to predict further declines in most schools' enrollment, possibly throughout the remainder of the decade (except in some elementary school situations).[53] Neither is there any sign that inflation will disappear. These factors have necessitated in many school districts the implementation of a program referred to as *reduction in force,* or RIF.

Nolte has defined RIF as policies and actions which cut, reduce, or trim down to size a group of employees.[54] In the vernacular this typically means employee lay-offs.

In order to determine whether or not a school district will need to plan for reduction in force, *local* enrollment studies should be conducted. Although national enrollment data may indicate prospective enrollment decline, Keller emphasizes that a school district should determine its own enrollment pattern rather than depend on regional, state, or national figures, which might not be representative or predictive in a local situation.[55] Certainly, not all school districts will experience declining enrollment, and some districts are encountering personnel shortages in certain fields.[56] Therefore, it is imperative that school districts analyze their own enrollment and program data rather than rely on the data of others. Shaw describes and recommends a number of worthwhile approaches to this task.[57]

Even though declining enrollments may make it impossible for a school district to avoid employee lay-offs, such personnel actions are seldom easy to implement and they generally result in negative side-effects. For example, Fowler contends that no administrative decision causes so much ill will and feeling among teachers.[58] In addition, Divoky believes that RIF tends to cause staff morale to plummet and make teachers' unions focus their efforts on greater security provisions than on pay raises.[59] And Weldy maintains that reductions in force can result in a staff of aging teachers who no longer want to sponsor or coach extracurricular activities; faculty members may also be more sensitive to unfavorable personnel evaluation and may be more likely to contest anything of a negative nature which could be placed in their personnel file, fearing that such information may later be used against them in a lay-off situation.[60] Furthermore, teachers may be prone to greater uncertainty and apprehension at the time of student course selection and the awarding of teacher contracts.[61]

The picture which emerges from these and other reports is one of anguish and regret on the part of administrators faced with difficult decisions, juxtaposed with insecurity, apprehension, and lower morale on the part of the staff.

For these reasons, numerous recommendations have been offered to reduce the need for and to cushion the negative impact of employee lay-offs. Ornstein has suggested that districts take advantage of declining student enrollment and the teacher shortage by expanding course selections and initiating programs to respond to the special needs of students, although he recognizes that public acceptance and financing for these changes will not be easily gained.[62] Thomas has advocated six strategies for staff reduction that could decrease the number of lay-offs a school district must make due to declining enrollment:[63]

1. Initiate aggressive evaluation procedures for the termination of teachers who are not performing satisfactorily.
2. Encourage all school personnel to become more aggressive in seeking additional financial support from the government and private sources.
3. Utilize laid-off teachers for substitute teaching.
4. Investigate the possibility of cooperative reassignment of teachers to neighboring school districts that are experiencing enrollment growth.
5. Adopt an attractive early-retirement plan.
6. Retrain teachers with high lay-off potential so that they will be qualified for a teaching assignment in a needed area.

One task force has also suggested that expenses should be cut in the areas of administration, maintenance, and other services before teaching staff reductions.[64]

Research thus far has been limited regarding the extent to which school districts are utilizing these kinds of recommendations, but one study has provided some insight. Averett studied 27 school districts identified by publications of the California Teachers' Association as experiencing a declining student population of more than 5 percent.[65] He learned that all the districts depended on normal attrition to offset lay-offs. Twelve school districts reduced clerical and custodial staff in order to postpone teacher lay-offs; fifteen school districts retrained teachers; six school districts granted extended leaves of absence; and all the districts had initiated early retirement incentive plans. The rationale for early retirement, its advantages and disadvantages, and examples of various retirement programs have been described in considerable detail by Ellsworth,[66] and the fiscal consequences of early retirement for teachers have been examined in a study by Montgomery.[67]

One particularly innovative retraining program which has been planned as an alternative to staff lay-offs and which may serve as a model for the future has been implemented in Greece, New York.[68] Negotiated by the teachers and the school board, the retraining provisions of the master contract offer every member of the bargaining unit an opportunity to gain new skills and new certification in the areas of greatest educational need. The training is financed by the school district and, in addition, during the training period the teacher also works for the district in some capacity for a few hours each week, receiving *full* pay and benefits. It is estimated that this particular retraining program will prevent the need to lay off forty-four teachers in the district.

Of course, employee lay-offs are frequently unavoidable. When they occur, Weldy stresses the importance of implementing a reduction in force (RIF) plan as humanely as possible, by recognizing the pain and anguish that is usually involved and taking appropriate action to reduce such costs.[69] The latter would include, according to Bishop, trying to help the laid-off personnel to find employment themselves.[70] This may be more easily recommended than accomplished, but given the right kind of concern and commitment on the part of a school district, it can be done. For example, the Nicolet School District has introduced a program of career counseling for teachers due to be laid-off, financed by the school district.[71] The program includes providing the services of a professional career counselor who assists the teachers to (1) assess their vocational training, experience, skills and interests; (2) develop an effective resume; (3) develop an effective marketing strategy, and (4) make contacts with possible employers and/or placement agencies. While some may question whether or not career counseling is a legitimate expense for school districts, such a service could offer the potential benefit of reducing or eliminating the need for paying unemployment compensation for laid-off personnel.

In order to minimize problems of staff reduction, it is essential that a school district establish a RIF policy and plan long before the need becomes urgent. Reducing staff is likely to be difficult under any circumstances, and there is evidence that teacher associations and unions will resist lay-offs.[72] Obviously, without a prior policy and plan, a school district will only be asking for trouble.

Berryman found that the following factors appear to affect staff reduction planning:[73] enrollment projections, statuatory requirements for dismissal of teachers, civil rights of individuals, teacher certification, school district interests, negotiated agreements, and staff/public relations.

A number of questions which should be considered by a school district in the development of its reduction in force policy have been raised by Educational Research Services:[74]

1. Has the school district considered alternatives to lay-offs, such as early retirement?
2. Is the policy being developed consistent with state laws on lay-offs, particularly state tenure laws?
3. To what extent does the collective bargaining master agreement need to be considered in developing the policy on staff reductions?
4. What criteria should be used in determining lay-offs, and what role should seniority and performance evaluation play in decision-making?
5. What are important dates of notification that must be observed?
6. What provisions will be made for rehiring laid-off teachers?

Nolte has also advocated that school districts be certain that, in their policy on staff reduction, the lay-off of a teacher be clearly distinct from dismissal, if the cause is a decrease in student enrollment rather than a negative evaluation of the teacher's performance.[75]

In implementing a policy on reduction in staff, it has been recommended by the American Association of School Administrators that a preliminary meeting be held as soon as possible with potentially affected teachers; that letters be sent by registered mail to potentially affected teachers, informing that they may be excessed within the year; and that teachers be sent a letter by registered mail informing them that they will indeed be excessed, once that decision has been made.[76]

Although school districts' policies, plans, and actions are potentially subject to court challenge, Delon maintains that reduction in force decisions are more likely to survive judicial scrutiny if they are implemented in compliance with well-formulated policies adopted prior to need, kept separate from dismissal for cause decisions, implemented on a nondiscriminatory basis, supported by complete and accurate documentation regarding the need for action and the basis for selecting certain individuals, and when collective bargaining agreements as well as constitutional and statuatory requirements are followed.[77] Examples of a number of school board policies which have been developed in an effort to adhere to these guidelines may be examined in a document published by the National Association of Secondary School Principals,[78] and in another by Kelly.[79]

A major policy issue with respect to reduction in force programs is the criteria to be used in determining employee lay-offs. Morse, for example, asserts that though nontenured teachers may be the easiest to lay off because they have little legal recourse, such a decision may be unfortunate since in many instances the nontenured teachers will be better teachers than those retained.[80] He further contends that a RIF policy based solely on seniority could result, over a number of years, in a staff that is neither progressive nor energetic. He concedes that experienced teachers do provide a school system with many benefits but that they may become burned-out over a period of time and may resist change. Seifert also points out that administrators who base RIF policy on seniority will face problems of an older and higher-salaried faculty.[81] Johnson believes that the criterion of seniority may result in a faculty with insufficient diversity, flexibility, and range of teaching skills.[82]

Perhaps the most serious criticism of the use of seniority as the sole or primary basis for decisions on employee lay-offs is that it conflicts with the goals of affirmative action, a policy adopted by many school districts in order to increase the number of women and minorities in the educational work force.[83] Since the policy has been in effect a relatively short time, women and minorities who have been hired in recent years have little seniority and are likely targets for an employee lay-off plan that is based on seniority.[84]

On the other hand, arguments have been advanced that the complete disregard of seniority would, in effect, insulate women and minority members from the national problems of the work place and could lead to reverse discrimination against white males.[85] The issue is whether the goal of an affirmative action policy aimed at reducing the vestiges of past discrimination against women and/or minorities by employing and retaining them can be achieved without infringing on the individual rights of members of majority groups or males. Various efforts have been made to resolve the issue, including extra seniority points to employees who have suffered from past discrimination.[86] However, at least one court has ruled that school districts with lay-off policies based on seniority must adhere to that criterion unless there is convincing evidence that past discrimination warrants considering factors other than seniority.[87]

Whether or not factors other than seniority can be used in in employee lay-offs will depend on a number of legal considerations including state law.[88]

However, research suggests that, even in those situations in which school districts are *permitted* to consider other factors than seniority, policy implementation may be a problem. For example, Johnson studied four school districts that were attempting to use teacher performance criteria as the primary basis to determine the order of teacher lay-offs.[89] While the policy of using performance evaluations as the basis for teacher lay-offs was clear, Johnson found incomplete and uneven implementing of the policy. The extent to which administrators in the district were implementing the policy seemed to depend on their attitude toward the policy, past evaluation practices, and leadership by the school board and administration. In the absence of a positive attitude toward the policy by principals, effective evaluation procedures, and strong leadership from the school board and district administration, the implementation of the policy suffered. Johnson also discovered resistance among the principals toward the role of evaluator of teachers because of the possibly negative effects on their relationship with staff members. In addition, the principals expressed concern about the effects of performance-based lay-offs on the morale of teachers. Although teacher opposition to a policy of relying on performance evaluations rather than seniority as a basis for layoffs was anticipated, it failed to develop. Johnson did find, however, that many teachers lacked confidence in the school districts' evaluation procedures, and they feared that evaluation related to lay-off decisions might be made on political grounds.[90]

Though it seems possible that the substitution of performance evaluation criteria for seniority (or at least considering the former) may address a number of the issues discussed earlier, particularly regarding affirmative action, the findings of the Johnson study suggest that the implementation of such a policy may be difficult and may raise additional personnel problems which will need to be resolved.

A FINAL NOTE

The special personnel problems discussed in this chapter are all too frequently not addressed until they develop into serious crises. The approach which this text recommends is early problem identification, diagnosis, and appropriate corrective action. The following Review and Learning Activities should provide the reader with experience in utilizing such an approach.

Review and Learning Activities

1. How does your school district determine whether staff absences are legitimate? How reliable and valid are those methods?
2. Discuss the causes of employee absenteeism presented in the text. What implications do these causes carry for the school administrator?
3. Develop a district policy and plan, based on the ideas presented in the text, for improving employee absenteeism. What obstacles would the policy and plan have to overcome before they could be implemented successfully?
4. Develop a district policy and plan, based on the ideas presented in this chapter, for addressing the possible problem of chemical dependency on the part of employees. What obstacles would the policy and plan have to overcome before they could be implemented successfully?
5. Discuss the arguments, pro and con, in regard to merit pay for teachers and reduced fringe benefits.
6. Develop a district policy and plan, based on the ideas presented in the text, for reduction in staff. What obstacles would the policy and plan need to overcome before they could be implemented successfully?

Notes

1. Major sections of this chapter represent an adaptation and expansion of an entry by the author entitled, "School Personnel Policy," in *The Encyclopedia of Educational Research,* ed. Harold E. Mitzel (New York: Macmillan, 1982).

2. D. E. Taylor, "Absent Workers and Lost Work Hours, May 1978," *Monthly Labor Review* (August 1979): 49–53.

3. Educational Research Service, *Employee Absenteeism: A Summary of Research* (Arlington, Va.: Educational Research, Inc., 1980).

4. American Association of School Personnel Administrators, *Conference Reports: Employee Absenteeism* (Seven Hills, Ohio: American Association of School Personnel Administrators, 1979.)

5. D. C. Manlove, "Absent Teachers . . . Another Handicap for Students?" *The Practitioner* (1979) 5 (4): 3–6.

6. Pennsylvania School Boards Association, *Teacher Absenteeism: Professional Staff Absence Study* (Harrisburg Pa: Pennsylvania School Boards Association, 1978.)

7. "Here's How to Reduce Teacher Absenteeism," *The Executive Educator* (April 1979): 11–12.

8. J. H. Capitan and B. J. Morris, "The Ohio Report on Teacher Absenteeism" (Paper presented at the annual meeting of the American Association of School Personnel Administrators, October 1978).

9. P. M. Muchinsky, "Employee Absenteeism: A Review of the Literature," *Journal of Vocational Behavior* (June 1977): 317.

10. R. Harclerode, *Attendance Improvement Guide for Superintendents: How to Improve Staff Illness Absence.* (Newark, N.J.: Chamber of Commerce, 1979.)

11. R. D. Johnson and T. O. Peterson, "Absenteeism or Attendance: Which Is Industry's Problem?" *Personnel Journal* (1975): 568–72.

12. Educational Research Service, *Employee Absenteeism.*

13. E. M. Bridges, "Job Satisfaction and Teacher Absenteeism," *Educational Administration Quarterly* (Spring 1980): 41–56.

14. *Teacher Absenteeism and Related Policies for Supplementary Remuneration,* produced by the Philadelphia Suburban School Study Council and the South Penn School Study Council Group (Philadelphia Suburban School Study Council and the South Penn School Study Council Group (Philadelphia: University of Pennsylvania, Graduate School of Education, 1970).

15. Pennsylvania School Boards Association, *Teacher Absenteeism.* Also see *Teacher Absenteeism: Experience and Practices of School Systems* (Arlington, Va.: Educational Research Service, 1981).

16. D. R. Winkler, "The Effects of Sick Leave Policy on Teacher Absenteeism," *Industrial and Labor Relations Review* (January 1980): 232–40.

17. D. L. Bundren, "The Influence of Situational and Demographic Factors on the Absentee Patterns of Teachers." Report to the Clark County, Nevada School District, 1974.

18. M. E. Redmond, "The Relationship of Selected Factors to Illness in the Fort Madison Community School District—A Case Study" (Diss., University of Iowa, 1978).

19. The Academy for Educational Development, *Report on Teacher Absenteeism in the Public Schools of Illinois to the State Board of Education, Illinois Office of Education* (Indianapolis, Ind.: The Academy for Educational Development, Public Policy Division, 1977).

20. R. M. Steers and S. R. Rhodes, "Major Influences on Employee Attendance: A Process Model," *Journal of Applied Psychology* (August 1978): 391–407.

21. Ibid.

22. American Association of School Personnel Administrators, *Employee Absenteeism.*

23. The Academy for Educational Development, *Report on Teacher Absenteeism.*

24. W. Clark, "How to Cut Absenteeism and Turnover," *Administrative Management* (March 1971): 64–65.

25. L. Olfson, "How to Use Fewer Substitutes and Save School Dollars," *Education Digest* (February 1978): 27–29.

26, Capitan and Morris, "Teacher Absenteeism."

27. *Teacher Attendance Improvement Program: A Joint Business-Education Project* (Newark, N.J.: Greater Newark Chamber of Commerce, 1975), p. 10.

28. *A Program to Improve Teacher Attendance* (Newark, N.J.: Greater Newark Chamber of Commerce, 1974), p. 168.

29. Educational Research Service, 1980, *Employee Absenteeism* pp. 114–39.

30. National Institute on Alcohol Abuse and Alcoholism, *Alcohol and Health* (Rockville, Md.: National Institute on Alcohol Abuse and Alcoholism, 1978), p. 77.

31. R. D. Russell, "Problem Drinking in the Eduation Profession," *The Kappan* (March 1979): 506–9.

32. J. Cramer, "The Alcoholics on Your Staff: How to Find Them, How to Help Them, and Why You'll Profit from Doing Both," *The American School Board Journal* (August 1977): 45–50.

33. P. Saltman, *Drinking on the Job* (New York: Public Affairs Pamphlets, 1977), p. 3.

34. A. Brooks, "Room for Recovery: Helping the Alcoholic Teacher," *Teacher* (October 1980): 38–40.

35. National Institute on Alcohol Abuse and Alcoholism, *Alcohol and Health, p.* 77.

36. Richard M. Weiss, *Dealing with Alcoholism in the Work-Place* (New York: The Conference Board, 1980), pp. 10–11.

37. Ibid., pp. 16–17.

38. Martin Shain and Judith Groeneveld, *Employee Assistance Programs* (Lexington, Mass.: Lexington Books, 1980).

39. Public Service Research Council, *The Effect of Collective Bargaining on Teacher Salaries* (Vienna, Va.: Public Service Research Council, 1978).

40. W. B. Castetter, *The Personnel Function in Educational Administration* (New York: Macmillan, 1976), p. 325.

41. "Merit Pay Research Action Brief." An ERIC Report: Ed–199–828.

42. Educational Research Service, *Merit Pay for Teachers* (Arlington, Va.: Educational Research Service, 1979), p. 1.

43. Ibid., pp. 5–7.

44. Educational Research Service, *Merit Pay for School Administrators* (Arlington, Va.: Educational Research Service, 1979).

45. Educational Research Service, *Merit Pay for Teachers,* pp. 4–7.

46. Ibid., p. 32.

47. National Center for Educational Statistics, *The Condition of Education* (Washington, D.C.: National Center for Educational Statistics, 1979).

48. Educational Research Service, *Fringe Benefits for Teachers in Public Schools, 1977–78* (Arlington, Va.: Educational Research Service, 1979).

49. C. W. Fawcett, *School Personnel Systems* (Lexington, Mass.: Lexington Books, 1979), pp. 158–59.

50. "Workers Get Paid for Staying Well Under New Health Insurance Plan," *Milwaukee Sentinel* (August 7, 1980), Pt. 2, p. 5.

51. "Another Way to Cut Health Bills, *Education U.S.A.* (November 10, 1980), p. 84.

52. "New Jersey Schools," *Education U.S.A.* (June 29, 1981), p. 344.

53. National Center for Educational Statistics, *A Favorable Job Market Foreseen for Teacher Graduates in the Late 1980's* (Washington, D.C.: National Center for Educational Statistics, 1980.)

54. C. M. Nolte, "Follow These How to's When You Must Cut Your Staff," *American School Board Journal* (June 1976): 26–27.

55. W. Keller, *Enrollment Trends: Programs for the Future, A Planning Guide for Districts with Declining Enrollments* (Albany: New York State Education Department, 1976), p. 2.

56. "The End of an Era: Teacher Surplus Is Gone," *Education* U.S.A. (September 1980), p. 9.

57. Robert C. Shaw, "How Accurate Can Enrollment Forecasting Be?" *NASSP Bulletin* (November, 1980): 13–20.

58. D. H. Fowler, "Effects of Declining Numbers: Poverty? Procastination? Planning? *NASSP Bulletin* (November 1979): 1–6.

59. D. Divoky, "Burden of the Seventies: The Management of Decline, *Phi Delta Kappan* (October 1979): 87–91.

60. G. R. Weldy, *Enrollment Decline and Reduction in Force—What Can Administrators Do?* An ERIC Report: Ed–150–371.

61. Linda Averill, "Managerial Techniques Which Promote Staff Motivation in Declining School Populations" (Ed.D. diss., Seattle University, 1981).

62. A. C. Ornstein, "Teacher Surplus? Trends in Education Supply and Demand," *Educational Horizons* (Spring 1979): 115.

63. D. Thomas, *Declining Enrollments: A People Problem.* An ERIC Report: Ed–136–375.

64. Illinois State Office of Education, *Report of the Illinois Task Force on Declining Enrollments in the Public Schools* (Springfield, Ill.: State Office of Education, 1975.)

65. R. L. Averett, "Alternatives to Layoffs in Education" (Diss., University of Southern California, 1979).

66. D. P. Ellsworth, *Early Retirement: A Proposal for Adjustments to Declining Enrollments* (Springfield, Ill.: Illinois State Office of Education, 1977).

67. Gerald W. Montgomery, "Analysis of Fiscal Consequences of Early Retirement Options for Indiana Teachers" (Ed.D. diss., Indiana University, 1978).

68. "Innovative Greece T. A. Bargains Retraining with Full Pay." *NEA Reporter* (October 1980): 10.

69. Weldy, *Enrollment Decline,* p. 8.

70. L. J. Bishop, "Dealing with Declining School Enrollments," *Education and Urban Society* (May 1979): 285–94.

71. J. Reiels, "Nicolet Board Offers Teachers Job Counseling," *Wisconsin School News* (September 1980): 10.

72. B. F. Sinowitz and C. Hallam, "Fighting Reductions in Force," *Today's Education* (March/April 1975): 32–34.

73. J. R. Berryman, "Staff Reduction Due to Severe Enrollment Decline: Guidelines for Planning in the State of Illinois" (Diss., University of Illinois at Urbana, 1979).

74. Educational Research Service, *Local Policies for Reduction in Force* (Arlington, Va.: Educational Research Service, 1975).

75. Nolte, "When You Must Cut Your Staff."

76. American Association of School Administrators, *Declining Enrollment: What to Do* (Arlington, Va.: American Association of School Administrators, 1974), p. 31.

77. F. G. Delon, "Reduction in Force: Legal Implications," in *Contemporary Legal Issues in Education,* ed. M. A. McGhehey (Topeka: National Organization on Legal Problems of Education, 1979), pp. 136–37.

78. National Association of Secondary School Principals, *Reduction in Force: Working Policies and Procedures* (Reston, Va.: National Association of Secondary School Principals, 1978).

79. E. Kelley, *Reduction in Force: Policies, Practices and Implications for Education.* An ERIC Report: Ed–150–371.

80. H. O. Morse, "Whom Shall We Fire?" *NASSP Bulletin* (February 1977): 76–77.

81. E. H. Seifert, "Declining Enrollments and New Staffing Patterns for the Eighties" (Paper presented at the annual meeting of the National Association of Secondary School Principals, 1979).

82. S. M. Johnson, "Performance Based Staff Layoffs in the Public Schools: Implementation and Outcomes," *Harvard Educational Review* (May 1980): 214–33.

83. S. McCune and M. Matthews, *Programs for Educational Equality: Schools and Affirmative Action* (Washington, D.C.: U.S. Government Printing Office, 1975), p. 1.

84. *Retrenchment in Education: The Outlook for Women and Minorities* (Denver: Education Commission of the States, 1977.)

85. G. W. Downey, "What School Boards Do When That Irresistable Force Called RIF Meets That Immovable Object Called Affirmative Action," *The American School Board Journal* (October 1976): 35–39.

86. Ibid.

87. Bacica v. Board of Education of the School District of Erie, 451 F. Supp. 882 (W. D. Pa. 1978).

88. Delon, "Reduction in Force."

89. Johnson, "Performance Based Staff Layoffs."

90. Ibid., p. 220.

9

Administrator-Staff Relations

The school administrator works with a variety of people, including students, teachers, and parents. Although no single individual or group should be considered by him to be more important than another, there is little doubt that his relationship with the staff will significantly influence his effectiveness as a leader. While a positive relationship won't guarantee effective administrative leadership, it is difficult to conceive how an administrator could continue to function successfully as a leader if his relationship with the staff were a negative one.

In the sections which follow, two aspects of administrator-staff relationships are explored: (1) staff satisfaction and morale, and (2) collective bargaining and contract administration.

STAFF SATISFACTION AND MORALE

DEFINITION AND PURPOSE

Most administrators recognize the importance of developing and maintaining high staff satisfaction and morale, even if they are not sure how to achieve these goals.

Satisfaction and morale are attitudinal variables which reflect positive or negative feelings about a particular situation or person(s). The two concepts are often used synonymously in the educational literature, and it is easy to understand why. The state of one's morale reflects the extent of his satisfaction with a situation or person. Satisfaction can also refer to one's feelings about himself or the situation in which he finds himself, although most studies of the concept have concentrated on the latter. Both terms can refer to the attitudinal characteristics of either a group or an individual. (While research seems to focus on teachers, the school administrator should take a broader view of staff as including support personnel as well as noncertificated workers, all of whose morale and satisfaction are important.)

Many attempts have been made to define the terms "satisfaction" and "morale." The term *satisfaction,* as it applies to the work context seems to refer to the degree to which an individual can meet his personal and professional needs in the performance of his role.[1] *Morale,* on the other hand, as defined in the educational literature seems to hold a broader meaning. Gross, for example, in his study of staff leadership in the schools, identified the following six indices of morale:

1. Displays a sense of pride in the school
2. Enjoys working in the school
3. Displays a sense of loyalty to the school
4. Works cooperatively with fellow teachers
5. Accepts the educational philosophy underlying the curriculum of the school
6. Respects the judgment of the school administrators.[2]

However one chooses to define satisfaction and morale, it seems clear that they are viewed as desirable goals for school organizations. A basic principle of personnel relations has long been the idea that a satisfied employee, one with high morale and satisfaction, is likely to get along better with co-workers, will be more accepting of management's directives, will be more committed to achieving organizational goals, and in general will be more productive. This belief persists despite rather limited supportive research.[3] Studies generally have been correlational in nature, and there is little hard evidence to support the basic premise regarding the purported outcomes of high staff satisfaction and morale. In fact, at present there is no conclusive evidence that a satisfied employee with high morale is necessarily a motivated or productive employee.[4] Nevertheless, it seems reasonable to assume that a dissatisfied employee with low morale is not likely to be a maximally motivated and productive worker.

High staff satisfaction and morale can be considered either as ends in themselves or as necessary conditions for achieving the educational objectives of a school. If the two are considered as ends in themselves, then the administrator is assuming that high staff satisfaction and morale are intrinsically valuable. Although, high satisfaction and morale are certainly desirable, it may be necessary in *some* circumstances for an administrator to actually create some temporary dissatisfaction in order to improve a stagnant situation. Such action would be based on the realization that important and needed changes generally will not occur as long as people are satisfied with the status quo and should be initiated only on a selective basis, and with considerable thought and care.

The writer's position is that high staff satisfaction and morale may be desirable as ends in themselves, but their primary value is in helping to achieve other kinds of worthwhile goals. These goals would include staff stability, cohesiveness, and increased effectiveness. Although research on the consequences of high or low staff satisfaction and morale is not conclusive, it would appear that the extent of staff satisfaction and morale can influence the degree to which the goals previously mentioned can be achieved.[5] For these reasons then, the administrator needs to understand better the factors which contribute to low or high staff satisfaction and morale, and based on that understanding he should develop conditions which will build and maintain the latter.

CONCEPTUAL BACKGROUND

The question of how to develop and sustain high morale and satisfaction on the part of workers is one that has long attracted the attention of theorists. While no single conceptual framework seems to answer totally such a complex question, several theories or models have been advanced which the administrator ought to consider.

Perhaps the most important initial factor which will influence an administrator's priorities and approach to developing staff members' morale and satisfaction is his attitude toward them and what motivates them. In this connection, McGregor has formulated a useful theory about administrators' attitudes toward people which is relevant to this discussion. He postulated that administrative behavior is influenced by two basic attitudes which he referred to as Theory X and Theory Y. The main characteristics of these two attitudes as they apply to decision-making are described below.[6]

Theory X

1. "The average human being has an inherent dislike of work, and will avoid it if he can."
2. "Because of this human characteristic of dislike of work, most people must be coerced, controlled, directed, and/or threatened with punishment in order to get them to put forth adequate effort toward achievement of organizational objectives."
3. "The average human being prefers to be directed, wishes to avoid responsibility, has relatively little ambition, and wants security above all."

Theory Y

1. "External control and the threat of punishment are not the only means for bringing about effort toward organizational objectives. Man will

exercise self-direction and self-control in the service of objectives to which he is committed."

2. "The average human being learns, under proper conditions, not only to accept but to seek responsibility. Avoidance of responsibility, lack of ambition, and emphasis on security are generally consequences of experience, not inherent human characteristics."

3. "The capacity to exercise a relatively high degree of imagination, ingenuity and creativity in the solution of organizational problems is widely, not narrowly, distributed in the population."

It should be obvious that Theory X and Theory Y administrators differ markedly in their attitudes toward people. A major implication of McGregor's Theory and the supporting research is that the administrator's attitude toward other people is likely to influence his selection of an approach to motivating them. (It should be noted that the attitude of many administrators is a synthesis or combination of Theory X and Y, referred to by some authorities as "Theory Z.")

A second conceptual model, which has greatly influenced the thinking of many educators, was developed by Maslow.[7] Maslow asserted that there are basic needs that everyone seeks to satisfy. These needs are identified in figure 9.1.

The two central ideas in Maslow's theory are (1) that a hierarchy of needs exists, and that low level needs, such as physiological needs, must be satisfied before higher level needs, such as self-esteem or self-actualization, will assume importance for an individual, and (2) once a need is satisfied, it becomes less important as a motivator. While the terms utilized in Maslow's theory are often sprinkled in the conversations of school practitioners, there is little evidence that school personnel policies are based on the theory to any great degree. It might also be noted that a review of the research on Maslow's theory,

---

Self-actualization Needs
↑
Self-esteem and Respect from Others Needs
↑
Love and Belonging Needs
↑
Safety Needs, e.g., Security, Order
↑
Physiological Needs, e.g., Food, Shelter

Figure 9.1. Maslow's Need Hierarchy

conducted by Wahba and Bridwell,[8] concluded that research had not confirmed the theory, although the reviewers emphasized that the lack of evidence did not necessarily invalidate the theory.

A useful reformulation of Maslow's theory has been proposed by Porter,[9] and was later adapted by Sergiovanni and Carver for use with teachers. The latter researchers defined the basic needs of teachers as those presented in figure 9.2.

This model of needs advances the idea of need deficiency which is determined by ascertaining the difference between the *desired* level of need fulfillment in a particular area, compared with the *actual* level of fulfillment. The lower the difference, the greater the satisfaction; the higher the difference, the greater the dissatisfaction. Several studies using this model have found that need deficiencies tend to be greater for the higher level needs, especially esteem and self-actualization.[10]

A somewhat different model of teacher satisfaction has been proposed by Chapman and Lowther.[11] Based on earlier research, they have concluded that teacher satisfaction (or the lack of it) is influenced by four major factors. These factors are identified in figure 9.3, which has been adapted from their model.

Basic Needs	Desired Fulfillment	Actual Fulfillment
• **Self-actualization:** the teacher perceived need for personal and professional success, achievement, peak satisfaction, and working at full potential	_____	_____
• **Autonomy:** the teacher perceived need for authority, control and influence	_____	_____
• **Esteem:** the teacher perceived need for self-respect, respect by others as a person and as a professional	_____	_____
• **Social:** the teacher perceived need for acceptance, belonging, friendship, and membership in formal and informal work groups. Affiliation is another term for this need	_____	_____
• **Security:** the teacher perceived need for money, benefits, and tenure associated with one's job	_____	_____

Figure 9.2. Basic Needs of Teachers.[12] (In this particular conceptualization physiological needs have been dropped and autonomy needs added.)

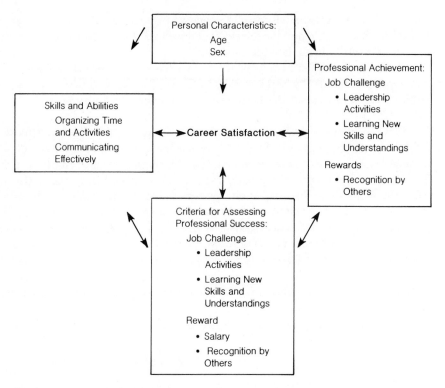

Figure 9.3. Factors Influencing
Teacher Satisfaction

The model presented in figure 9.3 suggests that the career satisfaction of a teacher is influenced by (1) the teacher's personal characteristics, (2) the teacher's skills and abilities, (3) the criteria a teacher uses to evaluate his or her professional success, and (4) the teacher's actual career accomplishments. The model also indicates that several of these factors influence each other. For example, the criteria for assessing professional success could influence how much professional achievement is attempted, and the actual achievement could cause one to revise the criteria for determining professional success.

Research by Chapman and Lowther has tended to support the model, although further evidence is needed.[13] One finding of particular interest was revealed by these researchers, namely, that while actual achievement by a teacher had a strong positive relationship to satisfaction, career satisfaction was also significantly related to assigning little importance to possible activities and accomplishments that might be difficult to achieve because of the structure of a school.[14] The latter finding suggests that acceptance and realism may be important personal characteristics related to career satisfaction.

Satisfaction Motivators	*Dissatisfaction Hygienes*
1. Achievement	1. Salary
2. Recognition	2. Possibility of growth
3. Work itself	3. Interpersonal relations (subordinates)
4. Responsibility	4. Status
5. Advancement	5. Interpersonal relations (superiors)
	6. Interpersonal relations (peers)
	7. Supervision—technical
	8. Company policy and administration
	9. Working conditions
	10. Personal life
	11. Job security

Figure 9.4. Herzberg's Satisfaction/
Dissatisfaction Factors

Another major theory on employee satisfaction which has tended to influence many school administrators was developed by Herzberg and his colleagues.[15] Herzberg theorized that the factors which satisfy employees and the factors which dissatisfy employees are mutually exclusive and are not aligned along a continuum. He found, for example, in his study of accountants and engineers that the factors presented in figure 9.4 contributed to satisfaction *or* dissatisfaction, but not to both.

Herzberg found that the existence of the five factors listed in figure 9.4 under "Satisfaction" tended to affect the employees' attitudes in a positive direction. However, interestingly, a reduction of these same factors did *not* result in job *dissatisfaction*. On the other hand, an improvement in one or more of the eleven factors listed under "Dissatisfaction" in figure 9.4 tended to reduce employee dissatisfaction, but this change did not ensure employee satisfaction.

A major implication of Herzberg's research would appear to be that the administrator cannot assume that modification of a factor creating dissatisfaction will automatically result in job satisfaction, nor can it be assumed that failure to maintain a satisfactory condition will inevitably result in staff dissatisfaction. Different factors seem to be involved in creating satisfaction or dissatisfaction on the part of employees.

Following Herzberg's work several studies in education have been initiated in an attempt to verify his findings. Sergiovanni, for example, conducted a study of 3,382 teachers and discovered that achievement, recognition, and responsibility contributed predominantly to staff satisfaction.[16] Advancement was not a factor which was associated with satisfaction of teachers, or, for that matter, with dissatisfaction. The work itself was a potential source of either satisfaction or dissatisfaction.

As revealed in Sergiovanni's investigation, those factors which seemed to contribute primarily to teacher dissatisfaction were poor relations with peers and students, unfair or incompetent administrative and supervisory policies and practices, and outside personal problems. The remaining factors associated with dissatisfaction in Herzberg's study (see fig. 9.4) turned out to be potentially significant for creating either satisfaction or dissatisfaction. It should be noted that the conditions affecting satisfaction or dissatisfaction, or both, as reflected in Sergiovanni's study, did not vary with the sex, teaching level, or tenure status of the teacher.

It would appear then, that by and large the same factors do not hold equal potential for creating staff satisfaction or dissatisfaction: the conditions which create staff satisfaction seem to be associated with the work itself, while the conditions which contribute to dissatisfaction seem to be associated with the environment of work, particularly the interpersonal relations aspect of that environment. These findings are consistent with Maslow's theory that individuals have a hierarchy of needs and that lower level needs such as security must be met before the higher level needs such as achievement or responsibility become important. It should be noted that some theorists have attempted to refine and elaborate on Herzberg's theory. For example, Hoy and Miskel modified the theory in several respects. First, they reformulated the theory to include three factors instead of two: motivators, hygienes and ambients.[17] Ambients, which function as either satisfiers or dissatisfiers, may include such variables as salary, professional growth possibilities, status, relationships with superiors, and risk opportunities. Hoy and Miskel have also suggested that, while the motivators contribute more to job satisfaction than to job dissatisfaction, a lack of adequate motivators *can* contribute to dissatisfaction. Finally, they contend that, although hygiene factors contribute more to job dissatisfaction than to satisfaction, an abundance of hygiene factors can contribute to job satisfaction.

Argyris[18] and Vroom[19] have proposed additional theories on motivation, satisfaction, and morale, providing useful ideas worthy of further investigation on the part of the reader.

RESEARCH FINDINGS

Extent and Symptoms of Dissatisfaction and Low Morale

Do school personnel possess high morale, and are they satisfied in their work setting? If one were to believe the newspaper headlines emphasizing teacher strikes, teacher burnout and stress, and assaults on school personnel, it would be difficult to answer affirmatively. In fact, a number of studies conducted through the '70s and into the '80s have indicated a gradual reduction in teacher satisfaction. For example, although Fuller and Miskel found in the early '70s that about 89 percent of the teachers participating in their study were "satisfied" or "very satisfied" with their jobs,[20] Bentzen and colleagues conducted a similar investigation in the late '70s and reported that the percentage of teachers satisfied with their jobs was a little over 75 percent.[21] In the latter study elementary school teachers expressed more satisfaction with their jobs than did secondary teachers.

In another study the National Education Association conducted a nationwide poll of teachers in 1980 and found that 35 percent of all public school teachers were dissatisfied with their current jobs.[22] Forty percent of the teachers said they would probably not go into teaching if they had it to do all over again; 10 percent were planning to leave teaching as soon as possible, and 20 percent were undecided about how long they would remain in teaching. These studies, along with continuing reports from the field, suggest a moderate trend in the direction of increasing dissatisfaction on the part of teachers, although thus far a majority of them continue to express satisfaction with their work.

A review of the literature reveals that possible symptoms of teacher dissatisfaction and low morale include questioning and criticizing of school goals and policies, lack of enthusiasm for teaching, rejection or lack of follow-through on administrative directives,[23] absenteeism,[24] and fragmentation, that is, a general feeling of being pulled in different directions.[25] Stapleton and his colleagues, who also identified some of these symptoms in their study, reported a positive relationship between teacher job dissatisfaction and brinkmanship, which they defined as teacher behavior that attempts to challenge the authority structure of the school while at the same time trying to avoid negative sanctions.[26]

Dissatisfaction and low morale are also believed to be manifested in employee stress and burnout. Werner perceives psychological stress as a combination of such feelings as frustration, great pressure, and a lack of control over one's emotions and environment,[27] whereas Maslach has defined burnout as emotional exhaustion caused by the stress of the job.[28] An instrument originally developed by Maslach for measuring burn-out has been adapted by Iwanicki and Schwab for use with teachers.[29]

It would appear that, among the more important indicators of teacher burn-out, are the following characteristics: loss of concern and detachment from the people with whom one works, a cynical and dehumanized perception of students, accompanied by a deterioration of the quality of teaching; depression, increased use of sick leave, and efforts to leave the profession.[30] According to Maslach and Jackson, the development of burn-out is progressive. In the initial stage the affected personnel develop increased feelings of emotional exhaustion and fatigue, and as emotional resources become depleted, they feel that they are no longer capable of giving of themselves as in the past. In the second stage they develop negative, cynical attitudes toward their students.

Finally, affected personnel turn against themselves and begin to evaluate themselves very negatively.[31]

Despite the fact that stress and burn-out are typically viewed as symptoms of dissatisfaction, it would appear that the relationship may not be as strong as assumed. A study by the American Academy of Family Physicians reported, for example, that two-thirds of teachers felt their jobs to be stressful, but 86 percent said that they usually or always liked their work.[32] Research indicates that excessive stress can be harmful, however,[33] so it is important that educators try to understand the causes of stress and burn-out.

Possible Causes

Not only are the causes of employee stress and burn-out frequently difficult to ascertain; they are also not easily distinguished from the symptoms. Nevertheless, numerous ideas have been advanced on possible causes. The Quicks believe that four groups of factors contribute to stress at work: (1) role factors, (2) job factors, (3) physical factors, and (4) interpersonal factors, and they have recommended a number of techniques for reducing stress created by the various factors.[34] It has been contended by the New York State United Teachers Organization, based on a survey of members, that the most important factor contributing to stress is disruptive children, followed by incompetent administrators.[35] In that study urban teachers reported more stress than teachers working in suburban or rural areas.

In a study by Feitler and Tokar, the five most frequent sources of stress reported by teachers were individual pupils who continually misbehaved, too much work, trying to uphold/maintain values and standards, noisy pupils, and a difficult class.[36] In a study of Chicago teachers, Cichon and Koff found the more important causes of teacher stress centered on problems of disruption and threats to the teachers' physical, professional, and personal well-being.[37] Such threats constitute a serious problem inasmuch as a National Education Association survey of members concluded that 113,000 of the country's school teachers were physically attacked during a twelve-month period.[38]

Suggested causes of teacher burn-out are generally believed to be similar to those associated with stress. Schwab and Iwanicki, for example, found that role conflict and role ambiguity were significantly related to teacher burn-out.[39] Anderson and Iwanicki discovered that teacher burn-out was significantly related to the extent to which a teacher felt that the need for professional respect and self-actualization was not being met,[40] and Sweeny reported similar findings in his study.[41] In a personal account of teacher burn-out, Bardo described several symptoms and perceived causes.[42]

Numerous investigations have also been conducted into the causes of teacher dissatisfaction. An NEA survey identified several factors which had been cited by a majority of the teachers polled, as exerting a negative effect on their job satisfaction: public attitudes toward the schools, treatment of education by the media, student attitudes toward learning, salary, and status of teachers in the community.[43] In addition nearly half the teachers surveyed indicated that student behavior affected their job satisfaction negatively. Teacher workloads are also believed by Ford to be related to dissatisfaction,[44] and in at least one important study the relationship between class size and teacher satisfaction is being investigated.[45] Moreover, Chapman and Hutcheson found that teachers' satisfaction was linked to the extent to which they felt locked into their jobs and unable to participate in organizational decision-making.[46]

Pagel and Price found in their study of 130 teachers that the factors contributing most to job dissatisfaction were, in order of importance, (1) lack of planning time, (2) tedious paper work and clerical work, (3) an out-of-touch and autocratic administration, (4) disruptive and unmotivated students, (5) extra-teaching functions, such as faculty meetings and "time-wasting" workshops, (6) uncooperative parents, (7) lack of autonomy to prescribe curriculum, (8) feelings of failure, and (9) low occupational prestige.[47] Interestingly, a study by Kulpa and Steitz revealed sex differences in regard to job satisfaction (men were more dissatisfied), but the primary factor affecting satisfaction was the extent to which a teacher felt control over the work environment.[48]

In a study of teachers in two communities, Schackmuth noted a positive relationship between the professional self-image of the elementary school teacher and the level of satisfaction with work,[49] while Rugus and Martin concluded from their review of the literature on school culture, that certain aspects of school culture impact negatively on teacher satisfaction and morale.[50] These cultural elements included physical, emotional and psychic demands of teaching; uncertainty of teaching because of a lack of validated technical procedures, and isolation from other teachers, which can result in loneliness. Bredo has also discussed the problem of isolation in a presentation of findings on the degree of collaboration among elementary teachers,[51] and Sarason[52] and Lortie[53] have treated the topic of isolation in greater depth.

An additional cause of employee dissatisfaction and low morale may be the different frames of reference that administrators and teachers possess. This is typically conceptualized as a conflict between the bureaucratic orientation of the administration and the professional orientation of the staff.[54] A bureaucratic orientation is one which emphasizes staff compliance with rules and regulations, and loyalty to the administration; on the other hand, a professional orientation emphasizes a desire for autonomy, control over one's work environment, and allegiance to one's subject matter and/or clients rather than to the organization itself. In this type of conceptualization teachers are assumed to be professionally orientated, while administrators are believed to have a bureaucratic orientation.[55] However, some writers have questioned whether all teachers possess a professional orientation and all administrators are characterized by a bureaucratic orientation.[56]

Several studies have indicated that teachers and administrators may possess different frames of reference and perceptions of problems and situations, however. Reineke and Welsh found significant differences between teachers and administrators in regard to how each group viewed the adequacy of teaching conditions.[57] Principals tended to perceive teaching conditions as satisfactory or better, while teachers tended to rate conditions as unsatisfactory. And, while teachers and principals have been found to generally agree on which school problems are serious, they differ greatly in their perceptions as to the magnitude of these problems, with teachers believing the problems to be more serious.[58] Furthermore, Ignatovich and his colleagues found in their study of the value and belief patterns of teachers and those administrators engaged in attempts to influence teaching, that the two groups differed in important respects.[59] Teachers tended to emphasize such aspects as humanistic orientation to instruction and positive relations between teachers and students, whereas administrators stressed factors such as student achievement on standardized tests and administrative evaluation. That a difference in orientation or frames of reference on the part of teachers and administrators can contribute to some forms of dissatisfaction and conflict has been shown in studies by other researchers as well.[60]

The relationship between personal satisfaction and motivation, and the extent of bureaucracy in school organizations has been the focus of several studies, but thus far confirming evidence of such a relationship has been limited. Patton and Miskel found no significant relationship between teacher motivation and school district bureaucracy,[61] but in a related study, Miskel and his colleagues discovered that increased centralization of decision-making power *reduces* job satisfaction while increased formulation of school rules *improves* teachers' attitudes toward their job.[62] Schackmuth's findings also failed to support the hypothesis that, as the level of bureaucracy increases, teachers' work satisfaction decreases.[63] Apparently the relationship between the level of bureaucracy and job satisfaction (if one exists) is complex and yet to be defined by research. In this connection, Packard has even questioned whether the concept of bureaucracy is appropriate for schools and school districts since, he points out, classroom teaching seems to be regulated little by administrators, rules, or other formal operating procedures. He also contends that the job of teaching does not possess the characteristics that are normally included in defining a profession.[64]

PROPOSED PROGRAMS

Although research on the causes of employee dissatisfaction, low morale, stress, and teacher burn-out is still in progress and it is premature to draw any definite conclusions about causality, a number of suggestions have been offered to help cope with these negative conditions. Weiskopf[65] believes, as do Pagel and Price,[66] that teachers need to become more aware of the overall symptoms and causes of stress and burn-out in the teaching profession, particularly those that pertain to their specific areas of responsibility. These writers also recommend that teachers try to develop more open and supportive interaction with colleagues and superiors, and to set realistic goals and expectations for themselves and their students.

Inservice programs and counseling services should be provided by school districts for teachers who may experience or are experiencing stress or burn-out, according to Cichon and Koff.[67] The role of the principal in ameliorating such distress on the part of teachers has been put forth by Werner as (1) gaining more awareness of indicators of stress and burn-out on the part of teachers, (2) communicating to the staff that asking for and accepting assistance in times of stress do not indicate weakness, (3) providing emotional support to teachers in times of stress, and (4) taking appropriate action wherever possible.[68] Boudewyn has described a meeting format which appears useful for employees to voice their concerns and frustrations.[69] In addition, Alschuler has offered numerous ideas for conducting workshops on teacher burn-out;[70] Hanley and Swick's workshop ideas have focused on reducing teachers' stress.[71]

While many writers have emphasized the role of the school administrator with respect to developing high satisfaction and morale, the research on the relationship between that role and the satisfaction and morale of school personnel has been limited. Duncan found that teacher morale was significantly higher in schools with employee oriented administrators than in schools with task oriented administrators, but he recommended that a combination of the two styles be utilized by administrators in working with teachers.[72] Ingle and Munsterman observed that teachers in high satisfaction schools described their principals as more democratic than did teachers in low satisfaction schools.[73] Group-centered leadership has been advocated by Degenfelder, based on a review of the literature on managing motivation, as most effective in promoting a healthy motivational climate for teachers.[74] She also concluded that teachers needed employment security, high interaction opportunity, institutional supportiveness, and high perceived contribution opportunity, for a healthy motivational climate to be maintained. One study found, however, that while teachers tended to rate the potential costs of decision-making involvement as low and the potential benefits as high, many teachers were reluctant to become involved because they saw little likelihood that the administration would provide them with meaningful involvement in which they could make a significant contribution.[75]

An often recommended approach to increasing staff satisfaction is that of providing greater incentives and recognition. Spuck has contended, however, that administrators exercise little control over organizational incentives for school personnel.[76] He has pointed out that most extrinsic rewards, such as salaries, are limited by legal and collective bargaining constraints, and that intrinsic rewards or incentives are controlled for the most part by the teachers' colleagues, students, and the teachers themselves. In this connection Lortie believes that teaching continues to be rather limited in the extrinsic rewards that can be made available, and that if teacher satisfaction is to be increased, then efforts will need to be applied to improving the teaching situation itself.[77] He feels that the problematic nature of teaching will make this objective challenging, however, since goals are intangible and unclear, assessment difficult, and the expectations and behavior of the clientele diverse. Nevertheless, Chapman and Lowther found in their study that the recognition actually received from administrators and supervisors had a strong positive relationship to the career satisfaction of teachers. Greater recognition by administrators and supervisors was related to greater job satisfaction.[78]

Miller and Swick have proposed a large number of incentives and reward systems which they believe will motivate teachers to perform better, such as (1) acknowledgement of efforts by teachers for self-improvement, (2) compensation to encourage teacher self-improvement, (3) rewards for teacher accomplishments, and (4) community recognition of teacher efforts.[79] An example of community recognition of teachers was briefly described in *Education USA* which involved a special day to honor the teachers and included a banquet and commendations from parents and citizens.[80] Moreover, research by Fuller and Miskel identified fifty-two specific incentives that teachers said were important, such as the school system's support of teachers, working conditions, salary and fringe benefits, and personal and professional relationships with teachers and students.[81] In a study of the intrinsic reward structure of the classroom, McDonald found that the most important satisfaction reported by teachers was the knowledge that they had induced students to learn.[82]

RECOMMENDATIONS

Research studies on staff satisfaction and morale can be instructive. However, unless the findings are translated into recommended courses of action, they will represent little more than interesting reading. Therefore, based primarily on the findings presented in the previous sections, the following guidelines are offered to the administrator who wishes to develop and maintain high staff satisfaction and morale in the school.

1. **Attempt on a regular basis to obtain systematic feedback from the staff as individuals and as a group, on their perceptions of the problems, concerns, and issues which they feel affect them personally or the school generally.**

   The administrator cannot hope to develop and maintain high satisfaction and morale on the part of the staff unless he knows what is on their minds; and he cannot realistically hope to arrive at this knowledge without actually asking the staff periodically for this information. Two procedures for achieving this goal would be the administering of anonymous questionnaires each semester, asking the staff to identify what they see as the main problems and issues affecting the school, and a principal-teacher *open discussion* scheduled at least monthly for teachers who want to discuss problems and issues on a more direct basis. It should be emphasized that an important prerequisite to the provision of feedback by staff is their belief that the administrator is sincerely interested in obtaining it, and that there will be constructive follow-up.

2. **Exert a major effort toward improving the satisfaction which staff derive from their work.**

   The research on teacher satisfaction and morale indicates that when staff feel a sense of accomplishment from teaching and receive due recognition for their efforts and performance, staff satisfaction and morale are high.

   Improving the conditions under which the staff works—size of class, type of facilities, quantity and quality of teaching materials, problem nature of the class, the quality of administrative and supervisory supporting services, and increasing opportunities for initiative, responsibility and achievement—are administrative contributions which should increase the likelihood that staff can obtain a sense of accomplishment from their endeavors.

   While in many school districts the master contract and/or local financial circumstances will limit or reduce the opportunity for an administrator to improve working conditions, the key factor is administrator effort. If an administrator is perceived by the staff as at least *trying* to improve working conditions, that effort is likely to positively affect staff morale. Certainly, at the minimum, administrators can provide appropriate recognition and positive reinforcement to staff members for their accomplishments. Such recognition could take the form of a personal tribute at a faculty or PTA meeting, an individual letter with a copy for the teacher's personnel file, or a recommendation for advancement on the salary scale. All too often teachers complain that administrators take them for granted. Almost all human beings need periodic expressions of appreciation of their worth, and this frequently requires no more than simply providing verbal positive reinforcement.

3. **Strive to improve the operation of the school and the overall quality of the educational program of the school.**

People feel pleased and proud to work in a school that is efficiently administered and that offers a quality educational program.

A poorly organized school with a limited or mediocre educational program is bound to affect adversely the morale and satisfaction of its teachers. According to Redefer, one of the major factors associated with faculty morale is the quality of the school's educational program.[83] Consequently, the administrator who improves the quality of a school's educational program will concurrently be improving the morale of the faculty. Again, the key is for the administrator to be *striving* to improve the operation of the school and the quality of the educational program. Not every administrator will find himself in a situation where it will be possible to have an outstanding program, but every administrator can at least be aspiring to this standard of excellence and striving to achieve it.

4. **Try to be sensitive to problems of an interpersonal nature between and among teachers, students, and parents, and try to mediate these problems when appropriate.**

Problems of interpersonal relations seem to be one of the main factors which contribute to low teacher satisfaction and morale, according to research. The administrator will probably experience difficulty in ascertaining these kinds of problems, however, because in many instances the people involved may be reluctant to talk to him about them. He can partially overcome this handicap by becoming more aware of what is going on in the school and by showing understanding and compassion when such problems are brought to his attention. The administrator himself may not always be in the best possible position to mediate these kinds of problems, but he should at least be knowledgeable of appropriate agencies for purposes of referral.

5. **Provide meaningful participation for teachers in the decision-making processes of the school.**

There is considerable evidence that teachers desire a more active and meaningful role in school decision making. Research evidence also suggests that increased teacher involvement can result in higher faculty morale. Leiman, for example, concluded in his study that teachers who participated in school administration manifested:[84]

a. Higher morale than teachers who did not participate
b. More positive attitudes toward their principals, their colleagues, and their pupils, and
c. Higher regard for themselves and for the teaching profession.

In addition, Thierbach found, in a study of middle and junior high school teachers that job satisfaction was related to perceived level of influence in decision-making and to the extent to which teachers were participating in school decision-making at the level they desired.*

The key word in this recommendation is "meaningful" participation. It makes little sense for an administrator to involve staff members in school decision-making unless he is prepared to fully utilize their knowledge and expertise, involve them at their expected level of involvement, and accept the consensus of the group, provided their decision does not result in a violation of school board policy, the master contract, or the law. Lesser involvement, while perhaps necessary in certain situations, runs the risk of being perceived unworthy of teachers' time and efforts, and can result in reduced morale and satisfaction. An indepth discussion of concepts, methods, problems, and issues associated with staff involvement in school decision-making may be found in the book, *School Administration and Supervision: Important Issues, Concepts, and Case Studies.*[85]

6. **Practice good human relations in your own interactions with the faculty as a whole and with individual faculty members.**

The type of relationship between the faculty and the school administrator is probably one of the most important factors affecting faculty morale. If that relationship is perceived as a good one, faculty morale is likely to be high; if it is perceived as a poor one, faculty morale is likely to be low.

A major factor influencing the type of relationship that exists between a faculty and the administrator will be the kind of human relations that he practices. Although obviously many different ingredients contribute to good human relations, the following seem essential for any administrator:

a. Be sensitive to the needs of others.
b. Attempt to explain the reasons for your actions.

---

*Gail L. Thierbach, "Decision Involvement and Job Satisfaction in Middle and Junior High Schools" (Ph.D. diss., University of Wisconsin-Madison, 1980).

    c. Try to involve others in decisions about the school.
    d. Be open to criticism; try not to be defensive.
    e. Be willing to admit mistakes and to make changes.
    f. Be honest and fair in your interactions with others.

A critical review of twenty-five years of research on morale concluded that whether or not teachers were satisfied depended primarily on the quality of the administrative relationships in which teachers were involved and the quality of the leadership they received.[86] And a study of education in an urban setting found that significant improvement in reading skills was related to high teacher morale which was associated with principal leadership behavior.[87] Therefore, a major key to high faculty morale and satisfaction seems to be the leadership behavior of the school administrator.

COLLECTIVE BARGAINING AND CONTRACT ADMINISTRATION

Beginning in the 1960s a new element entered into the relationship between the faculty and the school administrator: collective bargaining.[88] Although previously many school boards and administrators, on their own initiative, had informally consulted with teachers about conditions of employment, and the operation of the school, introduction of the concept of collective bargaining meant that the school board and administrators were required to consult and negotiate with the teachers about these matters. As a result, school boards and administrators were no longer as free to make unilateral decisions affecting the faculty's welfare, but had to share decision-making authority with the teachers. Since most, if not all, of the decision-making authority which teachers wanted to share had traditionally been considered management's prerogatives, teachers' attempts to gain and expand their rights under collective bargaining were certain to affect the role of school administrators, particularly the school principal.[89]

For the building administrator, collective bargaining has raised four basic questions: (1) What should be the role of the school principal in collective bargaining? (2) What should be his role in contract administration? (3) What should be his role in grievance procedures? and (4) What should be his role in a teachers' strike? The following sections will discuss recommendations and problems associated with each of the four roles.

THE PRINCIPAL'S ROLE IN COLLECTIVE BARGAINING

At the outset of collective bargaining between school boards and teacher groups, most principals seemed uncertain as to whether or not they should participate.[90] Early opinions among principals ranged from a desire to remain detached from collective bargaining for fear of jeopardizing their relationship with teachers, to a preference and concern that building administrators be involved in all aspects of collective bargaining lest they lose significant decision-making authority to the faculty. Eventually, the latter conception of the role of the building administrator in collective bargaining prevailed, as evidenced by a statement by Benjamin Epstein in an official document of The National Association of Secondary School Principals:

> The members of NASSP feel very strongly that principals and other administrators must be included in every phase of collective decision making whenever their fate and that of the schools for which they are responsible are to be determined.[91]

Statements published by The National Elementary Principals Association during the 1960s showed that it, too, supported the concept of involving the principal in all aspects of collective bargaining that affect his role.[92]

While the official position of the principals' associations and the eventual opinion of most principals was that the principal should be involved in all aspects of collective bargaining between school boards and teachers that affect his role, this concept was not immediately accepted by either of the latter two groups.

In the early years of collective bargaining, many teachers and school boards seemed to feel that the building administrator should be excluded from the process of collective bargaining; surprisingly, most superintendents seemed to concur.[93] It was not until later that district administrators and school boards began to recognize the desirability of involving principals in the process of collective bargaining. Not only could principals contribute useful ideas and perceptions to the formulation of a district's bargaining proposal, but their reactions to the teachers' bargaining demands were essential for the development of an educationally sound and enforceable master contract.

Although the degree to which building administrators receive opportunities to become involved in the collective bargaining process may vary, it would appear that the following guidelines would make greatest and most effective utilization of a building administrator's experiences and insights:

1. Building administrators should be involved in the *formulation* of the school board's bargaining position. Specifically, *all* building administrators should be asked (prior to the development of the board's bargaining proposal to teachers) to submit suggested items which relate to education at the school building level for consideration during the bargaining process.
2. Building administrators should be represented on the negotiation team for the school board or on an advisory committee which gives

counsel to the negotiation team during the bargaining process. The most appropriate way of involving the building administrators in the bargaining process is not easy to determine, and will depend to a large extent on school board and administrative philosophies, along with conditions within the local district. Obviously, not all building administrators can be involved equally, and different forms of participation may be appropriate. However, the key factor is that regardless of the form of involvement, it is essential that the building administrators' point of view be presented and adequately considered during the bargaining process.

3. Building administrators should, as a group or through their representative, be given an opportunity to evaluate the implications of any item considered during collective bargaining which may affect the operation of the school, their role in the school, or their relationship with others associated with the school. Building administrators are usually the ones who are primarily responsible for interpreting and enforcing the provisions of the master contract. Many of the items which are negotiated affect them and the operation of the school. They should therefore be given an opportunity to evaluate the effect of these factors on the school and its administration.

The extent to which building administrators are involved in one or more of the ways identified above will depend on local conditions and personalities. However, it is clear that building administrators can and should play an important role in the formulation of the school board's bargaining position and during the bargaining process itself. Unfortunately, available research suggests that their role is a limited one.[94] Nevertheless, it should be emphasized that, if a school board and a superintendent choose to ignore the building administrators' abilities and perceptions, they run the risk not only of alienating an important component of their management team, but also of failing to capitalize on a valuable source of ideas and insights.[95] (Since entire books have been devoted to the topic of collective bargaining, this chapter cannot possibly do justice to the subject. The reader who is interested in an excellent analysis of the literature is referred to Bruce Cooper, *Collective Bargaining, Studies and Financial Costs in Public Education* (Eugene, Ore.: The ERIC Clearinghouse on Education, 1982).

THE PRINCIPAL'S ROLE IN CONTRACT ADMINISTRATION

The final product of the bargaining process is a master contract between the school board and the teachers' group. The master contract contains in essence the various agreements which were reached during collective bargaining, to which management and employees alike are expected to adhere. Now the negotiations are over and the administration of the contract begins, and as Troxell points out, ". . . A contract is only as good as its administration."[96]

The school principal is usually viewed by the school board and the district administration as their main agent in administering the master contract, since the vast majority of the teachers are located at the school building level. The principal is the chief administrator at this level, so he is the one who is expected to interpret and enforce the master contract for management. He may be able to secure assistance from the district office when significant questions or problems arise, but he typically has the main responsibility at the building level for administering the master contract.

Contract administration at the building level usually consists of two major tasks: (1) interpreting the language and intent of the provisions of the contract, and, (2) enforcing the terms of the contract. A third task, implementing the grievance procedures, can be considered a part of contract administration but is sufficiently important to warrant separate treatment in the next section.

Interpreting

The role of the principal in interpreting the language and intent of provisions of the master contract can be a difficult or easy one, depending on the precision with which the contract was written and the degree to which he received adequate orientation about the contract before he was expected to begin administering it.

Master contracts which contain such phrases as, "if at all possible," "when feasible," and "every effort will be made," may provide the school board and/ or teachers with desired flexibility but also place a large interpretative responsibility on the school principal. It is true that he may, if in doubt, be able to seek guidance from the district administration. However, the guidance which he receives from this source, although usually helpful, may not arrive in time, may *not* be useful, or may not agree with the teachers' interpretation of the contract. As a result, in too many situations the school principal is forced to make his own interpretation of the language of the contract or else he finds himself in the middle between the district office's interpretation of the contract and the teachers' interpretation of the master contract.

A related problem which some principals have encountered in administering the master contract arises from the fact that they received inadequate orientation to the provisions and intent of the contract *prior* to its implementation.[97] They were given a copy of the master contract, sometimes even *after* the teachers in the building received their copies, and were then instructed to administer it to the best of their ability. There have been occasions when the principal did not even receive a copy of the master contract until after the opening of school in the fall, although the master contract had been finalized earlier.

If the principal is to administer the master contract effectively, he should be provided with a comprehensive orientation to the contract *prior* to its implementation, and he should have an opportunity to ask questions about any of its features. An orientation of this nature would minimize incorrect interpretations of the contract and should result in more uniform and consistent applications of its provisions. Certainly, such an orientation program would make it easier for the principal to effectively administer the master contract in the school.

Enforcing

Interpreting the master contract is one aspect of contract administration. Enforcing the provisions of the contract, particularly in regard to teachers, is a second important responsibility of the school principal. While some may assume that there is only one way to enforce the rules of a contract, a research study of rule enforcement by principals revealed three approaches, each with its consequences for administrator-faculty relations.[98]

Utilizing the Gouldner model of bureaucratic administration, Lutz and Evans investigated the effects of three types of rule administration by principals: "mock," "representative," and "punishment-centered." *Mock* administration was defined as nonenforcement of the rules when teachers failed to observe them. *Representative* administration was defined as the cooperative acceptance of the rules by principal and teachers, accompanied by enforcement by the principal and obedience by the teachers. *Punishment-centered* rule administration was characterized by the principal's use of threat or punishment in order to achieve rule adherence by teachers. It should be noted, however, that no school was run solely through the use of one type of rule administration.

After spending a considerable length of time making observations, conducting interviews with the personnel, and collecting questionnaire data in six schools, the researchers succeeded in documenting the effects of each type of rule enforcement.

Positive feelings between the principal and the teachers seemed to be associated in most instances with mock administration of the rules. Nonenforcement was usually associated with such rules as board policy on smoking, the use of school telephones, teacher time cards, and the use of sick leave. In most of the situations when the principal ignored a rule, he felt that extenuating circumstances surrounded its violation by a teacher. (In one research study "mock" rule administration was associated with superintendents who behaved in an authoritarian manner, e.g., high control methods.[99]) Nevertheless, it appeared in some cases that the administrator was concerned about the lack of rule enforcement.

In those instances when the principal engaged in representative rule administration, tension between teachers and the principal developed intially but subsided over time. With few exceptions, warmth and friendliness were observed in the relationship between the principal and staff, and a high rating of principal leadership was given by teachers whose principal exhibited representative rule administration as his dominant style. The researchers further discovered that when the principal engaged in representative rule enforcement, he initiated considerable informal, as well as formal, contact with teachers. As a result, complaints and problems frequently were resolved informally before they ever reached the grievance stage.

The key to effective representative rule enforcement seemed to be *intensive and extensive communication,* that is, explaining the rule and the reasons for it, and working with teachers on interpretation of the rule. Regular meetings between the principal and the teachers' building representative also appeared to be particularly helpful in reducing initial tensions and avoiding problems.

Data from the study indicated that punishment-centered administration was likely to produce negative consequences. Principals who tended to adhere to every rule and who used or threatened punishment in order to enforce the rules were regarded as "running a tight ship" but were usually given low leadership ratings by their teachers. More important, perhaps, was the fact that the tension and hostility which developed as a result of punishment-centered rule enforcement persisted beyond the original disagreement, thereby creating an atmosphere for potential future conflict between the administrator and the teachers.

Although the results of any study cannot be generalized for situations which are different, a school principal should realize that the quality of the relationship between himself and the staff will be affected by the approach he takes in enforcing the provisions of the master contract. Whether or not he should enforce every rule may, of course, depend in many instances on factors beyond his control. But the available research suggests that representative rule administration, as defined earlier, results in the most positive consequences in principal-staff relations.

THE PRINCIPAL'S ROLE IN GRIEVANCE PROCEDURES

A major objective of collective bargaining by teacher groups has been to secure the inclusion of grievance procedures in the master contract of the district. Although prior to collective bargaining, many school districts had informally mediated teacher grievances, these procedures did not, in the eyes of the teachers, sufficiently safeguard or guarantee their rights to a fair hearing and appeal.[100] Therefore, teachers' associations and unions have concentrated on gaining formal grievance procedures in the master contract and, at the present time, most master contracts contain some type of formal grievance procedure for teachers.

A grievance procedure is, essentially, a method or process which requires the parties to a dispute to discuss and try to resolve the dispute, with an opportunity for appeal to a higher authority by either of the parties in disagreement with the initial resolution of the matter.[101] The two main purposes of such a procedure are to prevent either party to a dispute from acting unilaterally to resolve the matter, and to guarantee the right of appeal. If a master contract contains a grievance procedure, the administrator must respond to a teacher grievance by attempting to work out a cooperative solution.

Although there can be considerable disagreement over what constitutes a grievance under a master contract, grievances typically arise under the following conditions:[102]

1. a misinterpretation or incorrect application of the provisions of the master contract
2. an intentional violation of the provisions of the master contract
3. a practice contrary to school board policy
4. unfair or discriminatory behavior which may not be prohibited by the contract or school board policy, but which causes someone to feel that he has been wronged.

The latter condition listed above is, in many contracts, defined as a complaint rather than a grievance, and it may be handled informally by the administrator rather than by going through formal procedures and appeal.

Whether a teacher actually files a grievance with the administration will depend on many factors. First of all, one of the four conditions previously identified will need to be alleged. Second, the teacher will have to feel strongly enough about his grievance to lodge a formal protest to the administration. At this point the role of the building representative for the teachers' group will become very important. Sometimes referred to as "chapter chairman," this is an individual at the building level who represents the teachers in matters involving the master contract. The teacher with a grievance will normally go to the building representative before registering a protest to the principal. If the building representative is supportive, then the teacher is likely to file the grievance. If, on the other hand, the building representative indicates to the teacher that he doesn't have a legitimate grievance, or if the building representative attempts to persuade the teacher to resolve the matter informally rather than going through formal procedures, the teacher may never initiate the grievance with the administration. The role of the building representative can be crucial in determining whether or not a grievance should be or will be filed with the administration.

In examining research on the role of the building representative, it would appear that whether or not a building representative will encourage a teacher to file a grievance will depend to a large extent on the building representative's relationship with the administration of the school.[103] A study of this relationship showed that building representatives who felt that the administration had not communicated with them sufficiently and had not consulted with them frequently enough in school decision making tended to file more teacher grievances than those building representatives who were satisfied with the communication and participation provided by the administration. A negative attitude by the building representative toward the administration was also likely to increase the number of teacher grievances filed. The main implication of this research is that the school principal would be well advised to develop a good working relationship with the building representative for teachers. A positive relationship may not prevent *all* grievances, but it should do much to reduce unnecessary ones.

If a teacher and the building representative decide to file a grievance, they should follow the procedures specified in the master contract, which usually include the following steps:[104]

1. The teacher submits his grievance directly to the principal, within five days after the teacher knows about or experiences the conditions giving rise to the grievance. (The time limitations specified in the contract may vary slightly from one district to another.)
2. If the grievance is not resolved to the satisfaction of the teacher within five days, the teacher can appeal the principal's decision to the superintendent or his representative.
3. Within five days of receipt of the written appeal, the superintendent or his representative, the teacher, and all other relevant parties, e.g., principal, building representative, meet in an attempt to resolve the matter. The administration must give its position on the grievance within five days after the meeting.
4. If the administration's response is not satisfactory to the teacher, he can appeal the matter to the school board. The school board or a subcommittee of the board then meets and must render a written decision within twenty days of the hearing.

Finally, arbitration by an outside agency may be part of the grievance procedure if the school board and the teachers have agreed to this previously, or if it is required by law. Nicholson and Simons provide a number of useful guidelines for minimizing problems in the area of grievance arbitration.[105]

The principal's role during grievance procedures, particularly in the initial stages, is crucial. Many, if not most grievances can be resolved at the building level without going through additional steps of appeal—*if* the school principal performs his role effectively. While his role will vary somewhat, depending on the specific circumstances, the principal should carry out the following steps in relation to grievance procedures.

1. **Study all the provisions of the master contract in order to understand them completely and accurately.** Resolving a teacher grievance will require that a principal possess a good understanding of the master contract. If he is not knowledgeable about the master contract, he may give the teacher an incorrect interpretation, or, worse yet, challenge a teacher's correct interpretation of the contract. During a grievance procedure the principal must be able to interpret the master contract correctly, and to do this, he must be knowledgeable about all aspects of that contract.

2. **If possible, attempt to resolve teacher concerns prior to their reaching the stage of formal grievances.** Many grievances can be resolved before they are formally filed with the principal of a school. A principal should try to be aware of teacher complaints and attempt to resolve them before they develop into formal grievances.

He should also attempt to be sensitive to the concerns of the teachers and make every feasible effort to improve working conditions and education in general in the building. These actions will not only help to reduce the number of grievances filed in a building but will also create a more positive attitude on the part of the teachers and the teachers' representative toward the principal if a situation ever reaches the formal grievance stage.

3. **The administrator should maintain his poise upon receiving a teacher grievance and no one should automatically assume that the filing of a grievance constitutes a personal attack on the administrator of the school.** If the principal views the grievance in personal terms, he is less likely to be objective in his response to it, and his emotions may adversely affect the possibility of successfully resolving the grievance. (It is recognized that in some instances the filing of a grievance *will* constitute a personal attack on the principal. However, even in these cases, becoming defensive is unlikely to contribute to the effective resolution of a grievance.)

Neither should the district administration and school board use the number of grievances filed in a school during the year as a major basis for evaluating a building administrator's effectiveness. A large number of grievances in a building could indicate something about a principal's effectiveness, but it may only reflect a very militant faculty in that particular building. Grievances are filed for many reasons, and more investigation and study will be needed before a fair conclusion can be reached about their relationship to administrator effectiveness.

It also needs to be recognized by administrators that grievances are not necessarily "bad." They can represent positive opportunities to correct misunderstandings and to improve school conditions.

4. **If a teacher's concern reaches the grievance stage, try to understand the grievance from the teacher's point of view.** This does not mean that a principal should necessarily agree with a teacher or forget that he is representing management during a grievance proceeding. However, if the principal is to avoid any invalid assumptions or interpretations about the teacher's grievance, he must do everything possible to understand how the teacher views the situation which caused the grievance. While this type of understanding may not in itself resolve the grievance, it will reduce unnecessary conflict and appeals of the principal's proposed resolution of the grievance and it should result in a more positive attitude on the part of the teacher toward the principal.

5. **Consult with the district administration if there is doubt about how to proceed before and during the grievance conference.** Usually someone in the district administration has the responsibility of helping principals when grievances arise. This individual can be a source of considerable assistance to the principal who is unsure about some aspect of the master contract or about what course of action he should take in trying to deal with a teacher's grievance. Consultation between the principal and the district administration when a grievance arises is usually desirable and sometimes essential for appropriate resolution of the grievance.

6. **Set a conducive atmosphere for communication during the grievance conference, and provide and seek information which will help both parties to decide on the best course of action to take.** The principal should try to provide a quiet, private setting for the grievance conference, and during that conference he should try to facilitate communication as much as possible. He should avoid interrupting the teacher or responding defensively. If appropriate, he should consider letting the teacher and the teacher's representative tell their view of the grievance first.

Under no circumstances should the principal attempt to negotiate with the teacher or make any precipitous decisions during the conference. The principal should offer whatever remedy is available under the master contract, but should not go beyond that. His basic task should be to provide and seek information that will enable him to make a proper decision on the disposition of the grievance, and that will give the teacher and the teacher's representative an adequate basis upon which to reach a decision about how they will proceed with the grievance.

7. **Give a response in writing to the teacher, concerning the disposition of the grievance after the conference(s).** The principal should not attempt to communicate to the teacher any final decision about the disposition of a grievance until there has been time after the grievance conference to think about the situation and, perhaps, to consult with the central administration. Then, when he has reached a final decision, it should be communicated in writing to the

teacher, in order to minimize any inadvertent or intentional misinterpretations of the principal's decision. A written record of the principal's disposition of a grievance could become very important should the teacher decide to appeal the decision.

8. **Make every effort to maintain a positive relationship with the teacher and the building representative, even if the grievance is appealed by the teacher to the principal's supervisor.** Obviously, this recommendation will frequently be difficult to implement. No one likes to have his decision challenged and appealed, and it would be perfectly normal for the principal to experience some negative feelings toward the teacher and the building representative if they should appeal his decision. However, the principal should remember that he will probably still be working with both of them long after the grievance is finally settled. For this reason, he should attempt to maintain as positive a relationship with the teacher and the building representative as possible during the appeal process, regardless of behavior on their part which may be upsetting to him at the time.

9. **Make sure that the solution is implemented fully, no matter what the final resolution of the teacher's grievance may be.** Regardless of whether the final resolution of the teacher's grievance supports or rejects the original decision by the principal, it is his responsibility to see that the solution is implemented promptly and fully. Lack of follow-through, particularly if the grievance is decided in favor of the teacher, can negatively affect relationships between the principal and other teachers and may result in future unnecessary grievances.

It is recognized that in some situations it may be difficult to implement all of the guidelines recommended. It is also conceded that there may be times when the grievance filed is frivolous or represents a personal attack on the administrator. Certainly, most grievances hold potential for being personally upsetting to an administrator. Nevertheless, it will be important in such situations for an administrator to maintain his poise and perspective, and to resist adopting the tactics of the other party or viewing the latter as an enemy. Such self-control may not come easily but it will be necessary in order to avoid exacerbating the problem.

THE ADMINISTRATOR'S ROLE IN A TEACHERS' STRIKE

Not all teacher grievances and collective bargaining can be resolved to the satisfaction of the teachers, and in some cases they may use the strike as their ultimate strategy for achieving their objectives. A study by the National Elementary Principals' Association found that about one-fifth of all the principals who participated in the study reported that they had been involved in a strike within the last five years.[106] Although binding arbitration of the issues unresolved by collective bargaining appears to be on the increase, strikes are likely to continue to occur, if for no other reason than a lack of total acceptance of the concept of binding arbitration, particularly by local school boards.[107]

Teachers' strikes usually put a severe strain on the relationship between the school administrator and the faculty. Unfortunately, the building administrator will in most cases be placed in an adversary relationship with teachers in the school. Although the building administrator may not be without sympathy for the teachers' cause, he will be expected by the school board and the district administration to represent management during the strike. Their main expectation for the principal will be that he carry out all the school board's directives, even if their implementation may impair his current or even future relationships with the staff.

Although the specific role of a school administrator in a teachers' strike will vary, depending on particular circumstances, it would appear that in most situations he will need the ability to anticipate problems accurately, to plan thoroughly, to be resourceful, and to maintain a sense of humor and perspective. In addition, the administrator's school system will (ideally) have developed a strike contingency plan which will provide guidance to the administrator during the pre-strike, strike and post-strike stages. (Examples of such plans are available from the American Association of School Administrators, Arlington, Va.) While the presentation of the many details of such a plan go beyond the intended scope of this text, the reader is referred to sources containing a number of excellent recommendations, largely from people who have been through a strike.[108]

Obviously, the various problems that may occur during a teachers' strike cannot always be accurately anticipated in advance. However, to the extent to which the administrator can accurately anticipate problems and plan thoroughly for avoiding or ameliorating problems, the strike is less likely to be a disruptive force. If unanticipated problems do occur during a teachers' strike, the administrator will be dependent on his ability to respond quickly to rapidly-moving events. Certainly, he should not act impetuously. But failure by the administrator to move quickly and imaginatively during a teachers' strike could put him on the defensive and limit his options. In many situations the administrator will need a high degree of resourcefulness if he is to avoid being overcome by events which he did not adequately anticipate.

Finally, the administrator will need to possess a good sense of humor and a long-range perspective, if he is to come through a strike successfully. Many events during the strike will be frustrating and irritating to him.[109] Teachers' motives may seem questionable, and it may be difficult not to perceive the teachers and anybody who agrees with them as "the enemy." Nevertheless, the administrator should avoid taking himself too seriously or questioning the motives of others.

He should, of course, do whatever he thinks is right in a strike situation, but before he acts, he should remember that he will still need to work with many of those same teachers long after the strike has been terminated. While he may be forced during the strike to take steps that will temporarily impair his relationship with them, he should refrain as much as possible from taking action which will permanently make it difficult to work successfully with the faculty after the strike.

A FINAL PERSPECTIVE

With the advent of collective bargaining and grievance procedures, the relationship between the school administrator and the staff has changed. The relationship is now frequently a frustrating and uneasy one in which both the administrator and the staff are unsure of each other's intentions and reliability. As a result, polarization and conflict between the administrator and the staff have increased in many schools.

Despite the frustrating and irritating aspects of some staff actions, the administrator should not forget that the staff represents the most important resource in the school for helping to educate students, and without its support and commitment there is very little the administrator will be able to accomplish in regard to bringing about educational improvement. Therefore, the administrator needs to work to build and maintain high staff satisfaction and morale without becoming disillusioned or bitter when members of the staff behave in ways which the administrator feels are undesirable. This obviously will not always be easy but will be necessary for a cooperative, productive relationship.

Review and Learning Activities

1. Why are high staff morale and satisfaction thought to be important in personnel relations? When would high staff satisfaction and morale be undesirable, and how should the administrator respond?
2. What are the implications for the administrator of each of the theories of satisfaction, morale, or motivation presented in the text?
3. Assess proposed programs to deal with employee dissatisfaction and low morale. Indicate how you would change current staff personnel practices in your school as a result of the research on the extent, symptoms, and possible causes of staff dissatisfaction and low morale.
4. What is the role of the principal in the collective bargaining process in your school district? Is that role capitalizing sufficiently on the contributions that principals could make to this process?

5. What should be the role of the building administrator in administering the master contract? What problems might be encountered, and how should these problems be approached?
6. Discuss those factors that may influence a teacher with regard to whether or not a grievance is filed. What should be the role of the administrator in responding to a grievance?
7. Identify those characteristics an administrator should possess before, during, and after a strike.

Notes

1. G. Strauss, "Job Satisfaction, Motivation and Job Redesign," in *Organizational Behavior: Research and Issues,* eds. G. Strauss, R. E. Miles and A. S. Tannenbaum. (Madison, Wis.: Industrial Relations Research Association, 1974), pp. 19–49.
2. Neal Gross and Robert E. Herriott, *Staff Leadership in Public Schools: A Sociological Inquiry* (New York: John Wiley & Sons, 1965), p. 35.
3. J. F. Cooper, *The Relationship of Morale and Productivity: An Historical Overview.* ERIC Report: Ed–147–985.
4. Richard A. Gorton, "Job Satisfaction and Morale," in *Encyclopedia of Educational Research,* ed. Harold Mitzel (New York: Macmillan, 1982). A major portion of this section on staff satisfaction and morale has been adapted from this source.
5. Ibid.
6. D. McGregor, *The Human Side of Enterprise* (New York: McGraw Hill, 1960), pp. 33–34, 47–48.
7. A. H. Maslow, *Motivation and Personality* (New York: Harper & Row, 1970).
8. M. A. Wahba and L. G. Bridwell, "Maslow Reconsidered: A Review of Research on the Need Hierarchy Theory," *Organizational Behavior and Human Performance* (April 1976): 112–40.
9. L. W. Porter, "A Study of Perceived Need Satisfaction in Bottom and Middle Management Jobs," *Journal of Applied Psychology* (1961): 1–10.
10. For example, see G. Goldsberry, R. Henderson, and T. J. Sergiovanni, *Perceived Need Deficiencies of Teachers in 1978 as Compared with 1968.* (Urbana, Ill.: Department of Educational Administration and Supervision, University of Illinois, Urbana-Champaign, 1978.)
11. David W. Chapman and Malcolm A. Lowther, "Teachers' Satisfaction with Teaching" (Paper presented at the annual meeting of the American Educational Research Association, Los Angeles, 1981).
12. T. J. Sergiovanni and F. D. Carver, *The New School Executive: A Theory of Administration* (New York: Harper & Row, 1973).
13. Ibid., pp. 8–9.
14. Ibid, p. 12.
15. Frederick Herzberg et al., *The Motivation to Work* (New York: John Wiley & Sons, 1959), p. 114.
16. Thomas Sergiovanni, "Factors Which Affect Satisfaction and Dissatisfaction of Teachers," *Journal of Educational Administration* (May 1967): 66–82.
17. W. K. Hoy and C. G. Miskel, *Educational Administration: Theory, Research and Practice* (New York: Random House, 1978.)
18. C. Argyris, *Personality and Organization* (New York: Harper & Bros., 1957).
19. V. R. Vroom, *Work and Motivation* (New York: Wiley, 1964.)

20. R. Fuller and C. Miskel, "Work Attachments and Job Satisfaction Among Public School Educators" (Paper presented at the annual meeting of the American Educational Research Association, Chicago, 1972).

21. M. M. Bentzen, R. C. Williams, and P. Heckman, "A Study of Schooling: Adult Experiences in Schools," *The Kappan* (February 1980): 394–97.

22. "Teacher Opinion Poll: Job Satisfaction," *Today's Education* (November/December 1980): 8.

23. D. H. Cook, "Teacher Morale: Symptoms, Diagnosis and Prescription," *Clearing House* (April 1979): 355–58.

24. Educational Research Service, *Employee Absenteeism: A Summary of Research* (Arlington, Va.: Educational Research Service, 1980).

25. E. Klugman et al., *Too Many Pieces: A Study of Teacher Fragmentation in the Elementary School.* An ERIC Report: Ed–178–515.

26. J. C. Stapleton, J. C. Croft, and R. G. Frankiewicz, "The Relationship between Teacher Brinkmanship and Teacher Job Satisfaction," *Planning and Changing* (Fall 1979): 157–68.

27. A. Werner, "Support for Teachers in Stress," *The Pointer* (Winter 1980): 54–60.

28. C. Maslach, "Job Burn-out: How People Cope," *Public Welfare* (1978): 56–58.

29. Edward F. Iwanicki and Richard L. Schwab, "A Cross Validation Study of the Maslach Burnout Inventory" (Paper presented at the annual meeting of the American Educational Research Association, Los Angeles, 1981).

30. D. Walsh, "Classroom Stress and Teacher Burn-out," *The Kappan* (December 1979): 253.

31. C. Maslach and S. Jackson, "The Measurement of Experienced Burn-out" (Unpublished research report, Department of Psychology, University of California, Berkeley, 1979).

32. American Academy of Family Physicians, *Lifestyle/Personal Health Care in Different Occupations: A Study of Attitudes and Practices* (Kansas City: American Academy of Family Physicians, 1979).

33. D. E. Girdano and G. S. Everly, *Controlling Stress and Tension* (Englewood Cliffs, N.J.: Prentice-Hall, 1979).

34. J. C. Quick and J. D. Quick, "Reducing Stress Through Preventative Management," *Human Resources Management* (Fall 1979): 15–22.

35. "Urban Teachers Report More Stress," *Compact* (Spring 1980): 61–64.

36. Fred C. Feitler and Edward B. Tokar, "Teacher Stress: Sources, Symptoms and Job Satisfaction" (Paper presented at the annual meeting of the American Educational Research Association, Los Angeles, 1981).

37. D. J. Cichon and R. Koff, "Stress and Teaching," *NASSP Bulletin* (March 1980): 91–103.

38. "Teacher Opinion Poll: Attacks on Teachers," *Today's Education* (September/October 1980): 21.

39. Richard L. Schwab and Edward F. Iwanicki, "The Effect of Role Conflict and Role Ambiguity on Perceived Levels of Teacher Burn-out" (Paper presented at the annual meeting of the American Educational Research Association, Los Angeles, 1981).

40. Mary B. Anderson and Edward F. Iwanicki, "The Burn-out Syndrome and Its Relationship to Teacher Motivation" (Paper presented at the annual meeting of the American Educational Research Association, Los Angeles, 1981).

41. Jim Sweeney, "Responsibilities and Fulfillment of Needs—Burn-out Remedies?" *The Kappan* (May 1981): 676.

42. P. Bardo, "The Pain of Teacher Burn-out: A Case History," *The Kappan* (December 1979): 252–53.

43. "Teacher Opinion Poll: Job Satisfaction."

44. J. D. Ford, "Faculty Workload in Public Schools," *Journal of Thought* (January 1979): 15–16.

45. G. V. Glass, L. S. Cahen, M. L. Smith, and N. N. Filby, "Class Size and Learning—New Interpretations of the Research Literature," *Today's Education* (April/May 1979): 42–44.

46. D. W. Chapman and S. M. Hutcheson, *Attrition from Teaching Careers: A Discriminant Analysis* (School of Education, State University of New York at Albany, 1980).

47. S. Pagel and J. Price, "Strategies to Alleviate Teacher Stress," *The Pointer* (Winter 1980): 45–53.

48. Carol M. Kulpa and Jean A. Steitz, "Powerlessness, Job Satisfaction and Teachers' Perception of Administrative Management" (Paper presented at the annual meeting of the American Educational Research Association, Los Angeles, 1981).

49. T. G. Schackmuth, "Creating Job Satisfaction in a Static Teacher Market," *Clearing House* (January 1979): 229–32.

50. J. F. Rugus and M. Martin, "The Principal and Staff Development: Countering the School Culture," *Clearing House* (September 1979): 27–31.

51. E. Bredo, "Collaborative Relations Among Elementary School Teachers," *Sociology of Education* (October 1977): 300–309.

52. S. B. Sarason, *The Culture of the School and the Problem of Change* (Boston: Allyn & Bacon, 1971).

53. D. C. Lortie, *Schoolteacher: A Sociological Study* (Chicago: University of Chicago Press, 1975).

54. P. M. Blau and W. R. Scott, *Formal Organizations: A Comparative Approach* (San Francisco: Chandler, 1962).

55. R. G. Corwin, "Professional Persons in Public Organizations," *Educational Administration Quarterly* (1965): 1–15.

56. A. J. DeYoung, "Professionalism and Politics: Toward a More Realistic Assessment of the Issue," *Clearing House* (February 1980): 268–70.

57. R. Reineke and W. Welsh, *Adequacy of Teaching Conditions as Perceived by Administrators and Teachers* (Washington, D.C.: National Science Foundation, 1975).

58. W. Sandefur and H. W. Smith, "A Comparison of the Perceptions of Classroom Teachers and Principals in Texas Concerning the Instructional Problems of Teachers," *Texas Study of Secondary Education Research Journal* (Fall 1979–80): 11–13.

59. F. R. Ignatovich, P. A. Cusick, and J. E. Ray, *Value/Belief Patterns of Teachers and Those Administrators Engaged in Attempts to Influence Teaching*. An ERIC Report: Ed–181–007.

60. J. Sweeny, "Principals versus Teachers: Where Will We Bury the Victims?" *Clearing House* (1980): 309–11.

61. M. S. Patton and C. Miskel, "Public School Districts' Bureaucracy Level and Teachers' Work Motivation Attitudes" (Paper presented at the annual meeting of the American Research Association, Washington, D.C., 1975).

62. C. G. Miskel, R. Fevurly, and J. Stewart, "Organizational Structure and Processes, Perceived School Effectiveness, Loyalty, and Job Satisfaction," *Educational Administration Quarterly* (Fall 1979): 97–118.

63. Schackmuth, "Creating Job Satisfaction."

64. J. S. Packard, "A Questionnaire Method for Measuring the Autonomy/Equality Norm" (Paper presented at the annual meeting of the American Educational Research Association, San Francisco, 1976).

65. P. E. Weiskopf, "Burn-out Among Teachers of Exceptional Children," *Exceptional Children* (September 1980): 18–23.

66. Pagel and Price, "Strategies to Alleviate Teacher Stress."

67. Cichon and Koff, "Stress and Teaching."

68. Werner, "Support for Teachers in Stress."

69. A. G. Boudewyn, "The Open Meeting in a Confidential Forum for Employees," *Personnel Journal* (April 1977): 192–94.

70. Alfred S. Alschuler, *Teacher Burn-out* (Washington, D.C.: National Education Association, 1980).

71. Patricia Hanley and Kevin J. Swick, *Stress and the Classroom Teacher* (Washington, D.C.: National Education Association, 1980.)

72. E. M. Duncan, *Task and Employee Oriented Styles of Behavior in Selected Minnesota School Administrators*. An ERIC Report: Ed–116–279. Also see Martha Leveilbe, "Characteristics of High and Low Teacher Morale" (Ed.D. dissertation, University of Southern California, 1981).

73. E. B. Ingle and R. E. Munsterman, "Relationship of Values to Group Satisfaction" (Paper presented at the annual meeting of the American Educational Research Association, New York, 1977).

74. P. Degenfelder, "Managing Motivation," *Planning and Changing* (Spring 1979): 7–11.

75. D. L. Duke, B. K. Showers, and M. Imber, "Teachers and Shared Decision Making: The Costs and Benefits of Involvement," *Educational Administration Quarterly* (Winter 1980): 93–106.

76. D. W. Spuck, "Reward Structures in the Public Schools," *Educational Administration Quarterly* (1974): 18–34.

77. Lortie, "Schoolteacher."

78. David W. Chapman and Malcolm A. Lowther, "Teachers' Satisfaction with Teaching" (Paper presented at the annual meeting of the American Educational Research Association, Los Angeles, 1981).

79. L. G. Miller and J. Swick, "Community Incentives for Teacher Excellence," *Education* (Spring 1976): 235–37.

80. "Teachers Have Their Day in Iowa Community," *Education U.S.A.* (July 21, 1980): 348.

81. Fuller and Miskel, "Work Attachments."

82. R. A. McDonald, "A Study of the Intrinsic Reward Structure of the Classroom for the Teacher" (Diss., University of Toronto, 1978).

83. Frederick L. Redefer, "Factors That Affect Teacher Morale," *Nation's Schools* (February 1959): 59–62.

84. Harold Leiman, "A Study of Teacher Attitudes and Morale as Related to Participation in Administration" (Ph.D. diss., New York University, 1961). For more recent research on this point, see Michael Buckley, "The Relationship of Philosophical Orientation, Participation in Decision Making, and Degree of Fulfillment of Expectations about Participation in Decision Making to Elementary School Teachers' Attitudes toward Leaders, Leader-Teacher Interaction and Membership in the Organization" (Ph.D. diss., University of Connecticut, 1981).

85. Richard A. Gorton, *School Administration and Supervision: Important Issues, Concepts and Case Studies* (Dubuque, Iowa; Wm. C. Brown Company Publishers, 1980), chapter 8.

86. C. E. Blocker and R. C. Richardson, "Twenty-five Years of Morale Research—A Critical Review," *Journal of Educational Sociology* (January 1963): 200–210. For more recent research on this point, see Bruce Q. Buerkens, "The Relationship between Job Satisfaction of School Teachers and Their Perceived Conflicts with School Officials, Principals, Other Teachers, and Parents" (Ed.D. diss., University of Missouri, 1973).

87. First National City Bank, *Public Education in New York City* (New York City: First National City Bank, 1969).

88. Thomas W. George, "The Principal and Collective Negotiations," in *The School Principal and the Law*, ed. Ralph Stern (Topeka: National Organization on Legal Problems of Education, 1978).

89. Richard C. Williams, "The Impact of Collective Bargaining on the Principal: What Do We Know?" *Education and Urban Society* (February 1979): 168–80.

90. C. Taylor Whittier, "Intervention between Administrators and Teachers," *Educational Leadership* (October 1969): 44–47.

91. Benjamin Epstein, *The Principal's Role in Collective Negotiations between Teachers and School Boards* (Washington, D.C.: The National Association of Secondary School Principals, 1965.), p. 6.

92. See, for example, Department of Elementary School Principals, *Professional Negotiations and the Principalship* (Washington, D.C.: Department of Elementary School Principals, 1969), p. 126. See also, "Proposed 1970 Resolutions," *National Elementary Principal* (February 1970): 64–65.

93. See John A. Thompson, "The Principal's Role in Collective Negotiations between Teachers and School Boards (Ph.D. diss., University of Wisconsin, 1968). For a somewhat more positive but generally similar perception of the role of the principal in collective negotiations, see Stephen Milton Poort, "Attitudes of Selected Kansas Superintendents, Principals, and Teachers toward the Involvement of Principals in a Collective Negotiations Environment" (Ed.D. diss., University of Kansas, 1968).

94. John F. Neill, "The Principal's Role in Collective Bargaining" (Paper presented to the Congress on Education at Toronto, Ontario, 1978).

95. William E. Caldwell, "Perceived Job Satisfaction of Secondary School Principals as Related to the Collective Bargaining Process" (Paper presented at the annual meeting of the American Educational Research Association, Los Angeles, 1981).

96. Raymond R. Troxell, "What Are the Ingredients of Successful Negotiations?" *NASSP Bulletin* (January 1977): 105.

97. Gregory Benson, *The Principal and Contract Management*. An ERIC Report: Ed–175–151.

98. For the total report of this study, see Frank W. Lutz and Seymour Evans, *The Union and Principal Leadership in New York City Schools.* An ERIC Report: Ed–029–400. For later studies on the topic, see Susan Moore Johnson, "Collective Bargaining and Leadership," *R and D Perspectives, University of Oregon* (Summer 1981): 3.

99. William Caldwell and James Easton, "The Relationship between the Superintendents' Management Behavior and Teachers' Perceptions of the Principal's Rule Administration Behavior" (Paper presented at the American Educational Research Association annual meeting, 1974).

100. National Education Association of the United States, *Addresses and Proceedings of the One Hundred and Fifth Annual Meeting* (Washington, D.C.: National Education Association, 1967), p. 500.

101. Marc Gaswirth, *Administering the Negotiated Agreement* (Trenton, N. J.: New Jersey School Boards Association, 1980), chapter 1.

102. Ibid, chapter 2.

103. Allan M. Glassman and James Belasco, "Grievance Procedures in Public Education: An Empirical Case Study" (Paper presented at the annual meeting of the American Education Research Association, 1972). Also see Estella Gahala, "An Ethnocentrific Study of Grievance Handling Procedures by Principals and Teachers' Association Representatives" (Ph.D. diss., Northwestern University, 1980).

104. Adapted in part from William Smith, "Coping with Grievances: Guidelines for Administrators," *NASSP Bulletin* (May 1981): 80–83.

105. Everett W. Nicholson and Philip D. Simons, "School District Defenses Used in Grievance Arbitrations," *NASSP Bulletin* (December 1978): 95–100.

106. *National Elementary Principals' Study* (Arlington, Va.: National Elementary School Principals Association, 1979), p. 91.

107. "Interest Arbitration," *Education USA* (January 26, 1980): 169.

108. Samuel L. Dolnick, "What to Do in the Event of a Strike," in *The School Principal and the Law*, ed. R. D. Stern (Topeka: National Organization on Legal Problems in Education, 1978); Robert Heller, "The Principal's Role in Planning for a Teacher's Strike," *NASSP Bulletin* (May 1978) 98–105; Contingency Planning for Teacher Strikes (Arlington, Va.: Educational Research Service, 1976.)

109. J. M. Gonroff, "The Effects of a Teachers' Strike on Principal Behavior," *Texas Study of Secondary Education Research Journal* (Fall 1979–80): 45–48.

10

Staff Evaluation

Staff evaluation and supervision represent two interdependent means for improving the professional resources of a school. Staff evaluation is a process whereby the strengths and limitations of an individual or group are identified and defined. Supervision is a process designed to capitalize on the strengths and correct the weakness of an individual or group.

Evaluation and supervision are interdependent, in that one cannot usually achieve maximum effectiveness without the other.[1] Staff evaluation without supervision can lead to anxiety, frustration, and resistance on the part of the recipient of the evaluation. The individual or group may have been informed through evaluation about certain areas which need to be improved but, in the absence of appropriate follow-up supervision, may not be able to remedy the deficiencies. On the other hand, staff supervision without adequate prior evaluation tends to lack focus and is often misdirected. The individual (or group) in such a situation is the recipient of assistance which is not based on an accurate diagnosis of need and, as a result, is not likely to accept or profit from the supervision. Because of a continuing concern on the part of the public about teacher competency, administrators will be expected to give a high priority to staff evaluation and supervision.

In the sections that follow, various aspects of staff evaluation will be discussed; the next chapter will focus on staff supervision.

PROGRAM CHARACTERISTICS

There is no uniform program of staff evaluation which operates in all school districts. However, there are some basic program characteristics which most districts share in common.

The staff evaluation program in most districts is formally designed, that is, its purposes, procedures, and schedules are usually officially established, and approved by the school board. The main purposes of the program are to identify needs for staff supervision and to reach a determination on whether staff, particularly new members, should be retained or dismissed.[2] These purposes are realized through a process of evaluating the staff on the extent to which they meet criteria for effectiveness, as previously defined by the district.

The typical evaluation program is usually initiated in the late spring or early fall in every building in the district and is conducted by the principal, perhaps with the assistance of another administrator or supervisor. The principal visits the classroom of each staff member who is to be evaluated during the year, and then holds an individual follow-up conference to present and discuss observations and conclusions. During the conference the principal reviews with the staff member the district's rating scale on which the principal has recorded her evaluation of the strengths and weaknesses of the individual. The rating scale, along with comments and recommendations, forms the basis for identifying needs for supervision and for reaching a determination on whether or not a staff member should be retained for the following year.

An example of the type of rating scale used in many school districts is presented in figure 10.1. (It should be noted that the instrument presented in figure 10.1 was developed after an examination of many districts' teacher evaluation forms and does not represent any one *particular* district.)

Teacher Rating Form

Instructions: Please evaluate the teacher on the following characteristics. The evaluation should take place on the basis of classroom observation and a follow-up conference.

Characteristics (Check appropriate space)

Personal Factors	*Outstanding*	*Satisfactory*	*Unsatisfactory*
Appearance	_____	_____	_____
Cooperation	_____	_____	_____
Sense of humor	_____	_____	_____
Tactfulness	_____	_____	_____
Health	_____	_____	_____
Attendance and punctuality	_____	_____	_____

Comments _____

Professional Factors			
Flexibility	_____	_____	_____
Loyalty to school system	_____	_____	_____

(continued)

Figure 10.1. A Sample District Evaluation Instrument

Professional Factors	Outstanding	Satisfactory	Unsatisfactory
Judgment	————	————	————
Professional ethics	————	————	————
Rapport with staff	————	————	————
Rapport with students	————	————	————
Rapport with parents	————	————	————

Comments _____

_____

*Teaching Performance and
Classroom Management*

	Outstanding	Satisfactory	Unsatisfactory
Classroom organization and appearance	————	————	————
Mastery of subject matter	————	————	————
Teaching techniques	————	————	————
Command of English language	————	————	————
Reports and records	————	————	————

Comments _____

_____ Teacher's Signature (Does not indicate approval of evaluation,
                       only that teacher has reviewed the evaluation with the principal.)
_____ Principal's Signature
_____ Date
cc: Personnel File

Figure 10.1. Continued

A number of questions could be raised about the validity and reliability of the factors included in the sample district evaluation instrument and about the format of the instrument itself. As Cook and Richards point out, such teacher ratings may ". . . reflect the expectations of the evaluator more than the actions of the teacher."[3] However, the purpose of presenting the sample at this stage is only to show the type of rating instrument that is frequently used in staff evaluation. More will be said later about the *desired* composition and format of a staff evaluation instrument.

STAFF EVALUATION: PROBLEMS, ISSUES AND RECOMMENDATIONS FOR IMPROVEMENT

It would appear that the staff evaluation program is perceived by many teachers and administrators as a "mixed blessing."[4] Most teachers and administrators accept evaluation as inevitable and potentially valuable, but many question its usefulness and value in practice because of the presence of certain basic problems and issues that will be discussed shortly.[5] These problems and issues do not, of course, exist in all schools, but wherever they are prevalent, they impair the usefulness of the staff evaluation program. The point that needs to be emphasized, however, is that they are not inevitable or irresolvable. The administrator can, by concentrating on developing a better understanding of the problems and issues associated with staff evaluation, and by initiating needed reforms, maintain an effective program of staff evaluation. (Moreover, the public's emphasis on school accountability will undoubtedly require school administrators to give a high priority to maintaining such a program.) Both of these aspects will be addressed on the following sections. Basic problems and issues of staff evaluation will first be presented, followed in each case with specific recommendations for improvement. The recommendations, included for the purpose of stimulating thought and discussion, are not intended to represent prescriptions for success or leave the impression that they represent the only alternatives for improving teacher evaluation. It is hoped that, after reflecting on and discussing the ideas presented in the following sections, school administrators and other concerned parties will view the various problems and issues as challenges and opportunities for leadership.

PURPOSES

As indicated previously, the main purposes of the district evaluation program are (1) to identify needs for supervisory assistance and (2) to reach a determination about whether or not a staff member should be retained or dismissed.

In the eyes of many teachers, these objectives are incompatible and in direct conflict. To achieve the first objective, staff members should be open, candid, and cooperative about revealing or confirming their limitations with the administrator. On the other hand, however, if staff members want to be retained or promoted, they will naturally want to be seen in the best light, and it may be to their disadvantage to willingly reveal their limitations or confirm the perceptions of the administrator about specific deficiencies.

Several consequences can result from this conflict in the purposes of the district's staff evaluation program. First of all, achieving the objective of identifying needs for supervisory assistance is impaired because of the reluctance of staff members to identify their weaknesses, for fear that they won't be retained or promoted.

Secondly, since many staff members feel that there are risks to participating cooperatively in the district's evaluation program, they tend to fall back on informal evaluation by their colleagues. While informal evaluation can be helpful, its effectiveness is limited by its sporadic and isolated nature. The one important advantage of colleague evaluation is that it typically possesses few risks for the staff member being evaluated, and it can give a teacher assistance which he may not be receiving from the district evaluation program. (Drummond discusses such a program in the *National Elementary Principal*, Vol. 52, #5, pp. 30–32.)

A third consequence of conflict in the purposes of the district evaluation program is that it has a poor image in the eyes of many teachers. They view the program as threatening, punitive, of little help, and not in their best interests. Consequently, they are often not very receptive to attempts by administrators to evaluate them.

If administrators are to avoid these consequences, they will need to concentrate on resolving the apparent conflict in purposes in many staff evaluation programs.

> **Recommendation:** The two main purposes of the staff evaluation program should be separated to the extent possible through the use of separate personnel.

The primary problem associated with the purposes of staff evaluation is that the use of evaluation as a basis for personnel decisions, such as dismissal or promotion, is viewed by many teachers as antithetical to the objective of using evaluation as a means for improving an individual's performance. Compounding the problem is the fact that in most schools the administrator is placed in the position of conducting both kinds of evaluation.

One solution is to utilize different personnel in order to accomplish each purpose. An example of this approach is the teacher evaluation program at Newport-Mesa, a unified school district in southern California.[6] In this district the principal, aided by representatives from the staff, evaluates the teacher in regard to the degree to which he has achieved predetermined student learning objectives, and this evaluation becomes the basis for personnel decisions such as teacher retention or promotion. Evaluation for the purpose of staff improvement, however, is separated entirely from the purpose and process just described, and is carried out by a team of colleagues who observe the teacher and work with him on self-improvement activities. The principal is not involved at all in evaluating for improvement; the perceptions and judgments made by the team of teachers are not communicated to her nor are they used for decisions related to retention or salary increase.

A disadvantage of this approach is that it appears to exclude the school administrator and her insights from the use of evaluation for staff improvement. However, it is possible that an administrator cannot reasonably expect the staff to respond openly and candidly if she attempts to evaluate them in order to identify areas for self-improvement *and* as a basis for making crucial personnel decisions. One feasible solution seems to be the separation of those two purposes and the designation of different people to accomplish each. McGee and Eaker describe one apparently useful peer approach in the 49th volume, issue #1 of *Contemporary Education.*

STAFF INVOLVEMENT

A major complaint of many teachers is that they have not been involved to any significant degree in the development of the district staff evaluation program, particularly as it relates to criteria and process of evaluation. As a result the evaluative criteria and procedures designed by the administrators in such a district do not reflect teachers' ideas. In such situations the professional staff members are being evaluated by criteria and a process on which they had little to say and about which they may disagree.

The consequences of a lack of staff involvement in developing evaluation criteria and procedures can be deleterious to efforts by a school administrator to suggest improvements to the faculty. If the staff members have not participated in the development of the evaluation criteria and process, the likelihood is increased that many of them won't accept or be receptive to either. Also, there is evidence that if the staff is not sufficiently involved, teachers could begin to pressure for negotiating into the master contract their involvement.[7]

Recommendation: Staff members need to be involved in the formulation, assessment, and appropriate revision of the total district evaluation program, including the definition of evaluative purposes, criteria, and procedures.

To facilitate acceptance of the district's evaluation program and to improve the program, the staff members themselves need to be involved by the school administrator in developing, assessing, and revising the program. (The key word in this recommendation is *involvement;* the administration and the school board should retain final authority in these matters.) To implement this idea, the administrator should establish a standing committee of the faculty to examine the present evaluation program and to suggest revisions. The committee should be composed of nontenured as well as tenured teachers, and the administrator should chair the committee. Its recommendations would probably be only advisory to the central office, but if its members did their homework, the committee could be a powerful force for changing and improving the staff evaluation program in the district. Part of its function should be to secure periodic and systematic feedback from the entire staff on the perceived strengths and weaknesses of the evaluation program, with recommendations for improvement. The alternative to encouraging this kind of voluntary involvement could be *required* involvement negotiated by the teachers through collective bargaining.

SELF-ASSESSMENT

The primary emphasis in many school districts' evaluation programs appears to be on external evaluation. With few exceptions, little attention is given in the evaluation plan to the need for teachers to engage in *self*-evaluation (as well as external evaluation) for professional growth. The implicit assumption seems to be that teachers are either unwilling or unable to participate in a program of self-evaluation. It is also possible that administrators in these districts feel that the perceptions of teachers about their strengths and limitations are not important.

Recommendation: The staff evaluation program needs to emphasize self-evaluation as much as external evaluation by the administrator.

All teachers to be evaluated by the administrator should be given the opportunity to evaluate themselves on the criteria used by the district. If the other recommendations in this chapter are implemented, then the administration should have the trust and confidence of the teachers, necessary prerequisites for any program of self-evaluation. In-service training to help the teachers become more competent and objective in analyzing their behavior may also be necessary.

Ideally, teachers would be engaged continuously in self-evaluation, but formal efforts in this regard should begin at and proceed through the same time period during which the administrator is conducting evaluations of the teachers. At the end of the self-evaluation process, a teacher's evaluative perceptions should be shared with the administrator who, in turn, should discuss her perceptions with the teacher. As a result of this sharing of evaluative data, the principal or the teacher, or both, may decide to revise the original perceptions and conclusions or engage in further investigation and analysis.

The potential advantages resulting from self-evaluation as a parallel activity to external evaluation are (1) a lessening of defensiveness by teachers regarding evaluation, and (2) the identification of areas in need of improvement and/or strengths which external evaluation might not ascertain. However, whether teachers would be willing and able to engage in a program of self-evaluation for professional growth would appear to depend on their degree of trust and confidence in the administration, and the extent to which the administration has provided in-service training for the teachers to help them become more competent and objective in analyzing their own behavior. If these conditions can be met, then self-evaluation by teachers can and should be a valuable activity for teachers and administrators alike. (Busmann describes three self-evaluation systems for teachers, in *The Bulletin* of the National Association of Secondary School Principals, Vol. 58, pp. 25–37.)

EVALUATION CRITERIA

The selection of criteria to be used for staff evaluation is undoubtedly one of the most important decisions in designing an evaluation program. The criteria are standards against which the teachers are to be evaluated and can usually be found in the district's instrument for evaluating members of the staff.

The question that many teachers raise about a district's evaluation form is, to what extent are the criteria presented based on personal preference, and to what degree are they based on research which supports their importance in teaching effectiveness and student learning? Although the answer to this question may vary, depending on the school district, it would appear from an examination of numerous evaluation forms that the selection of criteria is based more on personal preference than on any research evidence or theoretical foundation.[8]

Part of the problem is that administrators who select the staff evaluation criteria frequently have not adequately investigated the research on teacher effectiveness. However, another equally important aspect is the likelihood that uniform criteria penalize teachers with different personalities who can teach effectively with different classes, using different methods and/or materials, under different classroom conditions.[9] If true, then there should either be different evaluation criteria for different teachers and situations, or the criteria should emphasize the outcomes of teaching more than the personality of the teacher or the process of teaching.[10]

In any regard, the administrator needs to realize that, to a large extent, the criteria used in the district evaluation program are probably based more on personal preference than on research or theory. The disadvantages of this subjective approach to teacher evaluation were pointed out by Medley who found in his studies that, "teachers who looked most effective to supervisors were not actually the most effective in helping pupils learn."[11]

> **Recommendation:** The staff evaluation criteria and evaluation instrument should be based primarily on research on teacher effectiveness rather than on personal preference.

To implement this recommendation, the school administrator with appropriate staff involvement will need to investigate the research on teacher effectiveness and then propose to the central office a revision in staff evaluation criteria that will be based more on research and less on personal preference. This does not mean that the criteria cannot reflect some philosophical orientation, but it is recommended that the majority of the criteria should not rest on that subjective foundation.

It is recognized that for the most part research has not been very productive in identifying the characteristics of effective teachers. As Bloom has noted, "In general, the relationship between teacher characteristics and student learning has typically been represented by correlations of less than +.20. [Therefore] we may conclude that the characteristics of teachers have little to do with the learning of students."[12] On the other hand, there have been some major breakthroughs when the focus has been on the *behavior* of teachers, meriting the administrator's consideration.

For example, several studies have shown that effective teachers demonstrate the following behaviors to a far greater degree than do ineffective teachers.[13]

1. Ascertain current skill level and level of knowledge and understanding of students before establishing learning objectives and assigning work.
2. Set and articulate specific learning goals for each lesson.
3. Plan carefully and thoroughly for each lesson, taking into consideration students' needs and involving them in planning when appropriate and feasible.
4. Make presentations at the most appropriate level of difficulty for most pupils.
5. Assign tasks to students appropriate to their ability level so that chances of success are high and failures low.
6. Spend more time than ineffective teachers on the actual task of teaching. Spend more time structuring the lesson, giving directions, clarifying what needs to be learned, and how best to perform the work and illustrating how to do the assigned work.
7. Assess regularly student progress.
8. Keep students focussed on and engaged in the task at hand.

9. Provide regular feedback to students which informs them of their progress and indicates how they can improve.
10. Reinforce correct student behavior and responses with positive rewards, e.g., teacher praise.

While it might appear from an examination of this list of behaviors that what is being described is the "super teacher," such is not the case. As Salganik has emphasized, "Contrary to popular myths, most teachers at schools that are effective are not charismatic figures generating unforgettable experiences. They are simply hard-working, organized teachers moving crisply through a well-planned day."[14]

It should be pointed out that most of these behaviors of effective teachers that have been identified in this section have been categorized under the term, "direct instruction," which stresses being well-organized and task-oriented.[15] However, it has been observed that "direct instruction" may not be appropriate for all kinds of teaching situations. Peterson feels that the central question is, "For what educational outcomes is direct instruction most effective, and for what kinds of students?"[16] She seems to believe that direct instruction is most effective if one intends to teach *basic skills,* but it may not be as effective in teaching, for example, inquiry skills. Also, she asserts that direct instruction may be less effective in working with high-ability students who may need less direction, than with average and low ability students. Perhaps Rouk expressed it best: "Teaching strategies and methods that work best with all pupils all the time simply don't exist."[17] Nevertheless, the research reviewed for this section strongly suggests that the teaching behaviors previously identified are associated with effective teaching in most situations.

One of the more important variables which research has shown to be associated with increased learning is "academic learning time" (ALT).[18] ALT is the time that a student actually pays attention to and is engaged in the task of learning. Therefore, teaching styles or behavior which involve the student in the task of learning and *keep* the student engaged are likely to be effective in increasing student learning. In the implementation of ALT it is important to avoid extreme teaching styles. As one researcher noted, "A student's ALT falls off when classrooms are too casual and nondirective, and ALT also falls off when schools are too authoritarian."[19] (Stallings emphasizes that student learning depends not just on how much time is devoted to it in the classroom, but *how* the teacher structures the time. See *Educational Researcher,* December 1980.)

While it might appear that the teacher's *behavior* is the only critical variable associated with effective teaching (and clearly, it is the most important variable), the *attitude* of the teacher about his subject matter and toward students is also very important. Teachers who believe strongly that instructing students in the curriculum of the school is basic to their role and who believe that the students under their charge *are* capable of learning new skills or subject matter are more likely to be successful in increasing student learning.[20] That students are also interested in this type of teacher is supported by Sabine's study which found that students felt that the two most important characteristics of a teacher were (1) that the teacher was "demanding," and (2) that the teacher cared.[21] Apparently most students want a teacher who will not only challenge them and make them work, but will also be interested in them as individuals. Certainly, teacher attitude about teaching and students is a crucial variable which is likely to influence a teacher's predisposition and decision to utilize those behaviors previously identified as associated with effective teaching.[22]

From the studies reviewed for this section, it would seem that there are a number of indicators of staff effectiveness which are based on research that should be considered for inclusion in a district's staff evaluation criteria and evaluation instrument. In developing and deciding on these criteria the administrator should avoid including any *high inference* variables. High inference variables such as teacher enthusiasm, for example, require considerable inference by the observer as to whether or not the behavior has occurred; low inference behaviors require little or no inference by the observer regarding whether or not the particular teaching behavior has occurred. Although the criteria for evaluating teaching should contain as few high inference behaviors as possible (because of the resulting problem that observations of the same teacher behavior may lead to different inferences), high inference variables can be useful in staff evaluation if they are further analyzed into more precise measures.[23]

In addition to the importance of the relevance and validity of the criteria for staff evaluation, the instrument or rating scale which is used to apply the criteria to teacher performance should possess the following characteristics:[24] (1) It should be reliable, that is responses to it should be consistent; (2) it should be reasonable in cost; (3) it should be efficient to use and easy to understand; and (4) it should be diagnostic in nature, i.e., provide information which helps the teacher to improve rather than information which is confined to identifying weaknesses. The last factor is exceedingly important because a teacher's receptivity and perception of the evaluation's value are likely to be limited if the evaluation instrument only makes judgments about his performance without helping the teacher to understand how he can improve.[25]

The school administrator needs to realize that bringing about changes in the staff evaluation criteria and the evaluation instrument will not be an easy task, particularly if the selection of criteria and instrument is viewed by the central office administrators and supervisors as their responsibility, and if they have considerable emotional investment in the use of existing criteria and instrument. Nevertheless, teachers deserve to be evaluated by criteria and an instrument which are directly related to their effectiveness in the classroom, and the school administrator should exert her leadership toward the achievement of that objective.

COMMUNICATION

In many schools the purposes, criteria, and process of staff evaluation are not adequately communicated to the staff.[26] It is not unusual in those schools for the staff, particularly new members, to be uninformed about the criteria and process of the district evaluation program until they actually encounter them. Although most staff members are aware that the process of evaluation involves observation by an evaluator and a follow-up conference to discuss the results of the evaluation, questions about the nature, time, and frequency of observations and conferences are often not resolved. And in many cases, teachers are observed for the purpose of evaluation without their possessing first hand knowledge of the criteria on which they are to be evaluated.

Poor communication about the evaluation process can result in uncertainty and anxiety on the part of staff members. They don't know exactly what to expect from the evaluation, and therefore, they may not participate cooperatively in the process or accept the administrator's findings.

Recommendation: The purposes, criteria, and procedures of staff evaluation need to be clearly communicated periodically to all staff members.

The administrator should not assume that staff members are familiar with or will remember from year to year the evaluation purposes, criteria, and procedures. At the very least, *new* members of the staff should be informed of these elements before evaluation proceeds.

The most desirable approach would be for the administrator to schedule a meeting, after the first few weeks of school, with all staff members who are to be evaluated during the year and to review with them the purposes, criteria, and procedures to be used in the evaluation program. At that meeting certain points can be emphasized or clarified, and questions can be answered. The objectives of such a meeting would be to develop understanding and acceptance of the evaluation program, and to relieve anxiety and apprehension, particularly on the part of new staff members.

Once the administrator is ready to begin the evaluation process, she should schedule a conference with each individual to be evaluated and attempt to reach agreement on objectives and the proposed means for reaching those objectives.[27] This agreement should then be the focus of the classroom observations and other techniques which the administrator employs in making her evaluation, as well as the main topic of the follow-up conference during which the administrator discusses with the staff member the evaluative judgments made. The primary advantage of this approach is that administrator and teacher agree in advance on those aspects that will be examined during the evaluation process.

EVALUATING TENURED TEACHERS

In previous periods of high teacher turnover and influx to the staff, it was understandable that staff evaluation would focus primarily on evaluating new and nontenured teachers. While it may have been recognized that experienced teachers also need to be evaluated periodically for purposes of assessing performance adequacy and professional growth, there frequently seemed to be little time or priority given by many administrators to achieving these purposes.[28]

Although it might be argued that experienced teachers do not need to be evaluated as often as nontenured teachers because the former, as a result of their experiences, are more capable, not all experienced teachers have profitted from their experience nor continue to perform competently.[29] While it is true that generally a tenured teacher must be provided with due process if dismissal proceedings are initiated, Coursen rightly emphasizes that, ". . . Even at their most stringent, tenure laws regulate, rather than prevent the dismissal of incompetent teachers."[30] Beyond the question of incompetent tenured teachers, there is the problem of burn-out and stagnation on the part of tenured teachers, discussed elsewhere in the text, which personnel evaluation could identify as the problem impacts on performance. As the composition of school staffs become more and more experienced and tenured, because of limited staff hiring and turnover, the evaluation of tenured teachers will require a higher priority on the part of administrators.

Recommendation: Tenured teachers should be evaluated rigorously, at least every other year.

Although many administrators appear to feel that evaluating tenured teachers can be difficult and troublesome, tenured teachers need to be regularly and rigorously evaluated, as any other teacher. Because of their experience, tenured teachers should be involved more by the administrator in their evaluation, and the approach to changing them will probably need to be more indirect and flexible. (Pellicer and Hendrix describe one such approach.[31]) However, it is only through evaluation that it can be determined or verified whether a tenured teacher is still performing up to district standards. And for that reason, as well as offering the possibility for continuing professional growth, tenured teachers need to be evaluated at least every other year.

CONSIDERATION OF SITUATIONAL VARIABLES

The primary basis for reaching evaluative conclusions about the performance of a faculty member is usually the classroom visitation, during which most if not all of the attention is typically given to the teacher's behavior. However, many factors can influence a teacher's performance and student learning in a school. These include the instructional materials, the curriculum, the school schedule, the physical conditions in the classroom, the size of the class, and the types of students in the classroom. All too often these situational variables are ignored in assessing teacher effectiveness or insufficiently taken into consideration by the evaluator.

Recommendation: The evaluation process should include an examination of all major relevant school factors which may be affecting the staff member's performance.

Teaching effectiveness can be influenced by a wide variety of possible situational variables such as those described above. Failure to consider these variables in evaluating a teacher may result in an inaccurate and unfair assessment of that person's effectiveness. The administrator who is evaluating teachers should attempt to develop a better understanding of the various situational factors that are affecting a teacher's performance and take these conditions into consideration in evaluation and supervision. (For a further discussion of these factors, see *Educational Environments and Effects,* ed. by Herbert J. Walberg; Berkeley: McCutcheon, 1979. Also see "Context/Environment Effects in Teacher Evaluation" by Bernard H. McKenna, in *Handbook of Teacher Evaluation,* ed. by Jason Millman; Beverly Hills: Sage Publications, 1981.)

EVALUATION EXPERTISE

In recent years teachers have become better prepared and more specialized in their subject matter and teaching methodology. Many teachers now question whether the administrator, who has, typically, been out of the classroom for several years, and who may have specialized in only one aspect of the curriculum as an undergraduate, has the expertise to evaluate them. As a result, administrators have sometimes experienced difficulty in evaluating teachers and, in particular, in getting them to accept administrative judgments about their strengths and weaknesses.[32]

It would make little sense to minimize the importance of expertise in evaluating a professional staff. If the administrator is to do a competent job of evaluating teachers and obtaining their acceptance of her findings, she will need to be knowledgeable and expert in the various areas of curriculum, teaching methods, learning theory, and other facets of the educational program. It will also be in her interest to capitalize on and utilize as much as possible the expertise possessed by department heads, unit leaders, and other sources of assistance within the school and school district. Staff evaluation today can no longer depend on the expertise of one individual, such as the principal. (For further discussion of this problem, see "Practical Applications of Research," in the March, 1982, *Phi Delta Kappan Newsletter*.)

Recommendation: The school administrator needs to utilize to the maximum extent possible the expertise of others in evaluating staff members.

It is recognized that some people may feel that the school administrator possesses all of the expertise she needs in order to evaluate teachers. However, the position taken by the author is that the school administrator cannot conduct evaluation with maximal effectiveness by herself, and that the staff evaluation program will be improved if she capitalizes on the expertise of others in the school or school district.

The specific approach recommended is that the principal organize a staff evaluation team,[33] composed of herself, the central office subject supervisor, and the appropriate department head or unit leader. The latter two individuals normally possess specialized expertise in the curriculum and teaching method of a particular subject area and should complement the administrator, who is a generalist and whose in-depth knowledge of those aspects is likely to be limited. The administrator has, however, much to contribute to the evaluation process, particularly in the areas of class management and total-school perspective, and of course, she is responsible for making the final evaluation decisions at the building level.

While the team approach to evaluation has much to recommend it, problems may arise, depending on the purposes for which the administrator uses the team. If she wants the team to evaluate teachers for personnel decisions, as well as for staff improvement she is likely to experience difficulty in securing the cooperation of the department head (or unit leader) and the central office supervisor. Both will probably be interested in the objective of staff evaluation for improvement, but they may not want to participate in the other kind of evaluation for fear of losing the confidence of the teachers with whom they work. Paradoxically, if the administrator uses the team only for the staff improvement objective, she loses their expertise for the other purpose of staff evaluation. There is no easy answer to the problem, and its final resolution will depend on the administrator's assessment of conditions in her own school and school district. However, it seems likely that there will be difficulties in utilizing the same personnel and approach for both objectives of staff evaluation.

FOLLOW-UP AFTER EVALUATION

As supervision without adequate prior evaluation tends to be misdirected, evaluation without immediate and constructive follow-up supervisory assistance can lead to anxiety, frustration, and resistance on the part of its recipients. And judging from the reports of many teachers, there is too frequently a lack of immediate and constructive supervisory assistance following the evaluation process. In such situations teachers are informed of their weaknesses or limitations but are given no specific help in improving. Informing a teacher that she needs "better class control" or "greater student participation" may identify a shortcoming, but unless the individual is given supervisory assistance in achieving better class control or greater student participation, she may be unable to improve. Worse yet, informing an individual of a weakness without giving her adequate help in correcting it may harm the person's self-concept and lead to a negative attitude toward evaluation on her part.

Recommendation: Following the evaluation, the school administrator and others working with her need to provide staff members with specific and constructive suggestions and supervisory assistance to help them improve.

A staff evaluation program which only points out strengths and weaknesses of an individual without helping her to correct her limitations or to capitalize on her strengths is professionally inadequate. In order to improve, a person will usually need to receive *specific* and *constructive* assistance and support, and she will also need appropriate time in which to make the necessary changes. An example of a possible format for a personnel improvement plan for accomplishing these objectives is presented in figure 10.2.

Components of a Personnel Improvement Plan

Objectives of the Plan
What are the specific changes that are to occur?

Prescribed Activities
What are the *specific* activities that the individual should engage in so as to accomplish the needed improvements?

Time Frame
At what point should *progress* in accomplishing the objectives of the plan be apparent? At what point should the objectives of the plan *be accomplished?*

Supervisor's Role
What kinds of assistance and monitoring activities will be provided by the supervisor?

Figure 10.2.

Whether the evaluation program is perceived by the staff in a positive light will probably depend as much on the adequacy of follow-up supervisory activities as on the perceived fairness and validity of the evaluation itself. Therefore, the various supervisory alternatives discussed in the next chapter should be utilized by the administrator whenever needed.

DUE PROCESS

There are two types of due process: procedural and substantive.[34] In staff evaluation, *procedural* due process means, at the minimum, that before any adverse action is taken against a staff member (such as dismissal or denial of salary increase), the individual is given written notification and documentation of the reasons for the action and is provided an opportunity to present evidence that might reduce the severity of the action or eliminate its need entirely.[35] It also usually means that before adverse action is taken, the individual must be given sufficient opportunity to remedy her weakness, and the supervisor must make every reasonable effort to help the person accomplish this goal.

Substantive due process in staff evaluation means that the criteria used in evaluating an individual are not arbitrary and are directly related to the job.[36]

Although there is no complete record on the extent to which schools follow standards of due process, it is worth noting that when teacher dismissal cases reach the courts, the court more often rules against the school if it has failed to follow standards of due process than for any other reason, and that more and more school districts are being required to provide due process as a result of collective bargaining. While schools are legally required to provide due process to tenured teachers, the law regarding nontenured teachers has not been conclusively established. Be that as it may, it seems clear that due process is consistent with professional standards, even if it is not legally required, and should be considered by the school administrator in the case of nontenured teachers as well as tenured ones.

Recommendation: Due process should be followed in the evaluation of all staff, nontenured as well as tenured, whenever it appears that an evaluation may result in an adverse personnel decision for an individual.

The main purpose of due process is to ensure that an individual has received a fair and just decision. In staff evaluation this means that the criteria must be legitimate, the individual must be informed of her shortcomings, she must be given sufficient opportunity to correct them, and she must be provided with adequate supervision to do so. These four conditions (legitimate criteria, notification of weakness, sufficient time to correct weakness, and adequate supervision) represent practices which are professionally sound—regardless of whether or not they are legally required. Neglect by the administrator of any of these aspects may not be prohibited by law in the case of nontenured teachers, but it is surely a professional inadequacy. The administrator who insists that due process be followed in *all* staff evaluations will not only avoid possible legal entanglements at a later date, but will also be meeting high professional standards in regard to staff evaluation.

The basic due process procedures recommended for *all* staff members who are being considered for dismissal are the following:

a. Written identification of strengths and diagnosis of weaknesses with specific recommendations on how to improve. The diagnosis and recommendation for improvement should be given to the staff member in sufficient time *before* any final personnel ratings or decisions are made for the year so that the individual has adequate opportunity to correct or ameliorate his weaknesses.

b. Intensive follow-up supervisory assistance by the administrator and others who are working with the administrator, to help the staff member improve. The administrator should maintain written documentation on all efforts made to improve the staff member and the latter's response to those efforts. Both kinds of information will be needed if, at a later date, the staff member should challenge a decision of school district in the case of dismissal or salary consideration.

    c. Advance notice in writing to the staff member, in circumstances involving an adverse personnel decision, of the reasons for the decision, and notification of an opportunity to have a hearing with the administrator in order to review the decision and the reasons for it.[37]

    d. A hearing with the administrator to review an adverse personnel decision, if requested, and the opportunity to appeal the administrator's decision to her immediate superior and, if necessary, to the school board and to the courts.

    e. Publication to all staff members of the previous four procedures. A major principle of due process is that those who are to be affected by an adverse decision should be informed of their right to these procedures. Although an administrator may be willing to adopt these procedures if *requested,* due process will not become a reality in an evaluation program unless the administrator takes the initiative to explain these procedures to all staff members and emphasize their availability.

Some readers may regard the recommended use of these procedures as controversial, particularly as they apply to nontenured teachers. Many administrators may feel that due process is awkward, time-consuming, and very inefficient, and that they should provide no more due process, at least for nontenured teachers, than required by law. However, the right to due process in the case of a decision perceived as unfair or invalid is basic to our democratic heritage and should cause the administrator no overwhelming concern if her personnel decisions are based on solid evaluation practices.

It is conceded that due process may be awkward, time-consuming, and inefficient; and it is agreed that it may not be legally required in all situations. However, the basic intent of the administrator should be to act fairly. Due process is designed to minimize the possibility of unfairness. It should also help the administrator to do a more *professional* and *competent* job of evaluating staff. (Of course, the administrator should also be sure to follow the provisions of the master contract.)

STAFF DISMISSAL

A major responsibility of a school administrator is to ensure an adequate learning environment for the students. If a member of the staff is not performing adequately in spite of supervisory efforts, then steps must be taken to remove that individual from the staff. This will not be easy, but the responsibility for initiating action is clearly that of the school administrator. It makes little sense to have a "good evaluation program" in all other respects if such a program permits incompetent or unsatisfactory teachers to remain on the staff.

> **Recommendation:** When supervisory efforts are not successful in improving sufficiently the performance of an incompetent or, for some other reason, an unacceptable teacher, the school administrator needs to initiate dismissal steps which include due process.

An important problem, of course, is defining valid criteria for incompetent or unsatisfactory behavior, but the research reviewed in the previous sections should be helpful in that regard. Also, state statutes should be examined for the legal grounds for dismissal in the school administrator's state.

Neill and Curtis found in their review of successful dismissal cases that the courts have supported the following grounds for dismissal: (1) incompetent teaching methods, including failure to adapt to current teaching techniques, poor lesson organization, and failure to maintain classroom control; (2) negative impact on students, including inability to get along with pupils, failure to maintain self-control, and low pupil achievement; (3) negative teacher attitude, including insubordination, and (4) inadequate knowledge of subject matter, including lack of knowledge of English grammar, spelling, and punctuation.[38] Also, Bendow identified eight most frequently reported effective administrative factors that were associated with successful teacher dismissal:[39] (1) observations were numerous and well documented, (2) definite goals for improvement were established and a specific time table was formed for the attainment of goals, (3) the administrator was willing and able to assist the teacher in areas that needed improvement, (4) the administrator informed the teacher early of incompetency, both verbally and in writing; (5) central administration was consistently informed of the situation, (6) the administrator held to initially established expectations, (7) the administrator was factual, truthful, consistent, and followed district policies and laws to the letter, and (8) the teacher was told, verbally and in writing, after all administrative support had failed, that termination was being recommended. While dismissal of a staff person is seldom easy, the previous guidelines should be helpful in achieving the objective.

ASSESSMENT OF THE PROGRAM

The staff evaluation program, like any other program, needs to be assessed regularly if it is to improve and meet the needs of the people involved. Regrettably, assessment of the strengths and weaknesses of the staff evaluation program is frequently haphazard and sporadic. Whatever assessment does occur tends to rely on the random impressions of administrators and usually includes limited or no feedback from the staff members themselves.

> **Recommendation:** The staff evaluation program should be assessed systematically every year or two for the purpose of identifying areas for improvement.

Perhaps the greatest need for improvement in a school's staff evaluation program is for periodic and systematic examination of the strengths and weaknesses of the program. The school administrator, with the help of the faculty, should play a major role in achieving this objective.

The way in which the assessment is to be accomplished may take a number of different forms, but one condition is essential: those who are being evaluated should be surveyed on their perceptions of the program's strengths and weaknesses and their ideas on how it could be made more effective.

ON-THE-JOB TRAINING FOR EVALUATORS

Most administrators who evaluate the staff have received only limited professional training for their role as evaluator and little if any on-the-job training for evaluating staff. Because of a lack of preparation, many administrators approach the task of evaluating staff with some apprehension, or with a false sense of security, feeling that they know everything there is to know about evaluating school personnel. Personnel evaluation, however, is a complex process involving technical skills, and educational and legal concepts. And there is evidence that many administrators are not performing the task of evaluation as well as they should.[40]

> **Recommendation:** All evaluators should receive in-service training at least every three years in order to sharpen their technical skills of evaluation and to update educational and legal concepts.

One in-service approach that appears to hold considerable promise is described in research by Woods.[41]

A FINAL PERSPECTIVE

The staff evaluation program has had a checkered past and continues to be perceived by many as a necessary evil. However, it *can* be an important means not only of improving the staff, but also for reaching specific personnel decisions—but only under certain conditions. Since it is likely that staff evaluation will continue to be one of the school administrator's major responsibilities, it is essential that she work to improve the program. The discussion and recommendations presented in this chapter have been designed to help achieve that goal.

Review and Learning Activities

1. Ascertain the objectives of your district's staff evaluation program and examine the achievability of those objectives in light of the discussion in the test on cross-purposes.
2. To what degree is the staff involved in the development of staff evaluation purposes, criteria, and procedures? To what extent in your district is a low priority given to staff self-evaluation? How could these situations be improved?
3. Assess the degree to which your district's staff evaluation criteria and form are based on research and recommendations presented in this chapter. Attempt to draft an improved staff evaluation form and criteria for your district.
4. What are your school district's policy and procedures for evaluating tenured teachers and dismissing teachers? Draft an improved policy for each of these situations, based on the recommendations and ideas presented in the text.
5. Ascertain your school district's policy and plan for helping teachers to improve after the need for such improvement has been identified through teacher evaluation. What are the strengths and weaknesses of the policy and plan? How could they be made better?

Notes

1. Madeline Hunter, "Six Types of Supervisory Conferences," *Educational Leadership* (February 1980): 408–12.
2. Ronald B. Kimball, "Six Approaches to Evaluating Teaching: A Typology," *NASSP Bulletin* (March 1980): 41.
3. Martha Cook and Herbert C. Richards, "Dimensions of Principal and Supervisor Ratings of Teacher Behavior," *Journal of Experimental Education* (Winter 1972): 13.
4. Carmelo V. Sapone, "Appraisal and Evaluation Systems: Perceptions of Administrators, Teachers," *NASSP Bulletin* (February 1981): 25–30; Harrison Crenshaw II and John Hoyle, "The Principal's Headache: Teacher Evaluation," *NASSP Bulletin* (February 1981): 37–45; S. M. Johnson, "Performance Based Staff Layoffs in the Public Schools," *Harvard Educational Review* (May 1980): 214–33; Robert A. Rotherg and Lila L. Buchanan, "Teacher Perceptions of Teacher Assessment," *The Kappan* (March 1981): 527.
5. One of the main sources for identification of the problems and issues associated with teacher evaluation is the periodic review of the literature and survey of the field conducted by Educational Research Service, Washington, D.C.

6. For a full description of the program, see Fred Niedermeyer and Stephen Klein, "An Empirical Evaluation of a District's Accountability Program," *The Kappan* (October 1972): 100–103. Also see Elmer C. Ellis et al., "Peer Observation: A Means of Supervisory Acceptance," *Educational Leadership* (March 1979): 423–26. In addition, the Salt Lake City, Utah school district involves teachers in a program of peer evaluation.

7. *Negotiating the Teacher Evaluation Issue* (Arlington, Va.: Educational Research Service, 1979).

8. Bruce W. Tuckman, "Judging the Effectiveness of Teaching Styles: The Perceptions of Principals," *Educational Administration Quarterly* (Winter 1979): 104–15.

9. This hypothesis is based on research by William G. Cunningham, "Teachability Grouping Revisited," *The Kappan* (February 1975): 428–29.

10. For a full description of the program, see John D. McNeil, "Politics of Teacher Evaluation," in *Handbook of Teacher Evaluation* ed. Jason Millman (Beverly Hills, Calif.: Sage Publications, 1981): 286. Also see Robert Madgis, "Increasing the Reliability of Evaluations by Using Classroom Products," *NASSP Bulletin* (March 1980): 12–15.

11. Donald Medley, *Indicators and Measures of Teacher Effectiveness: A Review of Research.* An ERIC Report: Ed–088–844, p. 6.

12. Benjamin S. Bloom, "The New Direction in Educational Research: Alterable Variables," *The Kappan* (February 1980): 384.

13. For a description of a number of these studies, see *Research on Teaching: Concepts, Findings and Implications,* eds. Penelope L. Peterson and Herbert J. Walberg (Berkeley, Calif.: McCutchan, 1979); *Handbook of Research on Teaching,* ed. Merlin Wittrock (New York: Macmillan, 1983). Also see Bloom, "The New Direction in Educational Research;" Thomas L. Good, "Teacher Effectiveness in the Elementary School," *Journal of Teacher Education* (March/April 1979): 52–64; E. Joseph Schneider, "Researchers Discover Formula for Success in Student Learning," *Educational R and D Report* (Fall 1979): 1–6.

14. M. William Salganik, "Researchers Team with Reporter to Identify Schools That Work," *Educational R and D* (Winter 1980): 3.

15. For a fuller description of this method and related research, see *Research on Teaching: Concepts, Findings and Implications,* eds. Peterson and Walberg, chapter 3.

16. Penelope L. Peterson, "Direct Instruction: Effective for What and for Whom?" *Educational Leadership* (October 1979): 46.

17. Ullik Rouk, "Separate Studies Show Similar Results of Teacher Effectiveness," *Educational R and D* (Spring 1979): 6.

18. *Time to Learn.* An ERIC Report: Ed–192–454.

19. Quote by David Berliner, Director of Beginning Teacher Evaluation Study Far West Regional Lab, San Francisco, Calif.

20. Jere F. Brophy, "Teacher Behavior and Student Learning," *Educational Leadership* (October 1979): 33. Also see Harris M. Cooper and Reuben M. Baron, "Academic Expectations, Attributed Responsibility and Teachers' Reinforcement Behavior," *Journal of Educational Psychology* (April 1979): 274–77.

21. Gordon A. Sabine, *How Students Rate Their Schools and Teachers.* An ERIC Report: Ed–052–533. Also see Robert Wright and Robert Alley, "A Profile of the Ideal Teacher," *NASSP Bulletin* (February 1977): 60–64.

22. Nate L. Gage, *The Scientific Basis of the Art of Teaching* (Columbia University, Teachers College Press, 1978).

23. For a good discussion on how to reduce the high inference variables, see M. L. Land, "Low Inference Variables of Teacher Clarity: Effects on Student Concept Learning," *Journal of Educational Psychology* (December 1979): 795–99.

24. For further discussion of these points, see Gaea Leinhardt, "Modeling and Measuring Educational Treatment," *Review of Educational Research* (Fall 1980): 404–14.

25. For examples of several diagnostic instruments which are currently being used in teacher evaluation, see G. D. Borich and S. K. Madden, *Evaluating Classroom Instruction: A Sourcebook of Instruments* (Reading, Mass.: Addison-Wesley, 1977).

26. Donald Grossnickle and William B. Thiel, "The Etiquette of Evaluation—What's Often Forgotten But Not to Be Ignored," *NASSP Bulletin* (February 1981): 1–4. Also see June Thompson et al., *Failure of Communication in the Evaluation of Teachers by Principals.* An ERIC Report: Ed–105–637.

27. Russell S. Beecher, "Staff Evaluation: The Essential Administrative Task," *The Kappan* (March 1979): 515–17. Carole Grews, "All Roads Lead to Evaluation Conference," *NASSP Bulletin* (February 1982): 64–66.

28. Patricia Palker, "Tenure: Do We Need It?" *Teacher* (May/June 1980): 36–40.

29. Shirly Neill and Jerry Curtis, *Staff Dismissal: Problems and Solutions* (Arlington, Va.: American Association of School Administrators, 1978).

30. David Coursen, *Dismissing Incompetent Teachers* (Eugene, Oreg.: ERIC Clearinghouse on Educational Management, University of Oregon, 1980), p. 1.

31. Leonard O. Pellicer and O. B. Hendrix, "A Practical Approach to Remediation and Dismissal," *NASSP Bulletin* (March 1980): 57–62.

32. "I Still Don't Know What I Did Wrong." *NEA Reporter* (October 1980): 3.

33. See, for example, Donald W. Dubois, *Teacher Evaluation: The Salem Public Schools Model* (Eugene, Oreg.: Oregon School Study Council, 1980).

34. F. G. Delon and R. E. Bartman, "Employees," in *The Yearbook of School Law,* ed. P. K. Piele (Topeka: National Organization on Legal Problems of Education, 1979), pp. 99–103. Also see Joseph C. Beckham, *Legal Aspects of Teacher Evaluation* (Topeka, Kans.: National Organization on Legal Problems of Education, 1981).

35. Larry French, "Teacher Employment, Evaluation and Dismissal," in *The School Principal and the Law,* ed. R. D. Stein (Topeka: National Organization on Legal Problems of Education, 1978), pp. 39–40.

36. Delon and Bartman, "Employees."

37. J. P. Mahon, "Giving Reasons for Terminating Employees," *NASSP Bulletin* (December 1979): 35–42.

38. Neill and Curtis, *Staff Dismissal.*

39. Larry K. Bendow, "Factors in Teacher Dismissal Situations" (Ed.D. diss., Walden University, 1979).

40. Judith Redwine and Robert A. Dubick, *Teacher Perceptions of Instructional Supervision and Teacher Evaluation Processes.* An ERIC Report: Ed–157–892. Also see citations in reference #4.

41. Margaret Woods, "A Study of the Effect of Teaching Human Relations Skills to Principals as It Affects Their Role in a Teacher Evaluation Conference" (Ph.D. diss., University of Pittsburg, 1980).

11

Instructional Leadership

Instructional leadership may be defined as those activities, engaged in by one or more individuals, which have as their main purpose the improvement of a person, group, or program. The emphasis in this definition is on *improvement,* not merely maintenance, and on *instructional* leadership, as opposed to other kinds of leadership.[1] While at the building level, an administrator is usually involved in a variety of situations that call for leadership, probably the most important area for which an administrator has leadership responsibilities is the instructional program.[2]

The instructional program comprises all of the factors and conditions within a school that influence student learning. Although the teacher is perhaps the most important instructional variable affecting student learning, other factors and conditions also play a role. They include the size of the class, the quantity and quality of curricular materials available, and the educational and socioeconomic characteristics of the students.[3] While the supervision of staff will be emphasized in this chapter, the administrator is also encouraged to examine and take into consideration other significant variables which influence student learning.

CAN THE ADMINISTRATOR FUNCTION AS AN INSTRUCTIONAL LEADER?

ADMINISTRATIVE CONSIDERATIONS

The role of the school administrator as an instructional leader has frequently been espoused, particularly by administrator organizations.[4] However, for some time now, evidence has been surfacing that teachers—the main recipients of an administrator's instructional leadership—do not always recognize him as the instructional leader of the school. (Although later in this chapter research evidence will be presented indicating that administrators *can* perform as instructional leaders, it is important that the reader understand that important problems and obstacles will first need to be addressed.)

Campbell, for example, has asserted that, "The educational administrator is working with professionals who feel, often rightly, that they know more about teaching and learning than he does."[5] Erickson has pointed out that, "With the influx of additional personnel, there is a tendency to look beyond the principal for help with classroom problems to persons such as colleagues, subject matter specialists, supervisors and professors."[6] And more recently, Bredo observed that, ". . . Many teachers feel that no administrator can understand as well as they do what really goes on in the classroom, and that they themselves can judge what teaching practices are best suited to the particular group of students in their classes."[7]

Several studies on the role of the administrator cast doubt on whether or not he can function as an instructional leader. For instance, Croft found that teachers will more often solicit help from colleagues rather than administrators on important professional issues.[8] Deal and Celotti discovered that, "Methods of classroom instruction are virtually unaffected by organizational or administrative factors at the school or district levels,"[9] and studies by Corwin,[10] Sharma,[11] and Bredo[12] indicate a lack of acceptance on the part of many teachers of the administrator's role as an instructional leader.

Apparently the main problem many school administrators face in this regard is that their instructional leadership is perceived as (and may *actually* be) no longer based on an expertise differential.[13] Most teachers are as well, if not better, prepared on subject matter and teaching methodology than the administrator. Articulating this view best is Ball, who states:

> They [the teachers] know their subject matter, they know how to teach, they know a great deal about pupil behavior and motivation, and are in the best sense professionals. Many teachers today know a great deal more about their jobs than even the best principal can, and it's been a long time coming for principals to recognize this fact.[14]

As a result of their increased expertise, many teachers have become more militant in their expectations for professional autonomy and less receptive to attempts by the administrator to exercise instructional leadership.[15] Their attitude is characteristic of the problems with which many administrators must cope if they try to exercise leadership over professionals without expertise as a source of leadership.[16] (It should be emphasized, however, that there is evidence that those administrators who are perceived by teachers as possessing instructional expertise will be sought out by teachers if they have an instructional problem.)*

*Richard A. Gorton, "The Importance of Administrative Expertise in Instructional Leadership." Research paper presented at meeting of American Educational Research Association, 1971.

While the problem of limited acceptance of an administrator's role as an instructional leader is a serious one for many administrators, there exist, unfortunately, additional constraints or obstacles. It should be emphasized that these additional constraints or obstacles are not inevitable but, if present in an administrator's school district, could restrict his motivation and/or his efforts to perform as an instructional leader. Although these potential constraints or obstacles may vary somewhat from one situation to another, the most typical ones appear to be the following:[17]

The Press of Other Duties. Exercising instructional leadership takes time and energy over and above that which must be spent on administering a school or school district. Responsibilities other than instructional leadership will frequently press for an administrator's time and drain his energy, leaving him with the feeling that he is spread too thin and, though he would like to be an instructional leader, he really doesn't have the time to function as one.

The Nature of the Situation. Some situations involve more instructional problems, crises, and major issues which necessitate the instructional leadership of the administrator than do others. If an administrator is in a very stable, problem-free situation with an excellent instructional program and staff, there may be less opportunity or need for instructional leadership.

The Extent of Resources. A lack of resources—financial, physical, or human—can be a serious obstacle to instructional leadership. An administrator may want to lead, and the situation and expectations of others may call for his leadership. But if the resources necessary to implement his leadership are inadequate, the administrator will be facing a significant constraint.

The Degree of Incentive. An administrator should not need much incentive to adopt the role of instructional leader, and yet, in school districts where one or more of the previously mentioned obstacles are operant, some type of compensatory incentive or reward will probably be needed. Unfortunately, in all too many school districts, there is very little incentive for an administrator to function as an instructional leader. Those who make the attempt seldom receive much recognition or sustained encouragement from their superiors and, in many cases, are subject to subtle (and sometimes not so subtle) pressure from colleagues to behave in a way not too much different from the other administrators. Also, when one considers the risks that are frequently associated with instructional leadership, it would appear that incentives are meager, in comparison.

The Personal Qualities of the Administrator. The administrator's own personality, vision, extent of commitment, human relation skills, etc., can serve to constrain the exercise of effective leadership. If the administrator does not possess the appropriate personal qualities needed (more will be said about this later), the absence of those characteristics can be self-constraining.

It is unlikely that any administrator would experience all of the constraints or obstacles identified above, nor is it likely that any administrator works in a constraint-free situation. However, it should be emphasized that the extent of constraints for any administrator who wishes to exercise instructional leadership will probably vary from one situation to another, and what may be viewed as a serious constraint by one administrator may be perceived as only a minor restriction by another. The approach an administrator should take when confronted by an apparent constraint is to seek more information about its nature and extent, and to attempt to diagnose and modify its causes. Constraints are frequently not insurmountable, and if an administrator really wants to exercise instructional leadership, he will find some way to ameliorate the limiting influence of constraints on his leadership. This will not be easy, but if an administrator has a *strong commitment* to functioning as an instructional leader, he will find a way to overcome or at least reduce the constraints operating in the situation. And available evidence indicates that administrators *can* function as instructional leaders.

For example, Clark and his colleagues, after a review of 1,200 studies of urban schools and urban education, concluded that in successful schools, "The behavior of the designated school or program leader is crucial in determining school success. Principals are particularly important."[18] Edmonds, in an investigation of elements that make schools effective, discovered that such schools have strong administrative leadership.[19] And a study in California found that in "schools where student achievement is higher than might be expected, principals provide strong leadership and support."[20] What these, and several other studies that will be mentioned later, strongly suggest is that an administrator *can* be an instructional leader, and that such leadership is necessary if a school is to be successful.

But what qualities should an administrator possess if he is to function effectively as an instructional leader, and in what activities should he engage? The rest of this chapter will attempt to address that important question. (For a further review of studies which show that the principal can be an instructional leader, see "What Principals Can Do: Some Implications from Studies of Effective Schooling," by John Shoemaker and Hugh W. Fraser, *Phi Delta Kappan,* November, 1981, pp. 178–82.)

RESEARCH ON EFFECTIVE INSTRUCTIONAL LEADERS

Research has not been notably successful in determining the personal qualities which a leader should possess. Based on a review of the literature on leadership, however, it would seem that certain basic personal characteristics are important.

One important personal quality needed for effective instructional leadership appears to be the extent to which an administrator perceives accurately the existence of an instructional problem or area in need of improvement.[21]

Leadership is usually stimulated by an awareness of the existence of a problem. Consequently, the administrator who perceives few problems or who tends to minimize or ignore their existence is unlikely to see the need for instructional leadership. Of course, this does not mean that the administrator who aspires to leadership should find or create problems where none exists. However, he should try to be accessible and nondefensive to the people who bring problems to his attention, and he should take the initiative to seek feedback periodically from students, teachers and parents on possible instructional needs. As one study revealed, ". . . Effective principals understand the school's educational program inside out. . . . [They] spend about half their time in the school's halls and classrooms, often teaching classes themselves. They are 'high visibility' leaders rather than spending most of their time in their offices."[22]

Closely related to the accurate identification of instructional problems is the need for an administrator to possess or develop *educational vision.* An administrator's analysis of local problems will certainly provide one kind of clue about the changes that are needed. But if he is to function as an instructional leader, the administrator must go beyond solving the daily problems he encounters to considering and implementing more basic changes which offer the potential for improving education throughout the organization, and which may represent significant departures from the status quo. Such a vision can be developed through a program of continuing professional improvement (as recommended in the last chapter), travel, and consultation with various leaders in education. The importance of educational vision to instructional leadership is underscored by three studies that found principals in successful schools to have clear points of views about schooling, instruction, and educational goals, and to possess definite ideas about what kinds of improvements were needed in instruction.[23]

Knowledge about the different aspects of the instructional and curricular program, and skill in introducing change in that program, as well as in the people who staff it, are key elements in the *expertise* that an administrator will need if he intends to exercise effective instructional leadership.[24] Earlier, research was presented which showed that many teachers did not accept the administrator in the role of instructional leader because of a perception (or the reality) that the administrator lacked the necessary expertise to help them. On the other hand, research has shown that teachers *will* accept the instructional leadership of principals who can demonstrate appropriate expertise, and that such administrators are associated with effective schools. As noted by Guditus and Zirkel, "The influence of principals depends to a considerable degree on their possession of special knowledge and skills which enable them to help teachers achieve their goals."[25] (Chapters 10, 11, and 12 focus on those special skills and knowledge.)

A fourth factor which greatly influences the type of leadership an administrator exhibits is the kind of needs which he possesses. Does he have a strong drive to set and achieve new goals? Does he seek out opportunities to exercise leadership? Does he derive satisfaction from solving problems?

In a study by Lipham[26] which was indirectly concerned with leadership, it was found that effective administrators possess strong needs to develop good interpersonal relations with others, to engage in different problem-solving situations that call for considerable emotional control, and to be well organized, active, and directed toward achievement of success or status. By contrast, ineffective administrators had low needs in these areas. Lipham's study implies that administrators who attempt to perform as instructional leaders possess a different set of needs than those who do not initiate leadership.

A *strong commitment* to improving instruction is another personal prerequisite to exercising effective instructional leadership. As mentioned earlier, obstacles and constraints must frequently be overcome if an administrator is to function successfully in the role of instructional leader. There will be pressures to divert him from instructional leadership activities to managerial duties, and it will often seem that there is insufficient time to focus on improving instruction. Nevertheless, if an administrator has a strong commitment to improving instruction, he will take the initiative and work hard to ameliorate those obstacles, and he will find the time to exercise leadership in the instructional program.

That a strong commitment is important has been demonstrated by several studies. Wellisch and her colleagues, for example, discovered in their research on successful schools that such schools were headed by a principal who had a deep concern about and commitment to improving instruction.[27] Roeber found in his investigation that in those schools which attempted to utilize assessment information for the improvement of instruction, the principal had a strong *commitment* to such use,[28] and Scofield concluded from her review of the literature, that in schools with successful reading programs, ". . . Leaders have a strong commitment to reading and high expectations of staff."[29] Perhaps the Institute for Educational Leadership's study best expressed the idea in their publication, *What Makes for an Effective School:* "There's no magic. All it takes is the commitment, the time, and the guts to stay with it."[30]

If an administrator only feels that it would be nice or desirable to be an instructional leader, then he is not likely to initiate much leadership. He will usually feel that there are too many obstacles or constraints. An administrator must really have a strong commitment to improving instruction if he is to function effectively as an instructional leader.

Even with a strong commitment to improving instruction, however, an administrator may not succeed as an instructional leader unless he possesses a *high energy* level. Instructional leadership is hard work, and it is time consuming. An administrator who doesn't have a high energy level may lack the stamina necessary to do the job. A careful reading of the publication, *What Makes an Effective School,*[31] reveals the importance of high energy, drive, and long hours on the part of those principals who are exercising instructional leadership. As noted by Clark and his colleagues, ". . . Effective leaders did more; they framed goals and objectives, set standards of performance, created a productive working environment, and obtained needed support."[32] All of this requires a high level of energy, and an administrator who is deficient in this regard is unlikely to sustain the effort necessary for effective instructional leadership.

A seventh factor which observation and experience would suggest is related to the probability that an administrator will engage in leadership is his willingness to take risks. As Lipham has pointed out, the leader is a disrupter of the status quo.[33] As a disrupter, he runs the risk of alienating people and even losing his job. If the changes which he seeks to introduce are basic to the way people think and behave, the educational leader will undoubtedly threaten certain existing values and vested interests. Many people dislike and even fear change, particularly when it upsets their way of thinking, life style, or work pattern. The administrator who perceives the need for change but is unwilling to run the risk of alienating some people is unlikely to engage in leadership behavior to try to bring about needed change.[34]

The administrator who is reluctant to take risks, however, should recognize that education today is badly in need of improvement, which frequently requires risk-taking. As Groom and his colleagues emphasize, "For too long, many principals have been survival experts and have neglected their major calling—that of changing and improving education for boys and girls."[35]

It is true that exercising instructional leadership will frequently require the courage to assume certain risks, sometimes at great personal and professional cost. But, as the study by the Institute for Educational Leadership points out, "Good principals tend to rock the boat. They forsake the desire to be loved for the hard work of monitoring students' progress. They set achievement goals for their students, and they judge their teachers and themselves by them."[36] The alternative of not attempting to exert leadership will no doubt result in fewer risks and greater security for the administrator, but it may also mean the loss of opportunity to bring about needed improvement in education.

Finally, an important personal prerequisite which an administrator needs, particularly in risk situations, is the ability to work well with people.[37] Effective leaders possess human relation skills and are generally likable individuals, even though their actions may not always be popular. People will generally respond to these kinds of leaders with trust and confidence. Although researchers and theorists are not of one mind about the particular attributes and skills which generate this type of reaction, it appears that effective leaders[38]

- Are sensitive to the needs of others.
- Explain the reasons for their actions.

- Involve others in important decisions.
- Are open to criticism, without being defensive.
- Are willing to admit mistakes and to make changes.
- Are honest and fair in interacting with others.

It is probable that no one possesses to a high degree all of the qualities necessary to be an effective instructional leader, and there is no reason why a single administrator should have to possess every quality described previously. In most schools and school districts there will be a number of people who, in one way or another, can make a contribution to improving the instructional program. An important leadership responsibility of the administrator is to identify and then organize these people into an instructional improvement team.

THE INSTRUCTIONAL IMPROVEMENT TEAM

An important objective of any administrator who is trying to improve instruction should be to organize and utilize effectively all appropriate and available sources of expertise. Personnel in a school or district who may (or could) be assigned supervisory responsibilities for improving instruction include the assistant principal, the department head or unit leader, and the central office subject matter supervisor. The degree to which all of these individuals are assigned supervisory responsibilities may vary somewhat from one district to another. However, each of these persons generally possesses special knowledge, skill, or insight which an administrator should attempt to utilize in improving instruction. The administrator can capitalize on the talents of these individuals in two ways: (1) by making explicit to them (and to the people with whom they associate) the nature and extent of their supervisory responsibilities, and (2) by organizing them into an instructional improvement team.

The instructional improvement team is a relatively recent concept in education and it has not been implemented in many schools.[39] Its basic purpose is to improve instruction by mobilizing and organizing the various kinds of expertise which exist in a school. The team usually includes the principal and the department heads (or unit leaders) but can—and perhaps should—also include district supervisors if the latter are available.

The main activities of the team should be to evaluate the effectiveness of the instructional program and to study, develop, and implement ways in which it can be improved. The team should not, however, become directly involved in the evaluation of staff for the purpose of making personnel decisions. That function should be left to the staff evaluation team, which was discussed in the previous chapter.

An example of the kinds of activities in which an instructional improvement team may become involved is shown by a team agenda, presented in figure 11.1 on the next page.

1. Presentation of the Iowa Test results.
2. Discussion of how the test results relate to the achievement of the educational objectives of the school or organizational units within the school.
3. Identification of needed improvements.

Figure 11.1. Instructional
Improvement Team Meeting Agenda

The agenda for meetings of the instructional improvement team should be developed on the basis of members' input and should be distributed several days before the meeting in order to give participants an opportunity to consider it and prepare for the meeting.

The instructional improvement team should be involved in all aspects of the supervisory process. Supervision no longer should be the sole province of one person, the principal. While the principal may be held ultimately responsible for supervision and the improvement of instruction in a school, he cannot accomplish the job alone. Therefore, in the rest of the chapter, references will be made to the role of supervisor, a role which can (and if feasible should) be performed by various members of the instructional improvement team.

A PROPOSED PROCESS OF INSTRUCTIONAL SUPERVISION

The ultimate goal of instructional supervision should be to improve student learning, but its more immediate objective is to improve the instructional program. To achieve the latter purpose, the supervisor should engage in a number of activities. If these activities are interrelated and sequential rather than random, they constitute a process. The process of supervision is really the supervisor's design to accomplish the objective of improving the instructional program.

The process of instructional supervision which will be recommended in this chapter is the problem-solving approach. This approach is not new, of course, but its utilization as the main process of instructional supervision has been limited, at least insofar as discussion in the educational literature is concerned.[40] The main steps in the process are presented in figure 11.2.

In order to help the supervisor better understand and utilize the problem-solving approach to instructional supervision as outlined in figure 11.2, the major aspects of the process will be discussed in some detail.

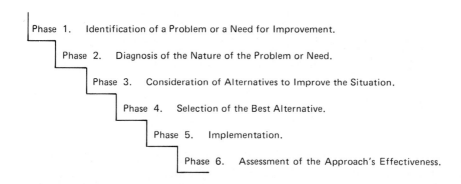

Figure 11.2. A Problem-Solving
Approach to Instructional Supervision

IDENTIFICATION OF A PROBLEM
OR A NEED FOR IMPROVEMENT

The supervisor's goal is to improve instruction. However, in order to accomplish that objective he must first determine which elements of the instructional program need to be improved. To arrive at that determination the supervisor should consider at least three major sources of assistance in the identification of problems or needs of the instructional program: (1) people who are associated with the school, (2) professional standards and/or recommendations, and (3) local research.

People Who Are Associated with the School
Students, teachers, parents, and the central administration all represent potentially excellent sources of assistance for identifying instructional program needs and problems. Since most of these groups are closely involved with the instructional program, they are in a good position to suggest areas needing improvement. Although some of these people may, on their own initiative, recommend instructional improvement needs to the supervisor, he should not depend on or limit his feedback to only those few individuals.

If a supervisor is really interested in securing input from students, teachers, parents, and the central office, he should survey these groups *regularly* to ascertain their perceptions and ideas on which aspects of the instructional program need to be improved. Such a survey would not have to be long and complicated, and it could provide useful information if it only included several questions. An example is presented in figure 11.3. Using a type of survey similar to the one in figure 11.3, the National Education Association found from a national sampling of teachers that the most important improvements the

---

1. What are the three *most* important classroom problems which you believe impair your effectiveness as a teacher?
2. What are three ways in which *each* of the problems listed above could be ameliorated?
3. Would you be willing to work on a committee to help resolve these problems?

Figure 11.3. A Teacher Survey to
Identify Instructional Problems

teachers wanted to see in education were (1) reducing the number of students in class, (2) educating parents on how to help with their children's education, (3) enforcing stricter discipline, (4) enforcing stricter requirements for school and class attendance, (5) devoting more attention to the basics—reading, English, etc., and (6) requiring higher standards of performance from students. Teachers in the survey were nearly *unanimous* in favoring these improvements.[41]

A supervisor may feel that the results of a national survey are not valid for his school. If so, then he should conduct a local survey. However, whether or not he agrees with the perceptions of teachers on which aspects of the instructional program need to be improved, feedback can help him to have a better understanding of their attitudes. And if a majority of teachers see too many discipline problems, for example, as a major impediment to teaching, it would probably be to the supervisor's advantage to investigate the validity of their perception.

Professional Standards and Recommendations

A second important source for helping to identify instructional improvement needs is the body of recommendations and standards proposed by professional organizations and educational authorities. For example, regional accrediting associations such as the North Central Association publish standards which member schools are expected to meet, and which can be used by an administrator to identify areas for instructional improvement.[42] The National Association of Secondary School Principals, The National Association of Elementary School Principals, and The Association for Supervision and Curriculum Development also publish recommendations for improving instruction in the schools. In addition, articles and books are written each year by educational authorities who advocate various improvements in the instructional program.

For example, one article which should be useful to supervisors who want to improve instruction is, "What Psychology Can We Feel Sure About?" by Goodwin Watson.[43] He has identified fifty different psychological principles on how students learn, established by research. Four of these are listed:

1. Behaviors which are rewarded (reinforced) are more likely to recur.
2. Reward (reinforcement) must follow almost immediately after the desired behavior and be clearly connected with that behavior in the mind of the learner in order for the reward to be most effective.
3. Sheer repetition without indication of improvement or any kind of reinforcement (reward) is a poor way to attempt to learn.
4. Threat and punishment have variable and uncertain effects upon learning; they may make the punished response either more or less likely to recur; they may set up avoidance tendencies which prevent further learning.[44]

These and the other forty-six psychological principles described in Watson's article represent valuable criteria which a supervisor could use to identify aspects of instruction which need to be improved. By observing the extent to which a teacher bases his instruction on sound psychological principles, a supervisor can identify ineffective or counterproductive teaching styles and take appropriate supervisory action.

Another publication that contains helpful ideas for improving instruction is *Research on Teaching: Concepts, Findings and Implications,* commissioned by the National Society for the Study of Education.[45] This book presents a comprehensive review of research regarding the improvement of instruction and is full of good ideas. For example, Rosenshine's analysis of the research on instructional time and student achievement suggests that the concept and activities of *direct instruction* seem to have merit. Although the concept is not easily defined, it seems to focus on those teacher behaviors that *directly* attempt to improve learning in reading and mathematics, and includes the following elements: (1) making clear to students the goals of the lesson, (2) spending sufficient time on instruction, (3) extensively covering content, (4) continuous monitoring of student performance, (5) asking questions that are within the capacity of the student to answer, and (6) providing immediate and academically oriented feedback to the students.[46] While Rosenshine's ideas on direct instruction are certainly worth examining, other chapters in the National Society for the Study of Education book also provide additional ideas and approaches to improving instruction.[47] Another equally valuable source of ideas is the *Handbook of Research on Teaching,* which contains many clues and hypotheses for instructional improvement.[48]

Local Research

A third source of assistance for identifying instructional improvement needs is local research, initiated or coordinated by the supervisor. The purpose of this type of research is to ascertain the effectiveness of the instructional program and the various conditions which influence its effectiveness. Although some supervisors may shudder at the mere mention of the term "research," it can legitimately include a variety of activities which most supervisors should be able to conduct with appropriate assistance.

Three suggestions for local research are

1. Follow-up study of graduates; follow-up study of dropouts. Both studies can yield useful information about the effectiveness of the instructional program and the conditions affecting it. These kinds of studies should be initiated on a regular basis and can be conducted through the use of questionnaires and in-depth interviews.

2. A study of how much time is spent in the classroom on direct teaching and learning as opposed to other kinds of activities which may occur in a classroom. There is now considerable research suggesting that instructional time is an important variable associated with student learning.[49] A research question which the supervisor could explore through classroom observation is, "What kinds of activities, e.g., direct teaching, are occurring in the classroom, and how much time is actually being spent on instruction?" A useful technique for answering that question has been developed by the Wisconsin Research and Development Center, and the reader is encouraged to pursue additional information about the method.[50]

3. An analysis of test data to ascertain progress toward or the achievement of the educational objectives of the school. Although an evaluation of the extent of achievement of educational objectives should not be *limited* to an examination of test data, these data can be helpful in suggesting possible areas in need of instructional improvement. The supervisor should, of course, be cautious in drawing firm conclusions about the instructional program based solely on test data, and it probably would be well to secure consultant assistance in interpreting the relationship between the test results and the achievement of educational objectives.

These are only a few examples of local research which could be helpful. By organizing such research efforts a supervisor can begin to pinpoint weaknesses in the instructional program so that corrective action can be taken. In the absence of this kind of research activity, the supervisor will frequently lack the data necessary to ascertain the effectiveness of the instructional program.

In concluding this section on the identification of needs for improving instruction, it should be emphasized that the improvement of instruction depends on ideas of what instruction *should* be and data on what it *is*. If the supervisor does not possess or seek both kinds of information, he is dependent on his own subjective preferences for improving instruction, surely a weak basis for exercising *professional* judgment.

DIAGNOSIS OF THE NEED FOR IMPROVEMENT

Identification of a need for improving instruction should be followed by diagnosis of that need. Diagnosing a need simply means determining its nature and the reasons for its existence.

For example, suppose a supervisor observes that a teacher doesn't seem to provide much direct instruction, and students appear to be left on their own to a large extent. The initial question that should be asked in attempting to diagnose the situation is, why is the teacher behaving this way? To obtain an answer to that question, the supervisor may need to explore several alternative explanations and questions:

1. The subject matter or skill being taught doesn't lend itself to direct instruction but, rather, requires a more indirect teaching style that provides for considerable student self-instruction. (Is this the case? Why?)
2. The students are quite mature, responsible, and have a high level of ability; therefore, a more "open" classroom with less direct instruction is appropriate. (Do data support this hypothesis?)
3. The teacher's particular approach to teaching is meeting certain needs of his personality or value system. (Is this possible? What specific teacher needs are being met, and how likely is it that they could be changed?)
4. There are few or no rewards or incentives for the teacher or the students to participate in a more structured situation.

In examining a problem situation the supervisor may find that a single factor explains the undesired behavior or condition. Frequently, however, there will be more than one reason. Therefore, in the initial stages of diagnosis, the supervisor should concentrate on identifying a broad range of possible explanations for a problem, and then attempt to focus on the more important and relevant factors that best explain why the problem exists. Once a problem has been completely and accurately diagnosed, the supervisor will be in a position to consider possible solutions.

Accurate diagnosis of a problem is an important prerequisite for successful problem solving, since a proposed solution to a problem is likely to be based on its diagnosis. Inaccurate diagnosis is frequently the reason why an instructional problem is not satisfactorily resolved. Usually in such a situation the wrong solution has resulted from failure to properly diagnose the problem. Until instructional problems are properly diagnosed, the supervisor cannot expect to improve instruction to a significant degree.

IMPROVING INSTRUCTION: MAJOR ALTERNATIVES

After an instructional problem has been accurately diagnosed, the supervisor is in a position to consider possible solutions for improving the situation. In the following sections, rather than examining alternatives for a *particular* problem, which would limit our consideration, a wide range of supervisory techniques, procedures, and programs available to the supervisor will be described in order to develop greater awareness and understanding of the main options for improving instruction. Discussion of supervisory alternatives will be divided into two parts: (1) working with an individual and (2) working with a group.

IMPROVING INSTRUCTION: WORKING WITH AN INDIVIDUAL

Classroom Visitation and Conferencing

Perhaps the supervisory techniques used most frequently by supervisors are classroom visitations, preceded by and followed by individual conferences. Although these techniques can be treated as separate supervisory activities, they are usually employed in conjunction with each other; seldom will a classroom visitation hold much value for a teacher without a preobservational conference and a follow-up consultation. The entire process has been referred to as clinical supervision, and a comprehensive review of books and articles on the topic has been published by the Association for Supervision and Curriculum Development.[51] The purpose of the following discussion is to introduce the reader to the concept, process, and activities of clinical supervision.

The three components of clinical supervision, conceptualized as a cycle, are depicted in figure 11.4.

The pre-observational conference, which involves the supervisor and the teacher who is to be observed, is very important to the effectiveness of the classroom observation.[52] The objectives and activities of the pre-observational conference include:

1. Developing rapport between the supervisor and the teacher who is to be observed.
2. Establishing the purposes and function of the classroom observation.
3. Agreeing on the aspects of the instructional program that are to be observed.*

*For a particularly good discussion of goal setting during the pre-observational conference, see Thomas L. McGreal, "Helping Teachers Set Goals," *Educational Leadership* (February 1980), 414–19.

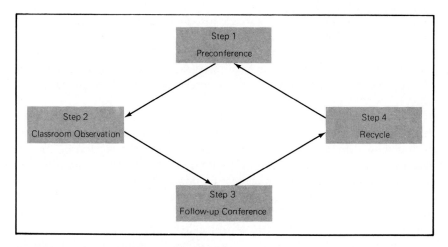

Figure 11.4. The Process of Clinical
Supervision

4. Developing procedures which will be used during the observation.
5. Identifying the roles that the supervisor and the teacher will perform during the observation.
6. Indicating the purposes and nature of the follow-up conference to be held after the classroom observation.
7. Answering the teacher's questions about the classroom observation and the follow-up conference.

It should be emphasized that numbers 1 through 6 should be agreed upon cooperatively rather than imposed by the supervisor. At the end of the pre-observational conference the teacher should feel that he has been meaningfully involved in the supervisory process and that the supervisor has the teacher's best interests at heart. The interpersonal relationship that develops between the supervisor and the teacher will in most cases significantly influence the effectiveness of the supervision, perhaps more than any other factor. As Blumberg has noted, ". . . The results of research on supervisory behavior styles in the school support the notion that more open, collaborative and nondefensive is the interpersonal climate created by the supervisor, the more teachers are satisifed with their supervision and feel that it is productive for them."[53]

Following the pre-observational conference the supervisor should initiate the classroom observation(s). The classroom observation or visitation should be used to identify and diagnose strengths and areas in need of improvement. Through classroom visitation the supervisor can identify teacher and classroom improvement needs and can observe conditions which may be impairing student learning. The supervisor should also find the classroom visitation useful in identifying effective teaching and for gaining a more complete and accurate picture of the total instructional program in the school. (Several sources that describe observational systems or instruments which should be of help to the supervisor in conducting classroom observations are listed at the end of this chapter.[54])

The supervisor will need to recognize, however, that classroom observations may not be viewed by many teachers as a positive and constructive contribution to their effectiveness.[55] Poor planning by the supervisor for the classroom visitation, little or no follow-up on the observation, and a lack of constructive suggestions to the teacher on how to improve have all cast considerable doubt for many teachers on the value of the classroom visitation. Added to these factors is the anxiety created by the classroom observation when it is conducted for the purpose of teacher evaluation.

Since most of these negative factors associated with the classroom observation can be corrected by the supervisor, he should not reject the classroom visitation as one of his supervisory alternatives, despite possible teacher opposition. It would be to his advantage, though, to be aware of the attitude of many teachers about classroom visitations and to try to make the visitations positive experiences. (An excellent source for ideas on the purposes of classroom observations and how to conduct them is *Responsive Supervision for Professional Development: An Overview of the Process,* by Nicholas Rayder and Trent Taylor. San Francisco: Far West Laboratory for Educational Research and Development.)

After the supervisor has completed his classroom observations and has identified and diagnosed a teaching problem, which is impairing the effectiveness of the instructional program, a follow-up conference with the teacher will probably be needed in order to improve the situation. (A follow-up conference can be useful for discussing a teacher's strengths and should not be limited only to the discussion of the teacher's weaknesses.)

The follow-up conference can be a useful supervisory technique for accomplishing the following objectives:

1. Developing a better understanding on the part of the participants in the conference of the way each person sees the classroom situation, and the reasons for those perceptions.
2. Exploring possible solutions to an instructional problem.
3. Designing and agreeing upon a plan of action to improve the classroom situation.
4. Reviewing progress made by the teacher in attempting to improve the classroom situation.

Whether any particular follow-up conference between a supervisor and a teacher should include all four of these objectives will depend on the conditions which brought about the conference. However, accomplishing all four purposes will obviously, in most cases, take more than a single meeting.

It should be pointed out that the success of the follow-up conference will depend in large part on the extent to which the teacher feels secure with and trustful of the supervisor, and the amount of planning invested by the supervisor in preparation for the meeting. If the teacher does not feel comfortable with the supervisor and does not feel that the supervisor has the best interest of the teacher at heart, then the latter is unlikely to be very cooperative. Also, factors such as the time and location of the conference, the seating arrangement, establishing and maintaining rapport during the conference, the objectives of the meeting, identifying and sequencing questions to be asked, anticipating questions the teacher may raise, and deciding how to close the conference—all will need to be considered by the supervisor.* Successful conferences cannot take place without adequate planning, and there is evidence that many supervisory conferences are not successful.[56]

The value of the supervisory conference is not restricted to its use in conjunction with the classroom visitation. An individual conference can be used by the supervisor to discuss with the teacher a variety of items which may be impairing instruction: class scheduling, the homework policy, grading, or nature of the text material, for example. However, since the classroom observation and the preobservational conference and follow-up conference are generally linked in people's minds, as well as in practice, the discussion has focused for the most part on the purpose and planning for those types of conferences.[57]

VIDEOTAPE ANALYSIS AND MICROTEACHING

A problem in trying to improve the instructional program that is encountered by most supervisors at one time or another is created by the difference in the way that the teacher and the supervisor perceive what has occurred in the classroom. An approach to this difficulty is for the supervisor to utilize, in cooperation with the teacher, a videotape machine to help both of them analyze the classroom situation.[58] This equipment can capture on tape for both teacher and supervisor the actual dynamics of what has happened in the classroom, thereby enabling them to review and study the tape, and to analyze it for the identification of strengths and areas needing improvement in the instructional program. Recent developments utilizing split-screen videotaping,

---

*For an earlier but still relevant discussion of these points see George C. Kyte, *The Principal at Work* (New York: Ginn & Co.), pp. 274–76. Also see Mary Acevedo et al., *A Guide for Conducting an Effective Feedback Session* (Austin, Texas: Department of Educational Administration, University of Texas).

allowing both the teacher and the students to be observed on the screen at the same time, make this technology even more valuable for improving instruction.[59]

In addition to helping a supervisor and teacher develop a better understanding of and agreement on the specific aspects of the instructional program needing improvement, the videotape machine can also be used by a teacher to examine videotapes of colleagues or outside experts demonstrating effective employment of instructional techniques and procedures.* Through this kind of study a teacher can observe a model of how a particular teaching technique should be employed and learn how he might use the same technique in his classroom. While undoubtedly many teachers could benefit from studying the videotapes without supervisory assistance, it is recommended that, at least in the beginning, the supervisor work with the teacher in analyzing the tapes.

Although studying videotapes should prove to be of value to a teacher who is trying to improve his methods and skills, a supervisor or a teacher may feel that there is a need to *practice* a teaching skill before it is incorporated in classroom procedures. Again, the videotape equipment can play an important role in increasing the effectiveness of the teacher's practice sessions. Prior to use of the video equipment, the major problem an individual faced in deriving significant benefit from practice was that he normally could not observe how well he was accomplished a task while it was being performed. Once the event had occurred, it was too late to observe it; therefore, he was dependent on the perceptions of others who described it to him. However, by utilizing a video machine a teacher can now tape his practice session with students and then view the tape to see how well he performed a particular skill and how he might improve in the next practice session. This process is referred to as "micro-teaching."[60]

The video recorder's essential function in supervision is to capture the reality of a situation for later study, analysis, and evaluation. It can be used by the supervisor and teacher to identify strengths and limitations in the instructional program, to analyze model teaching to gain ideas for self-improvement, and to provide feedback on progress that is being made in developing a particular teaching skill.[61] It is without question a very useful supervisory tool for improving the instructional program, and any school lacking access to a videotape machine should investigate the possibility of obtaining one.

INTERCLASS AND INTERSCHOOL VISITATION

Too many supervisors attempt to improve instruction by *telling* the teacher what needs to be changed in the classroom situation. While the technique of telling may work in some cases, a much more successful supervisory approach

---

*For further information on materials and procedures, write NEA, Publishing, 1201 16th St., N.W., Washington, D.C. 20036.

is to *show* the teachers a more effective way of conducting instruction. In some cases the supervisor himself might demonstrate the change he is advocating. It may be more realistic and likely, however, for him to identify individuals in (or outside) the school who can most appropriately and effectively demonstrate a new technique or procedure.

For example, one teacher in the school may be particularly skillful in leading a class discussion; another person might be good in the area of establishing student self-discipline, and another in evaluation techniques. The supervisor should attempt to capitalize on the talents of these people and others by organizing a program of interclass and interschool visitation for teachers who would like to improve their skills in a particular area. The interclass visitations might take place during a teacher's released period, or another type of accommodation might be made by the supervisor. Interschool visitations could take place during an in-service day or, if necessary, a substitute teacher might be hired in order for a member of the staff to view a class in another school. (A good example of an intervisitation program is described in Gersten's article in *Phi Delta Kappan.*[62])

Organizing a program of interclass and interschool visitations will not be an easy task for the school supervisor. It can be accomplished, but it requires effort and resourcefulness. There will be scheduling problems to be resolved, and the cooperation of those who are to be visited must be secured. However, interclass and interschool visitations are two excellent means by which teachers can actually see a technique or procedure demonstrated, instead of listening to a supervisor talk about it. For this reason, then, both kinds of visitations are recommended as desirable components of a good supervisory program.

USE OF THE PROFESSIONAL LIBRARY

Most schools have some type of professional library. The primary purpose of the professional library is to provide an opportunity for staff members to improve themselves through reading or viewing various kinds of print and nonprint materials.

Undoubtedly some members of the staff use the professional library on their own initiative and derive great benefit from it. However, observation and experience would suggest that many members of the faculty of a school seldom, if ever, use the professional library except in completing a university course or for other special reasons.[63] It would appear that in most schools the professional library plays a minimal role in the improvement of instruction.

Whether the professional library can play an important role in improving instruction in a school will depend on many factors. However, two factors appear to be critical.[64] First of all, the faculty should be involved by the librarian in selecting materials and in deciding on the location of the professional library. Secondly, the supervisor must demonstrate to the faculty that he feels the professional library is an important part of the school. If he tends to ignore the library in his own reading or is unfamiliar with the collection, he will not only fail to provide a good model for the faculty but will also be in a poor position to utilize the library's resources in working with the staff.

The materials in a professional library can, if properly selected, be useful in helping a teacher to improve himself. But before they receive much use, the supervisor must show that he is interested in the professional library's resources, and he must become sufficiently familiar with the resources to recommend them appropriately to others.

IMPROVING INSTRUCTION: WORKING WITH GROUPS

Most instructional leadership activities that involve working with groups come under the rubric of in-service education. Harris defines in-service education as ". . . any planned program of learning opportunities afforded staff members of schools, colleges or other educational agencies for the purposes of improving the performance of the individual in already assigned positions."[65] He believes that, "The improvement of instruction is the essential focus of in-service education."[66]

Although in-service education has been frequently advanced by educators as a corrective to many problems,[67] like so many other aspects of education, it comes under periodic attack. Rubin, for example, asserts that, "The typical [in-service] program has suffered from a lack of energy, precision, direction, and imagination."[68] He goes on to conclude that, "Put bluntly, the methods used in in-service education have been for the most part, bad educational practices. With few notable exceptions, most of the programs are sporadic and disorganized."[69]

Harris, on the other hand, takes a more optimistic view toward in-service, based on a fairly comprehensive review of the effectiveness of in-service programs.[70] He feels that research has shown that in-service education *can* be successful under the right conditions. (These will be discussed later.)

Whether or not in-service education has been successful is a debatable question. What is clear, however, is that, "Significant improvement of education cannot be accomplished, it would seem, without a major programmatic effort at the in-service education of personnel in all elementary and secondary schools and colleges."[71] As Harris emphasizes in connection with the need for in-service education, "The staff is the heart of the operation of the schools. Money, materials, time, space, facilities, and curricula—all of these are important, too. But initially, in process, and ultimately, the ability of the staff to perform is crucial."[72]

If in-service education is important but in need of improvement, how can it be improved? Based on an analysis of various recommendations for improving in-service programs,[73] it would appear that the following conditions must be met:

- The staff needs to be *involved* in the establishment of the need for in-service education and in the development, implementation, and evaluation of the program.
- The in-service program eventually initiated must be viewed by teachers as contributing to *their* professional growth rather than only meeting administrative needs.
- The school board, administrators, and supervisors of the school/district must be *committed* to the importance of in-service education, and the latter two groups must *plan carefully* with the staff for the development, implementation, and evaluation of in-service activities.
- Objectives of the in-service program need to be stated *clearly* and *specifically,* and be reasonably *attainable,* given the constraints of the situation.
- In-service activities need to be *varied* and should involve the participants *actively,* as opposed to the more passive role of listener, observer, or reader.
- In-service activities should be planned and scheduled so there is continuity and articulation between what goes on in the program and what occurs before and after the instructional program.
- The leader or presenter of the in-service activity needs to show how (by demonstrating, if possible) new content, materials, or skills can be applied to the staff member's situation.
- The incentives for participating in an in-service program should emphasize both intrinsic (e.g., professional improvement) as well as extrinsic rewards (e.g., credit on the salary schedule.)
- Participants in in-service education need periodic feedback during the program on their progress.
- Adequate time and funds must be provided by the administration to plan, carry out, and evaluate the in-service activities.

While the presence of these ten conditions may not *guarantee* a successful in-service program, their absence would seem to limit its chances of success. Additional factors that the supervisor will need to take into consideration in planning and implementing particular in-service activities are discussed in the following sections.

DEPARTMENTAL OR UNIT MEETINGS

Most schools hold departmental or unit meetings periodically during the year. These meetings offer an important opportunity for a supervisor to improve instruction by working with a group of teachers. Unfortunately, such meetings usually take place after a long day of school, and frequently only items of a "housekeeping" nature are discussed. However, the potential for discussing and exploring issues, problems and new approaches to instruction is definitely present at a departmental or unit meeting. The key people for capitalizing on that potential are the supervisor and the department heads or unit leaders.

If the departmental or unit meeting is to become an important means of improving instruction, the supervisor will need to work with the department heads or unit leaders to extend their vision of the purposes and uses of these meetings, and should hold the chairmen or unit leaders accountable for focusing their meetings to a larger extent on instructional improvement purposes. Most department heads and unit leaders, because of a lack of training or vision, do not take the initiative to utilize their meetings for discussion of instructional improvement activities. They need help and encouragement from the supervisor.

There is a wide variety of possible instructional improvement topics which could be explored during department or unit meetings. The following four examples should illustrate the range of possibilities:

1. Examination of departmental or unit objectives to ascertain the degree of understanding and consensus on overall objectives and the objectives for each grade level.
2. Consideration of an assessment program to provide data on the extent to which departmental or unit objectives are being met.
3. Presentation and demonstration of available supplementary resources from the instructional materials center.
4. Development of a uniform grading or homework policy for the department or unit.

These four topics are only suggestive of the kinds of instructional improvement activities which a department or unit could consider during its meetings.[74] This does not mean that the supervisor can realistically expect that *all* departmental or unit meetings can be devoted entirely to instructional improvement topics. There are admittedly legitimate housekeeping tasks, such as requisitioning and budgeting, which a department or unit must accomplish during its meetings. However, one of the primary purposes of these meetings should be to focus on instructional improvement.

FACULTY MEETINGS

The faculty meeting is probably one of the most abused and most often criticized of all group supervisory activities. It is generally scheduled at the end of the school day when teachers are tired, it is frequently informational in nature and dominated by the principal, and it seldom provides for much teacher participation and involvement. Also, since the advent of the master contract for teachers, the time allowed for faculty meetings is frequently of such short duration that little of an instructional nature can be discussed. On the other hand, the faculty meeting represents one of the few vehicles available to the supervisor during the year for bringing the total faculty together to consider instructional concerns. By correcting the abuses of the faculty meeting, it can be used profitably for instructional improvement purposes.

One of the major constraints which a supervisor must overcome in order to utilize the faculty meeting effectively is that, with the exception of very small schools, the size of the faculty usually limits the amount of participation which can take place.[75] Recognizing this limitation, it would appear that faculty meetings should be used primarily for problem identification and decision making, and that the investigation of a problem and exploration of alternative solutions should be carried out by subcommittees of the faculty, who would report their recommendations to the total faculty and administration for a final decision. This would make possible a more effectively conducted faculty meeting, and yet the administrator (with the faculty, if appropriate) could make the final decision on a matter. The alternative is for 40 to 100 people to attempt to determine the nature of a problem, the reasons for its existence, and possible alternative solutions—under conditions of apathy, fatigue, large group size, and limited time frame.

If a supervisor is to utilize the faculty meeting more productively, he should try to follow rather simple but important principles:[76]

1. **The meeting should be scheduled during school time, if possible, rather than at the end of the day.** Some schools dismiss students early on one afternoon every week or two in order to provide greater time for faculty consideration of a topic.
2. **Faculty input should be sought in developing the agenda.** This may mean establishing a faculty meeting planning committee (required by some master contracts) or simply requesting the faculty to submit items for the agenda. In any regard, faculty members' input is important in the development of the agenda if they are to play more than a passive role at the meetings.
3. **The agenda and all related materials for the faculty meeting should be distributed to the staff at least two days before the date of the meeting.** If faculty members are to react, discuss, and make decisions on agenda items at the meeting, they will need an opportunity to become aware of and think about the topics to be discussed, and to study the related material prior to the meeting. It is conceded that some faculty members—perhaps even a large proportion—won't take or find time to consider the agenda and related materials before the meeting, even if they receive them in advance. However, many teachers *will* find this procedure helpful.

4. **The supervisor should employ as much as possible the group leadership skills identified in chapter 3.** His role during the faculty meetings should be to[77]

   a. Create an atmosphere which is friendly and nonthreatening but task-oriented.
   b. Guide the discussion in such a way that as many people as possible who would like to and should participate during the meeting have an opportunity to do so.
   c. Clarify questions, comments, or statements so that intentions, meanings, and implications are not left ambiguous.
   d. Keep the group focused on the topic under consideration, and limit wandering from the subject.
   e. Summarize periodically where the group appears to be, relative to the topic, and what remains to be done.
   f. Mediate differences of opinion.

5. **Minutes of the meeting should be maintained that will indicate important points made, questions raised that are yet to be resolved, commitments made, and decisions reached.** The minutes are a useful record of what transpired during the meeting and can be used for self-improvement analysis and for providing continuity from one meeting to another.

6. **Minutes of the meeting should be disseminated to the total faculty and other relevant parties, e.g., the immediate superior in the central office.** Each member of the faculty needs a record of what transpired during the meeting, if understanding of and commitment to decisions reached during the meeting are to be maintained. It is also useful to provide space at the end of the minutes for reactions by faculty members for the purpose of obtaining feedback from individuals who, for one reason or another, did not comment during the meeting itself.

7. **Follow-up activities need to be initiated after the faculty meeting in order to implement decisions which were reached and to investigate questions or problems that were raised.** A fairly common complaint of many teachers about faculty meetings is that there is no follow-through afterwards. If the faculty is to feel that their meetings are worthwhile, the supervisor will need to initiate and coordinate appropriate follow-up activities after the meetings.

Faculty meetings can be a valuable group activity for the improvement of instruction if the previously described principles are followed. New approaches to teaching can be demonstrated, instructional problems can be identified, and/or recommendations from subcommittees on school philosophy, objectives, grading, and grade level articulation, for example, can be considered and decided upon. The value of the faculty meeting is limited mainly by the size of the faculty and the degree of resourcefulness and organizational skills possessed by the supervisor.[78] (For additional good ideas on how to make a variety of different kinds of group meetings more effective, see "Making Meetings More Effective" by John Lindelow, ERIC Report # Ed–189–680).

COMMITTEE WORK

Committee work is an appropriate problem-solving procedure for improving instruction as well as an excellent group activity for staff development. As a result of committee interaction and investigation of an instructional problem, each member of a committee can benefit in terms of increased awareness, understanding, and (possibly) new skills.

A supervisor should attempt to utilize committees in the improving of instruction whenever it appears that a situation would be more thoroughly investigated and considered if several people were involved rather than only one individual. The primary rationale for establishing a committee, rather than assigning only one person, should be that the other people whom the supervisor might involve possess additional knowledge, skill, or insight which will be helpful in the accomplishment of a task. That task may be investigating a possible instructional problem, identifying alternative solutions, or gaining acceptance from the entire faculty on a recommended course of action.

Although committee work can be an excellent method for improving instruction and capitalizing on the expertise of various staff members, the experience of those involved with committees has not always been positive. Frequently, teachers have felt that they were not "meaningfully involved" on a committee, and that the supervisor had his "mind already made up" before the committee was appointed. Supervisors, on their part, have sometimes felt that teachers expected too much from their involvement and tried to exceed their authority. And, of course, there frequently arise problems of insufficient time, role ambiguity, and inadequate incentives for committee work.

While the supervisor will probably not be able to avoid all problems in regard to committee work, difficulties can be minimized if the following procedures are followed:

1. Clearly define and communicate to all committee members, in advance, the objectives, function, scope, and authority of the committee. If it is only an advisory committee to develop recommendations to submit to the supervisor, then that function should be made clear to all participants.
2. Keep all members of the committee well informed before, during, and after meetings, as to what is transpiring. Advance agendas and minutes of each meeting are minimum requirements.

3. Utilize to the greatest extent possible the individual interest and talents of the members of the committee. There is little to be gained by either the school or the participants if the latters' potential contributions are not fully utilized.
4. Reward members of the committee for their individual and total contributions at every available opportunity. Committee work is frequently tedious, and periodic recognition of the value of the committee's work will pay important dividends.

A significant factor which has contributed to ineffectiveness of committees and the disillusionment of committee members is the ambivalence or vagueness of the supervisor in regard to the objectives and role of the committee, and the role of the supervisor in relationship to the committee. A precise understanding of these points on the part of everyone involved will do much to avert serious problems at a later date.

(For additional ideas and conceptual tools for working with groups, see Richard A. Gorton, *School Administration and Supervision: Important Issues, Concepts, and Case Studies.* Dubuque, IA: Wm. C. Brown Company Publishers, 1980, chapter 13.)

WORKSHOPS AND INSTITUTES

Three main types of school workshops or institutes are: (1) the preschool workshop for staff before classes formally begin in the fall, (2) the in-service workshop held during the school year on in-service days or Saturdays, and (3) the summer workshop.* Since the preschool workshop has already been discussed in conjunction with orientation for new staff, this section will concentrate on the other two types of workshops.

The primary purpose of in-service workshops that take place during the school year should be to explore a problem, topic, or new approach to instruction in greater depth than would be possible during a faculty or committee meeting. A workshop can include a combination of activities for the total faculty, small groups, or individuals. Figure 11.5 presents a typical format for an in-service workshop scheduled during the year.

The success of an in-service workshop will depend in large part on the degree of administrative planning, organization, and faculty input which have been invested in the design and implementation of the workshop. The last factor, faculty input, is tremendously important. If the faculty members or their representatives have not been involved in choosing the theme and in planning for the workshop, its success will be uncertain. The supervisor needs faculty

*Since there are more similarities than differences between workshops and institutes, the discussion will focus on workshops and refer specifically to institutes only when appropriate.

Workshop Theme: Improvement of Reading

8:15-8:30	Coffee and socializing in Room 201
8:30-8:45	Welcome and an overview of the Workshop
8:45-9:45	Presentation by Dr. Hiller, "Data on the Effectiveness of the School's Reading Program and Ways to Improve It."
9:45-10:00	Break
10:00-11:45	Small Group Discussions about the implications of Dr. Hiller's presentation
11:45-1:00	Lunch
1:15-4:00	Team and individual teacher planning of instructional techniques and materials that might improve our Reading Program

Figure 11.5. Sample Format for In-Service Workshop

involvement so that in planning the workshop he can capitalize on the thinking and insight of the staff members and increase their receptivity to it. In most cases the faculty will not be very receptive to unilateral administrative decision making and planning in regard to an in-service workshop.

The first step in planning for an in-service workshop is to conduct a needs assessment.[79] Ideally, this procedure will not be initiated *only* prior to a workshop, but as an ongoing process, utilizing the sources for identifying needs described in the previous section on "Identification of a Problem or Need for Improvement." The essential question that a needs assessment is trying to answer is, "What aspect of the instructional program needs to be improved?" The typical approach to answering that question has been simply to survey teachers as to their perceptions of areas to be improved in the instructional program, or in other aspects of the school program. Unfortunately, in many instances this approach has led to a superficial assessment of needs which has tended to reflect current interests and fads, rather than *basic* needs of the instructional program.[80] While teachers should be involved in any needs assessment, the approach to determining the needs for improvement should include additionally related sources for identifying needs (see earlier section in this chapter). The approach should also be one which fosters objectivity in identifying needs, and should emphasize basic and future needs, as well as apparent and current needs.*

Once a comprehensive needs assessment has been completed, then the supervisor (working with others who are involved in planning, implementing, and evaluating the workshop) should initiate a series of planning and organizing steps which are necessary if the workshop is to be successful. These include (1) specification of the objectives to be achieved; (2) analysis of the extent to which the proposed objectives are *clear* and reasonably attainable, given the limits of time, resources, etc.; (3) identification and assessment of relevant workshop formats and activities which would facilitate achieving the objectives; (4) identification of relevant and available resources needed; (5) identification and assessment of possible problems or obstacles which could impair the chances of conducting a successful workshop; (6) decisions on the most effective workshop format and activities, given the availability of resources, and the possibility of certain obstacles or problems; (7) identification and assignment of needed personnel for implementing the workshop; (8) preparation of a master schedule of events, detailing when, where, and for how long activities are to occur; (9) agreement, before implementing the workshop, on criteria and methods for evaluating its activities; (10) review of Murphy's Laws that "Most things are more complicated than they initially appear to be," and that "Most things take longer than originally anticipated;" and a re-examination of the previous nine steps before beginning the workshop.

While the steps recommended above may seem like a lot of work and perhaps an overemphasis on detail, they should be viewed as only *general* guidelines for planning and organizing a workshop. That the actual planning and organizing can be and may need to be much more detailed is evidenced by an example in Bishop's book in which 56 separate steps were listed for planning a summer workshop.[81]

After the workshop has been conducted, it should be evaluated; and herein lies one of the major weaknesses of workshops or institutes. Frequently they are not evaluated at all, or they are evaluated in terms of what the participants *thought* of the speeches, materials, or activities. Seldom is there an evaluation of the extent to which the workshop has achieved its objectives. In addition, it seems that, regardless of the ideas, questions, or discussions explored during a workshop, there is very little indication two days later that it has had any discernible effect on what is taking place in the school. Part of the problem,

*A good resource for conducting a needs assessment for the purpose of in-service education has been published by the California State Department of Education, *A Kit of Materials for Needs Assessment and Evaluation* (Sacramento: Bureau of Inter-Group Relations).

of course, may be that little was accomplished during the workshop; but another hypothesis is that no one has assumed the responsibility of following through on what was achieved.

Certainly, all school personnel have a professional responsibility for workshop follow-up activities. But the supervisor himself must shoulder the major responsibility for initiating, coordinating, monitoring, and evaluating the activities. If he does not assume this responsibility, it is unlikely that anyone else will, and the value of the workshop will be quite minimal.

While evaluation methods are beyond the scope of this text, some sample evaluation questions that should be asked following a workshop or institute are:

1. To what extent were the workshop objectives achieved? What is the evidence for this?
2. To what degree did the workshop improve the knowledge, understanding, attitudes, or skills of the participants? What is the evidence for this?
3. How effective were the speakers and materials utilized during the workshop? What is the evidence for this?
4. How effective were the workshop format, activities, and schedule? What is the evidence?
5. What problems or obstacles were encountered that had not been anticipated, and why?
6. What was learned from this workshop experience that should be taken into consideration in planning and organizing the next workshop?
7. How can changes in the participants' understanding, attitudes, or skills be best sustained?

These evaluation questions are, of course, only a representative sample of the kinds of questions that need to be addressed, but they should give a supervisor some useful ideas for evaluating a workshop or institute.[82]

The points which have been made about in-service workshops held during the year also apply to summer workshops. Recently, participants in summer workshops have been remunerated, and problems of motivation and receptivity to workshop topics and activities have been correspondingly reduced. However, careful planning, systematic organization, considerable faculty input, and adequate follow-through after the workshops are just as important for summer workshops as for those held during the year. Both types offer an excellent mechanism for staff development and for improving instruction if the conditions recommended in this section are present.

TEACHER CENTERS

In reaction to the poor quality of the typical in-service education program, a different type of in-service for teachers has come on the scene in recent years. Referred to as "teacher centers" or "teaching centers," the in-service education activities which take place in these centers emphasize teacher decision-making on policy matters, self-direction, and colleague assistance, in regard to improvement, and voluntary as contrasted with required participation.[83] The centers seem to be based on several assumptions, according to Burrell:

> First, there is the notion that basic and effective innovation and reappraisal of work in the classroom will come about mainly through the efforts and activities of practicing teachers, assisted by whoever can contribute in some way. The second assumption is that there exists among teachers a vast reservoir of untapped expertise and experience. If they are given the opportunity, good teachers are capable of drawing on these and using them as a starting point for professional renewal and growth. The good practitioner is seen to have great potential as the trainer of other teachers. Third, it is assumed that centers can be effective instruments for reconsideration or development of current practice in the schools. The fourth assumption is that centers can provide a neutral arena in which teachers can work relatively free of constraints and pressures and the hierarchical assumptions often present in other training institutions. Many would argue that the rejection of the latter is the initial decisive factor in the development of true professionalism among teachers. It is certainly associated with the idea of teacher control of in-service planning, for the fifth assumption is that centers should be organized and controlled as far as possible by the teachers themselves through the centers' programs and other decision-making committees.[84]

Teaching centers have been implemented in a variety of locales, but they tend to be established in larger school districts and/or near universities. Their programs usually deal with the basic concerns and issues facing teachers, such as teacher burn-out.[85] The centers are often supported by federal funds, although school district funding is not unusual. The effectiveness of teaching centers is still being ascertained and their merits debated.[86] Some people are concerned about the centers' heavy emphasis on teacher control of policy-making, the voluntary nature of participation, and the assumptions behind self-directed improvement.[87] While these represent important issues, it does appear that teacher centers or some variation of them are probably here to stay, and the supervisor should learn how to work *with* them rather than against them. The reader who is interested in pursuing this topic further is encouraged to read additional material identified at the end of the chapter.[88]

A FINAL NOTE

The last step in the recommended approach to instructional supervision is assessment. No program can be significantly improved without assessment, and there is considerable evidence (referred to previously) that the instructional supervision program currently in operation in many schools is badly in need of improvement. Therefore, in addition to implementing the various suggested procedures described in this chapter the supervisor should, with the involvement and help of the faculty, periodically assess the effectiveness of the different components of the school's instructional supervision program. (Ideas for accomplishing program assessment may be obtained from Sage Publications, Beverly Hills, California.)

Review and Learning Activities

1. What factors limit and what factors enhance the role of the administrator as an instructional leader? Based on these factors, what improvements would have to take place before you could be an instructional leader in your current school or district?
2. Evaluate the concept of an instructional improvement team. What are its advantages and disadvantages? Does an instructional improvement team operate in your school? If not, why not?
3. What sources of assistance can a supervisor utilize in identifying a need for instructional improvement? Assess the utility of each source of assistance. To what extent are the sources of assistance recommended being used in your school?
4. Evaluate the concept and procedures of clinical supervision. Are the concepts and procedures of clinical supervision being practiced in your school? If not, why not?
5. Utilize the recommendations for improving in-service education, and ascertain the extent to which each of the suggested guidelines is being implemented in your school. Also, attempt to diagnose reasons for a lack of implementation of guidelines.
6. Evaluate each type of in-service education described in this chapter. What are its advantages and disadvantages?

Notes

1. For the historical roots of this definition, see Ross Neagley and N. Dean Evans, *Handbook for Effective Supervision* (Englewood Cliffs, N.J.: Prentice Hall, 1970), pp. 1–7.
2. Based on an examination of numerous job descriptions.

3. For an excellent review of research on the impact of these variables, see *Educational Environments and Effects,* ed. Herbert J. Walberg (Berkeley, Calif.: McCutchan, 1979). Also see John A. Centra and David A. Potter, "School and Teacher Effects," *Review of Educational Research* (Summer 1980): 273–91.

4. Owen Kiernan, testimony given to Senate Select Committee on Equal Education Opportunity, 1974. Also see "Principals Can Be Leaders If They Learn to Take Charge," *Education U.S.A.* (April 28, 1980): 265, 269.

5. Roald F. Campbell, "What Peculiarities in Educational Administration Make it a Special Case," in *Administrative Behavior in Education,* ed. Andrew Halpin (Chicago: Midwest Administration Center, University of Chicago), p. 172.

6. Donald Erickson, "Changes in the Principalship," *National Elementary Principal* (April 1965).

7. Anneka E. Bredo, "Teacher Legitimation of Principal Control as a Situational Contingency in Principal-Teacher Influence Relations" (Paper presented at the annual meeting of the American Educational Research Association, San Francisco, California, April 1979), p. 2.

8. John C. Croft, "The Principal as Supervisor: Some Descriptive Findings and Important Questions," *Educational Administration Abstracts* (Spring 1969).

9. Terrence E. Deal and Lynn D. Celotti, "How Much Influence Do (and Can) Educational Administrators Have on Classrooms?" *The Kappan* (March 1980): 471.

10. R. G. Corwin, "Teacher Militancy in the United States: Reflections on the Sources and Prospects," *Theory into Practice* (April 1968): 96–102.

11. G. L. Sharma, "Who Should Make What Decisions?" *Administrator's Notebook* (April 1955).

12. Bredo, "Teacher Legitimation of Principal Control," 7–21.

13. Ibid.

14. L. B. Ball, "Principal and Negotiations," *High School Journal* (October 1968): 22–29.

15. Edward H. Seifert and John Beck, "Elementary Principals: Instructional Leaders or School Managers?" *The Kappan* (March 1981): 528. Also see Gordon Cawelti and Charles Reavis, "How Well Are We Providing Instructional Improvement Services?" *Educational Leadership* (December 1980): 236–40.

16. A. Etzioni, "Administrative and Professional Authority," in *Complex Organizations: A Sociological Reader* (New York: Holt, Rinehart and Winston, 1961).

17. Identified in part from Elizabeth D. Conklyn, "Role Definitions by the Principal: Effect and Determents" (Paper presented at the annual meeting of the American Educational Research Association, April 1976).

18. David L. Clark et al., "What Aids Success in Urban Elementary Schools?" *The Kappan* (March 1980): 467.

19. Ronald Edmonds, "Effective Schools for the Urban Poor," *Educational Leadership* (October 1979): 16–17.

20. California State Assembly, Assembly Education Committee Task Force for the Improvement of Present In-Service Training for Public School Administrators, *The School Principal: Recommendations for Effective Leadership,* (Sacramento, Calif., 1978), p. 5.

21. Andrew Halpin, "A Paradigm for Research on Administrative Behavior," *Administrative Behavior in Education,* ed. Roald F. Campbell and Russell T. Gregg (New York: Harper & Row, 1957), pp. 166–67.

22. Institute for Educational Leadership, *What Makes an Effective School?* (Washington, D.C.: George Washington University, 1980), p. 89.

23. Sandra Scofield, "Principals Make a Difference: The Role They Play in Quality Reading Programs," *OSSC Bulletin* (June 1979): 2; Jean B. Wellisch et al., "School Management and Organization in Successful Schools," *Sociology of Education* (July 1978): 211–26. Beverly Glenn, *What Works? An Examination of Effective Schools for Poor Children.* (Cambridge, Mass.: Center for Law and Education, 1981).

24. Richard A. Gorton, *School Administration and Supervision: Important Issues, Concepts and Case Studies* (Dubuque, Iowa: Wm. C. Brown Company Publishers, 1980), pp. 285–86, 293–310.

25. Charles W. Guditus and Perry A. Zirkel, "Bases of Supervisory Power Among Public School Principals" (Paper presented at the annual meeting of the American Educational Research Association, 1979), p. 16.

26. James Lipham, "Personal Variables of Effective Administrators," *Administrator's Notebook* (September 1960): 1–4.

27. Wellisch et al., "School Management and Organization," 211.

28. Edward D. Roeber, "Development of Single Ways for Using State Assessment Results" (Paper presented at the Tenth Annual Large Scale Assessment Conference, June 1980).

29. Scofield, "Principals Make a Difference."

30. Institute for Educational Leadership, *What Makes an Effective School?*, p. 101.

31. Ibid.

32. Clark et al., "Success in Urban Elementary Schools," 467.

33. James M. Lipham, "Leadership and Administration," in *Behavioral Science and Educational Administration,* ed. Daniel Griffith, Sixty-third Yearbook of the National Society for the Study of Education (Chicago: University of Chicago Press, 1964), p. 122.

34. Cecil Miskel and Donald E. Wilson, "Goal Setting Behavior and Shift: Two Studies of Risk Propensity" (Paper presented at the annual meeting of the American Educational Research Association, 1976).

35. Billy H. Groom, "The Principal: Meeting Instructional Needs in an Urban School," *Educational Leadership* (March 1977): 458. Robert Benjamin, "The Rose in the Forest: A City Principal Who Beats the Odds," *Principal* (March 1981): 10–15.

36. Institute for Educational Leadership, *What Makes an Effective School?* 102.

37. Richard A. Gorton and Kenneth J. McIntyre, *TheEffective Principal* (Reston, Va.: The National Association of Secondary School Principals, 1978).

38. Gorton, *School Administration and Supervision,* 274.

39. For an example of where it is happening, see Gary Freeman et al., "Team Building for Supervisory Support," *Educational Leadership* (January 1980): 356–58.

40. For a somewhat similar attempt to utilize the problem-solving approach, see Leslee J. Bishop, *Staff Development and Instructional Improvement* (Boston, Mass.: Allyn & Bacon, 1976).

41. "Teacher Opinion Poll," *Today's Education* (September/October 1979): 10.

42. North Central Association, 5454 South Shore Drive, Chicago, Illinois.

43. Goodwin Watson, "What Psychology Can We Feel Sure About?" *Teachers College Record* (February 1960): 253–57.

44. Ibid., 254.

45. *Research on Teaching: Concepts, Findings and Implications,* ed. Penelope L. Peterson and Herbert J. Walberg (Berkeley, Calif.: McCutchan, 1979).

46. Ibid., pp. 28–53.

47. *Research on Teaching,* ed. Peterson and Walberg.

48. *Handbook of Research on Teaching,* ed. Merlin Wittrock (New York: Macmillan, 1983).

49. Diana B. Hiatt, "Time Allocation in the Classroom: Is Instruction Being Shortchanged?" *The Kappan* (December 1979): 289–90.

50. "Timely Techniques: How Teachers Can Tell Where the Time Goes," *Wisconsin R and D Center News* (Spring 1980): 2.

51. Cheryl Sullivan, *Clinical Supervision—A State of the Art Review* (Alexandria, Va.: Association for Supervision and Curriculum Development, 1979). See also, Carolyn J. Snyder, "Clinical Supervision in the 1980s," *Educational Leadership* (April 1981): 521–24.

52. Yvonne M. Martin et al., "Supervisory Effectiveness," *Educational Administration Quarterly* (Fall 1978): 74–88.

53. Arthur Blumberg, *Supervisors and Teachers: A Private Cold War,* 2nd ed. (Berkeley, Calif.: McCutchan Publishing Co., 1980).

54. G. D. Borich and S. K. Madden, *Evaluating Classroom Instruction: A Sourcebook of Instruments* (Reading, Mass.: Addison-Wesley, 1977).

55. D. John McIntyre, "Teacher Evaluation and the Observer Effect," *NASSP Bulletin* (March 1980): 36–39.

56. Seifert and Beck, "Elementary Principals"; also, Cawelti and Reavis, "Providing Instructional Improvement Services."

57. For additional discussion of classroom observation and evaluation, see Richard A. Adamsky et al., "Conducting an Observational Session: Professional Preparation Module." An ERIC Report: Ed–195–056. Also see P. T. Mariton and L. M. Borchardt, "Review of Literature and Research: Bias in Teacher Observation." An ERIC Report: Ed–193–22.

58. C. H. Gardner, *Videotaping in a Naturalistic Classroom Setting* (Austin, Tex.: Texas University Research and Development Center for Teacher Education, 1980).

59. William Moritz and Jo Anne Martin-Reynolds, "The Genie in the Bottle," *Educational Leadership* (February 1980): 396–99.

60. For additional information on this topic, write for a copy of *Microcourse Work* (Superintendent of Documents, U.S. Government Printing Office).

61. An excellent review of research on the effectiveness of using the videotape recorder was conducted by Jo Anne Martin, "A Study of the Effects of a Self-Evaluation Model on the Focus Reaction of Student Teachers during Split Screen Video Feedback" (Ph.D. diss., Bowling Green State University, 1977). Also see G. Bailey, "Maximizing the Potential of the Videotape Recorder in Teacher Self-Assessment," *Educational Technology* (1979): 34–44.

62. Leon Gersten, "Intervisitation: A Process of Growth and Enrichment," *Phi Delta Kappan* (March 1979): 532–33. Also see Thomas W. Clapper, "The Effects of Peer Clinical Supervision on In-service Teachers" (Ph.D. diss., Pennsylvania State University, 1981).

63. In fact, there is evidence that teachers are neither regular readers of professional literature or aware of what is written. See Thomas George, "Teachers Tend to Ignore Professional Journals," *The Kappan* (September 1979): 69–70.

64. Betty Martin and Ben Carson, *The Principal's Handbook on School Library Media Center* (Syracuse N.Y.: Gaylord Professional Publications 1978).

65. Ben Harris, *Improving Staff Performance through In-Service Education* (Boston: Allyn & Bacon, 1980), p. 21.

66. Ibid., p. 15.

67. *Staff Development* (Eugene, Oreg.: ERIC Clearinghouse on Educational Management, 1980).

68. Louis Rubin, *The In-Service Education of Teachers* (Boston: Allyn & Bacon, 1978), p. 4.

69. Ibid., p. 7.

70. Harris, *Improving Staff Performance,* 31–38.

71. Ibid., p. 13.

72. Ibid., p. 13.

73. See Fred H. Wood and Steven R. Thompson, "Guidelines for Better Staff Development," *Educational Leadership* (February 1980): 374–78; Bruce Joyce and Beverly Showers, "Improving In-Service Training: The Message of Research," *Educational Leadership* (February 1980): 379–85; Harry Hutson, "PAR in In-Service," *Phi Delta Kappa Newsletter* (June 1979): 1; Robert L. Taylor and Robert C. McKean, "Staff Development in Los Angeles," *Educational Leadership* (March 1979): 447–48. Also see books by Rubin, Harris and Bishop, identified earlier, and Harry M. Hutson, "In-service Best Practices: The Learnings of General Education," *Journal of Research and Development in Education* (November 1981): 1–10.

74. For a description of several interesting approaches to making these meetings more interesting and productive, see Harris, *Improving Staff Performance,* chapters 7 and 8. Also see Vicki S. Dean, "Simulation: A Tool for In-service Education," *Educational Leadership* (April 1981): 550–52.

75. Association for Supervision and Curriculum Development, *Group Processes in Supervision* (Washington, D.C. National Education Association, 1948): 49. Also see Steven H. Larson, "The Behavioral Side of Productive Meetings," *Personnel Journal* (April 1980): 292–96.

76. Anthony P. Williams, "Management for More Effective Staff Meetings," *Personnel Journal* (August 1979): 547–50.

77. Association for Supervision and Curriculum Development, *Group Processes in Supervision,* 128.

78. For further ideas, see *Making Meetings More Effective* (Burlingame, Calif.: Association of California School Administrators, 1980).

79. See Leslee J. Bishop, *Staff Development and Instructional Improvement* (Boston, Mass.: Allyn & Bacon, 1976), chapter 2.

80. Harris, *Improving Staff Performance,* pp. 218–19.

81. Bishop, *Staff Development and Instructional Improvement,* 237–40.

82. For further ideas, see Leslee Bishop, ibid., 153.

83. Roy Edelfelt and Tamar Orvell, *Teacher Centers: Where, What and Why?* (Bloomington, Ind.: Phi Delta Kappa, 1978).

84. David Burrell, "The Teacher Center: A Critical Analysis," *Educational Leadership* (March 1976).

85. See Dennis Sparks, "A Teacher Center Tackles the Issue," *Today's Education* (November/December 1979): 37–39.

86. Roy A. Edelfelt, "Critical Issues in Developing Teacher Centers," *Phi Delta Kappan* (February 1982): 390–93.

87. Rubin, *In-Service Education of Teachers,* 14–18.

88. *Building a Teachers' Center,* ed. Kathleen Devaney (San Francisco: Far West Laboratory, 1979). Also, write Teachers' Centers Exchange at the Far West Laboratory, and ask to be put on their mailing list. In addition, see *Teacher Centers and Needs Assessment,* ed. Roy A. Edelfelt (Washington, D.C.: National Education Association, 1981), and Robert Luke et al., *Teacher-Centered In-Service Education: Planning and Products* (Washington, D.C.: Institute of Education, 1980).

12

Administrator's Role in Curriculum Improvement

An understanding of the administrator's role in curriculum improvement is essential for any administrator who wishes to increase educational opportunities for students. *Curriculum improvement* will refer to any change in the subject matter content or in its organization and objectives which results in increased student learning.[1] The emphasis on curriculum improvement rather than administration of the curriculum reflects the priority given in this book to the leadership dimensions of the administrator's role.[2] However, effective leadership also requires in-depth study of the curriculum itself, which is beyond the intended scope of this text. Therefore, it is recommended that readers include in their education at least one, and preferably, two or three curriculum courses which deal with the content and design of the elementary and/or secondary school curriculum.[3]

The following sections will focus on the role of the school administrator in bringing about curricular improvement. Three aspects of this role will be analyzed: (1) *assessing* the need for curricular improvement, (2) *planning* for curricular improvement, and (3) *implementing* curricular improvement.

DISTRICT-WIDE VERSUS SCHOOL-SITE APPROACH TO CURRICULUM IMPROVEMENT*

THE DISTRICT APPROACH

The district-wide approach to curricular improvement usually involves teacher and administrator representatives from different schools within a district, serving on a committee or curriculum council to investigate and develop ways

---

*It is recognized that curriculum improvement efforts can also take place at the county, state, and national levels, but the emphasis in this chapter will be on intradistrict approaches.

in which some aspect of the district's curriculum can be improved.[4] As a part of this method, subcommittees are established for each discipline in the curriculum, and members of the superintendent's staff provide direction and supervision for the various committees. Generally, the major intended outcome of the district-wide approach to curriculum improvement is to bring about needed curricular change in all of the schools within the district. A concern for curriculum articulation and correlation among subjects, grades, and schools also characterizes this method.

The extent to which a school administrator becomes involved in district-wide curriculum improvement efforts will vary with her own vision and capabilities, the size of the district, the district's concept of curriculum improvement, and its perception of the administrator's role. However, in situations wherein an administrator's potential contribution to curriculum improvement is recognized, a district may expect her to perform a number of responsibilities. These include (1) serving as a member of the district's curriculum council or on one of the district's curriculum subcommittees, (2) keeping informed about major curricular trends and innovations, (3) working on curriculum improvement projects with the curriculum director and/or the director of elementary or secondary education, (4) involving the school's teaching staff in problem identification and curriculum committee work at the district level, and (5) working in a staff relationship with K-12 subject matter area coordinators and with fellow elementary and secondary principals in the exchange of curriculum improvement ideas.[5]

The district-wide approach to curriculum improvement offers several advantages.[6] It tends to result in greater coordination of activities and promotes better curricular articulation and correlation between subjects, grades, and schools. It also provides access to a broader array of resources and expertise than might be possible with another method. And, since the superintendent's staff is usually directly involved in the curriculum council and committees, there is greater likelihood that a proposed curricular change will receive her and the school board's ultimate approval.

On the other hand, the district-wide approach to curriculum improvement has several weaknesses, according to its critics.[7] It can stifle creativity and diversity at the building and classroom levels because of its emphasis on coordination and uniformity of curriculum in all schools. In addition, it can lead to teacher apathy about curriculum improvement at the building level, as a result of limited involvement in the district-wide approach and a feeling that little can be accomplished unless the central office directs the change. In response to these criticisms, the school-site approach has been advanced as an equally valid means of curriculum improvement.

SCHOOL-SITE APPROACH

The school-site approach to curriculum improvement differs from the district-wide approach primarily in that the *impetus* for change occurs at the school rather than at the district level. As Caswell and his colleagues have pointed out:

> . . . the 'grass roots' [school site] approach which views the individual school as the operational and planning unit . . . means that problems which are dealt with on a system-wide or partial-system basis should arise out of work done by individual staffs and feed back into use through these staffs. The channel is from the individual school to the system and back to the individual school, rather than from the top down as under the traditional system-wide approach.[8]

It is generally assumed in the school-site approach that a curricular change which is initiated in one school in a district need not always be implemented in the other schools in that district. The premise is that, to some extent, the schools of a district serve different student clienteles and, for that reason, should be permitted to develop different curricula if appropriate. This does not mean, however, that each school should be permitted to "go it alone." Underscoring this point, the Association for Supervision and Curriculum Development emphasized in one of its yearbooks:

> Building principals, however, must not assume that the individual schools within a school system are completely autonomous. Some attention must be given to the need for a system-wide program. . . . The problem to be solved is how the building units can be stimulated to develop the best program possible for the neighborhoods which they serve, and at the same time, make their appropriate contributions to the total system of which they are parts.[9]

While there can be several advantages to the school-site approach to curriculum improvement, including greater involvement of personnel, more responsiveness to the needs of the local student clientele, and improved opportunities for the proposed curricular change to be implemented in the classrooms, the method is not without its limitations. The performance of school-site administrators and staffs in generating and maintaining the impetus for curricular change has been spotty.[10] In addition, sole reliance on the building-level approach to curriculum improvement has in many instances resulted in a patchwork district curriulum with poor articulation and correlation between grades and among schools.

Although the potential disadvantages, like those of the district-wide approach, are not necessarily inherent in the school-site approach, it seems clear that for an administrator to rely on a single method would be a mistake.[11] *Both* the district-wide and the school-site approaches are needed for effective curriculum improvement, and the goal for the administrator should be to capitalize on the strengths of each method while minimizing its disadvantages.

Regardless of which approach to curriculum improvement is utilized, the involvement of the school administrator would appear to be essential. Perhaps Spalding put it best when he said,

> The principal has much to contribute to the curriculum program. He is the one person who is concerned with every aspect of the life of his school. His interest in its success provides a strong and direct motivation for his efforts to secure curriculum improvement. He is better able than anyone else to discover the needs of his school. He knows best the contributions that the members of his staff can make. . . . His interest in the growth of his teachers requires that he should have responsibilities for the best single means for securing that growth—work on the curriculum.[12]

THE IMPORTANCE OF ADMINISTRATIVE COMMITMENT

Although Spalding obviously felt that the school administrator could make an important contribution to curriculum improvement, there are others who question whether that is possible because of various obstacles and the lack of certain personal qualities. These obstacles and personal qualities have already been discussed in the chapter on instructional leadership, but the factors of available time and competency in curriculum improvement merit additional attention in this section.

Certainly, available time can be an important potential constraint limiting curricular leadership initiatives by a school administrator. However, at least one study found that it was not so much whether or not a principal felt she had the time to devote to curriculum improvement that determined the extent of her involvement, but the degree to which a principal perceived that her superiors wanted her to give a very high priority to improving the school curriculum.[13] In addition, while competency in curriculum evaluation and planning is undoubtedly an important prerequisite to whether or not a school administrator becomes involved in efforts to improve the curriculum,[14] Novotney asserts that *commitment* may be even more important.[15] For example, if a principal believes that it is *essential* that she become involved in efforts to improve the school curriculum, then she is likely to take steps to become more competent in curriculum evaluation and planning. On the other hand, if a principal thinks that it would just be *nice* or *desirable* to become involved in curricular improvement, she is not as likely to increase her competency and, perhaps more important, she is likely to get sidetracked into routine administrative tasks that should have a lower priority or be delegated to someone else.

Commitment is the key. A school administrator must feel that it is essential that she become involved in curriculum improvement efforts. If she possesses this commitment, then it is probable that perceived insufficient time and competency or other constraints will become obstacles that she will strive to overcome, rather than resign herself to them as insurmountable barriers. It seems likely that an administrator with sufficient commitment will become competent (through study and application of the ideas in this chapter and related activities) and find the time to become involved in curriculum improvement. The question next becomes, in what ways can she make her best contribution?

ASSESSING THE NEED FOR CURRICULUM IMPROVEMENT

The school administrator who is interested in curricular improvement should, with the assistance of relevant others, initially concentrate her efforts on assessing the need for improvement. There is little reason to begin changing the curriculum until the nature of the need for improvement has been fully and accurately assessed. All too frequently, proposals for curriculum improvement are advanced and implemented without an accurate assessment of the real need for such improvement. As a result, curricular change occurs but not necessarily improvement.[16] The only valid criterion for ascertaining whether a curricular change results in significant improvement is whether the change better enables the school to achieve previously defined educational objectives. As Caswell has noted, "No matter how elaborate a program may be or how enthusiastic the staff, unless in the end the experiences of pupils are changed so that the educational outcomes are better than before, the work cannot be considered successful."[17]

An administrator can assess the need for improvement in at least two ways: (1) by evaluating a school's current program of studies, utilizing previously defined and accepted criteria, and (2) by studying and evaluating various proposals which are offered for the improvement of the curriculum. In either case, the administrator must develop or utilize a comprehensive set of evaluative criteria for assessing the need for curricular change. Without previously defined criteria, the administrator's assessment of the need for curricular improvement is likely to be unsystematic, idiosyncratic, and superficial. Using well-defined, comprehensive criteria, an administrator will be better able to assess the need for improvement in a current program of studies as well as to evaluate the potential of curriculum improvement proposals advanced by others.

Fortunately, there is no shortage of recommended criteria for assessing the need for curricular improvement. Over the years, a number of educational authorities have proposed criteria for evaluating the school curriculum.[18] A synthesis of their main points has been developed and is presented below in question form, with accompanying discussion.

1. Has the school established clearly stated, operationally-defined, educational objectives?

The school curriculum should be based on the educational objectives of the school.[19] If a school lacks clearly stated, operationally-defined educational objectives, its curriculum is more likely to be based on tradition and/or fad than on desired student learning outcomes. Most schools have educational objectives of one kind or another, but these objectives are frequently not stated in a form which facilitates assessment of the need for curricular improvement. Therefore, the administrator should begin her efforts to improve the curriculum by working with others to develop clearly stated, operationally-defined educational objectives for the school. (See Chapter 2 for further discussion of these tasks.)

2. Is each course in the curriculum related to and supporting the achievement of school objectives?

No course in the curriculum is an end in itself. It should relate in some demonstrable way to the achievement of school objectives. Undoubtedly, some courses exist in a curriculum for reasons other than their contribution to achieving the objectives of the school. The administrator needs to identify these courses and attempt to develop their relationship with overall school goals or consider the elimination of the courses from the curriculum.

3. Does the planned curriculum take into consideration sufficiently the "hidden curriculum" of the school?

Teachers, supervisors, curriculum developers, and relevant others plan the curriculum—facts, concepts, generalizations, skills—that they want or intend students to learn.[20] However, students may have needs and experiences which result in learning "facts," concepts, generalizations and skills other than those intended, representing a "hidden curriculum" in that school personnel may not be aware of these learnings.[21] Two excerpts from the writing of a former student will serve to illustrate the nature of the "hidden curriculum."

> In First grade, all I remember is that a new lady came
> To our Room for awhile and then went away and I learned years
> Later that was because she was only a practice teacher and
> She didn't like us much anyway you could tell but we'd sit
> On the floor in front of her while she sat on a chair sort of
> Board reading us a story and we could see up her dress.

> In eighth grade I wrote a funny theme about money and read
> It in front of English class and the kids liked it a lot but
> Mono Rynning told the teacher I copied it from Life Magazine
> And he believed him and when he got to be a high school
> Teacher years later I still hated him and wondered how he

Got promoted and that year I broke a drill bit in shop class
And went to the dime store to buy a new one because Mr. Noble
The teacher used to work in a reform school and he scared me
Because I saw him hit Suggy one day really hard and Suggy
Didn't cry but I was glad it wasn't me.[22]

It will, of course, be difficult at best to anticipate the exact nature of the "hidden curriculum" because of the individual differences of students. However, in identifying the need for curriculum improvement, it is important that the school administrator attempt to ascertain the extent to which the planned curriculum is compatible with the "hidden curriculum" because incongruities are bound to affect negatively the successful implementation of the planned curriculum.[23]

4. **Does the curriculum meet the needs of all students? Is it comprehensive?**

A comprehensive curriculum should meet the needs of the noncollege-bound as well as the collegebound students. It should provide for the needs of low-ability and average students, as well as the academically talented. It should also provide for the needs of students with special handicaps, as well as the needs of other kinds of exceptional students. In addition, the school should recognize that students have immediate as well as long-range needs, and that both should be accommodated through the curriculum. For example, the immediate need of a student to develop a healthy self-concept is as important as his long-range need to gain knowledge and skills for a career. (Perhaps the most useful conception of the needs of students has been advanced by Havighurst who postulates that people have particular tasks which need to be mastered at certain stages in their development.)[24]

A second way of raising the question about the comprehensiveness of the school curriculum is to ask. "To what extent does the curriculum help students to deal successfully with the various social influences which are or will be affecting their lives?" These social influences may include but are not limited to television, racial problems, poverty, war and peace, marriage and divorce, interpersonal relations, and urbanization. For example, in a society in which the typical student spends almost as much time at watching television as at studying in school,[25] the curriculum should help students to utilize more effectively this important medium of information and attitude change.*

The essential point is that if the school is to prepare students for a constructive and productive life, the curriculum should reflect the realities of that life. The alternative may be what Noyes and McAndrew have observed: "The

---

*Two sources of curriculum materials to accomplish this objective are The Learning and Media Research Division of the Southwest Educational Development Laboratory (for elementary level materials) and the Far West Laboratory (for high school level materials). Both of these labs have developed curriculum materials for teaching students critical viewing skills.

student is filled with facts and figures which only accidentally and infrequently have anything to do with the problems and conflicts of modern life or his own inner concerns."[26]

5. **Does the curriculum reflect the needs and expectations of society, as well as the needs of the students?**

The school does not operate in a vacuum. It is an agent of society and therefore its curriculum must reflect to a reasonable degree societal expectations and needs.[27] Although our society is a pluralistic one and is frequently in a state of flux, it is still possible for an administrator to ascertain general expectations in regard to what the school should be teaching. The Gallup survey presented in chapter one is an example of the type of information which an administrator should obtain.[28]

6. **Does the content of the curriculum provide for the development of student attitudes and values, as well as knowledge and skills?**

Whether this question can be answered affirmatively will largely depend on whether or not the educational objectives of the school emphasize the development of student attitudes and values, as well as knowledge and skills. While some authorities seem to feel that the school should limit its role to developing knowledge on the part of its students, others assert with equal conviction that the school can and should help students to develop attitudes and values.[29]

In reality, of course, the school already teaches attitudes and values, directly and indirectly, through its emphasis on punctuality and neatness, its penalties for cheating, and its response to certain styles of dress and grooming. The pertinent question would appear to be *not* whether the school *should* teach attitudes and values but *which* attitudes and values should the school attempt to develop, and how should the school curriculum provide for their development?

7. **Are the curriculum materials appropriate for the interests and abilities of the students?**

The major assumption behind this question is that, for successful learning to occur, the curriculum materials must be at the interest and ability level of the students using them. If materials are too difficult for students to read or understand, learning will be impaired; if the materials are too easy and insufficiently challenging, the teacher will have difficulty in motivating students to learn.[30] Moreover, if the curricular materials fail to take into consideration students' interest levels and attention spans, learning will be adversely affected.[31]

One approach an administrator can take is to utilize the help of a reading consultant to ascertain the reading level of materials used by each grade, and compare those levels with the reading levels of the students. The author once conducted such a study in a school and discovered that in a ninth grade class the reading level of the biology materials was at a 12th grade level. Since in any class there is a range of student reading abilities, there will, in situations like this one, be problems in learning for a number of students as long as only one textbook is used for the entire class.

A possible solution to this kind of problem is the use of multiple texts and nonprint media to accommodate the different interests and abilities of students within a class. A good indicator of the need for curricular improvement in a school is the extent to which a single text approach is being utilized in the classrooms.

In selecting curricular materials the administrator needs to keep close watch on the type of "free and inexpensive" items that are frequently made available to the school. Seldom are such materials without bias.[32] Even textbooks may be a source of bias, particularly racial and sexual bias, and the administrator should make sure that the resource guide provided by the Commission on Civil Rights is utilized before selecting any materials for the curriculum.[33]

8. **Are the educational objectives for each subject in the curriculum clearly stated and operationally defined?**

Earlier, the point was made that the school curriculum should be based on the overall educational goals of the school. However, even though the subjects included in the curriculum should relate directly to overall school objectives, each subject should have specific objectives of its own which represent interpretations of the more general school goals.

The objectives for each subject should be stated clearly and should be operationally defined if they are to provide direction and guidance to both teachers and students in the learning situation, and if the objectives are to be helpful in evaluating the extent to which a subject is achieving preëstablished goals.[34] The achievement of educational objectives, whether they be school or subject objectives, is very difficult to assess if the objectives are stated vaguely, or if, as is the case in some situations, they are nonexistent.

9. **Is there subject matter articulation between grade levels, and correlation among the various subjects of the curriculum?**

The curriculum content introduced at each grade level (at each phase in nongraded schools) should be built upon and be articulated with the subject matter introduced in the previous grade. Gaps or omissions in the sequencing of the content of the curriculum tend to cause problems for the learner. In each curricular area the subject matter content should be composed of sequentially-linked building blocks which the learner masters as he proceeds through the school system.

In addition, efforts should be made to correlate wherever possible the subjects offered at a particular grade level. The correlation may take the form of what is referred to as "core curriculum" or it may only represent an effort to relate certain topics within two or more subjects.[35] The school curriculum has often been criticized for its fragmentation, and there is little doubt that there needs to be better correlation between its various subjects.

10. **Are the various subjects in the school curriculum achieving their proposed objectives?**

Probably one of the most important efforts that an administrator can make in identifying the need for curricular improvement is to investigate the extent to which each of the subjects in the curriculum is achieving its proposed objectives. While the administrator cannot do this alone, she can initiate the investigation and can organize and coordinate the expertise of others, in an evaluation of the achievement of course objectives. Methods of assessment could include the use of criterion-referenced tests, teacher-constructed tests, interviews, and questionnaires. While each of these evaluation methods possesses certain limitations as well as strengths, the most serious deficiency of all would be incurred as the result of an administrator's failure to initiate any assessment merely because an evaluation tool could not be found that would accomplish exactly what she wanted.

CURRICULUM EVALUATION

Identifying appropriate criteria is only the first step in evaluating the curriculum. The next step is to apply the criteria, which will involve the collection, analysis and interpretation of data. Since an administrator may in many situations lack technical skills and/or time necessary to carry out these evaluation processes she will need to identify and involve people who do have the skills and time for evaluation. She will also need to become familiar enough with the basic concepts and techniques of evaluation so that she can monitor the work and its outcomes. In regard to methods, there are a variety of approaches for carrying out curricular evaluation. These include the use of tests, interviews, questionnaires, and content analysis studies. A discussion of the various concepts and techniques of curriculum evaluation is included in several good sources listed at the end of this chapter.[36]

However, one curriculum evaluation method that merits attention at this point, since it tends to be overlooked, is the technique of curriculum mapping.[37] Curriculum mapping is essentially a process of verifying what curriculum is *actually* being presented in the classrooms of a school, as contrasted with the curriculum which is *supposed* to be implemented in the school. Too often the curriculum of a school is viewed as a written document or set of curriculum guides that specify the objectives and content to be taught. Any administrator who attempts to evaluate a curriculum based on this view of curriculum is unlikely to obtain a very realistic or valid picture of the school's curriculum.

To ascertain the actual curriculum—that curriculum which is really being implemented in a school—the administrator will need to engage teachers and others in the technique of curriculum mapping. It can occur in two ways: (1) involving teachers and/or students in recording on paper the actual curriculum content being taught; and (2) involving independent observers in the classroom recording the kind of curriculum which is actually being implemented.[38]

The primary advantage of curriculum mapping is that it provides the evaluator with a more accurate picture of the actual curriculum in use, so that there is a more valid basis for determining the extent to which the criteria for needed improvement are being met. While, as mentioned earlier, this approach is only one of various tools for curriculum evaluation, it represents a very useful technique, particularly in the initial stage of evaluation.

In selecting a particular approach to be used in evaluating the curriculum, it is important at the outset for the administrator to ask certain basic questions: "What do I need to evaluate? Why do I want to evaluate? What do I intend to do with the results of my evaluation?"[39] As House points out, "For the evaluation to be effective [the administrator] must know precisely what she wants from it."[40] Unless the administrator is clear in her own mind as to the answers to the questions above, she is unlikely to be satisfied with the results of the evaluation.

THE ADMINISTRATOR'S ROLE IN PLANNING CURRICULAR IMPROVEMENT

In many school situations the school administrator is too busy with other aspects of managing the school to become directly involved in planning curriculum improvement.[41] Also, her major role in relation to curriculum is too often perceived as implementing a proposed curricular change which has been prepared or planned by someone else. Be that as it may, the school administrator can still play an important role in planning for curricular improvement if she possesses commitment, educational vision, group leadership skills, and initiative. A twofold role is recommended: (1) working directly with groups or committees who are planning curriculum improvement, and (2) encouraging and evaluating proposals for improving the curriculum.

THE COMMITTEE APPROACH TO PLANNING CURRICULUM IMPROVEMENT

It should be noted that planning for curricular improvement can be accomplished by individuals, and sometimes the best way to *begin* planning for a curricular change is on a limited scale, with one individual. However, most of the planning for curricular improvement will probably be done by committees, so the concepts and issues discussed previously (chap. 3) in conjunction with group leadership skills, should be considered.[42]

In utilizing the committee approach to curricular improvement, the administrator will need to adopt a plan of action to guide the committee's efforts. Although there are undoubtedly several ways to proceed, a proposed process for an administrator and a curriculum improvement committee to follow is presented in figure 12.1.

The process identified in figure 12.1 intentionally goes beyond *planning* for curricular improvement so that the reader can receive an overview of the total recommended process of curriculum improvement. There may be additional steps that could be added to the process, but an attempt has been made

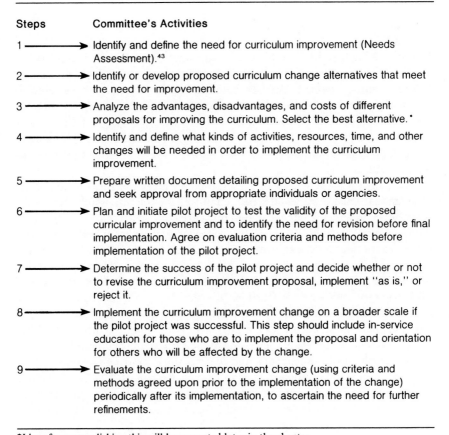

Steps	Committee's Activities
1	Identify and define the need for curriculum improvement (Needs Assessment).[43]
2	Identify or develop proposed curriculum change alternatives that meet the need for improvement.
3	Analyze the advantages, disadvantages, and costs of different proposals for improving the curriculum. Select the best alternative.*
4	Identify and define what kinds of activities, resources, time, and other changes will be needed in order to implement the curriculum improvement.
5	Prepare written document detailing proposed curriculum improvement and seek approval from appropriate individuals or agencies.
6	Plan and initiate pilot project to test the validity of the proposed curricular improvement and to identify the need for revision before final implementation. Agree on evaluation criteria and methods before implementation of the pilot project.
7	Determine the success of the pilot project and decide whether or not to revise the curriculum improvement proposal, implement "as is," or reject it.
8	Implement the curriculum improvement change on a broader scale if the pilot project was successful. This step should include in-service education for those who are to implement the proposal and orientation for others who will be affected by the change.
9	Evaluate the curriculum improvement change (using criteria and methods agreed upon prior to the implementation of the change) periodically after its implementation, to ascertain the need for further refinements.

*Ideas for accomplishing this will be presented later in the chapter.

Figure 12.1. A Curriculum Improvement Process

here to focus on the most important components. Although the proposed process emphasizes the group approach, it should be noted that the method proposed can be utilized on an individual basis as well.

The administrator's role in working with a curriculum improvement committee should be that of consultant and facilitator.[44] Generally the administrator will be interacting with committee members who possess greater expertise than she in the particular curricular area under consideration.* Therefore, it is unlikely that she will be able to contribute much subject matter knowledge. However, the administrator can assist other people on the committee by helping them to define their function, to follow a process such as the one presented in figure 12.1, and to work together cooperatively and productively as a committee. She can also facilitate their actions by securing necessary resources, removing obstacles, and helping them to increase their problem-solving capabilities.

Problems

In establishing a committee for curriculum improvement, the administrator should be aware of teacher attitudes toward committee work. While not all teachers can be assumed to possess identical attitudes, studies have revealed that many teachers have had negative experiences while serving on committees. For example, McQuizz found that teachers encountered three basic problems in trying to perform committee work: (1) lack of time, (2) lack of recognition or rewards, and (3) lack of follow-through on the committee's recommendations.[45]

Perhaps the most serious of these problems is lack of time, which is one problem that must be resolved if the committee is to be successful. During the school year, teachers, students, and parents are busy and, for all practical purposes, their only available time is after school or on weekends. Neither of these times is particularly desirable, due to the fatigue factor in late afternoon and evening, or to potential conflicts with other commitments. A partial resolution of the time problem, as it affects teachers and students, is to dismiss school early one day each week, if feasible, in order to permit curricular planning and other kinds of professional activities to take place. A number of schools have adopted this procedure, apparently with good results. Other possibilities include preschool workshops, better use of faculty and departmental meetings, utilization of substitute teachers, and in-service days during the year.

Another partial solution to the problem of inadequate time is to schedule committee meetings during the summer to plan for curricular improvement. This can be an ideal time since school is not in session, and people are more

---

*Expertise should not be narrowly defined. Students, for example, have a particular expertise that might be helpful in curriculum planning. See an example of this in "Involving Students in Curriculum Planning," by Arthur E. Garner and Leila A. Acklen in *Clearing House,* September 1979, pp. 36–39.

available to work on the curriculum. But the administrator should keep in mind that some of the individuals whom she might select to work on committees may prefer to attend summer school or take vacations. The administrator should also consider the possibility that she may be unable to secure a very high level of participation without remunerating committee members for their summer work for the school. Assuming that these problems can be avoided or resolved with careful advance planning and resourcefulness by the administrator, the summer months may indeed provide an excellent opportunity for a school administrator and a curriculum committee to engage in planning for curricular improvement.

Consultants

In formulating a curricular improvement committee, an administrator should give some attention to the need for outside help. The teachers, students, and parents on the committee and even the administrator may be familiar with the current program and associated problems, but they may not be fully aware of new approaches to the improving of a particular curricular area. A consultant from the district's central office, a university, the state department of public instruction, or another agency or organization might be able to offer valuable ideas and insights.

If the administrator and the committee decide that a consultant would be useful, they should define as precisely as possible, before employing the individual, the nature of the consultant's contribution and his relationship to the committee. Frequently, when these factors are not adequately defined by the committee or communicated to the consultant, his expertise is not properly utilized or his performance does not meet the expectations of the committee. Consultants can often make an excellent contribution to a committee, but the expectations of the committee and the role of the consultant must be clearly defined in advance.

Approval

The school administrator should recognize that any proposed curricular changes which result from committee work must ultimately be approved by the superintendent and the school board before implementation can proceed. It is important, therefore, to keep the superintendent and school board informed at each stage of the planning process. This might be done through periodic progress reports and/or by actually including a representative from the central office and/or the school board on the committee which is doing the planning for curricular improvement. Regardless of the method used to keep the superintendent and the school board informed, the importance of effective communication cannot be overemphasized. Many potentially good curricular improvement plans have encountered resistance or have even been rejected because they caught the superintendent or school board by surprise.

ENCOURAGING AND EVALUATING PROPOSALS FOR CURRICULUM IMPROVEMENT

A second major role of the administrator in planning for curriculum improvement should be to encourage and evaluate proposals from various individuals or groups, both inside of and outside of the school system. The administrator can encourage proposals for the improvement of the curriculum from people within the school system by (1) making known her interest in receiving such proposals, (2) trying to secure released time for individuals or small groups to work on curriculum improvement proposals, and (3) by giving recognition to those who develop curricular improvement proposals. To be effective these kinds of encouragement cannot be limited to a single announcement or indication of interest. Instead, the administrator must demonstrate an *active, ongoing, visible* commitment to receiving proposals for curriculum improvement.

In addition to encouraging the generation of curriculum proposals from within the school or district, an administrator needs to become better informed about those proposals that are advanced from the outside, by state and national organizations, agencies, and groups. As mentioned earlier, much curriculum change has originated with national curriculum committees. If the administrator is to capitalize on the ideas and thinking of people outside the school in regard to curricular reform, she will need to make a conscious effort to keep well informed about new proposals for improving the curriculum.*

Encouraging others to develop proposals and attempting to become better informed herself about various ideas which are proposed for improving the curriculum, however, are not the only dimensions to the administrator's role in curriculum improvement. She also has a responsibility to evaluate curriculum improvement proposals carefully as to their appropriateness and feasibility. A sample work sheet which should be helpful to the administrator in reaching a determination on the merits of curricular improvement proposals is presented in figure 12.2. Anderson also provides additional help for evaluating curriculum proposals.[46]

Although the suggested work sheet is recommended especially for evaluating the merits of curriculum improvement proposals, it could be used to assess the strengths and weaknesses of various other kinds of proposals, as well. It is primarily designed for helping the administrator and those who are assisting her to focus on a number of important questions that should be addressed by any proposal. By seeking answers to these kinds of questions, an administrator should be better able to assess the strengths and weaknesses of a proposal and make a judgment about its overall worth. (If an administrator

---

*An excellent way to accomplish this is by joining the Association for Supervision and Curriculum Development. This organization publishes many valuable articles and books on curriculum improvement and proposals.

Name _____ Date _____

Title of Proposal _____

1. What diagnostic methods or procedures were used to identify and define the problem or need?
2. What are the characteristics of the target population to which the proposal is addressed?
3. To what extent are the understandings, skills, attitudes, or values which the proposed program seeks to improve (the desired outcomes) clearly identified and stated in terms that will make evaluation possible?
4. To what degree does the proposal make clear *how* the recommended program will accomplish the objectives which are set forth?
5. To what degree is there evidence that potential problems (as well as strengths) of the proposed program have been identified, assessed, and possible solutions recommended?
6. To what extent does the proposal recognize the need for and make provision for in-service education for faculty and/or orientation activities for students and parents, to help ensure successful implementation of the proposed program?
7. Have the costs of the different aspects of the proposed program been fully assessed?
8. What procedures have been included in the proposal for ascertaining the progress/effectiveness of the program on a nine-week, semester, or yearly basis?

Summary

Strengths of the Proposal

Limitations of the Proposal

Priority Rating Assigned the Proposal

Figure 12.2. A Proposal Assessment
Work Sheet

adopts this work sheet, it would be advisable to distribute copies of it, in advance, to those who are thinking about preparing a proposal so that they may be aware of how their proposal will be evaluated, and so they can use the work sheet themselves in evaluating their proposal.)

THE ADMINISTRATOR'S ROLE IN IMPLEMENTING CURRICULAR IMPROVEMENT

It has already been noted that a major obstacle to curriculum improvement, from the teacher's point of view, is the lack of follow-through on committee recommendations. The occurrence of this problem is often a result of the administrator's failure to understand the process of and barriers to implementing a proposed curriculum change.

Implementing curricular improvement usually necessitates a modification in the *attitudes* and *role* of the staff, as well as in subject matter or its organization. For example, a proposed social studies curriculum which emphasizes student analysis and discussion of major problems and issues in American history may require, if the new curriculum is to be successfully implemented, that the teacher change her attitude about how American history is best taught and learned, and her conception of the role of the teacher and the student in the classroom.

The teacher who continues to lecture and limits the students' role to merely responding to questions may implement the proposed curricular change to the extent that she uses different subject matter and materials, but full effectiveness will not be achieved unless the teacher's and students' roles also change. Therefore, in attempting to implement curricular improvement, the administrator must recognize that curricular change also involves *people* change in order to be totally successful.[47] Too often this point has been ignored, or given insufficient consideration, and the implementation of curricular improvement has correspondingly suffered.

POSSIBLE BARRIERS TO CURRICULAR CHANGE

When implementing a proposed curricular improvement the administrator should perform the role of change agent. In this role, the administrator should be trying to bring about a modification both in the curriculum *and* in people's attitudes and roles in regard to the curriculum. People whose attitudes and roles may need to be modified and who may present resistance or obstacles to change include faculty, students, parents, central office staff, and school board members. Of course, different people resist change for different reasons, and it is often rather difficult to ascertain the real reasons for their opposition. However, the major barriers to implementing curricular change (or, for that matter, most kinds of change) that may be inherent in a specific situation and of which the administrator should be aware include the following:[48]

Habit. Habit is the tendency of people to behave in the same way that they have always behaved. Proposed change challenges habit, and the challenge is frequently met with resistance.

The bureaucratic structure of the school district. The school district as a bureaucratic institution emphasizes the maintenance of order, rationality, and continuity. Uniformity of educational programs and procedures among the schools of the district seems to be valued, whereas diversity does not. Attempts by individual schools to introduce new programs or procedures are often viewed with suspicion. Because of these attitudes and the hierarchical structure of the district, proposed change may be diluted before it is finally approved, or it may be rejected because it threatens the stability of the institution.

The lack of incentive. Change can be a difficult and frustrating experience for the individuals or groups involved. Although the administrator may be personally convinced of the benefits which will accrue if a proposed change is adopted, she can seldom guarantee those benefits or offer incentives (monetary or otherwise) to persuade others to adopt the innovation. As a result, she is dependent upon her own ability to influence others to adopt a proposed change for which there may be high personal costs in terms of time and frustration, and no immediate gain.

The nature of the proposed change. Innovations can vary according to complexity, financial cost, compatibility with the other phases of the school's operation, and ease of communicability. Some innovations, because of these factors, are more difficult to introduce into a school system than other proposed changes. Therefore, the characteristics of the innovation itself may constitute a major obstacle or problem in securing its adoption.

Teacher and community norms. Teacher and community norms can act as significant barriers to innovating in the schools. There is evidence that a teacher may receive disapproval from her colleagues for adopting an innovation; and efforts by the administrator to bring about change in a teacher's role or methods may be viewed as a challenge to that teacher's professional autonomy. Research has further revealed that community groups may feel threatened by change because of its implications for upsetting the stability of the power relations within the community. Both sets of norms—teacher and community—can act as a powerful source of resistance to the administrator who is trying to introduce a particular innovation.

Lack of understanding. People may resist a proposed change because they don't possess an adequate or accurate understanding of it. Their deficiency may be caused by a failure on their part to pay close attention at the time that the proposed change was explained, or, on the other hand, information about the change may have been poorly or inaccurately communicated. In any respect, a lack of understanding of a proposed change can act as a significant deterrent to its successful implementation.

A difference of opinion. A proposed change may be resisted because of an honest difference of opinion about whether it is needed, or whether it will accomplish all that its proponents claim. The difference in opinion may be based on conflicting philosophies and values of education in regard to teaching and learning, or it may result from variant assessments of how much improvement would actually occur if the proposed change were implemented. If the difference of opinion centers on the amount of improvement that will take place, resistance may be reduced with the introduction of new evidence of potential success. However, if the difference of opinion is based on conflicting educational philosophies and values, the administrator will probably find it extremely difficult to remove this source of resistance.

A lack of skill. A proposed change may be resisted by any individual or group that will be required to perform new skills and roles. The change from traditional roles and skills to new ones is viewed as an unsettling experience to many people. Therefore, any innovation which will require new skills or roles on the part of the participants should be accompanied by an in-service program that will enable them to develop the new skills or roles.

Resistance to change is a complex phenomenon, and the administrator should spend a considerable amount of time in diagnosing its source(s) before drawing any conclusions about how it might best be reduced.[49] In many situations there will be more than one reason for resistance to change, and the administrator should assess the validity of each of the possible factors identified above. By accurately diagnosing the reasons for resistance, the administrator will be in a better position to ameliorate it and smooth the way for successful implementation of proposed currricular improvement.

THE PILOT PROJECT APPROACH TO CURRICULAR CHANGE

If an administrator is unable to overcome people's resistance to a proposed curricular change, she might attempt to initiate a pilot project, i.e., a scaled-down version of the originally proposed change. The proposed innovation might be reduced in terms of size, length of operation, or number of participants involved. For example, rather than introducing a new school-wide language arts curriculum, the change could be implemented on a pilot basis at only one grade level. Or, perhaps, rather than implementing a curricular change at one grade level, several units of the curriculum could be introduced by all of the teachers of the school during the first semester of the school year. Other variations of the pilot project approach are also possible.

The pilot project approach to curriculum improvement implementation has several definite advantages. It can be conducted with a fewer number of participants and can involve those who would be more willing to try out new curricular ideas. If the pilot project is successful, its results may favorably influence other people who initially resisted the proposed change.

A pilot project can also be useful in identifying and refining defects or weaknesses in the original curriculum proposal which were not perceived earlier. Most proposed curricular changes, whether emanating from study and planning within a district or from other school situations, require adaptation and refinement before they can be used successfully by an entire grade level, department, or school. And finally, a pilot project may prove useful in demonstrating that a proposed change will *not* work, either because of a defect in the proposal's concept or because local conditions make it impossible to implement.

The pilot project approach is not the only approach to curriculum implementation, nor is it a panacea for resistance to change. But it does offer important advantages, and it should be considered by the administrator.

KEY FACTORS IN CURRICULUM IMPLEMENTATION

Despite thousands of dollars and untold hours expended each year by districts in the development of curricular improvement plans or guides, the limited evidence available indicates that those plans are poorly implemented. For example, in Krey's study of thirty-six elementary schools, thirteen junior high schools, and five senior high schools, teachers reported very little classroom implementation of district curriculum guides.[50] The modal response of the teachers about the extent of curricular implementation was, "No implementation."

Krey discovered in his investigation that four major factors were directly related to the degree to which curricular plans for improvement were actually implemented in the classroom:

1. The extent to which teachers felt a need for some kind of orientation and in-service activities to help them implement curricular plans
2. The extent to which teachers received an opportunity to participate in the *planning* of orientation and in-service activities to help them implement curricular plans
3. The extent to which teachers received an opportunity to participate in the *evaluation* of those orientation and in-service activities
4. The extent to which teachers felt they had a professional obligation to participate in curriculum implementation.

Krey's study emphasizes the need for orientation and in-service activities to help teachers implement curriculum improvement proposals and plans. It also suggests the importance of faculty *involvement* in the planning and evaluation stages if orientation and in-service activities are to be perceived by teachers as worthwhile.

An important implication of the study is that the school administrator should not assume that a curriculum improvement proposal or plan can be successfully implemented in the classroom without appropriate orientation and in-service activities for the teachers of the school. Such activities might include: (1) workshops to familiarize teachers with all aspects of the curricular plan; (2) clinics to provide teachers with an opportunity to practice using the materials or techniques contained in the curricular plan before implementing them in the classroom; and (3) evaluation sessions for teachers, held after the curricular plan has been implemented in the classroom, for the purpose of identifying strengths and weaknesses of the plan and making appropriate revisions. Although the degree of implementation of proposed curricular improvement would also seem to depend on the merits of the particular proposal or plan (a factor not studied in the research), it would appear from Krey's investigation that little curriculum implementation will occur without adequate orientation and in-service activities for the staff.

In working with teachers on implementing proposed curricular improvements, the administrator should also be aware that their perception of her own attitude toward implementing a particular plan is important. Edwards, for example, found in his study of essentially the same schools examined in Krey's research, that the more the teachers perceived the principal as personally accepting the curriculum improvement plans and *holding teachers responsible* for implementation, the more likely were the teachers to report a higher level of curriculum implementation, in their classrooms.[51] The key factor seemed to be the teachers' perceptions of the administrator's attitude, rather than the administrator's *actual* feelings about the importance of curriculum implementation. Teachers who perceived that their principal personally accepted the curriculum improvement plans and intended to hold teachers accountable for implementing the plans, reported a higher implementation level than those teachers who perceived the opposite—regardless of how their principal actually felt about the implementation of the curriculum plans.

It would appear, then, that if the administrator is interested in increasing classroom adoption of proposed curricular improvement plans, it will not be sufficient for her to hold a positive attitude about those plans; she must also accurately communicate to teachers her feelings about the importance of implementing the proposed curriculum improvement.

A FINAL NOTE

The main thrust of this chapter has been on the administrator's role in curricular improvement. Curricular improvement is seldom an easy task, and it will be difficult for the school administrator to resist pressures to concentrate on more manageable activities. However, it needs to be recognized that the school administrator is a pivotal person in any attempt to improve the curriculum. She can either be an initiator and facilitator, or she can be a resister and a rejector. For as McNally and others earlier pointed out,

> . . . changing the curriculum in order to keep it abreast of current demands for education is a difficult undertaking. The success with which the task can be discharged is directly related to the administrative provisions in a school system. Administrative arrangements may either facilitate curriculum change or make it difficult, if not impossible.[52]

Review and Learning Activities

1. Discuss the main characteristics, and the advantages and disadvantages of the district approach to curriculum improvement; the school-site approach. Describe your district's approach.
2. Attempt to apply the criteria for determining the need for improvement (as presented in this chapter) to the curriculum in your school or school district. Then draft recommendations for improvement.
3. Describe the committee process used in your school or district to improve the curriculum. How does it compare with the process identified in figure 12.1? Draft a new committee process for your school or district, taking into consideration the ideas and problems described in this chapter.
4. Ascertain the approach your administrator employs to encourage and evaluate curriculum improvement proposals. How does it compare with the ideas presented in the text? Specifically, how would you improve the approach used by your administrator?
5. To what extent are the barriers and obstacles to implementing curriculum improvement that are described in the text present in your own school or school district? How might you use the pilot project approach to help ameliorate these problems?
6. Utilize the findings in the studies by Krey and Edwards in order to evaluate your own district's approach to curriculum implementation. How would you improve this approach?

Notes

1. Douglas Christensen, "Curriculum Development: A Function of Design and Leadership." An ERIC Report: Ed–207–213.
2. J. Lloyd Trump and Delmar F. Matter, *Secondary School Curriculum Improvement* (Boston: Allyn and Bacon, 1979), chapter 1; J. G. Duerr, "How to Improve Your Reading Program Without Going into Hock," *National Elementary Principal* (March 1980): 61–63.

3. For a good introduction to this study, see *Curriculum: An Introduction to the Field,* eds. James R. Grass and David E. Purpel (Berkeley, Calif.: McCutchan, 1978).

4. J. Galen Saylor, William M. Alexander, and Arthur Lewis, *Curriculum Planning for Better Teaching and Learning* (New York: Holt, Rinehart and Winston, 1981).

5. Ronald Dahl, *Curriculum Improvement: Decision Making and Process* (Boston, Mass.: Allyn and Bacon, 1978), pp. 257–59.

6. Dennis Kelly, "The Effects of Curriculum Organization Structure on Curriculum Innovation" (Paper presented at the annual meeting of the American Educational Research Association, 1977). An ERIC Report: Ed–137–94.

7. For added discussion of these criticisms, see Daniel Tanner and Laurel Tanner, *Curriculum Development* (New York: Macmillan, 1975), pp. 589–92.

8. H. L. Caswell et al., *Curriculum Improvement in Public School Systems* (New York: Columbia University Teachers College Bureau of Publications, 1950), p. 72.

9. Association for Supervision and Curriculum Development, *Leadership for Improving Instruction, 1960 Yearbook* (Washington, D.C.: Association for Supervision and Curriculum Development, 1960), pp. 62–63.

10. Fenwick W. English, "Management Practice as a Key to Curriculum Leadership," *Educational Leadership* (March 1979): 412.

11. Hollis L. Caswell, "Persistent Curriculum Problems," *Educational Forum* (November 1980), p. 108.

12. Howard G. Spaulding, "What Is the Role of the Principal in Curriculum Work?" *NASSP Bulletin* (April 1956): 388.

13. Allan Vann, "Can Principals Lead in Curriculum Development?" *Educational Leadership* (March 1979): 404–5.

14. William Georigiades, "Curriculum Change: What Are the Ingredients?" *NASSP Bulletin* (March 1980): 70.

15. Patricia B. Novotney, "Principal as an Instructional Leader," *Educational Leadership* (March 1979): 405.

16. Eleanor Farrar et al., "The Lawn Party: The Evolution of Federal Programs in Local Settings," *The Kappan* (November 1980): 167–71.

17. Caswell et al., *Curriculum Improvement in Public School Systems.*

18. For example, see Saylor, Alexander, and Lewis, *Curriculum Planning.*

19. W. James Popham and Eva L. Baker, "Establishing Instructional Goals," in *Curriculum Development: Issues and Insights,* eds. Donald E. Orlosky and B. Othanel Smith (Chicago: Rand McNally College Publishing Company, 1978), pp. 14–16.

20. M. Francis Klein, "A Study of Schooling: Curriculum," *The Kappan* (December 1979): 244–45.

21. Benson Snyder, *The Hidden Curriculum* (New York: Alfred A. Knopf, 1970).

22. Richard Larson, "Curriculum Scope and Sequence," *Forward* (Spring 1980): 53.

23. Philip L. Hosford, "Improving the Silent Curriculum," *Theory into Practice* (Winter 1980): 45–50.

24. Robert J. Havighurst, *Developmental Tasks and Education* (New York: David McKay, 1972), pp. 43–82.

25. Marie Winn, *The Plug-in Drug: Television, Children and the Family* (New York: Viking, 1977).

26. Kathryn J. Noyes and Gordon L. McAndrew, "Is This What Schools Are For?" *Saturday Review* (December 1968): 65.

27. For further discussion of some of these influences, see William L. Boyd, "The Changing Politics of Curriculum Policy-making for American Schools," *Review of Educational Research* (Fall 1978): 577–628.

28. George H. Gallup, "The 13th Annual Gallup Poll of the Public's Attitudes toward the Public Schools," *Phi Delta Kappan* (September 1981): 38–40.

29. For an example of what employers say they need, see "Attitudes, Not Skills, Sought by Youth Employers," *Education USA* (June 2, 1980): 305+.

30. For help in this area, see Meredith D. Gall, *Handbook for Evaluating and Selecting Curriculum Materials* (Rockleigh, N.J.: Allyn and Bacon, 1981).

31. An excellent resource which every administrator should utilize to help the school determine the effectiveness of curriculum materials, particularly those that are commercially produced, is the Educational Products Information Exchange Institute, New York City. Also see *The Kappan,* June 1980, for a good example of a textbook selection guide.

32. See Sheila Harty, *Hucksters in the Classroom* (Washington, D.C.: Center for Responsive Law, 1980).

33. U.S. Commission on Civil Rights, *Fair Textbooks: A Resource Guide* (Washington, D.C.: U.S. Commission on Civil Rights, 1980).

34. For assistance in doing this, see Robert J. Kibler et al., *Objectives for Instruction and Evaluation* (Rockleigh, N.J.: Allyn and Bacon, 1981).

35. Orlosky and Smith, *Curriculum Improvement: Issues and Insights,* chapters 11 and 12. Also see Theodore J. Kowalski, "Organizational Patterns for Secondary School Curriculum" *NASSP Bulletin* (March 1981): 5–6.

36. A good *beginning* source for the administrator would be Sharon Tumulty, *Curriculum and Instruction: Planning Improvement* (Philadelphia: Research for Better Schools, 1978). Then turn to Bruce W. Tuckman, *Evaluating Instructional Programs* (Boston: Allyn and Bacon, 1979), and John J. Bowers, *Planning a Program Evaluation* (Philadelphia: 1978). For a good example of the application of evaluation methods to an actual evaluation of the curriculum, see Donald C. Wilson, "Curriculum Evaluation" (ERIC Report: Ed–175–928). Also, Sage Publications, South Beverly Drive, Beverly Hills, California, offers a number of good publications on program evaluation.

37. Fenwick W. English, *Quality Control in Curriculum Development* (Arlington, Va.: American Association of School Administrators, 1978).

38. Ibid., pp. 27–35.

39. D. A. Erlandson, "Evaluation and an Administrator's Autonomy," in *School Evaluation: The Politics and Process,* ed. E. R. House (Berkeley, Calif.: McCutchan, 1973), p. 22.

40. E. R. House, "A Tenuous Relationship," in *School Evaluation: The Politics and Process,* p. 8.

41. *National Elementary School Principals Study* (Arlington, Va.: National Association of Elementary School Principals, 1979); *The Senior High School Principalship* (Reston, Va.: National Association of Secondary School Principals, 1979), p. 17; Richard A. Gorton and Kenneth E. McIntyre, *The Effective Principal* (Reston, Va.: National Association of Secondary School Principals, 1978), pp. 20–24.

42. Also see an older but still relevant work by Kenneth D. Benne and Bozidar Muntyan, *Human Relations in Curriculum Change* (New York: Dryden Press, 1951). This book presents excellent ideas on working with groups in introducing change. Also see Richard A. Gorton, *School Administration and Supervision: Important Issues, Concepts and Case Studies* (Dubuque, Iowa: Wm. C. Brown Company Publishers, 1980), chapter 13.

43. For further discussion on utilizing a needs assessment for curriculum improvement, see Fred D. Williams, *School District Needs Assessment for Curriculum Development* (ERIC Report: Ed–137–95). Also see Willard Crouthamel and Stephen Preston, *Needs Assessment, User's Manual* (ERIC Report: Ed–181–562).

44. T. J. Kowalski, "Principal's Role in Curriculum Development: What Are the Barriers?" *Contemporary Education* (Spring 1979): 159–61.

45. Thomas McQuizz, "Participation in Curriculum Committees by Classroom Teachers in Selected Colorado Schools" (Unpublished document, University of Colorado, 1962), p. 180. For a more recent study, see Gill Schofer, "Analysis of the Qualifications, Selection and Behavior of Teachers on District-Wide Committees," *Education* (Summer 1978): 426–29.

46. D. C. Anderson, *Evaluating Curriculum Proposals: A Critical Guide* (New York: John Wiley and Sons, 1980).

47. For the early recognition of this point, which many administrators still seem to ignore, see G. Sharp, *Curriculum Development as Re-education of the Teacher* (New York: Columbia University, Teachers College, 1951), p. 2.

48. Gorton, *School Administration and Supervision,* pp. 300–301.

49. For further ideas and discussion about how to diagnose the reasons for resistance to change, and how to introduce and implement successful changes in the curriculum, see Gorton, chapter 11.

50. Robert D. Krey, "Factors Relating to Teachers' Perceptions of Curriculum Implementation Activities and the Extent of Curricular Implementation" (Ph.D. Dissertation, University of Wisconsin, 1968). For more recent evidence on this problem, see R. W. Common, "Managing for Curriculum Change: An Empirical Investigation," *Manitoba Journal of Education* (Fall 1979): 11–14.

51. Conan S. Edwards, "The Principal's Relationship to the Implementation of Official Curriculum Plans" (Ph.D. diss., University of Wisconsin, 1968). That curriculum implementation continues to be a problem is made clear in an article by J. L. Patterson and T. J. Czajkowski, "Implementation: Neglected Phase in Curriculum Change," *Educational Technology,* (December 1979): 204–6.

52. Harold McNally et al., *Improving the Quality of Public School Programs* (New York: Columbia University, Teachers College, 1960), p. 28.

4

STUDENT PROBLEMS, SERVICES, AND ACTIVITIES

13

Student Discipline Problems

The majority of students in most elementary and secondary schools do not misbehave. However, a minority of students do misbehave and their behavior is one of the major problems that confront administrators and their professional staffs. Since an examination of a number of books on school administration revealed little or no attention to this topic, an attempt will be made to treat this important subject in some detail.

FACTORS AFFECTING THE PREVENTION AND REDUCTION OF STUDENT MISBEHAVIOR

The prevention and resolution of student discipline problems have long been responsibilities of the school administrator. In the early days of education these were *major* responsibilities.[1] Through the years, other duties–particularly in the area of instructional improvement–have been added to the administrator's job, but maintaining appropriate student discipline has continued to rank as one of his more important responsibilities. Recent surveys of the public and of educators, which have identified student discipline as one of the most significant problems facing the school, suggest that it will continue to occupy much of the administrator's time.[2]

The amount of time that an administrator should spend on discipline problems will depend on many variables, including the nature of the student population, the capability of the faculty, and the willingness of teachers to work with the administrator in a team approach. However, it would appear that two factors which will influence the effectiveness of the administrator and the faculty are: (1) their perception of the causes of discipline problems, and (2) the approaches they utilize to prevent or resolve them. In this chapter, an emphasis will be placed on careful classification and diagnosis of student discipline problems, and organizational considerations for preventing and reducing them. Although the focus of most of the discussion will be on student misbehavior, the administrator and the staff should always keep in mind that their ultimate objective should be to develop *self*-discipline on the part of all students. In this connection it should be stressed that the place to begin the process of careful classification and diagnosis of student discipline problems and the development of self-discipline is in the elementary school. By beginning at this level, many potential and actual student discipline problems can be identified, diagnosed, and ameliorated before they become worse in the secondary school.

DEFINING THE PROBLEM

All schools do not experience the same kinds of discipline problems, but the differences seem to be mainly a matter of degree rather than type. For example, at one time, vandalism was thought to be a problem only for large city schools, and of little concern to rural, suburban, or elementary schools. Recently, however, this particular problem has been encountered in a variety of locales.[3] At present, there are probably few student discipline problems which are unique to only one kind of school or school setting, though in general elementary schools probably encounter fewer *overt* discipline problems than do secondary schools.

Although schools report a wide variety of student discipline problems, they seem to fall into four general categories. These categories are identified in the classification system presented in figure 13.1.

A difficulty encountered in designing any system of classifying problems is that one's definition of what constitutes a problem will largely determine what is included in the system.[4] In the classification system presented in figure 13.1, the areas included are those which are most typically reported by the schools as student discipline problems.[5] However, it should be noted that it is possible for an administrator to narrow or broaden the scope of problems included in a classification system (thereby reducing or increasing his responsibilities) merely be changing the definition of what constitutes student misbehavior.

For example, under the category "Misbehavior Outside Class," many schools have a rule against gum-chewing. While gum-chewing may be objectionable to some people, the question that needs to be raised is, "Is this the type of student behavior that teachers and administrators should be spending time and energy to eliminate?" If the answer to the question is "Yes," then the scope of responsibility for disciplining students has been broadened, and some of the time and energy of teachers and administrators is less available

Misbehavior in Class	Misbehavior Outside Class (But in School or on School Grounds)	Truancy	Tardiness
1. Talking back to the teacher	1. Fighting	1. Cutting class	1. Frequently being late to class
2. Not paying attention	2. Vandalism	2. Skipping school	2. Frequently being late to school
3. Distracting others	3. Smoking		
4. Gum chewing	4. Using illegal drugs		
5. Vandalism	5. Student dress		
6. Profanity	6. Theft		
7. Cheating	7. Gambling		
8. Assault	8. Littering		
	9. Student activism		
	10. Located in unapproved area		

Figure 13.1. Types of Student Discipline Problems

for other activities. Although it is true that the amount of time and energy devoted to the elimination of gum-chewing is probably not great, the cumulative effect of a number of such rules can be considerable. A reasonable guideline for determining whether certain student behavior should be considered a problem is whether or not the behavior is disruptive or only distractive. (These terms are defined later in the chapter.) It is the former rather than the latter which merits the time and energy of the administrator and the faculty.

In considering the types of student misbehavior for which the school should assume responsibility for disciplining, the administrator and staff should also try to make a distinction between student misbehavior which is within the appropriate jurisdiction of the school and student misbehavior which is more properly handled by outside agencies. Vandalism and using illegal drugs, for example, are student behavior which in most schools are subject to disciplinary punishment. However, since these particular student actions are also violations of the law, it is debatable whether the school has a legitimate role in disciplining students, in addition to whatever consequences are imposed upon them by the police or the courts. As the publication *Guidelines for Student Rights and Responsibilities* points out, "Standards of Conduct . . . need not prescribe school discipline for offenses committed within the school which are already adequately provided for by criminal law, unless the presence of the student in school would constitute a danger to the student himself, to other members of the school community, or to the continuation of the educative process."[6]

It should be emphasized that the school needs to play a role in *referring, counseling,* and *educating* students who break the law. But whether a school should also act as an institution for determining guilt and administering punishment is doubtful. The school that decides to determine guilt and administer punishment for student misbehavior which is *unlawful* will not only add immeasureably to the number and difficulty of the discipline problems with which it must deal, but may also be subjecting the student to double jeopardy. Therefore, in fairness to the student and in the best interest of the school, the administration and faculty should limit themselves to defining and punishing only student behavior that tends to disrupt education, and which would not be handled more appropriately by some outside agency, such as the police or the courts.

DIAGNOSING DISCIPLINE PROBLEMS

After a school has defined the types of behavior which will be considered as representing student discipline problems, the faculty's and administration's initial approach when encountering such behavior should be to diagnose the reasons for it. Admittedly, there will be cases in which diagnosis of a problem must follow punishment for the misbehavior. But if the intent is to prevent that misbehavior from occurring again, punishment alone will probably not prove to be very effective in most situations. All behavior is caused, and until the administration and faculty can better understand and deal with the causes of student misbehavior, it is likely to recur in the future.

In attempting to diagnose the causes of student's misbehavior, the administrator is really trying to understand the reasons for the student's actions. Such reasons are typically complex and may not be understood even by the student himself. However, it is essential that the administrator and staff conduct a thorough investigation into the causes of the problem if it is to be resolved successfully. The conclusions which the administrator and staff draw about why the student acted as he did will greatly influence their decision on whether or how the student should be punished, and will also determine further steps that should be taken to prevent the problem from happening again.

Possible Causes

To diagnose a discipline problem accurately, the administrator and staff should investigate the validity of several alternative hypotheses or explanations for the student's misbehavior. Although the nature of the hypotheses will vary for

School-Related Factors	Personal Factors	Home and Community Environment
1. Poor teaching	1. Student doesn't understand the rules	1. Poor authority figures and relationships within the home
2. Irrelevant curriculum	2. Student doesn't understand why the rules exist	2. Crime-infested neighborhood
3. Inflexible school schedule	3. Poor educational background	3. Student's activities after school, e.g., work, other activities that keep him up late at night
4. Insufficient adaptation and individualization of school's programs to a student's educational background	4. Undesirable peer relationships	
	5. Student is psychologically disturbed	
	6. Personality conflict between student and teacher	

Figure 13.2. Diagnosing Student Misbehavior: Some Alternative Hypotheses

different types of discipline and attendance problems, a taxonomy of hypotheses is presented in figure 13.2.

As an examination of figure 13.2 shows, diagnosing the causes of student misbehavior is a complex task. Any or several of the factors listed could contribute to a student's misbehavior in a particular situation. Since the administrator cannot hope to investigate all of the possible hypotheses at the same time, he must make some decisions about how to proceed. In general, it would appear that his first line of approach should be to investigate the first three hypotheses listed under "Personal Factors" and then those under "School-Related Factors." These are factors more subject to the influence of the administration and faculty and more within the responsibilities of the school.

For example, the following school-related factors may account for a student's behavior and should be investigated.[7]

1. The subject matter may be too difficult.
2. The subject matter may be too easy.
3. The subject matter or the class activities may not be relevant to the student's interests or needs.
4. The class assignment may be too heavy, too light, badly planned, poorly explained, or unfairly evaluated.

5. The course content or activities may not be properly sequenced for this student.
6. The seating arrangement for the student may be poor from a learning point of view.
7. There may be a personality conflict between the student and the teachers.

Each or any combination of these conditions may cause considerable frustration, boredom, anxiety, or hostility in a student, which could be expressed in misbehavior. However, if an administrator can ascertain the particular underlying reasons for a student's misbehavior, he will then be in a position to know which approach to take in remedying the problem.

Although one or more of the other hypotheses listed in figure 13.2 under "Personal Factors" (i.e., B-4, B-5, and B-6), and under "Home and Community Environment," may be valid for a given situation, the school frequently has little or no control or influence over these conditions. This is particularly true in respect to the factors associated with "Home and Community Environment." The school seldom has much control over a student's situation in either his home or neighborhood. Both factors may be important in causing a student's misbehavior in school, but school authorities will probably find it difficult to bring about change in these areas.

On the other hand, in some situations the school has a responsibility to respond immediately to a student problem caused by the home or the community. For example, it has been observed that some children misbehave in school because of their neglect or abuse in the home.[8] Child abuse is now recognized as a serious problem in the United States, and it is estimated that each year approximately half a million children suffer from abuse in the home.[9] Public Law 93–247, the Child Abuse Prevention and Treatment Act, requires individuals or agencies suspecting possible child abuse to report it to the proper authorities. In addition, Fossum and Sorensen recommend that school districts provide in-service education for all personnel to help them recognize symptoms of child abuse and to obtain knowledge of resources available in the community to deal with the problem.[10] Several national organizations that provide literature on the topic of child abuse are identified in the notes at the end of this chapter,[11] and the administrator is encouraged to keep well informed about this problem. (Possible approaches for working with parents and community groups on other kinds of student misbehavior are described in the next chapter.)

While there will be situations for which the school should look at the home or the community for possible causes of a student's misbehavior, in most instances the administrator and staff will find that the most productive approach is to concentrate initially on diagnosing those possible causes of a student's misbehavior which may operate *within* the school and for which the school can offer a remedy. As Howard and Jenkins point out, "Many causes of pupil behavior are deeply rooted in the nature of the institution itself. . . . Progress can best be made in improving discipline through changing the nature of the school itself."[12]

Process of Diagnosis

Although diagnosis in situations involving student discipline problems has yet to be fully developed as a concept or skill, it would seem to include the following kinds of behavior on the part of the administrator and staff:[13]

1. Conferences with the student to ascertain his attitude toward school and his feelings about those aspects of the school environment which make it difficult for him to perform as he should and as he would like.
2. Conferences with the student's teachers to ascertain their analyses of the problem.
3. Examination of the student's cumulative record for clues suggesting possible learning problems that might be frustrating him and causing his misbehavior. Examples of such clues would be low reading scores, poor grades in the past, underachievement.[14]
4. Examination of the student's program and schedule. Is it an appropriate program and schedule, considering his background, interests, and attitudes?
5. Review of the curriculum and teacher lesson plans in those areas of the student's program where he appears to be experiencing the greatest difficulty, academically and behaviorally.
6. Conferences with the student's parents to ascertain their attitudes and perceptions of the problem and to evaluate the extent to which they may provide assistance.
7. Observation of the student and his interactions with others in various school settings, e.g., classroom, cafeteria, extracurricular program.

Engaging in all of these procedures for one student would admittedly represent a major investment of an administrator's and/or faculty's effort and time. (They should by all means utilize the help of the school counselor, psychologist, or other pupil personnel workers.) But in many situations it will not be necessary for the administrator and staff to complete all of the steps outlined above in diagnosing the causes of a discipline problem. Sometimes the root of a problem may be uncovered after completing only two or three steps.

However, if the administrator and staff want to avoid inaccurate diagnosis of problems, they will be as thorough and comprehensive as possible. They should always bear in mind that if they fail to invest sufficient time and effort in diagnosing the causes of a problem, the time and effort that they have "saved" will need to be reinvested as the problem reoccurs time and again. There is no good educational substitute or shortcut to comprehensive, in-depth diagnosis of a problem.

In engaging in the process of diagnosis the administrator and staff should be aware that certain subjective factors could compromise the objectivity and effectiveness of the process. According to attribution theory, individuals who are judging other people tend to attribute the actions of the latter to their personal characteristics and attitudinal dispositions rather than to situational factors.[15] Therefore, the physical characteristics, appearance, or attitude of a student who has misbehaved could subconsciously affect an administrator and/or staff member, limiting the process of diagnosis as well as influencing the final disposition of the problem. For example, Porter found that the disciplinarians' view of the circumstances surrounding student misbehavior and their choice of disciplinary responses were more influenced by the students' physical appearance than by the students' previous disciplinary record or even the violation of rules for which the punishment was supposedly being given.[16] The Frashers report similar findings in regard to the influence of a student's attitude during the conference with the assistant principal and the severity of punishment recommended by the assistant principal, irrespective of the nature of the offense.[17] These findings, based on attribution theory, suggest that the individuals participating in the process of diagnosis need to pay special attention to how the characteristics of the student who has misbehaved are influencing their diagnosis and selection of corrective measures.

ORGANIZATIONAL CONSIDERATIONS

Responding to student misbehavior has thus far been viewed from a problem perspective. There is value, however, in examining student discipline from an organizational point of view. To maintain appropriate order in the school, roles need to be defined, procedures specified, relationships between roles coordinated, and the effectiveness of these various organizational elements needs to be assessed periodically.

RESPONSIBILITY FOR DISCIPLINARY POLICIES AND PROCEDURES

Disciplinary policies and procedures tend to be promulgated at both the school board and the building level. Policies and procedures at the school board level are frequently rather general, and may be no more specific than to delegate to the building administrator the authority to make those rules and regulations which will facilitate learning and maintain order and safety in the school. Some school boards, however, are very specific in defining disciplinary policies and procedures, even to the extent of specifying the type of student conduct which will (or will not) be permitted in the school district. Such specificity is usually for the purpose of maintaining a degree of uniformity throughout the district. It also results in lessening the authority of administrator and staff in the defining of rules and regulations which they may feel are appropriate for their students.

If the responsibility for defining specific disciplinary policies and procedures is delegated by the school board to the building administrator, he will have greater flexibility in developing particular policies and procedures which are appropriate for his own student clientele.[18] But he should always keep in mind that policies and procedures at the building level must be logically related to the initial mandate given by the school board at the time of delegation. So, if the school board has delegated to the building administrator the authority to "make those rules and regulations which will facilitate learning and maintain order and safety in the school," the specific policies and procedures defined at the building level should not go beyond this delegation of authority. It is clear that the administrator is not totally free to make whatever rules and regulations he thinks are best for the school; all school rules and regulations must be based on school board policy, and be compatible with state and federal law.

THE TEACHER AND STUDENT DISCIPLINE

While the administrator is primarily responsible for administering a school's disciplinary program, the classroom teacher performs one of the most important roles in the program. The teacher is the key person to interpret and implement the school's rules and regulations concerning student behavior, and is the one who typically first identifies, defines, and reacts to a particular student behavior as a problem. Also, as Brown has pointed out, the classroom teacher can play a major role in reducing student misbehavior. The better the teacher's preparation, teaching techniques, personality, and other classroom aspects, the less likely are student misbehavior problems to arise.[19]

Probably the most important step that an administrator can take to decrease the number of discipline problems referred to his office by teachers is to work with the staff, particularly new teachers, in regard to their role in student discipline. Apparently the first three weeks of class represent a critical time for teachers to establish appropriate classroom management. Emmer and his colleagues found that effective classroom managers establish their credibility as well as classroom procedures during the first three weeks rather than waiting until a crisis develops.[20] Specifically, these teachers

- Developed a workable system of rules and procedures that they then spent time teaching to their students

- Made explicit the consequences of inappropriate classroom behavior
- Stopped inappropriate behavior quickly and were consistent and predictable in their response to inappropriate behavior.
- Gave careful directions to students and monitored their behavior carefully.

Other research reviewed by Emmer and Evertson underscores the importance of teacher behaviors which help the student keep engaged in the task of learning.[21] A number of these teacher behaviors are identified in the chapter on Staff Evaluation.

The administrator can work individually or in groups with teachers who need help in classroom management. The latter approach can take the form of in-service activities which might begin with a review of the school's student discipline policies and procedures and the rationale upon which they are based. Such a review at the beginning of the year would be helpful for clearing up any misunderstandings and might even identify the need to revise some of the policies and procedures. Included in the review could be a discussion with the faculty on their expectations for student behavior.

A good approach to stimulating faculty thinking on discipline would be to give out a short questionnaire in order to secure teachers' perceptions of various factors which affect how they react to different kinds of student behavior. The administrator could develop his own questionnaire or use one of several instruments which are available, such as the Pupil Control Ideology instrument.[22] This questionnaire is composed of twenty statements which suggest factors that may be related to student control and discipline problems. Four sample statements from the instrument are:

- Teachers should consider revision of their teaching methods if these are criticized by their pupils.
- Being friendly with pupils often leads them to become too familiar.
- Pupils can be trusted to work together without supervision.
- Pupils often misbehave in order to make the teacher look bad.

Respondents to the Pupil Control Ideology instrument indicate the extent to which they agree or disagree with each statement. The instrument does not take long to administer, but can provide considerable useful information about the attitudes and philosophies of the faculty toward students, and may pinpoint the direction that an in-service program for the faculty should take. For example, responses to the instrument might show that many of the faculty are either creating discipline problems through their own actions, or that they are overly concerned about certain kinds of student behavior and insufficiently concerned about other kinds of student behavior. (Numerous studies through the years have suggested that teachers tend to overemphasize control problems and give inadequate attention to problems of a more psychological nature.) A major objective of an in-service program for the faculty, then, might be to develop a more positive philosophy and attitude on their part toward student behavior, with emphasis on the role that a teacher needs to play in promoting student *self*-discipline. An excellent approach for teaching students self-discipline has been developed by the Dobsons.[23]

Although research has shown that most school districts do not provide in-service training for teachers to help them manage discipline problems more effectively,[24] there is no shortage of in-service materials on the topic. The following examples illustrate several types of materials and approaches:

1. *Assertive Discipline in the Classroom* (two cassettes, two filmstrips, and one teacher's guide) is published by Media Five, 3211 Cahuenga Blvd., West Hollywood, CA 90068.
2. *Glasser on Discipline.* William Glasser, a well-known psychiatrist and author *(Schools Without Failure)* sets forth five basic steps to achieving effective discipline. This twenty-eight minute film can be ordered from Media Five, Film Distributors, Hollywood, CA.
3. *The First Day of School: Effective Classroom Management in the Elementary School* (videotape) can be purchased or rented from the Association for Supervision and Curriculum Development, 225 N. Washington Street, Alexandria VA 22314.
4. *Classroom Discipline* (case studies and viewpoints book) can be ordered from the National Education Association, Washington, D.C.

In-service activities for teachers should concentrate on the use of case studies, role playing, simulations, and videotape analysis (rather than more traditional methods such as guest speakers or open group discussions) in order to provide teachers with a greater opportunity to practice the application of new concepts and techniques.

REFERRAL PROCEDURES

A student should not be referred to the administrator for disciplinary action until the teacher has first conferred with the student about his behavior, unless it is such that class cannot continue as long as the student is in the room (i.e., disruptive behavior). The person who is best able to resolve discipline problems arising in the classroom setting is the teacher, and the administrator should attempt to foster this approach with the faculty.

However, the experienced administrator knows that not all discipline problems can be resolved at the classroom level, and that some student behavior problems will have to be referred to the administrator for appropriate action. It is at this stage that the administrator needs to call on his organizational and administrative abilities to develop procedures which will facilitate careful consideration of the problems, and accurate and full communication to all concerned. Usually some type of a referral and feedback form will be necessary. Although there are many examples of such forms, the one presented in figure 13.3 has much to commend it.[25]

Several provisions of the form presented in figure 13.3 should be included in any referral procedure. First of all, there should be a *written* record of the initial diagnosis of the problem and the action taken by the teacher and the administrator. Written communication, as opposed to verbal, tends to be more thoughtfully prepared and is less subject to misinterpretation and forgetfulness at a later date. Written communication is particularly important as part of the documentation which may be required later, if more severe disciplinary action taken by the school is challenged at a school board hearing or in the courts. (An option to reduce the amount of writing would be to identify and code the various kinds of student misbehavior on the back of the referral form, and request that the teacher use the appropriate code.)

Secondly, the referral procedures should require the teacher to specify in as much detail as possible the nature of the problem and the action that the teacher has taken to remedy the situation. These two requirements are designed to encourage the teacher to give some thought to why the problem has occurred and how it might be resolved at the classroom level, and to provide the administrator with information on these aspects. Unless the administrator has this information when a student is referred, he is likely to waste time or take the wrong approach with the student. Therefore, before the administrator will be in a reasonable position to take disciplinary or remedial action with the student, he must obtain information about the nature of the problem based on the teacher's perception, and on what the teacher has already tried to do about the situation.

The school's referral procedures should also include a mechanism (similar to the one in figure 13.3) by which the administrator can communicate to the teacher the action that has been taken. Most administrators have good intentions in this regard, but for one reason or another, the job frequently doesn't get done, at least according to teacher reports.

Probably the most efficient and certain way for an administrator to communicate back to the referring teacher is to use a procedure similar to the feedback portion of the form in figure 13.3. This kind of a system not only provides feedback to the teacher, but also provides for the maintaining of a written record of the action taken, which can be very useful in building documentation or in conducting an analysis of trends in discipline problems and the types of action initiated by the administrator.

Student _____ Section _____ Time _____.

Teacher _____ Date _____.

Nature of Problem _____.

	Teacher/Student/	
Action Before Referral	**Administrator Conference**	**Action by Administration**

Action Before Referral	Teacher/Student/Administrator Conference	Action by Administration
Conference with pupil _____	My planning period	Date _____.
Detention _____	is _____	Conference with pupil (warning/reprimand)
Phone call home _____	Student is in room	_____.
Parent conference _____	_____	
Letter to parents _____		Detention _____.
Guidance _____		Phone call to parents
Other _____		_____.
		Formal letter (copy in
		your mailbox) _____.
		Conference with parent
		being requested _____
		Referral to pupil personnel
		department _____
		Suspension (until
		conference) _____
		Corporal punishment
		_____
		Other _____

Initials _____

Figure 13.3. Referral and Feedback Form

UTILIZING SPECIALIZED RESOURCES

In attempting to prevent and ameliorate student misbehavior, the administrator should organize all of the professional resources that are available to the school. The school counselor, psychologist, social worker, and nurse, as well as personnel in law enforcement and family assistance agencies, all possess specialized knowledge and skill which an administrator should try to utilize in working with students who are discipline problems. These specialists should not be involved in administering punishment to the student, but they certainly can make a valuable contribution to diagnosing the nature of a problem, and in the making of recommendations for remedial action.[26]

For these specialists to make a maximum contribution, the administrator should consider organizing them into a pupil personnel committee for the purposes of studying and diagnosing severe student disciplinary problems and for offering suggestions about possible remediation. A deficiency in most approaches to student misbehavior is that they do not capitalize in an organized way on the various kinds of professional expertise which exist within the school and the community. The type of approach to student misbehavior that is needed is one in which the administrator takes responsibility for organizing and utilizing all of the different kinds of expertise which are available. Until the administrator assumes this organizational responsibility, the school's approach to student discipline problems is likely to be piecemeal, uncoördinated, and not very effective.

EVALUATING DISCIPLINARY POLICIES
AND PROCEDURES

The disciplinary policies and procedures of many schools have been attacked in recent years by students, parents, and the courts. At the same time, the number and severity of discipline problems in the schools have increased. Both of these factors have made the job of trying to prevent or deal constructively with discipline problems a very difficult and frustrating one for the school administrator. As Ladd has noted, "Being an administrator trying to keep order in school must sometimes seem like being a modern physician trying to practice medicine in a country that has outlawed scalpels and hypodermic needles."[27]

While some administrators may feel that, on the basis of court rulings, there is little student misbehavior that they can regulate, the courts have never taken the position that the schools have no authority in this area. In fact, in the famous Blackwell case the court reaffirmed that "It is always within the province of school authorities to provide regulation, prohibition, and punishment of acts calculated to undermine the school routine."[28] In ruling *against* school disciplinary policies and procedures, the main thrust of the courts' decisions has been that the policies and procedures were not fair, reasonable, or clear. Therefore, every administrator (with the assistance of relevant others) should periodically evaluate the school's disciplinary policies and procedures to ascertain the extent to which they meet these criteria.

Since *specific* discipline policies and procedures are frequently made at the building level, the school administrator is most likely to be concerned with evaluating the validity and effectiveness of these policies and procedures, rather than the ones established by the school board. However, there may be situations in which he will be requested to evaluate school board policies on student discipline, and suggest changes. In either case, the administrator will need defensible criteria upon which to make his evaluation. Due to the paucity of research on disciplinary policies and procedures, the criteria presented below are primarily based on a synthesis of recommendations in the professional literature and should therefore be discussed and analyzed before they are accepted. (One particularly useful document in this regard is *Resource Handbook on Discipline Codes* (Cambridge, Mass.: Oelgeschlager, Gunn and Hain Inc., 1980).

CRITERIA FOR EVALUATING STUDENT DISCIPLINE POLICIES AND PROCEDURES

1. **A school's discipline policies and procedures should be based on school board policy.*** School building policies and procedures, particularly those presented in student and faculty handbooks, should be examined to determine the extent to which they are in conformity with school board policies. In situations where there is doubt about a school policy or procedure, clarification should be obtained from the district administration and, if necessary, from the school board.

2. **There should be overall agreement among students, teachers, parents, and administrators about the philosophy and objectives of the disciplinary policies and procedures of a school.** If most people don't agree about the purposes of a school's disciplinary policies and procedures and why they must exist, they will be very difficult to enforce. This is particularly true for classroom "misbehavior." Unless the administrator has secured from the staff an agreed-upon, uniform, explicit designation of the kinds of behavior which can legitimately be considered discipline problems, some members of the faculty may feel free to provide their own interpretations. In the latter case there will undoubtedly be teachers who view students who question and argue as disrespectful and arrogant, while other members of the faculty will perceive the

---

*The National School Boards Association has periodically published surveys of school board policies and procedures on discipline and attendance which are worthy of the administrator's consideration. For more information, write National School Boards Association, Waterford, Conn.

same behavior as stimulating and challenging. In circumstances involving student tardiness, some teachers may feel that if a student is late to class two or three times, the student's behavior is excessive; other teachers may not concern themselves at all with this kind of behavior. In the absence of a definitive discipline policy which has been developed with faculty, student, and parent involvement, identical student behavior may be viewed by some people as a problem, and by others as unimportant; as a result of this type of inconsistency, students may be treated unfairly.

Discipline policies and procedures are seldom popular. But if those who are going to be affected by the policies and procedures and those who are expected to implement them can understand and generally agree with their purpose and justification, then the possibility of adherence to them should be significantly increased.

3. **The school should maintain only disciplinary policies and procedures which have an educational purpose, are administratively feasible, and are legally enforceable.** The more rules and procedures, the more difficult it will be to gain acceptance and adherence by students and teachers, and the more likely it will be that the administrator will have to devote a larger and larger portion of his time to interpreting and enforcing disciplinary rules and procedures.

In the past, schools have attempted to enforce rules on such items as hair length and style of clothing. These rules were unacceptable to many students and parents, for one reason or another, and ultimately, through court actions, have proved to be unenforceable in most situations. Therefore, it is important for the school to confine its regulations and procedures to those that are generally accepted and can be enforced. Three criteria which the New Jersey School Board has recommended be applied to every proposed rule should be considered by the administrator: "(1) Is the rule necessary for the orderly and effective operation of the school? (2) Does the rule involve some suppression of freedom? (3) If so, is the incidental restriction on . . . freedom any greater than is reasonably necessary for the orderly functioning of the school?"[29]

In determining which student behavior should be regulated, the faculty and administration should initially try to make a distinction between behavior which is disruptive and behavior which is distractive. *Disruptive* behavior may be defined as any action which prevents the continuation of an activity currently in process, such as teaching or learning. Fighting in class, throwing erasers, or refusing to keep quiet are examples of behavior which tends to disrupt a class.

Distractive behavior, on the other hand, may temporarily slow down a class activity but does not actually prevent it from continuing. Chewing gum while the teacher is lecturing, is an example of behavior which may be distractive but certainly not disruptive.

Although a school may choose to regulate and punish distractive behavior, the administrator should recognize that this decision will significantly increase the number of discipline problems with which he and the faculty must cope. It should also be understood by all concerned that in discipline cases the courts have, by and large, tended to apply the criterion of disruption rather than distraction. Although a school could, if it chose, administer minor punishments, e.g., chastening, to those students who engage in distractive behavior, more extreme measures such as suspension would probably not be upheld by the courts.

4. **Policies and procedures on student behavior should be stated in positive form as much as possible, and student responsibility rather than misbehavior should be stressed.** The emphasis on student behavior should be on that which is desired, not on behavior which is unacceptable. Two examples of this kind of emphasis is a statement in a student handbook disseminated by Barrington Consolidated High School, entitled "Bill of Rights and Duties" and a statement by the Detroit Public Schools on elementary students' rights and responsibilities.

Bill of Rights and Duties[30]

1. Because it is my right to elect student representatives to govern the student body . . .   it is my duty to elect those who can lead us wisely and to give them my full cooperation.

2. Because it is my right to have free speech, assembly, press, and religion . . .   it is my duty to allow others the same privilege.

3. Because it is my right to have free education and to choose subjects which interest me . . .   it is my duty to use my privilege to the best of my ability.

4. Because it is my right to act with freedom . . .   it is my duty to conduct myself so that I will not interfere with others.

5. Because it is my right to participate in school activities . . .   it is my duty to do my best in these activities and to uphold the name of the school at all times.

6. Because it is my right to use school and public property . . .   it is my duty to care for and respect this property.

7. Because it is my right to enjoy all of these rights . . .   it is my duty to accept the responsibility of preserving these rights.

Elementary School Students' Responsibilities and Rights[31]

Student Responsibilities   *Student Rights*

What You Can Do

1. Take Part
   • Come to school every day.
   • Come to school on time.
   • Go to all classes. Do the classwork.
   • Ask your teachers for help.

2. Control Self
   • Obey all school rules.
   • Act in a way that will help you and the other students to learn.
   • Help care for books, supplies, and all school property.

3. Respect School Workers
   • Be polite to all teachers, principals, aides and the school workers.
   • Obey all teachers, principals, aides, and other school workers.
   • If you do not see why you should obey at the time you are asked, talk it over later with the principal and your parents.

4. Respect Other Students
   • Be fair with other students.
   • Treat other students in a way that will not hurt them. Avoid fights.
   • Speak kindly to other students. Avoid name calling.

1. You have the right to take part in all programs of the Detroit Public Schools without regard to race, creed, color, or national origin.
2. You have the right to know all charges made against you. You also have a right to explain what happened and why. Any final records on you must state whether or not the charges were proven.
3. You have a right to privacy. No one can search or take things that belong to you unless there is an emergency or a good reason. If you are not present, you must be told as soon as possible that the things that you own have been searched or taken.
4. You and your parents have a right to choose your style of clothing. You may be denied this right when your style of clothing presents a safety or health hazard or interferes with learning.
5. You have the right to ask for changes [in school procedures] by writing a letter to your principal or teacher.

5. **The policies and procedures governing student behavior should be written in clear, understandable language and be presented in student, teacher, and parent handbooks which are reveiwed at the beginning of each school year.** Rules and procedures which are not written are more easily misunderstood or

forgotten. And rules and procedures which are not written in clear and understandable language can be misinterpreted or incorrectly applied.

Compounding these problems would be failure by a school to periodically review its rules and procedures with students, teachers, and parents. Every school should review its policies and procedures on student behavior at the beginning of each school year in order to refresh people's memories, clear up misunderstandings, and identify the need for change in current policies and procedures.

6. **The consequences of violating a rule or regulation should be made explicit and commensurate with the nature of the violation.** Students should not have to guess or infer what the consequences will be for violating a rule or regulation. The consequences should be made explicit at the time that the rule or regulation goes into effect. Students need to know what will happen if they violate a rule or regulation so they will have the opportunity to take that information into consideration. An administrator may want to leave himself a certain amount of latitude in stating the consequences of minor offenses for first-time violators by using such words as "could result in . . ." but for serious offenses and for repeated violations, language such as "will result in . . ." is more appropriate. It should be emphasized that the consequences of violating a rule or regulation need to be commensurate with the nature of the violation. Consequences that are too lenient will not generate sufficient respect, but overly severe consequences will raise questions of harshness and fairness. Also, there is the problem that what is too lenient or too harsh to one person may appear otherwise to another individual. Obviously, the administrator will not be able to satisfy everyone as to the appropriateness of a specific punishment. However, by involving representative teachers, students, and parents in the development of a statement of consequences, an administrator is more likely to end up with a more defensible and acceptable statement.

7. **The rationale supporting the rules, procedures, and consequences governing student behavior should be clearly communicated to students, and should be enforced fairly and consistently.** An understanding of the rationale behind the rules, and fairness and consistency in enforcement of rules and consequences are essential prerequisites to students' acceptance and compliance. In a study by Vredevoe, students reported that the following factors (in order of frequency) were important:

1. Interpreting the reasons and purposes of the rules
2. Fairness in enforcement
3. Treatment which recognizes maturity of student
4. Consistency in enforcement
5. Enforcement without embarrassment, whenever possible
6. Observance of rules by teachers
7. Opportunity to participate in making rules in areas where students are capable.[32]

It is interesting to note that students felt that if there were to be rules, they should be observed by the adults working in the school as well as the students. Of course, this may not always be feasible in school, but clearly it is a factor that is important to the students.

After an administrator has utilized the seven general criteria for evaluating the school's discipline policies and procedures, he may want to make certain changes in them. The types of changes will depend on his particular situation, but should not be made without faculty, parent, student, and school board involvement. Participation by all parties who may be affected by revisions in a school's disciplinary policies and procedures is the key to successful implementation of needed changes.

A FINAL NOTE

Studies show a dramatic increase in recent years in certain kinds of criminal acts in the schools, such as assaults, vandalism, and narcotics[33] although there is some evidence that this may be leveling off.[34] In response to this troubling situation a growing number of schools have employed their own security officers[35] and some have experimented with various forms of technology, such as closed-circuit television and walkie-talkies.

Even though the "good old days" were far from idyllic, there is little doubt that school discipline problems are becoming more numerous and severe.* Whether school security officers or technological aids will be successful in the long run in preventing student misbehavior is open to question. It is conceded that these measures may be temporarily necessary in some schools in order to control a bad situation. A book by Blauvelt is probably the most useful in that regard.[36] However, by their very nature these techniques tend to deal more with the symptoms of the problem than with its basic causes, and such methods run the danger of infringing on the civil rights of students.

It would appear that if a school is to make a significant reduction in student misbehavior, the administrator and faculty will need to identify and correct the basic causes of that misbehavior. Diagnosis is the first step; then alternative approaches to preventing misbehavior should be instituted. These approaches will be discussed in the next chapter.

---

*In Clifton Johnson's, *Old Time Schools and Schoolbooks* (New York: Macmillan Co., 1907), p. 21, it is reported that in 1837 over 300 schools in Massachusetts alone were broken up by rebellious pupils.

Review and Learning Activities

1. Explain how it is possible for an administrator to narrow or broaden the scope and nature of his responsibilities by changing the definition of what constitutes student misbehavior in school.
2. What are the purpose and steps of diagnosis in responding to student misbehavior?
3. Identify the main hypothesized causes of student misbehavior. What is the rationale for investigating certain of these causes first, and others later?
4. How can an administrator work with teachers and other specialized personnel to reduce or prevent student discipline problems?
5. Apply the criteria recommended in the text to an evaluation of your own school's disciplinary policies and procedures.
6. What are the implications of Vredevoe's findings on student expectations insofar as your own school's disciplinary policies and procedures are concerned?

Notes

1. Ellwood P. Cubberly, *Public Education in the United States,* rev. ed. (Boston: Houghton Mifflin, 1934), p. 328.
2. See recent September or October issues of *The Kappan* for Gallup Poll data on this topic.
3. National Institute of Law Enforcement and Criminal Justice, *School Crime: The Problem and Some Attempted Solutions* (Washington, D.C.: Department of Justice, LEAA, 1979).
4. Robert A. Stebbins, "The Meaning of Disorderly Behavior: Teacher Definition of a Classroom Situation," *Sociology of Education* (Spring 1971): 217–36.
5. George M. Usova, "Reducing Discipline Problems in the Elementary Schools: Approaches and Suggestions," *Education* (Summer 1979): 419–22; John F. Feldhusen, *Behavior Problems in Secondary Schools* (Washington, D.C.: National Institute of Education, 1978).
6. *Guidelines for Student Rights and Responsibilities* (Albany, N.Y.: New York State Education Department, n.d.), p. 30.
7. This list represents an adaptation and extension of factors suggested by George V. Sheviakov and Fritz Redl in *Discipline for Today's Children and Youth* (Washington: Association for Supervision and Curriculum Development, 1956).
8. Jeanne Rowe, "How Teachers Can Help Victims of Child Abuse," *Today's Education* (April/May 1981): 18–22.
9. Lynn Fossum and Lauralee Sorensen, "The Schools See It First: Child Abuse/Neglect," *The Kappan* (December 1979): 274. Also see Stephen W. Stile, *The School's Role in the Prevention of Child Abuse* (Bloomington, Ind.: Phi Delta Kappa, 1982).
10. Ibid.
11. National Center on Child Abuse and Neglect, U.S. Children's Bureau, HEW, P.O. Box 1182, Washington, D.C. 20013; National Committee for Prevention of Child Abuse, Suite 510, 111 East Wacker Drive, Chicago, Ill. 60601.

12. Eugene R. Howard and John M. Jenkins, *Improving Discipline in the Secondary School* (A CFK Ltd. Occasional Paper, 1972), pp. 2, 12.

13. Most of the conceptual work on diagnosis in the school has occurred in the field of counseling, and its application to administration has been extracted from the pioneer work of Francis P. Robinson. See Francis P. Robinson, "Modern Approaches to Counseling Diagnosis," *Journal of Counseling Psychology* (Winter 1963): 325–33. See also G. A. Koester, "The Study of the Diagnostic Process," *Educational and Psychological Measurement* (1954): 473–86. For a good discussion of how diagnosis can be used in responding to classroom discipline problems, see Boron Gil and Philip Heller, *Classroom Discipline: Toward a Diagnostic Model Integrating Teacher Thoughts and Actions.* An ERIC Report: Ed–167–514.

14. For a description of how such records might be used, see William S. Amoss, "The Use of School Records in the Identification of Juvenile Delinquents" (Ed. D. diss., University of Tulsa, 1970).

15. E. E. Jones et al., *Attribution Perceiving: The Causes of Behavior* (Morristown, N.J.: General Learning Press, 1972).

16. Edward Porter, "The Effects of the Type of the Offense Committed, Appearance, and Previous Behavior on Discipline Decisions Rendered by Public School Disciplinarians," *Dissertation Abstracts International,* 1973, 34 (1927–A).

17. James M. Frasher and Ramona S. Frasher, "Attribution Theory and Disciplinary Action in Schools" (Unpublished paper, Georgia State University, n.d.).

18. For an excellent study of the discretionary authority of the principal in this area, see Edward Casimis, "The Exercise of Administrative Discretion in Secondary Schools" (Diss., University of Chicago, 1976).

19. Edwin J. Brown and Arthur T. Phelps, *Managing the Classroom—The Teacher's Role in School Administration* (New York: Ronald Press, 1961), pp. 121–24.

20. Edmund T. Emmer et al., "Effective Classroom Management at the Beginning of the School Year," *The Elementary School Journal* (May 1980): 219–31.

21. Edmund T. Emmer and Carolyn M. Evertson, "Synthesis of Research on Classroom Management," *Educational Leadership* (January 1981): 342–47.

22. John S. Packard, *Pluralistic Ignorance and Pupil Control Ideology.* An ERIC Report: Ed–055–054, pp. 109–11. Another instrument specifically designed for the elementary school which might be of interest to the elementary school administrator is described by Priscilla Pitt Jones, "A Method of Measuring Discipline Expectations," *Journal of Experimental Education* (February 1967): 39–45. See also, "Clarifying Teachers' Beliefs about Discipline," *Educational Leadership* (March 1980): 459–62.

23. Judith E. Dobson and Russell L. Dobson, "Teaching Self-Discipline: An In-service Model," *Humanist Educator* (June 1979): 172–81.

24. *Student Discipline, Problems and Solutions* (Arlington, Va.: American Association of School Administrators, 1979).

25. Reported in *NASSP Spotlight,* October 1972, a publication of the National Association of Secondary School Principals.

26. For a model policy and rules for maintaining a productive relationship between the school and law enforcement officials in regard to student discipline, see *School Administrators and Law Enforcement Officials* (Reston, Va.: National Association of Secondary School Principals, 1979).

27. Edward T. Ladd, "Regulating Student Behavior without Ending up in Court," *The Kappan* (January 1973): 305.

28. Blackwell v. Issaquena, 363F. 2 and 749 (5th Cir. 1966).

29. *Policies That Clarify Student Rights and Responsibilities* (Waterford, Conn.: National School Boards Association, 1970), p. 6. Also, for minimum legal essentials of enforceable rules, see E. Edmund Reutter, "Student Discipline: Selected Substantive Issues," in *The School Principal and the Law,* ed. Robert Stern (Topeka, Kansas: 1978), pp. 68–69.

30. *The Roundup* [Student Handbook] (Barrington, Ill.: Barrington, Consolidated High School, n.d.).

31. Detroit Public Schools, *Elementary School Student Responsibilities and Rights.* An ERIC Report: Ed–193–359.

32. Lawrence E. Vredevoe, *Discipline* (Dubuque, Iowa: Kendall/Hunt Publishing Company, 1971), p. 24.

33. National Institute of Law Enforcement and Criminal Justice, *School Crime*. Also see National Institute of Law Enforcement and Criminal Justice, *Crime and Disruption in Schools* (Washington, D.C.: NILECJ, 1979).

34. Francis A. Ianni and Elizabeth Reuss-Ianni, "What Can Schools Do About Violence?" *Today's Education* (April/May 1980) 20G–23G.

35. Joseph Grealy, *School Crime and Violence: Problems and Solutions* (Fort Lauderdale: Institute for Safe Schools, 1979).

36. Peter D. Blauvelt, *Effective Strategies for School Security* (Reston, Va.: National Assn. of Secondary School Principals, 1981). Also see "School Security." An ERIC Report: Ed–199–829.

14

Responses to Student Discipline Problems

By implementing the recommendations discussed in the previous chapter, the school administrator should gradually be able to reduce the number and the severity of student misbehavior problems with which she is confronted. But despite this improvement, it seems reasonable to assume that in most schools there will continue to be student misbehavior of some type and degree. Two basic questions, then, are how should the administrator respond to student misbehavior after it occurs, and how can it be prevented from occurring again? The following sections will address these questions by analyzing punisment alternatives typically utilized by the school administrator, and by presenting several nonpunitive approaches for ameliorating student misbehavior and preventing its recurrence.

ANALYSIS OF PUNITIVE APPROACHES

In making a decision about punishing a student, an administrator generally chooses among several alternatives identified in figure 14.1.*

There are several reasons why an administrator might choose one of the alternatives identified in figure 14.1. She may feel that given the violation of a rule, she should punish the student—if for no other reason than to indicate that the student's behavior is not condoned. Or the administrator may face strong expectations by a teacher or a parent that a student be punished for his misbehavior. Teacher and parental expectations that the administrator be

---

*Other alternatives could also be listed, but the ones which seem to be mainly utilized by administrators are identified. Such actions as holding a parent conference or referring the student to a social agency should not be considered as punishment but as nonpunitive approaches to helping the student to deal with the causes of his misbehavior.

1. Verbal Punishment ("Chewing Out")
2. Detention (Student Must Stay After School)
3. Assigned Work Around the Building After School
4. Suspension
5. Corporal Punishment
6. Recommendation of Expulsion

Figure 14.1. Punitive Responses to
Student Misbehavior

a strong disciplinarian undoubtedly influence the decisions of many administrators regarding discipline alternatives.[1] Also, an administrator may punish a student based on the belief that punishment will deter the student from violating the rule again.

However, the school administrator should understand that, whatever else is achieved by punishment (and its effectiveness is debatable), it does not treat the basic *causes* of student misbehavior. While punishment may act to repress the misbehavior temporarily, and that may be necessary in certain situations, it does not deal with its underlying causes.[2] An administrator may need or want to punish a student to set an example or to meet teachers' or parents' expectations. But she should not operate under the illusion that punishment will somehow remove the roots of a problem or that the student misbehavior will not recur. There is little affirmative evidence to show that punishment is an effective technique for preventing misbehavior from recurring, and much evidence to show the contrary.[3] In addition, there is the possibility that punishment may lead to undesirable side effects, such as an even more negative attitude on the part of the student toward school.[4]

On the other hand, it is recognized that removal of all negative consequences associated with the violation of a rule or regulation could, over time, render such rules and regulations meaningless. Also, students need to know that they are accountable for their behavior and that negative consequences will result from inappropriate behavior. Therefore, the imposition of certain punitive measures may be necessary. However, the decision as to whether or not to punish should be based on an accurate diagnosis of the cause of the student's behavior (in addition, of course, to an investigation of whether the student actually was in the wrong in violating the rule), and the selection of the type of punishment should take into consideration the following factors: (1) the cause of the misbehavior, (2) the severity of the offense, (3) the habitualness of the offender, that is, the number of times he has committed the offense, and (4) the personality of the offender, e.g., certain individuals may respond to punishment better than others. Also, in punishing a student, the school administrator would do well to heed the recommendation of the O'Learys:[5]

1. Use punishment sparingly.
2. Make clear to the student why he is being punished.
3. Provide the student with an alternative means of meeting his needs.
4. Reward the student for utilizing the alternative means.
5. Avoid physical punishment if at all possible.
6. Avoid punishing while you are in a very angry or emotional state.

Moreover, for punishment to be effective, it needs to be applied as soon after the offense as possible. Delay in administering the punishment tends to reduce the association between the punishment and the violation of the rule.

The following sections contain a discussion of some of the more significant punishments used in response to student misbehavior, and the subject of due process.

CORPORAL PUNISHMENT

The U.S. Supreme Court has ruled that corporal punishment does not constitute cruel or unusual punishment to students.[6] However, the court also pointed out in its ruling that persons imposing corporal punishment could be sued for liability if they used unreasonable force. Unfortunately, the Supreme Court did not define "unreasonable force," and state and federal courts have had difficulty with this concept.[7]

While the use of corporal punishment in the schools may be legal if state law and school board policy permit it, there continues to be considerable disagreement on the part of teachers, parents, and educational authorities about its desirability and effectiveness. The arguments supporting the use of corporal punishment usually contains the following points:[8] (1) nothing else has worked, and something with more impact is needed; (2) some students only respond to physical punishment, usually because that is what they experience in the home; (3) physical punishment is effective because it makes students think twice before commiting the same offense, and (4) the use of physical punishment can be a deterrent to other students who might violate a rule in the absence of such punishment. Those opposing physical punishment often present the following reasons:[9] (1) regardless of what the Supreme Court said, corporal punishment is cruel and inhumane, and the fact that it is no longer permitted in prisons and in most other countries of the world confirms its impact; (2) "unreasonable" corporal punishment is too difficult to prove in court, and many affected students and parents lack either the knowledge of court remedies or the resources to pursue them; (3) corporal punishment holds considerable potential for child abuse; (4) the use of corporal punishment tends to be discriminatory, in that it is used more often with younger students, non-white students, and with boys; (5) there are more effective nonphysical alternatives to correcting student misbehavior.

It is unlikely that the debate over corporal punishment will be easily resolved. It should be noted that firm evidence supporting the effectiveness of corporal punishment is lacking, although it is conceded that corporal punishment may act as a temporary suppressor of behavior in certain situations.[10] In spite of the lack of evidence supporting its effectiveness, corporal punishment continues to be used in the schools in a wide variety of situations. One study, for example, found that corporal punishment was being used as a solution to nineteen different student discipline problems, ranging from chewing gum to bodily assault on teachers.[11] Obviously, *if* corporal punishment is to be employed as a disciplinary technique, it should be used on a more selective basis and only for very serious offenses.

Although surveys have shown that more than two-thirds of the states authorize school districts to utilize corporal punishment in the schools,[12] no school district is *required* to permit corporal punishment, and districts in such states which decide to use corporal punishment must first promulgate a policy. Certainly, no teacher or administrator should apply corporal punishment in the absence of a policy or go beyond the spirit and letter of the policy.

In developing a policy on corporal punishment, the administration and school board should involve representative students, teachers, and parents, and should consider the following guidelines, extracted from various court decisions and recommendations by educational authorities.

1. Corporal punishment should not be used at all except when the acts of misconduct are so antisocial in nature or so shocking to the conscience that extreme punishment seems warranted.
2. The particular offenses that will result in corporal punishment should be specified. Also, the nature of the corporal punishment which will be permitted should be made explicit.
3. Evidence that other nonphysical methods were used earlier in an attempt to help the student improve his/her behavior should be required before corporal punishment is employed.
4. Corporal punishment should not be used in those situations where physical restraint is more properly called for. For example, a teacher or administrator should not employ corporal punishment, but should be permitted to use physical restraint in order to protect herself, the pupil, or others from physical injury, obtain possession of a weapon or other dangerous object, and to protect property from serious damage.
5. If possible, a neutral party should administer the punishment, rather than the person who was in conflict with the student. The

person who *is* to administer the corporal punishment should be specifically identified.

6. Corporal punishment should be administered only in the presence of another teacher or administrator as witness, an individual who was *not* in conflict with the student.

7. Exempt from receiving corporal punishment those students who have psychological or medical problems.

8. Provide due process before administering the corporal punishment, including informing the student of the rule that has been broken, presenting the student with the evidence indicating that the student has violated the rule, and providing the student with an opportunity to challenge the allegation and/or the evidence.

9. Specify the kinds of documentation that will be required for administering corporal punishment, including those items specified in #8 above, and the details of the situation, including the student's name, age, racial background, nature of the offense, nature of the corporal punishment, etc. Provide the option for parents to request a written explanation of the reasons for corporal punishment and the reasons why nonphysical alternatives were not appropriate.

10. Forbid corporal punishment to be used on a continuing basis for those students whose behavior does not improve after it has initially been administered.

In addition, any administrator or teacher who employs corporal punishment should follow the legal prescriptions offered by Hamilton: (1) act from good motives, and not from anger or malice; (2) inflict only moderate punishment; (3) determine what the punishment is, in proportion to the gravity of the offense; (4) convince herself that the contemplated punishment is not excessive, taking into account the age, sex, and physical strength of the pupil to be punished; (5) assume the responsibility that the rule she seeks to enforce is reasonable.[13]

Although these particular guidelines were written for teachers, it seems safe to assume that they also apply to the school administrator.

SUSPENSION AND EXPULSION

Suspension and expulsion are two other punishment alternatives utilized by school administrators in cases involving extreme misbehavior. *Suspension* can be defined as the temporary removal of a student from school for a certain period of time, generally from one day to several weeks, depending on the offense. *Expulsion* involves removing a student from school on a more permanent basis, usually for at least a semester or longer, depending on the severity of the misbehavior.

Administrators employ the procedure of suspension in cases of repeated minor offenses by students, and for more serious student misbehavior such as smoking in school, or truancy. Expulsion is usually applied only to the *most* serious student misbehavior and is generally used by administrators as a last resort. In the case of either suspension or expulsion, however, there is considerable doubt about the effectiveness of removing a student from school as a method of disciplining her. As Phay and Cummings have observed, "School separation is a poor method. Students who misbehave usually are students with academic difficulties, and removal from the school almost inevitably adds to their academic problems."[14] Therefore, although suspension and expulsion may occasionally be necessary to protect the interests of other students, these methods are probably counterproductive in their effect on the students who are removed from school.

Though it seems clear that suspension and expulsion are disciplinary methods which may adversely affect the student who is removed, there undoubtedly will be times when an administrator may need to initiate these procedures in the case of emergency or extreme situations. The nature of these situations has been defined by the National Juvenile Law Center at St. Louis University as including the following types of student misbehavior:

1. Assault or battery upon any other person on school ground
2. Continual and repeated willful disobedience of school personnel legitimately acting in their official capacity, which results in a disruptive effect upon the education of the other children in school
3. Possession or sale of narcotics or hallucinogenic drugs or substances on school premises.

The Center also suggests that consideration for suspension be given to occurrences of the following kinds of student behavior: (1) academic dishonesty, e.g., cheating or plagiarism, (2) theft from or damage to institution premises or property, (3) intentional disruption or obstruction of the educational function of the school, and (4) possession of firearms.[15]

It should be noted that most of the student misbehavior identified by the National Juvenile Law Center represent violations of the law, and an argument can be made that in such cases law enforcement agencies should administer punishment rather than the school. In general an administrator should suspend students from school only when there would be clear and present *danger* to the student or others in the school if the student remains in school.

Administrators should also proceed very carefully in making a decision to suspend or expel special education students. Two legal questions can arise with such punishments: first, is a student being punished for misconduct that is related in some way to a handicap? and, second, does the punishment result in a change in the educational placement of the student?[16] If the answer to the first question is affirmative, the suspension or expulsion may not be legal unless the administrator can demonstrate a clear and present danger to keeping the student in school. If the answer to the second question is affirmative and the suspension is a lengthy one or the punishment is expulsion, the school may need to provide the due process safeguards mandated by federal law,[17] as well as a new individualized educational plan. If the suspension of a special education student is a very brief one and the school is sure that the behavior of the student is unrelated to his/her handicap or can demonstrate that the student's removal from school is necessary in order to protect the student or others, the suspension will be on firmer legal grounds, although a question may still be raised regarding whether other less punitive alternatives might have been more appropriate.

In those situations involving a suspension of a special education student or expulsion of a student from school, additional due process safeguards will probably be required. Generally, these are specified in state law, and the reader is encouraged to examine these laws, and to consult with the school district's attorney before proceeding with any action.

IN-SCHOOL SUSPENSION

Because of the limitations and general ineffectiveness of the procedure of suspension from school, enlightened administrators and educators have developed the concept of in-school suspension. This program differs from traditional suspension in that the latter procedure resulted in a student's removal from school for a specified number of days, while the former procedure removes the student from the regular school schedule while keeping the student in school, usually in a self-contained room under adult supervision. The characteristics of an in-school suspension program vary considerably among schools, ranging from a small isolation room where the student is not permitted to do any school work, to a large, well equipped room staffed by professionals who provide academic assistance and personal counseling.[18]

The type of in-school suspension program found in a school seems to depend primarily on the purpose it is meant to serve. If the main purpose is to punish the student for some offense or to use the program as a deterrent to misbehavior, the isolation aspects of the program will be emphasized. If, on the other hand, the main purpose of the program is to diagnose and remediate the cause of the misbehavior, then the nature of the facility where the program is housed, the nature of the activities and the staffing will emphasize student appraisal, and educational and psychological counseling. Some in-house suspension programs, of course, attempt to achieve both the purpose of isolation and the goals of academic and social assistance.[19] However, according to Chamberlain, "The main emphasis during the in-school suspension time should be to assist the student to analyze his previous behavior, to consider alternative behaviors available to him, and to select a more appropriate behavior to be implemented after returning to the normal school setting."[20]

Research findings on the effectiveness of in-school suspension programs are limited and inconclusive, revealing both successes and failures.[21] Those programs which serve primarily as isolation rooms with little or no thought or activities designed to help a student understand and change behavior are apparently not likely to succeed. However, those programs that emphasize helping the student, which are capably staffed in well equipped rooms, have greater potential for success. Two in-school suspension programs which appear to possess the latter characteristics are described by Winborne[22] and Sklarz,[23] Further, Grayson and her colleagues discuss the use of a "time out" room which is similar in a number of respects to many in-school suspension programs but is also different in important ways worthy of further consideration.[24] (For another excellent study identifying key factors associated with an effective in-school suspension program, see "Organizational Variables Affecting In-school Suspension" by Adele H. Corbett, a Ph.D. dissertation at the University of North Carolina at Chapel Hill, 1980.)

DUE PROCESS

Suspension and expulsion from school are severe punishments. Although they may be necessary in certain situations, the decision to impose these punishments generally must be preceded by a careful and thorough process of investigation into the factual basis for the alleged offense with an adequate opportunity for the student to refute the charges, or to challenge the legitimacy of the violated school rule. This is referred to as "due process." It means that an individual is entitled to a certain specified process or set of procedures, the objective of which is to assure that the individual is treated fairly and justly. Although some educators may view due process as unnecessarily burdensome, its essential rationale is presented below:

> A basic tenet of the American system of government as provided by the United States Constitution is that any individual who is threatened or becomes subject to serious or adverse action by public authorities must be provided with full rights of due process of law. Such procedures provide to the individual the opportunity to contest the proposed action within a series or proceedings which insure that fairness and good judgement govern the entire decision-making process.[25]

The two types of due process are termed "substantive" and "procedural."[26] *Substantive due process* examines the question of whether the *purpose* of the rule or regulation which the student violated is fair, reasonable, and just. *Procedural due process* focuses on the question of whether the *procedures* used to remove the student from the school were fair, reasonable, and just.

Prior to 1975, due process was required primarily for expelling a student, but in some instances it had been required for suspension as well, particularly if the suspension was for an extended period of time. However, in 1975, the U.S. Supreme Court ruled that school administrators could not suspend students for any periods up to ten days without "minimum due process."[27] Minimum due process was defined by the court to consist of the following elements:

- The student should be given oral or written notice of the charges against her.
- If the student denies the charges, she is entitled to an explanation of the evidence the school has as the basis of the charge.
- The student shall have an opportunity to tell her side of the story.
- There need be no delay between the time notice is given and the time of the hearing. In a majority of the cases the principal may informally discuss the alleged misconduct with the student minutes after it has occurred.
- Since the hearing may occur almost immediately following the misconduct, generally the notice and hearing should precede the suspension.
- In cases where the presence of the student poses a continuing danger to persons or property, or an ongoing threat of disrupting the academic process, the student may be immediately removed from school. In such cases, the notice and hearing should follow as soon as practicable.

The major import of the Court's decision was a change in the status of due process for students, in the case of short term suspension, from a recommended practice by some to a legal requirement. While it was recognized that this legal requirement could pose unforeseen problems for some administrators, Justice White (speaking for the majority of the Court) stated, "We have imposed requirements which are, if anything, less than a fair-minded school principal would impose upon himself in order to avoid unfair suspension."

After the Supreme Court decision there were various reactions and predictions as to how the "minimum due process" requirements would impact on the schools. While reports differ, there seems to be evidence to suggest that the due process requirements have not unduly complicated the lives of most school administrators, and the procedures have brought an increased degree of fairness and equality to disciplinary decisions.[28] However, it needs to be emphasized that research in this area is very difficult to conduct and is generally dependent on the self reports of participants in the studies. Since whatever due process that occurs generally takes place behind a closed office door or in some other relatively private setting, we really don't have very much objective data on how due process for students is working in the schools.

In the case of a longer suspension or expulsion, a more elaborate and comprehensive set of due process requirements usually apply. The publication, *The Reasonable Exercise of Authority,* describes these procedures:

> A notice of the time and place of the hearing and of the exact nature of the charge must be given to the student a reasonable time in advance. . . . In all cases the accused must be allowed to be represented by someone of his own choosing. The hearing may be informal, though it need not be open; and the accused must be allowed to cross-examine witnesses and to present witnesses on his own behalf. The student's parents or guardian may attend. The panel [a committee formed to conduct the hearing] should be instructed to make findings of fact and submit these, together with its recommendations, to the principal promptly after the close of the hearing. The principal and subsequently the board of education should be guided by the report and the practical recommendations of the panel. Also, if the accused believes he was not accorded a fair hearing, he must be allowed to appeal on this ground; any other plan of action may result in school authorities being brought into court.[29]

NONPUNITIVE APPROACHES TO STUDENT MISBEHAVIOR

A major implication of the data and statements discussed in the previous sections is that the school administrator and faculty will need to concentrate more on the in-depth diagnosis and remediation of student discipline problems and less on the punishment of student misbehavior. While punishment may still have to be utilized at times in order to *temporarily* control or suppress misbehavior, or to meet teachers' or parents' expectations, it is at best a short-term solution to a problem which requires alternative methods. A model which has been designed to provide the administrator with an overview of several alternative approaches to student misbehavior is presented in figure 14.2.

As figure 14.2 indicates, the first step that an administrator should take cooperatively with teachers, parents, and others in response to student misbehavior is to try to diagnose the cause(s) of the misbehavior. (Possible causes of student misbehavior, and the process of diagnosis were discussed in the preceding chapter.) Student misbehavior doesn't just happen; it is caused by some condition(s).

It is important for an administrator to recognize that her diagnosis of the cause(s) of student misbehavior will greatly influence her choice of approaches to preventing the problem from recurring. If an administrator decides that the cause(s) of a problem rests within the student, then attempts

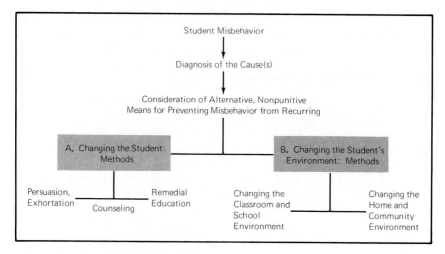

Figure 14.2. A Model for Responding
to Student Misbehavior

to change the student will probably be made through one or more of the means identified in figure 14.2, part A. If, on the other hand, the administrator diagnoses the cause(s) of the problem as lying within the student's environment (either the school environment or the home and community environment), the administrator will try to change that environment. The essential point is that an administrator's perception of the causes of the misbehavior will determine to a large extent her selection of an approach to be employed in an effort to prevent the misbehavior from recurring.

A second factor which will influence the administrator's choice of the best approach to prevent student misbehavior from recurring is her *awareness* of alternative methods of responding to student misbehavior. Since punishment has already been discussed, the focus now will be placed on analyzing nonpunitive approaches.

CHANGING THE STUDENT

Persuasion and Exhortation

Most administrators who are confronted with the "first instance" of a student's misbehavior (if minor in nature) respond with an approach other than punishment. Even in the case of repeated misbehavior, many administrators attempt to change the student by trying to persuade her that it is not in her best interest to misbehave and by exhorting her to "do a better job."

An investigation of the educational literature uncovered no research evidence on the effectiveness of these disciplinary tactics. Undoubtedly, for some administrators, these approaches "work"—at least with certain students. For the most part, however, persuasion and exhortation do not appear to be very effective with students who are discipline problems, if one can judge by their repeated misbehavior. These methods typically are employed by administrators because the "let us reason together" approach is commonly valued in American society, and they are frequently unaware of any other type of non-punitive techniques.

It would seem that before persuasion and exhortation could be effective in preventing student misbehavior from recurring, a correct diagnosis of the factors causing the misbehavior would have to be made, and the administrator employing these tactics would have to be perceived by the student as possessing a high degree of credibility.[30] If the causes of the student's problem have been incorrectly diagnosed, an administrator may be trying to persuade or exhort a student to do something which will not remove the basis of the misbehavior. And if an administrator is not perceived by a student as someone who can be believed and trusted, the student is unlikely to be persuaded or exhorted to do anything the administrator wants (if the student can avoid it).[31] Therefore, while persuasion and exhortation by an administrator in response to student misbehavior may be preferable to punitive measures, the former techniques are dependent on certain conditions which may or may not be present in a specific situation.

Counseling

Many administrators attempt to counsel students who have misbehaved. Desirable as that approach may appear, its success depends on the administrator's possession or acquisition of adequate knowledge and skill in counseling techniques, and on the perception of the students that the administrator is a counselor rather than a disciplinarian. Unfortunately, seldom is either of these conditions met. This does not mean that a school administrator should not use counseling techniques in working with student discipline cases, and Mitchell describes one administrator who is attempting to utilize counseling techniques in working with students who misbehave.[32]

But most school administrators probably need to become more knowledgeable about these techniques before much success will be achieved. Perhaps a more realistic and effective approach for an administrator would be to utilize whatever counseling resources exist within the staff or school district.

Counselors and teachers have been utilized in a number of individual counseling and group guidance situations for working with students who engage in misbehavior. For example, Tewel and Chalfin describe an apparently successful guidance program for students who have engaged in misbehavior which in most schools would result in suspension.[33] Neill reports on another program which is referred to as crisis counseling, an approach which focuses on "hard-core crisis students . . . [who] frequently display hostility or passive resistance, and they are prone to drug addiction and truancy."[34] Also, Manning presents findings of a study which showed that a systematic group guidance program at the elementary level could reduce the drop-out *potential* of a number of elementary school students.[35] And Hamberg describes a particularly innovative counseling program which involves the use of high school students to counsel junior and elementary school students who engage in misbehavior.[36]

These reports strongly suggest that individual counseling and group guidance can be successful in improving student behavior.[37] The degree of expertise of the pupil services team, the availability of their time, proper facilities and the extremity of the student misbehavior problems seem to be important considerations in determining counseling effectiveness. However, probably the most significant factor is the degree to which the counselors and other members of the pupil services team understand and accept the principle that they possess specialized expertise which can make a valuable contribution to ameliorating student behavior problems. Unless the pupil personnel workers wholeheartedly accept this concept, it is unlikely that they will make any significant contribution to improving student behavior.

Since the attitude of the pupil personnel specialists may be the most significant variable affecting the success of a counseling program for students who misbehave, it is important that the school administrator work with the pupil services team to help them develop an appropriate understanding of and attitude toward the contribution they can make to ameliorating student misbehavior. To achieve this objective the administrator will need to study and utilize the concepts in the next chapter which focuses on pupil personnel services.

Remediation of Learning Problems

It is probably accurate to say that learning problems of one kind or another are associated with most student misbehavior. Whether the learning problems result from the misbehavior or cause it has long been a subject of debate among educators. Unfortunately, research has not resolved the debate.

It does seem reasonable to assume, however, that learning problems play some role in regard to student misbehavior. The process seems to occur in either of the two ways presented in figure 14.3.[38]

As figure 14.3 suggests, learning problems might cause, as well as result from, student misbehavior. Students who do not initially engage in misbehavior or encounter learning problems may eventually become discipline problems if sufficiently bored with school or if experiencing personal problems, and as a result of conflict with the school or of a loss of time, may develop learning disabilities. Also, students who possess learning disabilities of one kind or another and who experience resultant failure in the classroom are more likely to feel frustration, anger, or boredom, and then engage in misbehavior in order

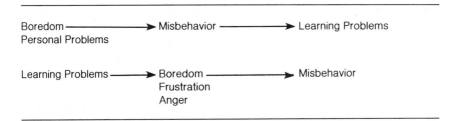

Figure 14.3. Some Possible
Relationships between Learning
Problems and Misbehavior

to vent their emotions. The misbehavior may consist of talking back to the teacher, "fooling around" in class, or skipping class or school. That the latter misbehavior has its roots in learning disabilities was poignantly brought out by one probation officer: "I found that the biggest problem with youngsters getting into trouble, boys in particular, was that they didn't want to face not being able to read in class. They would stay out of school, and their truancy would lead them into more serious trouble."[39]

A constructive approach, therefore, to ameliorating student misbehavior would be for the administrator to investigate the possibility that the student who is engaging in misbehavior is handicapped by some type of learning disability or motivational problem. This investigation should include the utilization of reading and special education specialists as well as other pupil personnel workers in an attempt to screen and diagnose the student's problem.[40] Depending on the nature of the problem and its diagnosis, the student may require individual and small-group work, different materials, special classes, or other remedial alternatives.[41]

It is conceded that remediation of student learning problems may be a long-term solution to a problem (i.e., student misbehavior) that demands some kind of immediate response from the administration. It is also possible that the administrator will be pressured by the expectations of teachers and others to take more immediate and punitive action when student misbehavior occurs. However, if the administrator hopes to have any significant success in preventing student misbehavior from recurring, she will need to investigate the possibility that student learning problems are causing or are a result of the misbehavior, and organize remedial assistance to correct these conditions.

CHANGING THE STUDENT'S ENVIRONMENT

Thus far, attention has been focused on nonpunitive approaches to changing the student in order to reduce or eliminate his misbehavior. However, it should be recognized that it may be difficult or even impossible for a student to change unless his environment changes. And, for many students, their environment may be the basic cause of their misbehavior.

A student's environment can be considered as composed primarily of two elements: (1) classroom and school conditions, and (2) home and community conditions. Figure 14.4 presents some possible variables in the student's environment which individually or collectively may be causing her misbehavior and which may need to be changed before the misbehavior can be reduced or eliminated.

The list of variables identified in figure 14.4 does not, of course, exhaust all of the possibilities, but it should give the administrator a good indication of the numerous environmental factors which may be causing a particular student's misbehavior.

In general, it would appear that an administrator will be more likely to achieve success in trying to modify a student's classroom and school environment than the home and community environment. An administrator has more contact with and control over the school environment, and in many cases, there is very little that she can do about a student's home and community environment. This does not mean that efforts should not be made to influence the student's home and community environment in positive ways, and specific suggestions will be discussed later in the chapter. Nevertheless, it would appear that the highest priority for changing a student's environment (if that is what is needed) should be given to attempts to bring about changes in the classroom and school environment. The nature of the changes would depend on the

---

Classroom and School Environment

1. Teacher's attitude toward and expectations for the student.
2. Teacher's style or methods of teaching.
3. Classroom rules and policies
4. Content of the subject being taught
5. Textbook and other reading materials
6. Size and composition of the class
7. Student's seating assignment in the class
8. School's schedule and total program of studies

Home and Community Environment

1. Parents' attitude toward and expectations for the student and for the school
2. Extent of crowdedness in the home
3. Attitude toward school held by siblings in the family and by the neighborhood peer group
4. Availability of alternative pursuits which are more attractive and rewarding to the student than is school

---

Figure 14.4. Examples of Environmental Variables Affecting Student Misbehavior

school's diagnosis of the causes of the problem, but two approaches which seem particularly promising for changing the student's school environment are discussed in the following sections.

Changing the Student's School Environment:
Behavioral Modification

One approach to preventing student misbehavior from recurring is behavioral modification. Behavioral modification, defined simply, is an attempt to change the behavior of an individual who has misbehaved by changing the response of the person or persons who are reacting to the misbehavior.[42] The method is based on the premise that it is the response to the misbehavior which is the key factor that determines whether or not the misbehavior persists, rather than any antecedent or internal cause.

In the school situation a student's misbehavior typically provokes a response from a teacher or administrator. The response may range from a form of punishment to a suggestion of possible rewards for correct behavior. The behavioral modification method is based on the assumption that certain responses to student misbehavior will tend to prevent the misbehavior from recurring, while others will only encourage the student to persist in misbehaving.[43]

The behavioral modification approach would change the role of the teacher or administrator from that of punishing misbehavior to one of reinforcing correct student behavior. Advocates of the approach do not entirely reject the use of punishment, but question its effectiveness unless used sparingly. They also believe in clear and consistently applied rules, preferably kept to a minimum.

Perhaps the best means to understanding the behavioral modification method would be to examine the instructions given to classroom teachers who were asked to employ this approach in working with student discipline cases:

GENERAL RULES FOR TEACHERS

1. Make explicit the rules as to what is expected of children for each period. (Remind of rules when needed.)
2. Ignore (do not attend to) behaviors which interfere with learning, unless a child is being hurt by another. Use punishment which seems appropriate, preferably withdrawal of some positive reinforcement.
3. Give praise and attention to behaviors which facilitate learning. Tell child what he is being praised for. Try to reinforce behaviors incompatible with those you wish to decrease. Example of how to praise: "I like the way you're working quietly." "That's the way I like to see you work." "Good job, you are doing fine." Transition period: "I see Johnny is ready to work." "I am calling on you because you raised your hand." "I wish everyone were working as much as 'X'," etc. Use variety and expression. In general, give praise for achievement, pro-social behavior, and following the group's rules.[44]

As can be seen by examining the instructions given to teachers, behavioral modification places a great emphasis on the teacher's rewarding students for behaving correctly, rather than paying attention to and punishing misbehavior. One of the underlying premises of the behavioral modification approach is that when a teacher or administrator reacts negatively to a student's misbehavior, that response only provides the student with the attention she is seeking, and therefore her misbehavior is likely to be repeated. On the other hand, if the student's misbehavior is ignored and the teacher's attention is focused instead on identifying (and rewarding) the response that is desired, the misbehavior will eventually be eliminated and the correct response will be strengthened.

It would appear that the behavioral modification approach offers school administrators a method they might use in working with students or one which they might try to encourage their teachers to utilize.[45] The approach has been tested empirically in a number of classroom situations, and it seems to be generally effective.[46] Moreover, several studies have shown that the principal can use behavioral modification techniques in reducing student misbehavior.[47]

It should also be emphasized that behavioral modification has been criticized in some circles.[48] Probably the greatest obstacle to its effective utilization is that, when faced with student misbehavior, teachers and administrators will not find it easy to accentuate the positive and to ignore rather than punish the misbehavior. (Caldwell describes several effective approaches to ignoring student misbehavior, as well as other nonpunitive behavioral modification techniques for shaping a student's misbehavior in the desired direction.[49]) Nevertheless, there is now sufficient evidence of the merits of this approach to student misbehavior to motivate the school administrator to at least investigate it further for possible use in her own school. (For further readings in this area, see *Progress in Behavior Modification,* edited by Henson and his colleagues.[50])

Changing the Student's School Environment: Alternative Educational Progarms

The use of behavioral modification is an attempt to change the school environment of a student who has misbehaved by changing the teacher's or administrator's immediate response to the misbehavior. While this approach appears to show promise, many schools have tended to turn to alternative education programs for those students who persistently engage in misbehavior.[51] Three educational alternatives which have been introduced are (1) work-study programs, (2) alternative classes or schools for chronic misbehavers, and (3) the development of individualized educational programs.

Work-Study. Participation in work-study programs is, of course, not restricted to students who have misbehaved; many types of students participate in this forward-looking educational alternative which combines study in school with work on the job.[52] But for students who are not motivated by standard classroom activities and who, because of their boredom and frustration get into trouble, a work-study program seems to offer an alternative way of learning from which they can derive greater meaning and satisfaction.[53] Students in such a program usually attend formal academic classes in the morning and work at a job in the afternoon. An attempt is often made to relate the job to the academic activities being pursued in school, and vice-versa.

Although the work-study program seems to be a constructive alternative to punishment as a means of reducing student misbehavior, it is not without limitations.[54] Sometimes, due to child labor laws, participation in the program cannot begin until the junior year of school, and by that time a student may have dropped out of school, or her behavior may have become so chronic that she could not qualify for the program. Also, since there is careful screening of applicants for the work-study program in order to maintain cooperative relationships with employers, the problem students who are most in need of this experience may not qualify for admission because of their extreme behavior. In addition, the program suffers because there are frequently insufficient jobs available in which to place students, or insufficient funds and other resources to do an adequate job of administering and supervising a large program.

For these reasons the work-study program has not totally met the need of an alternative educational experience for students who are turned off from school and who engage in misbehavior. But work-study programs still represent valid options in reducing student misbehavior and should be explored and utilized by the administrator to the greatest extent possible.[55]

Alternative Classes or Schools. Another approach to changing the school environment of students who have engaged in misbehavior is to provide them with alternative classes or, in some instances, placement in an alternative school.

Ability-grouping has in many circumstances resulted in alternative classes for students who misbehave, because of the strong relationship between learning problems and student misbehavior. In other situations, alternative classes or in-school suspension programs have been specifically designed for "problem students." Many of these classes and programs emphasize the development of reading and study skills, and frequently include opportunities for individual and group counseling and discussion of vocational opportunities.[56] The classes are generally smaller than regular classes and are taught by teachers who have been trained to work with these kinds of students. In addition, the school schedule set up for the students is usually more flexible. (The same characteristics are true of alternative schools for chronic misbehavers.)

The limited research that has been conducted on the merits of alternative classes or schools for students who engage in misbehavior suggest that they can be effective if the right conditions are present.[57] The "right conditions" include

1. **A teacher who wants to work with these kinds of students and who understands their strengths and limitations.** Although a teacher who has been especially trained for this type of work is desirable and may be required in certain states, the teacher's attitude and commitment to working with these students is probably the most important prerequisite.
2. **Careful screening and assignment of students.** Probably not every student who misbehaves can benefit from alternative classes or an alternative school, so potential applicants should be screened to make sure that the classes have a reasonably good chance of succeeding. In assigning students to alternative classes care should be taken to avoid putting people together who will stimulate or feed upon each other's misbehavior.
3. **Adequate resources to insure small classes (9–12), a good-sized room and sufficient materials and supplies.**
4. **Reasonable flexibility to depart from the school schedule, curriculum, and rules and regulations when it seems desirable in the eyes of the teacher and administration to do so.** Alternative classes should be treated differently, and should not be expected to adhere to everything that the regular classes need to do.
5. **A relevant and worthwhile curriculum in the eyes of the students, teachers, and parents.** Whatever is going to be accomplished in the alternative classes has to be viewed first of all as interesting and worthwhile by the students. Unless that objective is achieved, the rest of the program will make little difference.
6. **Interested and cooperative parents.** The interest and cooperation of the parents are desirable, if not essential conditions for an effective program. Whether the parents are interested and cooperative will depend, of course, on their perceptions of whether the school is REALLY interested in them and their child, or is merely trying to "get rid of" a troublemaker.
7. **Interested and cooperative administration.** Unless the administration understands the purposes of this kind of program and is committed to securing the resources necessary for making it work, there is little possibility that such a program can be effective.

In some situations it may not be necessary for each and every condition to exist for a special class or school to succeed, but in general most of the conditions should be viewed as prerequisites to success. There will no doubt be problems (particularly, financial ones) that must be resolved in providing these conditions, but the school administrator is the one who is responsible for resolving these problems and moving ahead with the introduction, maintenance, and improvement of the alternative program. It should be emphasized that the ultimate effectiveness of an alternative program should be judged according to the percentage of students who can successfully be integrated back into the regular school program. A useful book for those who are thinking about establishing an alternative program is *Alternative Education: Planning and Implementing Successful Programs,* published by Florida's Department of Education.

Individualized Educational Programs. Individualized education is a concept which has been discussed in education for many years. However, with the passage of the Education of All Handicapped Children Act (Public Law 94–142), the concept took on new importance and became much more widely implemented in the schools. Public Law 94–142 mandates that each school district desiring to receive federal funds must develop written individualized education programs for each handicapped student.[58] While obviously not all handicapped students misbehave, nor are all students who misbehave handicapped in some way, the passage of the law has forced school districts to take a closer look at students for possible handicaps than had been thus far attempted, and in the process many students who had misbehaved were found to possess handicaps of one kind or another.

In those cases in which a student has been diagnosed as possessing a handicap, the law requires that the school district, in cooperation with the parents, develop an individualized education program (IEP) for the student. An IEP consists of a written statement of the objectives, content, implementation, and evaluation of a student's educational program and process.[59] The basic rationale for the IEP has been summarized by Reynolds and Birch:

> Most pupil behaviors called learning disabilities and behavioral
> disorders are best acknowledged as the consequences of failure to
> provide enough high quality individualized instruction. The problem
> does not reside in the child, hidden in some mysterious physiological or
> psychological recess. It sets squarely in the hands of teachers, and its
> resolution depends on the degree to which they design and carry out
> personalized teaching.[60]

(The specific details of the IEP and possible problems in developing and implementing it are discussed in the next chapter.)

It should be emphasized that the law does not presently require an IEP for students without a handicap, even if they misbehave frequently. And it is possible that the law could change, even in the case of handicapped students. However, it would seem that most, if not all students who misbehave could benefit from an individualized education program. While it is recognized that the development and implementation of such a program for those misbehaving students who don't possess a handicap could add greatly to the time demands

and responsibilities of school personnel, an effective IEP could reduce significantly the time and energy currently being invested by school personnel in
dealing with repeated student misbehavior. In any regard, the IEP does seem
to offer the school a worthwhile nonpunitive alternative for responding to student misbehavior.

Changing the Student's Home and Community Environment

Many educators seem to believe that the causes of student misbehavior can
be found in the student's home and/or community environment.[61] While this
theory has a certain amount of evidence to support it,[62] the administrator who
tries to change a student's home or community environment is frequently likely
to encounter difficulties. For example, the administrator and the professional
staff are typically occupied with myriad tasks at the school and may not have
sufficient time to become well acquainted with a student's home and community environment. In addition, in many situations the administrator and
many of the teachers don't even live in the community from which the school
draws its students.

But the basic difficulty that an administrator will probably face in trying
to change a student's home and community environment is that the school has
very little control or influence over that environment. It may be that the following conditions in a student's home and community contribute to his misbehavior in school, but the school may be limited in what it can do about any
of these conditions.

1. Large family living in a crowded home.
2. Both parents work and don't have much time to supervise children.
3. Older brothers and sisters did not finish school.
4. Street gangs exist in the neighborhood.
5. Undesirable influences on the student, such as drugs, exist in the
   neighborhood.[63]

Any or all of these home and community conditions may be causing a
student's misbehavior at school, but the likelihood that an administrator and
the professional staff can change any of them is small. This is not to minimize
the importance of efforts to work with parents and various neighborhood groups
to improve conditions in the home and/or community. For example, individual
and group counseling of parents of children with behavioral problems has been
effective in some situations ultimately improving school behavior.[64] Hilling
describes one pre-school conference program involving the student, parents,
administrator, teachers, and counselor, which appears to be particularly
worthwhile.[65] Other schools have been successful in working out cooperative
programs with community groups to improve the community.[66] Also, some

principals have become directly involved with the community with apparent success in reducing student misbehavior.[67]

In addition, Anker has identified at least fifteen ways that schools can work with the community to provide students with more positive opportunities, such as [68]

- Additional recreational facilities with longer hours
- Conferences with parents
- Meetings with local political, religious and civic leaders, as well as representatives from influential citizen and ethnic groups
- Street workers to provide a bridge between school and community
- Community relations programs to keep schools aware of local problems, including an intelligence network to alert administrators to gang activities.

In a book published by the American Friends Service Committee a list of fifty approaches to improving home-school cooperation has been compiled.[69]

One approach in particular which potentially could be of assistance in reducing student misbehavior, if the program was initiated in the elementary school, would be parenting classes offered by the school. Many of today's parents need help in raising their children, and the school could assist parents in identifying at an early stage emerging problems of students and offer appropriate assistance.[70]

While it can be argued that there is much that the school can do in working with parents and the larger community to reduce student misbehavior, the administrator will need to recognize that, in attempting to change a student's home and community environment, progress may be slow and limited. Consequently, her main efforts and those of the professional staff should be focused on diagnosing and taking action on possible environmental conditions existing within the classroom and the school which may be causing the student's misbehavior and over which the administrator has better control and can more easily bring about change.

OTHER APPROACHES

In addition to the methods discussed thus far, some schools have experimented with several other approaches to preventing and reducing student misbehavior. For further information on these approaches, consult the sources listed under this note[71] at the end of the chapter.

A FINAL NOTE

Ladd has observed that "A sad but no longer rare spectacle is the school principal who used to keep order with reprimands, threats, and punishment but who finds them ineffectual today and becomes frustrated and angry."[72] The discussion and analysis in this chapter should have shown the school administrator that punitive responses to student misbehavior are largely ineffective in preventing that behavior from recurring—even though they may be temporarily necessary—and that nonpunitive remedies are available to prevent and reduce student misbehavior. Although the nonpunitive methods suggested may be perceived by some administrators as too time-consuming or not immediate enough in their impact, every administrator needs to recognize that there are few shortcuts to or panaceas for the prevention and reduction of student misbehavior. The nonpunitive approaches recommended in this chapter may not *eliminate* student misbehavior, but if implemented they could eventually reduce its recurrence significantly. And as Graham emphasizes, the key is leadership by the principal.

> By far the most significant factor with regard to school discipline is the leadership role of the principal. Weak leadership is likely to produce increased discipline problems, and strong leadership is likely to reduce them."[73]

Review and Learning Activities

1. Define the function of punishment. What are its advantages and disadvantages?
2. Identify the punishment alternatives that an administrator has available to him. What guidelines should an administrator follow in deciding on and implementing a punishment alternative?
3. Discuss those factors and guidelines that an administrator should consider in using corporal punishment with students who misbehave.
4. Under what circumstances are suspension and/or expulsion appropriate or inappropriate methods of responding to student misbehavior?
5. Define the terms "substantive due process" and "procedural due process" as they apply to student suspension or expulsion. Explain what is meant by "minimum due process."
6. Identify several nonpunitive approaches to changing a student who has misbehaved. Describe the advantages and disadvantages of each approach.

Notes

1. For an example of this type of influence by teachers, see Donald Willower, *The Teacher Subculture and Curricular Change.* An ERIC Report: Ed–020–588.

2. William W. Purkey, *Self-Concept and School Achievement* (Englewood Cliffs, N.J.: Prentice-Hall, 1970), p. 55.

3. Anthony F. Bongiovanni, "An Analysis of Research on Punishment and Its Relation to the Use of Corporal Punishment," in *Corporal Punishment in American Education,* edited by Irwin A. Hyman and James H. Wise (Philadelphia: Temple University Press, 1979). Also see G. C. Wathers and J. E. Gruser, *Punishment* (San Francisco: W. H. Freeman and Co., 1977). For a contrary view, see R. G. Gaddis, "Punishment: A Reaffirmation," *Clearing House* (September 1978): 5–6.

4. Timothy Heron, "Punishment: A Review of the Literature with Implications for the Teacher of Mainstreamed Children," *Journal of Special Education* (Fall 1978): 243–52.

5. K. Daniel O'Leary and Susan G. O'Leary, *Classroom Management: The Successful Use of Behavioral Modification* (Elmsford, New York: Pergamon Press, 1972), p. 152.

6. Ingraham v. Wright, 430 U.S. 651, 1977.

7. For example, see Leblanc v. Tyler, 381 So. 908, 1980.

8. Lansing K. Reinholz, *A Practical Defense of Corporal Punishment.* An ERIC Report: Ed–132–733.

9. Roosevelt Ratliff, "Physical Punishment Must Be Abolished," *Educational Leadership* (March 1980): 474–76. For a more extended discussion of these issues and considerable background in the history of punishment, see "Practice and Alternatives to Corporal Punishment," in *Corporal Punishment in American Education,* ed. Hyman and Wise.

10. Adah Mauer, "All in the Name of the 'Last Resort,' " *Inequality in Education* (September 1978): 21–28. Also see Bongiovanni, "Analysis of Research on Punishment."

11. William T. Elrod, "Discipline and Corporal Punishment in Indiana Public Secondary Schools" (Unpublished paper, n.d.).

12. Tobyann Boonin, "The Benighted Status of U.S. School Corporal Punishment Practice," *The Kappan* (January 1979): 395–96.

13. Robert Hamilton, *Legal Rights and Liabilities of Teachers* (Laramie, Wyo.: Laramie Printers, 1956), p. 36. For a more recent source of essentially the same guidelines on administering corporal punishment, see Joseph J. Cobb, *An Introduction to Educational Law for Administrators and Teachers* (Springfield, Ill.: Charles C. Thomas, 1981), pp. 88–89.

14. Robert E. Phay and Jasper L. Cummings, Jr., *Student Suspension and Expulsions* (Chapel Hill, N.C.: Institute of Government, 1970), p. 9.

15. Ralph Faust, *Model High School Disciplining Procedure Code* (St. Louis, Mo.: National Juvenile Law Center, 1971), pp. 4–5. Also see Phay and Cummings, *Student Suspensions and Expulsions,* pp. 15–23.

16. Thomas J. Flygare, "Disciplining Special Education Students," *The Kappan* (May 1981): 668–69.

17. *Education for All Handicapped Children Act,* P.L. 94–142 and Section 504 of the Rehabilitation Act of 1973.

18. Antoine M. Garibaldi, "In-school Alternatives to Suspension," *The Urban Review* (Summer 1979): 97–103.

19. Claiborne R. Winborne, "In-School Suspension Programs," *Educational Leadership* (March 1980): 466–69.

20. Leslie J. Chamberlain, "How to Improve Discipline in Ohio Public Schools," *American Secondary Education* (December 1980): 6–13.

21. Winborne, "In-School Suspension Programs"; Roy Mendez and Stanley G. Sanders, "An Examination of In-School Suspension: Panacea or Pandora's Box?" *NASSP Bulletin* (January 1981): 65–69.

22. Ibid.

23. David Sklarz, "Helping the Disruptive Student," *NASSP Spotlight* (May 1980): 5–6.

24. M. Catherine Grayson et al., "Using Time-out Procedures with Disruptive Students," *The Pointer* (Fall 1979): 74–81. For a description of a different type of "time out" program, see John P. Caronis, "Grandview Heights In-School Suspension: The Time-out Room Works!" *American Secondary Education* (December 1980): 14–22.

25. *Federal Register,* December 30, 1976, p. 56972.

26. Alexander Kern, "Administrative Prerogative: Restraints of Natural Justice on Student Discipline," *Journal of Law and Education* (July 1978): 331–58.

27. Gross v. Lopez, 419 U.S. 565, 1975.

28. Louis A. Gomes, Jr. "Effects of Due Process Procedures in Public Schools" (Paper presented at the 1981 annual meeting of the American Educational Research Association, Los Angeles, Calif.).

29. Robert L. Ackerly, *The Reasonable Exercise of Authority* (Washington, D.C.: National Association of Secondary School Principals, 1968), p. 15.

30. Behaviors that might convey the credibility are identified in a study by Rosa Baggett, "Behaviors That Communicate Understanding as Evaluated by Teenagers" (Ed.D. diss., University of Florida, 1967).

31. The norms of the reference group to which the student belongs are a major factor in this regard. See Albert K. Cohen, *Delinquent Boys* (Glencoe, Ill.: Free Press, 1955), chap. 4.

32. Mark Mitchell, "Assistant Principals Can Be Effective Counselors, Mediators," *NASSP Bulletin* (May 1980): 29–32.

33. Kenneth J. Tewel and Fredda Chalfin, "Close Encounters in the Classroom: A Technique for Combating Irresponsibility Among Today's High School Youngsters," *The Kappan* (September 1980): 56–58.

34. Shirley B. Neill, "Crisis Counseling," *American Education* (January–February 1977): 17–22.

35. Daisey Manning, "The Effects of Systematic Guidance Programs upon School Attitudes of Potential Dropouts" (Ph.D. diss., Walden University, 1979).

36. Bernice Hamberg, "Peer Counseling Can Identify and Help Troubled Youngsters," *The Kappan* (April 1980): 562–63.

37. For a good description of the various roles the school counselor can play in helping reduce student misbehavior, see Frank Bickel and Maude O'Neil, "The Counselor and Student Discipline, Suggested Roles," *Personnel and Guidance Journal* (June 1979): 522–25.

38. For the model's theoretical basis, see John Dollard et al., *Frustration and Aggression* (New Haven: Yale University Press, 1939); that misbehavior is not the only outcome for aggression is suggested in a review of relevant research by Gerald R. Adams, "Classroom Aggression: Determinants Controlling Mechanics and Guidelines for the Implementation of a Behavior Modification Program," *Psychology in Schools* (April 1973): 155–67.

39. Statement of former probation officer Jessie Jackson, reported in *Ebony* (November 1972), p. 67.

40. Samuel M. Deitz and John Hummel, *Discipline in the Schools: A Guide to Reducing Misbehavior* (Englewood Cliffs, N.J.: Educational Technology Publications, 1978).

41. *In-School Alternatives to Suspension: Conference Report,* Antoine Garibaldi, ed. (Washington, D.C.: National Institute of Education, 1979).

42. For an easily understandable introduction to this topic, see Saul Arelrod, *Behavioral Modification for the Classroom Teacher* (New York: McGraw Hill, 1977).

43. Vivian Hedrich, "Rx for Disruptive Students," *American Education* (July 1972): 11–14.

44. Wesley C. Becker et al., "The Contingent Use of Teacher Attention and Praise in Reducing Classroom Behavior Problems," *Journal of Special Education* (Summer/Fall 1967): 287–307.

45. See Ronald E. Brown et al., "The School Principal as a Behavior Modifier," *Journal of Educational Research* (December 1972): 175–80. See also Rodney E. Copeland et al., "Effects of a School Principal Praising Parents for Student Attendance," *Educational Technology* (1972): 56–59.

46. Arelrod, *Behavioral Modification for Classroom Teacher.*

47. Howard A. Rollins, Jr., and Marion Thompson, "Implementation and Operation of a Contingency Management Program by the Elementary School Principal," *American Educational Research Journal* (Spring 1978): 325–30. Also, Ted J. Marble and David Marholin, "Behavioral Contracting: The Principal as a Resource," *The Pointer* (Spring 1980): 39–46.

48. *Classroom Discipline* (Eugene, Oreg.: ERIC Clearinghouse on Educational Management, August 1979), pp. 2–3.

49. Judith Caldwell, "Basic Techniques for Early Classroom Intervention," *The Pointer* (Fall 1979): 53–60.

50. *Progress in Behavior Modification,* ed. Michael Hensen et al. (New York: Academic Press, 1981).

51. There are several very worthwhile articles in the April, 1981, issue of *The Kappan,* which describe the history of and current approaches to alternative programming.

52. Eli Ginzberg, *School/Work Nexus* (Bloomington, Ind.: Phi Delta Kappa, 1981).

53. Jack Heffez, "Employment and the High School Dropout," *NASSP Bulletin* (November 1980): 85–90.

54. Lyndon G. Furst, "Work: An Educational Alternative to Schooling," *Urban Review* (Fall 1979): 149–57.

55. For a description of what appears to be a particularly worthwhile program, see Alexander G. MacNab and Richard J. Weiland, "Earn and Learn: An Uncommon Solution to a Familiar Problem," *The Kappan* (December 1980): 280–81.

56. Jeffrey Robbins et al., "Alternative Programs," *NASSP Bulletin* (May 1981): 48–56.

57. Barbara J. Case, "Lasting Alternatives: A Lesson in Survival," *The Kappan* (April 1981): 554–57.

58. See *Federal Register* (December 30, 1976), pp. 56966–98.

59. Maynard C. Reynolds and Jack W. Birch, *Teaching Exceptional Children in All America's Schools* (Reston, Va.: Council for Exceptional Education, 1977), p. 157.

60. Ibid., p. 351.

61. For a review of the theoretical basis for that point of view, see Clinard B. Marshan, *Sociology of Deviant Behavior,* rev. ed. (New York: Holt, Rinehart & Winston, 1964).

62. See R. Lynn, "Personality Characteristics of the Mother of Aggressive and Unaggressive Children," *Journal of Genetic Psychology* (1961): 159–64. Also see Naomi M. Serot and Richard C. Teevan, "Perceptions of the Parent-Child Relationship and Its Relation to Child Adjustment," *Child Development* (February 1961): 363–78.

63. Extracted from Sheldon Glueck and Eleanor Glueck, *Unraveling Juvenile Delinquency* (Cambridge, Mass.: Harvard University Press, 1950).

64. Lucretia G. Robinson, "Volunteer Counseling, Not Suspension," *The Kappan* (October 1978): 131.

65. Carl Hilling, *Pre-School Conference: A New Approach to Discipline.* An ERIC Report: Ed–135–095.

66. Pat Samples, "The Road to Better Neighborhoods," *American Education* (August/ September 1979): 29–33.

67. William B. Thomas, "Parental and Community Involvement: Rx for Better School Discipline," *The Kappan* (November 1980) 203–204. Also see Daniel Sheats and Gary E. Dunkleberger, "A Determination of the Principal's Effect in School-Initiated Home Contacts Concerning Attendance of Elementary School Students," *Journal of Educational Research* (July/August 1979): 310–12.

68. Reported in "Principal Roles and School Crime Management," by Lewis M. Ciminillo, *NASSP Bulletin* (February 1980): 83.

69. *Everybody's Business: A Book About School Discipline* (Columbia, S.C.: Southeastern Public Education Program, 1980).

70. Don Dinkmeyer and Gary McKay, *Parents' Handbook* (Circle Pines, Minn.: American Guidance Service, 1976); and Louise Guerney and Lucy Jordan, "Children of Divorce—A Community Support Group," *Journal of Divorce* (Spring 1979) 283–94.

71. Daniel L. Duke and Adrienne Maravich, *Managing Student Behavior* (New York: Teachers College Press, Columbia University, 1980); *Student Discipline: Problems and Solutions* (Arlington, Va.: American Association of School Administrators, 1980); *Student Discipline: Practical Approaches* (Washington, D.C.: National School Boards Association, 1979): Howard L. Millman et al., *Therapies for School Behavior Problems* (Washington, D.C.: Jossey-Bass, 1980).

72. Edward T. Ladd, "Regulating Student Behavior Without Ending Up in Court," *The Kappan* (January 1973): 308.

73. Quoted in an article by Stanley Fagan et al., "A Principal's Checklist for School Behavior Management," *The Pointer* (Fall 1979): 33.

15

ADMINISTRATION OF SPECIAL EDUCATION AND PUPIL PERSONNEL SERVICES

There are many different kinds of students who attend school, ranging from the academically talented student to the special education student. The major objective of education should be to help each of these students achieve his maximum potential; the primary function of special education and pupil personnel services should be to provide a set of specialized services which will aid the school and, ultimately the student, to accomplish that objective.

Since a special education and pupil personnel services program may be found in most schools, and the school administrator is usually the one who has overall administrative responsibility at the building level, he will need to be well informed about the many facets of this very important program. The intent of this chapter is to help the administrator better understand the objectives, personnel roles, administrative responsibilities, and issues and problems of the special education program, and the two main components of pupil personnel services: (1) the counseling and guidance program, and (2) the social, psychological, and health program.

THE SPECIAL EDUCATION PROGRAM

Special education has been part of the educational scene for many years.[1] However, until 1975, special education in most states was separate from the general school program. In 1975 Public Law 94–142, the Education for All Handicapped Children Act, was passed by Congress, providing for, among other things, a mandate to increase, where appropriate, the integration of special education with general education.[2] The law, according to McCarthy, has been characterized in a variety of ways: "A bill of rights for handicapped children, an administrative nightmare, a disaster, a paradigm of educational perfection, a remarkable piece of legislation, and a bombshell."[3]

Since 1975, the federal law has had its share of critics, as well as supporters, and its continuing existence is not certain. Nevertheless, it is important for school administrators to understand the basic concepts of this law because, whether or not the law is repealed or amended, its main tenets are likely to continue to play an important role in American education. Also, by understanding the basic concepts of the law, the school administrator will learn a great deal about special education.

The Education for All Handicapped Children Act (PL–94–142) requires the following:[4]

- That handicapped children receive a free and appropriate public education at no cost to parents or guardian.
- That state education agencies (through individual school districts) locate and aid all handicapped children who presently are not receiving public education.
- That nondiscriminatory, comprehensive testing and evaluation be used in determining a person's handicap and eventual placement in an educational program.*
- That an individualized educational program (IEP) be developed and maintained for each handicapped child.
- That special education be provided for each handicapped child in the least restrictive environment for that child.
- That there be regular parent or guardian consultation in the handicapped student's assessment, program placement, and IEP development process.
- That the child's parents be guaranteed due process.

The term, "handicapped," in the federal law is defined very comprehensively:

> The term "handicapped children" means mentally retarded, hard of hearing, deaf, speech impaired, visually handicapped, seriously emotionally disturbed, orthopedically impaired, or other health impaired children, or children with specific learning disabilities who, by reason thereof, require special education and related services."[5]

Perhaps the most innovative concept in the law is the individualized educational program, more commonly referred to as the IEP. The IEP is a "written commitment of resources necessary to enable a handicapped child to receive

---

*For an excellent monograph on concepts and methods of nonbiased assessment, see *Nonbiased Assessment and School Psychology* by Daniel Reschly (Des Moines: Iowa Department of Public Instruction).

needed special education and related services."[6] It should be noted that the IEP is not a binding legal contract between the school and the child/parents, but an explicit, systematic, cooperative planning process designed to provide the best education possible for the handicapped child.[7] The overall process leading to the development of an IEP includes the following:[8]

Phase I.
1. Referral of the student to a multi-disciplinary team to ascertain whether or not a handicap exists.
2. Assessment of the skills, abilities, interests, and present level of performance.
3. Diagnosis and decision on whether or not the student is handicapped.

Phase II.
1. Evaluation of the child's present program placement and appropriate alternative placements and a decision to place the student in the least restrictive educational program for that child.
2. Development of an educational program which will best serve the child.
3. Establishment of an effective monitoring system for ascertaining the extent to which the educational program is being implemented and maintained.
4. Identification of criteria and methods for ascertaining student achievement and program effectiveness.

Participants in Phase II of the process should include a representative of the educational agency, e.g., school district, who will supervise the administration of the plan; the child's teacher; one or both parents or guardian; the child, if appropriate; and one or more persons knowledgeable about the child or evaluation procedures.[9] As a result of the varied contributions of the participants involved in the process described, an individualized educational program for each handicapped student should be produced, that would contain (a) the child's present level of performance, (b) a statement of annual goals and short-term instructional objectives, (c) a description of special education and related services for the child, plus the extent of participation in regular educational programs recommended for the child; (d) specified dates for initiation of services and their duration, and (e) identification of objective criteria and evaluative procedures for assessing whether the instructional objectives are being achieved, on at least an annual basis.[10]

Although the federal mandate of required IEP's for all handicapped children has been criticized for a number of reasons, including the allegation that it is confusing, expensive, and time-consuming,[11] that aspect of the IEP which seems most in need of improvement is the involvement of parents. One study, for example, showed that parents generally knew their children had IEP's, but only 20 percent were thoroughly familiar with what was in them. In the same study, parents were less familiar with the IEP's of their children than the teachers believed they were.[12] In another study, it was discovered that only about half of the parents actually attended the meetings in which IEP's were developed but, interestingly IEP's were more accurate when parents were involved.[13] And, in a third study, 71 percent of the parents with learning disabled children remembered being informed about an IEP, but only one-fourth helped write it, and only one-fourth were satisfied with their involvement.[14] These studies strongly suggest the need for the school administrator, in cooperation with the IEP Team, to develop a better system of involving parents in the development of the IEP's. Such a system is further described by Gaines.[15]

Parent involvement is also important because if parents are not satisfied with the school district's response to the needs of their handicapped child, they have a right to due process. The specific procedural guarantees to parents are described by Barbacovi and Clellard, and include[16]

- The right to a timely, written notice of the place and time of the hearing
- The right to review all records and information that the school has available on the child
- The right to be represented by counsel, to bring witnesses, to cross-examine witnesses, and to present evidence
- The right to obtain an independent evaluation of the data being used to evaluate the child's possible handicap and eventual placement, at the expense of the school
- The right to a complete written report of the hearing proceedings and findings
- The right to appeal the assessment decision and the placement decision.

Obviously, this aspect of the law on the handicapped is complex and potentially troublesome. For further information, the reader is referred to an excellent monograph discussing major problems and issues with regard to due process, published by the organization, Research for Better Schools.[17]

Another important aspect of PL 94–142 is the requirement that special education be provided for each handicapped child in the least restrictive environment for the child. This has been interpreted to mean that a handicapped child is entitled to an environment that provides the greatest interaction with other, nonhandicapped, students in which satisfactory performance can still be assured. A decision to take a handicapped child from a special education setting and place the child in a regular classroom has been termed "mainstreaming."[18] The rationale for mainstreaming is best expressed in a statement by the Council for Exceptional Children:[19]

> Mainstreaming is a belief which involves an educational placement procedure and process for exceptional children, based on the conviction that each such child should be educated in the least restrictive

environment in which his educational and related needs can be satisfactorily provided. This concept recognizes that exceptional children have a wide range of special educational needs, varying greatly in intensity and duration, that there is a recognized continuum of educational settings which may, at a given time, be appropriate for an individual child's needs; that to the maximum extent appropriate, exceptional children should be educated with nonexceptional children; and that special classes, separate schooling, or other removal of an exceptional child from education with nonexceptional children should occur only when the intensity of the child's special education and related needs is such that they cannot be satisfied in an environment including nonexceptional children, even with the provision of supplementary aids and services.

It should be noted that the concept of mainstreaming handicapped students is one of the more controversial ideas in American education, and even some special educators question whether academically and socially many handicapped children will benefit more from integration with nonhandicapped students.[20] Certainly, it needs to be recognized that mainstreaming a handicapped child requires much more than merely placing that child in a regular classroom. Several studies have shown that, "Even though they [handicapped students] are physically in the mainstream, they often continue to be socially isolated."[21]

As Sowers points out, successful mainstreaming in a school requires[22]

- New perspectives and new skills for the staff
- Increased awareness and sensitivity on the part of each individual
- In-service for teachers, with emphasis on acquiring diagnostic and observational skills
- Supportive resources for the classroom teacher
- Acceptance by the faculty
- Understanding by resource teachers of their role
- Acceptance of children with special needs by other pupils
- Variety of instructional materials
- Efficient methods in diagnosing and prescribing for individual pupils.

The special education teacher can play a key role in assisting the regular classroom teacher at the time mainstreaming is introduced. Assistance that the special education teacher should provide includes[23] (1) discussion with the regular teacher on how the student will be prepared for the change in classes, (2) description of techniques used by the special education teacher that have proved to be useful in teaching the student to manage behavior and to establish work habits, (3) identification of limits and controls used by the special education teacher in order to help the student manage his behavior,

(4) description of behavioral and academic expectations used in the special education setting and how they could be adjusted for use in the regular classroom, and (5) provision of materials used in the special education classroom that might be used or adapted for the regular classroom. The goal of the special education teacher should be to make the transition from the special to the regular classroom as smooth as possible for both the student and the regular classroom teacher.

The classroom teacher also plays an important role in the success of a mainstreaming endeavor. The attitude of the teacher is apparently the key variable.[24] If the classroom teacher holds a positive attitude, the chances of success for a mainstreamed child are probably high. On the other hand, if the classroom teacher is negative or even ambivalent toward mainstreaming, the chances of successful mainstreaming are, at best, uncertain. Larrivee and Cook, in their study of variables affecting the teacher's attitude toward mainstreaming found three factors which had the greatest import: (1) the teacher's perception of the degree of success with special education students, (2) the availability of supportive services to the teacher, e.g., special reading teacher assistance, appropriate instructional materials; and (3) the level of administrative support received.[25]

That the school administrator can make a significant contribution to the success of mainstreaming, as well as other aspects of special education, has been documented in a number of reports.[26] The specific role the school administrator should play, however, is not always clear. But a study by Sivage found that it was important for principals to be advocates of mainstreaming and use a leadership style which is democratic and that stresses team planning.[27] And a study by Berry reported that the extent of success that was achieved by a mainstreaming project in California was directly proportionate to "the degree to which the building administrator was risk-taking and achieving personal growth."[28]

As far as the school administrator's specific responsibilities in administering a special education program are concerned, the Council for Exceptional Education has published a manual which identifies primary and support responsibilities of the building principal.[29] These include such contributions as

- Helping to design special education services delivery plan
- Helping to formulate long-term policies and objectives for special education programs
- Helping to recruit and select special education personnel
- Providing in-service training for professional staff
- Evaluating special education professional personnel
- Coordinating due process procedures for students and parents.

With regard to evaluating special education personnel and programs (a frequently neglected task), the New Jersey State Department of Education has developed comprehensive criteria, along with suggested documentation for meeting the criteria, for evaluating all aspects of special education services.[30]

While the role description of the Council for Exceptional Children defines considerable involvement for the school administrator in administering the special education program, research suggests that the actual role may be more limited. For example, a study by Lietz and Towle found that the school administrators in their sample wanted more responsibility in regard to administering the special education program than was occurring in actual practice.[31]

In carrying out his responsibilities for administering the special education program, the school administrator should attempt to keep knowledgeable about federal and state requirements concerning special education, establish reasonable expectations of the staff in implementing the requirements of the law, provide supportive services and staff development and, perhaps most important, try to provide a model of behavior which indicates to all observers that the education of the handicapped in the least restrictive environment is an important and desirable educational priority, rather than an unnecessary legal mandate.[32]

The preceding discussion should be viewed as merely a short introduction to the major concepts of exceptional education. The reader is encouraged to pursue the references identified at the end of the chapter for further background.[33]

THE COUNSELING AND GUIDANCE PROGRAM

Although the counseling and guidance program is only one of the two components of pupil personnel services, it may constitute the only pupil personnel services offered in many schools. While a counseling and guidance program is more typically found in the secondary schools, a strong case can be made that it is needed as much, if not more, at the elementary level.[34] Younger students tend to be more receptive to counseling and guidance, and problems can be addressed in their early stages before they become more complex and difficult. A young person does not suddenly develop a need for counseling and guidance when entering junior high school; often the need develops much earlier but does not receive the attention it deserves.

The basic purposes of the counseling and guidance program are to assist students to better understand themselves, and to realize their potentialities more fully.[35] In order to achieve these objectives the program should provide to the student, and to others who are working to help the student, a set of services, which are identified in figure 15.1.[36]

As an examination of figure 15.1 will show, the counseling and guidance program provides services to five groups. The first and undoubtedly the most important group is the student body. The counseling and guidance program

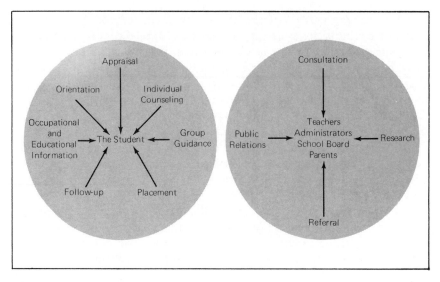

Figure 15.1. Counseling and
Guidance Services

offers a set of services designed to help students understand themselves (appraisal), as well as their immediate and future environments (orientation, educational, and occupational information), and to reach decisions which will fully utilize their present and future capabilities (individual and group counseling and guidance). In addition, a good counseling and guidance program provides assistance to those students seeking a job or a college which will be appropriate for them (placement), and checks with them periodically after they have left school to ascertain the effectiveness of the school's assistance to them and their need for further help (follow-up).

While students are probably the primary recipients of counseling and guidance services, the program also tries to provide help to other groups, as figure 15.1 indicates. These services include *consultation* on ideas for maximizing students' potentialities; a *referral* source on ways to prevent and ameliorate student problems; *research* on student aptitudes, interests, and problems; and *public relations* activities to help people better understand the counseling and guidance program. Teachers, administrators, school board members, and parents can and should utilize these services to help them do a better job in working with students. Frequently these groups do not make adequate use of the specialized resources which the counseling and guidance program can offer. Although the reasons for such underutilization are often complex, it is the responsibility of the building administrator, in cooperation with the guidance staff, to develop appropriate understanding and use of counseling and guidance services on the part of teachers, parents, the school board and other administrators.

THE ROLE OF THE COUNSELOR

Central to the effective utilization of counseling and guidance services is a broad understanding of the role of the counselor. The counselor is the transmitter of counseling and guidance services, much as the teacher is the transmitter of the curriculum. Though there have been many formulations of the role of the counselor, the most widely accepted conceptualization is the role description developed by the American Personnel and Guidance Association, presented in figure 15.2.

A. The Counselor's Responsibility to the Student
  1. Demonstrates respect for the worth, dignity, and quality of the student's human rights.
  2. Shows concern for and assists in the planning of the student's educational, career, personal, and social development.
  3. Aids the student in self-evaluation, self-understanding, and self-direction, enabling him to make decisions consistent with his immediate and long-range goals.
  4. Assists the student in developing health habits and positive attitudes and values.
  5. Encourages the student to participate in appropriate school activities with a view toward increasing his effectiveness in personal and social activities.
  6. Participates in the planning and designing of research that may result in beneficial effects to the counselee.
  7. Assists the student in the development of an awareness of the world of work and in the utilization of the school and community resources to that end.
  8. Helps the student to acquire a better understanding of the world of work through the acquisition of skills and attitudes and/or participation in work-related programs.
  9. Encourages the student to plan and utilize leisure time activities and to increase his personal satisfaction.
  10. Clearly indicates the conditions under which counseling is provided with respect to privileged communication.
  11. Assists in the student's adjustment to school and evaluates his academic progress.
  12. Makes referral to appropriate resources whenever his professional or role limitations limit his assistance.
  13. Assists the student in understanding his strengths, weaknesses, interests, values, potentialities, and limitations.

B. The Counselor's Relationship with the Teacher
  1. Views the teacher as a member of the guidance team.
  2. Serves as interpreter of the school's guidance program to teachers and familiarizes them with the guidance services available.

(continued)

Figure 15.2. The Role of the School
Counselor[37]

3. Shares appropriate individual student data with the teacher, with due regard for confidentiality, and assists the teacher in recognizing individual differences in students, as well as their needs in the classroom.
4. Assists the teacher in making referrals to other appropriate school personnel, such as the remedial reading teacher, the school nurse, the school's learning disabilities specialist.
5. Supports teachers of vocational and/or cooperative programs offering students on-site work experience.
6. Cooperates with efforts of the middle school/junior high school and senior high school teachers to articulate academic course work for the benefit of the student entering the senior high school.
7. Maintains an objective and impartial view in teacher-student relationships, endeavoring to understand the problems which may exist and to assist in their solution.
8. Assists in the planning of classroom guidance activities and acts as a resource person for obtaining appropriate up-to-date materials and information.
9. Makes current job information available to the teacher about the myriad of careers and job opportunities during and beyond school.
10. Involves the teacher in conferences with students and parents, promoting a better understanding of the student and his development.

C. The Counselor's Relationship with the Administration

1. Recognizes that the administrator is the major member of the guidance team whose outlook, leadership, and support create the atmosphere for success in his important school services.
2. Serves as interpreter of the guidance program to the administration, familiarizing it with the guidance services available.
3. Works closely with the administration in planning, implementing and participating in-service training and other programs designed to maintain and promote the professional competency of the entire staff in curriculum development, in adapting learning activities to pupil needs, and in effecting positive student behavior.
4. Serves as liaison between the guidance staff and the school administration by preparing pertinent information regarding student needs and abilities or other data related to the guidance program and curriculum development.

D. The Counselor's Responsibility to the Parent or Guardian

1. Provides the parent/guardian with accurate information about school policies and procedures, course offerings, educational and career opportunities, course or program requirements, and resources that will contribute to the continuing development of the counselee.
2. Makes discreet and professional use of information shared during conferences.
3. Assists the parent/guardian in forming realistic perceptions of the student's aptitudes, abilities, interests, and attitudes as related to educational and career planning, academic achievement, personal-social development, and total school progress.
4. Interprets the guidance program of the school to the parent/guardian and familiarizes him with the guidance services available.
5. Involves the parent/guardian in the guidance activities within the school.

(continued)

Figure 15.2. Continued

E. The Counselor's Relationship with Significant Others
1. Maintains good communication with the office of the probate judge and with law enforcement agencies.
2. Retains a cooperative working relationship with community and social agencies.
3. Consults with students' previous counselors in order to utilize valuable knowledge and expertise of former counselors.
4. Maintains a close and cooperative relationship with the admission counselors of post-high school institutions.

Figure 15.2. Continued

The APGA policy statement on the role of the counselor is a comprehensive one which should be useful to any school administrator. It clearly outlines the many facets and scope of the counselor's job, and identifies the various individuals and groups with whom the counselor works. It is a statement which should be studied by the school administrator and shared with teachers, parents, students, and other relevant groups to develop their further understanding of the guidance program and the role of the counselor. The role description should also be utilized by the administrator in discussions with the guidance department members on the extent to which the proposed role of the counselor is actually being implemented in the school and the degree to which improvement is needed.[38] For the administrator who is seeking direction on the role of the counselor in the school, the APGA policy statement should provide a valuable blueprint for identifying desired change.

While the role of the counselor is basically the same, regardless of the educational level of the students, there are some differences. Those differences become clear when one examines the role description for the elementary school counselor, presented in figure 15.3, with the role description in figure 15.2.

The Elementary School Counselor's Primary Functions

• Counsels individual students in order to facilitate their transition from home to school and to foster their self-understanding and self-reliance.

• Counsels groups of students for the purpose of offering individual students the opportunity to obtain greater self-understanding and confidence through interactions with their peers.

• Consults with teachers, other members of the faculty, and parents on child development and needs. In addition, the elementary counselor serves as a referral agent in regard to needed counseling and guidance resources outside of the school and home.

Figure 15.3. Role of the Elementary
School Counselor[39]

(continued)

The Elementary School Counselor's Primary Functions

• Evaluates self and program effectiveness continuously for the purpose of identifying possible problems and needed improvements.

The Elementary School Counselor's Supportive Functions

• Consults with teachers, administrators and relevant others on the testing program, grouping and placement, pupil evaluation, curriculum development, articulation of guidance program with pupil data, pupil screening, and impact of the instructional program on children.
• Serves on curriculum planning committees.
• Provides in-service education when appropriate.
• Serves on special school and community committees dealing with topics such as drug education and family living.
• Consults with faculty, administration, and parents on career education.
• Interprets the functions of the counselor, and objectives and activities of the guidance program to students, teachers, parents and the general public.

Figure 15.3. Continued

As can be seen by a careful examination of the two role statements, the elementary counselor's role seems to focus much more than does that of the secondary school counselor on group counseling in regard to the personal development of the student, with an emphasis on consulting with different groups on the guidance needs of children. That elementary school counselors place a high priority on these particular aspects of their role can be concluded from a study by Biggers, who asked elementary school counselors to indicate the amount of time they actually spent on various aspect of their job. Her findings are shown below.[40]

Elementary Counselor's Activities	*Percentage of Time Spent*
Group Counseling	20.6
Consulting (with parents, teachers, principal)	18.2
Individual Counseling	17.2
Testing (group and individual)	10.4
Planning	7.7
Case Conferences	6.1
Clerical/Nonguidance	4.9
Classroom Observation	4.7

Elementary Counselor's Activities	*Percentage of Time Spent*
Home Visitation	4.3
In-Service	2.7
Orientation	2.3
Miscellaneous	1.6

It seems clear that the elementary school counselor can make a major contribution to helping young children with their personal development, and to helping teachers, parents, and others to understand better the needs and potentialities of children. While there will undoubtedly be financial obstacles to establishing a counselor's position and a formal counseling and guidance program in elementary schools where none exists, every effort should be made to overcome those obstacles. In the final analysis, the money "saved" by deciding against establishing a position and program at the elementary level will be "spent" many times over on problems at the secondary level, which either could have been avoided or reduced in their severity. Readers who wish to explore further concepts and guidelines for introducing a counseling and guidance program at the elementary level should consult the references identified at the end of the chapter.[41]

THE ADMINISTRATOR'S ROLE IN THE COUNSELING AND GUIDANCE PROGRAM

Although in many schools the position of guidance director[42] has been created in order to accomplish certain administrative functions in relation to the counseling and guidance program, the school administrator is still responsible for providing overall leadership and administration to the program at the building level.

The leadership dimension of the administrator's role includes such responsibilities as:[43]

1. Assisting counselors to remove obstacles to the effective performance of their job, and helping them to utilize their specialized talents for improving education in the school.
2. Working with counselors to increase their awareness of unmet guidance needs of students, teachers, and parents; stimulating counselors to develop greater vision and creativity as to how these needs might be met.
3. Developing on the part of students, teachers, and parents a better understanding of the guidance program and the role of the counselor, and how these groups can best relate to that program and role.

4. Helping counselors to evaluate themselves and the guidance program on a regular basis in order to obtain information on effectiveness and to identify areas which are in need of improvement.

These are leadership functions which the building administrator should share with the guidance director, if the latter position has been established. However, the guidance director is frequently a counselor who may have little released time or professional training for carrying out the leadership functions identified above. Therefore, in many cases the administrator may need to assume a leadership role relative to the counseling and guidance program, even if a guidance director is available.

Aside from the leadership dimension of the administrator's role in the counseling and guidance program, there are administrative responsibilities that he must perform in order for the program to be established and maintained at an appropriate level of effectiveness.[44] These responsibilities include providing (1) sufficient and appropriately located office space, (2) an adequate budget for supplies, occupational and educational information, testing, and professional activities, (3) sufficient secretarial assistance, and (4) a reasonable counselor-student ratio. Of course, the definition of "sufficient," "appropriate," and "reasonable" will depend on local needs and conditions. However, the administrator should try to meet the standards covering these four areas of responsibility as recommended by authorities in the guidance field.

ISSUES AND PROBLEMS

The counseling and guidance program, like any other program in the school, is confronted periodically by issues and problems which, if not resolved, can reduce its effectiveness. The following three issues or problems seem common to many schools' counseling and guidance program.[45]

1. **The role of the counselor in resolving student discipline problems.**

This is an issue which periodically causes friction in many schools. Students who misbehave usually need help, and there is a belief on the part of many administrators that the specialized skills of the counselor should be utilized to help these students change their attitude and behavior.

Most counselors, on the other hand, seem to feel that they should not be involved at all in working with discipline problems, at least not immediately after the student has engaged in misbehavior. Their position is that they are not "disciplinarians" and any association with a student who is a behavioral problem would tend to give them the image of administrator rather than of counselor, thereby making it more difficult to work with other kinds of students.

In many respects it is unfortunate when the question of counselor involvement in helping to reduce student misbehavior becomes an issue or a problem in a school. In the first place, counselors should never be given the responsibility of disciplining students. That type of involvement is inconsistent with the role of the counselor and is a function which should be performed by the administration of the school. Neither should teachers and administrators refer for counseling any students who have *just* engaged in misbehavior. A referral to the counselor at that point is inappropriate and will make it unnecessarily difficult for him to work with the student later.

On the other hand, a counselor can and should be expected to contribute his specialized expertise so that misbehaving students can better understand themselves and the consequences of their behavior. Through individual diagnosis, counseling, and other guidance techniques, the counselor should also be able to help a student to develop a more positive attitude about himself and others, and ultimately to become a better school citizen.

But the means by which the counselor and the student come together and the timing of their first conference are key factors to the success of this approach. If the counselor is to work with a misbehaving student in the manner indicated, then he or the student should be the one to initiate the conference, and it should not occur while the student is still subject to disciplinary proceedings. If a teacher or an administrator refers a student to a counselor and the conference takes place while the student is being considered for disciplinary action by that same teacher or administrator, there is a real danger that, in the eyes of the student, the counselor could easily become implicated in the disciplinary proceeding. In order for a counselor to work effectively with student misbehavior cases, his involvement needs to be separated as much as possible from the school's disciplinary measures. (The administrator and the guidance staff might also consider utilizing student counselors. An apparently successful program is described in the June, 1980, issue of *The Kappan.*)

There is little doubt that counselors can play an important role in assisting students who have behavioral problems. Failure to utilize counselors to help these kinds of students would mean that a valuable resource would go untapped. But the administrator needs to recognize that many counselors object to working with student behavior problems, because of their counseling philosophy or due to negative experience in the past. So unless the administrator, in conjunction with the counselors in the school, develops sensible policies and procedures for counselor involvement in working with student behavioral problems, a major issue or conflict may occur.

2. **The role of the teacher in the counseling and guidance program.**

Before formal counseling and guidance programs were introduced, the classroom teacher was expected to perform many guidance functions. Now, in most schools, the guidance role of the teacher is minimized and this responsibility is considered to be the province of the counselor and the guidance department. For example, a review of counseling and guidance journals suggests that many counselors appear to believe that teachers lack the specialized training and skills to play an important role in the counseling and guidance program. Seemingly supporting this contention are many teachers who appear to feel that counseling and guidance is somehow separate from teaching, and that the school's formal counseling and guidance program obviates the need for them to become involved.

In spite of limited support for the guidance role of the teacher, it would seem that the classroom teacher could make a valuable contribution to the total counseling and guidance program, and his resources should be organized by the administrator in such a way that they can be utilized by the guidance department for the good of the student. Specifically, the classroom teacher can and should be expected to perform the following counseling and guidance functions:[46]

- a. Study the individual student and become more aware of his needs, problems, and characteristics.
- b. Counsel with students on educational problems and, when sought out by students, on minor personal problems.
- c. Refer to counselors any students with social, personal, and vocational problems.
- d. Administer appropriate measurement instruments, e.g., standardized tests, to ascertain students' strengths and limitations.
- e. Utilize data from the school's testing program, the cumulative record, and suggestions from counselors in modifying the instructional and curricular program to meet the needs of students more adequately.
- f. Interact on a regular basis with counselors for the purpose of pooling perceptions and knowledge about students and about how they might be helped to improve.

In many schools, the question of the extent to which teachers should be involved in the counseling and guidance program has not been satisfactorily resolved. Obviously, teachers have other responsibilities, and many teachers don't possess a great deal of time or inclination for performing guidance functions. However, teachers can make a valuable contribution to the guidance program, particularly in the area of helping special education students, and it is the responsibility of the school administrator to help teachers better understand and accept their guidance role and to remove the obstacles to their carrying out that role effectively.

3. **The role of the administrator in the evaluation of the counseling and guidance program.**

Evaluation of the performance of the school counselor and the effectiveness of the counseling and guidance program can present a problem. If the administrator tries to initiate evaluation procedures, he may encounter resistance. The counselors may infer that the administrator feels dissatisfied with their work, and may then become defensive. Or they may be opposed to any type of evaluation other than informal self-assessment.

Compounding these problems is the fact that much of the counselors' work is not conducive to evaluation. Counseling takes place privately and the nature of the conferences is usually kept confidential. Also, many of the outcomes of counseling and guidance, particularly in the area of vocational guidance, may not be realized until the students have graduated from school.

In spite of these problems, however, the school administrator has a responsibility to evaluate all personnel and programs, including the counselors and the counseling and guidance program. However, to carry out this responsibility effectively the administrator will need to be aware of the problems which may be associated with evaluation of counselors and the guidance program, and he will need to move cautiously and cooperatively with the counselors in developing evaluation criteria and procedures.

Standards for evaluating a counseling and guidance program have been developed by Carroll and approved for use by the governing board of the American School Counselors Association.[47] Although too detailed to be reproduced here, they appear to represent useful criteria for purposes of program evaluation. Aubrey[48] and Manarchev[49] have also developed criteria and methods for evaluating the effectiveness of counseling and guidance programs. (One approach referred to as "results management" which merits investigation by the administrator interested in counselor evaluation is described in ERIC Report Ed–086–914, "Progress Report: Pupil Personnel Services." This type of approach is described later in the chapter.)

PSYCHOLOGICAL, SOCIAL, AND HEALTH SERVICES*

Although in many schools the counseling and guidance services may represent the total pupil services program, a comprehensive program will also include psychological, social, and health services. These services are performed by the school psychologist, the school social worker, and the school nurse respectively, all of whom can offer specialized assistance to students, teachers, parents, and the administration, beyond that contributed by the school counselor.

The assistance which these members of the pupil services team can offer a school is potentially of great value (particularly in regard to the growing concern about the needs of special education students), but that potential is frequently not achieved. Part of the problem lies in an adequate understanding

*It is recognized that there are other aspects of pupil personnel services in the schools, such as speech services. However, only those services most frequently offered at the building level are emphasized in this section.

by administrators and teachers of the role of these pupil personnel specialists. A second important factor, though, is the way these services are organized and delivered. This section will attempt to develop a better understanding on the part of the school administrator of the role of the school psychologist, the school social worker, and the school nurse. Problems involved in the organization and delivery of their services will also be discussed.

THE SCHOOL PSYCHOLOGIST

Many school districts employ a school psychologist. He typically works out of the district's central office and divides his time among several schools. He may or may not be assigned a permanent office in each school building, and his schedule usually varies from week to week, depending upon the problems and needs of the schools with which he works. His role may be specifically defined and understood by the groups who could utilize his service, but this is frequently not the case. In too many schools the role of the school psychologist is not well defined, and it is certainly not well understood by the school administrator. For example, Hughes and Shofer found in their study that only 9 percent of the psychologists had access to a description of their role and functions within their assigned schools.[50] This is inexcusable, since there are excellent statements on the role of the school psychologist which, if studied and implemented by the school administrator and the staff, would help the school psychologist to achieve more of his potential usefulness to the school.

While there is not total agreement on the role of the school psychologist, and the role is somewhat in transition because of the impact of special education legislation,[51] one role description which merits review by the school administrator is presented in figure 15.4

As the role description in figure 15.4 indicates, the school psychologist should be involved in a wide range of diagnostic, counseling, and program consulting activities. His services should be utilized by students, teachers, parents, and administrators. One major problem, however, is that these groups are frequently not in agreement on the role the school psychologist should perform. When this problem occurs, it is usually based on a perception that the school psychologist is too involved in testing and assessment, and insufficiently involved in consultation and program development.[52] In many respects special education legislation has exacerbated this situation.[53] Unfortunately, there is no easy answer to this problem.

It should be noted, however, that whether or not the proposed role outlined in figure 15.4 is actually implemented fully will probably depend as much on a clear and complete understanding of that role by the administrator as on any other factor. If the administrator understands the role of the school psychologist and is committed to helping him fulfill that role, the potential for his making an important contribution to the school is more apt to be realized.

1. Counsels with individual students who are self-referred or referred by teachers, administrators, or community agencies, to help them develop behavior patterns and attitudes which are appropriate to students' environmental and developmental stages.
2. Gathers sufficient information from previous records and through observation and assessment, to determine how a student can best be helped.
3. Assists the school staff to develop criteria and referral procedures for identifying students who need the services of the school psychologist.
4. Assists teachers, administrators, and parents to develop a greater understanding of student behavior, and to create a special climate in the school which maximizes learning and personal growth for the student.
5. Consults with teachers, curriculum specialists, and administrators on possible ways to improve conditions necessary for effective student learning.
6. Encourages teachers and other professional educators to accept responsibility/accountability for (and to help students accept responsibility for) growth toward predetermined goals.
7. Identifies and utilizes remedial/corrective resources available within the school or community.
8. Serves as a liaison between school and community.

Figure 15.4 Role of the School Psychologist[54]

If, on the other hand, the administrator possesses an inadequate understanding of this role or is not committed to helping the psychologist carry out his role, it is unlikely that he can operate effectively. In the final analysis, the administrator holds an important key to the psychologist's success in a school. (For further ideas on planning and evaluating school psychology services, see Maker.[55]).

THE SCHOOL SOCIAL WORKER

The school social worker's employment situation and work schedule are similar to that of the school psychologist in many respects. The social worker usually works out of the district's central office, dividing his time among several schools. His work schedule may vary from week to week, and he is viewed by many as a primary liaison between the school and the home. His specific function is to provide assistance to "children who are having difficulties in using the resources of the school effectively."[56] The nature of his responsibility to the school can be conceived of as "a specialized service involving home and school case work with a minority of pupils whose school problems are primarily affected by family and neighborhood conditions."[57]

As with the school psychologist, the social worker's effectiveness has been hampered in many school systems by a poorly defined and poorly understood

1. Counsels with parents and students on problems of student adjustment to school.
2. Utilizes community resources in the process of working with children and parents.
3. Consults with staff members concerning community factors which may be affecting problems of student adjustment in school.
4. Collaborates with teachers, administrators, and noninstructional personnel in gathering and sharing information about students, designed to modify or resolve student adjustment problems.
5. Acts as liaison between the school and community agencies.
6. Cooperates with community agencies by providing pertinent information about a student's school adjustment and achievement.

Figure 15.5. Functions of the School Social Worker[58]

role. To partially remedy this problem a proposed role for the school social worker is outlined in figure 15.5 for the administrator's consideration.

The proposed role described in figure 15.5 suggests that the school social worker can perform a variety of useful services for students, teachers, parents, and administrators that can, in turn, help all groups understand and capitalize on the contribution that the home and the school together can make to the educating of the student. Again, whether these services are fully and properly utilized will depend to a great degree on the school administrator. Given a school administrator who understands and is committed to implementing the role proposed in figure 15.5, the influence of the school social worker should be a significant one. (For further ideas on evaluating the effectiveness of the school social worker, see Radin.[59])

HEALTH SERVICES

According to Warren Schaller, past president of the American School Health Association, "The basic premise for having a school health program, of course, is that if a child is not in a state of good health, he or she will not be able to learn as effectively."[60] Generally state laws require health education and, in the summer of 1977, Congress enacted a law (94–317) for the purpose of trying to improve the quality of health education and care for all children.[61] Nonetheless, the extent and quality of school health programs continue to vary considerably,[62] despite clear evidence of the growing health needs of students.[63]

The primary function of school health services is to assess and diagnose the health status of students in the school, and to work with teachers, parents, administrators, and others to promote better student health habits and practices.[64] The personnel for staffing a comprehensive school health services program should include a nurse, a physician, and a dental hygienist. (For an

1. Develops objectives and designs programs with the assistance of the school district (and public health agency) personnel and within school district philosophy and policy.
2. Assesses and evaluates the health and developmental status of students in order to identify those who should be referred for medical diagnosis or treatment.
3. Interprets the health and developmental status of the pupil to him, his parents, and school personnel.
4. Interprets the results of medical findings concerning the pupil to him, his parents, and school personnel.
5. Counsels the pupil, his parents, and school personnel regarding plans for eliminating, minimizing, or accepting a health problem that interferes with his effective learning.
6. Motivates and guides the persons responsible for pupil health to appropriate resources.
7. Recommends to the administration modifications in the educational program when indicated by the health or developmental status of the pupil.
8. Serves as health consultant and resource person in the health instruction curriculum by providing current scientific information from related fields.
9. Uses direct health services as a vehicle for health counseling.
10. Serves as liaison among the parents, school and community in health matters.
11. Serves as member of the placement committee for special education programs.
12. Evaluates program effectiveness and outcomes.

Figure 15.6. Role of the School Nurse[65]

example of this kind of staffing, see Cronin and Young.[66] Whether these personnel are employed full-time or part-time will depend on the size of the school or school district, availability of personnel, financial resources and—most importantly—the concept held by the educators of the district in regard to the role of each of these specialized workers.

Since the school administrator is, in most situations, more likely to have contact with the nurse than with any of the other health personnel, an understanding of the nurse's role is essential. Figure 15.6 presents a proposed role for the school nurse which defines the nature of his services.

It should be noted that the role of the school nurse seems to be changing. Long perceived as deliverer of services such as examining students with health concerns, the responsibilities of the nurse for acting as an advocate for the health rights of students and their families within the school setting and between the school and community, *and* as a health educator for the students, faculty, administration and the community seem to be assuming greater importance.[67] A major problem with this change in role emphasis, however, is that many people still do not understand what a nurse does in a school, and others hold conflicting expectations for the role. For example, one study discovered that many students didn't know what the nurse did in the school, didn't know when she was actually at the school, and perhaps most important, had a general aversion to seeking health care services.[68] In another study by Tosi it was found that students and administrators did not believe it was necessary to emphasize the nurse's role as a health counselor and educator for health rather than deliverer of services; teachers, on the other hand, believed that the former role should be emphasized but they perceived the latter as actually occurring the most.[69] These studies suggest some of the problems that must be addressed by the administrator and the school nurse if the potential contributions of the school nurse are to be realized in the school health program.

The importance of providing health services in the schools has long been recognized in education, but the implementation of a program to that end has frequently been limited. Although the extent and quality of health services in the schools varies widely throughout the country, thereby making generalization difficult, the program in many school districts consists of no more than a part-time nurse whose time is divided among several schools, with perhaps only 1½ days per week spent at each one.[70] This appears to be definitely inadequate for many schools, given the nature of the school nurse's proposed role. For example, research by Howell and Martin found that a majority of the principals interviewed believe that the time spent by health personnel in the schools is insufficient.[71] Perhaps this will change as the need for health services becomes better understood by those who allocate funds and make decisions about introducing or expanding health service programs.

In recent years the health problems of students have increased dramatically. Drug involvement, venereal disease, nutritional imbalance, obesity, adolescent pregnancy, dental decay, and other problems all strongly point to the need for a full-time nurse and a comprehensive health services program in the schools.[72] The program should probably emphasize referral rather than treatment, and it should help students experiencing health problems to secure proper medical assistance.

Administrators need to recognize that the condition of a student's health affects his educational motivation and performance in school. The school nurse and other health services personnel can and should play an important role in helping a school to ameliorate students' health problems. A useful description of a process for establishing the need for and introducing a more comprehensive school health program is provided by Gilman.[73] For an excellent book on the importance of this program at the elementary school level, see Ronald Rhodes, et. al., *Elementary School Health: Education and Services* (Rockleigh, N.J.: Allyn and Bacon, 1981).

ADMINISTRATOR RESPONSIBILITIES

Unlike the guidance counselor, the other members of the pupil-services team are typically part-time workers in a school. They divide their time among several schools, and their work schedule is sometimes unpredictable. The part-time nature of their assignment in any particular school frequently results in their not being considered as regular members of the school faculty. Therefore, when it comes to office space, secretarial help, and a budget for materials and supplies, the school psychologist, the social worker, and (to a lesser extent) the school nurse are likely to be left to shift for themselves. They may be able to rely on some secretarial help and budget assistance from the district office, but the support from that source may not be sufficient to meet their needs.

At the minimum, the school administrator is responsible for making sure that each of the pupil services specialists working in the building has an office, which may be shared with someone else but which should be available when the specialist needs it. It should be equipped with a file (which should not be shared), a desk, and sufficient side chairs so that the specialist may expeditiously proceed with his work. The administrator should also make available to each of the pupil personnel specialists sufficient secretarial assistance to supplement the clerical support provided at the central office. Reports and much of the correspondence can more easily be prepared at the school than at the district office. In addition, provision should be made within the school budget for purchase of those supplies and materials necessary for the psychologist, social worker, and nurse to operate effectively. Perhaps the best approach would be for the administrator to think in terms of a total pupil services program and budget.

Although the psychological, social, and health services components of the pupil services program cannot succeed without the administrator's carrying out the administrative tasks previously identified, the most important responsibility for the administrator is to provide *leadership*. Whether psychological, social and health services are administered by someone at the central office or at the building level, the program will not be successful without the leadership of the building administrator. Specifically, his leadership responsibility includes the following:

A. Help the school psychologist, social worker, and health workers to develop a better understanding of their roles and functions on the part of students, teachers, and parents. The functions and roles of these pupil services specialists are poorly understood in many schools. The building administrator who is willing to help develop an understanding on the part of others about these specialists' contributions to the school will do much to increase the effectiveness of the pupil services program.

B. Work with pupil services specialists to increase their awareness of the unmet psychological, social, and health needs of students, and stimulate the development of greater vision about how these needs might be met.

C. Work with pupil services specialists, guidance counselors, and other faculty members to help these groups see how they can work together more cooperatively and productively.

D. Assist each of the pupil personnel specialists to evaluate his own effectiveness and the overall usefulness of the pupil services program.

ISSUES AND PROBLEMS

The administrator needs to be aware of four major problems or issues that are associated with the delivery of psychological, social, and health services to the school. These are (1) inaccessibility, (2) underutilization, (3) inadequate coordination, and (4) difficulty of supervision.[74]

INACCESSIBILITY

Because the psychologist, social worker, and nurse are usually part-time members of a school staff and have somewhat unpredictable work schedules, they are often not available to students, teachers, parents, or administrators when a problem arises. However, a person who is experiencing trouble frequently needs help immediately, or at least during the same day, and doesn't want to be told to wait until the next day or later in the week when the pupil services specialist is scheduled to arrive at the school. Although it is true that the pupil services specialist might be called to the school in response to a problem (if he can be located at another school or at his office in the central administration building), such calls are not generally made unless an extreme emergency exists. Consequently, in the eyes of many students, teachers, and administrators, the limited accessibility of part-time pupil services workers poses a restriction which severely hampers the effectiveness of the program.

The ideal solution to this problem would be the full-time assignment of a school psychologist, social worker, and nurse to each school. While an argument could be made that there is sufficient work for these specialists, even in a small school, financial considerations and a limited vision of their potential contribution often rule out this possibility. Certain steps, though, should be taken by an administrator to alleviate the inaccessibility problem.

1. The administrator should try to secure from each of the part-time pupil personnel specialists a commitment to an established work schedule at the school. In too many situations these specialists do not keep any scheduled office hours at a school and, as a result, others at the school do not know when their services are available.

There may, of course, be times when a pupil services specialist will not be able to keep his office hours because of an emergency at another school. But generally it should be possible for all of the specialists to identify at the beginning of the year the hours when they will be at each school to make their services available.

2. The administrator should ascertain from each of the part-time specialists what their work schedule will be when they are not at the school so that they can be reached if an emergency arises. This information may be difficult to obtain because the pupil services specialist may not have his work schedule well organized, or he may be apprehensive that the information may be used for monitoring his performance. However, in spite of any resistance the administrator may receive when he seeks this information, he has an obligation to find out where the pupil services specialists are most likely to be located when they are not in the school.

3. The administrator should communicate at the beginning of the year to students, parents, and teachers the work schedule of the part-time pupil services personnel at the school and indicate the procedures to follow in order to reach these specialists at other times. If people in the school are to utilize the services of the pupil personnel specialists, then the schedule of their availability should be made common knowledge. And it is the administrator's responsibility to see that this information is communicated.

UNDERUTILIZATION

Judging from observation and comments by administrators and teachers, the services of the psychologist, social worker, and perhaps the nurse, are not being utilized to the extent that one might hope and expect. Many problems are not referred to these specialists simply because students, teachers, and administrators do not perceive that the specialists can be of any help, or because they are not sure how to work with them. In other cases these specialists are loaded down with testing or routine tasks which do not capitalize on their creative contributions. Part of the problem lies in an inadequate understanding about the role of pupil services specialists and what services they can provide. The administrator can help ameliorate this problem by becoming better informed about the role of each of the pupil services specialists. But beyond that, he should take the initiative in helping the pupil services specialists to develop a better understanding of their role.

The administrator will probably also need to take a look at the school's referral procedures to these specialists. Referral procedures represent the main mechanism for utilizing the services of the pupil personnel specialists. So if the referral procedures are inadequate or unclear, utilization of the pupil personnel specialists will be limited. In essence, a school's referral procedures should include the following characteristics:

1. The types of problems which can be referred to either the psychologist, the social worker, or the nurse should be explicitly defined to the school staff.
2. The person who makes the referral should be asked to state briefly the nature of the problem and his perception of its causes.
3. The faculty should know when the pupil services specialist will be at the school to receive the referral.
4. After the referral is received, there should be a preliminary conference between the individual submitting the referral and the pupil services specialist to determine the best plan of action for coordinating efforts.
5. An initial progress report by the pupil services specialist should be made within a week to the person who submitted the referral; a more complete report should be provided by the end of the semester during which the referral was initiated.

A referral form which incorporates most of these characteristics is presented in the chapter on student discipline and attendance problems.

INADEQUATE COORDINATION

Inadequate coordination of services is frequently a problem when two or more specialists are working with the same client. This problem is particularly prevalent in the pupil services program. All too often the psychologist, the social worker, the nurse, and the guidance counselor work independently, each specialist "doing his thing," with little or no attempt to coordinate efforts in a unified approach.

Although each of the pupil services specialists can make an independent contribution to the school, their efforts would be significantly strengthened through a coordinated, collaborative approach to delivering pupil services.[75] Methods for developing such an approach could include organizing the various specialists into a pupil services team, appointing someone to coordinate the efforts of the team at the building level (perhaps the guidance director), establishing regular meetings of the team to focus on collaborative efforts and using the case conference procedure in working with students who have problems. This type of an approach is especially appropriate for diagnosing and working with special education students.

It should be noted that the pupil services specialists may not be inclined or able to develop the team approach without administrative assistance. They may be used to working independently and may not see the need to work together in a collaborative effort. Therefore, the administrator, himself, may need to take the initiative to organize the specialists into a pupil services team and appoint someone to lead that team.

It should be reemphasized that the administrator would do well to involve the pupil services specialists in developing the concept of the team and how it will function, if he desires their cooperation. The idea of the team should not be imposed on its members. They may harbor mixed feelings about its merits, having previously worked independently. Those pupil services specialists who work out of the central office and spend only part-time in a particular building may also resist the notion of someone at the building level heading their team. It would be advisable, in this regard, for the administrator to define the main responsibility of the team leader as that of coordination rather than supervision. If the right team leader is chosen, he should be able to exercise supervisory responsibilities informally.

Once the team concept has been accepted, the team organized, and a leader appointed, then the scheduling of periodic meetings becomes important. Finding a time when everyone can be at the meetings will be a difficult task for a team primarily composed of part-time specialists with different work schedules. However, despite the problems that may be involved, the administrator should insist that the team meet at least monthly and more often as the need arises. A team cannot function effectively unless it meets often enough to develop a common frame of reference and cooperative efforts in problem solving. A good way for the administrator to keep himself informed of the operation of the team is to request that its leader provide the administrator with a copy of the agenda and minutes for all team meetings. This procedure should result not only in the administrator's becoming better informed of the functioning of the pupil services team, but may also cause the team leader to become better organized if he knows that this kind of information is expected.

An important team activity which the administrator should try to promote on the part of the pupil services specialists is the case conference. The case conference can be described as a meeting at which the various pupil services specialists, with relevant others, try to understand the problems of a particular student by examining the perceptions and data which each can contribute about the student. By utilizing and pooling the information and expertise of all appropriate parties, an insight into the student's problem and a possible resolution for it may be obtained—perhaps not possible had only one of the specialists been working with the student independently.

Most pupil services specialists know about the case conference method, but because it requires someone to take the initiative to organize the conference, it is not used often enough. In order to promote its use, the administrator might assign his pupil services team leader the responsibility for organizing such meetings and then request that the team leader report to him each semester about how many case conferences were held, and with what success.

Since tradition, current practice, and the varied work schedules of the pupil services specialists all mitigate against a coordinated, collaborative team approach, it will take considerable vision, commitment, and human relations skills on the part of the administrator to achieve this goal. However, there is little doubt that such an approach is necessary for a totally effective pupil personnel program.

SUPERVISION DIFFICULTY

Perhaps the most perplexing problem for the school administrator in regard to the pupil services specialists is how best to supervise them. The problem is three-fold. First of all, each of the pupil services workers possesses specialized knowledge and skills which most administrators have not acquired and probably would have difficulty obtaining. The problems involved in trying to supervise personnel who perform tasks for which the supervisor himself is not proficient is readily apparent to all who have been in such a situation.

Secondly, the work performed by pupil services specialists is typically not visible to the administrator since it is frequently carried out in privacy. This aspect of the problem is further compounded by the part-time nature of the specialists' work schedules.

Thirdly, the pupil services specialists probably perceive their superior in the district office as their only "legitimate" supervisor and may resist efforts by anyone at the building level to supervise them.

This set of problems has tended in many schools to result in little or no building-level supervision of pupil services specialists. Of course, some supervision of these specialists is conducted by their superiors at the district level. But the latter individuals' concept of supervision may be limited, or they may be "spread too thin" by reason of the considerable number of people they have to supervise. Therefore, it would appear that if the pupil services specialists are to be supervised at the building level, the school administrator himself will have to design a system to accomplish the task.

Since the administrator is not an expert in pupil services and is involved with many other kinds of supervisory responsibilities, his best approach with the pupil services specialists may be to establish a system of "supervision by objectives." This system of supervision would include the following steps:

1. Each pupil services specialist would be asked at the beginning of every semester to identify the objectives he hoped to achieve while working at the school. Proposed objectives might be requested for the areas of students, teachers, parents, and collaborative efforts.

Objectives could be up-dated during the semester as a result of new developments.

2. At the end of each semester all pupil services specialists would be requested to prepare and submit a short report indicating the progress which had been made in achieving the previously proposed objectives, the evidence for such progress, and the problems which were encountered in trying to achieve the objectives.

3. After the report is read by the administrator, he would meet with each pupil services specialist to review its contents and discuss the need for improvement. The report could be a vehicle for initiating follow-up supervisory activities.

In light of the problems previously discussed, it is unlikely that an administrator can or should engage in direct supervision of pupil services specialists. But he should institute a system of supervision which would help the specialist to evaluate his own performance and, at the same time, keep the administrator better informed of that performance. The supervision by objectives approach to evaluation and supervision is such a system.

Review and Learning Activities

1. Define the primary purpose of the pupil personnel services program and the counseling and guidance program.
2. Identify the kinds of services that the counseling and guidance program can provide to those groups who are associated with the school. What is the role of the administrator in developing appropriate use of those services?
3. Examine the special education program operating in your school, and compare it with the type of program described in the text. How could the special education program in your school be improved?
4. Define the primary purpose of the pupil personnel services program and the counseling and guidance program.
5. Identify the kinds of services that the counseling and guidance program can provide to those groups who are associated with the school. What is the role of the administrator in developing appropriate use of those services?
6. How should the school administrator make use of the counselor role description developed by the American Personnel and Guidance Association?
7. In what ways can the administrator make a leadership and an administrative contribution to the counseling and guidance program?

8. What are three major issues or problems that are frequently associated with the counseling and guidance program? How can the administrator best prevent or ameliorate these problems?
9. In what ways can the administrator make a leadership and an administrative contribution to improving the psychological, social, and health services of the school?
10. Describe the major issues and problems that frequently are associated with the psychological, social, and health services of the school. How can the administrator best prevent or ameliorate these problems?

Notes

1. Maynard C. Reynolds and Jack W. Birch, *Teaching Exceptional Children in All America's Schools* (Reston, Va.: Council for Exceptional Children, 1977), p. v.

2. Education of the Handicapped Act, 20 U.S.C. sec 1401 et seq.

3. Martha M. McCarthy, "Public Law 94–142 and Its Implications for Nonhandicapped Students," in *Contemporary Legal Issues in Education,* ed. M. A. McGhehey (Topeka: National Organization on Legal Problems of Education, 1979), p. 138.

4. "Education of Handicapped Children: Implementation of Part B of the Education of the Handicapped Act, Rules and Regulations," *Federal Register* (August 23, 1977), pp. 42474–518.

5. United States Congress, The Education for All Handicapped Children Act, P. L. 94–142, Sec. 4, November 29, 1975.

6. Education of the Handicapped Act, 20 U.S.C. sec 1401 et. seq.

7. Alice H. Hayden and Eugene Edgar, "Developing Individualized Education Programs for Young Handicapped Children," *Teaching Exceptional Children* (Spring 1978): 67–70.

8. Jacqueline Reeves, "An In-Depth Study of the Mainstream Individual Education Plan in an Urban School District" (Ed.D. diss., University of Massachusetts, 1980).

9. *Federal Register,* 41 (252), December 30, 1976, p. 56986; Section 121 or 432, p. 56991.

10. Hayden and Edgar, "Developing Individualized Education Programs," p. 68.

11. Oversight Hearings, U.S. Senate Subcommittee on the Handicapped, July 1980 (Comments by Albert Shanker, A.F.T.).

12. Reported in *Education U.S.A.* (December 22, 1980), p. 137.

13. Reported in *Education U.S.A.* (May 1980), p. 285.

14. Ibid.

15. Lawrence Gaines, "Parental Satisfaction with Evaluation and Planning Team Conferences" (Ph.D. diss., University of California, 1981).

16. Don R. Barbacovi and Richard W. Clellard, *Public Law 94–142: Special Education in Transition* (Arlington, Va.: American Association of School Administrators, 1978). 34–38.

17. Research for Better Schools, *Exploring Issues in the Implementation of PL 94–142* (Philadelphia: Research for Better Schools, 1979). Also see *Schools and the Law of the Handicapped* (Washington, D.C.: National School Boards Association, 1980).

18. Reynolds and Birch, *Teaching Exceptional Children,* p. 4.

19. *Mainstreaming: Origins and Implications,* ed. Maynard *Reynolds* (Reston, Va.: Council for Exceptional Education, 1976), p. 43.

20. Thomas E. Linton and Kristen D. Jual, "Mainstreaming: Time for Reassessment," *Educational Leadership* (February 1980): 433–37.

21. Barry Guinagh, "The Social Integration of Handicapped Children," *The Kappan* (September 1980): 27–31.

22. Ganelda Sowers, *Observations of a Primary School Principal after Four Years of Experience with Mainstreaming.* An ERIC Report: Ed–153–342.

23. Maureen A. White et al., "Returning Students from Special to Regular Classes," *The Pointer* (Fall 1979): 97–104.

24. Robert Williams and Bob Algozzine, "Teachers' Attitudes toward Mainstreaming," *The Elementary School Journal* (November 1979): 63–67.

25. Barbara Larrivee and Linda Cook, "Mainstreaming: A Study of Variables Affecting Teacher Attitude," *The Journal of Special Education* (Fall 1979): 315–24.

26. E. Kavanagh, "A Classroom Teacher Looks at Mainstreaming," *The Elementary School Journal* (March 1977): 318–32.

27. Carl A. Sivage, "Implementing a Mandate: Public Law 94–142 in the Schools" (Ph.D. dissertation, University of Oregon, 1979).

28. Keith Berry, *Project Catalyst* (Special Training Project OEG–0–71–0387, U.S. Department of Health, Education and Welfare, Office of Education, 1975).

29. S. Torres, *Special Education Administrative Policies Manual* (Reston, Va.: Council for Exceptional Children, 1977).

30. New Jersey State Department of Education, *Guide for Evaluation of Special Education Programs and Related Pupil* Personnel Services. An ERIC Report: Ed–181–060.

31. Jeremy J. Lietz and Maxine Towle, "The Principal's Role in Special Education Services," *Educational Research Quarterly* (Fall 1980): 12–20.

32. Richard Rumble, "Leadership Vital for Successful Implementation of New Law," *NASSP Newsletter* (March 1979), p. 6. Also see David Coursen, *Administration of Mainstreaming* (Burlingame, Calif.: Assn. of California School Administrators, 1981.)

33. Susan Hasazi, *Maintaining Momentum: Implementing the Least Restrictive Environment Concept* (Reston, Va.: Council for Exceptional Children, 1980); Dean Corrigan and Kenneth Howey, eds., *Special Education in Transition, Concepts to Guide the Education of Experienced Teachers* (Reston, Va.: Council for Exceptional Education, 1980); and *Clarification of PL 94–142 for the Administrator* (Philadelphia: Research for Better Schools, 1980).

34. William Van Hoose et al., *Elementary School Guidance and Counseling: A Composite View* (Boston: Houghton Mifflin, 1973), pp. 3–4.

35. American School Counselor Association, *Proposed Statement of Policy for Secondary School Counselors* (Washington, D.C.: American School Counselor Assn., 1964), p. 4; also see Edwin L. Herr, *Guidance and Counseling in the Schools: The Past, Present, and Future* (Falls Church, Va.: American Personnel and Guidance Association, 1980).

36. Figure 15.1 was developed from an extraction and synthesis of statements contained in *Policy for Secondary School Counselors* (Washington, D.C.: American School Counselors Association, 1964); and *The Development and Management of School Guidance Programs* by Robert L. Gibson et al. (Dubuque, Iowa: Wm. C. Brown Company Publishers, 1973), pp. 73–81.

37. "The Role of the Secondary School Counselor," *School Counselor* (May 1974) 380–86.

38. For an example of the process one school utilized to redefine the role of the counselor, see Jane Bebb, *A Model High School Counseling Program*. An ERIC Report: Ed–061–546.

39. Figure 15.3 was adapted from the role description presented in "The Unique Role of the Elementary School Counselor," *Elementary School Guidance and Counseling* (March 1974): 221–23.

40. Julian Biggers," The Elementary School Counselor in Texas: A Nine-Year Follow-up," *Elementary School Guidance and Counseling* (October 1977): 15–19.

41. Van Hoose et al., *Elementary School Guidance and Counseling;* Donald Kent, *Fundamentals of Child Counseling* (Boston: Houghton Mifflin 1974), and Norman Gysbers and Earl J. Moore, *Improving Guidance Programs* (Englewood Cliffs: Prentice-Hall, 1981).

42. William R. Watts, "What Can One Expect from a School's Guidance Director?" *National Association of Secondary School Principals Bulletin* (October 1981): 34–37.

43. For an excellent monograph which describes the administrator's responsibilities in detail, see William A. Matthes and Robert Frank, *Strategies for Implementation of Guidance in the Elementary School*. An ERIC Report: Ed–048–602), pp. 187–216.

44. Based on a number of interviews with professors of counseling and guidance.

45. Bruce Shertzen et al., *Fundamentals of Counseling* (Boston: Houghton Mifflin, 1980), pp. 125–30. Also see recent issues of *Elementary School Guidance and Counseling* and *School Counselor.*

46. Ruth S. Armstrong, *The Teacher as a Counselor.* An ERIC Report: Ed–187–663.

47. Marguerite R. Carroll, "Standards for Guidance and Counseling Programs," *The School Counselor* (November 1980): 81–86.

48. Roger F. Aubrey, "Counselor Effectiveness: How Good Are We Really?" *Guidelines for Pupil Service* (Spring 1979): 9–15.

49. Helen L. Mamarchev, *Program Evaluation and Accountability.* An ERIC Report: Ed–181–391.

50. Richard Hughes and Richard Shofer, "The Role of the School Psychologist: Revisited," *The School Psychology Digest* (Winter 1977): 22–29.

51. Irwin Hyman, "Debate: Will the Real School Psychologist Please Stand Up? A Struggle of Jurisdictional Imperialism," *School Psychology Digest* (Spring 1979): 174–80.

52. Jan Hughes, "Consistency of Administrators' and Psychologists' Actual and Ideal Perceptions of School Psychologists' Activities," *Psychology in the Schools* (April 1979): 234–39. Also see Steven Landau and Kathryn Gerken, "Requiem for the Testing Role? The Perceptions of Administrators v. Teachers," *School Psychology Digest* (Spring 1979): 202–6.

53. Gilbert Trachtman, "The Clouded Crystal Ball: Is There a School Psychologist in Our Future?" *Psychology in the Schools* (July 1979): 378–87. Also see C. A. Maher, "School Psychologist and Special Education Program Evaluations," *Psychology in the Schools* (April 1979): 240–45.

54. Adapted from *Guidelines for Training Programs in School Psychology* (Washington, D.C.: National Association of School Psychologists, 1972), pp. 27–34; and Noel LaCayo et al., "Daily Activities of School Psychologists: A National Survey," *Psychology in the Schools* (April 1981): 184–90.

55. Charles A. Maker, "Guidelines for Planning and Evaluating School Psychology Services," *Journal of School Psychology* (Fall 1979): 203–12.

56. John C. Nebo, *Administration of School Social Work* (New York: National Association of Social Workers, 1960), p. 17.

57. Robert H. Mathewson, *Guidance Policies and Practice,* 3d ed. (New York Harper & Row, 1962), p. 197.

58. Based largely on *NASW Standards for Social Services in Schools,* Policy Statement #7 (Washington, D.C.: National Association of Social Workers, 1978).

59. Norma Radin, "Assessing the Effectiveness of School Social Workers," *Social Work* (March 1979): 132–37.

60. Warren Schaller, "Positioning School Health as a National Priority," *The Journal of School Health* (September 1977): 393–95.

61. Georgia MacDonough, "School Health, 1977," *Journal of School Health* (September 1977): 425–27.

62. Eileen White, "Are You Ready to Provide the Health Services Demanded of the Schools?" *American School Board Journal* (June 1981): 25–28.

63. A. I. Rothman and N. Byre, "Health Education for Children and Adolescents," *Review of Educational Research* (Spring 1981): 85–100.

64. Charles C. Wilson, *School Health Services* (Washington, D.C.: National Education Association and American Medical Association, 1964).

65. Based in large part on *Guidelines for the School Nurse in the School Health Program* (Kent, Ohio: American School Health Association, 1974). Also see Sandra Dale, "Putting Health into School Nursing," *Health Values* (January/February 1980): 15–19.

66. Godfrey Cronin and William Young, *400 Navels: The Future of School Health in America* (Bloomington, Ind.: Phi Delta Kappa, 1980).

67. Judith B. Igoe, "Changing Patterns in School Health and School Nursing," *Nursing Outlook* (August 1980): 486–92.

68. Michael Resnick et al., "Adolescent Perceptions of the School Nurse," *The Journal of School Health* (December 1980): 551–54.

69. Charlene Tosi, "Role of the School Nurse as Perceived by Administrators, Teachers and Students" (Unpublished research study, University of Wisconsin-Milwaukee, 1979).

70. White, "Are You Ready to Provide Health Services?"

71. Keith Howell and Jeanne Martin, "An Evaluation Model for School Health Services," *Journal of School Health* (September 1978): 433–40.

72. Ellen Thornberg, "A Conceptual Basis for Health Education in the Secondary Schools," *The High School Journal* (March 1981): 239–42.

73. Susan Gilman, "Planning School Health Services in the Community," *Health Values* (January/February 1980): 38–42.

74. These problems or issues were identified in a review of the literature and in a supplementary interview survey of principals, teachers, and pupil personnel service specialists.

75. For an example of this approach, see Jeffrey Zdrale, *Pupil Personnel Committee Meetings in Our Schools.* An ERIC Report: Ed–177–446.

16

ADMINISTRATION OF THE STUDENT ACTIVITIES PROGRAM

The student activities program, also referred to as the "extracurricular" or "cocurricular" program* has been an accepted part of American education for many years.[1] Initially introduced in only a few schools, in an attempt to provide for the recreational and athletic interests and needs of students, it is now an integral component of the total educational program in the vast majority of schools in the United States.[†]

While the overall responsibility for administering the student activities program is sometimes delegated to a student activities director, in most schools the building administrator is assigned this responsibility directly, and certainly is ultimately accountable. Therefore, it is extremely important for the school administrator to develop a comprehensive understanding of the various facets of the activities program so that it can be operated with efficiency and effectiveness. Included in this understanding should be knowledge about the objectives, scope, and organizational dimensions of the program, as well as its major problems. The administrator should also be knowledgeable about criteria and a plan for evaluating the program, because without regular assessment, improvement of the program is likely to be limited.

---

*The term, "student activities" will be used in this chapter, rather than the other terms, because in practice it seems to be the one which authorities prefer.

†Although some people may feel that the student activities program is or should be confined to the secondary school, the program has been recommended for the elementary school for some time. See Harry C. McKown, *Activities in the Elementary School* (New York: McGraw-Hill Book Co., Inc., 1938).

PURPOSE, OBJECTIVES AND SCOPE

The primary purpose of the student activities program has been and continues to be that of meeting those school-related interests and needs of students which are not met—at least not to a sufficient degree—by the curricular program of the school.[2] The objectives of the student activities program may vary somewhat from school to school, depending on local conditions, but they should be logically related to the objectives of the overall educational program. Numerous statements of student activities objectives have been proposed during the years, and an examination of these statements would suggest that the objectives of the program should be to help *all* students[3]

1. learn how to use their leisure time more wisely
2. increase and use constructively whatever unique talents and skills they possess
3. develop new avocational and recreational interests and skills
4. develop a more positive attitude toward the value of avocational and recreational activities
5. increase their knowledge of and skill in functioning as a leader and/or as a member of a group
6. develop a more realistic and positive attitude toward themselves and others
7. develop a more positive attitude toward school, as a result of participation in the student activities program.

The key word in the statements is the word "all." The student activities program should be for *all* students, not just the more active and talented students; and the objectives of the program should reflect this priority.[4] While it may not be possible in some situations for all students to participate in the activities program, total participation should remain the objective to which a school aspires. A school that aims at a higher objective than may seem attainable is ultimately likely to accomplish more than the one with more "practical" goals.[5]

It should also be noted that the objectives listed above are stated so that the emphasis is on *helping* the students, not on just providing an opportunity for them. A school should be responsible for *more* than just providing an opportunity for students; it should be responsible for helping students *reach* whatever objectives that opportunity is supposed to engender. Those objectives should include the development of certain student attitudes, as well as knowledge and skills. Perhaps the most important objectives of a school's student activities program should be the development of a more positive attitude on the part of the student toward himself, others, avocational and recreational activities, and toward school in general. These attitudinal objectives will undoubtedly be difficult for the school to achieve but, if attained, are likely to show great carry-over value into the student's adult life.

Student Government and Publications	Performance Groups	Clubs and Organizations	Intramurals Boys' and Girls'	Athletics Boys' and Girls'
Student Council	Dramatics	Chess Club	Bowling	Basketball
Student Newspaper	Instrumental	Photography Club	Golf	Swimming
Student Yearbook	Vocal	Literary Club	Ping Pong	Tennis
Others	Debate	French Club	Others	Others
	Others	Others		

Figure 16.1. Major Activities Included In a Comprehensive Student Activities Program.*

To achieve the knowledge, skill, and attitudinal objectives of the student activities program, the school will need to provide a comprehensive range of student activities which includes the kinds of offerings presented in figure 16.1.

The activities identified under each major category in figure 16.1 are illustrative of possible types of student activities.[6] Of course, different schools offer different kinds of activities, depending on the needs and interests of the students, as well as other conditions. However, two factors which are extremely important are the *vision* and *commitment* of the administration and staff to a comprehensive student activities program. Unless the administration and staff of a school have the vision to develop comprehensive objectives for the total student activities program and the commitment to invest their own time and energy to achieve those objectives, the program will probably be limited in scope and in its impact on the student body.

The main purpose of a student activities program should be to meet students' interests and needs. Without the vision and commitment of the administration and the staff, this purpose cannot be achieved. It should be emphasized that the administrator is the one who is responsible for generating that vision and commitment on the part of the staff (if they do not already exist).

ORGANIZATIONAL DIMENSIONS

The emphasis thus far has been on the objectives and scope of the student activities program and on the vision and commitment of the administration and staff. However, if the program is to succeed, it must also be well organized. Good organization will not insure the success of a program, but without it a program is likely to flounder.

*The extent of these activities will differ according to whether the school is elementary or secondary.

In organizing the student activities program the administrator should consider the following principles.

1. **Each activity, as well as the total program, should have well-defined, written objectives.** The importance of establishing objectives for the *total* student activities program has already been noted. It is equally important for the administrator to work with teachers and students to define the objectives of each activity *within* the program. Activities without objectives lack direction and meaning, and are difficult to evaluate in terms of their effectiveness.

In developing the objectives for each activity in the student activities program, the administrator should make sure that they are stated in the form of outcomes, i.e., increased knowledge, skill, attitude, or participation, rather than in terms of the number of meetings of the activity.[7] The important thing is not how many meetings of an activity occur, but what the activity contributes in terms of increased student participation, knowledge, skill, or attitude change.

2. **Each activity should be directed by a well-qualified, interested advisor.** It is recognized that this is easier said than achieved, and that it may be stating an unattainable ideal for certain activities. However, obtaining well-qualified, interested advisers for the various components of the student activities program should be the objective to which the administrator is committed. She should do everything within her power to achieve, or at least be working toward, that objective.[8]

To a large extent, the adviser of an activity is the key to its success. A competent, interested adviser can provide leadership and spark to a student activity; a poorly-qualified, apathetic adviser can ruin it. Even a moderately-qualified and interested adviser may not be able to provide the leadership necessary for an activity to blossom and grow.[9] It is conceded that there are problems in securing competent, interested advisers, and this problem will be addressed later in the chapter.

3. **There should be a written role-description for each adviser, as well as a developmental in-service program to upgrade competencies.** Each adviser to a student activity should have a written role description specifying the qualifications and responsibilities of the position, and the individuals and groups to whom the adviser reports.[10] Such a role description will provide direction to the adviser and can serve as a basis for evaluating the effectiveness of her work. In the absence of this kind of a role description the advisers will have to create their own definition of their responsibilities, and an evaluation of their effectiveness by the administrator will become difficult.

A developmental in-service program to upgrade advisers' competencies is essential, particularly if the administrator has been less than completely successful in recruiting well-qualified advisers.[11] It seems peculiar that in-service education is provided for almost every other type of need, but apparently it is assumed that student activities' advisers are all well-qualified and are never in need of updating their skills.

A developmental in-service program for student activities' advisers should include learning opportunities for improving their skill in planning and organizing activities, decision making, communication, leadership, group dynamics and program evaluation.[12] The in-service program should also regularly provide opportunities for all the advisers to discuss problems and ideas, and to learn from each other.

The student activities' advisers also can benefit from the experiences and recommendations of experts outside of the school who are working in this field. Membership and participation in state and national associations of student activities' advisers are probably the best ways of acquiring this assistance. The administrator should assume the responsibility of encouraging and stimulating this kind of professional growth.

4. **There should be written role descriptions for the student officers of each activity, and an in-service program should be offered to help them improve their competencies.** In many schools the student activities program seems to be based on the implicit assumption that the students who are elected or appointed to office will already be familiar with all aspects of their job, and that they need no training to help them carry out their responsibilities effectively. Though there may be exceptions, in general this assumption is unwarranted.

Students are seldom familiar with the various responsibilities of the office to which they are elected or appointed, and they usually need on-the-job training. They should be provided with role descriptions which identify the qualifications and responsibilities of their positions, and with an in-service program which will help them improve their leadership skills.* Specifically, they need help in improving their knowledge and skills in planning and organizing activities, decision making, communication, leadership, group dynamics, and program evaluation.[13] They also need to participate in state and national student activities' associations, and the school should see that the professional literature which is available from these associations is accessible to the students.†

5. **The various organizational meetings that are held as part of the student activities program should be well planned.** With the possible exception of performance groups, intramurals, and athletics, there are many organizational meetings held during the year by various student organizations. Since students and advisers are usually busy, these meetings are frequently not well planned.

---

*An example of the type of role description needed for *all* student officers can be found in *Profiles of Student Council Officers* (Washington, D.C.: The National Association of Secondary School Pricipals).

†For example, the Office of Student Activities of the National Association of Secondary School Principals conducts workshops and publishes material for students involved in the student activities program of their school. The school administrator should see to it that representative students have an opportunity to attend these workshops and to receive materials published by the NASSP Office of Student Activities.

However, if the meetings of an organization are to be successful, then thought and time must be devoted to planning them. This includes a planning session between the adviser and the officers prior to the meeting, and a written agenda sent to the members of the organization before the meeting so that thought can be given to what will be discussed. Written minutes of the main points discussed and the actions taken during each meeting should also be sent to all members of the organization so that continuity between meetings is increased. The minutes will maintain a public record during the year (and from year to year) on what the student organization is accomplishing. These are basic management procedures which to some may seem like "red tape" but, if constructively applied, should increase the productivity of student organizations' meetings.

6. **A complete, written description of the total student activities program should be disseminated to students and other appropriate parties at the beginning of each school year.** The student activities program is for the students, and if they are to participate wisely, they need as much information as possible about the various aspects of the program. Perhaps the best approach for a school would be to publish a student activities handbook. Included in the handbook should be a description of each student group's purposes, objectives, types of activities, qualifications for membership and holding office, as well as the adviser's name, and who should be contacted about membership, or for more information.[14]

This type of handbook could be very helpful to students in choosing their participation in the student activities program, and could provide a valuable source of information to the student advisers, the administration, and the rest of the professional staff. It should be noted that the handbook would need to be updated periodically. This process would take time, and the cost of issuing the booklet at the beginning of each year may not be a minor expense. However, if the school is committed to informing its students about all aspects of the student activities program, ways will be found to resolve these problems.

7. **There should be a director of student activities and a student/teacher advisory council for the total program.** In too many schools the student activities program is composed of numerous groups and organizations, each seemingly going its separate way with very little overall program planning, coordination, or direction. As a result, there are conflicts in philosophy, use of facilities, membership criteria, and allocation of funds.

What is needed is a student activities director to take charge of the overall program, with an advisory group that can work with this individual in establishing policy for the total program and resolving significant disputes between student groups. The director should be an administrator or a teacher with released time, and at least one-third of her time should be devoted to carrying out leadership responsibilities.[15]

The activities director should chair the student activities advisory council and be responsible for calling meetings, stimulating discussion, and problem solving. The membership of the council should include representation from students, as well as from the activities advisors, and should function in an advisory capacity with the director. Through this kind of an organizational structure, better direction and coordination for the overall student activities program should result.

8. **The total student activities program and each of the component activities should be periodically evaluated to ascertain effectiveness and to identify areas which are in need of improvement.**[16] The student activities program is like any other program offered by the school in that it needs periodic evaluation. Ideally, the program should be evaluated yearly, but this may not always be possible. At the very minimum, however, the program and each of its constituent parts should receive a thorough evaluation every two or three years. For, as Frederick has observed, "It sometimes happens that particular activities are repeated year after year, not because of a genuine interest and need, but because we have always had them. The form lingers on after the spark of life has died."[17]

The school administrator (or the student activities director) is responsible for making sure that the student activities program is evaluated periodically, although she may not be the one who actually conducts the evaluation. In fact, the wise administrator will, in the evaluation of a program, involve advisers and student leaders who participate in that program. While it might become appropriate to call upon outside consultants in conducting the evaluation, the school administrator is the one who should initiate and bring to completion the periodic evaluation of the student activities program. If evaluation is neglected, it is the administrator who should be held accountable.

A number of excellent statements of recommended criteria are available to the administrator in evaluating a school's activities program.[18] Based on an examination of these statements, it would appear that the administrator should seek answers to the following questions in assessing the program:

a. Is the overall program and each specific activity meeting its objectives in terms of improving student knowledge, skills, attitudes and/or values? What is the evidence that objectives are being met?
b. What is the extent of student participation in the total program and in each activity? Are a majority of the students participating in the program? What is the evidence in regard to the degree of student participation?

c. What *kinds* of students are participating in the program, and what is the nature of their participation? Do the non-college-bound students participate to the same degree as the college-bound students, and if not, why not?[19] Do the girls participate to the same extent as the boys, and if not, why not? Do some students participate *too much* in the activities program?

d. Is the activities program well balanced and comprehensive, or do some activities dominate? Are there any student interests and needs that are not adequately met by the program?

e. Is the total program and each of the activities well organized? (Specific aspects of organization were discussed previously.)

f. Are all aspects of the program supported sufficiently in terms of availability of facilities, funds, school time, personnel, and recognition? Or are some activities disproportionately supported?

These are questions that administrators should be asking periodically about the student activities program, and which they should be able to answer if they are fully meeting their responsibilities for evaluating the program. The methods of evaluating the program will vary from situation to situation but could include student questionnaires, interviews, analysis of participation data, and observation of organizational factors.[20] If administrators do not feel competent in evaluation methodology, they should seek outside help, but they should not use their own lack of competency to avoid evaluating the program.

9. **Each of the student groups in the student activities program should be required to prepare an end-of-the-year summary status report to be disseminated to all appropriate parties.** If the student activities program is to be administered properly, information will be needed relative to the accomplishments of each student group. The general question that needs to be answered is, "What has happened to each student group during the year?" An end-of-the-year summary status report prepared by each student group would help answer that question.

The report need not be long (2–4 pages) and could be prepared cooperatively by the adviser to the group and the student officers. It should contain information on the progress, accomplishments, and major unresolved issues and problems evident at the end of the year. Copies of the report should go to the chief administrator of the school, the director of the activities program, and all members of the student group, for their information and reactions. Such a report would be valuable, not only in keeping people informed about the accomplishments and problems of each student group, but in pointing up the need for improvement or a new direction for a group to take. It would also give the administrator the kind of information she needs in order to administer the overall student activities program effectively.

MAJOR PROBLEMS OF THE STUDENT ACTIVITIES PROGRAM

It is difficult to generalize about the student activities program because of the variations among schools, but it is safe to say that in most districts the program has not operated without problems.[21] Some of the problems have been associated with a specific activity, while others have been rather pervasive throughout the program. In the latter category, the following three problems have persisted through the years: (1) Difficulty in obtaining well-qualified, interested advisers; (2) Apathy on the part of many students—overinvolvement on the part of a few students, and (3) Problems of financial support.

PROBLEMS IN THE RECRUITING OF ADVISERS

It was pointed out earlier that the adviser is a significant key to the success of any student activity. A well-qualified, interested adviser can resuscitate a dying activity and can help a mediocre one to reach greater heights of achievement. A poorly-qualified and barely interested adviser, on the other hand, will be of little help to a student group and may cause it to deteriorate. Despite the fact that most, if not all administrators recognize the need for obtaining well-qualified, interested advisers, many administrators experience difficulty in securing them.[22] This is particularly true for nonathletic student activities. What seems to be the nature of the problem?

Part of the difficulty in obtaining well-qualified, interested advisers is a result of the recent expansion of girls' athletics and other related activities along with, paradoxically, a reduction of resources due to declining enrollments and/or inflation.[23] While this type of an expansion of student activities was needed and, it could be argued, desirable, the result has been an even greater need for activity advisers with fewer potentially available. Complicating this situation is an apparent growing disinterest on the part of a number of teachers, particularly the more experienced ones, in supervising student activities. There has also been an increase in the number of collective bargaining agreements that limit an administrator's prerogatives in assigning the supervision of a student activity to a teacher.[24]

Another contributing factor is that in many schools certain advisers are paid for their sponsorship of a student activity, while advisers of other activities in the same schools receive no reimbursement for their time and effort. For example, advisers to special interest clubs and organizations are frequently unpaid, while coaches of athletic and other performing teams and the advisers to publications receive compensation. Although financial reimbursement should not be the sole motivating force in causing a capable individual to seek the advisorship of a student group, it is nevertheless an important factor, and the administrator should be realistic about it. Potentially well-qualified individuals who might be interested in sponsoring a student club or organization are likely to think twice before volunteering their time and effort for little or no compensation when they see other advisers receiving remuneration for their contribution to an activity.

Compounding the problem of compensation is the fact that in too many schools the salary differentiation among advisers seems to be based more on the status of the activity than on the extent of actual responsibilities. Coaches of athletic teams, for instance, seem to be paid at a higher rate than advisers for intramural sports; advisers to public performance groups such as band or dramatics seem to be paid more than advisers to nonpublic performing groups, such as debate. A forward-looking compensation plan for minimizing these problems has been developed by the Antioch, Illinois School District and is recommended for the reader's consideration.[25]

While there are additional steps that an administrator could take to secure more qualified and interested advisers for the student activities program (including the provision of better facilities and more funding and recognition for some of the groups), removal of the inequities in the advisers' salary structure would represent an important action toward improving the situation.

STUDENT APATHY VS. OVERINVOLVEMENT

A paradoxical situation which has plagued the student activities program over the years is the problem of student apathy vs. overinvolvement. In many schools a large percentage of the student body does not participate in the student activities program, and if one were to eliminate participation in athletics from the analysis, it might even be said that in most schools the majority of students do not participate in the activities program.

School administrators and student activities advisers usually attribute a lack of participation on the part of students to "student apathy," which may provide a label for the situation, but fails to explain the cause(s). The question that the administrator and the staff need to investigate is, "*Why* is there student apathy?" or, "What is there about our program which fails to attract students in larger numbers?" Underlying reasons may include lack of information about the activities, poor scheduling, low status of certain activities, limited activities, restrictive admission requirements for membership in a group, (e.g., "C" grade point average) and an inadequate understanding of the values to be obtained from participating in the student activities program.[26]

In investigating possible causes of student apathy or lack of participation, an administrator needs to concentrate on *correctable* causes rather than uncorrectable causes. Examples of the latter would be (1) outside interests such as television or the pool hall, (2) after-school jobs, (3) disinterest in certain activities, and (4) apathetic students. All of these reasons have been given at one time or another as alleged causes of student nonparticipation in school activities. The problem is that these factors are, for the most part, uncorrectable because they are not under the direct influence of the school, or they represent symptoms and labels rather than causes. Rather than focusing on or emphasizing these kinds of explanations, the administrator needs to examine those causes which are *correctable,* such as (1) unawareness by students of a particular activity, (2) inability to see how an activity might be beneficial or interesting, (3) lack of awareness or inability to envision how they could play a role in a particular activity, (4) uncertainty about how students can get started participating in an activity, (5) conflicts caused by scheduling an activity at a certain time of the day, and (6) lackluster leadership by the activity's adviser.

Perhaps the place to begin in analyzing reasons for student apathy is with the nature of the activities program itself. Such an examination might reveal, as Graham has observed, that "those young people who stand to benefit most from social experience in the activity program have the fewest opportunities to participate, whereas those students who have the least to learn from an activity program have the most opportunity to participate."[27]

Although student apathy is a much greater problem than student overinvolvement, the latter should also be of concern to administrators.[28] Overinvolvement manifests itself in two ways: (1) certain students get involved in too many activities, reducing the effectiveness of their participation, and (2) in some schools or during a particular period of time, a few students may capture many of the top leadership offices in the activities program, thereby reducing opportunities for leadership growth by other students. Most administrators and student activities advisers seem to be aware of these problems and some have taken steps to remedy the situation by restricting the number of offices which can be held by any one individual.

The problem of student overinvolvement in student activities is not an easy one to resolve.[29] Even the question of what constitutes "too much" participation is not readily determined. Obviously, the situation will vary, depending on the student and her circumstances.

Part of the problem is that most schools don't even have a mechanism for monitoring the deleterious effect on the student of excessive participation in the activities program, with the possible exception of grade reports. Though grade reports might be useful as one indicator of the problem, grades can be affected by many variables. Perhaps the best steps a school can take are to keep better centralized records of the number of activities in which each student is participating, and to ask advisers, counselors, and teachers to be especially observant of those students who are involved in several activities during a particular nine-week period of time.

PROBLEMS OF FINANCIAL SUPPORT

Although the public seems to feel that student activities are an important part of the total educational experience,[30] the student activities program is often one of the first programs reduced when budget cuts need to be made. One possible reason why this is true is that the student activities program is still perceived by many as an *extra*curricular program rather than an integral part of a student's education. Complicating the situation are the rising costs of student activities due to an expansion of girls' athletic opportunities, and across-the-board increases in inflation. Because of these factors a number of school districts have had to eliminate certain activities and have increased student fees to support other activities.

The problem of financing student activities is not likely to go away, and it is not a problem for which there are easy solutions. However, a major step in the right direction would be for the school to do a better job of demonstrating the value of student activities and keeping the public informed about the benefits. While this step will not eliminate the problem of financing student activities, it will certainly help, and it needs to be begun *before* a financial crisis, not during one. Recommended guidelines for administering a student activity budget are presented in the chapter on "Budget and Plant Management."

MAJOR PROBLEMS ASSOCIATED WITH SEVERAL SPECIFIC STUDENT ACTIVITY PROGRAMS

THE ATHLETIC PROGRAM

The athletic program has probably been the most successful of all the student activities, at least in terms of the number of students participating and the degree of esteem awarded it by the school and the community. It has undoubtedly maintained some students in school who would have dropped out without this interest,[31] and the program has made it possible for certain individuals to obtain scholarships to college, and other kinds of recognition. It has also been a source of school spirit for many students, and a means of entertainment for a large number of communities. However, the program has periodically been criticized and has had to face some serious problems.[32]

One problem that has continued to confront the athletic program is the matter of poor sportsmanship on the part of players and spectators.[33] Poor sportsmanship by players usually manifests itself when they argue with the officials or become involved in fights with the opponents on the playing field. Poor sportsmanship on the part of spectators includes booing the officials, throwing articles onto the playing field, or fighting among the fans during or after a game. While the extent of the problem varies from school to school and, sometimes, from sport to sport, such behavior represents a serious problem that should be of concern to the administrator and the school staff.

The approach to unruly behavior on the part of athletes and the student body should not be dependent solely on greater control or more security, but should also include a planned program of developing better student and player sportsmanship.[34] The objectives of the program should be to teach good, sportsmanlike attitudes and behavior to athletes and to the rest of the student body. A beginning step for achieving this goal would be for a school to develop a sportsmanship code similar to the one presented in figure 16.2.

The code in figure 16.2 and other aspects of the sportsmanship program should be implemented in physical education classes, assembly programs, after-school practices, and through the example of coaches and other adults in the

1. *Show respect for the opponent at all times.*
   The opponent should be treated as a guest; greeted cordially on arriving; given the best accommodations; and accorded the tolerance, honesty, and generosity which all human beings deserve. Good sportsmanship is the Golden Rule in action.
2. *Show respect for the officials.*
   The officials should be recognized as impartial arbitrators who are trained to do their job and who can be expected to do it to the best of their ability. Good sportsmanship implies the willingness to accept and abide by the decisions of the officials.
3. *Know, understand, and appreciate the rules of the contest.*
   A familiarity with the current rules of the game and the recognition of their necessity for a fair contest are essential. Good sportsmanship suggests the importance of conforming to the spirit as well as the letter of the rules.
4. *Maintain self-control at all times.*
   A prerequisite of good sportsmanship requires one to understand his own bias or prejudice and to have the ability to recognize that rational behavior is more important than the desire to win. A proper perspective must be maintained if the potential educational values of athletic competition are to be realized. Good sportsmanship is concerned with the behavior of all involved in the game.
5. *Recognize and appreciate skill in performance regardless of affiliation.*
   Applause for an opponent's good performance is a demonstration of generosity and goodwill that should not be looked upon as treason. The ability to recognize quality in performance and the willingness to acknowledge it without regard to team membership is one of the most highly commendable gestures of good sportsmanship. With the fundamentals of sportsmanship as the points of departure, specific responsibilities and expected modes of behavior can be defined.

Used with permission of the American Association for Health, Physical Education and Recreation Publications.

Figure 16.2. Fundamentals of
Sportsmanship[35]

school. The school administrator can "show the way" through her own example at games, and by making clear to the coaches and the student body the importance which is attached to good sportsmanlike behavior. In the final analysis the administrator and the staff need to view the success of the athletic program not just in terms of how many games are won or lost, but of equal importance, in the amount of progress made by the athletes and the student body in learning better sportsmanship.[36]

A second major problem with which the athletics program has been confronted is the introduction of girls' sports. Traditionally the athletic program has involved mainly boys, although girls have sometimes participated in certain sports, such as basketball. Since the passage of Title IX of the USOE, however, girls' athletics have expanded greatly, putting tremendous pressure on school budgets and facilities. The challenge for the school administrator is how to accommodate girls' as well as boys' athletics in existing physical facilities (which, in many localities, are already in short supply for boys' athletics and the intramural program), and within an athletic budget which has ballooned because of inflation and which is under attack by critics as being too large. This is not an unresolvable problem, and many schools have done a good job of accommodating girls' athletics through tighter scheduling and budgeting. Nevertheless, it is not an easy problem with which to grapple.

While probably most schools have done a good job in implementing Title IX, administrators are encouraged to perform periodic audits to ascertain the extent to which the regulations are being met and to which improvement is still needed. (A full description of such an audit is provided in the reference at the end of the chapter.[37]) Examples of questions asked during such an audit are (1) How many teams are available for girls, as compared with the number of teams for boys? (2) What kinds of uniforms and equipment are girls' teams using, compared with boys' teams? (3) Do girls' teams receive equal and desirable time on the practice field and gym? and (4) Do girls' teams receive the same kind of publicity as boys' teams?[38] The goal of administrative efforts in this area should be to make sure that the athletic needs of boys *and* girls are being *equally* met.

THE STUDENT COUNCIL

Most forward looking elementary and secondary schools provide an opportunity for students to participate in decisions about school affairs, usually through the mechanism of a group called the student council. It is generally comprised of student representatives who have been elected to their positions by the school's student population, and an adviser who is usually appointed by the principal. The council may meet during the school day, but frequently tends to hold its meetings after school. Meetings may consist of hearing reports from various subcommittees, passing motions recommending certain actions to the administration, and raising problems or questions which require discussion and possible further investigation.

Although the specific objectives of the student council are not the same in all schools, the following are recommended:

1. To promote the general welfare of the school.
2. To foster, promote and develop democracy as a way of life.
3. To teach home, school, and community citizenship.
4. To provide school experiences closely related to life experiences.
5. To provide learning opportunities through the solution of problems which are of interest and concern to students.
6. To provide training and experience in representative democracy.
7. To contribute to the total educational growth of boys and girls.[39]

There is little doubt that a student council can become an important and valuable force in the school. However, for it to be successful, certain problems and crises must be averted or resolved. One of the major problems or issues which many student councils and administrators encounter is how much authority should be granted to the student council. That is to say, should the student council be an advisory group with authority only to make recommendations, or should it be given decision-making authority? This question has troubled schools for a number of years, but it became a fundamental issue with the advent of student activism in the late 1960s and still surfaces periodically in many schools.

Actually, there should be no confusion in an administrator's mind about the answer to the question of the extent of the student council's authority. The building administrator is the one who is legally accountable to the school board for administering the school. Therefore, the student council can legitimately be given only the authority to offer recommendations in regard to how the school should be run. It is true that an administrator can delegate certain decision-making responsibilities to the student council, but final decision-making authority cannot be delegated to such a group unless the school board provides for a departure of this kind from normal procedure.[40]

An initial step that an administrator should take to avert the authority issue from coming to a head is to develop an understanding on the part of the entire student council and its adviser of the legal requirements and restrictions of the administrator's position, and the main function of the council in light of these factors.[41] This should be done in such a way that the importance of the recommending role of the council is stressed while at the same time it is being indicated that the council does not have a final decision-making role. Administrators should recognize, however, that regardless of the importance they attribute to the recommending role of the council, their reactions to its recommendations will communicate more than any statements they may make about the council's usefulness.

If the student council is to believe it plays an important role in the school, the administrator will need to exercise extreme caution in rejecting its recommendations. Of course, this does not mean that recommendations which are clearly illegal or not in the best interest of the school must be accepted, although discerning which recommendations to accept and which to reject because of the latter criterion will take considerable administrative judgment and wisdom. Administrators should realize that they will probably have to compromise sometimes, and in certain instances take risks in accepting recommendations which they believe to be impractical. At times however, the only way the students will appreciate the judgment of the administrator is if they are permitted to make their own mistakes.

The scope of many student council programs is another major problem. If one examines the general purposes of the student council set forth earlier, a rather broad mandate for taking action to improve the total environment of the school seems to be implied. However, if one looks at the actual activities of many student councils, the main thrust appears to be limited to fundraising, organizing and promoting social affairs, and occasionally coalescing to promote some particular school issue, such as a new smoking lounge.[42] What seems to be lacking on the part of these student councils—and, perhaps, on the part of the school administration as well—is a deep understanding of the potential purposes and scope of the student council in a school and the kind of program that would accomplish these purposes.

Administrators should assume leadership responsibility for helping to resolve this problem, if it occurs. They should, in their own minds, be clear about the purposes of the student council, and they should make equally sure that the student council and its adviser are also clear about the purposes of the organization. Then they should work with the adviser, who in turn should work with the members of the council to develop a program each year that will accomplish those purposes.

While it is probably true that some administrators prefer a student council that confines its program to organizing social events, the administrator who is truly interested in capitalizing on and encouraging the interests and skills of the students will help them to develop a more far-reaching program. Such a program should have as its main purpose the improvement of the educational and social environment of the school and the community. Included in this program might be the following kinds of activities:

1. Conducting remedial classes in a disadvantaged neighborhood
2. Refurbishing a community center for youth and adults
3. Setting up a city-suburb exchange program
4. Meeting with the principal to recommend new courses for the school's curriculum

5. Arranging for an after-school series of school lectures on "Black Militancy and White Power"
6. Developing a form for evaluating class instruction
7. Organizing a student-led seminar on contemporary issues to be offered in summer school, without grades or credits
8. Setting up a corps of student tutors to help slow learners in the school
9. Developing student-written individualized learning materials
10. Meeting with community leaders to plan for more effective use of community resources
11. Meeting with parents to explore school problems as parents perceive them
12. Making a proposal to the school board for the hiring of teacher aides.

Participation in these and similar activities by the student council should help it to achieve its general purposes, make a significant contribution to the school, and ameliorate the two-pronged problem of student apathy and criticism of the council that "it never does anything worthwhile."[44] Such a program should attract student participation, provide valuable learning experiences for students, and greatly improve the image of the student council in the school. Given a full understanding of its purposes and the nature of its authority in the school, as well as continuous encouragement and assistance by the administration and the staff, the student council can become an important force for school and community improvement.

THE STUDENT NEWSPAPER

Every elementary and secondary school should sponsor a student newspaper as a part of its activities program. A student newspaper can provide valuable learning experiences for those students who serve on its staff, and can act as a source of information about student perceptions, student functions, and school and community activities and problems. The newspaper's basic purpose, in addition to providing journalistic learning experiences for students, is to inform the student body and other school personnel about events in the school and community which may be of interest to students and to the professional staff.[45]

In spite of its potential and frequently realized worth, the student newspaper has been a source of considerable controversy in recent years.[46] Editorials attacking the administration and faculty and criticizing certain school practices and programs have appeared in some student newspapers. The use of obscene language, and pictures of questionable taste in some student newspapers have also caused problems for school administrators and newspaper advisers. And, finally, the initiation of an "underground" student newspaper in a number of schools has continued to trouble some administrators.

Administrators have tended to react to these problems in several different ways. Some administrators have tried to ignore such problems in the hope that they would eventually disappear. Their success has been mixed. Some administrators have responded by initiating procedures designed to censor in advance any undesirable (from the administrator's point of view) language, pictures, editorials, or articles.[47] These administrators have also tried to stop the distribution of student underground papers in school, and, in some instances, away from the school grounds. Other administrators have developed policies and procedures that have been designed to avoid or minimize problems.[48]

While it is difficult to assess the effectiveness of these efforts, it is worth noting that students have achieved considerable success in their court challenges of unnecessary administrative censorship and restriction of their publications. Although the case law is still in somewhat of a flux, the courts have generally upheld students' rights to publish material, with the following exceptions:[49]

1. *Libelous Material*—that which may result in defamation of character, such as a statement concerning a person which may unnecessarily expose him to hatred or contempt, or which could have a tendency to injure him professionally.
2. *Obscene and profane material.* Generally the courts have been more restrictive as to the language and pictorial representations from younger students than those from college students.
3. Material which would tend to *incite to disruption* the educational process of the school.
4. Material which would *clearly endanger the health and safety* of the students, teachers, and administrators.
5. Material which advocates destruction of school property.

Material that is critical of school officials[50] or discusses controversial issues[51] generally may not be legally restricted unless it meets one or more of these five criteria. Therefore, it appears that if an administrator or journalism adviser is going to attempt to censor some aspect of a student publication, that decision should be based on one or more of these standards.* It should be emphasized that any school requirement of administrative review of student material prior to actual publication and distribution must communicate in *advance* to students the *specific* and *understandable* criteria that will be used in the review, must include a *relatively* short time period for the review, and

---

*Administrators who are interested in keeping abreast of student thinking in this area should request to be placed on the mailing list of the Student Press Law Center, 1033 30th Street N.W., Washington, D.C. 20007.

must provide students with an opportunity to appeal an adverse decision.[52] While administrators can regulate the time, place, and manner of distribution within the school of a student publication, these regulations must be promulgated in advance of publication, must be clear as to their intent, and must be reasonable in their implementation.[53]

An approach employed by some schools which seems to be successful in resolving publication problems is to establish a publications advisory committee.[54] Such committees are generally composed of the advisers for the newspaper and yearbook, the student editors of each of these publications, one or more representatives from the faculty and from the administration, and sometimes a representative from the local newspaper. The committee membership should be broadly based in order to capitalize on the capabilities and insights of a number of people who can contribute valuable ideas for the improvement of school publications.

The main purposes of the advisory committee are to develop policies and procedures concerning student publications in the school, to evaluate various aspects of the publications program, and to act as a hearing board for people who have complaints about school publications. The committee's actions are advisory to the principal of the school, who may or may not be a member of the committee. The primary advantage of such a committee is that it serves as a focal point for the fostering of a continuous examination and upgrading of student publications, while providing a less emotional and more thorough process of resolving complaints and controversy surrounding student publications.

That such a committee is needed is made clear in a study by Broussard and Blackman who found that 80 percent of the schools they surveyed had no school publication committee, and that 74 percent of the school districts had no formal statement of policies covering the operation of student publications.[55]

Although there is little doubt that guidelines and committees can help to promote good journalism in schools—and to avoid controversy—, the administrator should recognize that all controversy is not necessarily bad, and in some instances it may represent a desirable learning experience for students. Perhaps this perspective has been best expressed by the Civil Liberties Union, which stated in its landmark pamphlet, *Academic Freedom in the Secondary School:*

> The student press should be considered a learning device. Its pages should not be looked upon as an official image of the school, always required to present a polished appearance to the extramural world. Learning effectively proceeds through trial and error, and as much or more may be sometimes gained from reactions to a poor article or a tasteless publication as from the traditional pieces, groomed carefully for external inspection.[56]

A FINAL PERSPECTIVE

The quality of a student activities program is primarily dependent on the vision and commitment of those people who are associated with the program. Any student activities program will, over a period of time, encounter certain problems. However, given proper leadership—particularly by the student officers, faculty advisers, and the principal of the school—these problems can be resolved, and the student activities program can make an important contribution to meeting school goals and student needs.

Review and Learning Activities

1. What are the purpose, objectives, and scope of the student activities program?
2. Cite two characteristics of the administration and the staff which are most important to the success of the student activities program. Why are these two aspects important?
3. What principles should the administrator follow in organizing or evaluating the organization of the student activities program?
4. Indicate the importance of continuous evaluation of the student activities program. What kinds of questions should the administrator be asking?
5. Define the major problems of the student activities program. What factors seem to contribute to the problems, and how can the administrator prevent or ameliorate the problems?
6. Discuss the major problems associated with the following student activities, the factors contributing to these problems, and ways that the administrator can prevent or ameliorate them.
   a. The athletic program
   b. The student council
   c. The student newspaper

Notes

1. For a description of the early evolution of the student activities program, see E. D. Grizzell, "Evolution of Student Activities in the Secondary School," *Educational Outlook* (November 1926): 19–31.
2. Robert W. Frederick, *The Third Curriculum* (New York: Appleton-Century Crofts, 1958), p. 58.
3. For examples of other statements of objectives, see Sharon Wegner, *"Extracurricular Activities Are an Essential Factor in the Student's Self-Concept, Socialization, and Future Success.* An ERIC Report: Ed–196–171.

4. Most studies have found that a majority of the students do not participate in school activities if one excludes the athletic program. See, for example, Robert C. Serow, "The High School Extracurriculum: Cui Bono?" *NASSP Bulletin* (April 1979): 90–94.

5. For an excellent and still relevant statement of the rationale supporting this position, see Ellsworth Thompkins, "Extra-Class Activities for All Pupils," *Federal Security Agency* (1950), pp. 1–3.

6. See J. B. Grady, "Middle School Activities: More Meaningful with More," *NASSP Bulletin* (December 1979): 74–78.

7. David Mosrie, "Well Planned Activity Program Benefits Middle School," *NASSP Bulletin* (November 1979): 114–15.

8. For an example of how to do this, see Douglas D. Christensen, *Planning and Evaluating Student Activity Programs* (Reston, Va.: National Association of Secondary School Principals, 1978).

9. William Neal and Jack Hoggartt, "Congratulations! You're the Adviser!" *Business Education Forum* (May 1979): 3–4. This article contains useful suggestions for the *new* adviser to an activity.

10. *A Handbook for the Student Activity Adviser* (Reston, Va: National Association of Secondary School Principals, 1979).

11. James Vornberg, "In-Service Training for Student Activity Sponsors," *Catalyst for Change* (Spring 1979): 6–7.

12. A useful booklet that discusses some of these needed competencies is authored by Russell D. Robinson, *Group Dynamics for Student Activities* (Reston, Va.: National Association of Secondary School Principals, 1977).

13. Sandy Young, *Developing a Student Leadership Class* (Reston, Va.: National Association of Secondary School Principals, 1977).

14. An excellent example of this type of handbook is the one developed by Princeton High School, Cincinnati, Ohio.

15. Russell Stokes, Jr., "What Hat Do You Wear as an A. P.?" *Catalyst for Change* (Spring 1979): 8–12; also see Dennis De Neve, "A Study of the Status and Role of Activities Directors in California High Schools" (Ed. D. diss., University of Southern California, 1981).

16. James A. Vornberg, "Auditing the Student Activity Program," *NASSP Bulletin* (April 1980): 83–88.

17. Frederick, *The Third Curriculum,* p. 121.

18. *Evaluation Criteria* (Falls Church, Va.: National Study of School Evaluation, 1980). Also see, *Auditing the Student Activity Program* (Reston, Va.: National Association of Secondary School Principals, 1980).

19. Joseph S. Yarworth and William Gauthier, "Relationship of Student Self Concept and Selected Personal Variables to Participation in Student Activities," *Journal of Educational Psychology* (June 1978): 335–44.

20. For examples of various evaluating methods, see Christensen, *Planning and Evaluating Student Activity Programs,* pp. 18–23.

21. Ronald E. Gholson, "Research Notes," *The Kappan* (September 1979): 67.

22. Ibid.

23. Vera J. Gordon, *Extra Curricular Programs–How to Survive in an Era of Austerity.* An ERIC Report: Ed–136–371.

24. Based on comments and individual reports from building administrators.

25. A. E. Blecke, "Compensating Teachers for Extracurricular Activities," *NASSP Bulletin* (October 1980): 78–86.

26. Gholson, "Research Notes."

27. Grace Graham, "Do School Activity Programs Build Better Intergroup Relations?" *School Activities* (February 1967): 6–7. Also, for an extensive review of various approaches for getting students involved, see *Models for Student Participation* (Reston, Va.: National Association of Secondary School Principals, 1977).

28. Gholson, "Research Notes."

29. For some still valid suggestions, see Neil F. Williams, "Encouraging and Limiting Participation in School Activities," *School Activities* (November 1964): 19–21.

30. George H. Gallup, "The 10th Annual Gallup Poll of the Public's Attitudes toward the Public Schools," *The Kappan* (September 1978): 40.

31. For a review of research on this point, see Charles W. Peck, "Interscholastic Athletics and Delinquent Behavior: Appraisal or Applause," *Sociology of Education* (October 1979): 238–43. Also see pp. 243–48 of the same issue.

32. A. E. Blecke, "High School Athletics—Some Straight Talk for Principals," *NASSP Bulletin* (November 1979): 119–21. Also see for due process problems: Donald F. Uerling, "High School Athletics and Due Process; Notice of Eligibility Rules," *Nebraska Law Review* (March 1978): 877–92.

33. Ellen Morrow, "Latitude of Sportsmanship Behavior Deemed Acceptable of Spectators of Basketball Games" (Ph.D. diss., Texas Women's University, 1981).

34. See Harold Meyer, *Crowd Control for High School Athletics* (Washington, D.C.: National Council of Secondary School Athletic Directors, 1970), pp. 9–14.

35. Ibid., pp. 10–11.

36. Everett Abney and Judith Green, "Senior High Athletes—Winners or Losers?" *National Association of Secondary School Principals Bulletin* (November 1981): 93–96. Also see Glen Potter et al., "Making Interscholastic Athletics a Winner," *National Association of Secondary School Principals Bulletin* (September 1981): 50–55.

37. Rita Bornstein, "The Principal's Role in Title IX Compliance," *NASSP Bulletin* (April 1979): 40–45.

38. Ibid., p. 44.

39. Based on a reading of Gerald M. Van Pool, *Improving Your Student Council* (Reston, Va.: National Association of Secondary School Principals, 1977).

40. James E. Ferguson, *Student Council Activity Resource Book* (Reston, Va.: National Association of Secondary School Principals, 1980), pp. 1, 3.

41. Van Pool, *Improving Your Student Council.*, pp. 1–14.

42. Based on an examination of agendas of various student councils.

43. Linda Mathes, "Student Activities—Who Needs Them? The Community, That's Who!" *Catalyst for Change* (Spring 1979): 16–17.

44. For information on additional Student Council projects, see James E. Ferguson, *Student Council Activity Resource Book,* pp. 8–39.

45. Any administrator who wishes to develop a better understanding of the purposes and role of the student newspaper and its adviser should subscribe to the journal, *Quill and Scroll.*

46. Patricia A. Shea, "The School Newspaper: A Challenge or Aggravation?" *NASSP Bulletin* (October 1981): 111–14.

47. E. Joseph Broussard and C. Robert Blackman, "Principals Think They Can Do What Congress Cannot—Abridge Freedom of the High School Press," *Quill and Scroll* (October/ November 1980): 15–17.

48. For example, see Thomas J. Flygare, "School Officials May Halt Distribution of Student Newspaper with 'Headshop' Advertisement," *The Kappan* (October 1980): 139.

49. For an excellent discussion of the court cases supporting these restrictions, see E. Edmond Reutter, "Student Discipline: Selected Substantive Issues," in *The School Principal and the Law,* ed. Ralph D. Stern (Topeka, Kans.: National Organization on Legal Problems of Education, 1978), pp. 71–87.

50. Sullivan v. Houston Independent School District, 307 Supp. 1328 (S.D. Tex., 1969).

51. Gambino v. Fairfax County Sch Bd., 429 F. Supp. 731 (E.D. Va., 1977).

52. Quarterman v. Byrd, 453 F. 2nd 54 (4th Cir. 1971). Also see Flygare, "School Officials May Halt Student Newspaper."

53. Grayned v. City of Rockford, 408 U.S. 104 (1972).

54. For further discussion on establishing and operating such a committee, see D. A. Staver, "High School Freedom of the Press," *NASSP Bulletin* (January 1979): 48–50.

55. E. Joseph Broussard and C. Robert Blackman, "Principals Think They Can Do What Congress Cannot."

56. American Civil Liberties Union, *Academic Freedom in the Secondary School* (New York: American Civil Liberties Union, 1968), p. 12.

PART

5

THE SCHOOL AND THE COMMUNITY

17

SCHOOL-COMMUNITY RELATIONS: COMMUNITY STRUCTURE AND INVOLVEMENT

A school is not an independent or isolated entity; it operates in a social context, an important element of which is the local community.[1] The school draws its students from the community and depends on the community for much of its financial and social support. The community attempts to exercise its power over the school primarily through the school board, which has authority to establish policies and approve financial expenditures. The community also tries to exert its influence on the school informally through parents' and special interests groups and individual contacts.[2] Because of these factors every administrator needs to develop a good understanding of and competency in building and maintaining effective school-community relations.

UNDERSTANDING THE COMMUNITY

THE SCHOOL ADMINISTRATOR'S COMMUNITY

The school community can be thought of as encompassing the total geographical area and population of a school district, or as comprised of the more immediate area and population within an individual school's boundaries. While a school administrator needs to understand the total community, he needs particularly to understand and develop good relationships with the local community that the school serves.[3] It is the local community that is sending its children to the school, and it is the people in this community with whom the administrator is likely to have the greatest contact. They are also the ones with whom the administrator needs to communicate the most, since their opinions about the school are likely to be most influential. And although school busing has stretched the meaning of the term "local community" for many schools and made the task of understanding the community more difficult, the task is no less important because of this factor. School busing will, however, require greater effort on the part of the school administrator and the staff to develop a good understanding of an expanded school community.

While many administrators may believe that they already possess a good understanding of the community, it would appear that, for the most part, this understanding is based on irregular, random contacts with parents and other members of the public, which occur through occasional telephone calls, parents' meetings, "open houses," and personal correspondence. Although these contacts are potentially valuable, they all too often tend to be casual, superficial, and unrepresentative in nature. They do not in most cases lead to a good understanding of the many dimensions of the community.[4]

Also contributing to an insufficient understanding of the community by many administrators is their personal residency in a community other than the one served by their school. While the author is not asserting that it is necessary for every administrator to live in the community his school services, such residence would make it easier to become more knowledgeable about the community, and it would certainly increase his accessibility. At the minimum, if an administrator chooses to live in another community than that served by his school, it would seem that he should have a systematic plan (such as the one described later) which he is implementing in order to gain knowledge about the community. This kind of a plan is recommended for all administrators, but it seems especially important for those who do not live in the community that their school serves.

The most important step that an administrator can take initially to develop good school-community relations is to study and better understand the school's local community.[5] A community is a very complex unit, but there are four elements to which the administrator should pay especially close attention. Those elements are presented in figure 17.1.

In trying to develop a better understanding of the local community served by the school, the administrator first needs to study the kinds of people who reside in that community.[6] Examples of questions which might guide his study include the following: What is the socioeconomic background of the people? What percentage are professional, in contrast to blue-collar workers? How many are on welfare? In how many instances are both parents working outside the home? Who are the informal leaders of the community? What percentage of the parents move each year? What percentage of the parents represent minority groups? What percentage of the people in the local community are parents/nonparents? In how many instances are both parents working outside the home? What percentage of families are headed by a single parent, and in how many of these situations is the parent employed?

Factor 1: People	Factor 2: Places Where People Meet	Factor 3: Methods of Communication People Use	Factor 4: Expectations and Attitudes
Examples	*Examples*	*Examples*	*Examples*
A. *Individuals:* Parents/nonparents Professional/laboring class Welfare clients Working mothers/ fathers Informal leaders B. *Groups:* Parents' organizations Social and fraternal groups Informal groups (coffees, bowling teams)	Homes Churches Supermarkets Cocktail parties; taverns Coffees Organizational Meetings	Face-to-Face Telephone Letter Newsletter Radio TV	Attitudes about children Expectations for the school Attitudes towards school effectiveness Interest in and availability for working with the school

Figure 17.1 Major Community Elements

Obtaining answers to the latter three questions is very important for developing a better understanding of the community. There is evidence from the national scene to indicate that the demographics of many local communities are changing. For example, due to a declining birth rate, the ratio of parents to nonparents has been significantly altered, and in many communities the parents of students are in the minority.[7] This change suggests that it will be important for schools to aim their community relations programs at nonparents as well as parents. The characteristics of the American family are also changing. While traditionally conceptualized as including two parents, one of whom was employed (usually the male), the situation now according to Bureau of Labor Statistics is that in most two-parent families, both parents have outside jobs, and there has been a dramatic increase in the number of one-parent families (and usually this parent is employed).[8] That the latter change in family structure can cause problems was revealed in a study, jointly sponsored by the National Association of Elementary School Principals and the Institute for the Development of Educational Activities, which found that, as a group, children in one-parent families presented more discipline problems, were more frequently tardy and absent, and achieved less in school than did their classmates.[9] (It should be noted that the design and findings of this study have been criticized by some reviewers.[10])

Although it is not inevitable or necessarily likely that these demographic changes will produce problems for the school, they do underscore the importance of the administrator's developing and periodically updating his understanding of the community through the use of a school census and supplementary school surveys. (More will be said later about responding to demographic changes.)

A school administrator also needs to become knowledgeable about the different groups and organizations to which the people in the local community belong. The particular groups and organizations about which an administrator needs specific information are those which have a special interest in education and in the school. These would be the groups or organizations who discuss education from time to time in their meetings and who may even have a subcommittee for educational matters. (For an understanding of the power structure of a community, an excellent source is *The Structure of Community Power,* edited by Michael Aiken and Paul Mott, and published by Random House.) Figure 17.2 identifies groups and organizations about which an administrator should be knowledgeable.

At the minimum, an administrator should try to meet the leaders of the major groups and organizations in the local community the school serves and learn their points of view about education and about the school.[11] The administrator should be well enough acquainted with each group so that he can communicate easily with its leaders in a time of crisis and can utilize whatever expertise the members possess for improving the school program.

In addition to studying the types of individuals and the major organizations in the community which the school serves, the administrator needs to become more aware of the different places where people in the community meet, and of the various methods of communication they use in discussing education and the school. These meeting places—whether they be churches, local barber shops, or coffee-klatches—are a part of the informal structure of the community. By familiarizing himself with the informal structure of a community, the administrator will be in a better position to ascertain what people are thinking and saying about the school, and he can also use the informal structure for communicating information about the school.[12]

The objective of an administrator in regard to the ways people receive information about the school is to be aware of these channels so that he can capitalize on them when *he* tries to communicate information about the school or needs to find out what people are thinking. For example, if people in a community pay more attention to news about the school that they hear on radio or television than information they receive from the school newsletter or the city newspaper, the administrator should be aware of this reality and take it into consideration in his communication practices. An understanding of the ways in which the people in a community receive information about the

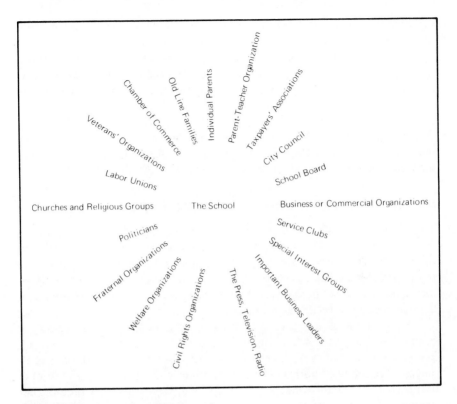

Figure 17.2. Community Groups and
Organizations with a Special Interest
in Education

school is essential for an administrator who wants to develop effective communication with the community.

The fourth and perhaps most important element of the community about which a school administrator needs to become knowledgeable is the educational expectations and attitudes of its people. In most situations the community is not, of course, a homogeneous entity, and the administrator is unlikely to discover that everyone holds identical educational expectations and attitudes. Most communities comprise diverse people and groups who are likely to hold somewhat different expectations and attitudes about education and the schools.

Regardless of this diversity, however, the school administrator should try to understand the expectations and attitudes of the people in the community, for community expectations constitute standards by which the people in the community evaluate the performance of the school. The current attitude of people in the community toward students and the school reflects citizens' feelings about how effectively the school is meeting community expectations. Therefore, the school administrator needs to become knowledgeable about both the educational expectations and the attitudes of people in the community. As a result of such knowledge, he will be in a better position to recognize the direction that the community would like to see education take in the school, and citizens' feelings about how successful the school has been in meeting their expectations. (For a useful manual on how to survey community attitudes, write Phi Delta Kappa, Bloomington, IN. Also see Bowles and Fruth for a description of indepth interviewing techniques.[13])

MAJOR PROBLEMS IN SCHOOL-COMMUNITY RELATIONS

The administrator should understand that school-community relations have never been completely trouble-free. From the very beginning of education in this country there have been periodic differences and conflicts between the school and the community. In most communities these differences and conflicts have usually not been severe, but in some periods school-community conflict has seemed to be rather widespread.

Although the basic causes of problems in school-community relations are complex and may vary according to the nature of a community and a school, it would appear that two general factors are at work: (1) professional challenges to community norms, and (2) community challenges to professional norms. The first factor concerns those efforts by educators to change the educational program—efforts which in many instances have conflicted with community norms. Integration, sex education, and open education are only a few of the innovations that educators have tried to introduce which have, in one way or another, challenged the norm structure of many communities. When a community feels that its schools are going beyond or against community expectations and norms, it tends to react negatively, thereby causing difficulties in school-community relations.

A second general factor which has caused problems in school-community relations is intensified efforts by many communities to ascertain and evaluate what is going on in the schools. These efforts have tended to challenge the professional norms of many educators, whose motto seems to be, "Trust us, we're the experts."

Increasing numbers of parents and other community citizens, however, have indicated that they no longer accept the word of educators that "everything is going all right." These community people want to see the *results* of the school's effectiveness, and in many cases, they want to be personally involved in the decision-making processes of the school. An administrator should not assume that all of the people of a community possess these attitudes. But he should recognize that there is a growing trend in this country toward greater expectations on the part of many citizens to become involved in school decision making and for the school to be held accountable for its educational effectiveness.*

These problems in school-community relations will not be easily ameliorated. It would appear, however, that more effective communication between the school and the community, and greater community involvement, are necessary prerequisites. The remainder of this chapter will focus on ways in which the school administrator might more effectively involve the members of the community in the school; the following chapter will discuss school communication and the school's public relations program.

COMMUNITY INVOLVEMENT**

Many observers believe that the key to improving school-community relations is greater parental and public involvement in school affairs. DeVault, for example, has stated, "Parent involvement is an essential ingredient of the effective American school."[15] And Thomas believes that "Parents will become equal partners with professionals to decide what schools can and cannot do."[16] He goes on to say, "The truth of the matter is that without parent participation and support, schools cannot succeed."[17] While few educators would argue that parent and public involvement is unimportant, there continues to be considerable confusion and uncertainty among school administrators about the concept of involvement and how to utilize it to improve school/community relations. The confusion and uncertainty seem to revolve around three basic questions: (1) What are the purposes of involvement? (2) What types of involvement are possible? and (3) What are the problems associated with parental and community involvement in the schools, and how can these problems be overcome? The following sections will take up each of these questions and attempt to discuss and analyze the ideas and issues involved.

*A group that recently organized for this purpose is the National Committee for Citizens in Education, which has its national headquarters in Columbia, Md., and local chapters in many communities. Another group is the Institute for Responsive Education, which has national headquarters in Boston, Mass.

**It should be noted that some authorities on school/community relations make a distinction between community involvement and participation, with the former stressing supportive activities while the latter emphasizes school decision-making.[14] However, an analysis of the rationale behind this distinction suggests that the difference may be a matter of semantics more than anything else, and that the key factors are the form and substance that involvement takes rather than the existence of a separate concept called participation. In the following sections the terms involvement and participation are used synonymously.

PURPOSES OF INVOLVEMENT

Many administrators have experienced difficulty in understanding the concept of involvement, and in implementing a program of parental and community involvement in the schools, because they were not clear about the purposes which such involvement should achieve. Involvement has been presented so positively in the educational literature that it has frequently seemed to be the main objective of school-community relations rather than a means of improving education.

Although involving parents and the public in the schools represents an important task, the school administrator should understand that in the final analysis, involvement should be viewed primarily as a means rather than an end. Any involvement of others—regardless of the form it takes—should ultimately result in improving education, if the involvement is to be judged worthwhile.[18]

While the reasons for involving parents and other groups in school affairs will vary somewhat, depending on the nature of the involvement, there appear to be three main objectives that advocates of involvement hope to achieve:

1. Through involvement, parents and other citizens will become more knowledgeable about school affairs, and as a result, they will become
   a. better informed about what students are learning in school
   b. more understanding of the problems that the school faces
   c. more supportive of efforts by the school to improve the educational program
2. Through participation by parents and other citizens, the school will receive ideas, expertise, and human resources, all of which will improve school decision-making and the educational program of the school.
3. Through involvement, parents and other citizens will be in a much better position to evaluate the school fairly and effectively.

Perhaps Don Davies made the best summary statement of these objectives when he maintained that, "Meaningful citizen involvement can strengthen confidence in and commitment to the school, while making schools more responsible to citizens' diverse concerns."[19] However, as he later emphasized, ". . . Parent involvement means more than cookie sales. It means helping to make the policies and carry them out."[20]

It should be pointed out that in the case of all three objectives, several assumptions are made. First of all, it is assumed that parents and other citizens need to become more knowledgeable about school affairs, that involvement of some kind is the best means of their becoming more knowledgeable, and that greater knowledge will result in more understanding and support on their part. (A Gallup Poll has found that those individuals having some in- volvement with the school hold more favorable attitudes toward the school than those who had no involvement.[21])

The second objective assumes that parents and other citizens possess ideas, expertise, or skills which would be helpful to the school, and that they are willing to make these contributions to the school. The third objective assumes that parents and other citizens need or want to evaluate the school, and that they will do a more accurate job of evaluating the school if they are in some way directly involved in what the school is doing. And finally, all of the ob- jectives assume a reasonable degree of cooperation and commitment on the part of the administrator, the faculty, and the community to the concept of involving parents and other citizens in the school.

The assumptions underlying the objectives of involvement may or may not be tenable, depending on the community and the school. Whether or not they are tenable will, of course, have a bearing on the success of any program of community involvement in the school.

BARRIERS

Unfortunately, in many situations there seems to be a large gap between the rhetoric of emphasizing community involvement and the reality of limited op- portunity for parents and other members of the community to become mean- ingfully involved in school affairs.[22] As Davies has observed, "While the rhetoric of participation is almost universally accepted now and few voices are ever publicly raised against it, the rhetoric is rarely put into practice with com- mitment."[23]

Although the reasons for the large gap between the rhetoric and the real- ity of community involvement in the schools are complex, it seems clear from analyzing the available evidence that before increased citizen involvement in the schools (and the improvement of other aspects of school/community re- lations discussed later) will occur, certain barriers or obstacles may have to be overcome. For example, the faculty, or particular segments of the school staff, may resist a proposed program of increased community involvement in the schools. These faculty members may take the position that parents are better left alone, are not capable of making a useful contribution to the school, and might only interfere in areas that are best handled by the professionals of the school. The motivation for such a stance against citizen involvement in the school tends to be complicated, but for many teachers who hold such views, citizen involvement represents an unconscious or direct threat to teach- ers' status as professionals, their job security, or their personal convenience.[24] Of course, it is entirely possible that the resistance may be based primarily on a lack of understanding on the part of the teachers about the purposes and advantages of increased citizen involvement. In any regard, it would seem essential for an administrator to work with the faculty to develop a better understanding of the objectives and values of increased community involvement *prior* to initiating any major community involvement activities in the school. Guidelines for accomplishing this are discussed by Safran.[25]

A second major barrier or obstacle to increased community involvement and improved school/community relations may be the community itself. Changing community demographics may be causing a problem for the school in this regard. In most two-parent families, both parents are employed, and in single-parent families the parent is likely to be employed or tied down with child care. As a result, parents are frequently no longer available for meetings during the school day, and may be too tired to go to meetings in the evening. Some of these difficulties can be alleviated through more creative scheduling of meetings and by moving the location of the meetings from the school out into the community. However, involvement in school/community activities will not be easy for many members of the community. Also, despite all the emphasis placed on increasing community involvement in the schools, the administrator may encounter considerable disinterest on the part of parents and other members of the community in becoming more involved with the schools. Confronted with a perceived lack of interest, the administrator who does not possess a deep commitment to involving the community could become easily discouraged and could give up on increasing community involvement, later rationalizing that parents and others really didn't want to get involved. However, the administrator who holds a strong commitment toward increased community involvement will not become easily discouraged, but will persist and in most cases will eventually diagnose the causes of the disinterest and take steps to ameliorate the problem. (The problem of community disinterest and apathy is addressed more fully later in the chapter.)

A lack of incentives and rewards is another barrier to increasing community involvement and improving other aspects of school/community relations.[26] It would appear that in many situations there are few incentives or rewards offered by the school district to a principal who is favorably disposed toward increasing community involvement. Such an individual may not be discouraged from pursuing this objective, but he is not likely to receive much encouragement or recognition either. Perhaps even more important, there does not seem to be any negative consequences imposed by most districts' bureaucracies or school boards if a principal exerts little effort in improving school/community relations, provided that parent and citizen complaints to the district office do not significantly increase. It would appear that in many school districts, as long as parents are quiet, community relations are taken for granted. It seems clear that unless the school board and the district administration have an explicit policy emphasizing the importance of community relations and provide appropriate incentives and rewards to promote school/

community relations (as well as imposing negative sanctions for those administrators who drag their feet), a comprehensive program of school/community relations is unlikely to flourish.

Finally, it takes time, a high degree of competency, and commitment on the part of the administrator in order to increase community involvement and improve other aspects of school/community relations. Although there is little doubt that the first two factors are important, the key seems to be *commitment*.[27] If an administrator believes strongly enough in the value of community involvement in the schools and feels it is essential (not just desirable), then in most cases he will find the time and develop the capabilities to increase meaningful community involvement.

If, on the other hand, he lacks a strong conviction about the importance of community involvement, he is likely to feel that its objectives are not necessary, possible, or worthwhile pursuing. The administrator's own attitude is a very significant factor.

TYPES OF COMMUNITY INVOLVEMENT

Up to this point, we have discussed the concept of involvement, without identifying various ways in which a school might involve parents and other local citizens. Although there are many ways to involve the community in a school, the six examples identified in figure 17.3 are illustrative of community involvement.

Each of the types of community involvement identified in figure 17.3 can potentially benefit both the school and the community. The school can gain from the contributions made by community members through their involvement; local citizens can derive satisfaction from their involvement. In order

---

1. Member of an organization such as PTA

2. Committee or council member to study problems, offer recommendations, or make decisions.

3. Parent education

4. Evaluation of some aspect of the school through responding to questionnaire or by observation

5. Resource person for classes; helper in media center, etc.

6. User of school facilities.

Figure 17.3. Types of Community Involvement

that the school administrator may better understand the nature of the types of involvement listed in figure 17.3, an introductory description of each is provided below.

Parents' Organizations

Probably the most typical type of formal parental involvement is membership in a school-related parents' organization, the best known of which is the Parent-Teacher Association (PTA). The PTA was organized in 1897 and now has local chapters in every state. Its overall objectives are to

> (1) promote the welfare of children and youth in home, school, church and community, (2) raise the standards of home life, (3) secure adequate laws for the care and protection of children and youth, (4) bring into closer relation the home and the school, that parents and teachers may cooperate intelligently in the education of children and youth, and (5) develop between educators and the general public such united efforts as will secure for all children and youth the highest advantages in physical, mental, and spiritual education.[28]

Until recently, the PTA was considered by many to be little more than a coffee-and-cookies group who met several times a year to hear speeches and to discuss buying additional equipment for the school. As Koerner observed, "It [PTA] is chiefly useful to the administrator for raising money for special projects and persuading parents who are interested enough to attend meetings that the local schools are in the front ranks of American education."[29]

This situation has changed to some extent, however, and many PTA's have become very active in trying to bring about improvement in the education of children. This change was exemplified, according to a recent president of the National Congress of Parents and Teachers, ". . . when we dropped a section of our bylaws that stated that local PTA units should '. . . cooperate with the schools to support the improvement of education in ways that will not interfere with the administration of the schools, and shall not seek to control their problems,' and substituted, 'PTA shall work with the schools to provide quality education for all children and youth and shall seek to participate in the decision-making process establishing school policy, recognizing that the legal authority to make decisions has been delegated by the people to Boards of Education.' "[30] The new statement makes clear that, while the PTA recognizes the legal right of the School Board to make policy decisions, the members of the PTA expect to participate in the process leading up to such decisions. The new motto of a number of PTA units is "PTA—Parents Taking Action!"

The PTA has also broadened its membership base in recent years. While traditionally composed primarily of parents (couples) and teachers, it now seeks to include single parents, senior citizens, and particularly, students.[31] Many groups have made a decided effort to include students, even changing their name to PTSA or Parent-Teacher-Student Association. It should be noted, however, that in some cases parents have organized parent *unions,* which have tended to exclude administrators, teachers, students, and other nonparents, perhaps because of prior poor experiences.[32]

Whether a parents' group refers to itself as PTA, PTSA, or simply PA (Parents' Association), it would seem that parental involvement in some type of an organization associated with the school is a desirable goal for the school administrator. Through such involvement, parents can develop a better understanding of what goes on in the school and can make a useful contribution to improving education. While the performance record of parents' organizations is mixed, and they can be an irritant to a school administrator if they overextend their authority, they can play a valuable role in helping the school and parents to improve educational opportunities for children. It is true that in a number of situations, especially at the high school level, the PTA has gone out of existence and most parents seem apathetic. However, there are still many strong PTA's and PTSA's at the secondary school level, and a number of these are further described by Gross[33] and Sparling.[34] (Successful PTA's at the elementary school level are also described by Horn[35] and Goens and Schulze.[36])

The key to a successful parent organization seems to be the principal, his vision and his commitment. As one principal emphasized, "The activities of the PTA are limited only by the principal's imagination and insight."[37] This observation was confirmed by one PTA president who noted, "The PTA in a school is just as good as the principal wants it to be."[38] Although both of these statements may somewhat oversimplify the task of initiating and sustaining a successful PTA, it seems clear that such a task is not likely to be accomplished without considerable vision and commitment by the school principal.

Committee or Council Member

Initiation of a school committee or a school advisory council is another type of community involvement which an administrator should consider. For example, parents or other members of the community could be asked to serve on advisory committees to improve the homework policy, extracurricular activities, school-community communication, or the development of school goals. Many parents and other members of the community possess resources and expertise which could be of assistance to the school, and their utilization on advisory committees is a good way to capitalize on this source of expertise and resources.

The establishment of a parent advisory council for the school should also be considered. Parent or community councils at the individual school level have been mandated in a number of states and have been initiated on a voluntary basis in other localities.[39] The basic assumptions behind the introduction of these advisory councils seem to be that the councils would act to improve the channels of communication between the public and the schools, and that students would learn more as a result of increased parental interaction with the school.[40] The council's main objectives seem to be[41]

1. Facilitating school communication with parents and community
2. Assisting in providing support to parents, teachers, students, and community members who are involved in school programs
3. Participating in the decision-making process
4. Informing and advising school staff regarding community conditions, aspirations, and goals.

Council activities seem to vary. In one state study it was discovered that 8 percent of the councils participated in faculty selection and evaluation; 29 percent recommended changes in the curriculum and assisted in textbook selection; 34 percent assisted the school with desegregation, zoning, and the development of comprehensive plans; 34 percent helped identify budgeting needs and assisted in the establishing of spending priorities; 45 percent recommended ways of responding to student problems, such as vandalism; 60 percent advised the school in regard to community conditions, aspirations and goals; and 73 percent of the councils participated in the development of the Annual Report of School Progress to parents. The latter activity involved the councils in conducting surveys to ascertain the attitudes of parents, students and teachers toward different aspects of the school's program.[42]

While the potential of school advisory councils seems to be sizeable, their performance has been uneven. Several studies of the effectiveness of parent advisory councils revealed that many of the councils were not realizing their potential.[43] Although the reasons are typically complex and vary somewhat from one situation to another, major barriers to parent advisory councils' effectiveness usually revolve around issues of lack of ownership, incentives, authority, resources, representation, and organizational maintenance capabilities.[44]

The school principal appears to be a key factor in whether or not a parent advisory council is successful. In a study by the Institute for Responsive Education, it was found that all too frequently school principals directed and controlled the meetings and permitted committee members little meaningful impact on decision-making.[45] In a related study by Paddock, it was observed that school principals attempted to control the purpose and flow of the meetings through the use of one or more methods: (1) establishing the agenda and setting the priorities for the council, (2) providing information *selectively* to members of the council, and (3) pushing their own proposed solution to any problem or issue. Paddock concluded from her research that, "Parent involvement in decision making through participation in advisory councils is a myth."[46] However, other research has documented the existence of a number of effective parent advisory councils where parent involvement in decision making is high.[47] In these situations, as a result of leadership by the school principal, ". . . The trust level was high and the interaction was open,"[48] and "on a substantial number of issues, the council had the authority to make the final decision or see that the final decision maker acted as directed."[49] A description of how one school district established and operates apparently effective parent-advisory councils is provided by Morgan;[50] Regalbuti briefly describes how one principal went about initiating a parent advisory council.[51]

Parent advisory committees and councils are probably perceived by many administrators as a mixed blessing. Perceived problems, according to Podemski and Steele, can include the following:[52] (1) citizen committees or councils consume too much administrative time; (2) they often lack needed background and perspective for solving school problems and addressing issues; (3) they may not understand how a school system or school operates; (4) members frequently have an axe to grind and may represent a very narrow or special interest; (5) members often lack experience in working as part of a group; and (6) citizen advisory committees and councils sometimes search for problems to justify their existence.

Although an administrator will not be able to eliminate all of the problems associated with citizen participation on school committees and councils, these problems can be either avoided or minimized if the administrator will adhere to the following guidelines:

1. *Don't* establish an advisory committee or council *unless* you sincerely believe that parents and other community members have something important to contribute, and you are prepared to implement those recommendations which are not in violation of school board policy or state or federal law. (In situations where committees or councils are mandated by law, the first part of this guidelines does not, of course, apply.) Unless you are willing to provide and facilitate meaningful citizen participation on important issues and problems, you are better off not establishing a committee or council, thereby avoiding citizen and administrator frustration and disillusionment.
2. If you establish a citizen advisory committee or council, then clearly define and communicate to all members, in advance, the objectives, function, scope, and authority of the committee or council. If it is only an advisory committee to develop recommendations to submit to the administrator, then that function should be made clear to all participants.
3. Provide *training* to members of the committee or council on how to function effectively in a group. Many citizens have had little or no experience or training in this kind of an activity. The administrator should consider utilizing an outside consultant to provide the training.

4. Keep all members of the committee or council well informed before, during, and between meetings, as to what is transpiring. Advance agendas and minutes of each meeting are minimum requirements.
5. Utilize to the greatest extent possible the individual interests and talents of the members of the committee or council. There is little to be gained by either the school or the participants if the latter's potential contributions are not fully utilized.
6. Reward members of the committee or council for their individual and total contributions at every available opportunity. Committee and council work is frequently tedious, and periodic recognition of the value of the group's work by the administrator will pay important dividends.

Citizen advisory committees and councils offer potentially major contributions to improving school-community relations and to assisting the school in improving the educational program. Whether that potential will be realized or not will depend as much on the attitude, vision, and leadership capabilities of the principal as on any other factor. (For further ideas on establishing and working with advisory committees, see Olivero[53] and New Jersey School Boards Association;[54] for further information on establishing and working with citizen advisory councils, see National Coalition of ESEA Title I Parents,[55] and Morris and Zerchykov.[56])

Parent Education

In recent years a number of schools and school districts have attempted to involve parents more directly in the learning of their children through programs of parent education. The basic assumption of such programs is that the school can teach parents how they can assist in the education of their children and, as a result, improve the motivation and achievement of students in school.[57] The main objectives of parent education programs usually include one or more of the following:[58]

1. To help parents acquire the understanding and skill to teach certain concepts and skills at home, e.g., reading readiness.
2. To help parents learn how to become educational managers of their children's work at home, e.g., monitoring homework.
3. To help parents become more effective in parenting, e.g., learning and practicing particular childrearing techniques.

The activities in a parent education program vary, depending on the objective(s) the school district is trying to accomplish. Examples of activities initiated by a number of school districts include special courses for parents on how to tutor their children, written materials and games to be used with children, in-home contact by school specialists to help parents with problem children, and facilitation of counseling or support groups for parents who are experiencing difficulty in rearing children. A rather comprehensive program developed by the Philadelphia School District consists of the following activities:[59]

- Parent workshops. Conducted throughout the school system twice a year, workshops help parents understand various aspects of child development and make use of learning materials in the home. Recent workshops have featured school discipline, testing, and other school-related topics.
- Mini Workshop Series. Schools can request to have one of almost sixty workshops presented at their regular Home and School Association meetings.
- Personalized reading and mathematics books. On request, parents may receive graded materials in reading and math. Computer-generated booklets are also available to strengthen reading comprehension. These stories include references to the child and his or her friends.
- Public awareness. Parents of school-age children are informed of the variety of program activities through print and broadcast media.
- Data Line. A telephone resource center which provides assistance and information to parents and pupils related to homework, program activities and school services. A Spanish language hotline is also available.

Another example of parent education by the school is presented below in the form of a letter to the parents of students in one school.[60]

Dear Parents of Townsend,

Do your children make you feel guilty when you discipline them? How do you handle temper tantrums? Do you react to them or do you take action?

Mrs. Lucia Halyard, our Title VII Guidance Counselor, is planning a workshop for any interested parent. The purpose of the workshop is to help parents develop skills in conflict resolution and to discuss ways of assisting children in establishing good relationships at home and at school.

The first workshop is scheduled for Tuesday at 7:00 p.m. at Townsend Street School, Teacher's Lounge.

If you are interested in attending, please fill out and return the slip below.

Sincerely,
(Signed)
Robert T. Johnson
Principal

Research on the effectiveness of parent education programs has been limited but, for the most part, positive. For example, Oinonen found that parental tutoring of their children was significantly related to increased student achievement.[61] Also, Weibly reviewed a large number of studies on parent involvement programs which indicated that when parents were instructed on methods of promoting their children's intellectual development, long-term improvement in the academic achievement of students was obtained.[62] And Callard's study showed that a program of parent education could raise the expectations of parents for their children's academic success and, as a result, produce increased student academic motivation and achievement.[63]

Despite these positive findings and the potentially positive benefits of parent education programs, the school administrator needs to be aware that initiating such a program may not be easy. The faculty may not accept the notion that parents can also be educators with something important to contribute to the total education process. Also, the parents may not see themselves as educators and may feel that education is the job of the school. And financial support for a program of parent education may be difficult to obtain and sustain. While these potential problems, if they occur, could represent serious obstacles to initiating or continuing a program of parent education, they are by no means inevitable and, for the most part, they can be overcome with appropriate leadership of the nature described earlier in this chapter.

Evaluator

Although some administrators may recoil at the prospect of involving parents in the evaluation of a school, it should be recognized that, in one way or another, parents evaluate the school all the time. They may not evaluate the school in any scientific or formal sense, but parents do make evaluative judgments on the worth of different aspects of the school program. The real question to which administrators need to address themselves, then, is whether it is better to allow parents to continue to make informal kinds of evaluative judgments (about which the school may not be aware and which in many instances are based on inadequate information and limited contact with the school), or to involve parents in some type of formal evaluation of the school's program. While the question is stated rhetorically and the answer is, hopefully, obvious, it is surprising how many administrators continue to behave as though the absence of a formal program of evaluation by parents means that parents are not evaluating the school.

An administrator and staff need periodic, systematic, evaluative feedback from parents (and other members of the community) regarding their perceptions, feelings, and ideas as to the effectiveness of the school and how the school program could be improved. "Periodic" evaluation means, in this context, at least once a year, and "systematic" means that an attempt should be made to secure representative parents' viewpoints in the evaluation. A school administrator needs this kind of information if he is to keep himself accurately informed on what parents are thinking and in order to correct any inaccurate perceptions on their part. He can also find such information helpful in identifying aspects of the school program which may need improvement. Despite the fact that most parents are not professionally trained in education, they can nonetheless contribute valuable ideas for improving the school. The administrator should attempt to capitalize on this potential source of ideas.

Although many administrators try to involve parents in evaluating the school, these efforts are often informal or initiated only after the development of a serious problem in school-community relations. Informal contacts with parents and the community are necessary and desirable, but they cannot adequately substitute for a formally organized program of securing evaluative community feedback. In addition, the best time to obtain community input is *before* a problem reaches the crisis stage, not at the point of crisis. Periodic surveying of parental and community sentiment can alert a school administrator to a developing problem and may suggest a possible means of avoiding a crisis.

Before initiating a formal program of parental evaluation of the school, an administrator should work with the staff. The faculty will need to understand the purpose and possible value of parents' evaluation of the school. The staff will also need to be reassured that the evaluation will not be directed at individual teachers. Although parent evaluation of teachers might have some value, it is potentially such a controversial area that the administrator would do well to steer the parent evaluation away from this topic—at least until the faculty better understands and accepts the program.

The administrator should also attempt to work with parents on their role as evaluators of the school. Most parents have not been involved in formal programs of evaluation and will need assistance if they are going to make a constructive contribution. An excellent booklet written for parents by the Texas Advisory Committee to the United States Commission on Civil Rights, entitled *Working with Your School,* contains a major section on school evaluations which provides many useful concepts and guidelines.[64]

After the administrator has provided appropriate preparation for his staff and parents, there are various alternatives which an administrator might consider for involving parents in evaluating the school, but two techniques particularly merit his attention. The first is the questionnaire method. Utilizing this approach, an administrator (perhaps with consultant help) can design a questionnaire which asks for parents' reactions to or perceptions of the school program. The questionnaire can be long and comprehensive or short and specific, covering only a certain aspect of the school. An example of a short questionnaire is presented in figure 17.4 (An example of a longer questionnaire is provided by Almen.[65])

Grade of your Child _____ School _____ Boy _____ Girl _____

    We would like your reactions to our new homework policy. Please indicate your feelings as to its good points and any areas needing improvement, and then mail this form back to the school.

Good Points

Areas Needing Improvement

(Please return by Monday. Thank you for your help.)

Figure 17.4. A Short Questionnaire
for Parents

A questionnaire can be sent to all parents or to only a random sample. In most cases a questionnaire study will provide the school with valuable information, although it should be noted that its usefulness will depend as much on the care with which it is designed as on the cooperation of the parents.

Another good technique for involving parents in the evaluation of the school is the interview. An interview might be used as a follow-up to a questionnaire, or it may be used instead of the questionnaire, depending on the administrator's objectives. Usually it will not be possible to interview all parents on a single matter, but through sampling procedures and in-depth interview techniques, the administrator should be able to secure representative views from parents. Interviews may be conducted either at the school, in the home, or by telephone. Provided with in-service training, teachers, counselors, and administrators should be able to conduct the interviews and obtain valuable information for the school.

Regardless of the particular technique or approach used, it is important for the administrator to recognize that securing parents' assessment of the school on a regular basis is essential. Parents will be evaluating the school whether or not the administrator thinks it desirable for them to do so. The task for the administrator is to plan, design, and implement evaluative procedures for parents which will aid in eliciting information and ideas for the improvement of the school program.

Resource Person, Helper

An excellent means by which the school can involve parents and the community at large is by encouraging them to serve as resource people or helpers. There are many people in most communities who possess skills, knowledge, or ideas which might be made available to the school. Professional workers, craftsmen, individuals who have traveled, and those who have a particular area of expertise could serve as resource people and offer a great deal to supplement a school's curriculum. In addition, many housewives and older or retired people have time available and are willing to serve as helpers or aides to the school in the classroom, library, cafeteria, or guidance office. According to the executive director of the National School Volunteer Program, there is generally a large number of people in every community who possess resources of expertise, time, and energy, and who are willing to volunteer their services to make a major contribution to the school.[66]

Schools which have initiated community volunteer programs have involved citizens in a wide variety of ways. In one school citizens were involved in a tutorial program to help students cope with the new pressures of competency testing.[67] In a Virginia school volunteers make daily calls to the homes of absent students, and assist teachers and office staff by typing, filing, collating and other clerical duties.[68] In the Dade County, Florida school system volunteers work in the library, operate audio-visual equipment, tutor students in math, listen to students read, prepare instructional materials, read stories to youngsters, and play learning games with children.[69] As one principal observed, "Just having another adult in the classroom who cares about a child is a marvelous asset. I wish we could have the senior volunteers five days a week."[70]

While utilizing community volunteers can potentially provide the school with additional resources and help, the school should approach the task of initiating a program carefully and thoughtfully. Perhaps the Fairfax County, Virginia, Public School's Volunteer Handbook put it best. "Volunteer programs should arise out of a clearly felt need for assistance in some area of the school program. A principal and a school staff must genuinely desire a program, and the community must be willing to serve and to accept orientation and training. And, however high the enthusiasm, experience in volunteer programs clearly indicates the wisdom in beginning with a limited, carefully run project, and expanding slowly."[71]

In all too many situations the community is still a relatively untapped source of knowledge and assistance. The school administrator has the responsibility of surveying the community to discover the different types of resource people and helpers that might be available. Then, through careful planning and appropriate training for staff members, as well as community volunteers, he should institute a program for capitalizing on these resources for the improvement of the school program. Materials on how to initiate and administer a school volunteer program can be obtained from the National School Volunteer Program, 300 North Washington Street, Alexandria, Va. 22314.

User of School Facilities

Possibly one of the best ways to gain parents' and other citizens' support for the school is to involve them in the use of school facilities. People who use the school building are usually more likely to support the school than those who have little or no opportunity to use the facilities maintained by their tax money.

The imaginative administrator can find a variety of ways in which to involve parents and other members of the community in the use of school facilities. Probably the most widely known method is the "lighthouse school" approach.[72] In this approach the school building is kept open and *lighted* at night, and educational and recreational programs are offered by the school to members of the community. Participants may be charged a minimum fee, or the entire expense may be assumed by the school district as an investment in community goodwill and adult education. The objectives of this type of program are to provide

1. An educational center where members of the community can study and learn.

2. A neighborhood center for cultural and recreational activities.
3. A center for social services.
4. A center for utilizing school and community resources to help citizens solve neighborhood problems.[73]

Although such programs are usually administered by the district office, the building administrator can help make them a success through his cooperation and leadership. In addition, by periodically making himself visible at the school while these programs are in process, the administrator can extend his knowledge of and acquaintance with the community, and indicate his support of this type of community involvement.

In a more direct sense, an administrator has an opportunity to involve community groups in the use of school facilities when he responds to their requests for the use of rooms in the building, (at the end of the school day or on weekends). Many groups, such as scouts or local drama players, may request the administrator's permission to use school facilities after school hours. The ultimate authority for granting this permission may be the central office, depending on school board policy. However, the school administrator can act as either a facilitator or an impediment in securing permission for use of the facilities. Certainly, the school administrator's attitude and behavior in this kind of a situation can either evoke considerable good will or create ill will on the part of these community groups.

Another opportunity for community use of school facilities on which more administrators should capitalize, is that of inviting retired people to view student activities as the school's guests. Retired people often have limited financial resources and social outlets, and appreciate complimentary passes to watch athletic, dramatic, and music activities at the school. Some schools issue a "Golden Age School Activities Pass" to retired people in the community. This type of effort by a school can deliver dividends in increasing community good will, and it offers at the same time, a service to the retired people of the community who have supported the schools for so many years with taxes.

It should be noted that involving the community in the use of school facilities will not always be an easy task for the school administrator. Financial problems on the part of the district, lack of vision on the part of the school board and teachers, and inadequate cooperation from the custodial staff are three major obstacles which may have to be overcome by the school administrator. However, if an administrator really believes that the schools are for all the people in the community, and if he is willing to exert his energy and time to resolve serious problems, then a program of community use of school facilities should be possible and, in any event, remains desirable.

INVOLVING PARENTS: PROBLEMS

PARENTAL APATHY

Although community participation in the school has value, the administrator should recognize that it is not without attendant problems. An initial barrier which may confront a school administrator who wishes to involve parents in the school is parental apathy. Ironically, despite the great emphasis recently on parental involvement, many administrators who have tried to involve parents report that they have encountered considerable apathy. For example, questionnaires sent to parents may not be returned, and meetings of parents' organizations are often poorly attended. A common complaint of many administrators is that parents are indifferent about school unless a controversial issue arises; otherwise, most parents seem to prefer to remain uninvolved in school affairs.

Realistically, a school cannot accommodate the active involvement of *all* parents and there will always be a number of them who simply do not care to participate in school affairs, regardless of how much effort the school expends in that direction. The school administrator should also realize that many parents are occupied with full-time jobs and, at the end of a long day, various leisure activities compete with the school for the available time of parents. (For example, how many school administrators, if given a choice, would decide against a relaxing evening at home, watching television, reading, or engaging in another type of leisure time activity with the family, in favor of attending a meeting at the school?) Although most parents are interested in the school and many of them might be willing to become more active in working to improve it, the administrator needs to recognize that a number of alternative activities are competing for parents' available time.

A school administrator who is faced with parental apathy needs to approach this situation as he would any other problem: by attempting to define more precisely the nature of and reasons for the problem. A thorough diagnosis may reveal that parent apathy is only a symptom, rather than the problem itself.

The initial question which the administrator needs to ask is, "Why are parents apathetic?" Until the administrator attempts a systematic investigation of the reasons for parental apathy, he is unlikely to make much progress in ameliorating it, and any actions he takes may be based on an incorrect diagnosis of the causes of the problem. An effective solution to a problem must be preceded by a correct diagnosis of the causes. The administrator, by trying to hypothesize as to the causes of parent apathy and then collecting data from parents on the hypotheses, is engaged in the process of diagnosis.[74] This process should provide direction for a possible solution to parent apathy.

Figure 17.5 presents a questionnaire based on several analyzes of parent apathy, which an administrator can use to ascertain the reasons for parental apathy and the perceived importance of those reasons.[75]

As figure 17.5 suggests, the reasons behind parental apathy may be complex. Parental apathy should be viewed as a *symptom* of limited parental involvement in the schools, but not as its cause. Actually, parental apathy may be only a convenient label which many administrators have used to affix blame

	Parent's Response				
Reasons from Parent's Perception	Not Important	Of Some Importance	Fairly Important	Very Important	Extremely Important
1. Not enough time	_____	_____	_____	_____	_____
2. Not sure how to get involved	_____	_____	_____	_____	_____
3. Not sure the school really wants parents to get involved	_____	_____	_____	_____	_____
4. Not sure that I have the necessary skills and knowledge to get involved in school affairs	_____	_____	_____	_____	_____
5. No need to get involved; teachers and administrators already know what is best	_____	_____	_____	_____	_____
6. Have previously had poor or bad experience when I became involved in school decision making	_____	_____	_____	_____	_____
7. No one has ever encouraged me to become involved	_____	_____	_____	_____	_____
8. _____	_____	_____	_____	_____	_____
9. _____	_____	_____	_____	_____	_____

Figure 17.5. Factors Which May Restrict Parental Involvement in the Schools

on parents for not responding better to the school's attempts to involve them. Again, the basic question that the administrator needs to ask is, "*Why* are parents apathetic?"

A related question which also should be raised by a school administrator as he investigates parental apathy is, "Do the professional staff and I really want parents to become *significantly* involved in school affairs, and if we do, are we willing to work *hard* to secure that kind of involvement?" Involving parents is a time-consuming, demanding, and at times frustrating task. Unless the administrator and the staff are truly committed to parental involvement, it is not likely to be successful.

Many parents believe, rightly or wrongly, that the school wants them to be involved only in busywork or in providing support for the school, rather than in evaluating the effectiveness of the school or participating in school decision making. If an administrator wants to combat parental apathy, he will probably need to provide more meaningful opportunities for parents to participate in school affairs. Most people are apathetic about taking part in a given activity unless they feel that they can make a significant contribution. (For further ideas on how to deal with the problem of parents' apathy, contact the National Committee for Citizens in Education, Columbia, Md., and the Institute for Responsive Education, Boston, Mass.)

PARENTAL "OVERINVOLVEMENT"

Although parental apathy can be a troublesome problem for a school administrator who is sincerely committed to participation by parents in the schools, an equally difficult (though opposite) problem for some administrators is parental overinvolvement.[76] The latter problem can take many forms, but it may be defined as parental involvement which tends to interfere with the operation and administration of the school by the professional staff and the administrator. Figure 17.6 presents some examples of parental overinvolvement, as perceived by many administrators.

---

1. Censorship of books or materials in the school by individual parents.

2. Efforts by individual parents or by groups of parents to become "excessively" involved in decision making about school policies and procedures.

3. Attempts to modify the school curriculum (e.g., ban on sex education) by pressure groups.

4. Regular or constant complaints by individual parents or parents' groups.

Figure 17.6. Types of Parental Overinvolvement

It should be noted that parental overinvolvement is a value judgment that is in "the eyes of the beholder." What is considered to be "overinvolvement" by one administrator may be seen as appropriate or justifiable involvement by other observers. For example, community efforts to become involved in the collective bargaining process between the school board and the teachers' union—a growing trend[77]—may be perceived as legitimate and reasonable by many parents, and yet may be regarded by the school administrator and the faculty as representing "overinvolvement" on the part of citizens and interference with the management of the school district.

As problems of the schools have recently attracted increased attention from the media, parents have become more concerned about the quality of education and, as a consequence, many of them have tried to become actively involved in school affairs. Depending on the nature of that involvement and the concept of parental involvement held by the school administrator and the professional staff, conflicts are possible.

Part of the problem is that active involvement by parents who have tended to question the school's effectiveness or who have attempted to develop a larger role for themselves in school decision making represents a threat to many school administrators and their professional staffs, and they respond negatively. In some cases, much of the administrator's concern about parental overinvolvement is caused by his own lack of willingness to be evaluated by parents and to share decision-making responsibilities with them. On the other hand, there is legitimate administrative concern in connection with certain types of parental involvement, such as attempts at censorship or the use of protest tactics by special interest groups.[78]

According to Wirt and Kirst, the following factors are characteristic of special interest groups who use protest against the school:[79]

1. The use of protest indicates that regular channels for handling grievances and complaints are not functioning effectively for the special interest group.
2. The special interest group that uses pressure will try to publicize their demands through communications media in hopes of attracting allies and supporters.
3. The special interest group that uses pressure will try to dramatize issues and problems rather than to present "objective" data.
4. Working with a special interest group that uses pressure can be a difficult and frustrating task for the school administrator.

Despite the difficulties in working with a special interest group that uses pressure tactics, the administrator should not assume that the demands of the group are without merit or that pressure by a group is necessarily bad. Historically, in our society necessary change has frequently been brought about *only* after the use of pressure. While not every kind of method can be justified, pressure tactics may be needed in certain situations in order to bring about needed change. And, regardless of the methods used, the demands of a group should be considered on their own merits, separately from the tactics employed.

If an administrator is concerned about special interest groups who use pressure tactics, or any other type of parent overinvolvement, the following possible causes of that overinvolvement should be investigated:

1. The regular channels for parental involvement and resolution of grievances and complaints are not functioning effectively.
2. A misunderstanding. Perhaps the parents were not briefed clearly enough by the school as to the limits of their or the school's authority.
3. An unrealistic or inappropriate notion of the value and concept of parental involvement on the part of either the parents or the administration, or both.
4. An honest difference of opinion between the school administration and the parents on the role of parents in school affairs.

Parents' overinvolvement can create serious problems for the school. The school administrator's role in response to parental overinvolvement should be to investigate its possible causes and take whatever action seems appropriate and feasible in light of local circumstances.

A CLOSING PERSPECTIVE

Effective community involvement will not be an easy objective to achieve. There will be frustrations and problems which must be overcome, and little success will be experienced without considerable hard work and persistence on the part of the administrator. However, given an administrator with a strong commitment to and broad vision of the potential usefulness of community involvement, a successful program of community participation in the schools is attainable.

Review and Learning Activities

1. Why is it important that a school administrator maintain up-to-date knowledge about the community? Ascertain the extent to which your school has reliable and valid information about each of the factors in figures 17.1 and 17.2. How could this information be better utilized for instructional, curricular, and administrative purposes?

2. Why is it important for the school to involve parents and other citizens in school affairs? What should be the main purpose of this involvement? Ascertain the degree to which the possible barriers to community involvement exist in your school situation. If you were the principal, how would you overcome these barriers, using the concepts presented in chapters 3 and 4?

3. If you were the principal of your school, to what extent would you introduce (or improve) each of the types of community involvement presented in the text? What obstacles and/or problems would have to be overcome?

4. What are the two main problems that an administrator might encounter in trying to involve parents? How can he best prevent or ameliorate these problems?

Notes

1. William O. Stanley et al., *Social Foundations of Education* (New York: Holt-Dryden Books, Henry Holt Co., 1955), p. 81.

2. Frederick Wirt and Michael Kirst, *Schools in Conflict* (Berkeley: McCutchan, 1982).

3. Eugene Litwak et al., *School, Family and Neighborhood: The Theory and Practice of School-Community Relations* (New York: Columbia University Press, 1974).

4. Joel Milgram and John Hill, "The School Official Who Can Best Estimate Parental Approval or Disapproval of New Programs," 1972. N.P.M. Also see Gary L. Kesl, "Perceptions of the Community Power Structure of Selected Communities" (Ph.D. diss., University of Miami, 1972).

5. Richard W. Saxe, *School-Community Interaction* (Berkeley, Calif.: McCutchan Publishing Corporation, 1975).

6. For a good description of how to carry out this study, see Gene C. Fusco, "Working with Organized Groups: Improving Your School-Community Relations Program." An ERIC Report: Ed–021–328.

7. Michael W. Kirst and Walter I. Garms, *The Demographic, Fiscal, and Political Environment of Public School Finance in the 1980s* (Stanford, Calif.: Institute for Research on Educational Finance and Governance, 1980). Also see Beth J. Soldo, "America's Elderly in the 1980s," *Population Bulletin* (November 1980): 1–42.

8. Beverly L. Johnson, "Marital and Family Characteristics of the Labor Force," *Monthly Labor Review* (April 1982): 48–52.

9. "One-Parent Families and Their Children," *Principal* (September 1980): 31–39.

10. "Single-Parent Study Is Misleading, Critics Say," *Education U.S.A.* (September 1, 1980): 2.

11. An excellent description of the objectives and influence of a number of these groups can be found in Roald Campbell et al., *The Organization and Control of American Schools* (Columbus, Ohio: Charles E. Merrill, 1970), chaps. 12, 13.

12. An interesting study which revealed that the people in a community received their information more from informal than from formal channels was conducted by Donald G. Marcotte, "The Dyadic Relationship of Selected Variables in the Process of Communication from the School to the Public" (Ph.D. diss., Purdue University, 1971).

13. Dean Bowles and Marvin Furth, *Depth Interview Handbook* (Madison, Wis.: Wisconsin R and D Center, 1979).

14. For a discussion of the rationale for this distinction, see Hillel I. Haskas, "The Relationship Between School-Community Relations, Community Support and Student Achievement in Communities of Different Socio-Economic Character" (Ph.D. diss., University of Wisconsin, 1979).

15. M. Vere DeVault, *Parent Involvement in Your School* (Madison, Wis.: Wisconsin Department of Public Instruction, 1977), p. 1.

16. M. Donald Thomas, "Parent Participation in Education," *NASSP Bulletin* (January 1980): 1.

17. Ibid.

18. For a review of evidence which shows that parental involvement can, under the right circumstances, exert a positive influence on children's academic achievement, see Gary W. Weibly, "Parent Involvement Programs: Research and Practice" (Paper presented at the annual meeting of the American Educational Research Association, San Francisco, 1979). Also see Don Davies et al., *Patterns of Citizen Participation in Educational Decision-Making* (Boston, Mass.: Institute for Responsive Education, 1978) and Mario O. Fantini, *Community Participation: Alternative Patterns and Their Consequences on Educational Achievement.* An ERIC Report: Ed–191–167.

19. Don Davies, "The Emerging Third Force in Education," *Inequalities in Education* (November 1973): 5.

20. Quoted by Patricia F. Story in "Parents Can Cause Change in Special Education," *Citizens in Action* (March 1979): 3.

21. George H. Gallup, "The Eleventh Annual Poll of the Public's Attitudes toward the Public Schools," *The Kappan* (September 1979): 33–45.

22. Kathleen Huguenin et al., "Narrowing the Gap Between Intent and Practice." An ERIC Report: Ed–180–084.

23. Don Davies, "A Useful But Bland Book That Ignores Profession/Lay Conflict," *The Kappan* (April 1978): 566.

24. Robert Byrne and Edward Powell, *Strengthening School-Community Relations* (Reston, Va.: National Association of Secondary School Principals, 1976), pp. 5–6.

25. Daniel Safran, "Preparing Teachers for Parent Involvement," in *Community Participation in Education,* ed. Carl A. Grant (New York: Allyn and Bacon, 1979).

26. David Hollister, "School Bureaucratization as a Response to Parents' Demands," *Urban Education* (July 1979): 221–35.

27. Kerry L. Moyer, "Four Steps to Effective Community Involvement," *Educational Leadership* (January 1982): 285–87.

28. *PTA Magazine* (September 1971); also see The National PTA Urban Task Force, "The PTA in the Urban Context: Phase II: An Action Plan." An ERIC Report: Ed–186–530.

29. James Koerner, *Who Controls American Education?* (Boston: Beacon Press, 1968), p. 148.

30. Virginia Sparling, "PTA Involvement in the 80s: New Concepts, New Directions," *NASSP Bulletin* (January 1980): 25.

31. Ibid., p. 24.

32. Happy C. Ferandez, "Empowering Parents," *The Urban Review* (Summer 1979): 92–96.

33. Richard A. Gross, "The Parent Teacher Association—A Personal Encounter," *NASSP Bulletin* (January 1980): 52–54.

34. Sparling, "Pta Involvement in the 80s."

35. Yvonne M. Horn, "Saving a Neighborhood School," *American Education* (March 1981): 13–15.

36. George Goens and Gary Schulze, "School Organization: Creating Islands or Building Bridges," *Wisconsin School News* (May 1980): 18–20.

37. James A. Sandfort, "The PTA—Is It the Forgotten Community Resource?" *NASSP Bulletin* (January 1980): 4.

38. "The Value of the PTA," *Today's Education* (May 1969): 30.

39. Ross Zerchykov and Don Davies, *Leading the Way: State Mandates for School Advisory Councils in California, Florida and South Carolina* (Boston, Mass.: The Institute for Responsive Education, 1980).

40. Miriam Clasby et al., "Improving Education in Florida: A Reassessment." An ERIC Report: Ed–172–353.

41. Nelson Price, "School Community Councils and Advisory Boards: A Notebook for Administrators, Why? Who? What? When? How?" An ERIC Report: Ed–145–583.

42. Gordon E. Greenwood et al., "Citizen Advisory Committees," *Theory into Practice* (February 1977): 12–16.

43. Marilyn Gittell, *Citizen Organizations: Citizen Participation in Educational Decisionmaking* (Boston, Mass.: Institute for Responsive Education, 1980).

44. Jim Stanton and Ross Zerchykov, *Overcoming Barriers to School Council Effectiveness* (Boston, Mass.: Institute for Responsive Education, 1979).

45. Donald Davies et al., *Sharing the Power? A Report on the Status of School Councils in the 1970's* (Boston, Mass.: Institute for Responsive Education, 1978).

46. Susan C. Paddock, "The Myth of Parent Involvement through Advisory Councils" (Paper presented at the annual meeting of the American Educational Research Association, San Francisco, California, 1979).

47. Clasby et al., "Improving Education in Florida."

48. A quotation by John Shadgett (who studied school-based advisory councils in Florida) which appeared in *Education USA* (March 10, 1980): 213.

49. Clasby et al., "Improving Education in Florida."

50. Stanley R. Morgan, "Shared Governance: A Concept for Public Schools," *NASSP Bulletin* (January 1980): 29–32.

51. Armand Regalbuti, "In Support of Parent Advisory Councils," *NASSP Bulletin* (September 1978): 113. Also see Mary C. Fedler, "Local Elementary School Advisory Committees" (Ph.D. diss., University of Florida, 1980).

52. Richard S. Podemski and Ruth Steele, "Avoid the Pitfalls of Citizen Committees," *The American School Board Journal* (April 1981): 40–42.

53. James Olivero, "Working with Advisory Committees . . . Promising Practices" An ERIC Report: Ed–146–665.

54. New Jersey School Boards Association, *Working with Advisory Committees* (Trenton, N.J.: New Jersey School Boards Association, 1981).

55. National Coalition of ESEA Title I Parents, *Organizing an Effective Parent Advisory Council* (Washington, D.C.: National Coalition of ESEA Title I Parents, 1980).

56. Richard Morris and Ross Zerchykov, *Working Papers: Community Councils* (Boston, Mass.: Institute for Responsive Education, 1980).

57. James Filipczak et al., "Parental Involvement in the Schools: Towards What End?" An ERIC Report: Ed–143–104.

58. Oliver Moles and Carter Collins, "Home School Programs of Urban School Districts" (Paper presented at the annual meeting of the American Educational Research Association, Los Angeles, April 1981).

59. Ibid. Also see Nicholas Criscuola, "Parent Involvement in the Reading Program," *Phi Delta Kappan* (January 1982): 345–46.

60. Townsend Elementary School, Milwaukee Public School System, Milwaukee, Wisconsin.

61. Charlotte Oinonen, "The Relationship between School-Community Relations and Student Achievement in Elementary and Secondary Schools" (Ph.D. dissertation, University of Wisconsin, 1980).

62. Gary W. Weibly, "Parental Involvement Programs: Research and Practice" (Paper presented at the annual meeting of the American Educational Research Association, San Francisco, 1979).

63. Rosemary Callard, "A Study of the Effects of Increasing Parental Expectations for Student Achievement" (Ed.D. diss., State University of New York at Buffalo, 1979). Also see "Parent Involvement in Education," *Phi Delta Kappan Newsletter* (December 1981): 1–4.

64. Texas Advisory Committee to the United States Commission on Civil Rights, *Working with Your School* (Washington, D.C.: Government Printing Office, 1977).

65. Roy Almen, "SEA Parent Opinion Survey." An ERIC Report: Ed–115–683.

66. John W. Alden, "Citizen Participation in Education: School Volunteers Broaden the Definition," *Compact* (Spring 1980): 11–14.

67. Allen L. Huggins, "Community Helps Boost Students' Test Scores," *The American School Board Journal* (June 1980): 23–24.

68. William C. Parrish, "Volunteers in the Secondary School," *The Practitioner* (January 1981): 6.

69. Georgia Slack, "Volunteering Is In," *American Education* (April 1978): 6–10.

70. Ibid., p. 10.

71. Quotation from Parrish, "Volunteers in the Secondary Schools," p. 3. For further guidelines on planning and operating an effective volunteer program, see Corrine Paxman Hill, "A Comparative Study of Formal Volunteer Programs in Educational Settings" (Ed.D. diss., University of Utah, 1980).

72. For the early roots of this approach, see Clarence A. Perry, *Wider Use of the School Plant* (New York: Russell Sage Foundation, 1910). For a more contemporary concept of this approach, see Jack D. Minzey and Clyde E. Le Tarte, *Community Education: From Program to Practice* (Midland, Mich.: Pendell Publishing, 1980).

73. John R. Hughes, ed., "The Community School and Its Concept." An ERIC Report: Ed–073–531.

74. This process is further described in chapters 3 and 13.

75. Ted R. Urich and Judith P. LaVorgna, "A Parent Involvement Program—Giving Opportunity a Chance," *NASSP Bulletin* (January 1980): 34–38. Also, James Smith, "The Relationship between Parents' Attitudes toward School and Their Involvement in School Decision Making." A Specialist Field Inquiry, University of Wisconsin-Milwaukee, 1973.

76. Roy R. Nasstrom, "Principals View Parents as Enemies," *Educational Communication* (July 1981): 35.

77. For an excellent review of this issue, see *Public Access: Citizens and Collective Bargaining in the Public Schools,* ed. Robert E. Doherty (Ithaca, N.Y.: Institute for Labor Relations, Cornell University, 1979).

78. For an excellent book on the censorship problem, see Edward Jenkinson, *Censors in the Classroom: The Mind Benders* (Carbondale, Ill.: Southern Illinois University Press, 1979). Also, for some excellent guidelines on how to deal with censorship problems, see "How to Handle Censorship Issues," *Education U.S.A.* (August 10, 1981): 377.

79. Frederick M. Wirt and Michael W. Kirst, *The Political Web of American Schools* (Boston: Little, Brown and Company, 1972): 57–59. For a good discussion of the theoretical dimensions of special interests groups, see Wirt and Kirst, *Schools in Conflict.*

18

SCHOOL-COMMUNITY RELATIONS: COMMUNICATION AND PUBLIC RELATIONS

Most administrators have long recognized the importance of effective school-community communication and the desirability of maintaining good public relations. Unfortunately, in too many situations, communication has been primarily *from* the school *to* the community (with little attempt to secure feedback), and the objective of the school's public relations activities has been to "sell" the school program.

School-community communication and public relations should be cooperative processes which are both honest and responsive. In the case of school-community communication, each party has something of value to communicate to the other and needs to seek feedback on whether its own message is being received and understood accurately. A school's public relations program must reflect honesty and integrity in all of its interfaces with the community in order to retain its credibility, and the confidence and support of the community. In the following sections, a number of different aspects of school-community communication and the school's public relations program will be explored.

SCHOOL COMMUNICATION

TYPICAL PRACTICES

Traditionally the school has, for the most part, used two main methods of communicating with its immediate community: (1) the school newsletter, and (2) the PTA or parents' meeting. (The telephone and individual conferences are two other means of communication used by the school on a *limited* basis to communicate with individual parents or other members of the community.)

The school newsletter has taken several forms, depending on the school and the school district. It may be an informational bulletin developed and disseminated by the district office, describing noteworthy activities occurring in all the schools in the district. Or an individual school may publish its own newsletter, describing in more detail and to a greater extent than would be possible in a district newsletter, the major activities and happenings in that school that might be of interest to parents. The newsletter may be a semi-monthly commercially printed news bulletin mailed to parents, or it may consist of an occasional, mimeographed information sheet sent with the students to the home. The school newsletter may be perceived by parents and the community as informative and worthwhile, or it may be perceived as containing little or nothing that is newsworthy or important. (For ideas on how to improve building level publications, see Gelms.[1])

A second major means by which schools try to communicate with parents and the community is through PTA or parents' meetings. At parents' meetings, information about some aspect of a school's program is usually disseminated, and there are some opportunities for two-way communication between school personnel and parents. The meetings may be scheduled on a regular basis or they may be scheduled only irregularly. The meetings may be well attended by both teachers and parents, or by only a small percentage of parents and teachers. The programs at the parents' meetings may be informative to parents, or they may be perceived as presenting little or no real information about what is happening at school.

Regardless of the type of school newsletter and parents' meetings, it is clear that they reflect an attempt by the schools to communicate with the parents and the community.* The questions which need to be raised, however, are: to what extent are the school's communication practices with parents and the community effective, and how could they be improved?

Although there is a paucity of research data on the effectiveness of school communication practices with parents and the community, observation and analysis of available studies would suggest that many schools are engaging in ineffective communications practices.[2] Criticisms have generally focused on the following aspects.

1. **Information disseminated by many schools has tended to be primarily self-promoting and not relevant to the immediate needs and concerns of the parents and the larger community.** This criticism is directed in part to the practice of communicating only the "good news" (e.g., National Merit Scholarships, the latest federal grant), while omitting the less desirable news (such as the truancy rate, or problems of vandalism or litter at the school).

---

*It is recognized that there can be innumerable variations of the newsletter and parents' meetings described.

A school should attempt to communicate to the home *both* favorable news and information about general problems. As Wherry emphasizes, "Admitting a problem is not a weakness. It takes some courage, but it's seen as a strength. The public knows we are not perfect, and is reassured to know that we are aware of our shortcomings as well. . . ."[3]

In most situations, news about problems will reach the home one way or another, regardless. Therefore, for purposes of increasing accuracy, and informing parents of steps that are being taken to alleviate troublesome conditions, the school should be as candid about its "blemishes" as possible. This would include factual information about the *nature* of a problem, what the school is trying to do about the problem, and what contributions parents and the community might make toward ameliorating the problem.

Criticism is also directed at the tendency of schools to disseminate predominantly that information which school officials *think* parents and the community should receive, without securing *feedback* from these groups on what they *actually want to receive.* In a good school-community communication program *both* types of information are disseminated.

2. **Communication from the school to the community is limited to those special instances when a school needs the community's support, such as in a bond referendum, or when a major crisis or problem occurs.** Otherwise, most schools' communication to parents and the community is sporadic. That the public would like to receive more information about the schools was indicated by a Gallup survey which revealed that the majority of both public and nonpublic school parents were desirous of knowing *more* about the schools in their community. Specific areas included were: (1) the curriculum, (2) qualifications of teachers, (3) current methods of teaching, (4) how the schools are administered, and (5) problems of discipline.[4]

3. **The school's dissemination procedures are not reliable in many instances.** School newsletters which are not mailed directly to the home are frequently lost or destroyed by students, who are being used by the school as information carriers. Parents' meetings and parent-teacher conferences are often poorly attended and are an ineffective means of communicating with a large number of parents. Consequently, unless the information which a school wishes to communicate to parents is actually *mailed* to them, it is, in many cases, unlikely to be received.

4. **The school has not sufficiently utilized means of communication in addition to the newsletter and parents' meeting for transmitting information to parents and the larger community.**[5] Other means of communication include radio, television, the newspaper, and regular parent and community visitations to the school. More will be said about this later.

5. **The school has not tried hard enough to ascertain the extent to which its messages are being received, understood, and acted upon by parents and the community as intended by the school.**[6] Conspicuously absent in many school

situations is a plan for systematically and periodically seeking feedback from parents and the community on how they are reacting to the information which the school is communicating to them.

While poor communication practices are not characteristic of all schools, ineffective or inadequate messages and methods exist to a sufficient degree to cause concern among many parents, members of the community, and educators. Therefore, in the following section, ideas and recommendations will be presented to help school administrators improve their communication effectiveness with parents and the community. (For an example of a comprehensive public information program, see Salman.[7])

IMPROVING COMMUNICATION

THE MESSAGE

One of the most important aspects of communication is the message. In school-community communication there are potentially several types of messages. There is the message that the school wants to communicate, there is the one that the community wants to receive, and there is the actual message received by the community. Conversely, there is the message that the community *wants* to communicate to the school, there is the message the school wants to receive from the community, and there is the actual message received by the school. Complex? Perhaps, but school administrators should be aware of these six types of messages, and they should recognize that, to the extent to which the various messages within each set are congruent with each other, communication may or may not be effective.

For example, a school may have a message that it would like to communicate to the community. However, the community may not be interested in that particular topic and may want the school to communicate with it on a different topic. When this happens, communication between the school and the community becomes impaired. Too often this kind of situation exists because the school is not sending to parents and the larger community the types of information they would like to receive. (Of course, there are times when a school *should* send a particular message to the community regardless of whether or not the community wants to receive it, if the message is in the community's best interests.)

An important first consideration in improving school-community communication is for the school administrator to find out what kinds of messages and information parents and the community wish to receive. She can begin developing a better understanding of the types of messages she should send by means of a study of community expectations for communication from the school. (A survey periodically administered to all or a sample of parents and other people in a school's immediate community would ascertain many of their communication needs.)

In conducting such an investigation the administrator should be aware of existing research studies on parental expectations for school communication. For example, in a fourteen-school study Anderson found that parents from the central city, city fringe-suburban, rural and urban areas all agreed that they wanted to receive "frequently" from the school eight different types of information. These categories listed in order of their importance to the parents were: (1) the grades and achievement of the parents' son or daughter, (2) discipline problems involving their child, (3) the child's personal weaknesses or physical handicaps, (4) the child's talents and abilities, (5) a schedule of school events, (6) graduation requirements (7) career information, and (8) information on the school's rules and regulations.[8] In addition, parents' responses pertaining to desiring information on "the needs and shortcomings of the school" tended toward "frequently." In a related study by McGeever and Wall, most parents indicated that they wanted more information from the school about school board decisions, possible careers for their children, the regular classroom, special education, student test scores, adult and community education, and class size. Those parents who reported receiving an adequate amount of information (which was accurate and reliable) also rated the quality of education highly and had a high degree of trust and confidence in public education.[9]

School administrators who are seeking insight into parents' expectations for information from the school should find the results of Anderson's and McGeever's investigations helpful. Their research revealed the kinds of information that parents, regardless of population setting, want to receive from the school, as well as specific types of information particularly valued by parents in certain areas. However, their findings should be used only as a general guide to parental expectations for school communication, not as a substitute for the administrator's own specific investigation. Any school administrator who is interested in improving a school's communication effectiveness should conduct her own study of parents and other residents in the school's immediate community to ascertain their communication needs. This study should include an effort to discover any special language or cultural barriers, e.g., Spanish background, that might make it difficult for some parents to understand the message the school is trying to send.[10]

THE MEDIUM

According to Marshall McLuhan, "The medium is the message." Even if McLuhan's observation was overstated, the administrator who wants to improve a school's communication effectiveness with parents and other citizens should examine the means by which the school is trying to send its message.

The best way to start would be to review the research on parents' preferences for how information about the school should be communicated to them. For example, according to a Gallup Poll, when parents were asked, "What is your best source of information about the local public schools?" 70 percent of the respondents reported that word of mouth and personal involvement were their best sources, 37 percent identified the local newspaper, 16 percent mentioned local television programming, and only 7 percent identified school publications and newsletters as their best source of information about the school.[11] In a related study by McGeever and Wall, parents were asked to identify the single information source by which they would prefer to receive all their information about the schools. While there was no majority trend in the responses, those sources identified most frequently, in order of priority, were (1) school staff members, (2) newspapers, and (3) school publications.[12]

While the findings from research studies should not be generalized as referring to all school settings, they can serve as a guide to parental preferences for certain channels of communication. (It should be noted that parents' use of or preferences (or lack of them) for a particular medium of communication are dependent, at least in part, on the degree to which the school has utilized that method. If, for example, a school never uses television for communicating school news, parents may not be aware of its potential.) However, as valuable as research might be, the school administrator should still conduct her own investigation on parental preferences for school communication methods. This study might include ascertaining parents' preferences for the alternative channels of communication identified in research. The important question which the administrator should try to answer is, by what methods would parents prefer that the school communicate information to them?

In considering possible methods of communicating, the administrator should investigate several innovative ways of communicating with parents and other members of the community which have been developed in recent years. These include

1. The identification and utilization of "key communicators" who can help the school communicate important messages and reduce the incidence of rumors. Their use by one school has been described by Litwin.[13]
2. Utilization of newspaper supplements to provide additional information about the school and to discuss school problems. Cangelosi and his colleagues discuss one such approach.[14]
3. Use of taped telephone messages which give parents information about homework, school activities, and services. Brasch relates how several such programs operate.[15]
4. Utilization of radio talk shows to answer questions from the public and to act as a forum for discussing educational issues and problems.[16]

5. Use of cable television to present information to parents on school programs, activities, and services. One school district that has made extensive use of cable television for these purposes is the Irvine Unified School District.[17]

These alternative approaches for communicating with parents and other members of the public offer great potential for improving understanding of the school and what it is trying to accomplish.

As the administrator examines various means by which the school communicates information to parents, she should also investigate to determine whether the information is attractively packaged and the degree of reliability with which it reaches the intended recipients of the message. The "printed word" is one of the principal methods by which most schools try to communicate a message of general interest to parents. Frequently, the information to be communicated is mimeographed or dittoed, and copies are given to the students to be taken home to the parents at the end of the day. Parents complain that all too often the information does not reach them because it is lost or thrown away before the students reach home. Even in those cases in which the information arrives at the home, however, the format, typing, and quality of reproduction of the message may be unattractive, perhaps illegible, and not conducive to stimulating the parents to read the school's message.

While there are times when a school probably cannot avoid communicating printed information through a dittoed sheet or by the student carrier, the administrator should try to limit their use. If the information which the school would like to communicate to parents is important and represents something that parents definitely should read, then the school should make every effort to communicate this information in an attractive, readable form. A publication which the administrator should find useful for improving the format and packaging of the information she sends home to parents is *Putting Words and Pictures About Schools Into Print.*[18]

A case can also be made that a school should make every effort to *mail* important printed information which it wishes to communicate to the home. Utilizing the student as a messenger to the home has not been a particularly successful practice in most school situations, for the reasons mentioned above. By mailing a message to the home, the school can be assured that the information will probably reach the parents. A bulk mailing permit is not an expensive item for a nonprofit organization such as the school, and the total cost of mailing information home from the school should not result in an exorbitant expense. The main question the administrator needs to ask is, "How important is it that the information the school is trying to communicate to the parents be received by them?" If it is important, then the administrator should strongly consider mailing the information to the home. (For further ideas on how to improve school communications, see *School Communication Workshop Kit.*[19])

FEEDBACK

School-community communication should be a two-way process. The school has something important to communicate to parents and other residents of the immediate community, and the school's professional personnel should recognize that the community and parents have something important to communicate to the school.

While there are many kinds of information which a school should be seeking from parents and other citizens, it should attempt to obtain the following information on a regular basis:

1. What are the expectations of parents and other citizens in regard to the types of educational programs the school should offer?
2. What elements do parents and other citizens perceive as the strengths of the school?
3. Which aspects of the school program would parents and other citizens like to see changed?
4. To what extent are parents and other citizens receiving the types of information they desire from the school?
5. To what degree are parents and other citizens satisfied with the *means* by which the school communicates information?

Too often the school seems to be interested primarily in getting its message across to parents and other citizens while giving little or no priority to ascertaining the message they want to receive or the message they would like to communicate to the school. For example, in a study by Gorton and Strobel, most principals gave lip service to the importance of seeking feedback from parents and other members of the community, but in practice their efforts were quite limited.[20] If the school is to improve its communication effectiveness with the community, the administrator must give as much priority to developing a better understanding of the communication needs of the community as she does to communicating what the school wants the community to know.

While there are numerous approaches which administrators could employ to seek feedback, three methods in particular will be recommended. (For ideas on additional methods of obtaining feedback, see Lordeman[21].)

One is to include space for feedback comments, suggestions, or questions in the printed information which the school disseminates. An example of this method is presented in figure 18.1.

The administrator can tailor this approach to the kind of feedback she desires. If she wants specific feedback on the content of a message she is sending to the parents, she can design her questions accordingly. If, on the other hand, she is interested in more general or open-ended feedback, a portion of the newsletter can be designed with that purpose in mind. Using part of the

How Come?

Do you ever wonder why certain things are done or are not done? Or why some things are done the way they are?? If so—and you have never had the time or opportunity to find out—use the form below and a reply will be mailed to you.

How Come: _____
_____
_____
_____

Name: _____
Address: _____

Mail to: School District No. 1
         8060 N. 60th Street

Figure 18.1. An Example of a Method
for Obtaining Feedback[22]

school's information bulletin for the purpose of seeking feedback from parents and other interested parties would seem to be a relatively easy, low-cost means.

A second approach which a number of schools have utilized in order to secure feedback from parents is the Parents' Invitation to Visit the School Program. This method differs from the traditional Parent-Teacher Conference Program or the Back-to-School-Night Program in that a smaller group of parents is involved, the discussion is less formal, and the meeting does not focus on the problems of specific children. The primary purpose of the Parents' Invitation to Visit the School Program is to provide an opportunity for a small group of parents to meet with the school administrator in an informal atmosphere to share ideas and perceptions. The meetings usually take place during school hours (or at night to accommodate working parents) on a biweekly basis and an attempt is made by the school to schedule as many of these meetings as possible during the year. An example from the elementary level of how such meetings are organized and implemented is presented in figure 18.2. Sink describes how these meetings occur at the secondary level.[23]

Reports from schools and parents who have employed this approach are generally favorable. One thing, though, that the administrator herself should try to avoid during these meetings is dominating the discussion and concentrating too much on "selling" the school's program. The primary purpose of this kind of meeting should be to provide an opportunity for parents to present *their* ideas, questions, and concerns—not just a forum for the administrator.

While the previous two methods can provide useful feedback to a school, they do have shortcomings. The feedback portion of the newsletter allows only a limited amount of space for a response, and visits to the school are not convenient for all parents. This does not mean that the administrator should reject these means of obtaining feedback. They should definitely be employed. However, the administrator may need to utlize, in addition, a more comprehensive and systematic method of obtaining feedback from parents and the general public. If an administrator really wants to know what parents or other relevant groups in the community think about some aspect of education, an attempt should be made to survey them periodically through some type of a formal questionnaire, followed by a sample of in-depth interviews. An example of such a survey is presented in figure 18.3.

The school survey is perhaps the most systematic and complete feedback approach. It can be designed for a variety of purposes, and it can provide a great deal of useful information. It is probably the most costly of the feedback methods recommended in this chapter, but its expense can be justified on the basis of the valuable information it generates. The administrator who would like assistance in designing a survey should see *How to Conduct Low Cost Surveys* and *Policy and Survey Research,* both published by the National Public Relations Association, Washington, D.C. For ideas on how principals,

---

Care to spend an hour or so at Dean School on a Thursday morning, sipping coffee and sharing your ideas and opinions with the principal? Want to offer a parent's perception of the school scene? Looking for answers to questions raised by some educational trend or practice or development?

Starting Thursday, February 24, and continuing through May, small groups of parents will be invited to Thursday morning coffees with the principal. These "sip and share" sessions will be held in the main lobby of the Dean School and will begin at 10:00 a.m. If you would be interested in attending one or more of these meetings, please indicate below and have your child return the slip to school. You will then be contacted by phone to arrange for a specific date convenient to you.

Figure 18.2. Parents' Invitation to Visit the School[24]

Presurvey

Objective: To improve the present public relations and communications program between home and school.

Survey Data:
1. Person completing survey: Mother _____ Father _____ Guardian _____
2. In what grade level(s) are your children? 7 _____ 8 _____ 9 _____

- -

Instructions:
Place a check (√) on the line indicating your preference with regard to the following questions and statements:

3. Have you received our November school newsletter? Yes _____ No _____

4. If "yes," how effective do you think it is in getting information about our school to our parents? (Check one.)

   1 _____ 2 _____ 3 _____ 4 _____ 5 _____

   very poor   poor   average   good   very good

5. When your child started junior high school, did you attend the orientation meeting for parents? Yes _____ No _____

6. If "yes," how useful do you think the orientation was for parents?

   1 _____ 2 _____ 3 _____ 4 _____ 5 _____

   very poor   poor   average   good   very good

7. Do you know about the Jerstad-Agerhold Junior High School Advisory Council of parents, teachers, and administrators? Yes _____ No _____

8. If "yes," please rate their effectiveness in getting information to our parents. (Check one.)

   1 _____ 2 _____ 3 _____ 4 _____ 5 _____

   very poor   poor   average   good   very good

Figure 18.3. Jerstad-Agerhold Junior
High School[25]

teachers and parents can plan and conduct feedback interviews, write to the Wisconsin Research and Development Center in Madison, Wisconsin for the publication, *Depth Interview Handbook.*

RELATIONSHIP WITH THE NEWS MEDIA

The relationship between the school administrator and the news media has frequently been one of ambivalence and suspicion. As Gorton has noted, often the administrator perceives the reporter as a nuisance who is interested only in exposing the school's shortcomings.[26] On the other hand, the reporter may see the administrator as one who is secretive, defensive, and less than responsive to the public's right to be informed about what is happening in the schools.[27]

---

*Only sample questions are used to illustrate the nature of the survey.

While neither point of view is valid, there is enough truth in both perceptions to create grounds for a poor relationship. This is unfortunate, since the news media does have a responsibility to obtain accurate information about the schools for the public, and administrators could more effectively utilize the news media to provide the public with information about various aspects of the educational enterprise.

The problem of a poor school-news media relationship does not lend itself to any simple solution. However, it would appear that greater openness and candor by the administrator would be helpful. Specifically, she should attempt to adhere to the ten guidelines that follow, which were extracted from an examination of several proposals for improving school-press relationships.[28]

Guidelines for Working with the News Media

1. Don't wait for reporters to call you. Take the initiative and call the reporter first, especially when there is a crisis.
2. Regularly and systematically offer news and feature story ideas to the press. Don't be discouraged because your first half-dozen or dozen ideas are brushed off with no coverage or only a few lines. Keep trying. Not only is the law of averages on your side, but if you are alert, you will be sharpening your skills in identifying what makes a good story. Also, don't limit yourself to the newspaper. Initiate contact with radio and television sources of news as well.
3. Get to know the reporters and editors covering your school. If you don't have a speaking relationship with them, pick up the phone and introduce yourself. Let them know that you would be happy to discuss educational issues with them.
4. Find out the reporter's time-deadline requirements and try to cooperate. You need not drop everything for the press and, indeed, often you have more pressing responsibilities. But perhaps you can spare sixty seconds before his deadline, or assign someone else to help, or decide when you have time for the press before it's too late.
5. Be patient with reporters so that you know they have all the facts and understand them in the context of your interpretation.
6. If you don't know an answer, say so. If you know who does know, refer the reporter to the source, but don't shuttle him just because you don't want the responsibility for the answers. If you don't know and don't know who does, agree to try to find out and call back, and do it.
7. Spend as much time as necessary explaining an idea or program to get it understood. A percentage of the people who feel they are misquoted are really people who didn't make clear what they were trying to say.

8. Be credible. Don't distort the facts even if they hurt. The media will usually believe what you say until you give them cause not to believe you.
9. Keep your head about errors. If a story has an error, decide whether the error invalidates the main idea of the story. If it doesn't invalidate the whole thing, you would probably still want to let the reporter know about it so the mistake won't reoccur on subsequent articles—but don't make a federal case out of it. A correction or a retraction on this level does more harm than good. If the mistake does serious harm (says the school play will be Friday when it is Thursday) or makes the whole story erroneous (says the school board is thinking of closing down one of the high schools when they have decided not to do so), ask for a correction. You'll probably get it. If a reporter does a good job on a story, tell him.
10. Maintain your composure. Even though the reporter might call you during a crisis, be "calm, cool, and collected." This type of image helps create credibility and a favorable impression of the administrator and the school.

These recommendations may not be easily implemented in all situations, but they are basically sound. While some administrators may feel that reporters are the ones who need to improve and not themselves, it seems clear that as administrators we need to put our own house in order before turning our attention to others.

FINAL COMMENT ON IMPROVING SCHOOL-COMMUNITY COMMUNICATION

Communication between the school and the community should be on a regular basis. The school has frequently been criticized because its communication with the community has been irregular, and then only at times of importance to the school, e.g., a bond referendum. Many administrators behave as though it is not too important for the school to communicate regularly with parents and the rest of the community. However, as Bortner has observed, "The community will acquaint itself with and express opinions about its school whether the school attempts to keep the people informed or not."[29] Regular and full communication between the school and the community is an important prerequisite for developing more accurate information on the part of both and, as a result, a more positive attitude toward each other.

THE SCHOOL'S PUBLIC RELATIONS PROGRAM

PURPOSE AND OBJECTIVES

Most administrators would agree that it is essential that a school and school district maintain an effective program of public relations with the community. An initial problem, however, is that the term "public relations" in this context is subject to different interpretations, three of which are presented below:

1. The purpose of a public relations program is to *sell* the educational program to the people of the community, so that they will take pride in and support their schools. (To do this, the public relations program should widely publicize the strengths of the existing school program.)
2. The purpose of a public relations program is to *interpret* to the people of the community the educational program that is in operation so that the people will have a better understanding of what the schools are doing and will support the school program. (To do this, the public relations program should explain purposes and procedures in reporting both the strengths and weaknesses of the existing school program.)
3. The purpose of a public relations program is to encourage community interest and *participation* in the school program. (To do this, the public relations program should solicit and utilize appropriate information, advice, and assistance of interested community groups and individuals in many aspects of school operations. It should also report and explain both the strengths and weaknesses of the existing school program.)[30]

Although there are probably few administrators who would *publicly* admit to subscribing only to the first concept of school public relations, the behavior of many administrators suggests that the other concepts have little appeal to them. Seldom does one find an administrator who reports to the community both strengths *and* weaknesses of the existing school program. While the concept of encouraging community interest and participation in the school program has received considerable attention in the educational literature and at conventions and conferences, the number of schools implementing the concept in full measure is less than overwhelming. The fact of the matter is that in practice most administrators have not accepted fully the concepts of public relations as defined in nos. 2 and 3.[31]

Perhaps the failure by most administrators to endorse and implement the latter two concepts can be attributed to a misunderstanding of how one gains support of the school by the public. If administrators are really interested in community pride in and support of the schools, the most effective way to achieve this objective is to be completely open and candid in reporting to the community on the effectivenss of various aspects of the school program and to encourage and utilize community participation whenever appropriate and feasible. Attempting to "sell" the educational program to the people of a community by publicizing only the strengths of the existing school program will strain the believability of a school's communication and will eventually seriously erode its credibility. As Hughes has perceptively observed, ". . . To expect people to 'buy' simply because educators are selling is unrealistic. The terms buying and selling are used advisedly; it is recognized that any successful program will have to be the result of mutual planning, mutual understanding, and mutual trust."[32]

This does not mean, of course, that schools should not attempt to stress the positive. An example of a rather innovative way of stressing the positive was developed by the Pequa, Ohio, school district for its annual report to the community. In the report the school district indicated:

99.9% of the students were not suspended or expelled.
97.3% of the students were not tardy for class.
98.2% were not issued offenses or detentions for misbehavior in school.
98.1% did not cause trouble on the school buses.
93.4% were well behaved on the playground.
98.7% were not disciplined for fighting.
99.4% were respectful of the staff.
99.8% were not admonished for having drugs and/or alcohol on school premises.
99.6% were not involved in school vandalism.

(See Armistead for other ideas on how to stress the positive.[33])

However, if a school continues to emphasize only the strengths of its program while covering up the weaknesses and isolating itself from community involvement, the risk increases that the public will begin to ignore, suspect, or fail to believe what the school says. As noted in the publication, *Ideas for Improving Confidence in Public Education,* "School officials must report successes and failures honestly and realistically. This must be an on-going policy."[34] The administrator should keep in mind that an essential requirement for effective communication and public relations is credibility.

The best kind of public relations program is one based on an open dialogue with the public on the strengths, weaknesses, and problems of the school, creating and maximizing opportunities for community groups and individuals to give information, advice, and assistance to the school. The specific objectives of such a program have been identified by Kindred:

1. To develop intelligent public understanding of the school in all aspects of its operation.

2. To determine how the public feels about the school and what it wishes the school to accomplish.
3. To secure adequate financial support for a sound educational program.
4. To help citizens feel a more direct responsibility for the quality of education that the school provides.
5. To earn the good will, respect, and confidence of the public in professional personnel and services of the institution.
6. To bring about public realization of the need for change and what must be done to facilitate essential programs.
7. To involve citizens in the work of the school and the solving of educational problems.
8. To promote a genuine spirit of cooperation between the school and community in sharing leadership for the improvement of community life.[35]

ORGANIZATION OF THE PUBLIC RELATIONS PROGRAM

Public relations is not something that just happens. As Bortner has noted, ". . . the school does have a choice: between unplanned and planned public relations, between disregarding or developing an organized public relations program designed to promote community understanding and support."[36]

In order to achieve the objectives of a planned public relations program, people and resources will have to be organized. The final organizational design should clearly identify the various individuals and groups who are involved in the public relations program and the nature of their responsibilities.

While administrators in small school districts are primarily responsible for their school's public relations program, in many medium-to-large school districts a public relations or public information officer directs and coordinates the school district's public relations program. The public relations role of the school administrator in a district that has a public relations officer may be significant or quite limited, depending upon how she and the public relations officer conceive of that role. Generally, the public relations officer will view the school administrator as playing a potentially important role in public relations, although a role definition or in-service training to carry out the administrator's responsibilities in this area may be lacking. Regrettably, there is also some tendency on the part of school administrators in larger districts to feel that public relations is something that is solely in the public information officer's province and should involve other administrators only if a problem develops at their school.

Regardless of whether or not a district employs a public relations officer, the building administrator should be a key figure in the public relations program. It is at the building level that the success or failure of the public relations program is likely to be determined, and the school administrator is a crucial variable influencing that determination.

Although there are many different facets to the school administrator's role in public relations, she should attempt to perform the following tasks in cooperation with other members of the professional staff and representatives of the school community:

1. Develop or update the philosophy and objectives of the school's public relations program. Without clear specification and an understanding of the philosophy and objectives of the program on the part of everyone, it will tend to flounder or go off into different directions.
2. Identify and define the public relations role of the administrative team, the professional and certified staff, the students, and the community. Public relations should be the responsibility of all people who are associated with the school. However, the administrator will need to define the precise nature of that responsibility, particularly for the personnel who work in the school.
3. Plan and implement a set of public relations activities which will accomplish the goals of the program. The nature of these activities will depend on the type of objectives adopted for the program, but a well-planned, comprehensive set of activities will be needed. (For an excellent description of examples of public relations activities which can be initiated at the building level, see Jones[37] and Swedmark.[38]
4. Concentrate your primary efforts in public relations on developing and sustaining the best possible educational program. A good educational program will do more to improve public relations than any other factor. As Armistead emphasizes, "If we are to build public confidence in education, certain things must take place. First and foremost, all educators must try to do the best job possible, for nothing replaces a good performance.[39]
5. Evaluate the school's current public relations program on a periodic basis to ascertain the need for adding, modifying, or eliminating public relations activities. The questions which the administrator should ask about the school's public relations program are, "What are we now doing that we could be doing better?" "What new activities are needed?" "What activities are unproductive?"

In conceptualizing the type of public relations program most desirable for a school, the administrator needs to recognize that there are many factors which affect the public's attitude toward the school.[40] In a broad sense, almost everything that happens in or to a school can potentially affect the public's attitude. While the administrator cannot always control or influence events or forces in the larger society which may affect the public's attitude toward the school, she can at least try to do something about those conditions that are associated with the school and which may affect public relations. A number of school-related factors which can potentially influence the public's attitude toward the school are presented in figure 18.4.

An examination of figure 18.4 suggests almost everything that the school does may affect the public's attitude toward it. As Charters has noted, "Every aspect of the school, every remark by an employee of the school, every communication with the home, every subject taught, every service to the community, even the janitor's appearance is believed to affect public relations either favorably or unfavorably."[41]

Three factors which can particularly affect a school's public relations image are the ways in which parent-teacher conferences are conducted, the manner in which the school responds to telephone calls, and the general receptivity of the school office to visitors, whether they be parents or other adults. A courteous, friendly, and helpful approach in these situations will contribute greatly

Classroom Factors	*General School Factors*	*School-Community Factors*

1. Teacher-student relationship
2. Homework policy
3. Grading policy and procedures
4. Classroom discipline
5. Friendliness and communicability of the teacher to the parents
	1. Type of educational program
	  a. program of studies
	  b. teaching staff
	  c. student activities program
	2. General school discipline
	3. General atmosphere in the school
	4. Appearance of the school building, inside and outside
		1. Receptivity and friendliness of school personnel to parents and visitors
		2. Effectiveness of the school in resolving school-community issues and problems
		3. The accuracy and completeness of information about the school as it is transmitted to parents
		4. The accuracy and completeness of information the school has about the community

Figure 18.4. School-Related Factors
which Affect the Public's Attitude
Toward the School

to a favorable public perception of the school; the expression (whether intended or not) of an impersonal, condescending, or disinterested attitude will lead to a negative view of the school. It is the administrator's responsibility to impress on all school employees the importance of positive contacts with parents and the community.*

While the contribution of school employees to public relations can be significant, probably the single most important public relations agent for the school is the student.[42] Most of the factors identified in figure 18.4 affect the student in some way, and it is through the student that parents and the larger community gain many of their impressions about the school. Therefore, the school administrator should give high priority to policies, procedures, and programs that will result in the development of positive student attitudes and accurate student information about the school and its personnel.

EVALUATING THE SCHOOL'S PUBLIC RELATIONS PROGRAM

An important step an administrator should take to improve a school's public relations program is to evaluate the current program's effectiveness, since periodic evaluation of any program is required for continued improvement. To evaluate a school's public relations program the administrator will need criteria and assessment procedures. Of the many attempts to design criteria for evaluating a school's public relations program, those developed by the National School Public Relations Association would appear to be among the most useful for a school administrator.[43] Examples of criteria questions from the NSPRA's Evaluation Instrument are presented below.

- Does the district have a written, clear and concise policy statement regarding its public relations program?
- Is the policy statement approved by the school board, published in its policy manual and revised annually?
- Does the policy statement express the purposes of the public relations program and provide for the delegation of such authority as necessary to achieve the purposes to an appropriate administrator?
- Is the policy statement included in the district personnel handbooks so that all staff members are aware of the purposes of the public relations program?
- Is the public relations program allocated sufficient human and financial resources to accomplish its goals?

---

*An excellent filmstrip and tape cassette which identify the public relations role of everyone in the school, and which could be used in an in-service program is *A School Is People,* produced by the National Public Relations Association, Washington, D.C.

- Does the public relations unit utilize feedback continuously to modify its activities to meet the information needs of its audiences?
- Does the public relations program include inservice training for other members of the school staff in the areas of school/community relations?
- Does the program encourage community involvement in the schools?
- Is there provision for continuous and systematic evaluation?

Whether the administrator uses a checklist such as the one by the National School Public Relations Association or another assessment procedure, it is important that she recognize the need for periodic, systematic evaluation of the school's public relations program. In evaluating the program, the administrator should try to secure representative perceptions from every group associated with the school, including students, parents, teachers, and classified employees. If public relations is the responsibility of everyone in the school, and if the public is considered to include everyone in the community, then representatives of these individuals and groups should all be actively involved in assessing the effectivenss of the school's public relations program.

However, the leadership and impetus for evaluating a school's public relations program should come from the administrator. She must feel strongly about the need for periodic and systematic evaluation, or it probably will not occur. And if a school's public relations program is not evaluated and upgraded, it is the school administrator who should be held accountable for the consequences of a negative or apathetic public attitude toward the school.

A FINAL NOTE

School-community public relations and communication are important tasks for the school administrator. These activities should focus on giving an accurate, candid, and complete picture of the school's strengths *and* problems, and should provide ways by which members of the community can communicate to the school their perceptions and needs. The goal of the school administrator in performing these tasks should not be to manipulate public opinion, but to develop understanding, perspective, and commitment on the part of the community. Only the achievement of the latter goal will maintain school credibility and community support over the long run.

Review and Learning Activities

1. Review the situation in your own school in light of the criticisms presented in the text regarding communication practices with parents and the community. To what extent are the criticisms valid for your school? How would you improve matters?

2. Based on the concepts presented in the text, how would you improve the "message" aspect of school-community communications in your school? What problems and/or obstacles would need to be overcome?
3. Based on concepts presented in the text, how would you improve the "medium" aspect of school-community communications in your school? What problems and/or obstacles would need to be overcome?
4. How does your school or school district secure feedback from parents and the larger community? Draft a policy and a plan for improving feedback from parents and the larger community.
5. Evaluate the merits of each of the recommended guidelines for working with the news media. In what ways will your own attitude and behavior need to change in order for you to develop a good working relationship with the news media?
6. Ascertain the extent to which your school and/or district has a formal, written public relations program. Based on the concepts identified in the text, draft a comprehensive public relations program for your school.

Notes

1. Kenneth J. Gelms, "The Overlooked Communications Tool: Building Level Publications," *National Association of Secondary School Principals Bulletin* (January 1979): 39–45.

2. One of the main sources of these criticisms comes from reports and studies published by the Institute for Responsive Education, Boston, Massachusetts, and the National Committee for Citizens in Education at Columbia, Maryland. Also see J. Cy Rowell, "The Five Rights of Parents," *Phi Delta Kappan* (February 1981): 441–43.

3. Donald Bagin and John H. Wherry, "Ten Ways to Improve Your Relationships with Your Public" (Paper presented at the annual convention of the American Association of School Administrators, 1982).

4. George Gallup, "Sixth Annual Gallup Poll of Public Attitudes toward Education," *Phi Delta Kappan* (September 1974): 25. See the September 1980 issue of the *Kappan* for a different (but not contrary) set of findings.

5. Nancy Seymour, "Community Radio in North Carolina," *Citizen Action in Education* (November 1979): 1, 7.

6. Dick Gorton and Paul Strobel, "Principals' Actions Fall Short of Stated Attitudes toward Community Relations," *Journal of Educational Communication* (July 1981): 35–36.

7. Daniel A. Salman, "Building a Strong Public Information Program in the School," *National Association of Secondary School Principals Bulletin* (December 1979): 111–15.

8. Reviewed by Richard A. Gorton, "Comments on Research," *National Association of Secondary School Principals Bulletin* (February 1972): 98–101.

9. James M. McGeever and Victor Wall, "The Origin of Ohio Household's Opinions about Public Education" (Paper presented at the annual meeting of the American Education Research Association, Los Angeles, 1981).

10. Robert L. Marion, "Communicating with Parents of Culturally Diverse Exceptional Children," *Exceptional Children* (May 1980): 616–23.

11. George H. Gallup, "The Eleventh Annual Gallup Poll of the Public's Attitude toward the Public Schools," *Phi Delta Kappan* (September 1979): 37.

12. McGeever and Wall, "Origin of Ohio Households' Opinions about Public Education."

13. M. Larry Litwin, "Key Communicators—They Lock Out Rumors," *NASSP Bulletin* (January 1979): 17–22. Also see Don Bagin, "Eleven Questions and Answers about Key Communicators," *Journal of Educational Communications* (July 1981): 15–16.

14. James S. Cangelosi et al., "Help for Parents on Their Doorsteps," *Phi Delta Kappan* (November 1978): 245–46.

15. Phyllis Brasch, "Recorded Classroom Reports Get High Marks," *CEMREL Reports* (Winter 1981): 5.

16. For a good background article on the possible uses of radio, see Bernard Caton et al., *Public Radio in Virginia* (Richmond, Va.: Virginia State Telecommunications Study Commission, 1979).

17. Educational Products Information Exchange Institute, "The Ultimate Wired Community," *New Technology* (January 1981): 5–6.

18. *Putting Words and Pictures about School into Print* (Washington, D.C.: National Public Relations Association, 1982).

19. National School Public Relations Association, *School Community Workshop Kit* (Arlington, Va.: NSPRA, 1981).

20. Gorton and Strobel, "Principals' Actions Fall Short."

21. Ann Lordeman et al., "Establishing and Assessing Two-Way Communication between Parents and School." An ERIC Report: Ed–143–103.

22. Edited from material employed by Brown Deer Public Schools, Brown Deer, Wisconsin. Used with permission.

23. Ed Sink, "Meeting with the Parents," *NASSP Spotlight* (January 1977): 1–2.

24. Brown Deer Public Schools.

25. Edited from material employed by Jerstad-Agehold Junior High School. Used with permission.

26. Richard A. Groton, "What Do Principals Think of News Media Coverage?" *NASSP Bulletin* (December 1979): 116–18.

27. Gene I Maeroff, "The Media and the Schools," *The Reading Teacher* (October 1980): 7–11.

28. Robert Krajewski, "Superintendent to Daughter: Why Don't You Reporters Shape UP?" *The American School Board Journal* (August 1980): 17–20; William E. Henry, "Working with the Media," *NASSP Bulletin* (January 1979): 10–16; Lew Armistead, "Working with Media Develops Good News," *NASSP Newsletter* (February 1981): 5–6; Betty Orsini, "Press Coverage Can Be Positive," *NASSP Newsletter* (February 1979): 8; and Al Bruton, "The School Administrator and the Press: Is Co-Existence Possible?" *Thrust for Educational Leadership* (1973): 15.

29. Doyle M. Bortner, "The High School: Responsibility for Public Relations," *NASSP Bulletin* (September 1960): 7.

30. First introduced in a study reported in *The Classroom Teacher and Public Relations* (Washington, D.C.: NEA Research Division, 1959), p. 10. Observation would suggest that these three purposes are still current.

31. For example, see Roy R. Nesstrom, "Principals View Parents as Enemies," *Journal of Educational Communication* (July 1981): 35

32. Larry W. Hughes, "Know Your Power Structure," *American School Board Journal* (May 1967): 33–35.

33. Lew Armistead, "Tips for Principals: Communicating the Positive," *NASSP Newsletter* (April 1981): 5–6. Also see William J. Jones, *Building Public Confidence for Your Schools* (Arlington, Va.: National School Public Relations Association, 1978).

34. *Ideas for Improving Public Confidence in Public Education* (Washington, D.C.: National Public Relations Association, 1971).

35. Leslie W. Kindred, *School Public Relations* (Englewood Cliffs, N.J.: Prentice-Hall, 1957); pp. 16–17, and *The Basic School Public Relations Kit* (Arlington, Va.: National School Public Relations Association, 1980).

36. Bortner, "High School: Responsibility for Public Relations."

37. Jones, *Building Public Confidence for Your Schools.*

38. Donald C. Swedmark, "Competencies and Skills for an Effective School Public Relations Program," *NASSP Bulletin* (December 1979): 79–84.

39. Lew Armistead, "Getting the Education Team Organized to Speak Up for Schools," *NASSP Newsletter* (December 1980): 13.

40. For an early analysis of this point, see W. W. Charters, Jr., "In a Public Relations Program Facts Are Never Enough," *Nation's Schools* (February 1954): 56–58.

41. W. W. Charters, Jr., "Public Relations," in *Encyclopedia of Educational Research,* ed. Chester Harris (New York: Macmillan Co., 1960), p. 1075.

42. Dorothy Dubia, "Students Are Your Best PR," *NASSP Bulletin* (January, 1979): 65–66.

43. National School Public Relations Association, *Evaluation Instrument for Educational Public Relations Programs* (Arlington, Va: NSPRA, 1978).

6

CAREER CONSIDERATIONS

19

CAREER ASSESSMENT

The pursuit of a successful career in school administration involves at least two major elements: (1) understanding and capitalizing on career and employment opportunities, and (2) possessing needed competencies and professional ethics. These aspects will be discussed in this chapter, along with factors involved in obtaining a position in school administration and planning for the first year.

CAREER AND EMPLOYMENT OPPORTUNITIES IN SCHOOL ADMINISTRATION

CAREER OPPORTUNITIES

When one considers career opportunities in school administration, the principalship is usually the first and most frequently cited position. Although the principalship is perhaps the most important position in the administration of a school, there are a number of other positions with administrative or quasi-administrative responsibilities with which the reader should also become familiar. Examples of these positions are identified in figure 19.1.

Entry Positions

Assistant or Vice-Principal	Dean of Students	Administrative Intern	Administrative Assistant	Department Head or Unit Leader
	Athletic Director		Grade Level Coordinator	

Advanced Position
Principal

Figure 19.1. Examples of Career Positions in School Administration

It should be noted that most people seeking their first job in school administration do not begin as principals.[1] An exception would be the person who moves from a teaching position to an elementary school principalship or a secondary school principalship in a small school district. The more typical career pattern is for an individual to begin a career in administration by assuming one of the entry positions identified in figure 19.1, e.g., administrative intern, assistant principal. These positions can offer valuable experience and training for more advanced roles in school or district administration and can in many instances provide sufficient personal satisfaction and reward so that they become permanent career positions.

The entry positions in administration represent important components of the administrative team of a school or school district, and the individuals occupying them should have opportunities to make useful contributions to the success of the school program. It should be emphasized that no one should consider an entry position as *merely* a stepping stone to a higher place in the administrative hierarchy. An entry position offers a potentially valid career in and of itself, rather than as a temporary stopping-off point before a move on to a more advanced position.

However, even if a person decides that it is really the *principalship* or a position in district administration to which he/she aspires, it would be desirable for that individual to first obtain as much experience as possible in one or more of the entry positions in school administration. For example, a person who is now a teacher might seek the position of department head or unit leader in a school. Such a position, quasi-administrative in nature, could give one considerable experience in the administrative processes of goal setting, planning, organizing, and working with adult groups. It could also provide practice in supervising and evaluating teachers, if such responsibilities are associated with the job. All of these experiences constitute potentially valuable training in administration. Certainly, the experiences gained through being a department head or unit leader could be useful later when a person becomes a principal and interacts with the people occupying those positions.

Or an individual might prepare for the principalship by seeking on-the-job training as an administrative assistant, an assistant principal, a vice-principal, or a dean of students.* Unlike the department head, who generally teaches three or more classes, these other entry posts are usually full-time administrative positions. Typically they differ in types of responsibilities associated with each position, but they all offer potentially useful training for more advanced careers in administration. The problem is that none of these positions itself offers the kind of *broad* on-the-job training that a principal really needs.

---

*See chapter 5, The Administrative Team, for a description of these positions.

For example, although there are exceptions, the administrative assistant's role is frequently managerial in nature, concerned with budgeting, plant management, or student discipline, with little or no responsibility in the areas of instructional improvement and curriculum development. The primary duties of the assistant principal, vice-principal, and dean of students are usually confined to student discipline and attendance. Instructional improvement, curriculum, and budgeting are responsibilities which are seldom associated with these positions, although that situation is changing to some extent. It is true that in larger schools with two assistant or vice-principals, one of them may be assigned responsibilities for instructional improvement and curriculum development, but in such cases the individual occupying that position receives little experience in the other aspects of the principalship.

Perhaps the best on-the-job training for the principalship, at least in terms of breadth, is the administrative internship. The internship has existed in education for a long time, in one form or another.[2] But it wasn't until the early 1960s, when Lloyd Trump and others proposed the administrative internship as an important training vehicle for those interested in school leadership, that it assumed major stature. Since then, thousands of individuals have used this approach as on-the-job preparation for the school principalship, and many school districts now sponsor their own internship program, often in cooperation with a nearby university. (It should be noted that financial problems have caused many school districts to reduce or eliminate their administrative internship program, thereby significantly limiting this type of preparation for administration.)

Although the nature of experiences which an intern receives may vary from district to district, the intent of most programs is to provide a person with as much exposure to and actual experience in the various facets of the principal's job, as possible. Therefore, anyone who plans to become a principal (or for that matter, any of the full-time administrative positions in the school) should investigate the possibility of securing an administrative internship in a school in the district or in another district which offers such an opportunity.

For further information on how to establish an administrative internship program and for a description of several examples of successful administrative internships, the reader is referred to the monograph, *The Administrative Internship.*[3]

EMPLOYMENT OPPORTUNITIES

Before one decides on a career in school adminstration, that individual should thoroughly investigate the employment opportunities.

Until recently, it was assumed by those entering the field of administration that if state certification could be obtained, there would be little or no problem in securing a job.* Many people, including those responsible for preparing administrators, believed that if an administrative aspirant was willing to move to a new situation or wait until a vacancy occurred in his or her own district, it would be simply a matter of time before a job in administration could be secured. It has also been implicitly believed by many that once a person acquired an entry position in administration, it would not be long before an opportunity to become a principal would present itself.

Whether there was ever a close relationship between these beliefs and reality is debatable. Unfortunately, there has been a paucity of data on employment opportunities, which has tended to encourage an optimistic viewpoint on job possibilities in school administration. One rather important booklet by Donald Mitchell, *Leadership in Public Education Study,* has been published, presenting statistics that cast considerable doubt on the previously optimistic beliefs about employment opportunities in administration.[4] (Although the study was conducted in the 1970s and has yet to be replicated in the 80s, this author could find no contrary evidence which would invalidate the relevance in the 1980s of the study's basic findings.)

On the basis of a questionnaire sent to state certification authorities across the country, the Mitchell study found that, in more than half of the thirty-nine states from which responses were obtained, more people were qualified to take the position of principal than there were openings. In fact, five states indicated that *many* more people were qualified for principalships than there were openings. Twelve states replied that there were a sufficient number of qualified people for the openings for princials; only four states indicated a shortage of qualified people for principalship vacancies. Although the data were not analyzed according to elementary or secondary openings, it seems fair to conclude from the findings of this study that most states have a surplus of individuals certified for the principalship, and that a person contemplating a career as a principal should therefore recognize that there may be extreme competition for a job. It should be noted that this situation has worsened as a result of the decline in student enrollment in the schools.

While the available data do not suggest a very rosy employment picture in school adminstration, several factors mitigate the severity of the overall outlook. First, observation would suggest that employment opportunities for a prospective principal appear to be better in certain states than in others. The Mitchell study did not report by state the employment opportunities for the principalship; as a consequence the reader will have to do some investigating in this regard. Usually state departments of public instruction are a good source of general information on employment opportunities in school administration,

---

*The reader who is interested in certification requirements for administrators and supervisors in the different states should check in a library for Elizabeth H. Woellner, *Requirements for Certification* (Chicago: University of Chicago Press, 1982).

and individual professors within a school of education may be especially good sources for such information. (Since Mitchell's study indicates that in most states there is a surplus of certificated people for available vacancies in the principalship, steps should be taken before an individual is very far along in a preparatory program to ascertain exactly what the situation is in a particular state or area.)

A second reason for investigating the local employment situation in school administration is that it may have changed since the Mitchell study. For example, there is some indication that the turnover rate in the principalship is increasing as a result of the many problems and pressures that have become a part of a principal's job. Consequently, there may be more early retirements, resignations, and advancements to central office positions than was formerly the case. Also, laws and court cases on sex and racial discrimination may provide greater job opportunities in school administration for women and members of minority groups. Although the evidence supporting these potential trends is fragmentary and contradictory, it is possible that conditions associated with the principalship, along with federal equal rights legislation, will create more employment opportunities (at least for certain groups) than the Mitchell data suggest.

On the other hand, several studies have shown that the growth in employment of women and minority administrators, especially women, has been much less than one might have predicted after a period of civil rights legislation, regulations, and court decisions.[5] This situation could change significantly in the 1980s, however, as more and more people responsible for the hiring of administrators become familiar with the research which identifies the leadership strengths of these underrepresented groups and as individual women and members of minorities become more assertive in demanding that they be treated fairly in employment decisions. (For a review of this research, see Adkison, and Ortiz;[6] for an excellent book which describes the problems of becoming and being a woman administrator and offers suggestions for coping with those problems, see *Women and Educational Leadership*.[7])

Finally, it needs to be emphasized that Mitchell's study refers only to a likely surplus of *certificated* people for available vacancies in the principalship. In other words, there is a surplus of people who meet the *minimum* employment standards to become a principal. This says nothing about employment opportunities for those individuals who *exceed* state standards, or who possess or acquire competencies and personality characteristics which would place them above the average candidate for a principalship. While there may be a surplus of minimally qualified people for the principalship, it would seem reasonable to assume that there will continue to be employment opportunities for those who possess training beyond that of the average candidate for an administrative position, or who reveal outstanding leadership capabilities.

NEEDED COMPETENCIES AND PROFESSIONAL ETHICS FOR SCHOOL ADMINISTRATION

RECOMMENDED COMPETENCIES

One important theory concerning the competencies needed by administrators has been advanced by Katz, who feels that the three basic skills needed by administrators are (1) technical, (2) human, and (3) conceptual.[8] Technical skills are those which the school administrator must possess to perform such tasks as budgeting, scheduling, staffings, and other similar administrative responsibilities. Human skills refer to interpersonal skills needed to work successfully with people in one-to-one or group settings. Conceptual skills are those which the school administrator needs in order to see the "total picture" and the relationships between and among its various parts. Katz believes that the relative importance of these basic skills depends on the level of administrative responsibility, with higher level administrators (e.g., superintendents) requiring more conceptual than technical skills, and lower level administrators, (e.g., principals) needing more technical than conceptual skills.[9] Human skills, however, are important at all levels of administration.

In another context, Gorton has proposed five types of competencies which appear to be essential for school administrators who want to function as leaders.[10] The five, identified in question form, are:

1. Does the administrator have the ability to identify accurately the problems which need to be corrected in the school?
2. Does the administrator possess vision as an educator? Does he/she recognize, understand, and see the implications of the various trends and social forces which are and will be affecting education and the larger society?
3. Does the administrator feel a strong need to be a leader? Does he/she have a strong drive to set and achieve new goals? Does he/she seek out opportunities to exercise leadership?
4. Is the administrator willing to assume a degree of risk in initiating leadership—and to face resistance, opposition, and personal or professional criticism?
5. Does the administrator possess good human relations skills, e.g., sensitivity to the needs of others?

In addition to the concepts described above, research on leadership and numerous personal reports from administrators are helpful in suggesting those competencies that a person should possess or acquire in pursuing a career in school administration.[11] Rather than reviewing all of these studies and reports, a self-assessment questionnaire has been developed, based on a synthesis of this information, and is presented in figure 19.2.

	Usually	*To a Large Extent*	*Improvement Needed*
1. Are you objective about yourself and about others? Evidence?	_____	_____	_____
2. Do you possess ideas and convictions about improvements needed in education and the direction that education should take in the future? Evidence?	_____	_____	_____
3. Are you a hard worker, stong on perseverance and a high energy level? Evidence?	_____	_____	_____
4. Do you possess a high tolerance for frustration, stress, challenges to self by others? Evidence?	_____	_____	_____
5. Do you possess considerable self-confidence? Evidence?	_____	_____	_____
6. Do you like responsibility? Evidence?	_____	_____	_____
7. Are you engaged in continuous self and professional improvement? Evidence?	_____	_____	_____
8. Do you have the ability to plan and organize a job? Evidence?	_____	_____	_____
9. Are you well organized in the use of your time? Evidence?	_____	_____	_____

Figure 19.2. Self-Assessment Questionnaire for Prospective School Administrators

(Continued)

	Usually	To a Large Extent	Improvement Needed
10. Do you have the inclination and the ability to solve or ameliorate difficult problems? Evidence?	_____	_____	_____
11. Are you a good decision maker? Evidence?	_____	_____	_____
12. Do you have the capacity to compromise and to be flexible? Evidence?	_____	_____	_____
13. Do you possess the ability to know when to compromise and to be flexible? Evidence?	_____	_____	_____
14. Are you able to influence others, to change their thinking? Evidence?	_____	_____	_____
15. Do you have the ability to mediate conflict, to reconcile differences among others? Evidence?	_____	_____	_____
16. Are you perceptive about the needs and problems of others, including those you don't like? Evidence?	_____	_____	_____
17. Are you an articulate and effective speaker in front of a group, or as a member of a group, or as a leader of a group? Evidence?	_____	_____	_____
18. Can you express yourself clearly, logically, and accurately in writing and speaking? Evidence?	_____	_____	_____

Figure 19.2. Continued   (Continued)

	Usually	To a Large Extent	Improvement Needed
19. Are you knowledgeable about the concepts and principles presented in this text?	_____	_____	_____
20. Do you possess a good capacity to learn, to "catch on"? Evidence?	_____	_____	_____

Figure 19.2. Continued

It should be emphasized that this self-assessment questionnaire is still in the process of being formally validated, and therefore should not be used as the sole basis for making a decision about a career in school administration. The questionnaire is primarily intended (1) to stimulate the reader to engage in some serious thinking about his/her potential for school administration, and (2) to help the reader identify possible areas in need of further improvement.

In responding to the questions in figure 19.2, the reader should pay particularly close attention to examining the evidence used in determining the rating of the extent to which he/she possesses each of the traits. It is usually difficult for anyone to be completely objective or knowledgeable about his/her own strengths and weaknesses. Therefore, before answering such a question as, "Are you well organized in the use of your time?" the reader should think about his/her experiences in situations which called for priority setting and efficient use of time, and perhaps even discuss performance and potential with others who may be more objective in their perceptions.

It should be pointed out that a prospective administrator is unlikely to possess *all* of the traits identified in figure 19.2. In fact, it is doubtful whether the vast majority of current school administrators possess all of these traits to a large degree. But each of the traits identified in the self-assessment questionnaire is an important characteristic for an administrator to possess or acquire. Without having a majority of these traits, he/she will not be likely to succeed in exercising leadership in the school. Therefore, the reader should make every attempt to complete conscientiously the Self-Assessment Questionnaire for Prospective School Administrators, and then seek improvement wherever needed.

In addition, the reader should explore the possibility of participating in one of the assessment programs sponsored by the national principals' associations and cooperating school districts; a description of one such program is provided by Hersey.[12]

PROFESSIONAL ETHICS

It was emphasized in the previous section that prospective school administrators should either possess or acquire certain basic competencies if they expect to pursue a successful career in school administration. However, competencies are only one prerequisite to success. If a person is to be successful in administration, that individual also needs a set of ethical beliefs or standards for guidance or direction in the appropriate use of competencies. Without such beliefs, a person's competencies may be misused or misdirected, and the school will not receive the best kind of leadership. Therefore, every administrator should attempt to maintain high professional ethical standards in order to make a more positive contribution to the improvement of education in the school.

Although there are various sources to which a prospective administrator might turn in an attempt to enhance his/her professional ethics, the national administrators' associations have developed a set of recommended guidelines which have much to commend them. The standards were developed on the basis of considerable involvement and input from school administrators throughout the nation, and represent the best thinking of practitioners on this important subject. They are presented in figure 19.3 for the reader's study and consideration.

The standards identified in figure 19.3 constitute a positive response to the need for ethical guidelines for school administrators. They should provide all administrators with a basis for directing their actions, and serve also as evaluative criteria by which administrators can determine whether or not they are acting ethically in profesional matters. The reader is also encouraged to use the standards to consider how they might apply in individual situations, and the possible problems as well as advantages involved in acting ethically.

THE NEW ADMINISTRATOR

The person who possesses the competencies and professional ethics already identified should be able to pursue a career in school administration successfully. However, because of a lack of knowledge about how to proceed, some individuals may experience difficulty in obtaining a position in school administration; and some may encounter problems during the first year on the job

An educational administrator's professional behavior must conform to an ethical code. The code must be idealistic and at the same time practical, so that it can apply reasonably to all educational administrators. The administrator acknowledges that the schools belong to the public they serve for the purpose of providing educational opportunities to all. However, the administrator assumes responsibility for providing professional leadership in the school and community. This responsibility requires the administrator to maintain high standards of exemplary professional conduct. It must be recognized that the administrator's actions will be viewed and appraised by the community, professional associates, and students. To these ends, the administrator subscribes to the following statements of standards.

The educational administrator:

1. Makes the well-being of students the fundamental value in all decision making and actions.
2. Fulfills professional responsibilities with honesty and integrity.
3. Supports the principle of due process and protects the civil and human rights of all individuals.
4. Obeys local, state, and national laws and does not knowingly join or support organizations that advocate, directly or indirectly, the overthrow of the government.
5. Implements the governing board of education's policies and administrative rules and regulations.
6. Pursues appropriate measures to correct those laws, policies, and regulations that are not consistent with sound educational goals.
7. Avoids using positions for personal gain through political, social, religious, economic, or other influence.
8. Accepts academic degrees or professional certification only from duly accredited institutions.
9. Maintains the standards and seeks to improve the effectiveness of the profession through research and continuing professional development.
10. Honors all contracts until fulfillment or release.

This *Statement of Ethics* was developed by a task force representing The National Association of Secondary School Principals, National Association of Elementary School Principals, American Association of School Administrators, Association of School Business Officials, American Association of School Personnel Administrators, and National Council of Administrative Women in Education. Used with the permission of the National Association of Secondary School Principals.

Figure 19.3. Statement of Ethics for
School Administrators[13]

because of inadequate planning and misplaced priorities. Guidelines for avoiding or, at least, ameliorating these problems will be discussed in the following sections.*

*It is recognized that, to some readers, the ideas discussed in these sections will seem obvious or rather pragmatic in nature. However, contact with new administrators indicates that many need practical guidelines on how to obtain a position in administration and what to expect during the first year.

OBTAINING A POSITION

The immediate objective of the person who has completed an administrator preparation program and obtained certification, and is ready to begin a career in administration, is to secure a position. Since employment opportunities in educational administration are limited in most states, obtaining a position will not be an easy objective for the prospective administrator to achieve. However, if one has performed well in a preparatory program, possesses the kinds of qualities necessary for success in school administration, and is *persistent,* that individual's chances of securing a position in administration should be greatly improved.

The first step that a person should take in seeking a position in educational administration is to register with a university placement office. Usually any student attending a college or any graduate of a college can register with its placement office and utilize the placement services. Once registered with a placement office, an individual will receive vacancy notices such as those shown in figure 19.4.

Seldom will a placement notice provide all the information about a position that one might desire. However, sufficient information is usually supplied for the applicant to make a decision on whether follow-up action should

---

1. Assistant Principal Vacancy in Medium-Size School District

   Requirements
   a. Master's Degree and certification as an administrator
   b. Three years of successful teaching experience
   c. Open and warm personality, ability to lead others, ability to work well under pressure

   Benefits
   a. Salary range is $23,000–$26,000 for a 40-week contract
   b. Full retirement contribution, health-and-life-insurance contributions

2. School Principal Vacancy in Small School District

   Requirements
   a. Master's Degree and administrator certification
   b. Five years of teaching experience; some experience as an assistant principal desired
   c. Competency in school management and human relations

   Benefits
   a. Salary commensurate with experience and responsibilities
   b. Friendly community with good opportunities for hunting and fishing

---

Figure 19.4. Examples of Placement Notices in Educational Administration

be taken regarding the notice. If the position is of interest, the individual should contact the placement office and request that a copy of his/her credentials be sent to the school district. The prospective administrator should also write to the school district expressing an interest in the vacancy, and advising that placement papers are being forwarded to the district's office. In the letter a statement of the reasons for the applicant's interest in the position should be included together with a brief description of his/her qualifications with reference to any special factors of which the school district should be aware. If the district is interested, the applicant will usually be contacted within several weeks about the scheduling of an interview.

Information on job vacancies in educational administration can also be obtained from the state employment office (which may have an educators' employment division); private employment agencies; the city newspaper, which may carry vacancy notices; and also from the personnel office in the beginning administrator's own school district. Another potential source of information on administrative vacancies may be the professor who served as the student's adviser in the university's administrator preparation program. The prospective administrator should take the initiative to explore and maintain contact with all possible source of information on administrative openings. Rarely will a school district contact the prospective administrator first; he/she will have to exert initiative and persistence to obtain a position.

An important factor which will greatly influence the number and type of vacancies available is the prospective administrator's geographic mobility. Many vacancies for beginning administrators occur in small school districts, and in districts located at a distance from metropolitan areas. An individual who, for whatever reason, is unable or unwilling to move to these districts, or who will consider a vacancy only if it is in his/her own district or in a metropolitan area, has significantly restricted opportunities for employment. The more mobile the prospective administrator can be, the more likely is the applicant to obtain a position.

Once a prospective administrator has applied for a vacancy and has been contacted by the school district for an interview, that person should take time to plan for the meeting. An individual who has been scheduled for an interview can usually assume that he/she is among several persons who are being strongly considered for the vacancy. Generally, the school district will give considerable weight to the results of these interviews in reaching a decision on candidate selection. It is therefore essential that a candidate plan carefully for the interview.

Planning for an interview is really no different than planning for any important conference or meeting. First of all the candidate needs information about the situation itself, in this case the school and the school district where the vacancy has occurred. Prior to the interview, the prospective administrator should attempt, if feasible, to visit the school, talk with the administrator who is leaving, and try to become familiar with the school district and the community. The information and impressions that are gained will be invaluable in the planning for the interview.

Secondly, the candidate should determine the objectives he/she wants to achieve during the interview, and then define the questions and comments which need to be offered in order to achieve those objectives. In addition to thinking about objectives and questions, time should be spent in trying to anticipate the kinds of questions which the *interviewers* may ask. While it will be impossible to anticipate every question that may be raised, the more questions that are anticipated and considered prior to the interview, the greater is the likelihood that the interview will be a success. For example, a study by Cook revealed that beginning administrators felt that interviewers were most interested in ascertaining the strengths of candidates in the areas of discipline, supervision and evaluation, and human relations.[14]

During the interview the prospective administrator should try to remain calm and poised. An individual may experience some nervousness, which is perfectly natural and shouldn't cause a problem as long as he/she doesn't overreact. The candidate should concentrate on listening carefully to the interviewer's comments and questions and if a question or comment isn't understood, the interviewer should be asked for clarification or elaboration. The candidate should not attempt to respond to a question or comment unless it is clearly understood.

In answering questions or making observations the prospective administrator should be perfectly candid. Rather than presenting what he/she thinks the interviewer would like to hear, the candidate's own views should be given. This approach may cost an individual a particular job, but it is far better that the applicant be candid at the outset, since discrepancies in philosophy or approach will probably surface later and cause difficulties. This does not mean that one should be dogmatic or argumentative during an interview. However, there should be a frank and full exchange of views.

At the conclusion of the interview the candidate will usually be told that he/she will be contacted in the near future with regard to the school district's decision. If the applicant does not hear from a representative of the district within two or three weeks, contact should be made with the district's office to inquire as to when a decision will be reached. During this interval, however, the prospective administrator should be exploring other alternative employment possibilities until an actual contract is received and the offer accepted.

THE NEW SITUATION: ORIENTATION

Having accepted a position, the new administrator will need to become oriented further to the school, school district, and the community (unless, of course, the position is in his/her own district). The administrator may already have had an opportunity to meet several associates, and to visit the community; but there probably remains considerable orientation to be acquired before school begins in the fall.

In this endeavor the new administrator should attempt to secure and thoroughly read student and teacher handbooks, and copies of the student newspaper. A careful examination should also be made of the school board policies, district office manual of procedures, and the district's master contract, if they exist. All of this information should contribute to the process of familiarizing the new administrator with current school and district problems, policies, and procedures.

Next, individual meetings should be scheduled with the superintendent, and relevant members of the central office staff. The new administrator's meetings with the superintendent and the central office staff should be for purposes of getting better acquainted and ascertaining how all parties can work together cooperatively. One topic for discussion might be the district's master contract.

The beginning administrator should also schedule individual meetings with the school's assistant principal, department heads and/or unit leaders, the cook, the head secretary, and the head custodian. It is particularly important that an administrator pay attention to becoming acquainted with the latter three individuals, since they can play a significant role in the administrator's success or lack of it, yet are frequently overlooked. And the new administrator should see student and parent leaders who are available and interested in conferring with him/her.

During these initial meetings the administrator should focus primarily on developing a good personal relationship with the people with whom he/she will be working at the school, reviewing proposed activities and possible problems, and also indicating a receptivity to meeting with them again whenever the need arises. One should not attempt to cover too much in these first meetings. For example, unless the subject comes up naturally, the administrator should wait until later to ascertain people's role expectations. It will be more appropriate to discuss these topics after the new administrator and the other school personnel have become better acquainted.

While becoming better informed about the school district and school personnel, the new administrator should also be trying to become better oriented to the school community. Although he/she may have toured the community when interviewing for the vacancy, the administrator's knowledge of the community at this point is probably rather superficial.

A good starting point for orientation to a community is a drive around the neighborhoods and commercial areas surrounding the school within a half-mile radius. Such a drive should yield valuable impressions about the types of neighborhoods that are adjacent to the school, potential safety problems for students, extent and kinds of recreational opportunities for students, and possible student "hangouts." The latter may include cafes, drugstores, poolhalls, and similar places where students might congregate before or after school. Such places frequently represent the "community" from the student's point of view, and the new administrator needs to become more aware of that community.

The administrator should also try to become acquainted with the neighborhoods of those students who have to travel a long distance to the school. These students and their parents may feel isolated from the school, and the administrator should become more knowledgeable about their situation. If school is still in session in the spring when the administrator is hired, riding a school bus might be considered to achieve this objective.

As the administrator visits various neighborhoods of the community, any opportunities to meet the residents, particularly parents, should be capitalized on. There probably won't be time to meet too many parents, but the administrator should take advantage of those opportunities that present themselves in the situation.

Perhaps one of the better ways for a new administrator to become informed about the culture, norms, problems, and personalities in a community is to read the local newspaper, back issues of which are generally to be found in the local library. By browsing through the copies of the newspaper published during the preceding year, the new administrator should be able to become familiar with many important aspects of the community, including its significant groups and leaders, its problems and issues, and dates of special local events. Also generally found in the library is pertinent information about the community's governmental structure. Without question, the local library is potentially a very useful source of material for orienting a new administrator to a community.

PLANNING FOR THE OPENING OF SCHOOL*

In one sense, the orientation activities that have been described can be considered a part of planning for the opening of school. However, before mid-August the administrator should make some additional plans in regard to the start of the school year.[15] Although "get-acquainted meetings" with student,

---

*Most of the ideas in this section are more germane for the principal than for the assistant principal, although the latter will need to be aware of a number of those recommended.

teacher, and parent leaders should already have been held by the administrator, it is important for him/her to meet with them again to plan activities to be held prior to the opening of school and during the first few weeks after school has started.

The administrator should also meet with the assistant principal (if one is assigned to the school) and with the department chairpersons or unit leaders to plan the workshop which usually takes place two or three days before school begins. Information should be solicited from these people about the type of workshop presented in the past at the school, and they should be encouraged to offer suggestions on how it could be improved. The new administrator will certainly have his/her own ideas on what should be included in the workshop, and these ideas should be presented and reactions sought.

Topics for inclusion in the workshop will depend to a great extent on local circumstances. However, the administrator should recognize that the total staff will be using this opportunity to "size up the new administrator," and will be listening carefully to what that individual has to say during the workshop. Although the new administrator will want to make a good impression, he/she should try to avoid raising people's expectations too much and should refrain from the temptation to promise more than can be delivered.[16] Also, it would be preferable to postpone reviewing one's own educational philosophy and expectations for the staff unless specific questions about them are raised. Until the new administrator and the total staff become better acquainted, discussions about educational philosophy and expectations could be misinterpreted.

During the workshop, the new administrator should be perceived as someone who will try to work cooperatively with people to resolve problems, who is friendly, warm and professional in interpersonal relationships, and who is well organized and a hard worker.

In planning for the workshop the beginning administrator should take into consideration the needs of new teachers who will be attending the meetings, and the needs of the total staff for enough time to do individual planning for the first day of school. He/she should also plan for some form of activity which will provide an opportunity for the members of the staff (and perhaps their families) to socialize with each other. The preschool workshop should consist of more than just professional meetings.

In planning for the opening of school, meetings should also be scheduled with the school secretary, head custodian, chief cook, and student and parent leaders (such as the president of the student council, the editor of the student newspaper, and the president of the PTA). These meetings should be devoted to a review of proposed activities for the opening day and the first month of school (with a discussion of problems to be resolved), and steps which need to be taken prior to those activities. Careful planning before school opens will eliminate many problems that might otherwise arise later.

The new administrator should also check on a number of important operational details at least several weeks prior to the beginning of school. These include ascertaining whether the items enumerated in figure 19.5 still require attention.

The checking on some of these details may be delegated to the assistant principal, if there is one. However, the principal still retains the ultimate responsibility for making sure that everything operates smoothly on the first day of school. While the new administrator may view himself/herself as an instructional leader, the staff's initial judgment will be based on their evaluation as to whether this "newcomer" is an efficient administrator. The events of the first day of school will greatly influence their evaluation.

PRIORITIES DURING THE FIRST YEAR

Regardless of whether or not the administrator is new, he/she will be expected to meet certain responsibilities. These include visiting classrooms; holding faculty meetings; conferring with individual students, teachers, and parents; developing a school budget, and many other tasks delineated in previous chapters.

The effectiveness with which these tasks are accomplished will depend in part on the type of role that the new administrator adopts. According to Lipham, the administrator is "the individual who utilizes existing structures or procedures to achieve an organization goal or objective."[17] Lipham goes on to state that "The administrator is concerned primarily with maintaining, rather than changing established structures, procedures, or goals."[18] The leader, on the other hand, is defined by Lipham as "concerned with initiating changes in established structures, procedures, or goals; he is a disrupter of the existing

---

1. **Development of the Master Schedule for the School.** Has it been completed? Does it need updating?
2. **Employment of Teachers.** Do additional teachers need to be hired?
3. **Allocation of Classroom Furniture and Textbooks.** Does each classroom have sufficient classroom furniture and textbooks to accommodate the number of students assigned to the room?
4. **Distribution of Teacher Supplies.** Has each teacher been allocated adequate supplies for the first week of school?
5. **Maintenance of the Building.** Have those aspects of the school which have been in need of repair been fixed? Has the school building itself been cleaned and floors waxed?
6. **Planning for the Cafeteria Program.** Have preparations been made to provide hot lunches on the first day of school?

Figure 19.5. Checklist: Planning for the Opening of School

state of affairs." Leadership, to Lipham, is "the initiation of a new structure or procedure for accomplishing organizational goals and objectives."[19]

A case can be made that, during the first year, a new administrator should *not* function as a leader, as defined by Lipham, but should concentrate on administering the school. A new administrator needs to complete at least one year on the job becoming familiar with the school situation, before being in a good enough position to know what changes should be made and how they might best be accomplished. Also, a new administrator should take the time to become competent in performing administrative tasks before beginning to initiate changes in existing procedures and policies.

Of course, a new administrator may be forced to institute changes during the first year in response to a problem whose solution cannot or should not be delayed. However, as much as possible during the first year, the administrator should avoid initiating major changes in established structures, procedures, or goals, or in any other way disrupting the existing order of affairs. To the extent feasible, such leadership activities should be postponed until the new administrator becomes more knowledgeable about the school situation.

The priorities that a new administrator should concentrate on during his/her first year are presented below.

1. *Obtaining a good understanding of all aspects of the educational program and the social context in which the school operates.* During the first year, the new administrator needs to become very familiar with what is going on in the school, and why things are done the way they are. He/she also needs to continue to learn about school district procedures and how the school relates to the total community.

2. *Developing a good interpersonal relationship with other people.* This includes students, parents, and central office personnel, as well as the teachers in the school. The new administrator's first year will be a busy one with many tasks to accomplish, but time should be set aside to see students, teachers, parents, and other relevant people. These individuals will determine the success of the beginning administrator more than any other factor.

3. *Attaining a well-organized and smoothly operating school.* Most of the people with whom the new administrator will have contact will tend to view him/her as an administrator, rather than as a leader. If both roles can be performed effectively, people will be pleased; but first of all competency as an administrator must be shown. This can be achieved by running a well-organized, smoothly operating school. Having obtained this objective, the new administrator can begin to function in the role of leader if he/she possesses the qualities needed for leadership.[20]

A CONCLUDING NOTE

For the individual interested in a new position in school administration, securing a job and planning and establishing priorities for the first year will require careful organization, persistence, and clear thinking.[21] The administrator's first year will undoubtedly be a useful learning experience but, at the same time, the new administrator should realize that people will expect effective performance regardless of whether or not the individual is new to the position. Two major factors which will tend to demonstrate the administrator's effectiveness are his/her response to the problems which are associated with the school situation, and the efforts made by the administrator to pursue continuing professional development. The next chapter will focus on problems of school administration and the need for continuous professional growth.

Review and Learning Activities

1. Analyze the advantages and disadvantages of various entry positions in school administration.
2. What is the nature of employment opportunities in school administration in your state? What are the implications of this situation for the individual who is interested in pursuing a career in school administration?
3. What are the implications of the administrator competencies recommended by Katz and Gorton for your professional development and performance as an administrator?
4. Assess yourself in regard to the extent to which you possess traits identified in figure 19.2 and the ethical standards identified in figure 19.3. What are the implications of your assessment?
5. What steps should an individual take and which factors should he/she be aware of in:
   a. Seeking a new administrative position?
   b. Becoming oriented to a new administrative situation?
   c. Planning for the opening of the school?
6. Why is it important for an administrator to determine his/her priorities in a new situation? What would appear to be reasonable first year priorities for a new administrator?

Notes

1. David R. Byrne, Susan A. Hines, and Lloyd E. McCleary, *The Senior High School Principalship* (Reston, Va: National Association of Secondary School Principals, 1978), p. 6. See also William L. Pharis and Sally Banks Zakariya, *The Elementary School Principalship in 1978* (Arlington, Va: National Assn. of Elementary School Principals, 1979).

2. For an excellent review of the origins and various aspects of establishing and administering an internship program, see Don R. Davies, *The Internship in Educational Administration* (Washington, D.C.: Center for Applied Research in Education, 1962). Also see T. F. Flaherty, "Theory and Practice Yields Qualified Administrators," *Education* 93 (November 1972): 128–29.

3. *The Administrative Internship,* eds. Judith A. Adkison and Andrea Warren (Lawrence, Kans: University of Kansas, 1980).

4. Donald P. Mitchell, *Leadership in Public Education Study: A Look at the Overlooked* (Washington, D.C.: Academy for Educational Development, 1972).

5. Byrne et al., *The Senior High School Principalship,* pp. 1–2; and William L. Pharis and Sally Zakariya, the *Elementary School Principalship in 1978,* pp. 4–8.

6. Judith A. Adkison, "Women in School Administration: A Review of the Research," *Review of Educational Research* (Fall 1981): 311–43; and Florence I. Ortiz, *Career Patterns in Education: Men, Women and Minorities in Public School Administration* (New York: J. F. Praeger, 1981).

7. *Women and Educational Leadership,* eds. Sari Knopp Bihlen and Marilyn B. Brannigan (Lexington, Mass.: D. C. Heath, 1980). Also see Dorothy Erinakes, "An Analysis of Women Elementary School Principals and Long Term Women Teachers in Relation to Selected Psychological and Situational Variables" (Ph.D. diss., University of Connecticut, 1980).

8. Robert L. Katz, "Skills of an Effective Administrator," *Harvard Business Review* 33, no. 1 (January-February 1955): 33–42.

9. Ibid., p. 42.

10. Richard A. Gorton: *School Administration and Supervision: Important Issues, Concepts and Case Studies* (Dubuque, Iowa: Wm. C. Brown Company Publishers, 1980), pp. 272–75.

11. For example, see Chad D. Ellett, *Results Oriented Management Education, Project Rome.* An ERIC Report: Ed–131–590; Paul W. Hersey, "What's Happening with NASSP's Assessment Center (Reston, Va: National Association of Secondary School Principals, 1980); and Donald Walters, *Perceptions of Administrative Competencies.* An ERIC Report: Ed–172–361. See also James A. Lipham, *Effective Principal, Effective School* (Reston, Va: National Association of Secondary School Principals, 1981); Arthur Blumberg and William Greenfield, *The Effective Principal* (Boston: Allyn and Bacon, 1980); and Richard A. Gorton and Kenneth E. McIntyre, *The Effective Principal* (Reston, Va: National Association of Secondary School Principals, 1978). The reader who wishes further information about administrative competencies should subscribe to *CCBC Notebook,* University of Utah, Salt Lake City, Utah.

12. See the *Bulletin of National Association of Secondary School Principals* (October 1980), pp. 87–117 for descriptions by Hersey and others.

13. National Association of Secondary School Principals and National Association of Elementary School Principals, *Ethical Standards for School Administrators* (Washington, D.C.: NASSP and NAESP, 1973).

14. Jerome Cook, "First Year Wisconsin Secondary School Principals: Their Opinions, Reflections and Frustrations" (Specialist Paper, University of Wisconsin-Milwaukee, 1979).

15. Some practical ideas on planning for the opening of school are given by Gary Funkhauser, "A Checklist for Principals," *National Association of Secondary School Principals Bulletin* (September 1976): 87–88.

16. Linda Robertson, "The First Year," *Principal* (September 1981): 54–55.

17. James A. Lipham, "Leadership and Administration," in Behavioral Science and Educational Administration, ed. Daniel Griffiths, 63rd Yearbook of the National Society for the Study of Education (Chicago: University of Chicago Press, 1964), p. 122.

18. Ibid.

19. Ibid.

20. For a discussion of approaches, constrains, and prerequisites to leadership, see Richard A. Gorton, *School Administration and Supervision,* pp. 263–76.

21. Edward H. Seifert, "How to Be a Successful New Principal," *NASSP Bulletin* (September 1981): 56–58.

20

NEED FOR CONTINUING
PROFESSIONAL DEVELOPMENT

This book has recommended a number of principles and concepts which, if appropriately utilized, should improve the administration of a school. The competencies that the school administrator will need to perform effectively have been suggested at various points and the many challenges confronting the administrator have been stressed. Certainly it should be clear to the reader by now that the job of the school administrator is not an easy one.

In order to demonstrate further the nature of the administrator's problem-filled job and the consequent need for continuous professional growth, the following two sections will discuss the problems of the new administrator and report on the types of problems faced by all administrators—new and experienced. The latter half of the chapter will then focus on several approaches to continued professional development for the school administrator.

THE NEW ADMINISTRATOR: FIRST YEAR PROBLEMS

Individuals who become school administrators are frequently not sufficiently aware of the scope of problems that can occur. As Blumberg and Greenfield note.

> Whatever the reasons for wanting to become a school principal (some are more noble than others), most aspirants to the role have a vague understanding of much it entails. The loneliness, the conflicts, the dullness of the routine, the "busy work," and the anguish that accompany having to solve complex educational and organizational problems with extremely limited resources are usually not part of teachers' conceptions of the principalship."[1]

While Blumberg and Greenfield quite properly emphasize the problem nature of the principalship, it should also be stressed that these problems are not insurmountable and their impact can, with appropriate understanding and leadership, be largely minimized. The purpose of the following discussion is to attempt to develop a realistic understanding on the part of the reader regarding major problems that the beginning administrator may face during the first year, and to suggest appropriate perspectives and/or strategies for dealing with these problems.

It is difficult to generalize about the types of problems that the beginning administrator may encounter, because these problems will vary according to the administrator's background, training, personality, and school situation. However, discussions with and observations of new administrators suggest that there are several problems which many of them faced during the first year.* It should be pointed out that a majority of these same problems are also encountered to a certain degree by experienced administrators who move to a new situation.

THE ACCEPTANCE PROBLEM

Many beginning administrators are initially concerned about how students, parents, and particularly teachers will react to them. As beginning administrators in a new situation, they naturally hope to gain acceptance by the groups with whom they will be working. But what type of acceptance should they be seeking? They want to be respected, but they wonder, "Is it important to be liked? And if you seek the personal approval of the people with whom you work, will they still respect you?"

These are normal questions for any beginning administrator to ask. In fact, many experienced administrators who change jobs feel some concern about being accepted in a new environment. However, the beginning administrator usually is new, not only to the work environment, but to the job itself, so being concerned about other people's reactions is understandable. Whether a beginning administrator will actually encounter difficulty in gaining the acceptance of others will depend in large part on the type of acceptance that is sought.

If the administrator decides that people must like him/her, or must approve all decisions before action can be initiated, there are likely to be problems. One frequently may have to make decisions or take actions which will result in a reduction of one's popularity, but it is better to do what seems right

---

*A particularly vivid account of the first year of a beginning principal is related by Margaret Nelson, *Looking Back at the First Year* (Eugene, Oreg.: Oregon School Study Council, 1979). For a good description of the first year for an assistant principal, see Lynne Miller and Anne Lieberman, "School Leadership Between the Cracks," *Educational Leadership* (February 1982): 363–67.

in a situation rather than what may be popular. Any administrator who makes a decision or initiates action based *primarily* on its potential for generating a favorable response from those who will be affected by the decision or action will soon learn that it is virtually impossible to please everyone. He/she will also discover that a decision or action which elicits an immediate, favorable response from those affected may not always lead to the best results in the long run.

On the other hand, the administrator who never makes any attempt to secure the approval or acceptance of a proposed decision by the persons whom it will affect cannot expect their continuing cooperation. While people may not need to *like* the administrator personally, or approve of all administrative actions, they generally must find the administrator or a majority of administrative acts acceptable, if they are going to implement fully what that individual wants done in the school. Therefore, if people's feelings and reactions toward the administrator and his/her decisions are not taken into consideration, a growing wave of discontent may emerge.

Probably the most appropriate response for a beginning administrator in regard to the "acceptance problem" is to concentrate during the first year on administering a well-organized, smoothly running school. The achievement of this goal will favorably influence most people's acceptance of the administrator, perhaps more than any other factor. Of course, he/she should also try to develop a warm and helping relationship with the staff, students, and parents. However, in all likelihood, their judgment of the administrator will depend primarily on whether the school is being administered effectively, and will be based only secondarily on personal considerations. Both factors may be influential but the former is the most important.

THE PROBLEM OF INSUFFICIENT TIME

During the first year the beginning administrator may frequently have the feeling that there is never enough time to do everything that needs to be accomplished. But the problem of lack of time is not limited to new administrators; it also frustrates experienced administrators, although perhaps to a lesser degree. For example, a study by Gorton and Frontier of elementary school principals revealed that a majority of respondents indicated that they frequently found it difficult to make time to accomplish what they really wanted to achieve in their job.[2] And a study by Byrne, Hines and McCleary of secondary school principals suggests a similar conclusion.[3] Also, research by Olson on elementary school principals[4] and by Martin and Willower on high school principals[5] found that principals spend most of their time on meetings, frequently of an unscheduled nature, dealing with organizational maintenance tasks rather than instructional and curricular improvement activities. These findings on principals' *use* of time contrasts with principals' reported *preference* for spending the most time on improving instruction and curriculum.[6]

The problem of having too little time can generally be attributed to four factors: (1) inexperience, (2) the absence of a system for organizing time, (3) the administrative job itself, which by its very nature is demanding and time-consuming, and (4) failure to delegate responsibility. Since there is little probability that the job of the administrator will become less demanding, and since most beginning administrators are initially employed in situations where the opportunity for delegating responsibility may be limited, we shall concentrate on analyzing the first two factors.

Due to inexperience, the new administrator usually takes longer to perform most administrative tasks. Despite having received excellent university training for the new role, and even having acquired previous experience as an intern, the administrator will be performing many tasks for the first time. These duties will take longer to accomplish until, with practice, shortcuts can be identified and errors eliminated. Therefore, until the beginning administrator gains more experience, the time problem will not be significantly ameliorated.

However, as indicated earlier, inexperience is not the only cause of a fledgling administrator's problem of seemingly never having enough time. Another major factor is the absence of a system for organizing time. Unless the administrator utilizes such a system, he/she will reach the end of many days and weeks, wondering why more wasn't achieved. The administrator may have been busy while at school, but at the end of the work period there may be little to show for the efforts.

One approach the administrator might use to organize time more effectively is to keep a time log each day for a week or two, and then analyze how the time is being spent and how it might be utilized more efficiently. According to a study by Weldy, the administrators spend a certain portion of their time on activities which might be better organized or restructured, and a time log may be helpful in spotlighting possible problems. In the publication *Time: A Valuable Resource for the School Administrator,* Weldy makes a number of practical recommendations for improving the administrator's use of time, including saving time in meetings, using clerical services more judiciously and planning work to save time.[7] (A second valuable source for ideas is *Time Management for Educators,* published by Phi Delta Kappa, Bloomington, Ind.)

Another approach which could be helpful to the administrator who is trying to utilize time better is Management by Objectives (MBO).[8] Originating in the business sector but now adopted by many school districts. Management by Objectives is a system by which an administrator defines objectives, establishes priorities, plans a course of action for achieving the objectives, and evaluates success. By requiring a beginning administrator to define what needs to be achieved and to establish priorities, MBO can help to organize time more efficiently. And by requiring the administrator to evaluate whether or not objectives have been achieved, MBO can be helpful in ascertaining effectiveness and making changes where desirable and feasible.

Although MBO has more frequently been used in connection with semester or yearly objectives, it can also profitably be employed by a beginning administrator to organize time on a daily and weekly basis. An example of a daily MBO format is presented in figure 20.1.*

It should be pointed out that, until the beginning administrator becomes proficient in using MBO, it may take *more* time rather than less.[9] However, the time spent in thinking and planning is an investment which should pay dividends in better decision making, even if it doesn't immediately save any time. In the final analysis, the administrator may never entirely eliminate the feeling of having insufficient time to accomplish all the responsibilities, but MBO should be helpful in utilizing time more productively.

THE AUTHORITY PROBLEM

Many beginning administrators seem to experience difficulty in exercising authority during their first year. They either try to exert authority they don't possess, or fail to utilize the authority they do possess and which needs to be

---

Name _____ Date _____ School _____
Objectives for Today:

Plan of Action for Accomplishing Each Objective:

Evaluation Plan for Ascertaining Success:

Figure 20.1. Daily MBO Format

*The format described in figure 20.1 can also be adapted for use on a weekly basis.

employed for the successful resolution of a problem. The consequence of exercising authority that one doesn't possess can be resistance and even outright noncompliance; failure to exercise authority which the individual possesses and which circumstances require can result in a deteriorating situation and loss of respect or confidence in the individual who is supposed to exercise the authority. In either case a general eroding of the perceived authority vested in an administrator's position can occur.

One reason why many beginning administrators encounter problems in the exercise of authority is that they have not examined carefully the nature and scope of their authority. Administrators should recognize that their basic authority is delegated to them by the school board and the superintendent of schools; therefore, they should understand clearly the policies and directives of the school board and the superintendent.

Unfortunately, in too many situations the authority of the administrator is not formally delegated or explicitly stated because it is believed to be inherent in the position or associated with the responsibilities which have been assigned. Therefore, a beginning administrator should attempt to secure as clear a reading as possible on the extent of authority actually possessed in the situation.

A second reason why many beginning administrators experience difficulty in exercising authority is that they don't seem to understand the limitations of authority or the conditions under which it is best employed.[10] Authority is not power. The administrator possesses *power* if people can be forced to do what he/she wants them to do, even when they resist or refuse to accept that individual's authority in a situation. The beginning administrator will soon discover that he/she has very little power in most circumstances.

Authority, on the other hand, is based on people's acceptance of an administrator's initiatives because they believe the administrator has the right to direct them by virtue of his/her position in the school organization and the authority vested in that position by the school board and/or the superintendent of schools. While this type of authority, typically referred to as "legitimate authority," has been severely eroded in recent years,[11] it still exists in large measure if appropriately utilized.

In exercising authority, the beginning administrator should keep in mind the following guidelines, based on Barnard's analysis of the authority problem in organizations:[12]

1. In deciding on the need for an order and in its formulation, presentation, and execution, the administrator should take into consideration how the order will affect the recipients personally, recognizing that people are likely to question or resist orders which they feel are not in their best interest.

2. The administrator should take into consideration the strengths and limitations of those who will be expected to implement an order, and should avoid, if possible, issuing orders for which people lack the necessary motivation, skill, or training to carry out.
3. The administrator should explain thoroughly the rationale behind each order and its relationship to the goals of the organization, and should not assume that people understand the reasons for an order or that they will necessarily see the logic or value of an order.
4. The administrator should leave room for modifying the original order or its method of implementation. Flexibility and a willingness to compromise when appropriate are key factors in exercising administrative authority successfully.
5. The administrator should issue only those orders that will with relative surety be obeyed, or that can be enforced if they are resisted. Orders which cannot be enforced in one situation weaken the administrator's authority for successfully issuing orders in other circumstances.

By following these guidelines and working within the authority limitations of his/her position, the beginning administrator should be able to avoid most of the difficulties associated with the "authority problem." In working with students, teachers and other school related groups the beginning administrator will probably find that the best approach is to utilize his/her expertise to *influence* or persuade people to take a particular course of action, rather than relying on his/her authority to direct them.[13]

THE EFFECTIVENESS PROBLEM

It is understandable that a beginning administrator may experience some concern about his/her effectiveness during the first year. After all, it is natural for an administrator who is new to the job, and to the school situation itself, to wonder how effectively he/she is performing in the new role. In spite of this concern, however, the administrator may encounter difficulty in ascertaining that effectiveness.[14]

In the first place, there may not be general agreement on the criteria to be used in evaluating an administrator's effectiveness. Superiors may make the evaluation based on one set of criteria, the teachers may use another set of criteria, the students another, and the parents still a different set. There may be a great deal of overlap in the criteria utilized by these groups, but the value they ascribe to each criterion may differ significantly. For example, both the teachers and the administrator's superiors might agree that maintaining "good school-community relations" should be considered in evaluating the administrator's effectiveness but may differ greatly on the importance they attach to this aspect.

A second difficulty that the beginning administrator may encounter is that, although the superiors and the other groups with whom he/she interacts may be constantly making evaluative conclusions, they may not explicitly communicate these conclusions to him/her. For example, it is still not unusual for an administrator to receive no *formal* evaluation from superiors. The latter may either fail to recognize the importance of yearly, formal administrator evaluation, or have no system for implementing it. In addition, unless the administrator actively seeks feedback from students, teachers, and parents, they also are unlikely to give their evaluation of his/her effectiveness. Most of these groups are in a subordinate role to the administrator, and there is little if any tradition of subordinates' *initiating* an evaluation of their administrator.

For these reasons then, many administrators receive little substantive feedback on their effectiveness. If an administrator is in this kind of a situation, however, there are certain steps that should be considered. First of all, administrator evaluation criteria and approaches *are* being used in a number of school systems, and that information should be brought to the attention of the administrator's superiors. Bolton, for example, discusses in his excellent book, *Evaluating Administrative Personnel in School Systems,* the purposes, roles, and methods of administrator evaluation.[15] Zakrajsek presents and analyzes fifteen discrete approaches to evaluating principals.[16] And the Educational Research Service periodically surveys the practices of school districts regarding administrator evaluation and publishes the results, as well as sample administrator evaluation forms.[17] Thus, it seems clear that there is no shortage of ideas on administrator evaluation. If administrator and superiors can agree upon appropriate criteria and on an evaluation approach, then perhaps periodic assessment of the administrator by superiors can occur.

One method which is being utilized with increased frequency in administrator evaluation is the "evaluation by objectives" approach.[18] It typically involves several steps:

1. The identification of specific, expected responsibilities and competencies of an administrative position
2. Joint assessment of the current performance of the administrator performed by the occupant of the administrative position and his/her superiors
3. The development and approval of a plan for improvement which includes objectives, activities, timetable, and standards and methods for determining progress or achievement of objectives
4. Periodic meetings between the administrator and superiors to review progress and problems
5. Final assessment of progress or achievement.

An excerpt from one school district's administrator evaluation program is presented in figure 20.2 to illustrate a number of the concepts of the evaluation by objectives approach.

**Intensive Evaluation Program
Target Setting Sheet**

Administrator's Name

Standard No. _____

Indicators (Indicate by letter) _____

Date   Target no.

1. What is to be changed? (List characteristics of present situation.)

2. What desired change do you want to achieve? (Identify performance to be acquired)

3. How will you know when you have achieved the desired change? (List level of achievement to be reached.)

4. What will you do to achieve the desired change? (Specify conditions under which change is to be made.)

5. What resources do you need to achieve the desired change? (Consider such resources as time, materials, training, supervision, etc.)

6. When should the change be completed? (Specify date for target assessment conference).

Signatures:

Administrator _____ Supervisor _____

Figure 20.2. Example of *Evaluation by Objectives* Approach

Evaluation of administrators by objectives, of course, does not lack critics.[19] It has been viewed by some as too time-consuming, anxiety-provoking, and subject to coercive manipulation by the administrator's superiors. An examination of these criticisms, however, suggests that, as with any method or technique, evaluation by objectives can be misused; nevertheless, the problems are not inevitable. Certainly, an essential prerequisite to the effective utilization of the evaluation by objectives approach is the presence of adequate trust and a supportive relationship between the administrator and the evaluator(s).[20] In addition, the administrator being evaluated must believe that the evaluation criteria and methods being used are valid and reliable. If both of these prerequisites cannot be met, it is unlikely that any evaluation system can achieve its stated purposes. One useful way to meet these prerequisites is to provide the administrators being evaluated with considerable input into the development of the evaluation system and with periodic opportunities to suggest improvements in the system.

Administrators should also consider initiating some type of effectiveness evaluation by teachers, students and parents. (Research has found that teachers, in particular, can be good evaluators of administrators.[21]) An administrator interested in evaluative feedback from various reference groups might adopt the evaluation form used by superiors, or develop a new evaluation form to be used specifically by teachers, students, and parents. A form which the author employed with the latter groups when he was a beginning administrator is presented in figure 20.3; an excerpt of a form which has been used in another situation for faculty evaluation of the principal is presented in figure 20.4.

Date _____

Instructions: Please be as candid and complete as possible. I am very much interested in your perceptions of my effectiveness as an administrator, particularly your suggestions for improvement. You need not sign your name to this evaluation.

Strengths (please identify three characteristics, or actions that I have taken this year which you view as positive, and which you would like to see me continue).

Weaknesses (please identify three characteristics or actions that I have taken this year which you think I should work on in terms of self-improvement, or which you think I should eliminate).

Figure 20.3. Reference Group
Evaluation of Administrator's
Effectiveness

The purposes of this survey are

1. To improve the school
2. To provide information that will help the principal improve in effectiveness.

Instructions

1. This survey is intended to be anonymous
2. Circle or check the appropriate response.
3. A response of "1" is lowest (never) and "5" is highest (always).
4. N/O means "I do not have enough information to form an opinion." (Note that N/O can be used in the "What Is" column. You can respond to the "What Should Be" column for every item.

A. Goal Setting

	What Is?					What Should Be?				
1. The principal guides faculty toward setting personal goals.	1	2	3	4	5	1	2	3	4	5
2. The principal guides faculty toward setting building goals.										
a. Long-range	1	2	3	4	5	1	2	3	4	5
b. Short-range	1	2	3	4	5	1	2	3	4	5
3. The principal has personal goals.	1	2	3	4	5	1	2	3	4	5
4. The faculty is aware of those goals.	1	2	3	4	5	1	2	3	4	5

B. Taking Charge

1. The principal guides development of school rules.	1	2	3	4	5	1	2	3	4	5
2. The principal supports enforcement of those rules (and personally enforces them).	1	2	3	4	5	1	2	3	4	5
3. The principal's disciplinary actions are fair and related to the rules.	1	2	3	4	5	1	2	3	4	5
4. The principal is not afraid to make a decision when necessary.	1	2	3	4	5	1	2	3	4	5
5. The principal takes command in "sticky situations."	1	2	3	4	5	1	2	3	4	5
6. The principal is viewed as an authority figure by the students.	1	2	3	4	5	1	2	3	4	5

(continued)

Figure 20.4. Principal Evaluation Survey[22]

C. Communications

What Is? *What Should Be?*

1. The principal has time to listen to me and help me.
   1 2 3 4 5   1 2 3 4 5

2. The principal tells people what is expected of them.
   1 2 3 4 5   1 2 3 4 5

3. I feel free to talk to the principal about my concerns, successes, etc.
   1 2 3 4 5   1 2 3 4 5

4. The principal is honest with me.
   1 2 3 4 5   1 2 3 4 5

5. The principal communicates clearly.
   a. Written communications 1 2 3 4 5   1 2 3 4 5
   b. Verbal 1 2 3 4 5   1 2 3 4 5

6. The principal communicates effectively with parents.
   1 2 3 4 5   1 2 3 4 5

7. Parents feel free to approach the principal about a problem or concern.
   1 2 3 4 5   1 2 3 4 5

8. The principal establishes and maintains favorable relationships with local community groups.
   1 2 3 4 5   1 2 3 4 5

D. Teacher Supervision

1. The principal discusses my teaching methods with me.
   1 2 3 4 5   1 2 3 4 5

2. The principal allows my input in the supervision process.
   1 2 3 4 5   1 2 3 4 5

3. The principal has adequate background information and input before he evaluates my work.
   1 2 3 4 5   1 2 3 4 5

4. The principal considers my teaching as a whole.
   1 2 3 4 5   1 2 3 4 5

5. The principal emphasizes specifics that are valuable to my growth.
   1 2 3 4 5   1 2 3 4 5

6. I know how the principal feels about me, as a teacher.
   1 2 3 4 5   1 2 3 4 5

7. The principal spends adequate time visiting my classroom to be a supervisory leader.
   1 2 3 4 5   1 2 3 4 5

(continued)

Figure 20.4. Continued

E. Decision-Making	What Is?	What Should Be?
1. The principal is capable of making decisions.	1 2 3 4 5	1 2 3 4 5
2. The principal examines alternative solutions.	1 2 3 4 5	1 2 3 4 5
3. The principal seeks input before making important decisions.	1 2 3 4 5	1 2 3 4 5
4. The principal makes decisions and follows through promptly.	1 2 3 4 5	1 2 3 4 5
5. The principal permits shared decision-making in some areas.	1 2 3 4 5	1 2 3 4 5

Optional

1. If I were principal of this school, I would _____

_____

_____

2. I would like the principal to be more _____

_____

_____

3. I'd like the principal to be less _____

_____

_____

4. General comments _____

_____

_____

_____

Figure 20.4. Continued

The evaluation form presented in figure 20.4 was developed by the principal of a school and five teachers who had volunteered to assist the principal. The results of the evaluation were shared with the faculty by the principal, and attention was given to those items on which there was a significant discrepancy between responses to "What Is?" and "What Should Be?"[23] Obviously, such an evaluation system requires a secure principal who respects the judgements of the faculty.

Whether the administrator uses the types of evaluation forms presented in figures 20.3 and 20.4, or a different one, he/she should initiate some form of evaluation by students, teachers, and parents each school year. These are important groups to the administrator, and their effectiveness perceptions can provide excellent feedback on performance, with suggestions for improvement.

Regardless of the type of evaluation system used, the key questions, according to Bolton, are the following:[24]

1. Is the evaluation system helping administrators to do their jobs better?
2. Is sufficient time being spent to implement the evaluation procedure?
3. Is the evaluation of administrators cyclical and self-correcting?
4. What results can be attributed directly to the administrator evaluation system?

THE SOCIALIZATION PROBLEM

Many, if not most beginning administrators finish their university course work and start their first job in administration with a certain degree of idealism. Once on the job, however, they are typically exposed to a socialization process which, in many cases, diminishes much of the idealism they may have acquired.[25]

Although this process starts on the day that the administrator is employed, it will most clearly be felt when he/she makes the first effort to introduce change in the school. In many situations the bureaucratic red tape that the administrator must overcome before change can be introduced will discourage him/her from implementing the improvements envisioned. He/she will quickly discover that there are few incentives and sometimes considerable personal risk for trying to initiate school improvements. The new administrator who attempts to introduce procedures that differ from those employed in the other schools in the district may be viewed as a maverick by the central office, and as a "loner" by colleagues. Informal pressures by both may be brought to bear in order to make the new administrator and the school become "a part of the district." The result may be a conflict between the personal needs of the administrator and the school and the expectations of the school district or, even more likely, a compromise of the administrator's idealism.[26]

That the socialization process is important was demonstrated in a study by Bridges, who found that the longer an administrator was exposed to the role expectations of the school district, the more his/her behavior was influenced by those expectations rather than by personal needs.[27]

In essence, the socialization process that beginning administrators will be exposed to in a district is designed to encourage them to emphasize institutional expectations rather than personal needs. Regrettably, these expectations often don't leave much room for idealism or for different approaches to administering a school.

In spite of its potentially negative effects, the socialization process of the school district should not be completely rejected by beginning administrators. The process can be a positive one in acquainting them with the role expectations, norms, and sanctions of the district, and several factors may minimize the possibly negative consequences of the socialization process. (Licata and Hack,[28] and Wolcott[29] provide insightful discussions of the influence of role expectations, norms, and sanctions.)

First of all, simply recognizing that the process does exist should be helpful. Secondly, if beginning administrators follow an earlier recommendation to delay introducing change until they learn more about their job and their new situation, they probably will not be exposed to the negative aspects of the socialization process until they are more secure, and therefore will be in a better position to withstand certain pressures when they are ready to introduce change.

Finally, new administrators should not assume that there is no flexibility in the role expectations, norms, and sanctions operating in a school district. There may be room in the district for an idealistic administrator who wants to do things differently in the school, if he/she knows how to "bend" the role expectations, norms, and sanctions without breaking them. This will require knowledge, understanding, and, perhaps most important, risk taking to find out what is possible—but it can be done.[30] And, if beginning administrators hope to retain the idealism that they possessed when they started in administration, that effort will indeed need to be made.

CONTINUING PROBLEMS OF MIDDLE MANAGEMENT

While the problems reported by one administrator may not be perceived as problems by another, attempts have been made to identify a common set of problems faced by most school administrators—both new and experienced.

For example, in a study by Pharis and Zakariya for the National Association of Elementary School Principals, a representative national sample of elementary school principals was asked about the extent to which each of thirty-three possible problem areas was currently or potentially (within the next year) troublesome.[31] Close to half of the elementary school principals identified the following five problems as the most serious:

1. Dismissing incompetent staff
2. Managing student behavior

3. Declining enrollments
4. Staff reductions
5. Evaluating teachers.

Other problems identified by between 25 percent and a little over 40 percent of the responding principals were vandalism by school-age outsiders, pupil absenteeism, pupils' disregard for authority, declining test scores, complying with student records regulations, dealing with teachers' due process problems, stealing by pupils, and staff morale.

An examination of the problems identified by elementary school principals reveals two main categories of concern: (1) evaluating and relating to the professional staff, and (2) diagnosing and responding effectively to student misbehavior. Both of these areas of concern are treated extensively elsewhere in this text. The subjects of teacher evaluation and personnel problems are discussed in chapters 8, 9 and 10; student misbehavior problems are examined in chapters 13 and 14.

Elementary school principals, of course, are not the only administrators who experience problems in their jobs. In a study for the National Association of Secondary School Principals a team of researchers found that a majority of the respondents in a national sample of high school principals cited the following problems, listed in order of importance:[32]

1. Time taken up by administrative detail
2. Lack of time
3. Variations in the ability of teachers
4. Inability to obtain funds
5. Apathetic or irresponsible parents
6. Problem students
7. Insufficient space and physical facilities
8. Inability to provide teachers time
9. Tendency of older teachers to frown on new methods
10. Defective communication
11. Teacher tenure
12. Compulsory school attendance.

While it appears that some of the problems identified by the high school principals are different from those reported by the elementary school principals, the differences probably reflect dissimilar methods of questioning the two groups of principals. Certainly, there is adequate evidence that elementary principals also experience time problems, although the problem of apathetic or irresponsible parents may be more serious on the secondary than on the elementary level. In any case, this text has offered a number of suggestions for responding to these kinds of problems.

ADMINISTRATOR STRESS AND BURN-OUT

One problem which appears to be common to both elementary and secondary school principals is administrator stress, sometimes resulting in burn-out.[33] Stress is believed to be manifested by feelings of frustration, great pressure, and a lack of control over one's emotions and environment,[34] while burn-out has been defined as emotional exhaustion caused by the stresses of the job.[35] Although most elementary and secondary school principals do not experience high levels of continued stress or become burned out, the problem of administrative stress and burn-out is perceived to be a serious one for an increasing number of administrators. For example, there is research which suggests that more individuals are leaving the principalship at an earlier age than would be expected.[36] In trying to ascertain the reasons for premature retirement from the principalship, it was found that a majority of the respondents identified *excessive time demands, stress,* and *heavy work load* as the three main factors that caused them to leave.[37]

It should be noted that studies have shown that excessive time demands and heavy work load are some of the possible causes of stress. Gorton found in his investigation of factors associated with administrative stress that the following six conditions contributed the most stress to high school principals:[38]

- Feeling that I [the principal] have too heavy a work load that I cannot possibly finish during the normal work day
- Imposing excessively high expectations on myself
- Feeling that I have to participate in work activities outside of the normal working hours at the expense of my personal time
- Having to make decisions that affect the lives of individual people that I know (colleagues, staff members, students, etc.)
- Complying with state, federal, and organizational rules and policies
- Trying to resolve parent-school conflicts.

In a related part of his study Gorton attempted to ascertain those factors that contributed to the stress of elementary school principals. The five most important factors identified by the respondents were:[39]

- Complying with state, federal and organizational rules and regulations
- Trying to resolve parent/school conflicts
- Imposing excessively high expectations on myself
- Feeling that meetings take up too much time
- Trying to complete reports and other paper work on time.

An examination of the two sets of factors that contribute to the stress of principals reveals that at least half the factors are common to both elementary and secondary school principals. (It should be noted that factors not in one list but in another were rated as contributing at least moderate stress.) It can also be seen from examining the various factors that stress is caused by both internally and externally generated pressures. For example, "Imposing excessively high expectations on myself" is a type of internally generated stress, while "Complying with state, federal and organizational rules and policies" is a response to external pressure. And stress from "Feeling I have to participate in school activities outside of the normal working hours at the expense of my personal time" may be caused by a combination of internal and external pressures. Psychologists have long recognized that to some extent (and for some individuals to a large extent) people generate their own stress in addition to that which the external environment itself may be contributing.[40]

On the other hand, there is evidence to suggest that the school principalship itself has perhaps become more difficult. For example, the Herlihys review studies which suggest that the principalship has become a lonely occupation.[41] Also, Blumberg and Greenfield conclude from their study of effective principals that "A general malaise seems to have come over the principalship in recent years; the present and the immediate future hold more uncertainty than anything else."[42] In reference to possible causes, these two researchers state, "Principals frequently take the brunt of multiple and usually conflicting expectations over issues ranging from student discipline to the problem of personnel administration, compliance with increasing numbers of state and federal policy mandates, and maintaining a smooth-running educational program that serves the needs of a school community that has become less and less homogeneous in the character of students' abilities and parent aspirations for themselves and their children."[43]

In another study of school principals by Hill, Wuchitech, and Williams, it was found that school principals have busier days, do more night work, endure more scrutiny and criticism, and have a good deal less discretionary authority than they did five years ago.[44]

Whether the school principalship today is more difficult than it was five years ago or earlier can be debated. Certainly, the problems of the late '60s and early '70s such as student and parent activism, teacher militancy, racial strife and drug abuse seem to be as serious as today's problems. However, even if today's principalship is not more difficult than in past years, the *perception* that it is contributes to the reality for many principals and observers. Fortunately for the administrator who is experiencing stress, there is no shortage of recommended programs and materials for understanding and ameliorating causes of stress.[45] Nevertheless, it would be useful for any individual to keep in mind that stress is inevitable in most jobs of an administrative nature and that a stress free job is probably not only unlikely but may not even be desirable for maximum productivity. Most people need at least some pressure to motivate them to aspire to a higher level of performance. It should also be emphasized that the fact that administrators face many problems need not discourage those considering a career in school administration. Despite these problems, there is research which shows that a large majority of elementary and secondary principals' morale or satisfaction is high.[46] And, although any position has problems associated with it, if a person can become an effective problem-solver, administration can represent a rewarding and successful career.

ADMINISTRATIVE TRANSFERS AND REDUCTION IN STAFF

Declining student enrollments, persistent inflation, and tax-payer revolts have caused many school boards to transfer some of their school administrators to other schools or other assignments within the district and, in some cases, to reduce the size of the administrative staff by laying off principals. While these school board actions do not appear to be on the same scale as those taken with teachers, the impact on the individual administrator affected can be the same. An administrator who has been an elementary school principal but is reassigned to a junior high school as an assistant principal because of the closing of an elementary school experiences a major change in his/her professional career, which will probably require considerable adjustment. Nevertheless, at least in this situation, the administrator still has an administrative position in the school district. In another situation it may become necessary for a school board to reduce the size of the administrative staff and actually lay off some administrators and reassign others to administer more than one school. Administrative reduction in staff raises all of the problems and issues that were discussed in chapter 9, Special Personnel Problems, and the reader is encouraged to review that discussion.

Administrative transfers and reductions in administrative staff may be inevitable in a growing number of school districts. It is important in such situations that there exist a policy and plan developed by the school board with considerable involvement and input of the building administrators and supervisors, the two groups who are likely to be most affected by transfers and lay-offs. Such a policy and plan should make clear the criteria to be used in determining the need for transfers and lay-offs, as well as determining who should be transferred or laid off. Appropriate due process safeguards also need to be defined adequately. A model policy and plan has been developed by the National Association of Secondary School Principals that seems worthy of consideration.[47]

CONTINUING PROFESSIONAL DEVELOPMENT

After a person has completed a preparation program, obtained state certification, and secured a position as a vice-principal or principal, there is a natural tendency to feel that he/she has "arrived." At this point the administrator has probably invested considerable time and effort in preparation for school administration, and now, having a job, continued professional development may be one of the least attractive things to contemplate. The administrator may realize that there are still a few remaining deficiencies in his/her background and may acknowledge the need to keep up-to-date on new approaches in education. But the administrator thinks, "*More* education or professional development? Never! At least, not for the moment. There are too many things going on in school and there just isn't time to engage in further professional development."

Fortunately, most school administrators eventually recognize and accept the fact that they must engage in continuing professional development in order to remain effective in their schools, and they find ways to organize their time better so that they can pursue such activities. Finding enough time will always be a problem for the practitioner. But an individual who feels strongly about the need for self-improvement will somehow find time for it, while the person without such strong convictions will "never seem to have the time" for continued professional growth and eventually will experience professional stagnation or regression.[48]

For the administrator who is sincerely interested in continuing professional development, a variety of opportunities exist. Too often professional development has been perceived as representing only more course work. Although additional courses can make a contribution toward the further professional growth of an administrator, there are other kinds of activities that are equally valuable. These can range from membership on committees of state and national professional associations to a planned program of reading certain of the professional journals and books published during the year.

Identified below and discussed briefly are a number of professional growth activities, including additional course work, which are recommended for the administrator's consideration.

PARTICIPATION IN PROFESSIONAL ORGANIZATIONS

Every school administrator should belong to and participate in local, state, and national professional administrator organizations.* These organizations can offer many opportunities for professional growth and development, and the administrator can benefit greatly from active participation.

At the district level, a forward-looking local school administrators' association will organize in-service meetings for its members, sponsor trips and visitations to schools where innovative programs are being implemented, and

---

*At the national level the professional association to which most elementary school administrators belong is the National Association of Elementary School Principals; most secondary school administrators belong to the National Association of Secondary School Principals.

involve its members extensively in making recommendations for the improvement of eduction in the district. All of these activities can contribute to the continuing professional development of an administrator.

If, for some reason, an administrator's local professional association does not have a professional improvement program similar to the one described, the administrator can exercise leadership in the interest of initiating such a program. Professional improvement activities should not be left solely to universities or to the state or national administrators' associations. There should be an ongoing program of professional development for administrators within every district, and the local administrator's association should play a large role in planning for and implementing this program.*

At the state and national association levels, an administrator will find a wide variety of opportunities for professional growth. While the administrator may not feel either ready or possessing enough available time to become an officer of a state or national association, there is no reason why that individual shouldn't be able at least to try to participate in one or more of the committee activities of the professional associations.

Most school administrators' state and national associations have standing committees for the areas of curriculum, student personnel, and research, among others, and are frequently anxious to involve members of the association in these activities. By participating on a committee, the administrator will have an opportunity to develop leadership skills and to exchange ideas with colleagues. From such involvement the administrator should be able to broaden his/her perspective beyond the local situation, and at the same time make a useful contribution to the professional associations.

In addition to office-holding and committee work, the state and national professional associations offer potentially significant opportunities for the professional development and improvement of any administrator through annual conventions. At each convention there are presentations and discussions about problems, issues, and new approaches in education, and there is considerable time for school administrators to interact informally. Certainly the chance to "get away from it all" and to recharge one's emotional and professional batteries before facing again the trials and tribulations of the job is a legitimate part of the need to attend a convention.

But whether attendance at state or national conventions will result in the further professional development of an administrator will depend primarily on the extent to which he/she actively pursues the available opportunities. If

---

*An excellent in-service program for school administrators which utilizes an individualized, personal approach combined with a principal support group has been developed by the Kettering Foundation and has been implemented in a number of school districts. For more information, see James LaPlant, *Principals' In-service Program* (Dayton, Ohio: Institute for Development of Educational Activities).

the administrator spends most of the time socializing, he/she may "enjoy" the convention, but probably will not derive much professional growth. This is not to say that there should be no socializing at a convention or that such activities are without value. Quite the contrary.

However, if the administrator is to benefit fully from the convention in terms of professional growth, he/she will need to plan and organize time judiciously so that it will be possible to attend and participate in meetings covering a wide range of professional topics, as well as to examine the various convention hall exhibits of new materials or technology which could be utilized in the school. A state or national convention represents a tremendous opportunity for additional professional development and improvement, if the administrator capitalizes on it.

As a supplement to their annual conventions, the national associations and many of the state administrator associations have recently initiated a series of professional development seminars or institutes which appear to offer considerable opportunity for the continuing education of administrators. At the state level these seminars or institutes frequently take the form of a workshop scheduled for two consecutive weekends, and may be cosponsored by the state association and a cooperating university. Participants are usually able to obtain university credit for their work, and the topics explored at the meetings are typically very timely and relevant. Because the practitioner doesn't have to spread such activities over an entire semester, as is generally the case in university courses, he/she is better able to arrange a schedule in order to participate in the kinds of programs sponsored by the administrators' associations.

The format and advantages of the institutes offered by the national associations are similar in many respects to the state associations' programs. The main differences lie in the greater variety of topics explored, greater availability of nationally renowned speakers and resource people, and more numerous options in regard to the time schedule of the institutes. Figure 20.5 shows the kind of topics that have been explored in institutes sponsored by national administrators' associations.

As figure 20.5 shows, the national institutes and conferences represent a significant opportunity for the continuing professional development of an administrator. The topics are relevant and cover a wide range of professional issues and new approaches. The meetings are scheduled so that the administrator is seldom away from the job for too long a period of time. Without a doubt, the national institutes and conferences offer the school administrator a tremendous opportunity to continue professional development with a minimum of disruption to the everyday work schedule.

MIDDLE LEVEL FRONTLINE CONFERENCES
(Junior High/Middle Principals)

Specific conference speakers listed on registration pages

FIRST DAY
4:30 p.m.	Registration
6:00 p.m.	Reception (Cash Bar)
7:00 p.m.	Dinner
8:00 p.m.	*Brain Growth Periodization: Implications for Middle Grades Education*
10:00 p.m.	Adjourn

SECOND DAY
8:00 a.m.	Continental Breakfast
8:30 a.m.	*Update on National Study of Schools in the Middle* (NASSP, Dodge Foundation)
10:15 a.m.	Swap Shop Session— Share schedules and curriculum programs. Participants bring materials to share
11:30 a.m.	LUNCHEON

1:00 p.m.	CONCURRENT WORKSHOPS I
	a) *Evaluation of Middle Level Schools, Staff, Students*
	b) *Appropriate Programming in Junior High or Middle Schools*
	c) *Changing from Junior High School to Middle School*
2:30 p.m.	Refreshment Break
2:45 p.m.	CONCURRENT WORKSHOPS II Topics repeated from above
4:00 p.m.	Adjourn

THIRD DAY
8:00 a.m.	Continental Breakfast
8:30 a.m.	*Middle Level Schools: Making the Ideal a Reality*
11:15 a.m.	Conference Summary
11:30 a.m.	Adjourn

NASSP INSTITUTE

DATE:	January 28–30
PLACE:	Gainesville, Florida
HOTEL:	Gainesville Hilton
SPEAKERS:	Roy Bolduc, Professor
	Mary Kantowski, Associate Professor
	Vincent McGuire, Professor
	David Smith, Dean, College of Education

TOPIC: Microcomputers for the Principal: Instructional and Management Applications (in cooperation with the University of Florida, College of Education)

- De-mystifying computers
- Providing an understanding of computer operations

Figure 20.5. Professional Development Programs[49]

(continued)

SPEAKERS: Gene Todd, Chairman,
Department of
Subject
Specialization

*(All from University of
Florida,
Gainesville)*

NASSP Staff Member,
Reston, VA

TOPIC:
• Introducing
instructional and
school management
applications of
microcomputers

• Suggesting methods
for faculty
involvement in
classroom usage of
microcomputers

• Providing extensive
"hands on"
participation

Figure 20.5. Continued

SCHOOL DISTRICT PROFESSIONAL DEVELOPMENT PROGRAMS

There is no hard, comprehensive evidence on the extent and quality of professional development programs for administrators sponsored by local school districts. The evidence that exists suggests that most professional development programs offered by school districts for their administrators suffer from the same defects and problems associated with teacher in-service programs, a topic addressed in chapter 10.[50] Such defects and problems typically include the lack of a formal policy and plan for the continuing professional development of school administrators, insufficient involvement by the administrators in the development of in-service programs, inadequate incentives for participating in continuing professional development, an superficial evaluation of what was learned during the in-service programs.

It should be emphasized, however, that inadequate and ineffective professional development for administrators at the local school district level is not inevitable. Good professional development programs at the local school district level are in operation. Administrator Training Academies have been established by school districts, frequently with the assistance of university professors, in such places as Little Rock, Arkansas, and Dade County, Florida. Also, in California, legislation has been passed which encourages the establishment of District Professional Development Centers in all school districts for the training of administrators as well as teachers.[51] Nudson and Devries have described the development and operation of an Academy for Management and Organizational Development in one California school district.[52] In addition, in some areas local[53] and regional consortiums[54] have been established which provide for the sharing of expertise and resources. It seems clear that there are sufficient ideas and examples of good programs for any administrator who would like to bring about improvement in a school district's professional development program.

PROFESSIONAL READING

Most school administrators usually work a ten- to twelve-hour day, and many of their evenings are occupied with various kinds of school-related meetings. School administration is a demanding job and seldom is the evening when the administrator does not arrive home weary and fatigued. Therefore, when an administrator finally gets a rare evening or weekend free from the demands of the position, professional reading may be the last activity that person would like to pursue. It isn't that the administrator doesn't realize the benefits of professional reading. It's just he/she has neither the energy or the motivation to do so, and other alternatives may seem more attractive.

While it will not be easy for a school administrator to engage in a program of professional reading, he/she must make the effort in order to keep informed and avoid falling into a "professional rut." Although an administrator may find the summer months more convenient for reading, particularly books, there should also be an attempt to set aside three or four hours a week during the regular school year, perhaps on weekends, for reading professional journals. A planned program and regular schedule of reading professional journals during the school year and summer months is a "must" for the administrator who is serious about maintaining professional growth and development.

In addition to professional journals, the administrator should try to read several books each year that are concerned with education or related matters. A book can provide a deeper understanding of a subject than would a journal article, and will frequently contain data and information that one could not easily derive from an article.

The problem for the administrator who contemplates reading a book is that the task may require an extended period of concentration and time that is not normally available during the regular school year. However, the winter and spring holidays and the summer months should be convenient times for the administrator to delve into several books. By setting a goal of reading one book during each holiday period and at least one each month during the summer, the administrator could maintain a program of reading five to six books a year. Although such a program cannot be represented as extensive, it is at least a beginning upon which the administrator can expand, depending on available time and developing interest.

The types of books an administrator should read will vary, of course, according to interests and needs. But insofar as possible, an attempt should be made to read broadly, rather than only books on education. The administrator who is unsure about which books to select for reading, can consult the book review section of *The Kappan* for books on education and the book review section of the *New York Times* for those dealing with various aspects of our society. The important factor, though, is not *how* the administrator makes the selection, but that he/she does become committed to scheduling some time during the school vacation periods and the summer months for reading books which will provide professional and personal benefits.

RESEARCH

Many administrators shudder at the sound or sight of the word, *research*. They may have gone through a preparatory program in which they were required to read research articles or to undertake a research study. In pursuing these activities administrators have sometimes had experiences with research which were not pleasant. As a result, many administrators are "gun-shy" about research and certainly do not perceive it as a means of furthering their professional growth and development.

This is regrettable, since research is only a systematic method for seeking an answer to a question or a possible cause of a problem. Although some methods are more complex and sometimes more difficult to understand than others, research—reduced to its essential elements—is simply a means of investigating something about which one would like to learn more. It is true that the utilization of research procedures will force an administrator to become more systematic and objective in investigating a question or problem, but the primary advantage of using research methods is that the information ultimately obtained is likely to be more valid and trustworthy than if such methods were not used.

At this point, the reader may be thinking, "But what kind of research could I do in my school?" Actually, the school setting doesn't lend itself to conducting all types of research studies, and it must be remembered that the administrator's main job is not that of researcher. However, the four examples presented below illustrate the kinds of research studies that are usually possible in a school and which an administrator might consider initiating or becoming involved in at some stage:

Follow-up Studies. Combination questionnaire-personal interview studies to gather information from graduates on career and further training patterns and their recommendations for improving the school program.
Feedback Studies. Combination questionnaire-personal interview studies to obtain information from students, teachers, and/or parents on their perceptions of the effectiveness of some aspect of the school program, e.g., the curriculum, and their recommendations for improvement.
Current Status Studies. Standardized testing and/or questionnaire studies to obtain current information, on, for example, student achievement and ability, dropout rate, or percentage of students participating in student activities.
Diagnostic Studies. Studies designed to shed light on why, for instance, some students underachieve and are truant; why some teachers aren't as effective as they should be; or why certain curricular programs aren't working the way

they should be. The research methodology would depend on the area being investigated, the availability of instruments, and the flexibility of the school in permitting such research to be conducted.

Each of the types of studies identified above can generally be conducted within a school setting, and should provide the administrator and others with useful information for improving the educational program of the school. It might be further emphasized that these kinds of research studies may be *necessary* if the school program is to be improved in any substantial sense. As a result of participating in research studies, the administrator will not only make a contribution toward improving the school program, but should also become more knowledgeable about the school and ways to improve it, thereby increasing his/her own professional growth and development.

PROFESSIONAL WRITING AND PUBLIC SPEAKING

Most textbooks that discuss continuing education recommend professional writing and public speaking as means of professional development. However, the observable evidence shows that relatively few administrators engage in these activities.

There is little doubt that an administrator can further develop professionally through writing and public speaking. The self-discipline, concentration, planning, and organizing required for professional writing and public speaking are valuable for the school administrator. But many administrators lack not only time to engage in writing and speaking, but also the confidence or skill for performing these tasks. Neither their undergraduate nor graduate training has prepared them well for professional writing or public speaking. Therefore, although they may recognize the need to do more professional writing and public speaking and may even feel remiss, many administrators simply choose to avoid these tasks when opportunities present themselves.

In light of the problems previously discussed, it may not be realistic to recommend that an administrator engage in professional writing and public speaking as means of further professional development. Still, these are useful activities if an administrator is willing to invest the extra time and effort necessary for accomplishing them. An administrator who lacks confidence or skill in public speaking should consider joining a "Toastmasters" group or taking a speech course. The way for an administrator to start professional writing may be by describing an aspect of the school program which would be of interest to other administrators in the state and could be included in a state publication. Later, as skill and confidence develop, the administrator can try to write articles for national publications. (An excellent book on how to write for professional publication has been authored by Van Til.[55])

Writing and speaking well are difficult tasks for most people, not just for administrators. But if an administrator has ideas, convictions—in other words, something to say—an attempt should be made to communicate those thoughts to people through professional writing and public speaking.

ADVANCED COURSEWORK

Most administrators quickly discover after they take a job that their initial administrator preparation program did not prepare them for every aspect of school administration. The preservice preparation program is usually designed to meet state certification requirements for administrators (which are minimum standards) and to provide a foundation of knowledge and skills on which they can continue to develop building blocks of competency. Some of these building blocks can be achieved through on-the-job experience and others as a result of pursuing the activities already discussed in this section on continuing professional development.

One important way in which a person can continue to develop professionally is by taking additional courses. By this means an administrator can fill in gaps in his/her preparation program and become better informed about some of the newer approaches and ideas in education.

If an administrator would like to develop further professionally by taking additional course work at a university, the first step might be to write or call the chairperson of a department of educational administration for an appointment. Before conferring with the chairperson however, the administrator should spend some time analyzing his/her particular strengths and limitations, and the challenges currently confronting the school. As a result of this analysis, the administrator will be better able to identify and define his/her special needs for further professional development, and the university department chairperson or an assigned adviser will be in a much better position to help plan an appropriate program of course work and related learning experiences.

The administrator might also give some consideration to whether or not the course work is to lead to an advanced degree or certificate. For many administrators, the main reason for seeking additional university course work seems to be to obtain an advanced degree. Actually, there is no evidence that possession of a doctor's degree or specialist's certificate will make it any easier to obtain, hold, or succeed in a job in school administration. Although some school districts prefer that applicants possess a doctorate or specialist's degree, the final decision on candidates is usually based on factors other than their degree, as long as they have been certified by the state. Many if not most school districts include provision for an increase in salary for those who obtain a specialist's certificate or doctor's degree, but the increase is usually slight and hardly justifies the time, effort, and money invested by the individual.

The only truly legitimate reason for an administrator's taking advanced course work is that he/she wants to increase professional knowledge and skills. If this is the main motivation, it is perfectly reasonable to plan a program in such a way that it leads to an advanced degree. The primary goal of an administrator, though, should be to increase his/her learning so that a more effective leadership contribution can be made toward improving the school program.

A FINAL NOTE

Throughout the book and particularly in this chapter the problem dimensions of school administration have been emphasized. The school administrator who is not able to anticipate and prevent or resolve problems sucessfully is not likely to perform effectively as an administrator nor provide the leadership needed to improve educational opportunities. However, if an individual possesses or can acquire and maintain through continuous professional development the personal qualities and competencies discussed in various places in this book, he/she should be able to respond effectively to present and future challenges and opportunities for leadership.

Review and Learning Activities

1. Define the nature of each of the five typical problems which many new administrators face during their first year. Describe how each of the problems might be avoided or resolved.
2. Analyze the similarities and differences between the problems of the elementary school principal and the problems of the secondary school principal. What are the implications of these problems for the school administrator?
3. Identify and define the possible obstacles that an individual may encounter in the contemplation of a need for continuing professional development.
4. Describe the kinds of professional growth opportunities that are possible by participating in the following activities and indicate what the administrator needs to do to capitalize on these opportunities:
   a. membership in professional organizations; school district professional development programs
   b. professional reading
   c. research
   d. professional writing and public speaking
   e. advanced course work.

Notes

1. Arthur Blumberg and William Greenfield, *The Effective Principal* (Boston: Allyn and Bacon, 1980), pp. 9–10.

2. Dick Gorton and Mike Frontier, "Research on Time Management Problems," *Association of Wisconsin School Administrators Bulletin* (February 1980): 12–14.

3. David R. Byrne, Susan Hines, and Lloyd E. McCleary, *The Senior High School Principalship* (Reston, Va.: National Association of Secondary School Principals, 1978).

4. Julia Ann Losby Olson, "A Time Use Study of Male and Female Elementary Principals" (Ph.D. diss., University of Minnesota, 1980).

5. William J. Martin and Donald J. Willower, "The Managerial Behavior of High School Principals," *Educational Administration Quarterly* (Winter 1981): 69–90.

6. Byrne et al., *Senior High School Principalship,* p. 20.

7. Gilbert R. Weldy, *Time: A Resource for the School Administrator* (Reston, Va.: National Association of Secondary School Principals, 1974.)

8. The credit for the origination of the concept of MBO is usually given to Peter F. Drucker, *The Practice of Management* (New York: Harper & Row, 1954).

9. For an excellent review of the concepts of MBO and their practical application, see George S. Odiorne, *MBO II: A System of Management Leadership for the 80s* (Belmont, Calif.: Fearon Pitman, 1979).

10. For an extensive discussion of the ideas in this section, see Richard A. Gorton, *School Administration and Supervision: Important Issues, Concepts and Case Studies* (Dubuque, Iowa: Wm. C. Brown Company Publishers, 1980), Chapter 10.

11. For an analysis of this problem, see ibid., pp. 278–79.

12. See Chester Barnard, *The Function of the Executive* (Cambridge, Mass.: Harvard University Press, 1948), p. 165.

13. For a further discussion of this type of influence, see Gorton, *School Administration and Supervision,* pp. 285–86.

14. Richard G. Hess, "Evaluation of the Secondary School Assistant Principal." Specialist Field Inquiry Report, University of Wisconsin-Milwaukee, 1979. Also see William L. Pharis and Sally Banks Zakariya, *The Elementary School Principalship in 1978* (Arlington, Va.: National Association of Elementary School Principals, 1979), p. 81, for data on what appears to be a less serious problem.

15. Dale L. Bolton, *Evaluating Administrative Personnel in School Systems* (New York: Teachers College Press, 1980).

16. Barbara Zakrajsek, "Evaluation Systems: A Critical Look," *National Association of Secondary School Principals Bulletin* January 1979): 100–110.

17. Educational Research Service, Washington, D.C.

18. For further reading on this approach, see *How to Evaluate Administrative and Supervisory Personnel* (Arlington, Va.: American Association of School Administrators, 1977) and George Redfern, *Evaluating Teachers and Administrators: A Performance Objective Approach* (Boulder, Colo.: Westview Press, 1980).

19. Jan Muczyk, "Dynamics and Hazards of MBO Application," *The Personnel Administrator* (May 1979): 51–62.

20. Gary P. Latham and Lise Saari, "Importance of Supportive Relationships in Goal Setting," *Journal of Applied Psychology* (April 1979): 151–56.

21. Chad Ellett, "Teacher Assessment of Principals' Performance: Their Validity and Independence of School Size and Other Characteristics," *CCBC Notebook* (October 1977): 4–21.

22. Developed and used by principal Curtis Kittleson at Manitou Springs Elementary School, Manitou Springs, Colorado.

23. Personal correspondence from Mr. Kittleson.

24. Bolton, *Evaluating Administrative Personnel in School Systems,* pp. 123–24.

25. For an interesting discussion of the effects of the problem, see Thomas W. Wiggens, "What's in the Script for Principal Behavior?" An ERIC Report: Ed–057–445. Also see Flora I. Oritz, "Scaling the Hierarchical System in School Administration: A Case Study of a Female Administrator," *The Urban Review* (Fall 1979): 111–26.

26. Jacob W. Getzel, "Conflict in Role Behavior in the Educational Seeting," in *Readings in the Social Psychology of Education,* ed. W. W. Charters, Jr., and N. L. Gage (Boston: Allyn and Bacon, 1963).

27. Edwin M. Bridges, "Bureaucratic Role and Socialization: The Influence of Experience on the Elementary Principal," *Educational Administration Quarterly* (Spring 1965): 19–29.

28. Joseph W. Licata and Walter G. Hack, "School Administrator and Grapevine Structure," *Educational Administration Quarterly* (Fall 1980): 82–99.

29. Harry F. Wolcott, *The Man in the Principal's Office: An Ethnography* (New York: Rinehart and Winston, 1973).

30. *The Principal in Metropolitan Schools,* eds. Donald Erickson and Theodore Reller (Berkeley, Calif.: McCutchan, 1979), chapters 3 and 4.

31. Pharis and Zakariya, *Elementary School Principalship* pp. 95–97. Also see, "What Kind of Principal Reads *Principal?" Principal* (January 1981): 48.

32. Byrne et al., *Senior High School Principalship,* p. 25.

33. Maurice Vanderpol, "School Administrators Under Stress," *Principal* (March 1981): 39–41; Boyd Swent and Walter Gmelch, *Stress at the Desk and How to Creatively Cope* (Eugene, Oreg.: Oregon School Study Council, 1977).

34. A. Werner, "Support for Teachers in Stress," *The Pointer* (1980): 54–60.

35. C. Maslach, "Job Burn-out: How People Cope," *Public Welfare* (1978): 56–58.

36. Nancy DeLeonibus and Scott D. Thomson, "Pushout Principals: Why They Leave and Where They Go," *National Association of Secondary School Principals Bulletin* (December 1979): 1–10.

37. Ibid., p. 2

38. Richard A. Gorton, "Administrator Stress: Some Surprising Research Findings," *Planning and Changing* (Winter 1982): 358–59.

39. Richard A. Gorton, "Elementary Principals and Stress" (Unpublished paper, 1981).

40. Meyer Friedman and Ray Rosenman, *Type A. Behavior and Your Heart* (New York: Alfred A. Knopf, 1974).

41. Barbara Herlihy and Dennis Herlihy, "The Loneliness of Educational Leadership," *National Association of Secondary School Principals Bulletin* (February 1980): 7–12.

42. Blumberg and Greenfield, *The Effective Principal,* p. 15.

43. Ibid., p. 9

44. Paul Hill, Joanna Wuchitech and Richard Williams, *The Effects of Federal Educational Programs on School Principals* (Santa Monica, Calif.: The Rand Corporation, 1980).

45. Michael C. Giammateo and Delores M. Giammateo, *Executive Well-Being: Stress and Administrators* (Reston, Va.: National Association of Secondary School Principals, 1980); Randall S. Schuler, "Managing Stress Means Managing Time," *Personnel Journal* (December 1979): 851–54; Vanderpol, "School Administrators Under Stress," pp. 39–41; John Adams, "Guidelines for Stress Management and Life Style Changes," *Personnel Administrator* (June 1979): 35–38; and James C. Quick and Jonathan D. Quick, "Reducing Stress through Preventive Management," *Human Resources Management* (Fall, 1979): 15–22.

46. Pharis and Zakariya, *Elementary School Principalship* pp. 10–18; and Lloyd E. McCleary and Scott D. Thomson, *The High School Principalship, Vol. III: The Summary Report* (Reston, Va.: National Association of Secondary School Principals, 1979), p. 28; and Donna Domian, "Impact of Job Stress on Job Satisfaction of Iowa High School Principals" (Ph.D. diss., University of Iowa, 1980).

47. *Administrative Assignment and Transfer Policies Reflecting Due Process: Promotion, New Positions, Transfers, Demotions* (Reston, Va.: National Association of Secondary School Principals, 1979).

48. James L. Olivero, "Principals and Their In-service Needs: Facing the Realities of the Situation," *Thrust for Educational Leadership* (May 1981): 4–9.

49. National Association of Secondary School Principals: Institutes and Conferences, 1981–82.

50. James L. Olivero, "Basic Obstacles to the Effective In-service Program—and How to Overcome Them," *Thrust for Educational Leadership* (May 1981): 10–13.

51. Richard H. Ehrgott, "Administrators Face New Era Requiring Observational Skills," *Thrust for Educational Leadership* (March 1979): 8–10.

52. Henry M. Nudson and Robert T. Devries, "Meeting the Urban Principal's Needs," *Thrust for Educational Leadership* (March 1979): 22–24.

53. Robert E. Lowery, "School Management: Principals Assisting Principals," An ERIC Report: Ed–181–593.

54. Arthur L. Costa, "Project Lead—Staff Development for All Needs," *Thrust for Educational Leadership* (March 1979): 11–13.

55. William Van Til, *Writing for Professional Publication* (Rockleigh, N.J.: Allyn and Bacon, 1981).

Index